Ruins of Praça de Patriarcal, Le Bas series, Bibliothèque nationale, Colleção de algumas ruinas de Lisboa, 1755. Drawings executed by Messrs Paris et Pedegache. Paris, Jacques-Philippe Le Bas, 1757 (from original in private collection).

The Lisbon earthquake of 1755

Representations and reactions

Edited by

THEODORE E. D. BRAUN

and

JOHN B. RADNER

SVEC

2005:02

VOLTAIRE FOUNDATION

OXFORD

© 2008 Voltaire Foundation, University of Oxford

ISBN 978 0 7294 0857 8
ISSN 0435-2866

Voltaire Foundation
99 Banbury Road
Oxford OX2 6JX, UK

First printing 2005

A catalogue record for this book
is available from the British Library

The correct reference for this volume is
SVEC 2005:02

This series is available on annual subscription

For further information about *SVEC*
and other Voltaire Foundation publications see
www.voltaire.ox.ac.uk, or email svec@voltaire.ox.ac.uk

Printed and bound by CPI Antony Rowe, Eastbourne

Contents

Contents

List of illustrations

Avant-propos

Il n'est pas donné à beaucoup d'événements de devenir des moments de l'histoire des idées. Les catastrophes naturelles qui frappent le plus ne sont pas celles qui font le plus de victimes. Ce sont celles dont l'onde de choc est le plus large géographiquement et, surtout, symboliquement. Quantitativement le nombre des secousses et des répliques sismiques à travers l'Europe et le nord de l'Afrique au cours de l'année 1755 a élargi l'audience du drame. La catastrophe touchait une capitale et à travers elle l'ensemble du continent européen puis de proche en proche l'Afrique et l'Amérique. Symboliquement, elle engageait les grands problèmes métaphysiques et scientifiques de l'époque. Si le problème du mal hantait depuis longtemps la conscience religieuse, la pensée des Lumières s'accommodait de moins en moins facilement de l'arbitraire divin. Une humanité impuissante et fautive pouvait se soumettre à la violence d'une nature imprévisible, incompréhensible, la divinité n'avait de compte à rendre à personne. Une humanité qui se libère du péché originel et qui revendique une maîtrise progressive de sa condition par le savoir supporte plus difficilement d'être ramenée avec brutalité à la condition de victime passive des phénomènes naturels. Le développement du rationalisme et les progrès de la science classique avaient rapproché l'homme raisonnable de son Créateur. L'être humain se sentait capable de penser l'ordre universel, il participait à la rationalité providentielle. Raison et foi s'accordaient dans la compréhension et la célébration de la Loi divine dont les lois scientifiques étaient l'écho et le reflet. Une catastrophe comme le tremblement de terre de Lisbonne brise l'euphorie d'un tel accord. Elle oblige à repenser les relations des hommes à la divinité et celles du savoir rationnel à la foi.

Il se trouve encore des théologiens et des défenseurs de l'orthodoxie chrétienne pour renvoyer au mystère de la Providence et suspecter l'humanité de crimes provoquant le châtiment. Ils rappellent la disproportion entre le Créateur et les créatures. Les décisions divines ne peuvent être comprises par des êtres aussi limités dont la nature pécheresse explique forcément la punition, si atroce soit-elle. La science est impuissante devant la volonté divine, le savoir désarmé devant les questions de l'origine et de la fin. Il faut attendre Kant pour que ces questions soient découplées de la connaissance rationnelle. La violence du drame métaphysique est à la mesure du problème scientifique. Les navigations autour du globe et les explorations systématiques avaient permis de cartographier les mers et les continents, de réduire les *terrae incognitae*, de dresser le table des végétaux et des animaux. Mais si le microscope et le télescope démultiplient les capacités de l'être humain, la connaissance se heurte aux mystères de la génération et de l'histoire du monde. Comment naît la vie? comment s'est formée la terre? La nature profonde du globe terrestre dépend de son origine. Comment se sont constitués les continents? comment la planète va-t-elle continuer à évoluer? L'ordre naturel suppose une régularité, les volcans et les tremblements de terre seraient des exceptions ou des infractions. L'image familière à l'époque est celle de la montre ou de l'horloge. La discontinuité et la violence destructrice de certains phénomènes naturels obligent à concevoir une nature qui avance par à-coups brutaux. La belle machine dont les astronomes et les naturalistes se plaisaient à vanter l'ordonnance redevient sombre, inquiétante.

Le savoir scientifique s'est affermi et affirmé grâce à l'expérimentation et à l'enregistrement des phénomènes. Dans le domaine des catastrophes telluriques, les savants sont démunis, sans archives ni mémoire précise, sans possibilité d'expérimentation en échelle réelle. Bientôt le passage du modèle mécanique classique au modèle thermodynamique va permettre d'intégrer l'explosion à la continuité et de penser les cassures de l'histoire naturelle, en même temps que celles de l'histoire politique. Les révolutions qui exprimaient les cycles répétitifs du monde se mettent à désigner les sauts irréversibles et l'invention du nouveau. Les catastrophes ne sont plus simplement d'affreuses exceptions dans l'ordre universel, elles ont leur place et leur explication dans une nature contradictoire et dynamique, de même que les soulèvements de population et les invasions peuvent servir au développement de l'espèce humaine. L'idée d'énergie avec ses risques et ses excès est caractéristique de cette nature qui ne se confond plus avec la symétrie classique, mais suppose entraînement et débordement, tension et déséquilibre.

L'importance de l'intervention de Voltaire est d'être à la fois philosophique et littéraire, argumentée et imagée. A une époque qui distingue encore et hiérarchise les modes d'expression, le vers est noble et la prose plébéienne. Voltaire sait jouer de l'un et l'autre. Il pratique un grand genre comme l'ode et réinvente un petit genre qui se prétend simple amusement comme le conte. Le phénomène sismique devient événement et date de l'histoire intellectuelle, en touchant les élites et un public plus large, les savants et tous les lecteurs de *Candide*. Les Lumières se caractérisent par cette irruption du pathétique dans l'intellectuel. Le mélange de l'argumentation et de l'émotion est aussi ce qui fait du tremblement de terre de Lisbonne un des drames des siècles.

Si la discussion est métaphysique et scientifique, elle est aussi esthétique. La première moitié du dix-huitième siècle manque d'une catégorie pour rendre compte de la haute montagne et des tempêtes maritimes. En donnant un sens inédit à la catégorie ancienne du sublime, Edmund Burke offre à ses contemporains l'outil qui aide à penser les déchaînements de la nature, tout ce qui menace l'homme dans sa sécurité personnelle et peut l'enchanter dans son imaginaire. Le sublime réintroduit la distance que la compassion et l'indignation semblaient devoir exclure. L'esthétique aide à atténuer le coup moral et intellectuel. La profondeur de l'onde de choc se mesure aussi sur toute la seconde moitié du dix-huitième siècle. Le scandale se double de fascination trouble et l'expérience de la Révolution française déplace l'émotion, du phénomène naturel à l'événement politique, le premier devient métaphore du second. Des colorations nouvelles apparaissent dans le traitement du drame. Quarante ans après son évasion des Plombs, Casanova se remémore sa révolte contre l'Inquisition de Venise et sa volonté de retrouver la liberté, à n'importe quel prix. En pleine rêverie d'évasion, il sent la prison trembler: 'j'ai vu l'énorme poutre non pas branler, mais se tourner vers son côté droit, et se retourner d'abord comme elle était par un mouvement contraire lent et interrompu, en même temps ayant senti que j'avais perdu mon aplomb, je fus convaincu que ç'avait été une secousse de tremblement de terre.'[1] Nous sommes le 1er novembre 1755; Casanova, selon la reconstruction de la scène *a posteriori*, imagine le palais des doges ébranlé et, pourquoi pas, mis à bas par la secousse. Le tremblement de terre de Lisbonne devient une métaphore de sa révolte. Les deux chapitres qui suivent dans l'*Histoire de ma vie* opposent sans doute à ces rêveries excessives la lente préparation d'une évasion qui mobilise toutes ses ressources intellectuelles, psychologiques et physiques. Mais le jeu d'écho entre la révolte individuelle et les catastrophes marque l'émergence d'une idée nouvelle d'individu.

A la veille de la Révolution, un des chapitres du *Tableau de Paris* révèle l'ambivalence de Louis Sébastien Mercier qui rêve à la catastrophe capable de détruire la capitale. Sous le pathétique obligé perce discrètement un désir de palingénésie, de régénération par la destruction: 'Ceux qui commandaient le jour d'auparavant ne trouveraient personne qui leur obéirait; il n'y aurait plus ni maître ni sujet.'[2] Le moralisme et le sens du devoir recouvrent bien vite cette pulsion désorganisatrice, mais celle-ci s'épanouit et s'exacerbe chez Sade dont un personnage emblématique cherche à provoquer de véritables tremblements de terre. Le narrateur est un moine scélérat, il rencontre sur les flancs de l'Etna cet alchimiste misanthrope qui expose sa conception d'une nature criminelle. Les volcans et les tremblements de terre ne sont plus des exceptions à l'ordre, mais la règle même du monde. L'alchimiste prétend imiter la Nature et la battre sur son propre terrain. Il forme des pains de dix à douze livres, pétris avec de l'eau, de la limaille et du soufre, qu'il enterre de place en place, à travers la Sicile. 'Nous multipliâmes tellement ces dépôts, que l'île entière éprouva l'un des plus furieux bouleversements qui l'eût encore agitée depuis pluseurs siècles; dix mille maisons furent renversées dans Messine, cinq édifices publics écrasés, et vingt-cinq mille

---

1. Casanova, *Histoire de ma vie* (Paris et Wiesbaden 1962), iv.220.
2. Mercier, *Tableau de Paris* (Amsterdam 1782-1788), xi.8.

âmes devinrent la proie de notre insigne méchanceté.'[3] Ce qui était pour
Casanova la tranquille évidence d'un droit de l'individu à disposer de lui-
même devient chez Sade une provocation scandaleuse. On sait que le
tremblement de terre de Calabre qui a détruit Messine en février 1783
a brusquement libéré les moines de leur clôture et les jeunes gens
des contraintes de l'ordre moral. La catastrophe naturelle a provoqué à
sa façon une révolution des mœurs. L'imaginaire sadien radicalise
l'identification entre secousse tellurique et pulsions centrifuges. Mais il
postule une compréhension scientifique aussi bien que métaphysique du
phénomène. L'humanité peut acquérir la maîtrise technique des
tremblements de terre aussi bien que de la foudre. Une des nouvelles
des *Crimes de l'amour*, 'La double épreuve', offre une version mondaine et
souriante de l'entreprise destructrice: 'La terre tremble... les flammes
vomies du volcan avec mille fois plus d'impétuosité, se réunissant au feu
du ciel et aux secousses de la terre, brûlent, détruisent, renversent les
édifices de cette ville superbe qu'on voit s'abîmer de toutes parts... Les
tours qui tombent en ruine, les temps qui se consument... les obélisques
qui s'écroulent, tout glace l'âme, tout la remplit d'effroi.'[4] Et pourtant
tout n'est que spectacle, offert par un amant richissime à une femme qu'il
veut séduire. Cette mise en scène, digne du théâtre de boulevards qui
prospère alors, est caractéristique de l'effort pour dépasser le traumatisme.

Il est vrai que la Révolution française a été ce tremblement de terre qui
a mis à bas en France les institutions qu'on croyait les plus stables. Quand
elle ne partait pas à la recherche de métaphores antiquisantes, la peinture
de l'époque a montré des familles essayant d'échapper au cataclysme, le
tremblement de terre renouvelait les scènes de déluge biblique ou de fuite
sur fond de Troie en flammes. La musique n'est pas en reste. En 1804,
comme pour clore définitivement l'épisode révolutionnaire, on donne à
Paris *Le Désastre de Lisbonne*, drame héroïque en trois actes sur un livret de
Bouilly et une musique d'Alexandre Piccini. On savait que les hommes
étaient capables de provoquer des bouleversements comparables à ceux
de Lisbonne en 1755. Mais certains y voyaient désormais un spectacle
sublime ou une violence nécessaire au progrès historique. Le débat était
relancé sur de nouvelles bases.

Michel Delon

---

3. Sade, *La Nouvelle Justine*, dans *Œuvres* (Paris 1995), ii.781.
4. Sade, *Les Crimes de l'amour*, dans *Œuvres complètes* du marquis de Sade (Paris 1988),
x.172.

Introduction

THERE must be very few eighteenth-century scholars who are not aware that on 1 November 1755 an earthquake devastated Lisbon, then a city of 275,000 inhabitants and the fourth largest city in Europe (after London, Paris, and Naples). We know today that it was one of the most powerful earthquakes in recorded European history, and as depicted in art and literature it continues to affect people. According to Jan T. Kozak and Charles D. James, in an article placed on a website, 'Although not the strongest or most deadly earthquake in human history, the 1755 Lisbon earthquake's impact, not only on Portugal but on all of Europe, was profound and lasting.'[1] The earthquake that hit Lisbon and its inhabitants that day was truly and literally awesome.

Even though most of us know that this seismic event occurred, before 26 December 2004, very few of us could have imagined the terrifying power of the earthquake that created one of the greatest natural disasters of the eighteenth century. Centred in the Atlantic Ocean some 200km west-southwest of Cape Saint Vincent, along a fault line running from the Azores through the Strait of Gibraltar and into the Mediterranean, where the African and European plates meet, the earthquake began in Lisbon at 9.30 am and lasted ten minutes, with three distinct waves. By contrast, the Tokyo earthquake of 1923 lasted only four minutes, according to most witnesses; and the 1994 shock in Northridge, California, which brought about vast destruction, lasted only eight seconds. The Lisbon event is estimated to have been between 8.5 and 8.8 in magnitude (see the James and Kozak article in this collection). The Tokyo earthquake measured between 7.9 and 8.2, and swept away 140,000 lives; in Kobe in 1995, a 6.9 magnitude quake claimed 5400 lives and left tens of thousands of wounded; the Northridge incident was measured at 6.7, causing fifty-seven deaths and 5000 injuries; the 1999 Izmit temblor, in Turkey, with a magnitude of 7.4, took more than 30,000 lives and caused catastrophic damage, although it lasted only forty-five seconds. All of these pale before the force of Lisbon. Unfortunately, Lisbon itself pales in comparison with the terrible death and destruction recently caused in South Asia and the Indian Ocean by a massive underwater earthquake, estimated at magnitude 9.0, and the devastating tsunami that followed. We can perhaps

---

1. Jan T. Kozak and Charles D. James, 'Historical depictions of the 1755 Lisbon Earthquake', http://nisee.berkeley.edu/lisbon/index.html. Our descriptions of the earthquake are based on this study, augmented by their article in this collection, and by material generously supplied by Diego Téllez Alarcia, who has also written an article for this volume.

better understand the shock of our eighteenth-century forebears when faced with the destructive forces of nature.

Although Lisbon was the hardest hit of the cities, Spanish and North African towns were also severely affected. In Morocco, a large number of mosques, synagogues, churches, and other public buildings collapsed in Asilah, Rabat, Larache, Agadir, and Meknesh. Algiers and the southwest coast of Spain suffered severe damage as well. Tremors were felt as far away as France, Switzerland, and Italy. The earthquake was the cause of enormous tsunamis that brought destruction to coastal areas of Portugal and Spain, Morocco and Algeria, and whose effects were felt as far away as Ireland and Holland, North Africa and even in America: in the Antilles, twelve hours later, Antigua, Martinique and Barbados were hit by a three-foot rise in the sea and flooding by high waves.

In Lisbon, the destruction was widespread over a large portion of the city. It was fire, spread naturally or by thieves trying to cover up their crimes, and then raging for five days throughout the city, that destroyed the largest amount of property and took the greatest toll in human lives. But the tsunamis were also devastating. Many people in Lisbon had taken refuge in boats moored in the port on the Tagus river; but half an hour after the first tremor had struck, a twenty-foot wave carried off all these boats. Two similar waves followed the first one. In Tangier, thirty-foot waves killed many people. It was reported that along the Portuguese coast, some regions were struck by waves almost 100 feet high. Huelva in Spain, was also terrorised by the waves, as was Cádiz.[2] A good number of the articles in this volume examine various first-hand accounts of the earthquake, along with other attempts to represent in words or in images its devastating effects. Indeed, these narratorial and pictorial descriptions touched people all over Europe at the time and well into the nineteenth century.

Even though there was exaggeration at first concerning the loss of life (some early estimates claimed that 100,000 people lost their lives in Lisbon alone), and even though modern estimates for the number who died vary considerably, as the articles in this collection indicate, with some putting the figure at 'only' 10,000, most modern scholars argue that in Portugal's capital 30,000 people were killed. And severe damage, including loss of life, spread over a huge territory. The earthquake also affected countries that experienced no physical damage. England, for instance, was very hard hit economically because of its heavy investment in trade with Lisbon; various German states were also affected in this manner. Many wealthy investors in France were concerned because they had placed much of their fortunes in the Lisbon and Cádiz trade routes to

---

2. Cádiz was struck by tsunamis resulting in much death and destruction. It was here that French dramatist Jean Racine's grandson was drowned on his honeymoon, an event which inspired a poem discussed in Braun's article.

the Americas, and these were the two European cities most devastated by the shocks and tsunamis, and the fires that followed.

The earthquake itself was probably worse in its total effects than we can imagine. Eye-witness accounts and images drawn soon after the quake narrate and depict the damage, but always from a limited perspective. With the extremely long tremors, the fires that followed, and the triple tsunami, the devastation was far more severe than that described in Voltaire's *Candide*, for example, the text that offers most readers their first encounter with this earthquake. And to the impact on Lisbon must be added the destruction in the rest of Portugal, in Spain, and in North Africa. So it is easy to understand the far-reaching significance of this event.

Reactions to the Lisbon earthquake were immediate. As with similar natural disasters, there were sympathetic and charitable reactions from those not directly affected, even people from other countries. In addition, particularly in Lisbon, there were efforts at reconstruction unprecedented in their vision and scope. Another kind of reaction consisted of varied efforts to understand the event, to interpret its significance, to come to terms with it. The power and destructive force of this earthquake stimulated scientific debate about the nature and causes of earthquakes, speculation that had recently been modified by mid-century interest in electricity. This event also had a powerful effect on religious faith and on philosophical systems. Like violent storms, and smaller or more remote earthquakes, the Lisbon earthquake impressed some preachers throughout Europe as a clear sign of God's intervention in the world, a strong warning for people to change their ways. For others, the immense loss of life and property produced a formidable challenge to philosophical optimism, and to a belief in God's goodness. In many ways Lisbon was a watershed event, separating modern from older ways of reacting to disasters and interpreting natural events from a scientific rather than a theological viewpoint. It had a profound effect on European thinking for well over 100 years; and because the event made such an impact on the consciousness of people living at the time, it still remains potent in the European imagination.

The eighteen articles on the earthquake assembled for this special issue of *SVEC* focus on the event itself and on some of the reactions at the time and afterwards. Written by scholars from Canada, the Czech Republic, France, Germany, Portugal, Spain, Switzerland, the United Kingdom, and the United States, they represent many disciplines, including literature, history, philosophy, seismology, sociology, disaster studies, and political science.

We have adopted as an organising principle of this volume the image of the earthquake itself, as it moves physically from its centre outward and temporally as it sends out various aftershocks. The first three articles deal with the event itself and with its effect on Portugal. Drawing heavily on eye-witness accounts, Malcolm Jack depicts the physical city of Lisbon before and immediately after the earthquake, the damage caused to public buildings, collections, and private houses. He then describes the new city that was built on the ruins and the process that produced a new Portugal as well as a new Lisbon, largely owing to the enlightened despotism of the Marquis de Pombal. Charles James and Jan Kozak offer a physical description of the earthquake, its causes and its effects, compare the force of this earthquake with others, and then use their knowledge of the physical effects of earthquakes to assess the accuracy of various visual representations of Lisbon during and after this event, while also noting how various modern themes inform these engravings. Russell Dynes charts the unprecedented, systematic, state-regulated response to the earthquake in Lisbon, including food distribution, price controls, and even pre-fabricated materials for building earthquake-resistant structures. Pombal's handling of the crisis in these and other matters allows the Lisbon earthquake to be rightly thought of as the first modern disaster.

Spain, geographically closest to Portugal and therefore the next hardest-hit country, receives the attention of two articles. Diego Téllez Alarcia describes how interpretations of the earthquake in Spain shifted between 1755 and 1756, when Spanish interests were aligned with those of Portugal (perhaps in part because the Queen of Spain was Portuguese), and 1762, when the new Spanish king sought to justify invading this former ally. His article analyses diachronically the political, social and religious factors that conditioned the interpretations of the earthquake in the two eras. Carmen Espejo Cala surveys the large number of texts concerning the earthquake published in one affected city, Seville. She analyses these varied publications, mainly 'popular' *relaciones de sucesos* or journalistic accounts of the events following the temblor, examines the printers' strategies for arousing and maintaining the public interest in the subject, and speculates about the authors of these texts, and their readers.

Three articles discuss the British reactions to the Lisbon and the earlier, much less severe 1750 London earthquakes, focusing on the question of Providence, of God manifesting his will, and the relationship between this point of view and the growing importance of scientific explanations of seismic phenomena. Matthias Georgi details how in the English public sphere at mid-century earthquakes were generally described as natural spectacles of nature, caused by the laws of nature, and argues that this way of understanding and representing earthquakes affected debates about those in London and Lisbon, even though these debates were mainly conducted in sermons. Robert Ingram surveys British reactions to the London and Lisbon earthquakes by examining letters, memoirs, newspaper accounts, sermons, and other documents, finding strong indications of the importance of religious thought in contemporary interpretations of these seismic events, thus entering into a dialogue with Georgi's analysis. Finally, Robert Webster explains how both John Wesley and his brother Charles regarded the earthquakes in London and Lisbon, and also violent storms, as disasters that put rich and poor on equal grounds, as egalitarian events that served the evangelical agenda of the Methodist movement.

4

France is represented by seven articles. Two of these deal with the questions of scientific explanations and providence, thus providing a different perspective on the issues raised by Georgi, Ingram and Webster. Grégory Quenet explores the debates over competing scientific explanations and the diffusion of scientific knowledge to a broader public; the central problem was to discover how an event which occurred in a specific place could be diffused thousands of kilometres away. The debates engaged the public as well as the scientific community, therefore illustrating the growing popular interest in science. Theodore Braun contrasts the reactions to the event of Voltaire and Le Franc de Pompignan, especially Voltaire's arguments against a belief in providence in his 'Poème sur le désastre de Lisbonne' and Le Franc's point-by-point refutation of Voltaire's arguments in a book of religious odes published some years later. Two articles study various literary reactions to the temblor. Anne-Sophie Barrovecchio examines Jean-Henri Marchand's burlesque tragedy on Lisbon, inspired by Voltaire's poem and comically attributed to M. André, a wigmaker. She sees a many-layered text, including a story of two star-crossed lovers who die in Lisbon, an intertextual dialogue discreetly drawn between certain lines of Voltaire's poem and the action of the play, and the often witty non-dialogic echoing of Voltaire's work in a reply to it, often in anodyne and apparently unrelated contexts, by allusion and parody. Catriona Seth analyses three quite distinct works dealing with the earthquake: Ponce-Denis Ecouchard Le Brun's two odes, Marchand's tragedy, seen in a different perspective from that of the preceding article, and Stéphanie-Félicité Du Crest de Genlis's *conte moral*, *Alphonse et Dalinde, ou la Féerie de l'art et de la nature*, written near the end of the century. A close reading of Le Brun's poems reveals a style owing much to the psalms, a deeply emotional response to the earthquake in which he lost a close friend, and a celebration of the power of Nature and of God. Marchand's mock tragedy is seen more as a comic response to Voltaire than to the earthquake itself. Genlis's story, written years after the event itself, shows a father and son learning the true value of things when compared to the majesty of Nature and the friendship of their fellow human beings. There follow two studies of how the quake and its aftermath were reported in French-language journals, gazettes and other periodical publications. Anne Saada and Jean Sgard examine the gradual spread of the news of the earthquake and its effects in the French-language press (it took almost a month before reliable reports could be prepared and disseminated). Their analysis includes examinations of court mail as well as the ordinary post, official bulletins, and public and private correspondence, and personal first-hand accounts of events as seen by reliable sources. Interestingly, the science of earthquakes does not appear as important as the issue of providence in these publications. On the other hand, Jeff Loveland analyses the work of Philibert Guéneau de Montbeillard reporting the scientific side of this calamitous event (and others) in the *Collection académique*, of which he was editor, and in the 'Liste chronologique', a roster of highly selected facts concerning natural events that shows a fragmentary earthquake theory. Finally, Gilbert Larochelle raises the question of why Voltaire, who was so moved by the Lisbon event, virtually ignored the expulsion of the Acadians from their adopted homeland in what is now Nova Scotia, Canada, at the same time, around 1755 and 1756. The forces of Nature and the question of providence wrench Voltaire's soul; but the real harm inflicted on thousands of people by a single political decision seems hardly to affect him at all. Larochelle asks if this silence concerning the fate of the Acadians might suggest that Voltaire underestimated, or even failed to realise, the possible link between Reason and inhumanity.

The reactions of Swiss Protestants to Voltaire's poem, both as it was being composed and after its publication, receive attention in an article by Monika Gisler that naturally connects with the issues explored in the three articles on British Protestant reactions to the earthquake as well as with those by Quenet and Braun. These Swiss Protestant reactions were quite diverse, and Gisler's interpretation goes far beyond providential arguments relating to philosophical optimism and a study of the exigesis of sacred texts.

Spiralling forward (and backward) in time and also moving outward in space, the article by Luanne Frank focuses on *Das Erdbeben in Chile* ('The earthquake in Chile'), the German author Kleist's Lisbon-inspired, nineteenth-century story of a seventeenth-century event. Frank describes Kleist's earthquake-like shock at discovering that neither reason-based or feeling-based knowledge was certain, and presents Kleist as a transitional figure, inhabiting both the Foucauldian classical *epistème* and the contemporary *epistème*, and experiencing the conflict between them as unavoidable, tragic, and unacceptable.

We close with an article by Estela Vieira, which returns us to ground zero while continuing the spiral in time towards our own era. By surveying the immediate (mainly poetic) responses to the earthquake in Portuguese literature, the revival of the epic stimulated by the quake, novelistic representations of the earthquake in the late Romantic period, and allusions to the earthquake in modern Portuguese writing, this concluding article demonstrates the traumatic event's powerful and enduring impact on the country's literary and intellectual development.

We hope that this volume will inspire further study on all aspects of the Lisbon earthquake and its aftermath. The articles gathered here demonstrate that what happened early on 1 November 1755, and the various efforts both to recover from this disaster, and to assess, understand and come to terms with it, can still engage and inform us in the twenty-first century.

Theodore E. D. Braun and John B. Radner

MALCOLM JACK

Destruction and regeneration: Lisbon, 1755

THE morning of 1 November 1755 was bright and sunny in Lisbon. Being All Saints Day, congregations were gathering in the principal churches of a city renowned as much for its piety as its commercial wealth. Lisbon had long been famous for its concentration of ecclesiastical buildings. In the city centre stood the sumptuous Patriarchal building; up the slope from it was the Jesuit church of São Roque with its fine chapels; Rossio Square contained both the Convent of São Domingues and the Palace of the Inquisition (now the site of the National Theatre of Dona Maria II). To the west, in hilly Santa Catarina, was São Paulo. Numerous convents and monasteries such as São Vicente da Fora stretched out to the east just outside the old centre. Parish churches alone may have numbered forty.

Intermingled with the churches and convents were grand public buildings such as the Customs House and the colonial trading agencies described two hundred years earlier by Damião de Góis as the finest and most magnificent in Europe.[1] Many of these buildings reflected the growth of Portugal's overseas empire during the reign of King Manuel I (1495-1521), following the great voyages of discovery to India in one direction and Brazil in the other. The Paço da Ribeira, the royal palace, stood in the Terreiro do Paço, or central square, on the river's edge. It was crammed with stately furniture, tapestries and rare *objets d'art*, particularly of Oriental origin. Indian furniture was mingled with Chinese ceramics. As the Crown became the wealthiest in Europe, Dom Manuel was determined to create a court which would impress his fellow monarchs in Christendom. Other public buildings, such as the Casa da India, were built on a grand scale, with numerous wings and internal courtyards. They were decorated in ornate styles, reflecting the newly acquired imperial aspirations of the nation. A large complex of these buildings interlinked to the royal palace, physically uniting the administrative and commercial features of empire.

To this Manueline city, King João V, who reigned from 1706 to 1750, had added further ornate buildings in the prosperous years of the half century before the earthquake. He totally redesigned and enlarged the old royal palace. The reconstruction at the palace went on for years under the supervision of João Frederico Ludovice, who later designed the

---

1. See Damião de Góis, 'Urbis olisiponis descriptio', in *Lisbon in the Renaissance*, translated by S. Ruth (New York 1966), p.24.

7

church and palace at Mafra. If the royal collection had always shown an inclination to the exotic and eastern, King João wanted to create a setting of grandeur in which to show it off. Gilt, baroque features were created in the interiors; rare and valuable tapestries were hung; furniture was covered in fine brocades. Collections of works of art were purchased at home and abroad: a number of works by Rubens passed into royal hands in the 1720s and impressive architectural models of palaces and churches of Rome were acquired at the same time. The bibliophile monarch continued to add to his library throughout his reign. His agents scoured European markets in search of the latest scientific literature as well as rare manuscripts and engravings.

Meanwhile, the spendthrift king lavished attention and funds on the building of the Patriarchal church, with its adjoining palace, on a scale that he hoped would rival the Vatican and put Lisbon on a footing with Rome.[2] Other palaces in the area, the homes of the court aristocracy, were also sumptuous. Dom Luís de Sousa had amassed a library of 30,000 volumes displayed in four Italianate rooms with lavish gilded *stucchi* in his house near the cathedral. The conde de Vidigueira, who had been ambassador at the French court and had no doubt been impressed by its regal grandeur, installed another imposing library in spacious rooms, decorated with Italian paintings and statues, near São Roque church.[3] Important collections of art, and much gold and silverware, were scattered throughout other aristocratic houses in the central area.

As mass began on the fateful morning of 1 November in the midst of these splendours in what had become one of the most ornate cities in Europe, no one could have guessed that the events of the day would change the course of the country's history, as well as having a profound impact on the prevailing Enlightenment belief in progress. A letter from an anonymous English witness vividly sets the scene that fine autumn morning:

There was never a finer morning than the First of November, the sun shone out in its full lustre, the whole face of the sky was perfectly serene and clear, and not the least signal nor warning of that approaching event, which has made this once flourishing, opulent and populous city, a scene of the utmost horror and desolation except only such as served to alarm, but scarce left a moments time to fly from the general destruction.[4]

The first tremor was felt after 9.30 am. It took the form of a loud and sinister rumbling noise that shook buildings but did not cause immediate

2. For a detailed and absorbing account of the treasures of the royal palace, see A. Delaforce, *Art and patronage in eighteenth-century Portugal* (Cambridge 2002). For illustrations of furniture, silverware and paintings of the Joanine period see the Catalogue of the Exposição *Lisboa Joanina*, Palácio Galveis, Lisbon, 1950.

3. Delaforce, *Art and patronage*, p.71.

4. Anon., *An Account by an eye-witness of the Lisbon earthquake of 1 November 1755*, British historical society of Portugal (Lisbon 1985), p.5-6.

damage. The English correspondent records that the sound was like that of thunder and that it lasted for less than a minute.[5] It was followed by two more violent quakes which were of sufficient strength to bring down roofs, walls and, in some cases, entire buildings. Much of the central and western part of the city was affected. The English eye-witness, staying in Buenos Ayres (modern Lapa), slightly to the west of the old centre, describes the moment of impact:

The house I was in shook with such violence that the upper stories immediately fell and though my apartment, which was on the first floor, did not then share the same fate, yet was everything thrown out of its place, in such sort that 'twas with no small difficulty I kept on my feet and expected nothing less than to be soon crushed to death as the walls continued rocking to and fro, in the frightfullest manner; opening in several places; large stones falling down from every side from the cracks and the ends of most of the rafters starting out from the roof.[6]

When the shaking had stopped, a suffocating cloud of dust enveloped the whole city, choking the panic-stricken inhabitants who were crawling about in the debris. In this confusion, the recorder of these events attempted to make his way down towards the river to escape by water. But he found the entire street piled high with debris. Instead he turned eastwards towards São Paulo Church, which he found in ruins. The great church had collapsed into a pile of rubble after the second tremor, killing a large number of the congregation and others who had rushed into the building for safety.

The streets in the whole central area running from São Paulo Church to the Royal Palace were the most severely affected, with buildings reduced to complete ruins or standing semi-derelict with only the odd wall intact. A panoramic view of the destruction is recorded by another anonymous witness from his vantage point on a ship in the Tagus:

Ten minutes before ten I felt the ship have an uncommon motion, and could not help thinking she was aground, although sure of the depth of the water. As the motion encreased, my amazement encreased also, and as I was looking round to find out the meaning of the uncommon motion, I was immediately acquainted with the direful cause; when at that instant looking toward the city, I beheld the tall and stately buildings come tumbling down with great cracks and noise, and particularly that part of the city from St Paulo in a direct line to Bairroalto.[7]

There were scenes of chaos everywhere. Our first eye-witness reports seeing priests still clad in their vestments from celebrating mass, women half dressed and without shoes, screaming children and terrified animals jostling to escape. A similar account of the horrors was given by Thomas Chase, a young member of the British Factory, who fell from the fourth

5. Anon., *An Account*, p.6.
6. Anon., *An Account*, p.6.
7. *The Lisbon earthquake of 1755: some British eye-witness accounts*, ed. J. Nozes, British historical society of Portugal (Lisbon 1987), p.79.

floor of his house but managed to survive in the debris in the basement with a broken arm and bruises. First sheltering in the burnt-out ruins of the Royal Palace, he eventually managed to escape by river to an English merchant ship moored on the Tagus. Chase describes the stench, and the corpses burning in the flames, the devotion of the parish priests who tried to console their flocks and the rapacious boatmen who could not resist cashing in on the situation.

This was not the end of the misery, nor had the horror ended. Our first eye-witness commentary continues:

On a sudden I heard a general outcry. The sea is coming in, we shall all be lost. Upon this, turning my eyes toward the river, which at that place is near four miles broad. I could perceive it heaving and swelling in a most unaccountable manner, as no wind was stirring. In an instant there appeared at some small distance a vast body of water, rising, as it were like a mountain, came on foaming and roaring, and rushed towards the shore with such impetuosity that tho' we all immediately ran for our lives, many were swept away.[8]

This was the first of a series of seismic waves that hit the Lisbon–Cascais coast about two hours after the original tremors. Coming from a south-westerly direction, they would have gone along the river bank until reaching the slightly protruding lower-lying areas around the foreshore of the central area, always liable to storm damage and flooding. Starting out at sea, these waves may have been as high as twenty feet by the time they crashed against the shore. Buildings near to the Terreiro do Paço were badly hit – a marble quay in front of the Customs House, only recently restored after earlier damage, was smashed to pieces. The Customs House itself was damaged and later burnt to the ground. Ships were thrown against each other in the harbour; boats on the river were swept away in the current. Hundreds of people were drowned, including groups who had gathered to escape from the city across the river. By early afternoon, the waves had subsided, allowing vessels to cross the Tagus once more.

The next disaster to hit the stricken city was fire. Contemporary accounts seem to suggest that fire broke out in different parts of the city soon after the tremors had subsided. Whether these all arose from natural causes, or whether some were the work of arsonists who saw an opportunity for looting, is not clear. A French deserter was held responsible for the burning down of the Casa da India.[9] Other soldiers, including Portuguese ones, were implicated as the plundering increased. The exhausted and demoralised inhabitants who had survived the tremors made little effort to put out the fires. Fierce flames soon engulfed the central part of the city from the slopes of the ruined Carmo Convent to the eastern built up area under the castle walls. From Rossio Square southwards to the Royal Palace and westwards across to São Paulo, the entire area was

8. Anon., *An Account*, p.6.
9. D. Couto, *História de Lisboa* (Lisbon 2003), p.185.

gutted. A strong north-west wind spread the flames in an uncontrollable conflagration that lasted for nearly a week before being completely extinguished. Damage from the fire was as great as damage from the earthquake itself.

Lisbon had a long history of earthquakes. Several of those recorded in the sixteenth century had also caused severe damage and loss of life; a mild tremor in 1750 coincided with the death of King João V. The epicentre of the 1755 earthquake was off the coast of Morocco: many cities, including Rabat and Agadir, were damaged by it. Tremors were felt as far away as Brazil and the Antilles as well as in the south of France and Italy. The second two tremors registered 9 and 10 on the Mercalli scale, indicating considerable force likely to result in significant damage. Tremors continued to be felt for some weeks in the Lisbon area, adding to the panic and devastation.

The damage done to Lisbon on 1 November 1755 was extensive. Some of the finest civic buildings (including the great trading houses) were ruined: hundreds of smaller shops and homes were destroyed. One estimate suggests that only 3000 of Lisbon's 20,000 houses remained habitable.[10] At least half the city's churches were damaged or reduced to rubble. The riverside, around the Royal Palace in the Terreiro do Paço, was particularly badly affected. The Ribeira Palace itself, crammed with rich art work and a library that may have numbered 70,000 books, was swept away. The royal family, who were staying in Belém in order to attend solemn mass at St Jerónimos church, escaped uninjured.[11] The Bragança Palace, where the crown jewels were kept along with the royal family's fine collection of books and works of art, was totally destroyed. Nearby, the sumptuous Patriarchal church and the new Opera House, an ornate building with gilt interiors that had dazzled the foreign community and visitors to Lisbon when it opened the previous spring, were both burnt to the ground. The marquis of Louriçal's Renaissance collection of art and another fine library, which included ancient manuscripts and rare maps and charts relating to the early voyages of discovery, was also destroyed. Important collections of incunables in the Oratory sited in the Chiado disappeared in the flames. Gold and other valuables stored in the trading houses were also lost. Foreign traders, including the English and Hamburg merchants, lost large and valuable supplies. To east and west the slopes of the city exposed ruins; perhaps as many as half its buildings were either damaged or destroyed. Even the Palace of the Inquisition in Rossio Square had been swept away. Thomas Pitt, an English visitor soon after the earthquake, records his grim impression:

10. K. Maxwell, *Pombal, paradox of the Enlightenment* (Cambridge 1955), p.24.

11. A. Castres (1691-1757), British consul and then envoy, records being received by the king 'with more serenity than we expected' a few days later at court (*The Lisbon earthquake*, ed. Nozes, p.34).

A far more melancholy abode than Lisbon cannot be conceived, nothing strikes the Eye in the City but ruin and Desolation; the Fire having completed what the Earthquake began: Heaps of Rubbish; broken walls; Fragments of Churches, with the Paintings and Ornaments in many parts remaining, form although a Scene of Horror rather to be felt than described.[12]

T. D. Kendrick rightly said that the combined damage from land movement, flooding and fire amounted to as 'savage a gutting of the heart of a city as can be found anywhere in the previous history of Europe'.[13]

It is more difficult to determine how many people were killed in the disaster. Early reports, suggesting that hundreds of thousands of people had perished, were wildly exaggerated. In the first published report, which appeared only six weeks after the event, J. Trovão e Sousa claimed that as many as 70,000 people had been killed and much of Lisbon lay in ruins. His unscientific description and gross exaggeration provoked immediate reaction from other Portuguese writers, who were naturally annoyed at the impression that this first account was making across Europe. A number of pamphlets and other works appeared in the early months of 1756. One of the most reliable is the *Commentary* of António Periera who puts the death toll at about 15,000.[14] An attempt was made to count casualties by way of parish records but requests for information sometimes remained unanswered. J. J. Moreira de Mendonça, another of the more reliable historians, sets a figure of 5000 deaths on 1 November itself. T. D. Kendrick agrees that António Pereira's figure of 15,000 in total is probably as accurate a guess as possible.[15] That would have been more than five per cent of the total population of 275,000. Many of those killed were caught in churches either during the first quakes or in subsequent fires while they were seeking shelter. Of the large clerical population, only about 200 probably perished, a relatively small proportion. The British Factory or merchant community, many of whom lived in the suburbs where the damage was less serious, escaped with a small number of deaths – less than 100. D. Francis puts the number at seventy-four.[16] Misery and suffering were, of course, widespread. Many people were trapped in rubble, and the dying and injured were left unattended. Crowds of people roamed the streets, reluctant to go inside the buildings for fear of further tremors, of which many were recorded in subsequent days. Injured animals struggled to free themselves from the wreckage, and faced starvation when freed as there was no one to feed them. Anarchy and disease were the immediate threats to the city.

---

12. Maxwell, *Pombal*, p.24.
13. T. D. Kendrick, *The Lisbon earthquake* (London 1955), p.32.
14. *Commentario Latino e Portuguez sobre o terremoto e incendio de Lisboa* (Lisbon 1756).
15. Kendrick, *Earthquake*, p.32. Judite Nozes agrees with this estimate although cautioning against being too dogmatic. See *The Lisbon earthquake*, ed. Nozes, p.103, n.66.
16. David Francis, *Portugal* (London 1985), p.123.

Although it was important to spread word through Europe that Lisbon had survived a catastrophe and was open for trade, it was even more vital to take action to ensure that normal life in the city could be resumed as speedily as possible. António Pereira mentions the actions of four prominent citizens who contributed to restoring order and confidence, – namely the Duke of Lafões, who as head of civil administration worked tirelessly to preserve law and order and his younger brother Dom João de Bragança, who took a lead in rescue work, the old Cardinal Patriarch Manuel and Monsenhor Sampaio of the Patriarchal Church who, together with numerous other clergymen still in post, continued to administer to the spiritual needs of the citizens. Mendonça mentions[17] the generosity of the Royal Princes Palhavã (the bastard sons of King João V) and, most important of all, the Secretary of State, Carvalho e Melo, later the marquis of Pombal.[18]

Pombal was the real genius behind the impressive effort to get Lisbon functioning again. Brushing aside all suggestions of abandoning the capital, he realised that the administration had to seize the initiative if civil disorder on a serious scale was to be averted.[19] His ruthless realism is summarised in the advice given to the king to 'bury the dead and feed the living'. Pombal realised that to achieve success, government had to be directed to clear and precise policy objectives. Planning needed to be detailed and effective; policy would only gain widespread support if it appeared to apply to all citizens, whatever their station. Ironically, the minister's own house in the Rua Formosa had survived the earthquake, although in the first days of November, Pombal appeared to be operating from his carriage as he moved about the stricken city issuing proclamations and orders.

Pombal divided Lisbon into twelve administrative districts, each headed by a magistrate who was responsible for ensuring that the emergency measures were enacted. The first and most urgent need was to dispose of the dead. The most efficient method of disposing of corpses was to put them on barges and sink them in the Tagus. Strongly anti-clerical by instinct, the Secretary of State realised that he needed the support of the Church and got the Cardinal Patriarch's agreement to this unconventional method of burial. If the bodies had not been dealt with quickly, plague or other diseases would soon have broken out. Pombal's efforts on

17. J. J. Moreira de Mendonça, *Historia universal dos terremotos* (Lisbon 1758).
18. Sebastião José de Carvalho e Melo, Marquês de Pombal (1699-1782) was born in the ranks of the lower aristocracy. After a period managing the family's country estates in the north of Portugal, he began a diplomatic career that took him first to London and then Vienna from 1739 to 1750. His political career took a decisive turn when he was appointed a minister by King José in 1750. His experiences abroad, and a certain distrust of the British interest in Portugal, helped to shape his policies when he was in office.
19. A Portuguese biographer has described him as being 'perspicacious' rather than 'original'. See A. Bessa Luis, *Sebastião José* (Lisbon 1984), p.53.

public health were helped by the cool winter weather which followed the earthquake.

The central control of the administration was so tight that the next vital matter, securing a safe water supply, could be put into immediate effect. Of equal importance was ensuring sufficient food supplies. Warehouses and other places where food had been left were requisitioned; cooks, millers and others involved in catering were compelled to work in specially set up centres where ovens and soup kitchens were installed. Food prices were controlled, particularly by the lifting of tax on fish, the staple diet. The supply of fuel, particularly wood, was also controlled centrally. Response from abroad helped Pombal's energetic efforts. The British Parliament voted £50,000 of aid; supplies of fuel and provisions were sent from Spain and much needed timber from the Hanseatic League based in Hamburg.[20]

Practical measures were supplemented by strict enforcement of law and order. Chief magistrates had the power to order the summary execution of anyone who was caught looting or pillaging. At least thirty-four people were executed for such offences within the first few days of November. Pombal mobilised the army, under the command of the marquis of Abrantes, to take physical control of the city, guarding buildings of particular importance. The movement of individuals was also restricted so that people in particularly vital jobs – carpenters and builders for example – could be kept in the city, or brought back from the provinces if they were found to have fled from it. No one could leave the city without an official pass. Bands of workmen were forced to undertake the urgent job of removing rubble and flattening buildings that were too dangerous to leave standing. At the same time a survey of property was instituted, as disputes about ownership were likely to arise once the initial shock of what had happened had been absorbed. In some areas, of course, nothing remained to be recorded. In another clever decision, Pombal closed the port of Lisbon so that the many ships in harbour could be searched for looted goods. Not only were large amounts of booty recovered, but where there seemed to be an excessive supply of food aboard vessels this was confiscated for use in the city. These measures were seen to be just and gained the minister widespread support for his strict control of the lives of citizens otherwise accustomed to a degree of freedom in going about their business.

To help the economy stabilise, rents and wages were regulated and a massive programme of house building undertaken. This reconstruction moved on at a rapid pace. The king and his court had taken to living in tents soon after 1 November, but within months a wooden building was put up on the site of the Ajuda Palace. It remained the royal residence

---

20. A. H. de Oliveira Marques, *Historia de Portugal*, 3 vols (Lisbon 1984), ii.353.

until 1777.[21] As far as more modest housing was concerned, as many as 9000 wooden structures were put up in six months, housing a proportion of the 25,000 refugee population. The building programme was carefully planned from the centre; no construction work was allowed to proceed without permission. Pombal realised that the flattening of a large part of the riverside area and levelling of some of the hillside to the west would enable a new modern city to be built around the Baixa district. He was determined that this would be done in an orderly manner. The layout would be on a grid system, making downtown Lisbon one of the most up-to-date Enlightenment cities, a home fit for a new middle class on whom national prosperity would depend.

A team of engineers and architects including Manuel de Maia, Carlos Mardel and Eugénio dos Santos (all military officers) took as its starting point the great square or Terreiro do Paço where the Ribeira Palace had stood. Focusing the city centre on a great square at the waterfront was dos Santos' idea; significantly, it was to be renamed Commercial Square.[22] A grand equestrian statue in bronze of the king in triumphal mode, clutching the symbol of absolute power, his sceptre, was later erected in the square. From the square two parallel roads, the Rua Aurea and the Rua Augusta sweep straight up to Rossio, while just to the west, the grid leads through another set of streets, parallel with the Rua da Prata, to the Praça da Figueira. The whole area forms an impressive rectangle and has remained the commercial centre of the city. Street lighting and other modern conveniences were installed under the imaginative super-intendence of Pina Manique, one of Pombal's close allies.[23]

Pombal's policies were executed not only for the benefit of the citizens of Lisbon but to restore the confidence of the international trading community upon which Portugal depended for its economic welfare. The message for them was that not only would their interests be protected, but that in fact the reconstruction of Lisbon would enhance the possibilities of commerce. Pombal had been much influenced by his diplomatic career, especially his time in London. In 1739 he had replaced his cousin, Mario António de Azevedo, as the envoy to the court of St James's. Although Pombal was never entirely at home in England (his grasp of the language was not fluent even though he moved in erudite circles such as the Royal Society), he recognised the superiority of English commercial arrange-ments, particularly the organisation of the great trading companies whose

21. Beckford was not impressed when he visited the palace in 1787, describing it as shabby and barn-like. See *The Journal of William Beckford in Spain and Portugal*, ed. Boyd Alexander (London 1954), p.262.

22. Maxwell, *Pombal*, p.26.

23. Pina Manique (1733-1805) was sympathetic to the plight of the ordinary Lisbon people whom he, like Pombal, believed should be properly protected by an absolutist but benign authority. One of his lasting reforms was in setting up the charitable institution, the Casa Pia, for looking after orphans. A great political survivor, he managed to remain in office after Pombal's fall in 1777.

ships had the protection of the Royal Navy when carrying out their overseas enterprises.

English predominance in the Brazilian trade had been formalised by the terms of the Treaty of Methuen in 1703. In fact, British interests had been secured by an earlier treaty of 1654. Under the terms of that Cromwellian agreement, not only were privileges accorded to English traders but a provision prohibited the raising of customs duties on English goods above an agreed percentage. British merchants understood that the Brazilian trade was one that needed medium to long term investment. They had sufficient capital resources to fund credit over a number of years, giving them an edge over their Portuguese rivals. Average profits from this colonial trade could be as high as thirty per cent, double the already profitable fifteen per cent made in Portugal itself.[24]

Pombal resented the advantages that these treaties had given to the British. As the representative of his country at the court of St James's, he pressed hard for recognition of Portuguese commercial interests and gained some minor success for Portuguese residents in Britain.[25] His London days taught him how demanding the English could be when it came to trading terms, and the extent to which the 'old alliance' served British rather than Portuguese interests. When he returned to Portugal, Pombal began to consider ways of curbing British privileges without upsetting the cornerstone upon which Portuguese foreign policy had been firmly based for decades. British support was meant to be a guarantee against incursion by Spain, traditionally seen as a threat from the time of the unification of the two kingdoms (1580-1640). The Royal Navy also guaranteed the integrity of Brazil. Although Pombal would have had some sympathy with the view expressed by the French writer, Ange Goudar, who urged the Portuguese to take the opportunity afforded by the rebuilding of Lisbon to throw off oppressive British control, he was realistic, and accepted the need for the alliance with England.[26]

In his reconstruction of Lisbon after the earthquake, Pombal applied the lessons he had learned in London, giving due prominence to the interests of the commercial houses. The new grid system designed for the Baixa allowed for the orderly co-ordination of commercial, banking and government interests. Buildings were to be in a uniform style, with limited ornamentation on their façades. Arcaded elevations and pavilions echoed the neo-Palladian style in England. By keeping the design simple (the so-called Pombalese façades were plainer than previous styles) much of the work could be prefabricated and put into place speedily and more economically than would otherwise have been the case. This effect was

24. Maxwell, *Pombal*, p.46-47.
25. For a detailed account of his efforts see Francis, *Portugal*, p.89.
26. Goudar blamed much of the Portuguese weakness on superstition and the influence of the church, another sentiment that Pombal would have shared with him. See A. Goudar, *Relation historique du tremblement de terre* (The Hague 1756).

immediately apparent to visitors. William Dalrymple, staying in Lisbon in 1774, said 'Whole streets and adjoining squares were planned in a single sweep: there was no place for individual variation. In the New City there is great attention to uniformity, and the houses being built of white stone have a beautiful appearance.'[27] Plainer facades lent an air of harmony to the emerging clean-cut buildings. The uniform feeling was also achieved by strict measurement of the streets – sixty feet across for those running up the grid north to south, forty feet across for those crossing west to east. Pavements of exact proportions were laid out on each street. The military background of the engineers and surveyors in charge of reconstruction was clearly in evidence in this precision planning. The proximity and modernity of the quarter encouraged efficiency. Buildings were made safer by the invention of a flexible wooden frame, known as the *gaiola*, around which the structure was built; this reinforcement was intended to make them better able to withstand future tremors.[28] Other features included a new sewerage system and, wherever possible, fountains for the provision of clean water, amenities attractive to those commercial businesses that were largely to finance the rebuilding.

Meanwhile the ex-envoy turned his mind to ways of mitigating the trading advantages which he had seen the British enjoying so effortlessly. A careful reading of old treaties, particularly the treaty of 1654, proved fruitful. Pombal realised that under the terms of the agreement, the British Factory controlled the wine trade only in the absence of any Portuguese company. But if a Portuguese company were to be set up, it would have the right to deal exclusively with the wine trade between Portugal and Brazil. In 1756, Pombal set up the Douro Wine Company with a monopoly over the wine business, and thereby gained control of a trade which had always been controlled by the British.

Although scoring points over the British would not have upset the old court nobility, Pombal's radicalism at home led them to see him as a menace to their conservative way of life. Not only did they regard him as socially inferior, they also considered that meritocratic educational views would eventually loosen the grip which their own families held on privileged positions at home and in the colonies. For his part, Pombal was concerned for the progress of the nation and had no patience with those who did not share his ideal. But his position was still precarious as he depended entirely on royal favour. Although his success in tackling the considerable problems caused by the earthquake had put him in a powerful position, he needed to consolidate his power by removing opposition from the old aristocrats.

Pombal's chance came in 1758 when a group of conservative nobles attempted a *coup d'état*. An attempt was made to assassinate King José I,

---

27. Quoted in Delaforce, *Art and patronage*, p.289.
28. Maxwell, *Pombal*, p.25.

whom the rebels considered to be entirely under the minister's control. Although the king was only wounded, Pombal directed the setting up of a regency (under the queen) during his convalescence. Exact details of what had happened were suppressed for a while by the minister, who was determined to make the most of the incident to consolidate his own position. Dom José, enfeebled by years of sybaritic living (his two passions were hunting and the Italian opera on which he had lavished royal funds), had no idea how to handle a situation he had not anticipated. He could only turn to his first minister who had shown such steeliness in dealing with the earthquake.

Pombal acted ruthlessly. After an initial period of silence, a series of arrests were made. Members of the Tavora family, headed by the Duke of Aveiro, and the Count of Atouguia were the most prominent of those detained, but Pombal also took the chance to act against the Jesuits by confining leading members of the order to house arrest, following the discovery of a letter warning the king of divine punishment if he acted against the order. A tribunal with sweeping powers was set up. As the minister responsible for home affairs, Pombal sat on this tribunal and took part in the interrogation of the prisoners. Proceedings were conducted in secret. A panel of judges, over whom Pombal also had control, pronounced sentence for the crime of treason. All the leading conspirators, including the Duke of Aveiro, were tortured before being executed, some in the most brutal manner. Even the ageing Marchioness of Tavora was not spared; other members of the family were rounded up, tortured and in some cases left in prison for years. The noble houses were disgraced and their property confiscated by the Crown.

Acting against the Jesuits would take a little longer. Pombal had first clashed with the Jesuits in Brazil, setting up his company, the Junta do Comércio, to break the missionaries' stranglehold on the country. As he encountered the force of their resistance, the minister came to realise that only by removing the company altogether could he secure Crown interests. So he adopted a policy of expelling the order from various provinces in Brazil until it was no longer able to operate in the country at all. Once he had been successful in Brazil, Pombal turned his attention to the Jesuits' influence in metropolitan Portugal. He began with an approach to Rome, hoping to build on the envy of many clerics against a rich and powerful order. But progress was slow. Eventually the Pope agreed to allow the Patriarch of Lisbon, Saldanha, to act against the order by removing its rights and privileges. By 1759 Pombal had persuaded the king that the Jesuits were a menace to national security, and they were duly expelled. Pombal began a policy, which was followed in a number of European countries: in France in 1764 and in Spain in 1767. In 1773 Pope Clement XIV decreed a suppression of the entire order.

Pombal was not yet finished with the Jesuits. He despised Padre Gabriel Malagrida, leader of the order, for supporting the widespread theological view that the earthquake was a sign of God's wrath and a punishment for the hedonistic life led by the inhabitants of Lisbon.[29] In late 1756 Malagrida had published his views in a thirty-page tract, the *Juízo da verdadeira causa do terremoto*, in which he reiterated the message of damnation that he had been repeatedly preaching in highly publicised sermons. With his considerable personal authority, Malagrida flatly contradicted Pombal's view that the earthquake was a natural phenomenon. This was open defiance, something Pombal could not let pass if his authority was to remain intact. Malagrida's view undermined the entire reform programme, which was based on a rational response to a natural rather than divinely inspired happening. When his overtures to Rome failed, Pombal turned to the Portuguese clergy. Having installed his brother to head the Inquisition, he persuaded senior Portuguese clerics to press charges against Malagrida as both a heretic and a subject in rebellion against the Crown. Though the evidence was flimsy, the Inquisition found Malagrida guilty, and he was eventually garrotted and publicly burnt in Lisbon in 1761.

Pombal's action in the matter of the Aveiro conspiracy displayed the same ruthless *realpolitik* that he had employed after the earthquake. The decade which followed the quake marked the high point of his influence. He himself ascended to the rank of marquis and ruled the country as a dictator, although, as always, he depended on the seal of royal approval. He directed his energies at modernising Portugal along English and Dutch lines and set about reforming both the public service and the educational system on which it was founded. He was convinced that the public service needed to be more effective in a modern, commercial country.

A new class of bureaucrats, inspired by modernising ideals, would have to be educated to take control of the programme of modernisation. The Jesuit schools scattered throughout the country were taken over by the Crown; a number of free schools were opened so that talent from the lower classes could be channelled to the good of the state. Pombal also set up new institutions such as the Casa do Risco das Reis Obras – a school of architecture and drawing – and the Colégio Real dos Nobres where classes were held on the principles of military and civil architecture. In 1770 the Junta de Providência Literária began to formulate new statutes for the University of Coimbra. The emphasis of these reforms was to promote the study of science, and various buildings in the university were to be dedicated to this purpose.[30] Pombal continued to press on with his ambitious plans for changing Portuguese society by these measures.

29. Gabriel Malagrida (1689-1761) was an Italian who had become a celebrated missionary in Brazil. His pulpit eloquence was matched by alleged miraculous powers. He had been well received by King João V in 1749, whose confessor he became and at whose deathbed he was present. He was friendly with the Tavora family.

30. See Delaforce, *Art and patronage*, p.295.

The king allowed him a free hand in all matters of government. When the minister set about reforming the Treasury so that the nation's accounts could be put on a proper footing for the first time in decades, the king even acceded to his requests that royal expenditure itself should be more tightly controlled.

Although Pombal may have acted ruthlessly against those who opposed him while favouring those who supported him, on the whole his measures stabilised the Portuguese economy after the excesses of the first half of the century under King João V. In the two decades of his rule he did much to put Portugal on the path to being a modern state, capable of competing against its European rivals. The earthquake proved the decisive turning point in providing the opportunity for this short-lived period of enlightened despotism.

CHARLES D. JAMES
and JAN T. KOZAK[1]

Representations of the 1755 Lisbon earthquake

RECOLLECTIONS, representations and records of destructive earthquakes have long been kept by many cultures and societies. In western societies, non-sacred techniques to resist the damage to human life inflicted by earthquakes (other than running for your life) have been more widely considered only since the early eighteenth century.[2] Contemporary earthquake engineering concerns itself wholly with the effects of earthquakes on the built environment, primarily buildings and bridges. Like most modern natural sciences, earthquake engineering is highly computational in scope, but its empirical and analytical understanding of physical earthquake damage mechanisms can enlighten a review of older, artistic representations and recollections of historical earthquakes. Several artistic renderings of the great Lisbon earthquake of the mid-eighteenth century particularly lend themselves to such an examination. Applied to artistic representations of the historical Lisbon earthquake, modern earthquake engineering 'scales generally used to weigh the misfortune of men and estimate their sorrows'[3] might help to identify fanciful, factual, and ideological representations of this powerful natural phenomenon.

The 1755 Lisbon earthquake is perhaps the most notable in western history for its severity (an estimated 40,000 to 60,000 fatalities in Portugal and North Africa, up to 20,000 buildings partly collapsed or destroyed, at least one devastating tsunami wave, urban fires) and for the distance over which it was felt (believed to be at least 300,000 square miles and possibly up to one million square miles). The story of the earthquake is well known. On the feast of All Saints Day, 1 November 1755, starting at about 9.40 am when the majority of the citizens were in church observing the religious holiday, three comparatively large shocks in succession struck the city. Contemporary seismologists believe these were probably three 'substantial and separate earthquakes', not one main shock and two

---

1. This chapter is a much shorter version of a presentation at *Nature and artistry, the 34th annual meeting of the East-Central American Society for Eighteenth-Century Studies*, 2 October 2003, University of Pittsburgh at Greensburg, PA.

2. Stephen Tobriner, 'Earthquakes and planning in the 17th and 18th century', *Journal of architectural education* 33:4 (1980), p.11-15.

3. Voltaire, *Candide or optimism*, translated by John Butt (New York 1947), p.130.

aftershocks. Some scientists now believe that the first large shock might have triggered subsequent seismic activity in the Tagus river valley (see note 6, below).[4]

The second shock was the largest and produced shaking for as long as an estimated three and a half minutes in parts of Lisbon. There was, of course, no seismic measuring equipment in the Portugal of 1755, but seismologists now estimate that the shaking magnitude was likely to measure from about 8.5 to 8.8 on the Richter scale – these were powerful earthquakes.

Lisbon had experienced damaging earthquakes before, including one approximately 400 years earlier, when strong earth shaking had wrecked a new cathedral. But in 1755 Lisbon, built on low hills and some estuary land along the Tagus River close to where it meets the Atlantic Ocean, was among the largest cities of Europe, a centre of commerce and religion, with growing commercial trade in its harbour, many fine, stone buildings on its hillsides and little concern for earthquakes.

By all accounts, the earthquake's shaking was strong in Lisbon and the surrounding country, at least partially collapsing many of Lisbon's stone buildings into narrow streets and doorways, crushing citizens and often blocking escape. The strong shaking and destruction would have raised clouds of dense dust. To this dust would have been added the smoke from fires lit by tipped over church candles and household fireplaces and stoves, fuelled by dry building timbers and driven through the city by wind. Citizens fled to the city's main squares or wharves close to the river's edge, and many were soon crushed or swept away by a huge tsunami wave that arrived in Lisbon forty to seventy-five minutes after the original earth shock. Lesser waves followed.

The destruction and loss of life caused by the earthquake were enormous. Several of Lisbon's great churches, including its cathedral, all of which had probably been filled with people as it was All Saints Day, collapsed. The new marble quay and parts of the city's thriving waterfront disappeared into the water, battered by waves and weakened by softer earth subsidence and strong shaking. Fires raged out of control. Refugees swarmed from the city.[5]

The principal tectonic source of the great Lisbon earthquake is now generally believed to have been south and west of Lisbon in the Atlantic Ocean along the Azores–Gibraltar fault zone, an active tectonic interaction zone between the African and the Eurasian plates that is thought capable of generating large earthquakes and tsunamis. The large main shock may have triggered secondary fault rupture, and there is recent

4. Bruce Bolt, *Earthquakes*, 4th edn (New York 2000), p.1.

5. Accounts derived from several secondary sources include Bolt, *Earthquakes*; Thomas D. Kendrick, *The Lisbon earthquake* (London 1956); Harry Fielding Reid, 'The Lisbon earthquake of November 1, 1755', *The Bulletin of the Seismological Society of America* iv:2 (June 1914), p.53-80; Jan Kozak and Marie-Claude Thompson, *Historical earthquakes in Europe* (Zurich 1991).

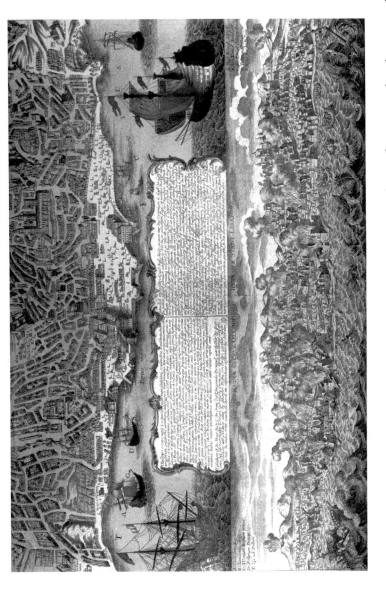

1. Hand-coloured copper engraving of Lisbon, late 1755 or early 1756, Augsburg, Germany, showing a precisely drawn map of Lisbon in a top panel, a legend in Latin and German in the middle panel over the harbour, and an imaginatively burning, post-earthquake Lisbon in the bottom panel (private collection, Prague).

speculation that one of the subsequent large shocks may have originated on-shore, closer to Lisbon.[6] There are some extraordinary claims about the effects of the Lisbon quake – reports of five-foot waves in Lake Ontario, strong shaking in Pennsylvania, tsunami run-up on the shores of the Atlantic coast of America, large waves in Finland, shaking in Sweden, Iceland, Greenland and the Cape Verde islands. The extravagant North American reports may have been aggravated by the occurrence of a significant earthquake in the general area of Boston in November 1755 (estimated at a magnitude of 7.0 but perhaps smaller), which was reported fairly widely in colonial America.[7] Reports of very distant shaking in parts of Europe and the Atlantic Ocean islands are nearly impossible to confirm or to rule out completely.

The 1755 earthquake appears to have been the largest in magnitude and most widely felt in historical Europe. But eighteenth-century Europe experienced other deadly earthquakes, and southern Italy and Sicily in particular have had a tradition of earthquake tragedy.

Earthquakes with significant mortalities in or near Europe, 1693-1908[8]

Earthquake name	Estimated (M) magnitude	Date	Fatalities
Val di Noto (Catania, Sicily), Italy	–	11 January 1693	~60,000
Tabriz, Iran	–	8 November 1727	~77,000
Lisbon, Portugal	8.5-8.8	1 November 1755	40-60,000
Calabria, Italy	–	4 February 1783	~50,000
Naples, Italy	6.9	16 December 1857	11,000
Messina (Sicily), Italy	7.5	28 December 1908	70-100,000

But none of these other significant earthquakes seems to have achieved the notoriety of the great Lisbon earthquake of 1755. This notoriety may be because of the magnitude and location of the Lisbon event and the great

6. Susana Vilanova, Cataraina Nunes and João Fonseca, 'Lisbon 1755: a case of trig-gered onshore rupture?', *Bulletin of the Seismological Society of America* 93:5 (2003), p.2056-68. Also M. A. Baptista (American Geophysical Union, San Francisco, CA, 8-12 December 2003) recently developed geophysical tsunami modelling of the 1755 earthquake for a large subduction zone earthquake.

7. The Boston earthquake was popularly reported in newspapers and church pulpits and discussed scientifically by, among others, Professor John Winthrop of Harvard in the *Philosophical transactions* 50, p.1-18, Royal Society of London, 1757. A useful compendium of accounts was assembled by Weston Geophysical Research for its publication of 'Historical seismicity of New England' (Westborough, MA 1976) and selected contemporary accounts have been reported recently by Christopher Ellis and Pedro de Alba, 'Acceleration distribution and epicentral location of the 1755 "Cape Ann" earthquake from case histories of ground failure', *Seismological research letters* 70:6 (1999), p.758-73.

8. Table adapted from United States Geological Survey (USGS), *Information about past and historical earthquakes*, http://earthquake.usgs.gov/activity/past.html.

loss of life and goods that it occasioned, not just in Lisbon but also in many parts of Portugal, Spain, Morocco and other parts of north Africa.

At least as important for its posterity are the visual representations and interpretations of the Lisbon earthquake. Images of powerful natural disaster kindle both the scientific and the poetic imagination. Many representations of the quake blend a sometimes very precise rendition of building ruins with poetic views of human struggle and nature's power. These large themes, though probably quite separate in modern imaginations, intersect in contemporary disaster studies.

Modern earthquake engineering can classify, in general, six direct causes of damage resulting from large earthquakes: fault rupturing, earth shaking, structural pounding, soil liquefaction and failures, tsunamis and seiches, and nonstructural damage to buildings. Two collateral causes of damage from earthquakes are also identified: fire and flood. It might be expected that any factual representation of the Lisbon earthquake should provide evidence of at least one of these mechanisms, with the possible exception of fault rupturing (since we have already seen that the fault rupture responsible for the 1755 earthquake is likely to have occurred at some distance from the city). This categorical earthquake damage offers one interpretive path through at least two representations of the Lisbon earthquake, both executed shortly after the event and illustrated here.

Figure 2, overleaf, is a reprint from a series of copper engravings made in Paris in 1757 by Jacques-Philippe Le Bas from drawings executed in Lisbon by Messrs Paris and Pedegache (Paris, Jacques-Philippe Le Bas, 1757). Figure 3 is a reproduction of a copper engraving produced after the 1755 earthquake and now in the possession of the Museu da Cidade, Lisbon. Both digital images are from the Kozak Collection of Historical Earthquake Images at the Earthquake Engineering Research Center, University of California, Berkeley.[9]

Historical reports of the shaking being felt throughout Portugal and also in south-eastern France and parts of Spain and Italy indicate that it must have been very strong. Switzerland and southern Germany also reported feeling it. Morocco and parts of northern Africa were strongly shaken and structural damage occurred in many towns there. Strong shaking of the earth's softer soils, especially wet soils – such as might be expected to be present around a harbour or river – can result in a separation of solids and liquids, or liquefaction, severely weakening the soil's capacity to support structures. Even slightly sloping soils are quite prone to spreading and sliding when shaken strongly. Liquefaction and soil subsidence seem to have contributed to the disaster of Lisbon in 1755

---

9. Jan Kozak and Charles James, 'Historical depictions of the 1755 Lisbon earthquake' and 'Images of historical earthquakes: the Kozak collection', http://nisee.berkeley.edu/ used with the permission of the University of California, Berkeley.

2. Ruins of Praça de Patriarcal, Le Bas series, Bibliothèque nationale, Collecão de algunas ruinas de Lisboa, 1755. Drawings executed by Messrs Paris et Pedegache. Paris, Jacques-Philippe Le Bas, 1757 (from original in private collection).

3. Dramatic scene of Lisbon, copper engraving, late eighteenth century, Museo da Cidade, Lisbon. Reproduced in *O Terramoto de 1755: testamunhos britanicos* (Lisbon 1990).

and, in particular, the destruction of the new marble block wharf. The combined assault of soil liquefaction, soil subsidence, lateral spread, irregular shaking of largely unconnected, big stone blocks, and the impact of a large tsunami wave seems to offer a viable explanation for the disappearance of the wharf structure under water.

But these two engravings suggest quite different realities as well as different localities. The Le Bas engraving illustrates buildings damaged by shaking and perhaps gutted by fire. The hillside, probably largely harder rock, seems only slightly cracked at worst, and no obvious slides of large amounts of soil are in evidence, nor are any faulting or other soil failures clearly drawn. Pedestrians are seen walking in the square at the base of the hillside and the damaged wall and buildings in the foreground seem not to have sunk into the soil. Because of this realistic and empirical tone, it might be suggested that the purpose of the drawing and engraving was to show the damage to the built environment of Lisbon wrought by the events of All Saints Day, 1755 as accurately as possible without reference to deeper earthquake meaning. In contrast, the second engraving illustrates people and stone buildings, both seemingly nearly undamaged by strong shaking, sinking into the earth. The earth appears to be in a near-liquid state. This illustration could be egregiously depicting soil liquefaction of the softer soils near the harbour. It could be suggesting earthquake fissures caused by nearby faulting that have trapped people. It may also depict lateral expansion of the soils closest to the harbour, and sliding hillside soils covering the unfortunate victims. But its central representation of people suggests its probable purpose was to depict a human disaster; it focuses on the suffering of ordinary citizens rather than on an accurate portrayal of natural effects. The popular image might elicit curiosity and sympathy for the victims of the earthquake from an audience at some distance from the disaster.

As well as rendering views of the earthquake, these two illustrations may depict some broader themes of the English and French Enlightenment: a triumph of rational, scientific-empirical reason over superstitious or dogmatic interpretation of natural disaster and also a wider concern for the welfare of all citizens. The natural science strain of earthquake investigation is carried beyond Lisbon in treatises such as the Rev. John Michell's 1760 Royal Society reading of *Conjectures concerning the cause, and observations upon the phænomena, of earthquakes; particularly of that great earthquake of the first of November 1755, which proved so fatal to the city of Lisbon, and whose effects were felt as far as Africa, and more or less throughout almost all Europe.* In his conjectures, Rev. Michell avoided the strictly theological and suggested that earthquakes are caused by shifting masses of rock miles below the surface. Clearly a new scientific rationality, a natural world of Newtonian movement and mechanics, and a geological view of time are given some impetus by European speculation about the great Lisbon earthquake. It might be convincingly argued that this natural science of earthquake conjecture continues through to Robert Mallet's (the Irish engineer) study, commissioned (or at least sponsored) by the Royal Society of London, of the Neapolitan earthquake of 1857. Mallet produced *Great Neapolitan earthquake of 1857. The first principles of observational seismology as developed in the report to the Royal society of London of the expedition made by command of the Society into the interior of the kingdom of Naples, to investigate the circumstances of the great earthquake of December 1857,* a two-volume scientific report with precise, realistic drawings, which, for the first time, used photographs to record earthquake damage. This report set the standard for subsequent scientific earthquake investigation and for post-earthquake reconnaissance reports to this day.

The broad theme of wide concern for the welfare of all in society not only provided an intellectual backdrop for popular reporting of Lisbon's earthquake but also keyed speculation and debate concerning its social and metaphysical causes among some French writers of the late eighteenth century, most notably Voltaire and Rousseau. Wider concern for the well-being of all citizens after the Lisbon earthquake was particularly devastating to a Panglossian view that all is for the best in the best of all worlds. The suffering of all the citizens of Lisbon underlined some flaws in the deist, often optimistic, universe whether God, evil, nature itself, or social convention was seen as the real cause of the hardships inflicted by the earthquake.

Local representation of the 1755 disaster seems to have been slightly different from the more widely distributed European images of the earthquake, suggesting some of the intellectual and social dilemmas that were faced by late eighteenth-century thinkers.

Figure 4, an illustration of the damage to the Royal Palace following the earthquake, shows an architectural drawing of a collapsed roof (and dome), structural damage and partial collapse to the walls at one end of the palace. Under the administrative direction of the Marquês de Pombal this building was strengthened and re-opened as part of the reconstruction of Lisbon. The damage portrayed in this view and the precise quality of the illustration confirm that there was strong shaking, but there is no suggestion of ground failure or fire near this building. Although the illustration may symbolically denote a slightly damaged but restorable secular authority, there is little suggestion of suffering by the population in this architectural rendering, completed some time after the disaster. The image seems to present a damaged but well-ordered and scientific, post-disaster Lisbon.

João Clama's oil painting *The Destruction of Lisbon* (figure 5), provides a contrasting view of the earthquake, apparently dominated by religious symbolism, clerical figures, and heroic themes. The painting shows citizens injured and dying, massive structural damage, especially to the stone masonry church building in the background, fire, and a suffering, displaced population. The baroque style, combined with the busy

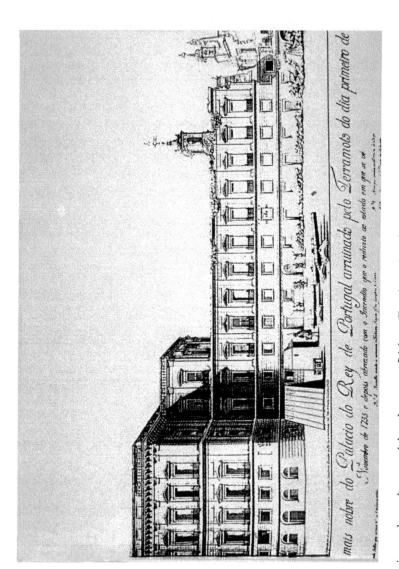

mais nobre do Palacio do Rey de Portugal arruinado pelo Terramoto do dia primeiro de Novembro de 1755 e depois abrazado com o Incendio que o reduzio ao estado em que se ve

4. Ribeira palace damaged by the great Lisbon Earthquake. Copper engraving, late eighteenth century.

5. João Clama, *The Destruction of Lisbon*. Oil painting, in the Museo Nacional de Arte Antigua in Lisbon.

ecclesiastical and angelic characters, may suggest that providential order is the source of the earthquake, and portrays the divine necessity of a greater good being accomplished through this seismic challenge to faith. Or perhaps the painting suggests that the disaster is retribution and punishment for the sins of Lisbon's citizens and a call to return to a hierarchically arranged, ecclesiastical good order. A clerically robed person occupies centre stage. Bathed in heavenly light, both he and his huddled flock appear largely unharmed. But his church, behind him, is severely damaged. Both religious leadership and religious interpretation of events may be taking a damaged back seat to human suffering, and to the nearly realistic renditions of building damage and fire that frame the painting.

The two disrobed gentlemen in the foreground may be there in figurative homage to the martyrs of the earthquake or perhaps to the saints associated with earthquakes in catholic Europe during the eighteenth century.[10] But these figures may also represent a newer sense of empowerment: a sense that human thoughts and feelings emerge from nature which, as exhibited by this powerful earthquake, gives them a new force and a new direction. Perhaps a new moral energy derived from releasing nature drives the emerging naturalist rejection of religious interpretation. To judge from the two gentlemen's expressions, however, this new naturalism first appears as bewilderment.[11]

It may also be that a secular authority is forming in the right foreground of the painting. The gentleman with the sabre and his cohort seem ready to leap into municipal action. This latent secular authority seems not quite, or not yet, a denunciation of religion and its replacement by a secular rationality. But the painting's portrayal of general suffering assumes the viewer's interest in the well-being of all citizens and deep sympathy with their misery. It may even be possible that this image offers a prophetic glimpse of an emerging revolutionary aspiration, drawn from nature's capacity to destroy an older, ecclesiastical, established order, and affirm a new sense of the ordinary human place in nature.

The images presented here help illustrate at least two important currents of thought that surfaced after the earthquake. The first is the scientific conjecture spawned by the enormous damage caused by the disaster, and the size of the area affected. This appeal to natural science encouraged an expert, detached interpretation of natural phenomena and may have led directly to the scientific understanding of earthquake engineering in technologically advanced, modern societies affected by a randomly shaken earth. The attention to precise scale, and detailed accuracy in

---

10. See for example the illustration of Saint Alexius in the 1765 Bohemia illustration depicted at http://nisee.berkeley.edu/images/servlet/EqiisDetail?slide=KZA60.

11. Our comments here derive crudely from Charles Taylor, *Sources of the self: the making of the modern identity* (Cambridge 1989), especially ch.8.

representing realistic damage to the environment, characterise this aspect of earthquake study.

A second current of thought is humanitarian concern, seen in the artistic presentation of ordinary citizens suffering death and misery as a result of a powerful natural disaster. These images pay less attention to the accurate rendition of natural catastrophe but resonate with a broad, modern, utilitarian sense of social responsibility for the welfare of ordinary citizens and suggest the latent power of nature and of human life freed from a predominantly religious interpretation. Since the Lisbon earthquake of 1755, this broad current of thought has travelled a twisted path of social revolution, romanticism, and modern social science in western societies.

RUSSELL R. DYNES

The Lisbon earthquake of 1755: the first modern disaster

THE timing of the Lisbon earthquake made it a topic of discussion and disputation among intellectuals involved in what has come to be known as the Enlightenment. In part, it challenged growing liberal views about the wonder of nature itself, and seemed to reaffirm the presence of God that many were trying to make abstract, distant and benign. The focus of this chapter is the way in which the earthquake on 1 November 1755 can be considered the first 'modern' disaster because it was the first to evoke a co-ordinated state emergency response as well as a forward-looking, comprehensive effort at reconstruction which included attempts to reduce the impact of future disasters.

Major earthquakes were not new. In 1693, for instance, there had been major earthquakes in Port Royal, Jamaica, in Catania, Sicily, in Naples. But most of northern Europe was seismically stable, and for most Europeans, earthquakes were events that happened elsewhere. The Lisbon earthquake was not the first to evoke governmental interest. At times, European governments had been involved in the process of reconstructing colonial towns and villages destroyed by earthquakes.[1] But when the Lisbon earthquake occurred, it became the focus of attention for the 'relevant civilized world'.[2]

i. The social and political context of the Lisbon earthquake

The Lisbon earthquake occurred in the context of Portugal's efforts to 'modernise' and to catch up with the progress neighbouring nations had already achieved. As a capital city, Lisbon was crucial to the development process. As the residence of the king, it was the location of nobility that could enhance or impede the development process. As a port, Lisbon was central to trade with the colonies, notably Brazil, itself crucial to the future economic fortunes of Portugal. In effect, the earthquake provided a

1. See for example, Stephen Tobriner, *The Genesis of Noto: an eighteenth-century city* (London 1982).
2. T. D. Kendrick, *The Lisbon earthquake* (London 1956), p.25.

serious threat to the continuity of the state and its chance to enhance its position in the global economy.

Woloch has suggested that the eighteenth century in Europe was characterised by a multiplicity of states linked together in a pattern of rivalry and mutual recognition[3] and that rulers sought to promote their sovereignty by amassing power over policy and resources within the state and by competing with other states for influence and territory. Most European countries were undergoing dramatic transformation during the eighteenth century. At the time of the Lisbon earthquake, George II ruled in England, Louis XV in France, Maria Theresa in Austria, Frederick II in Prussia and Elizabeth in Russia. Compared with these countries, Portugal was considered a backwater, an irrelevant country ruled by ineptness and indifference. For the first part of the century, Portugal was ruled by João V (1705-1750), who spent most of his reign building monuments and palaces, funded by gold from Brazil. Much of his wealth was distributed by gestures of largesse and prestige, but wealth made him independent of the court, which he rarely assembled. In 1742, his illness caused the affairs of state to fall increasingly into the hands of churchmen. The major governmental positions were filled by cardinals or priests, and the king's confidential advisor was a Jesuit. When João V died in 1750, he was succeeded by his son, José I, then thirty-six, whose main interests were riding, playing cards, attending the theatre and opera, and religious devotions.

In 1750, Portugal, with a population of fewer than three million people, had an army of clergy, perhaps as many as 200,000. Charles Boxer called eighteenth-century Portugal 'more priest ridden than any other country in the world, with the possible exception of Tibet'.[4] At mid-century, Portugal's colonial operations in Brazil and Paraguay were being undercut by Jesuit control and independent merchants. The British Factory, an association of British merchants with favourable trade agreements, had a major grip on port commerce and on Brazilian gold. Apart from the long-term but often uneasy alliance with British commercial interests, Portugal was not on good terms with France. It was traditionally suspicious of Spain and was not necessarily responsive to Vatican directives.

At the time of the earthquake, Lisbon, with a population of 275,000, was perhaps the fourth largest city in Europe, after London, Paris and Naples. Famous for its wealth, it was full of palaces and churches and, because of its commercial activity, was one of the best known cities in the world since traders, particularly English and German, did most of the business in town. But Lisbon was also known as a city of the Inquisition, and was characterised as being a centre of superstition and idolatry.

---

3. I. Woloch, *Eighteenth-century Europe: tradition and progress* (New York 1982), p.1.
4. C. R. Boxer, *The Portuguese seaborne empire: 1415-1825* (Oxford 1963), p.189.

The key to understanding Portugal in the last half of the eighteenth century and the response to the earthquake lies in the career of Sebastião José de Carvalho e Melo.[5] In 1770, he was made marquês de Pombal and, historically, that name is usually associated with him. Pombal was given the responsibility for the emergency response and reconstruction of Lisbon after the earthquake, but this was only one part of his overall effort to 'modernise' Portugal. From 1739 to 1743, which was a period of expansion and imperialism in England, he represented the Portuguese king in the court of St James's. In that capacity he came to distrust British ideas about expansion in South America, where Portuguese interests were critical. He was also offended at what he perceived to be British indifference to Anglo-Portuguese affairs, which were central to Portugal's economic and social future. From 1745 to 1750, Pombal was posted to Austria to Maria Theresa's court. He was irritated by the shift from London since he felt that this was intended to keep him away from economic and commercial issues, perhaps as a deliberate move by his 'enemies' in the court. But during this time he was able to observe Maria Theresa's attempt to reform the censorship system in Austria and to wrest the University of Vienna from Jesuit control.

Throughout his various experiences, Pombal sought to understand the economic and political weakness of Portugal. He was particularly concerned as to how a small country could maintain economic viability, especially in an international system composed of larger, more aggressive states such as Britain. He was interested in how the state might guarantee its economic interests. He was also distrustful of the Jesuits and of many members of the aristocracy. The Jesuits had set up their own economic empires in South America with the dual rationale of protecting their missions and converting the Indians. The Jesuits also had a monopoly on higher education in Portugal, which trained the aristocracy and rejected many new ideas, including scientific ones, through control and censorship. During his experiences outside the country, Pombal had also met many people whose talents had been lost to Portugal since they had been exiled for their opposition to the Inquisition, but whose skills could be important in revitalising its economic fortunes. Consequently he regarded Jesuits as a particular threat to Portugal's economic future, whose close ties to the aristocracy and to the king made them especially dangerous.

Pombal's experience outside the country came to an end when João V died in 1750, and José I became king. Three days after the death of João V, Pombal was appointed a minister and, three days later, was chosen to head the Department of foreign affairs and war. Given José's

---

5. My major source on the career of Pombal is K. Maxwell, *Pombal: paradox of the Enlightenment* (Cambridge 1995), and on the reign of José I, H. V. Livermore, *A New history of Portugal* (Cambridge 1976).

lack of interest in state affairs, Pombal in time gained almost complete power over foreign policy. The king spent most of his days at his country estate in Belém and returned to confer with his ministers in the evening. Whether such conferences actually occurred is perhaps moot, but Pombal was able to gain and utilise his power in the name of the king until 1777. In his activities, Pombal was aided by others, including family members: two of his brothers were close collaborators in his administration. Paulo de Carvalho, a priest, was elevated by Pope Clement XIV. Pombal appointed him Inquisitor General (he had previously transformed the Inquisition into an independent court, that is, a royal court) and president of the municipal council of Lisbon, a position to which Pombal appointed his son, Henrique, when his brother died. Another brother, Francisco Xavier Mendonça Futado, served as governor and captain general of the Brazilian provinces of Grao Para and Maranhao, an area which then covered the entire Amazon valley. Later, he worked closely with Pombal as Secretary of State for overseas dominion.

Of course the involvement of family members was not unique to Portugal, but it provided a significant clue to Pombal's aspirations for his country and the direction of his efforts to reform it. For example, an expatriate friend, Duke Silva-Tarouca, whom Pombal had known in Vienna, recalled their conversations there and, on hearing of his appointment as minister, recommended to Pombal that 'when new dispositions are necessary, they should always be put forward by ancient names and in ancient clothing'. In effect, he was characterising Pombal's future direction – 'a policy of reform disguised, when necessary, by traditional institutions and language'.[6] This stance of using tradition has often been misunderstood by historians who have generally excluded Pombal from discussions of the Enlightenment or have characterised him as a 'despot', without any limiting adjectives. Maxwell, however, accurately subtitled his biography of Pombal, calling him a 'paradox of the Enlightenment'.

ii. The initial actions of Pombal as minister

Pombal, in his new position of responsibility, initiated a number of actions intended to strengthen the nation's control of its colonial empire and its domestic economy. When he came into office, there was ambiguity over boundaries in Portugal's holdings in South America. In the Treaty of Madrid (1750), Portugal agreed to relinquish control of Colonia do Sacremento and the land north of the river La Plata, in exchange for Spanish recognition of Portugal's rights to its river transportation system. The acceptance of these boundaries placed the Jesuit's Seven Missions

---

6. Maxwell, *Pombal*, p.9.

and their pasture land, long a part of Spanish control, under Portuguese rule. This agreement required the relocation of the Jesuits and their Indian converts. Under the terms of the treaty, some 30,000 Indians would be expected to relocate. The Indians chose to resist, and it was not until 1756, when a joint Spanish-Portuguese military force invaded the territory of the Seven Missions, that their resistance was ended. This experience reinforced Pombal's distrust of the Jesuits whom he blamed for the resistance.

Pombal's efforts in South America were assisted by his brother, Francisco Xavier de Mendonça Futado, who had been a member of the Luso-Spanish boundary commission which had decided that the Jesuits must move some of their holdings to conform to the new boundaries. Pombal later appointed his brother governor of Para and Maranhao in northern Brazil, to enforce the implementation of a form of state capitalism, the Grao Para Company. This company was intended to monopolise the trade of Brazil. It was not greeted with enthusiasm by Portuguese merchants already trading in Brazil, nor was it seen positively by the Jesuits and British merchants. (Pombal also banned independent small merchants who often sold goods to the British.) Objections to these changes were met by immediate sanctions. A sermon preached in the Patriarchal church there criticised Pombal's action. Such criticism could now be labelled as treasonous since the changes were new royal laws. The preacher was banished; three merchants involved in the Brazil trade were exiled to Africa and four Jesuits, who arrived in Lisbon soon after the earthquake, were expelled.

Pombal's acquisition of power also provoked many of the aristocracy to oppose him. While the number of nobles in Portugal was relatively small compared to other neighbouring countries, they were often at the centre of activities to undercut the king or to cultivate his possible successor. Traditionally, the nobility expected to be appointed as ambassadors or governors and be given other responsibilities in the royal court. But Pombal often appointed his family members and friends and publicly suggested that titles should be a reward for service, not lineage. By the end of his tenure in 1777, Pombal had retired twenty-three titles and created twenty-three, usually to reward merit, and so had changed one third of the nobility.[7] He also tried to minimise status differences. As was the practice in other European countries, he allowed merchants to wear swords, which previously had been an obvious mark of nobility. On occasion, when state companies were formed, he would appoint some noblemen to boards of directors with the stated hope that they might learn some relevant commercial skills.

Opposition to Pombal's actions came principally from the Jesuits, whose international viewpoint clashed directly with Pombal's nationalism, from

7. Maxwell, *Pombal*, p.78.

merchants who previously had advantages in the colonial trade, and from the aristocracy, distrustful of Pombal's increased power. Opposition to his policies, particularly collaboration among his enemies, was sure to evoke action on Pombal's part. Those 'enemies' continued to bedevil Pombal when he had to assume responsibility for the response and reconstruction following the earthquake.

iii. The consequences of the earthquake

The earthquake occurred in Lisbon at 9.40 am on 1 November when many of the residents were at mass, causing the first of a series of problems. Some time later a tsunami created additional victims and new damage. There was also a fire that lasted five to six days, destroying many of the buildings that had not been damaged by the earthquake. And Lisbon was plagued by aftershocks, over 500 in the next nine months.

Estimates of the number of lives lost varied tremendously. Franca cites ten estimates (the lowest 10,000 and the highest 90,000), and settles on 10,000, four per cent of the population, a figure for which he makes a strong case.[8] The deaths cut across social categories. Certainly several hundred priests and nuns were killed, and some twenty or thirty of the forty parish churches damaged. As Kendrick noted, many died 'unconfessed and unforgiven'.[9]

The major impacts were in the centre of the city, which contained significant art works and libraries. Being an international city, foreign victims were often the focus of widespread attention. The deaths of the Spanish ambassador, the head of the English Seminary and the grandson of the French dramatist Racine, provoked concern in other European countries. Seventy-seven members of the British Factory, most of them women, were among the casualties.

The number of houses damaged was considerable. Some estimates suggest that perhaps only 3000 out of 20,000 dwellings were habitable. Most certain was the damage to landmark public buildings. The Royal Palace was destroyed, but the king and his entourage had been at Belém, outside town, where the earthquake caused minimal damage. The Royal Opera House, finished the month before, was destroyed. The Royal Mint, Arsenal, and Custom House were gone. The church of the Inquisition and the church of the Patriarch were damaged. Some of the facilities for the busy port no longer existed and many merchants, including those from foreign companies, suffered significant losses. It was estimated that of the 48 million Spanish dollars losses, 32 million was the British share and perhaps 8 million were losses by Hamburg merchants.

8. J. A. Franca, *Lisbon Pombalina e o Ilumimismo* (Lisbon 1983).
9. Kendrick, *Lisbon earthquake*, p.26.

Obviously, the extent of the destruction of Lisbon's resources was a severe blow to Pombal's aspirations for Portugal's economic renewal. The young king, whose behaviour had already evidenced a lack of interest in affairs of the state, is supposed to have asked, 'What should we do?' And Pombal is supposed to have answered, 'Bury the dead and feed the living.'[10] That exchange, perhaps apocryphal, indicates a significant shift in political responsibility. The principal minister was old and ill, so the king gave Pombal total responsibility for dealing with the emergency response and later for managing the reconstruction.

A few months later when the principal minister died, Pombal assumed his position and the king retreated further into his personal concerns. In effect, Pombal ruled Portugal until 1777 when the king died.

iv. The emergency response

Pombal's assumption of responsibility for the emergency leads to a series of decisive actions which could provide a model for subsequent disasters, including some modern ones. Pombal's initial action was to ask the Chief Justice to appoint twelve district leaders with overarching emergency powers. The most pressing task was the disposal of bodies, since there was considerable fear of the outbreak of plague. The day after the earthquake, Pombal suggested to the Patriarch (the head of the church in Portugal) that the best way to dispose of the bodies was to collect them on barges in the Tagus river. These could then be weighted down and sunk. Although this meant disregarding traditional rites associated with death, the Patriarch agreed, and instructed the clergy involved in collecting the dead bodies of this decision. A number of emergency measures were instituted to ensure a continuing food supply. The military provided transportation for produce from the countryside and the price of food was controlled. Fishing was encouraged. Some traditional taxes on fish were suspended, if the fish were sold within the impacted area. Ships which were in port at the time were not allowed to leave until it had been determined that their contents could not be used in the emergency.

Housing, of course, was at a premium. The king and his family lived for nine months in tents outside the city, until a wooden palace was finished. Pombal, although his palace was undamaged, also lived in a hut in Belém. By the end of November, plans for a massive reconstruction were beginning to take shape. A survey was planned, land rents were controlled, and laws passed which forbade landlords from evicting tenants. The debris was sorted to salvage materials that could be used in the reconstruction. Initial profiteering in wood was controlled and supplies were sequestered. Building that did not conform to the planned construction was stopped.

---

10. Kendrick, *Lisbon earthquake*, p.48.

Security became an issue. It is reported that gallows were set up in several parts of the city as warnings against looting. It was noted that at least thirty-four people were executed for looting, but as usual it was claimed that most of them were 'foreigners'. Early in 1756, the Patriarch announced that excommunication would be the sanction for those posing as priests or nuns in order to get special advantages. It was feared that many people would leave the city, so those in charge of outlying provinces were instructed to send refugees back, and a pass system was set up to regulate entrance and exit from the city. There was, as might be expected, a concerted effort to maintain normality. The weekly newspaper, published just before the earthquake, kept to its schedule.

v. On delayed economic development and the earthquake

Obviously his responsibilities for emergency response and reconstruction interrupted Pombal's attempt to make Portugal economically viable and politically strong. He was particularly concerned as to how the earthquake would be interpreted by others. The next day, when he asked the Patriarch for permission to initiate mass burials, he also asked him to stop 'alarmist' sermons which were suggesting that the earthquake was a form of divine retribution for the 'sins' of Portugal. He worried that calls for devotional repentance might lead to personal withdrawal at a time when the city needed everyone for the tasks remaining. In the succeeding months, he was continually concerned about the prediction of future earthquakes as continued punishment. A spate of new predictions came as the first anniversary approached. Throughout this period, however, much of the temporary housing and the provision of food became the responsibility of the church, surviving churches became temporary facilities for those displaced, and there were no indications that Pombal was not supportive of the impressive actions of most clergy during the response. This suggests Pombal saw danger only in those religious practices and interpretations that might inhibit or delay the reconstruction process.

There were several opportunities in the aftermath to further Portugal's economic viability. Warships were sent to Brazil, India and Africa to indicate to those lands that trade with Portugal was still secure. Troops were sent to the Algarve to prevent African pirates from taking advantage of trade opportunities during the preoccupation with reconstruction. While taxes were temporarily suspended, a four per cent 'donation' was levied on all imports. Members of the British Factory objected to that 'tax' on the basis that previous treaties would exempt them, but the tax held. Pombal also used the earthquake to press his conflict with Jesuits and the aristocracy.

41

vi. The role of Malagrida

One man who personified all that Pombal had come to dislike was Gabriel Malagrida. Born in Italy in 1689, he had gone in 1721 as a Jesuit missionary to Brazil where he had restored decaying churches, established convents, and become famous for his fervent sermons and for stories about his adventures with Indians. His fame preceded him when he came to Portugal in 1749. His reputation and his knowledge of the colonies allowed him access to the palace, where he became confessor to King João. Malagrida's reputation grew when it was reported that the king had died in his arms, and he informed the queen that he would also act as her confessor when her time came. Malagrida returned to Brazil in 1751, travelling on the same boat as Pombal's brother, who was going to assume his administrative duties; but in 1753 he returned to Portugal and attached himself to the Queen Mother. But his influence now evoked suspicion. When she fell ill, he was forbidden entrance to her apartments, and returned to his house in Setubal. On 14 August 1754 he interrupted a sermon to announce the death of the queen. When that prediction was verified, his reputation as a prophet was enhanced. Many of those who encouraged him were members of the court opposed to Pombal. Malagrida specialised in holding retreats, which he suggested were necessary for everyone. He espoused hopes of building a permanent retreat house in Lisbon.

In the autumn of 1756, Malagrida published *Juízo da verdadeira causa do terremoto* (An opinion on the true cause of the earthquake), a summary of the sermons he had been preaching for the last year which suggested it was scandalous to pretend that the earthquake was a natural event. As the first anniversary of the disaster approached, he insisted that the people of Lisbon had returned to their sinful ways, including their love for theatre, music, dancing and bull fighting, that their efforts to repent were short-lived, and that they had to change their ways.

Malagrida advised the citizens that by going to a retreat at a Jesuit house for six days they could be properly instructed about making peace with God. The pamphlet structured the debate in rather stark terms: 'Learn, O Lisbon, that the destroyers of our houses, palaces, churches, and convents, the cause of the death of so many people and the flames that devoured such vast treasures, are your abominable sins, and not comets, stars, vapours and exhalations, and similar natural phenomena.'[11] That argument undermined the work of the parish priests and those of other orders, who had provided a significant service during the emergency response. Malagrida sent copies of his sermon to Pombal and to members of the royal family. He continued his retreats at Setubal, exhorting those who attended with his view on the 'causes' of the earthquake.

11. Kendrick, *Lisbon earthquake*, p.89.

Malagrida presented a particular problem for Pombal. A papal dispensation was necessary if the state were to act against a Jesuit. But for religious orders, turning someone over to state authorities was usually interpreted as an indication of guilt. The route of administrative sanction was too risky for Pombal and he acted with considerable indirection. In May 1757 he ordered the secularisation of civil powers in Para, extinguishing the missions and declaring the Indians free. Jesuits were limited to the duties of parish priests. Then, when the priests removed sacred images from the churches, they were informed that these were now state property. There was also the charge that the Jesuits were armed, although they claimed that their small cannons were only ceremonial. In September, when the royal confessor in Lisbon had become sufficiently alarmed about this tension in the colonies between the state and the Jesuits, he found his access to the king blocked. Then the royal confessor and other Jesuits in the palace were ejected and forbidden to return without the king's permission. Their previous duties were reallocated to members of other orders – Franciscans, Augustinians and Carmelites.

Pombal later sent his cousin to seek a secret audience with the Pope to push for reform of the Jesuits, claiming that they were attempting to usurp the power of the sovereign and that they had an insatiable desire for wealth. Early in 1758, Pombal wrote a widely translated tract accusing the Jesuits of attempting to create their own state. And in April, the Pope (Benedict XIV) authorised the Cardinal-Patriarch to reform the Society in Portugal. In May, the Cardinal prohibited the Jesuits from engaging in illegal commerce, and in June Jesuits were forbidden to preach or hear confessions, and their superior was banned from Lisbon. Malagrida appealed to the new Pope, Clement XIII, in the following words:

What a fatal scene. What a grievous spectacle! What a sudden metamorphosis! The heralds of the word of God expelled from the Missions, proscribed and condemned to ignominy. ...and who does this? Not his most Faithful Majesty,... but the minister Carvalho, whose will is supreme at court. He, yes, he, has been the architect of so many disasters and seeks to darken the splendour of our Society, which dazzles his livid eyes, with a flood of bigoted writings that breathe an immense, virulent, implacable hatred. If he could behead all the Jesuits at one blow, with what pleasure would he do so?[12]

In September of that year, Pombal took advantage of an incident to weaken his traditional enemies further. The king was returning to Belém late in the evening after an amorous adventure when he was ambushed and shot several times. Although rumours were circulated that he had been ambushed by some of the nobility, nothing was done for over three months. In December, a royal decree was issued to create a special court to investigate the attempt. It waived customary legal protection and allowed the court to sentence and execute the guilty on the same day.

12. Livermore, *A New history*, p.227-28.

It also accused certain persons of prophesying the king's death and of conspiring to bring it about. Troops were sent to arrest six titled persons, their families and servants. Malagrida and twelve other Jesuits were arrested and all the Jesuit colleges were surrounded by troops. The two major conspirators were the Duke of Aveiro, the highest ranking noble after the royal family and head of the supreme court, and the marquês de Tavora, who had been a general and Viceroy of India.

A new voice was added to the political landscape when the Casa dos Vinte Quatro, an urban municipal council of the guilds, expressed the desire of 'the people' that the guilty should be punished, that the trial should be held in secret and that the king should be permitted to use torture. Later the Casa exhorted the king to 'withdraw unwonted clemency', in other words, to act harshly.

Sentence was pronounced and executions held on 12 January 1759. On a scaffold in Belém, various guilty parties were beheaded, broken on a rack and burnt. The whole scaffold was then set alight and the ashes of nobles and their servants scattered in the Tagus river. This event received considerable attention throughout Europe, since high-ranking nobles had seldom been punished in this way. The episode reinforced the view of outsiders that Portugal was 'backward'.

The ecclesiastical 'suspects' still presented a problem. The priests were confined to their colleges. The Pope agreed that any priests involved in the assassination attempt could be tried in secular court, but hoped the king would not condemn all for the offences of a few. But the Pope's message was never delivered to Pombal. On 3 September 1759, the anniversary of the assassination attempt, a royal edict was issued identifying the crimes of the Jesuits. It outlawed them from Portugal. Jesuits then in Portugal were sent to Rome and those in Brazil arrived in Rome by sea the following year. All, that is, except Malagrida and others in prison. Malagrida was to be condemned as a heretic by the Inquisition. Since the extant Inquisitor-General was not too keen to supervise this proceeding, Pombal's younger brother, Paulo de Carvalho, took his place. Pombal himself drew the first indictment, in which Malagrida was charged with planning regicide from his house in Sebutal. He was also charged with heresy for some of his writings, not, however, his discourse on the causes of the earthquake. He was found guilty on 12 January 1761 and publicly executed on 20 September, just under six years after the earthquake. The rather spectacular auto-da-fé lasted all day, two hours of which were devoted to reading his sentence. Malagrida was strangled and his body was later burned and his ashes thrown in the river.

vii. The reconstruction

One of Pombal's first actions after the earthquake was to appoint several military engineers and surveyors to make inventories of property rights and claims, and to assure that the sanitary and levelling operations were carried out safely and with dispatch. The engineers were also charged with drawing up plans for a new city. The waterfront area and the zone back from the river Tagus to Rossio Square were levelled and the rather steep western slopes reduced. Streets were fixed at 60 feet in width – 50 feet for the roadway and 10 feet for pavements. Street crossings were set at right angles. To speed up reconstruction and encourage local enterprises, efforts were made to prefabricate and standardise materials which would be needed: ironworks, wood joints, tiles and ceramics. A wooden frame, called a *gaiola*, which had flexibility in the event of future earthquakes, was mandated for all construction, and a standardised façade was required for the new buildings. These innovations were used later in the construction of new buildings at the University of Coimbra and in the construction of a new town in the Algarve on the Spanish border. The plans drawn for reconstruction included a great square on the waterfront which would be the centrepiece of the rebuilt city. The new square, placed on the old Royal plaza was, and still is, called the Praça do Comércio – the commerce square. Its name reflects the direction that Pombal intended for the future of Portugal.

The ongoing reconstruction of Lisbon was only one part of Pombal's transformation. Woloch has suggested that, in the eighteenth century, a ruler's success could be measured by the extent to which he or she developed a monopoly over coercion, taxation, administration and law-making.[13] In the 1760s, Pombal was concerned with a series of 'solutions' to continuing problems. In particular, there was the creation of a new system of public education to replace Jesuit education, and a new curriculum more attuned to educating people other than just the nobility. There was the assertion of national authority in religious and church administration. There was strengthening of the state's taxing authority, military capabilities and security. In the 1760s, Pombal established the office of general supervisor of police and of the court of the kingdom. The legislation necessary for these new measures was, in all cases, codified and systemised, with the reasoning outlined and justified. Attention continued to be given to colonial policy. Pombal's brother joined the cabinet as Minister of Overseas Dominion, and moved quickly to create a new commercial company to control the major centres of Brazilian commerce and production in the sugar-producing regions. In 1761, a royal treasury – a key element in Pombal's efforts to rationalise and centralise – was established. The aim of the treasury was to centralise jurisdiction for all fiscal matters and to be responsible for different sectors, from customs houses to the allocation of royal monopolies: Pombal appointed himself Inspector General. This completed his reform of revenue collection. Finally, certain changes were made in the Inquisition.

13. Woloch, *Eighteenth-century Europe*, p.4.

The Inquisition's police powers were given to the police in 1768 and its role in book censorship was assumed by a royal commission that year. In 1769, Pombal removed the Inquisition's power to act as an independent tribunal and all the property confiscated by the Inquisition was transferred to the national treasury. Public autos-da-fé were eliminated, as was the death penalty.

By June 1775 the reconstruction of Lisbon had progressed far enough to hold a dedication of the Praca, adorned with the equestrian statue of José I. For the three-day celebration, the unfinished buildings around the square were filled in with wood and canvas to give an impression of what the final effect would be. Several days after the celebration, Pombal sent José I a series of reflections in which he described their 'joint' accomplishments. These included improvements in literacy, industry and culture, and Pombal indicated that the square indicated prosperity – that 'observant foreigners did not fail to remark about the millions spent in public and private buildings after the earthquake. They saw a most magnificent square surpassing all others in Europe.'[14]

José died on 24 February 1777. The next day, when Pombal arrived at the palace, Cardinal de Cunha met him and told him, 'Your Excellency no longer has anything here to do.'[15] Twenty years before, as an archbishop, de Cunha had issued a pastoral letter against the Jesuits at Pombal's request. But with José's death, the opposition that Pombal had repressed during his tenure coalesced quickly and with certain vengeance. Pombal spent the rest of his life defending himself and his past accomplishments against charges of abuses of power. In 1781, Don Marie I intervened in the persistent attacks and declared that although Pombal deserved 'exemplary punishment', no formal proceedings would be initiated because of his age and feeble condition. Pombal died the following year. In one sense his enemies had finally won. But most of the changes he had made prepared the transition that was necessary for Portugal to move toward a modern state. Maxwell concludes that 'The story of Pombal's administration is, therefore, an important antidote to the overly linear and progressive view of the role of the eighteenth-century enlightenment in Europe and the relationship between the Enlightenment and the exercise of state power.'[16]

viii. Final comments

The Lisbon earthquake can be called the first modern disaster. It happened as Portugal was developing into a more centralised and 'modern' state. No other European country going through the state building

14. Livermore, *A New history*, p.237-38.
15. Livermore, *A New history*, p.238.
16. Maxwell, *Pombal*, p.161.

process had to deal with the destruction of its capital city. But Portugal has never been considered a useful case study of state building in the eighteenth century. The key eighteenth-century figures, of interest to later historians, were those whose actions seemed to strengthen liberty rather than those who used power. In this context, Pombal is usually identified with abuses of power rather than for his accomplishments in organising the first modern governmental response to a major disaster, as well as his insistence on defining the earthquake as a 'natural' event. His example suggests that a 'natural' explanation of disaster is closely tied to the state building process.

In his monumental work on the 'civilising' process, Norbert Elias focuses on generalised causes of state building.[17] In particular, he traces the struggles between the nobility, the church and the princes, and later the emergence of the bourgeoisie. In that struggle, Elias says, there is a gradual accumulation of land, then money, in fewer and fewer hands. This tends toward a monopoly, which he labels the 'royal mechanism'. In this process, what was previously the private power of individuals gradually becomes public or state power until one social unit, the state, is able to control more and more opportunities. This process is enhanced by the state's gaining control of both physical violence and taxation. The development of centralisation and monopolisation means that what was previously achieved by military or economic force becomes amenable to planning by the state.

We cannot infer that Pombal substituted a naturalistic interpretation of the earthquake since, at the time, no well differentiated 'scientific' theory existed. It is possible that Pombal was familiar with Thomas Burnet's *The Sacred theory of the earth* which argued that, since God operated through natural processes, the biblical flood could be explained in scientific terms.[18] Burnet's theory, which also had an explanation for earthquakes, was being widely discussed in England when Pombal was there, and it was also a topic of interest for Enlightenment intellectuals.

There are indications that Pombal did act to introduce new ideas and structures in his reforms. He was interested in movements such as gallicanism and regalism, which give more autonomy to 'national' churches against Rome and the Pope. In his educational reforms at the university, he sought to modernise the faculties of theology and canon law. Two new faculties were created, mathematics and philosophy, which included the new natural sciences, based on observation and experiment. In his transfer of censorship from the Inquisition to the state, he appointed persons more identified with reformist ideas, so that previously banned books by Locke and Montesquieu were released, although books that contained 'irreligion' were still not allowed. One of Pombal's closest col-

17. Norbert Elias, *Power and civility: the civilizing process*, vol.ii (New York 1982).
18. Thomas Burnet, *The Sacred theory of the earth* (1691; reprinted Carbondale, IL 1965).

laborators in educational and ecclesiastical reform, Antonio Ribeiro dos Santos, commented on the paradox of the authoritarian and enlightenment strains in his actions, writing that Pombal 'wanted to civilise the nation and at the same time to enslave it. He wanted to spread the light of the philosophical sciences and at the same time to elevate the royal power of despotism.'[19] This suggests that, in the context of institutional change, there is seldom a direct confrontation between equivalent ideologies. Instead some interpretations begin to erode, and over time other ideologies are substituted.

Extending these ideas, Stallings has recently explained the implications for sociological theory of the way disasters disrupt social routines.[20] The state has increasingly assumed control over such disruptions, since disasters create a threat to the social order. One of the state's major functions is to promote political order and social stability, since predictability is necessary for decision making and strategic planning. Stallings says that 'the state's' disaster role is to minimise the disruptions to economic routines as quickly as possible when they are disrupted.[21]

Unique turning points in history cannot be easily determined by comparative and/or longitudinal analysis, but the case study of the Lisbon earthquake suggests certain reasonable conclusions. With the development of the modern state in Europe in the eighteenth century, notions of the state's responsibility for the welfare of 'citizens' and for the continuity of society make the Lisbon earthquake a test case for these changes. Changes in the social structure in Portugal, especially changes in the political and economic sectors, made the earthquake especially problematic. The Lisbon earthquake was the first modern disaster in the sense that the state accepted responsibility for mobilising the emergency response and for developing and implementing a comprehensive plan for reconstruction. In order to support these efforts, traditional notions of supernatural causes were rather harshly opposed. This opposition was not directed toward the Portuguese Church itself, but toward those segments of the Church with more international and universal aspirations, in particular the Jesuits. This shift in interpreting disaster did not stem from those ideas concerning the nature of authority and liberty that have come to be identified as the Enlightenment, but from the efforts of Pombal to build a Portugal which was economically and politically more secure in the context of a competitive Europe.

In *Candide*, Voltaire uses the Lisbon earthquake as the backdrop for criticising optimism, which he saw as prevalent among intellectuals. The entire work is filled with ironic images and situations, and includes a discussion between Candide and Pangloss of the sufficient cause of the

19. Cited in Boxer, *The Portuguese empire*, p.191.
20. R. Stallings, 'Disaster and the theory of social order', in *What is disaster? Perspectives on the question*, ed. E. L. Quarantelli (London 1998), p.127-45.
21. Stallings, 'Disaster', p.142.

earthquake, as well as a discussion with a member of the Inquisition who is arguing for an interpretation of the earthquake as a consequence of sin. Voltaire says, 'After the earthquake, which had destroyed three fourths of Lisbon, the Portuguese pundits could not think of any better way of preventing total ruin than to treat the people to a splendid *auto da fe.*' Thus Voltaire missed the ultimate irony – that the last victim of the Inquisition was Malagrida who had insisted on a religious interpretation of the earthquake.

DIEGO TÉLLEZ ALARCIA

Spanish interpretations of the Lisbon earthquake between 1755 and the war of 1762[1]

Introduction

IT is clear that the shock waves produced by the 'first modern cata-strophe', as the Lisbon earthquake of 1755 has been defined,[2] demolished more than just buildings in the heart of enlightened Europe. As if the effects of these shock waves had filtered into the minds of the leading intellectuals and politicians of the time, the earthquake shattered old prejudices, prompting new and controversial interpretations of the dis-aster, stirring consciences and immersing the Old Continent in the troubled waters of scientific, political, moral and philosophical debate.

After Portugal, Spain – because of its proximity to the centre of the earthquake – was the area most affected by the phenomenon. Any assessment of the cultural impact of the disaster must start with a review of its physical impact.[3] Fortunately, we have an invaluable historical source which allows us to do this: the damage assessment report com-missioned by the government of Fernando IV. A total of 1273 Spanish towns and cities responded to the royal request, yielding an exceptional documentary corpus that can be used to prepare a detailed account of the true impact of the catastrophe.[4]

The survey consisted of eight questions, which can be summarised as follows: 1) Was the earthquake felt? 2) At what time? 3) How long did it

1. This article is included in the research projects entitled 'Redes clientelares a mediados del XVIII español', which is funded by the Spanish Ministry of Science and Technology and the University of La Rioja (Ref. BHA2003-07360) and 'El terremoto de Lisboa de 1755 en La Rioja', which is funded by the I Plan Riojano of I + D of the Government of La Rioja.

2. Russell R. Dynes, 'The Lisbon earthquake in 1755: the first modern disaster', p.34-49, of the present volume.

3. Charles D. James and Jan Kozak, 'Representations of the 1755 Lisbon earthquake', and Malcolm Jack, 'Destruction and regeneration: Lisbon, 1755', p.21-33 and p.7-20 respectively, of the present volume.

4. The replies to the survey are kept in the National Historical Archive (Madrid) and the Royal Academy of History (Madrid). Both sources of information complement each other because neither has preserved the documentation in its entirety. Martínez Solares has transcribed all the sources that he has managed to locate in both institutions: José Manuel Martínez Solares, *Los Efectos en España del terremoto de Lisboa de 1 de noviembre de 1755* (Madrid 2001).

last? 4) What movements were observed on the ground, walls, buildings, fountains and rivers? 5) What damage or financial loss was caused in factories? 6) Were any people or animals killed or injured? 7) Did anything else remarkable happen? 8) Before it happened, were there any warning signs?

Thanks to this information, we know that most deaths were attributable to the tsunami effects, which, in the Gulf of Cádiz, reached an intensity of 3-4 on the Imamura-Iida scale, killing around 1200 people (Martínez Solares' estimate for total deaths is 1275).

Material damage recorded, above all, in buildings (for example, 6.5 per cent of Seville's houses destroyed, 89 per cent damaged), has been estimated at 53,157,936 copper reales (old currency equivalent to one quarter of a peseta), rising to as much as 70,250,070. Converting these amounts into modern currency is not easy. Martínez Solares values the damage at somewhere in the region of 507 million euros.[5] To get a sense of the impact of the material damage, we can compare these figures with those documented at the time by the Royal Treasury of Fernando VI. According to Pieper, the expenses of the Spanish monarchy in 1755 amounted to 334,644,000 reales. Based on this figure, the cost would have amounted to nearly 21 per cent of the money spent in this year. If compared with the figure of 1756 we obtain the same 21 per cent (337,736,000 reales of expenses).

If this is compared to revenues (341,825,000 in 1755 and 358,150,000 in 1756), we obtain a figure of 20.5 per cent of revenue for 1755 and 19.6 per cent for 1756. Compared to specific expense or revenue items, the recorded damage costs would amount to the equivalent of the taxes collected from the provinces (one of the treasury's main sources of income) for both 1755 and 1756, whereas damage estimates would be similar to state naval expenses in 1756 (76,948,000 reales) and more than double the expenditure of the royal family over the same two years.[6] But only a portion of Spain suffered material damage from the earthquake and tsunami. If this damage was experienced in just one sixth of the nation (Andalusia above all), then the impact in these affected regions would have been much more significant than the 20 per cent figures mentioned above.[7]

Taking this data as a starting point, this study aims: to determine the nature of the cultural impact; to analyse the diachronic evolution of

5. Data obtained from Martínez Solares, *Los Efectos en España*, p.74-79. Unsatisfied, he made an even more daring assessment: he quantified the damage that would be caused by an earthquake of identical characteristics in the year 2000 at 2.4 million euros, excluding indirect damage to the economy.

6. Data obtained from Renate Pieper, *La Real Hacienda bajo Fernando VI y Carlos III, 1753-1788* (Madrid 1992), p.99 and p.161.

7. One regional example (Catalonia) is available in Pilar López, Miguel Arranz, Carme Olivera, and Antoni Roca, 'Contribución al estudio del terremoto de Lisboa del 1 de noviembre de 1755: observaciones en Cataluña', in *Materials of CEC project review of historical seismicity in Europe*, ed. P. Albini and A. Moroni (Milan 1994).

the interpretation of the earthquake in Spain between 1755 and 1762; and to highlight the political, social and religious factors that conditioned this interpretation between 1755 and 1762.

i. The Lisbon earthquake and Spain: cultural impact

Writing primarily about France, Russell R. Dynes reports that the cultural reaction to the disaster became immediately apparent through the 'generation of a popular literature which described the destruction, speculated on the causes and drew moral conclusions. This literature included newspaper discussions, entire books, essays, long poems, eye-witness accounts and theatre presentations.'[8] As we shall see, the same occurred in Spain.

Throughout Europe, one of the most interesting reactions in these cultural circles was philosophical. Towards the end of 1755 Voltaire wrote his famous 'Poème sur le désastre de Lisbonne', its subtitle – 'Un examen de cet axiome: "tout est bien" ' – indicating the direction that his verses would take. This axiom was the *leitmotiv* of the theorising of Leibniz and Pope, which attempted to reconcile divine goodwill and the evil caused to man at any cost. This theorising would be refuted using the same earthquake as decisive empirical evidence that 'God, the Christian God in particular, has no pity or excuse for this sudden, terrible catastrophe, the cause of so much gratuitous, undeserved and unjustified suffering.'[9] Voltaire's poem is a clear symptom that something had changed in the minds of Europe's intellectual elite, as a consequence of a complete cultural process that had already been set in motion. The Lisbon earthquake can be identified as a turning point in human history. It marked the transition from such physical events being regarded as supernatural signals to a more neutral or even a secular, proto-scientific view of their causes. It was the catalyst for an intellectual revolution that had been gestating for decades, 'a process that distances the new urban groups from the naive, fatalistic and superstitious faith of the past'.[10]

In certain circles – although not in all – the traditional explanations of divine punishment were being questioned, and other new theories began

8. Russell R. Dynes, 'The dialogue between Voltaire and Rousseau on the Lisbon earthquake: the emergence of a social science view', *International journal of mass emergencies and disasters* 18:1 (March 2000), p.97-115. On this subject, Dynes referred to Thomas Downing Kendrick, *The Lisbon earthquake* (London 1956).

9. Fernando Escalante, 'Voltaire mira el terremoto de Lisboa (1)', *Cuadernos hispanoamericanos* 600 (2000), p.69-82 (p.69). This article is continued in Fernando Escalante, 'Voltaire mira el terremoto de Lisboa (2)', *Cuadernos hispanoamericanos* 601-02 (2000), p.139-52.

10. Escalante, 'Voltaire mira el terremoto de Lisboa (1)', p.71. He concluded thus: 'old explanations are beginning to run out of steam, the mechanisms that allowed the daily transformation of pain into sacrifice', p.75.

to circulate. Rousseau's response to Voltaire seems to be a paradigm in this sense, because 'he introduced for the first time, a social science view of disaster [and he] launched into a discussion which can best be described as the first truly social scientific view of disaster':[11] 'Without departing from your subject of Lisbon, admit, for example, that nature did not construct twenty thousand houses of six to seven stories there, and that if the inhabitants of this great city had been more equally spread out and more lightly lodged, the damage would have been much less and perhaps of no account.'[12]

This type of reasoning was not exclusive to the French. In 1760 in England, Adam Smith published his article on the Lisbon earthquake, associating the tremors with wave movements in the earth's crust for the first time.[13] Kant would later approach the problem in metaphysical terms.[14]

Meanwhile in Portugal, the minister Pombal used the earthquake 'to consolidate his power and to move Portugal out of its backward status toward the beginnings of a modern state', using 'his political skill and the Church itself to undercut the traditional interpretation that the earthquake was a signal of God's displeasure'.[15]

But what happened in the second most affected country?

On the one hand, the Lisbon earthquake caused a great popular demand for published materials on the disaster. Spanish readers studied eagerly the 'Relaciones' on the catastrophe. There were plenty of 'accounts' or 'news items' which offered more or less accurate descriptions of what happened, mainly in Portugal. Some opportunistic authors seized the occasion to publish very poor works, which were still extremely profitable. The school established by Torres de Villarroel followed this line.[16]

Within the Spanish administration, a more pragmatic and social dimension of the earthquake can be identified, as in the case of Rousseau.

---

11. Dynes, 'The dialogue between Voltaire and Rousseau', p.103, 106. Voltaire's concern for the earthquake is famous (*Candide*, 1759). Less well known is the letter written by Rousseau to Voltaire on 18 August 1756.

12. Jean-Jacques Rousseau, *The Collected writings of Rousseau*, ed. Roger D. Masters and Christopher Kelly (Hanover, NH 1990), iii.110.

13. Martínez Solares, *Los Efectos en España*, p.91.

14. Gemma Vicente, 'El terremoto de Lisboa y el problema del mal en Kant', *Themata, revista de filosofía* 3 (1986), p.141-52.

15. Dynes, 'The Lisbon earthquake', p.3. Sebastião José de Carvalho e Melo was the Secretary of Foreign Affairs and War. In 1756 he was appointed Home Secretary of the Negotiations of the Kingdom, Count of Oeiras (1759) and Marquis of Pombal (1769). We use the latter title since this is the one that has been used most often in historiography.

16. A good example is Isidoro Francisco Ortiz Gallardo de Villarroel, *Lecciones entretenidas y curiosas physico-astrológicas sobre la generación, causas y señales de los terremotos y especialmente de las causas, señales y varios efectos del sucedido en España en el día primero de noviembre del año passado de 1755* (Salamanca, Antonio José Villagordo, 1756). Sánchez-Blanco said very cleverly about it that 'it is a pseudoscientific pursuit of somebody that takes advantage of the situation to sell printed papers' (Francisco Sánchez-Blanco Parody, *La Mentalidad ilustrada*, Madrid 1999, p.368).

Thus, for instance, the abovementioned 'survey' was organised to identify all the damage sustained in the country. A native of Lima was charged to draw a report on the earthquakes in this part of the world in order to know what buildings would survive and what measures might be taken to protect them. The text is part of the private archive of one of the main Spanish civil servants and intellectuals of the second half of the century, Pedro Rodríguez de Campomanes.[17]

Apart from popular curiosity and the concern of the government, the disaster also led to a debate between theologians and philosophers, between providentialistic and deistic postures, between natural and supernatural explanations. This debate was particularly relevant in Seville.[18] The main forums of this controversy were the Academia de Buenas Letras, the Tertulia Médica, the press, and, of course, the pulpits.

On the one hand, in a theistic or providentialistic line, there were 'pastoral notices summoning people to prayer', moralising 'sermons' or ecclesiastical 'circulars'. An example: 'Earth tremors are a clear indication of divine displeasure [...] The earth trembled, said David, and the mountains shook because God was angry with men. There is no reason to attribute the earthquake to the influence of the stars nor to fear their signs [...] Nor should we attribute it to insensitive creatures, which are merely instruments of Divine Justice.'[19]

These included more religious than scientific works, one particularly interesting variant being the miracle workings of saints devoted to protecting people from earthquakes. Francisco San Cristóbal, for example, proposes San Egmidio as main protector.[20] However, the Jesuits proposed a saint of their order, San Francisco Borja, as the 'perfect advocate',[21] whereas the Oratonians extolled the efficacy of San Felipe Neri in such cases.[22] The secular clergy, more in contact with the local traditions, highlighted the figures of Santa Justa and Santa Rufina, who, according to the local tradition, had already braced the Giralda with their hands

17. Madrid, Fundación Universitaria Española, Archive of Campomanes, bundle 38/5, *Sobre los terremotos (1755)*.

18. Francisco Aguilar Piñal, 'Conmoción espiritual provocada en Sevilla por el terremoto de 1755', *Archivo Hispalense* 56 (1973), p.37-44.

19. Francisco José Figueredo y Victoria, *Pastoral letter, exorting penitence, sent by Don Francisco Joseph de Figueredo, y Victoria, the Archbishop of this Holy Metropolitan Church, to the clergy, in the city of Guatemala, and to the people of his diocese, in connection with the earthquake that had such a devastating effect on the City of Lisbon, in Portugal, and on other parts of Europe and the Coasts of Africa last year on 1 November 1755* (Guatemala, Joachim de Arévalo, 1756), p.6-7.

20. Francisco San Cristóbal, *Vida, martyrio y milagros del apóstol de Ascoli, el sr. S. Egmidio, especialísimo protector en los terremotos* (Seville 1756).

21. *Relación de los patronatos que tiene San Francisco de Borja en varios Reynos y Ciudades de la Christiandad contra los Terremotos, y beneficios que con dichos Patronatos recibieron sus habitantes: sacada de varios autores* (Madrid, Imprenta de la viuda de Manuel Fernández, 1755).

22. *Patrocinio admirable del glorioso patriarcha y perfectíssimo modelo del Estado Eclesiástico San Phelipe Neri, segundo thaumaturgo y especial avogado en tiempo de terremotos. Sácalo a la luz pública la devoción de sus hijos para excitar al Pueblo Sevillano acudan a su Patrocinio en semejantes calamidades* (Seville, Imp. de los Recientes, 1755).

before, and in Cádiz, the Virgen del Rosario was the chosen one.[23] The frequency of earthquakes in Spanish America had already given rise to these types of works.[24] Sánchez-Blanco noted that 'several ecclesiastic groups compete to offer intercessors with God's will'.[25]

On the other hand, the Lisbon earthquake also generated, in Spain as well as elsewhere in Europe, huge controversy over its natural causes. After reviewing and ruling out the main explanatory theories since the time of Thales of Miletus, Nipho suggested that the ultimate cause of earthquakes was sun and 'gas' disturbance.[26] Meanwhile, Feijoo designed a new system ascribing the speed of the 1755 tremors to electrical phenomena.[27] This theory was based on rudimentary experiments with 'electrical machines', which were applied to the physical world by supposing the presence of sulphuric and bituminous substances in the subsoil. This is how Feijoo explained why two cities as far apart as Cádiz and Oviedo felt the tremors at the same time. The great earthquakes could therefore be explained, while smaller quakes were still attributed to collapsing underground caverns.[28]

López de Amezua defended the hypothesis of the underground fire. He thought that the earth had pockets of flammable materials linked by channels and caverns that facilitated their explosion and diffusion. He also believed that the original impulse was transmitted as a wave and that a relevant factor to explain the effects of earthquakes was the differences in consistency between the materials that made up the earth's crust. In other words, a purely mechanical explanation can be intuited in this theory of

23. Francisco García Colorado, *La Voz de Dios oída en el terremoto acaecido el día primero de Noviembre* (Madrid, Francisco Javier García, 1755).

24. An example: Fray José Cabezas, *Historia prodigiosa de la admirable aparición y milagrosos portentos de la imagen soberana de María Santísima Nuestra Señora de la Soterraña de Nieva, especialísima defensora de truenos, rayos, centellas y terremotos* (Mexico, Imp. del Nuevo Rezado, 1748).

25. Sánchez-Blanco, *La Mentalidad ilustrada*, p.247. Finally, this conflict was settled with a general consensus on the election of the Inmaculada Concepción de la Virgen María (Blessed Virgin Mary), which was ratified by the Pope Benedicto XIV some years later.

26. Francisco Mariano Nipho, *Explicación physica y moral de las causas, señales, diferencias y efectos de los terremotos: con una relación muy exacta de los mas formidables* [...] *que ha padecido la tierra desde el principio del mundo hasta el que se ha experimentado en España y Portugal el día primero de noviembre de* [...] *1755* (Madrid, Herederos de Agustín de Gordejuela, 1756).

27. Fray Benito Feijoo, *Nuevo Systhema sobre la causa physica de los terremotos, explicado por los phenómenos eléctricos y adaptado al que padeció España en el primero de noviembre de 1755. Su autor el Ilmo y Rmo Sr. D. Fr. Benito Feijoo. Dedicado a la Muy erudita, Regia y esclarecida Academia Portopolitana por D. Juan Luis Roche* (Puerto de Santa María, Casa Real de las Cadenas, 1756).

28. Other works by Feijoo: *Copia de carta escrita por el Ilmo y Rmo P. Mro. Fr. Feijoo a cierto caballero de la ciudad de Sevilla en que apunta algunas noticias pertenecientes a los terremotos* (Seville, José Navarro y Armijo, 1756); and *El Terremoto y su uso. Dictamen del Rmo P. M. Fr. Feijoo explorado por el Licenciado Juan de Zúñiga* (Toledo, Francisco Martín, 1756). For an analysis of his thought, see Nigel Glendinning, 'El padre Feijoo ante el terremoto de Lisboa', *Cuadernos de la Cátedra Feijoo* 18:2 (1966), p.353-65.

the fire.[29] Antonio Jacobo del Barco, professor of philosophy and member of the Academia de Buenas Letras in Seville, advanced with more precision than his contemporaries the 'vibratory' nature of earthquakes, and compared it to waves.[30]

This complex panorama offers a fairly accurate picture of Spanish society in the mid-eighteenth century; a society still imbued with old prejudices, where the Church was still all-powerful, but which was slowly opening its doors to the ideas and fruits of the Enlightenment.[31] Sánchez-Blanco summarised the situation to perfection: 'The "theist" position, according to which God intervenes voluntarily and consciously in natural phenomena, was upheld in the pulpits. On the other hand, the press represented, using the speech of that time, the "deist" position, according to which the Universe has its own eternal laws established by a Supreme Intellect who does not need to correct Himself all the time.'[32]

ii. The Lisbon earthquake and political power

Far beyond the philosophical disputes, the various ruling powers tried from the outset to use the catastrophe to their advantage. In Portugal it was Pombal who tried to suppress any providentialistic interpretations. One case that he failed to suppress was that of Malagrida, a Jesuit who took advantage of the pervading climate of fear and fervour in Lisbon to publish his *Juízo da verdadeira causa do terremoto* in October 1756. In it he stated his vision clearly: 'Learn, O Lisbon, that the only destroyers of so many houses and palaces, temples and convents, the slaughterers of so many inhabitants and the flaming devourers of so many treasures are not comets, they are not stars, gases or exaltations, they are not phenomena, nor are they hazards or natural causes, rather they are simply our own intolerable sins.'[33] But, in the end, Pombal was successful. He managed to banish Malagrida who ended up on the scaffold.

29. Fernando López de Amezua, *Historia de los Phenómenos observados en el terremoto que sintió esta Península el día 1 de noviembre de 1755*, in Juan Galisteo, *Diario philosóphico, médito, chirúrgico. Colección de selectas observaciones y curiosos fragmentos sobre la Historia Natural, Physica y Medicina* (Madrid, Antonio Pérez de Soto, 1757).

30. Antonio Jacobo del Barco, 'Carta del Doctor Barco satisfaciendo algunas preguntas curiosas sobre el terremoto del primero de noviembre de 1755', in Juan Enrique de Graef, *Discursos mercuriales* 3:13 (21 April 1756), p.566-605.

31. See the controversial work of Francisco Sánchez-Blanco Parody, *El Absolutismo y las Luces en el reinado de Carlos III* (Madrid 2002) for more information on the problem of the Enlightenment in Spain.

32. Sánchez-Blanco, *La Mentalidad ilustrada*, p.268-69.

33. Gabriel Malagrida, *Juízo da verdadeira causa do terremoto* (Lisbon, Offic. de Manoel Soares, 1756). The conflict between the church and the state had been latent in Portugal for some time (the same was true in Spain) and regalism was gaining followers in both countries. The disgrace of the Jesuits was to be the result of this struggle and the Lisbon earthquake helped to strengthen the power of the Jesuits' enemies (like Pombal) in Portugal.

But the most interesting work for us is the essay of the French adventurer Ange Goudar, a friend of Casanova, a work entitled *Relation historique du tremblement de terre survenu à Lisbonne le premier Novembre 1755*, which contains a *Discours politique sur les avantages que les Portugais pourraient retirer de leur malheur et dans lequel on développe les moyens que l'Angleterre avait mis en usage pour ruiner le Portugal.*[34] The first edition of the work was published in The Hague in 1756 (ed. Philantrope). Some copies of the *Discours*, which very soon began to be distributed as a separate unit, indicate Lisbon as the place of publication.

Since the Royal Academy of History (Madrid) keeps a handwritten copy in Portuguese that perhaps also travelled to Lisbon, it seems that someone attempted to publish this book in Portuguese, possibly in Portugal.[35] (The French government, then at war with England, was probably unaware of the whole operation.) But since Pombal managed to prevent its publication, the indication of Lisbon as the place of publication is false. The British Library corroborates this fact in its catalogued record of the work ('The imprint is fictitious, printed at The Hague').[36] Furthermore, Philantrope was located in The Hague. Indeed, no Portuguese version was available until 1808.

The contents of the *Discours* were particularly unfavourable to Pombal's interests, since it criticised the superstition of the people and the alliance between Portugal and England (p.4-5):

I found a monarchy that had run out of steam, weakened by revolutions, disturbed by hidden sects and impoverished by its own wealth. A people repressed by superstition, a nation whose customs bore a striking resemblance to those of Barbarians and a State governed by Asian half-breeds whose only Europeanness was in the form of a puppet monarchy [...] The mines of Brazil can be said to belong entirely to England. Portugal is merely an administrator of its own wealth.

These circumstances were blamed for all the ills that had befallen Portugal, including the earthquake: 'Finally Physics too became mixed up in this confusion, transmitting this confusion to generate political ineptitude. The Earth opened up and it can be said that everything that lay in its path was swallowed up.' But the conclusion to this account was even more striking: 'When this kingdom falls for the second time into the hands of the Spanish, would it lose more in political status? Certainly not.'

The author evidently wished to gain protection from the Spaniards in order to publish his manuscript, trusting that such statements would

---

34. 'Of the pre-physiocratic French writers who approached the population problem in terms of agricultural values and reforms, Ange Goudar was the most important', Joseph J. Spengler, *French predecessors of Malthus* (Durham 1942), p.23. For more on Goudar, see: Gianfranco Dioguardi, *Un Aventurier à Naples au XVIIIe siècle* (Castelnau-le-nez 1993), and Jean-Claude Hauc, *Ange Goudar. Un aventurier des lumières* (Paris 2004).
35. Madrid, Royal Academy of History, bundle 9/5585.
36. British Library Public Catalogue, see http://www.bl.uk.

please Madrid. But the political context in 1756 was wrong. Spain's relationship with Portugal was very different from that which had prevailed in the eighteenth century, and which would soon resume.

Portugal was in fact one of the courts with which the Spain of Fernando VI maintained cordial relations. This is shown by the steps taken by Fernando VI after the catastrophe. As Benjamin Keene, the English ambassador in Spain, reported:

[the Spaniards] send as much ready money every day as a messenger can carry, and the King's [Fernando VI] letter to his sister offers all her King can ask and he can send. The douanes are open on the frontiers for all necessaries to pass free without duties, and the administrator general of the customs at Badajoz will send you whatever you write for.[37]

This ready co-operation was the logical consequence of Fernando's marriage, in 1729, to Doña Bárbara de Braganza, the daughter of the Portuguese King Juan V. Doña Bárbara exerted a notable influence on her husband and also on the policy of his ministers. In 1750 she inspired the Treaty of Boundaries, which was designed to resolve problems relating to the borders of both crowns with respect to their American possessions.[38] She was also a force behind both the dismissal of the Marquis of Ensenada,[39] one of the most noteworthy eighteenth-century ministers in Spain, and the Spanish policy of neutrality during the Seven Years War, a decision that pleased England immensely.[40]

At the same time there were other causes for Spain's stance towards England. In Madrid, French acceptance of the preliminary peace treaty in Aix-la-Chapelle (1748) had been perceived as a serious setback for Spanish aspirations, which, coupled with previous unsolved squabbles

37. Benjamin Keene, *The Private correspondence of Sir Benjamin Keene*, ed. Richard Lodge (Cambridge 1933), p.434, Keene to Castres, 10 November 1755. Lodge states that Portugal received 150,000 dollars in aid from Spain (p.436). An example of Spanish interest is also the sending of relief personnel such as the Count of Aranda as Special Ambassador to Lisbon, replacing Peralada who had died during the earthquake. As regards England, it sent a subsidy of 100,000 pounds (p.440). The full text of Keene's dispatches may be read in London, The National Archives (formerly Public Record Office), State Papers, bundle 94/149.

38. In return for surrendering the Colony of Sacramento, a Portuguese establishment on Río de la Plata that caused serious commercial problems for Spain (due to smuggling), Portugal would receive a large territory in Paraguay occupied by a series of Jesuit missions. See Guillermo Kratz, *El Tratado hispano-portugués de límites de 1750 y sus consecuencias* (Rome 1954).

39. José Luis Gómez Urdáñez, *El Proyecto reformista de Ensenada* (Lérida 1996). According to the nuncio Spinola, 'Ensenada and Rávago's opposition to the Treaty of Boundaries was [...] the reason for the fall from grace of the Marquis, as well as for that of Father Rávago, after the Queen discovered that one of them, with the knowledge of the other, had stirred the opposition against something she was managing and desired' (Rome, Secret Vatican Archive, Home Secretary, Spain, bundle 431, Spinola to Torrigiani, 5 April 1759).

40. José Luis Gómez Urdáñez, *Fernando VI* (Madrid 2001) and Juan Molina Cortón, *Reformismo y neutralidad. José de Carvajal y la diplomacia de la España Preilustrada* (Badajoz 2003), p.476-91.

between France and Spain, prompted Spain's diplomatic *rapprochement* with England.[41] This external situation coincided with ministerial reshuffles in Spain following the accession of Fernando VI (1746) to the Spanish throne. The group of *vizcaínos* (Biscayans), led by the Secretary of State, the Marquis of Villarías, was ousted from power by the 'Spanish' or *castizo* group captained by José de Carvajal and the Duke of Huéscar (the future Duke of Alba). Moreover, the widowed queen, Isabel de Farnesio, who had designed a large part of her husband's policy, was exiled to the Palacio de la Granja.[42]

This institutional renewal (which included other noteworthy figures such as Wall and Grimaldi, both future Secretaries of State) coincided in London with Newcastle's ministry,[43] a cabinet that supported dialogue and the resolution of differences with Spain, and so was the most appropriate for the Catholic monarchy – as was highlighted at the time by the Spanish ambassador to London, Ricardo Wall:

Your Majesty will recall the reasons that I presented at the time to persuade you that it is in our interest for the Duke of Newcastle to remain in the ministry and my understanding of these disputes once again confirms my previous opinion; in this knowledge I believe that it would be very harmful for us to allow, due to delays on matters that do not benefit the monarchy, arms to be given to its enemies that may inflict damage on us despite their intention being solely to overthrow the duke.[44]

This *rapprochement* policy, albeit with fluctuations, remained stable in 1755. Wall had succeeded Carvajal as the Secretary of Foreign Affairs, precisely because of his supposed support of the English.[45] He was the hegemonic figure in the second government of Fernando VI, which was created as a result of Carvajal's death and the dismissal of the Marquis of Ensenada, the other great political figure until 1754.[46]

---

41. Molina Cortón, *Reformismo y neutralidad*, p.115-279.

42. José de Carvajal y Lancáster, *La Diplomacia de Fernando VI. Correspondencia entre Carvajal y Huéscar, 1746-1749*, ed. Didier Ozanam (Madrid 1975).

43. Peter David Garner Thomas, *George III. King and politicians, 1760-1770* (Manchester 2002), p.24-30.

44. Valladolid, Simancas General Archive, State Section, bundle 6.914, Wall to Carvajal, 9 June 1749.

45. Diego Téllez Alarcia, 'La supuesta anglofilia de D. Ricardo Wall. Filias y fobias políticas durante el reinado de Fernando VI', *Revista de Historia Moderna. Anales de la Universidad de Alicante* 21 (2003), p.501-36.

46. In fact it had been Wall, in collaboration with Huéscar and Keene, the English Ambassador in Spain, who had achieved the aforementioned dismissal; see Diego Téllez Alarcia, 'El caballero D. Ricardo Wall y la conspiración antiensenadista', in *Ministros de Fernando VI*, ed. José Miguel Delgado Barrado and José Luis Gómez Urdáñez (Córdoba 2002), p.93-138. For more information on Minister Wall, see the following web page: Diego Téllez Alarcia, *D. Ricardo Wall, el ministro olvidado*, http://www.tiemposmodernos.org/ ricardowall. In English, see Diego Téllez Alarcia, 'Richard Wall: light and shade of an Irish minister in Spain (1694-1777)', *Irish studies review* 11:2 (August 2003), p.123-36.

The Hispano-British *rapprochement* strengthened the close bond with Portugal. We can understand why the sermons that proliferated in Spain after the event denounced the vices of the Portuguese, the corruption of their customs or their lack of faith, but under no circumstances alluded to the role of their alliance with the English. Moral explanations were not banned, provided that they did not contain any 'political' allusions. When these appeared, the effect was immediate. A good example is the *Mercurio historico-politico*, one of the most important publications in the country, which was taken over and controlled by the state after the spread of different news stories relating to the Lisbon earthquake.[47]

iii. The Lisbon earthquake in Spain from 1762 onwards

The death of Doña Bárbara, in 1758, which helped to cause the death of Fernando VI the following year, produced a significant change in the direction of Spanish foreign policy.[48] Implementation of the Treaty of Boundaries had been delayed due to the Guarani Indian rebellion (1753-1756), and then the earthquake; and in 1761 this treaty was annulled once and for all by the signing of the Treaty of El Pardo. The neutrality maintained by the ministers of Fernando VI was gradually modified and turned into a warlike stance against England and an alliance with France (the Third Family Compact was signed in 1761).[49] War was declared against England at the beginning of 1762; and though Hispano-French diplomatic pressures delayed the breaking-off of relations with Portugal until May, Spanish troops then invaded Portugal through the province of Tras-os-Montes.[50]

This shift in relations with respect to Portugal was explained very clearly by Minister Wall to the French Ambassador, the Marquis of Ossun: 'This minister began by saying that Portugal should be seen as a province of England.'[51] The union between English and Portuguese resulting from the Treaty of Methuen (1703) had remained solid through-

---

47. Luis Miguel Enciso Recio, *La Gaceta de Madrid y el Mercurio Histórico Político, 1756-1781* (Valladolid 1957), p.27-28.

48. José Luis Gómez Urdáñez and Diego Téllez Alarcia, '1759. El "Año sin rey y con rey": la naturaleza del poder al descubierto', in *El Poder en Europa y América: Mitos, tópicos y realidades*, ed. E. García Fernández (Bilbao 2001), p.95-109.

49. Diego Téllez Alarcia, 'Guerra y regalismo a comienzos del reinado de Carlos III. El final del ministerio Wall', *Hispania* 209 (2001), p.1051-90.

50. Curiously it was the Count of Aranda who was sent in 1755 as special ambassador to Lisbon to transmit the condolences of Fernando VI to the Portuguese monarchs, who would direct the final part of the campaign, Antonio María Mourinho, *Invasão de Trás-os-Montes e das Beiras na guerra dos sete anos pelos exércitos bourbónicos, em 1762, através da correspondência oficial dos comandantes-chefes Marquês de Sarriá e Conde de Aranda* (Lisbon 1986).

51. Paris, Archive of the Ministry of Foreign Affairs, Political Correspondence, Spain, bundle 532, Ossun to Choiseul, 3 April 1761.

out the whole of the century, and in Wall's opinion, Portugal's neutrality in the war only concealed disadvantages for the Bourbons.[52] Early in 1762, he proposed forcing Portugal to declare itself friend or foe.[53] If it chose the latter, Spain would invade its neighbour, a military move that was deemed likely to succeed, given Portugal's weakness after the earthquake.[54]

The radical change in the political climate also marked a striking shift in the interpretation of the earthquake of Lisbon. It was in this new context that Goudar's pamphlet, which had been published in The Hague in 1756, but not published in either Portugal or Spain, was published in Spanish, under the tendentious title of *Profecía política verificada en lo que está sucediendo a los portugueses por su ciega afición a los ingleses. Hecha luego después del terremoto del año de 1755* (Madrid, Imp. de la Gaceta, 1762).[55] Although blaming foreigners – especially the English – for Portugal's misfortunes was not particularly original,[56] the printer's preface to this translation of the *Profecía* emphasises this feature of the argument:

Believing that I would only find a bare account of the damage caused by the Earthquake of 1755 [...] I admired how against this [...] its author wrote a discourse on the political system of that kingdom, unearthing its roots and the cause of all its miseries [...] letting itself blindly be governed by the

52. This is acknowledged in Portuguese historiography: 'Portuguese neutrality was certainly partial to England', in J. Lucio Azevedo, *O marquês de Pombal e a sua época* (Porto 1990), p.179.

53. This summed up the mission of O'Dunne: 'he will depart for his destination next Friday, he will take to our Ambassador the minutes of the Report that both must present in order to force that court to declare its support quickly and openly for us, or for the English [...] we will rescue it from its shameful dependence, protecting its purpose and conservation'. This manoeuvre was described by Wall as a 'sweet and bitter errand, a kiss concealing a bite', Valladolid, Simancas General Archive, State Section, bundle 6.092, Wall to Tanucci, 26 January and 9 March 1762.

54. Paris, Archive of the Ministry of Foreign Affairs, Political Correspondence, Spain, bundle 533, Choiseul to Ossun, 7 July 1761, attributing the authorship of the project to Wall: 'Mr. Wall has, by his side, two great merits: [...] the second one having designed, intelligently, were war to be declared, the project of Portugal, which is an enlightened plan.'

55. The official status of the pamphlet is confirmed because it was printed by the Printers of the Madrid Gazette, a state-controlled publication. In addition, the translators of the *Discours*, now called *Profecía política*, were Bernardo de Iriarte and Nicolás de Azara, both of them bureaucrats under minister Richard Wall's command, Agustín Millares Carlo, *Ensayo de una bio-bibliografía de escritores naturales de las Islas Canarias* (Madrid 1932), Bernardo de Iriarte a Francisco de Angulo, 9 February 1808. We have consulted a copy of the *Profecía política* in Rome, Secret Vatican Archive, Home Secretary, Spain, bundle 289.

56. The Count of Aranda had already mentioned this: 'The loss is irreparable in the life of those who knew Lisbon, and this kingdom will be destroyed for ever, because if the foreigners squeeze the little substance that remains out of it, they will contribute to its definitive demise', Madrid, Archive of the House of Alba, Box 151/123, Aranda to the Duke of Alba, 10 December 1755.

English, without realising that they sold their protection to it at the price of slavery.[57]

According to the *Profecía*, the 'Physical causes' concurred 'with moral causes, the elements have done what politics has been unable to achieve'.[58] The earthquake was just divine punishment for the inclination of the Portuguese towards the English and for their apathy, caused by the wealth of Brazil: 'the nation fell into a type of lethargy, idleness and laziness took over their hearts'.[59] Political considerations immediately came to the fore. Portugal 'was in the hands of the English, under their control and insensitively they had conquered it'.[60] What is more, 'after the Portuguese revolution [of 1640] this kingdom has been more a slave of England than ever was [a slave] of Spain'.[61] It was a blessing that 'the seizure of the wealth of Brazil has simply delayed, for at least one century, the domination so coveted by England'.[62] Viewed from this perspective, Portuguese neutrality was deceptive and harmful: 'There is no more wayward a policy than that of constantly maintaining peace, when all the powers in Europe are at war [...] A state is being very deceptive when it believes that victories achieved 200 leagues from its continent are of no interest to it.'[63] As can be seen, the ideas expressed in the *Profecía* coincide, point by point, with the programme designed by Madrid and Versailles to provoke Portugal's entry into the conflict, either on their side or on the English one.

The publication of the *Profecía* was part of a larger 'mediatic' war strategy extremely well orchestrated from the seats of power.[64] The war on Portugal must be popular in order to be prolonged. After more than a decade of peace, it was necessary to influence Spanish public opinion against Portugal. If something similar could be done with public opinion in Portugal, where it was suspected that the aggressive policies of the Marquis of Pombal had produced significant discontent, all the better.

During the early months of 1762 Portugal was hot news in Spain. The thirst of Spanish readers fostered the proliferation of 'geographic des-

57. *Profecía política verificada en lo que está sucediendo a los portugueses por su ciega afición a los ingleses. Hecha luego después del terremoto del año de 1755* (Madrid, Imp. de la Gaceta, 1762), p.1-2.

58. *Profecía política*, p.5.

59. *Profecía política*, p.20.

60. *Profecía política*, p.14.

61. *Profecía política*, p.22.

62. *Profecía política*, p.10.

63. *Profecía política*, p.23.

64. The *Profecía* would be translated into Portuguese, with a similar aim, in 1808, after the Napoleonic invasion of the Peninsula Iberica: *Profecía política, verificada no que está succedendo aos Portuguezes pela sua céga affeicão aos Inglezes. Escrita depois do terremoto do anno 1755 e publicada por ordem superior no anno de 1762, em Madrid, traduzida do hespanhol* (Lisbon, Typografia Rollandiana, 1808). One of the *Discours*'s Spanish translators, Bernardo de Iriarte, was an 'afrancesado' (Napoleon's partisans in Spain) and counsellor of José I Bonaparte, king of Spain.

criptions', 'historical reflections', 'cartographic' curiosities and even the reprint of old Hispanic conquests in the Portuguese kingdom. Once again we find prestigious writers taking advantage of what was fashionable at the time. The first to benefit from this situation was Campomanes, thanks to his close relationship with the Secretary of State, with whom he collaborated closely. In his *Noticia* he presented a descriptive compendium of Portugal's cities and provinces, its main fortifications, important buildings, population, roads, paths and distances between inhabited settlements, all 'to the benefit of the community'.[65]

Another illustrious figure, Francisco Mariano Nipho, reappeared on the scene a few weeks later with a similar publication. This is how the author himself justifies his book:

To coincide with the current war between Spain and Portugal, all those presumptuous politicians, out of sheer vanity, have purchased their map, without any knowledge of its magnitudes, climate, circles and cardinal points, simply pointing their finger to the conquered location, and like fools calculate the distances from one town to the next. This use of curiosity without any investigation other than the pastime neither warrants claims of a conquest or seizure of a location, nor invests glory on the victor; because to say that Moncorvo, Chaves and Braganza were taken without knowing the state of their defences or their population or walls is tantamount to achieving even less than half the objective.[66]

The plethora of works of this type is impressive, including texts by Juan González,[67] José de Torrubias y Ponce,[68] Juan Bravo,[69] or Pedro

---

65. Pedro Rodríguez de Campomanes, *Noticia geográfica del Reino y Caminos de Portugal* (Madrid, Joachim Ibarra, 1762), p.5. This work is dedicated to Minister Wall and was accompanied by some *Reflexiones históricas* [...] *de las razones con que el Rey puede reunir a la corona los países que conquisten las armas españolas en Portugal* which were eventually not printed, but can be consulted in Madrid, Fundación Universitaria Española, Archive of Campomanes, bundle 4-6. See Diego Téllez Alarcia, 'El joven Campomanes y el ministro Wall (1754-63)', in *Campomanes doscientos años después*, ed. María Dolores Mateos Dorado (Oviedo 2003), p.417-31.

66. Francisco Mariano Nipho, *Descripción historica y geographica del reyno de Portugal, con la serie y panegyrico de todos sus Reyes: La población repartida por provincias, comarcas, corregimientos, intendencias, y oidorías, dando circunstanciado el vecindario, y situación de sus ciudades, villas y lugares, que con un índice geográfico, para mayor claridad extracto de varios Autores y particularmente del P. Luis Cayetano de Lima, clérigo reglar, etc.* (Madrid, Gabriel Ramírez, 1762), p.4.

67. Juan González, *Nueva Chorographica Descripcion de todas las provincias, villas, obispados, arzobispados, puertos, fortalezas, y considerables lugares del Reyno de Portugal* [...] *con los Principales Rios, Bahías, Mares, Montañas, Llanuras, Sierras, y Collados, sobre que estàn situadas: Obra utilissima, para la inteligencia de la historia deste Reyno, y politico Systema presente* (Madrid, Joseph Padrino, 1762).

68. José de Torrubias y Ponce, *Descripcion geografica-historica del Reyno de Portugal: en la qual se dara mas gustosa y cabal inteligencia a los mapas* (Valencia, Joseph Estevan Dolz, 1762).

69. Juan Bravo, *Compendio geográfico y histórico del Reyno de Portugal, dividido en 5 provincias y el Algarve, en el que se da puntual noticia de todas las plazas y fortalezas que hay en dicho Reyno, su graduación, vecindario, parroquias y personas* (Madrid, Andrés Ortega, 1762).

Burillo.[70] But there are many others, including the reprint of the work by Mascareñas describing the successful campaign of Don Juan José de Austria in Portugal, exactly one hundred years earlier in 1662,[71] and the pamphlet drafted by the Home Secretary for distribution by Spanish troops in Portugal to justify their presence in the neighbouring country as friends and not invaders:

A poster or manifesto has been sent (to General Sarriá) that must be made public in the first place of that kingdom and in other places through which we pass. It states that the entry of Spanish troops is not intended as an act of war on the Portuguese; instead, it is designed to serve a useful and glorious purpose for the Portuguese crown and for vassals such as His Majesty has represented before His Loyal Majesty, who, in view of the peaceful intentions of the king [...], hopes that this will be corresponded through trust on the part of His Majesty and his vassals that the entry and passage of our troops will not unleash any violence on them nor stop them from being supplied with any supplies that are delivered to them.[72]

Though these papers do not refer directly to the earthquake, they reflect a change in the political context that earlier had restricted the interpretation of the Lisbon earthquake in Spain.

Conclusions

Every aspect of the Lisbon earthquake was interpreted politically. But this construction was not immutable. While the context of international relations evolved, this interpretation fluctuated between innocuous considerations and clearly war-like visions. While Spain was an ally of Portugal, and particularly when cordial relations were maintained with England, misfortune was not related to the cruelty of the Portuguese–British alliance. With the transformation of the international panorama the context changed radically. The earthquake was now seen as a divine punishment, and the sin that was being punished was none other than Portugal's friendship with England. The catastrophe was being used as

70. Pedro Burillo, *Descripción histórico-geográfica y chronológica del Reino de Portugal* (Zaragoza, Francisco Moreno, 1762).

71. Jerónimo Mascareñas, *Campaña de Portugal por la parte de Extremadura: el año de 1662: executada por el serenísimo señor. D. Juan de Austria, Gran Prior de Castilla, de la Orden de San Juan, del Consejo de Estado, de su Majestad, Gobernador y Capitán General de los Países Bajos, Gobernador de las Armas Marítimas y Capitán General del Ejército de la Recuperación de Portugal; y escrita por D. Gerónimo Mascareñas, caballero y difinidor general de la Orden de Calatrava, del Consejo de Estado de S. M. y del Supremo de la Corona de Portugal* (Madrid, Imp. de Francisco Javier García, 1762).

72. Valladolid, Simancas General Archive, State Section, bundle 6.092, Wall to Tanucci, 30 March 1762. The pamphlet in question is entitled *Razón de entrar en Portugal las tropas españolas como amigas y sinrazón de recibirlas como enemigas. Reducido a las memorias presentadas de parte a parte* (Madrid, Imp. de la Gaceta, 1762). This pamphlet was countered in Portugal by another pamphlet, entitled *Sem razão de entrarem em Portugal as Tropas Castelhanas como amigas, e razão de ferem recebidas como Inimigas: Manifesto reduzido as memorias presentadas de parte a parte* (Lisbon, Offic. de Miguel Rodrigues, 1762).

part of a programme of ideological justification for breaking off relations and the invasion of Portugal by Spanish troops, in order to rescue Spain's neighbours from their humiliating dependency on the English. The historical parallels could not have been more poignant and attempts were made to revive the revolution of 1640-1665, albeit with the countries playing different roles: Spain became the liberator rather than the oppressor, while England adopted a diametrically different role. The result of these events was negative for Spanish interests, since this initiative failed, although it left a magnificent paradigm of the way in which certain events, including natural catastrophes, may become corrupted to suit the interest of different states. This corruption, even if it is only temporary, is nothing new in our time.

CARMEN ESPEJO CALA

To Francisco Aguilar Piñal

Spanish news pamphlets on the 1755 earthquake: trade strategies of the printers of Seville

i. The earthquake as a news item

FEW, if any, events drew as much public interest as the Lisbon earthquake of 1755. Although the devastating effects were most severe in Portugal's capital, with a death toll of around 30,000 people and the virtual destruction of half of the city, the tremor also hit the south of Portugal and Spain and was felt in the north of Africa and even as far away as America. The intensity of the havoc coincided with a crisis of the mentality of the time, making the disaster an issue of intellectual concern throughout Europe, with leading intellectuals like Feijoo in Spain, Voltaire in France and Kant in Germany taking part in the public debate. Current studies have carefully examined this discussion, showing how scholars took sides, seeing the earthquake as a punishment from God, as a challenge to optimism, or just as a fact of life.[1]

Naturally enough, the earthquake hit the headlines at the time, and the journalists exploited this event as an issue that aroused much interest. One of the leading scholars of Spanish literature of the eighteenth century, Francisco Aguilar Piñal, came up with the very interesting fact that in Seville alone the total number of printed pamphlets on this subject reached more than fifty by the end of 1755, barely two months after the actual earthquake had occurred.[2] Our research, which will eventually be published in a catalogue, has so far discovered sixty-eight items printed in

---

1. Main works on the subject published in Spain and Portugal are: Francisco Aguilar Piñal, 'Conmoción espiritual en Sevilla por el terremoto de 1755', *Archivo hispalense* 171-73 (1973), p.37-53; María Luísa Braga, 'O terremoto de 1755: sua repercussão, a nível ideológico, em Portugal e no estrangeiro', in *História de Portugal e dos tempos pré-históricos aos nossos dias*, ed. Joao Medina (Lisbon 1997), p.347-70; Vicente Fombuena Filpo, 'El terremoto de Lisboa: un tema de reflexión para el pensamiento ilustrado', *Espacio y tiempo* 9 (1995), p.9-22; Francisco Sánchez-Blanco, 'El terremoto de 1755', in *La Mentalidad ilustrada* (Madrid 1999), p.241-75.

2. Aguilar Piñal, 'Conmoción espiritual', p.39.

Seville concerning the earthquake.[3] Most of these date from 1755, some from 1756 and a few from 1757. Several were further reprinted, both in Seville and other main towns.

When Aguilar Piñal attempted to account for the huge amount of printed material on this event, he pointed out that it resulted from three different attitudes towards the earthquake: 'una es el legítimo deseo de información; otra la mirada suplicante hacia la Divinidad, [...] una tercera actitud, la crítica, que se pregunta por la verdadera causa de tan lamentables efectos'.[4] Each of these attitudes led to a number of different texts. Whatever their purpose, most of the writings produced should be labelled in terms of genre typology as *relaciones de sucesos*, that is, popular news pamphlets. Thirty-six of the total of sixty-eight items we have come across are *relaciones de sucesos*. These are brief works, running for an average of four pages, carelessly printed, anonymous and openly informative about the facts following the earthquake as experienced or imagined in Lisbon, Seville and other locations in Spain and northern Africa. We find them both in prose and in *romance* verse.[5] In addition there are lyrical pieces, prayers and notices, all printed with the same low quality – and equally low prices – as well as a number of formally-styled short theological and moral essays. The printing presses in Seville and Madrid produced most of the information about the earthquake. Printers from both locations shared each other's works, reprinting or creating new versions.[6]

This sizeable production of cheap and popular works around the same issue seems to be a distinguishing feature of Iberian journalism in the eighteenth century, which might be called popular press. Such a label is hardly employed by journalism historians when they refer to the eighteenth century, despite its widespread use to define an important part of the press from the nineteenth century onwards and for naming the *relaciones* and other similar pamphlets in the early Modern Age.[7] Although

3. Although these works are scattered in libraries and archives around Spain, the National Library in Madrid, the University Library in Seville and the Capitular Library in Seville keep whole collections of works on the earthquake. In the years following the catastrophe, several collections were formed in Portugal, with pieces from different locations, including some from Seville (see note 10). For further information on the contents of these collections, see *Sismicidade de Portugal. Estudo da Documentação dos Séculos XVII e XVIII*, ed. M. R. Themudo Barata, M. L. Braga, M. Norohna Wagner, B. Guerra, J. F. Alves, J. Nieto (Lisbon 1989).

4. 'Firstly, the genuine desire for information; secondly, a begging attitude to God, [...] the third attitude is a critical one, pondering the rationale of the devastating effects', Aguilar Piñal, 'Conmoción espiritual', p.46.

5. *Romance* is the usual kind of verse for Spanish popular poetry.

6. Other cities with well-established printers severely damaged by the earthquake were Cadiz and Puerto de Santa María (Cádiz) in southern Spain. It took a while before printers in Lisbon could resume their activity, due to the severity of the havoc. By the time they got back to work, the event had been widely covered.

7. This concept is used by Henry Ettinghausen throughout his work on the Spanish press in the seventeenth century: Henry Ettinghausen, 'Política y prensa "popular" en la

the *relaciones de sucesos* were commercially successful in Spain throughout the eighteenth century, the mainstream history of journalism has neglected this product and has focused instead on the coming of age of the 'serious' press as the major event of the time. But our main claim here is that this so-called serious press can be fully understood only if the commercial and creative context of the popular press is appreciated.

This study will use the many items printed concerning the earthquake to examine the strategies of Sevillian printers in the mid-eighteenth century in producing cheap, informative printed products. In particular, we will explore the printers' and the authors' identities, and the social profiles of the readers, in order to consider how the former managed to obtain and promptly report updated information, and to assess the social usefulness of this information for readers.

ii. Production strategies of the Sevillian printers

There is little doubt that earthquake-related news was a boom that swamped the city with papers in a matter of days. When the earthquake actually occurred on 1 November 1755, there were only six workshops involved in the printing business in Seville. This shows the gravity of the cultural and economic crisis of the city, since 150 years earlier more than thirty printers had worked regularly in town.[8] As soon as the earth stopped trembling, the six remaining printers set to work to supply the high demand for information produced by the event. In fact they had to work round the clock, due to the continuous aftershocks that continued till the end of the year. All six in one way or another covered news of the earthquake, although different printers took different approaches to the same event.

The *relaciones de sucesos* as a genre were produced by only three printers. Two of these were specially fond of reporting this news and above all José Padrino, who printed at least thirteen *relaciones* on this issue – twelve of them before the end of the year, all of them anonymous and brief. But this printer also published an essay of around forty pages by an enlightened friar discussing Feijoo's theory on the cause of the earthquake, along with some other pamphlets.[9]

España del siglo XVII', *Anthropos* 166-67, special issue *Literatura popular*, ed. M. C. García de Enterría (1995), p.86-91; and Henry Ettinghausen, 'Hacia una tipología de la prensa española del siglo XVII: de *hard news* a *soft porn*', in *Studia aurea*, actas del III Congreso de la AISO (Toulouse 1993); *I. Plenarias. General. Poesía*, ed. I. Arellano, M. C. Pinillos, F. Serralta, M. Vitse (Navarra 1996), p.51-66.

8. From the end of the sixteenth century, the latest glory years of the city, the local population – which amounted to 150,000 people – declined sharply. By the mid-eighteenth century, the total population was about 70,000.

9. Only the works from which we have quoted are included in the footnotes; on the other hand, the titles of the popular works are long and rhetorical, so in this study we have

Had it not been for José Padrino, the soundest and most prosperous printer of the time, the information explosion would have been unlikely.[10] He had been working in the city years before the earthquake and he would work in the same location for twenty more years. Several generations of heirs followed in his footsteps until well into the nineteenth century. Also well known as a bookseller, with many connections in the social and educated circles in Seville and elsewhere in Andalucía, José Padrino had gained a well deserved reputation. He ran both of his activities from the same outlet located in Calle Génova, off the Cathedral, near the shops of four of the other five printers.[11]

Padrino's outstanding reputation explains why he published certain kind of works, such as the above mentioned letter, or the *relación* entitled *Copia de una carta, que escribió D. N. N. a un Amigo suyo, dándole cuenta del Terremoto, y Retirada del Mar, acaecidos en Cadiz Sabado primero de Noviembre de 1755.*[12] In the preface to this work, an anonymous sender states: 'Vea V. m. (que no podrà executarlo sin assombro) esta sincera Relacion, que *nada huele à Vulgo*, y es hija entera de la observación de un Jesuita, de quien yo la adquirí.'[13] The reliability of the story is further emphasised later in the document, when the narrator is presented as taking notes while the earth was still trembling, an instance of total scientific determination. The letter was a true success, partly because of Padrino's resourceful attempt to satisfy his customers' curiosity by relying on realistic narrative devices and abundant descriptions. So moving were some descriptive details of the narrative – swaying lamp posts, paintings coming off their hooks in the walls, bells jingling – that they appeared in many serious written accounts over the following weeks.

Another *relación* reports the effects in Ayamonte, a fishing village on the edge of the Portuguese border. This one uses casual, fully informative language. The author detaches himself from the event, the result being an impersonal narration with a wealth of details, including descriptions of

decided to shorten them. We have already undertaken the task of putting together a catalogue with the full citations, to be published shortly.

10. Actually his works were distributed internationally. In the *Collecção Universal de todas as obras que tem sahido ao publico sobre os effeitos que cauzou o terramoto nos Reinos de Portugal e Castella no primeiro de Novembro de 1755* at the National Library of Lisbon, which was compiled between 1756 and 1759, several items by Padrino appear, apart from other *relaciones* by the same printer in other volumes of the library.

11. By the eighteenth century, Calle Génova in Seville was the most common location for printers and booksellers, as attested by Francisco Aguilar Piñal, *Historia de Sevilla. Siglo XVIII* (Seville 1989), p.260 and ss.

12. [This is the copy of a letter, written by D. N. N. and sent to a friend of his, whereby full account of the earthquake and the withdrawal of the sea, as it happened in Cádiz on the 1 November 1755, is given] (Seville, Imprenta de Joseph Padrino, [1755]). This tentative translation is given only for the purpose of this paper.

13. Emphasis added. 'Notice Your Honour (you shan't do it without awe) this very honest *relación*, which *smells not like the mob*, and it's the entire account of a witnessing Jesuit from whom I purchased it.'

torn corpses after the tragedy. In reality the *relación* has two clearly differentiated parts, the first dating from 2 November and the second two days later, 4 November. It could hardly be more up to date. The *relación* entitled *Memoria funebre, y descripcion tragica de los inauditos formidables estragos que ocasionò en toda la Española Peninsula el violentissimo Temblor de tierra, experimentado en ella la mañana del dia primero de Noviembre del año 1755. Deducida, y extractada, con la mas critica veracidad, de diferentes noticiosas Cartas, que se han recibido en esta Imperial, y Coronada Villa de Madrid*[14] reports the same events in somewhat more expressive language. This focuses on the effects of the earthquake in Madrid, La Mancha, Toledo and its surroundings, Castilla la Vieja, Andalucía *alta* and *baxa*, Cádiz, Córdoba, Granada, and Portugal. The information is arranged geographically in different blocks with their corresponding headlines. The title gives the sense of a skilful journalist fully aware of how to present the news effectively. A similar edition published in Madrid with the same title also exists. We tend to think of the Madrid edition as the original, which Padrino read and then reprinted, knowing it was bound to sell well.

Another long and richly detailed *relación* on the havoc in Lisbon – split in two different parts and running for twenty-two pages in small print – is not only a vivid account but also an instance of the most elevated language, comprehensible only to the most educated class, still fond of the typical baroque rhetoric. The narrative starts as follows: 'Yace en el Lusitano Imperio la magnifica y de todos aplaudida en el Universo Ciudad de Lisboa'.[15] Curiously enough, this twofold *relación*, though printed by Padrino, was sold in another bookshop of the city, the one owned by Alonso Castizo, one of around fifteen bookshops in town. This shows Padrino's skills as an entrepeneur, printing both for himself and on behalf of other booksellers.

Despite Padrino's close acquaintances among the enlightened and other local scholars, and his ability to offer them very appealing reading matter, these were not his best customers. On the contrary, he is much better known for printing popular *romances*. In the catalogue *Romancero popular del siglo XVIII*, Aguilar Piñal collects and comments on thousands of these *romances*, mostly published in Andalucía, more precisely in Córdoba, Málaga and Seville. Several Sevillian printers stood out for

---

14. Seville, Imprenta de Joseph Padrino, [1755] [Tragic account of the outstanding havoc that the earthquake caused in Spanish Peninsula on 1 November 1755. As appears in letters received in this imperial city of Madrid].

15. 'There lies in the Lusitan Empire the magnificent and highly acclaimed around the globe city of Lisbon', *Breve compendio de las inumerables lamantables ruinas, y lastimosos estragos, que à la violencia, y conjuracion de todos quatro Elementos experimentó la Gran Ciudad, y Corte de Lisboa el dia 1. de Noviembre de este año de 1755* ([Seville], [Joseph Padrino], [1755]) [Brief account of the much regretted ruins and sad havoc caused by the sheer violence and joint action for all four elements in the Court of Lisbon on 1 November 1755].

their high production in this field, but José Padrino was second to none. Drawing on Caro Baroja's previous theory, Aguilar Piñal pointed out:

su evidente *andalucismo*. Si, como puede comprobarse, las imprentas de Sevilla, Córdoba, Málaga, con Madrid y Valencia, destacan por el número de los pliegos de cordel en ellas impresos, es lógico suponer que los habitantes de esas ciudades serían los máximos consumidores de esta popular literatura. Andalucismo, pues, en el público lector, que podríamos ampliar a la mitad sur de la península. Pero andalucismo también por los temas que tratan y por los autores conocidos, cuyo lugar de origen es Sevilla y su contorno.[16]

This being the context, Rodríguez's theory about the *relaciones* on the Lisbon earthquake kept at the National Library of Madrid, makes full sense: 'seguramente la abundancia y la inmediatez con que se publicaron tales pliegos no hubiera sido tal de no haberse tratado de un fenómeno fundamentalmente andaluz'; 'el éxito de las relaciones se explica sobre todo porque [...] difunden aquello que el público dieciochesco y, en particular, la sociedad andaluza deseaban escuchar'.[17]

This definitely seems to be the case. Though worthless by literary standards, the *romances* are very valuable for their informative efficiency, and are also a good vehicle for moralist propaganda. The *romances*, presumably distributed by blind sellers, were the main sources of information for the illiterate, who might find it hard to distinguish reliable accounts of the earthquake from the made-up anecdotes that were included in the reporting, like the story of how some lucky few had been saved thanks to the Virgin Mary's miraculous intervention.

Padrino published at least five *romances* on the earthquake before the year came to an end. All of them recounted the events as they were experienced in the main Andalusian towns close to Seville and some other important villages. It is not hard to imagine that these items aroused the interest of Sevillians as well as citizens from other towns, hence their distribution and consumption beyond the Andalusian capital city.

Unlike the primarily informative works written in prose, the *romances* aimed at enhancing popular religious feelings, which was better served by

16. '[The *romances*] have a clear Andalusian flavour. If the printers in Seville, Córdoba, Málaga, together with those in Madrid and Valencia are well known for publishing most of the *pliegos de cordel* (ballads), it follows logically that the people in these cities were the most eager readers of this popular literature. The audience is Andalusian (roughly speaking those living in the Southern part of the country), the topics are Andalusian too, and as far as we know the authors were from Seville and its surroundings', Francisco Aguilar Piñal, *Romancero popular del siglo XVIII* (Madrid 1972), p.xiii.

17. 'News would not have been so abundant and so promptly spread through if the ballads had it not been an essentially Andalusian event'; 'the huge success of the *relaciones* can be accounted for only by the fact that they touched on issues that the audience of the time, that is, the Andalusian society, wanted to hear about', M. José Rodríguez Sánchez de León, 'El terremoto lisboeta de 1755 en las relaciones de sucesos', in *Las Relaciones de sucesos en España (1500-1750)*, Actas del Primer Coloquio Internacional (Alcalá de Henares, 8-10 June 1995), ed. M. C. García de Enterría, H. Ettinghausen, V. Infantes and A. Redondo (Alcalá de Henares 1996), p.313.

literary means. Padrino's *romances* are essentially a coming together of both discourses, with the literary and the informative going hand in hand. Needless to say, they have no literary value, but that does not mean that there are not remarkable examples of popular poetry. Some *romances* are filled with references from classical mythology, while others show overtones of Góngora's poetry, which reveal the sophisticated education of the authors behind these works.

These *relaciones* in prose and the *romances* in verse catered to clearly differentiated audiences. Not only did Padrino meet the informative needs of the most educated minds, he also fulfilled the hunger of the majority for the superstitious and the macabre. Padrino's commercial expertise was unique, since despite severe competition from other printers working in the same area in town, he was the top printer in Seville.

José Navarro y Armijo, another well known printer, was also located in the Calle Génova, a few doors down from Padrino's. In 1755, when his career as printer was about to end, he enjoyed the best of reputations, proven by his being the *Impresor Mayor* – official printer – of the university. The official support of this award facilitated his printing works on the earthquake in a different style from Padrino's, such as a long treatise by a well-known *ilustrado* (enlightened person) paid for by the University. Also, Navarro's connections with groups of local scholars gave him the opportunity to publish two average length works (fifteen to thirty pages) on the natural disaster and a letter by Feijoo on the causes of the earthquake, the first in a series of four letters which were later put together under the title *Nuevo Systhema, sobre la causa physica de los terremotos*. Given Feijoo's reputation, this piece, which opened up a hot scientific controversy, sold very well even in the street markets. Its full title states that the letter was addressed to someone in Seville, even though the letter was actually addressed to an esquire living in Cádiz.[18] This might have been a mistake, or perhaps a rhetorical device to gain readers' sympathy.

Since the letter did not cover all the sides of the pages included, Navarro left the reverse of the cover blank, and used the back cover to announce further items on the earthquake to be published soon. This information comes under the headline: 'El impresor a los curiosos.'[19] This is one, among many, of Navarro's commercial strategies. The most common of these is the inclusion of imprints advertising his products and claiming to be the only one having exclusive news: 'En Sevilla, en la Imprenta de

18. *Copia de carta escrita por el Ilmo. y Rmo. P. Mro. Fr. Benito Feyjoo a cierto caballero de la Ciudad de Sevilla, en que apunta algunas noticias pertenecientes a los Terremotos, con la ocasión, del que se experimentó el dia de Todos Santos I. de Noviembre de 1755* (Seville, Imprenta de D. Joseph Navarro y Armijo, [1756]) [Copied letter written by Sir Fray Benito Feyjoo to some sevillian esquire, giving some news on the earthquake, regarding the one that took place on All Saints Day 1 November 1755]. The letter was actually addressed to Don José Díaz de Guitian, living in Cádiz.

19. 'From the editor to the curious.'

D. Joseph Navarro y Armijo, en Calle Genova; donde se vende este, y otros de varios Lugares, y el Papel en Prossa añadido de todo lo acaecido de resultas del Terremoto experimentado en esta Ciudad.'[20]

In addition to these works in prose, other publications, such as anonymous lyrical works on the earthquake in verse, made Navarro stand out from his colleagues in the city. But the bulk of his production is eleven brief anonymous *relaciones de sucesos*, the publication dates of which provide clear evidence that his printing press was working round the clock, since they were all published in 1755.

Much like the ones printed by Padrino, Navarro's four *relaciones* in prose are of two kinds: two of them use a literary style, filled with narrative details and moral overtones, while the other two fall into the category of informative pieces. Noteworthy among the *relaciones* by Navarro is the one entitled *Relacion de lo acaecido en la Ciudad de Granada*, which starts *in media res*: 'En la Cathedral, siendo una obra tan fuerte, quebrantò quatro Naves.'[21] On some occasions Navarro includes last minute news as an extra chapter following a piece composed earlier. Another romance on the earthquake in Seville ends with news on the well-being of the king and the queen as well as the minor consequences of the earthquake in the capital city of the kingdom, as had been reported by the official source of the Spanish royalty – the *Gaceta de Madrid* – on 4 November.

Navarro's strategies as a publisher included seeking well-informed and updated sources. But alongside this serious professional side, he also catered to the popular audience with macabre, sensationalist pieces that commonly reported on criminal events and the lives of saints and rogues. Navarro published seven *romances* of this kind concerning the earthquake, very similar in tone and layout to those by Padrino. The only difference worth mentioning is that the information provided referred to different locations. Seemingly, both printers agreed to cover different zones of the affected areas, hence avoiding straightforward competition in telling similar stories.

Their joint publishing of two *relaciones* is undeniable proof of their collaboration. For such publications, printers decided to split production expenses, resulting in works which were virtually identical, aside from small decorative details or imprints, and which were most likely to have been printed simultaneously in each printer's workshop. Their titles are *Nuevo, y Curioso Romance del estrago causado el dia de Todos Santos en la villa de*

20. 'In Seville, in the print office of D. Joseph Navarro y Armijo, in Génova Street, where this and others from different locations are sold. And other paper in prose that gives a full account of what happened as a consequence of the earthquake in this city.'

21. 'In the Cathedral, as strong as the building is, four aisles tore apart', *Relacion de la acaecido en la Ciudad de Granada el dia I. de Noviembre de 1755. con el Terremoto, que principiò entre 9. y 10. De la mañana, y durò 10. Minutos* (Seville, Imprenta de D. Joseph Navarro y Armijo, [1755]).

Huelva[22] and *Noticias de lo acaecido en el Reyno de Portugal de resultas del terremoto.*[23] There is little doubt that the same authors handed the manuscripts to both printers, who, confident of the success of the venture, decided to double the number of copies.

If one puts together Navarro's eighteen and Padrino's seventeen, the total amounts to thirty-five works on the earthquake. Still, the productions of another printer were even more numerous. The printer Viuda de Don Diego López de Haro took over her late husband's business in 1752, as was customary throughout the Modern Ages. By then, this firm had been established for over a hundred years in the city, its reputation being beyond any reasonable doubt, as proven by the fact that this printer had been awarded the highest credentials years before: 'Real', 'Tipografía Castellana y Latina', 'Impresor y Librero de la Reina' – that is to say, officially supported by the royalty. Her shop was also located in the Calle Génova.

Like Padrino and Navarro, Viuda de López de Haro augmented her mainstream production, aimed at the educated, with works for a wider audience. Her total production regarding the earthquake amounts to nineteen works. These include four average-length treatises, two of which focus on the scientific controversy around the causes of the tremor. A third attempts to arouse feelings of guilt with open references to the earthquake as a punishment that sinners had brought upon themselves. Finally, the fourth treatise thanks San Francisco de Borja and San Felipe Neri for their alleged intervention in saving citizens from more serious consequences. In addition to these works was a brief letter addressed to the king by a mathematician, who claimed to have experienced an earthquake before, in Peru. Despite the erudite tone of this work, the address to the throne was designed to attract public attention.

The firm's prestige, gained through the support of the official institutions of the city, led to Viuda de López de Haro's being asked to publish official flyers, like the one entitled *Distribucion de Iglesias, y predicadores, para la mission general, y reformacion a una nueva vida, que ha de empezar el domingo 30 de noviembre por nueve tardes continuadas.*[24] This work contains practical information that was bound to sell extremely well, considering the sudden

---

22. *Nuevo, y Curioso Romance del estrago causado el dia de Todos Santos en la Villa de Huelva* (Seville, Imprenta de D. Joseph Navarro y Armijo, [1755]) [New and curious ballad on the havoc that took place in Huelva on All Saints Day].

23. *Noticias de lo acaecido en el Reyno de Portugal de resultas del terremoto, experimentado el dia primero de noviembre de este presente año de 1755* (Seville, Imprenta de D. Joseph Navarro y Armijo, [1755]) [News on the events that occurred in the Kingdom of Portugal as a result of the earthquake occurred on 1 November 1755].

24. *Distribucion de Iglesias, y predicadores, para la mission general, y reformacion a una nueva vida, que ha de empezar el domingo 30 de Noviembre por nueve tardes continuadas* (Seville, Imprenta Real de la Viuda de D. Diego López de Haro, [1755]) [Preachers and churches allotted for the general mission and the making of a new life to start Sunday 3 November and will continue for nine evenings].

bout of superstitious fear which, according to many sources, seized the city immediately after the earthquake. More precisely, it contained a list of preachers and the schedule of religious services to be held in the most important churches of the town – services that were differentiated for men and women, as was the norm – and ended with a list of past earthquakes that had struck the city of Seville. She also printed some other cheap ballads and a chapbook with a curious title which urged the people to say their prayers. The chapbook featured a long-winded prayer, especially useful to keep earthquakes away; the reading of the pamphlet guaranteed the reward of 180 days of indulgences.[25]

The remaining works printed by Viuda de López de Haro are *relaciones*, more precisely ten pieces in poetry, or *romances*, the genre for which this printer was best known. A work also exists describing the effects of the earthquake on the San Jerónimo monastery, located on the edge of town, a work that was printed simultaneously by both Viuda and Navarro y Armijo, who as usual split the printing expenses. Also noteworthy is the publication of sequels of *relaciones* by this printer. Thus, one piece on the effects in Cádiz was published by Padrino, but only the first and the third part, whereas the second must be attributed to Viuda de López de Haro. The same pattern seems to apply to the publication of one *relación* on the earthquake in Córdoba, published at first by Padrino, with the sequel published by Viuda de López de Haro.

From what has been stated so far, it is clear that Viuda de López de Haro, Padrino and Navarro y Armijo were the main printers in town, who together account for fifty-four of the sixty-eight items published concerning the earthquake. This is not to say that they were the only ones exploiting news of the earthquake. Diego de San Román y Codina, who not long before 1755 had opened his shop on Colcheros Street, published two items on the subject: a chapbook of verses and a new treatise for scholars. Francisco Sánchez Reciente's workshop, established in the city for generations, added to the massive production a short book of verses and a brief discourse devoted to San Felipe Neri, as well as a long treatise giving credit to the (by then outdated) Aristotelian principles, which offered a physical explanation for the earthquake. In addition, Jerónimo de Castilla, the award-winning Mayor Printer of the city, published six works on the issue, all sermons that had been formerly preached in the important churches of the town. His production on the earthquake was limited because his official status blocked him from publishing vulgar comedies and ballads.

Finally, there was one further *relación* on the effects of the earthquake in several locations of North Africa. Although the publisher is unknown, it is

---

25. *Prevencion espiritual para los temblores de Tierra, dispuesta por un Devoto este presente año de 1755* (Seville, Imprenta Real de la Viuda de D. Diego López de Haro, [1755]) [Spiritual aid against earthquakes, composed by a man of God in this very year of 1755].

thought to have been printed in Seville in 1755. Two additional works on the earthquake, most probably published in the city, have also been found, but it is not clear who published them. These are a book with a poem and a flier with a pray devoted to San Emigdio, whom religious tradition held as protector against earthquakes.

iii. Notes on the writing and reading habits of the popular press in the eighteenth century

The output of the six Sevillian printing presses, as described above, gives a clear idea of the extent to which publishers managed to keep the public updated with the latest news. Having reviewed the main publishing strategies at the time, our attention should now shift to the remaining parts in the publishing process, namely the author and the reader. One of the obvious conclusions from a close look at the works published is that many different kinds of authors produced these 'minor products'. Many of these works were certainly written by what Amelang calls 'popular writers', but renowned scholars also attempted this genre.

Popular writers appear to have abounded in Seville at the time, if the complaints and queries of contemporary highbrow scholars are to be believed. But despite their popularity, the names of these authors are now unknown, except for a few such as padre Zacarías, a blind preacher whose *romances* were chanted all around Seville.[26] On the other hand, the academics who acted as journalists used to write brief essays, distributed throughout a well established network of colleagues. Within these circles, where contributors ultimately worked as influential lobbyists, all scientific and literary news was discussed and debated. Many of these works were supposed to be private correspondence, but all of them were finally sent by their authors to the printing press. In some cases, they may have tried to seek publicity as scholars; others may have considered it their duty to fight the lack of ethics of the time through their works. For many the purpose was pretty much in line with the mindset of the *Ilustración*, to educate the ignorant crowds with informative pieces. Apart from these two basic kinds of authors, there are other anonymous writers who produced journalistic pieces; little is known about them.

All the writers who contributed to the overall production on the earthquake had access to the letters, *avvisi*, gazettes and *relaciones* from Madrid sent to Seville twice a week via the mail. Unlike the educated or most professional authors, who relied solely on these sources, the popular

26. Francisco Aguilar Piñal, *Historia de Sevilla: siglo XVIII* (Seville 1989), p.339. A few studies deal with the activities of the so-called blind nightingales. Apart from the well known critical works by Botrel and García de Enterría, Pedro Cátedra's recently published *Invención, difusión y recepción de la literatura popular impresa (siglo XVI)* (Mérida 2002) will surely be definitive.

writers did not hesitate to echo public rumours and street gossip. The educated could do little about this, apart from making it clear that they deeply regretted the lack of sensibility of popular works, which at times were so sensationalist as to spread the false news that a plague had taken hold of the city.

Several further conclusions as to how people read and received these works can be drawn. It is again necessary to draw a line between the serious works, for which a single reading is feasible, and the *relaciones* – or at least the less vulgar of them – the reading of which was open-ended in nature. In fact, the cultivated authors sometimes cite the *relaciones* in their works as a source of information, although they normally do it with a wry comment, so as to distance themselves from the genre.

It would be interesting, but beyond the aims of this study, to browse the catalogues and indexes of the private libraries in search of *relaciones de sucesos*, however hard this task may be. While not intending such an in-depth study, we have looked into the libraries of four key *ilustrados* living in Seville in the eighteenth century: conde del Aguila, Jovellanos, Cándido M. Trigueros, and Francisco de Bruna. Only the last of these had *relaciones de sucesos* among the volumes in his library, which was donated to the Crown after his death. These items had been published in Seville in the sixteenth and seventeenth centuries, and dealt with religious festivals.[27] Trigueros also had in his library one *relación* on the martyrdom performed on Jesuits dating from the seventeenth century, although there might be more among the volumes labelled 'papeles varios', unidentified works.[28] Both authors had regular subscriptions to the most important national and foreign journals. During his short stay in Seville, Jovellanos put together a sizeable collection of books, most of which had been purchased from Jesuits sent into exile. In his personal library we can only find two items which appear to be *relaciones* on royal affairs printed in Madrid and Seville in the eighteenth century; but Jovellanos seemed to attach little importance to the local material printed in Seville. Rather, he would have booksellers, local or from elsewhere, order books printed in Madrid or abroad.[29]

This survey of these four libraries suggests that the educated considered the *relaciones* to be intellectually worthless, even if they happen to have read or bought them. At the other extreme as far as reading habits go, we should give the *romances* serious consideration. By the mid-eighteenth century, the clergy had disapproved time and again of their lack of morality; this mood eventually led to an official ban on these products for educational purposes in Seville in 1743. It was precisely at this time that

27. María Luisa López-Vidriero, *Los Libros de Francisco de Bruna en el Palacio del Rey* (Seville 1999).

28. Francisco Aguilar Piñal, *La Biblioteca y el monetario de Cándido M. Trigueros (1798)* (Seville 1999).

29. Francisco Aguilar Piñal, *La Biblioteca de Jovellanos (1778)* (Madrid 1984).

the sales of *romances* was at its peak. The *romances* included open references to the type of audience they would supposedly reach. From some notes in the works themselves:

> y al Auditorio le pido,
> que me preste su silencio[30]

we can learn that the *romances* were read in public with people gathering around the reader.

Recent studies have looked further into the situations where public readings occurred. Castillo Gómez mentions groups of people gathering together by the stairways of the cathedral in Seville to engage in public readings as early as the mid-sixteenth century.[31] In the same vein, Bouza refers to seventeenth-century sources that give full descriptions of the *relaciones* and authors putting them up on walls in public places, so that passers-by would read them. Quite often the news spread immediately after the events had taken place.[32] In any case, the available data show that the habit of the blind presenting *romances* in public had caught on to such an extent that blind singers had formed guilds. All through the Modern Age, and even as late as the nineteenth century, they appear reciting these long ballads which were easily learnt by heart due to their rhyming schemes. On many occasions, the blind were the authors of the works too. From this it follows that such public readings were instances of what Blanco and Rubalcaba have labelled 'escritura recibida': products that the popular classes appropriated.[33]

iv. Popular and serious press in the eighteenth century

The news business in an average-sized city like Seville reached high levels of activity because of the wide range of products coming off the printing presses. In one way or another, all members of the social fabric, either consumers or producers, were involved in the writing and reading process. We believe that the stages of the production process of this popular press can cast some light on the wider printing business.

In addition, we should point out that it was the existence of the cheap publications and news coverage of natural disasters that helped information about the 1755 earthquake to spread, since it was hardly mentioned in the quality press, such as the *Gaceta de Madrid*. As M. José Rodríguez

30. 'I request silence from the distinguished Audience.'

31. Antonio Castillo Gómez, '*No pasando por ello como gato sobre ascuas. Leer y anotar en la España del Siglo de Oro*', *Leituras. Revista da Biblioteca Nacional* 9-10, special issue *O livro antigo em Portugal e Espanha séculos XVI-XVIII* (2002), p.99-121

32. Fernando Bouza, *Corre manuscrito: una historia cultural del Siglo de Oro* (Madrid 2001), p.73-74.

33. Rosa M. Blanco Martínez and Carmen Rubalcaba Pérez, 'Sueño de una sombra: escritura y clases populares en Santander en el siglo XIX', in *Cultura escrita y clases subalternas: una mirada española*, ed. Antonio Castillo Gómez (Oiartzun 2001), p.128-31.

notices: 'Quien compraba uno de estos papeles deseaba conocer exclusi-vamente detalles relacionados con el suceso. Por el contrario, la prensa periódica ofrecía esta información acompañada de otras noticias de similar o incluso mayor interés público.'[34] The 4 November issue of the *Gaceta de Madrid* brought news from Vienna, Hamburg, London, The Hague, Paris and lastly, right before the adverts, from Madrid covering the earthquake very briefly. Actually, the news item tells us little, focusing primarily on the royal family and their being unaffected by the earth-quake:

Los Reyes nuestros Señores consiguen la mas perfecta salud en su Real Palacio del Buen Retiro, adonde se restituyeron de el de S. Lorenzo el Sabado primero de este mes por la tarde con motivo de un considerable Temblòr de Tierra, que el mismo dia à las diez, y diez minutos de la mañana se experimentò en aquel Real Sitio, haviendo durado por espacio de cinco à seis minutos; pero felizmente no ha causado novedad en la importante salud de sus Magestades, ni ocasionado daño alguno.[35]

A closer look at this issue of the *Gaceta* shows that the news is sequenced chronologically. The first item is dated in Vienna on 4 October and the last one addresses the earthquake, and is dated in Madrid one month later. As unbelievable as it may seem to contemporary readers, such an arrangement made perfect sense since the official gazette was a tool politically manipulated for the sake of the stability of the monarchy. Within this context, local or regional news was paid little heed, less so if it reported chaos and disorder, as was the case with natural disasters.[36] The distribution scheme, as André Belo points out, did not help either:

A *Gazeta* devia chegar a várias regiôes, dentro e fora do reino, mas era pre-sumivelmente lida sobretudo em Lisboa, meio urbano macrocéfalo de um ter-ritório largamente rural e analfabeto. Ela nâo informava o grande público. E numa época em que a informaçâo adquirida através de textos era menos importante do que aquilo que se via e do que aquilo que se transmitia oralmente pode começar-se por dizer que na capital do reino niguém soube do grande tremor de terra pelo jornal. O terramoto de 1755 nâo é noticia. O grande acontecimiento passa praticamente implícito na *Gazeta*: vivido por todos, ele é

---

34. 'Those who purchased these cheap publications were fond of learning all the details of the events. Readers had not the least interest in the updates of the general affairs; instead, the quality press covered all the news whatever their nature and location', Rodríguez Sánchez de León, 'El terremoto lisboeta', p.313.

35. 'Their Highness the King and the Queen are in good health in the Buen Retiro Palace, where they dwell now after leaving San Lorenzo Palace last Saturday evening following an earthquake which, on the same day, at exactly ten past ten in the morning hit the Royal estate. The tremor, which went on for five or six minutes, made no damages whatsoever and the health of their Majesties remained well.'

36. As a proof, the Lisbon earthquake and its consequences in Portugal and Spain were widely covered by French and German gazettes, as Hans-Jürgen Lüsebrink mentions. See André Belo, 'A *Gazeta de Lisboa* e o terramoto de 1755: a margem do nâo escrito', *Análise social* 151-52 (2000), p.619-37.

previamente conhecido, nâo assume estatuto de novidade quando passa ao periódico.[37]

Still, if we have to justify the lack of interest in the earthquake of the official press, it has to be admitted that the powerful popular news-trade, eager to spread local sensationalist news, left little room for serious journalism to tackle this event. The *relaciones de sucesos* and those other genres of the popular press make it clear that 'serious' newspapers were still far from the general public.

37. 'The *Gazeta* was distributed all around the kingdom, but it was mostly read in Lisbon, the urban spot within the rural and highly illiterate territory. The *Gazeta* was not aimed at the general public. At that time when information learnt by word of mouth was more important than information from actual texts, few if any knew about the earthquake from the newspaper. The 1755 earthquake is not a news item as such. The *Gazeta* takes it for granted, and in fact it was hardly new by the time the *Gazeta* covered the event', André Belo, 'A *Gazeta de Lisboa* e o terramoto', p.621.

MATTHIAS GEORGI

The Lisbon earthquake and scientific knowledge in the British public sphere

> In earth and air sulphureous vapours stor'd,
> Sleep mix'd by him, and wake but at his word[1]

Introduction: natural philosophy and the public in eighteenth-century England

IN *Recreations for gentlemen and ladies* the following recipe can be read:

To make an artificial earthquake
To twenty pounds of iron filings add as many pounds of sulphur; mix, work, and temper the whole together with a little water, so as to form a mass, half moist and half dry; this being buried three or four foot under ground, in six or seven hours time will have a prodigious effect; the earth will begin to tremble, crack and smoke, and fire and flame burst through.[2]

Originally the experiment, quoted here from the fourth edition of the book in 1759, was not devised for entertainment – it was not meant to be fun. Instead it was usually presented as proof of one theory concerning the natural causes of earthquakes in the mid-eighteenth century. Experts knew that earthquakes were caused by subterranean explosions of matter with ingredients similar to gunpowder. Why, however, do we find expert knowledge on earthquakes in a book on 'arithmetical sports' and 'fire-works'?

This chapter deals with the representation of earthquakes in the British public sphere in the mid-eighteenth century. The first section will show how earthquakes were portrayed in the 1740s and 1750s, and which epistemological rules the understanding of explanations for earthquakes had to obey. An analysis of the debate concerning the Lisbon earthquake forms the second section. In the public discussion of this disaster, which lasted for several weeks, we can detect how natural philosophical knowledge about earthquakes was presented, which theories and facts needed

---

1. [Richard] Carter, *An Ode on the late earthquakes to which is added a cantata and song. Sung by Master Thumoth at Ranelagh Gardens. Set to musick by Mr. Charter* (London [1756?]), p.3.

2. [Jacques] Ozanam, *Recreations for gentlemen and ladies: being, ingenious sports and pastimes. Containing the many curious inventions: pleasant tricks on the cards and dice: arithmetical sports: diverting experiments, natural and artificial: recreative fire-works: and other curiosities, affording variety of entertainment*, 4th edn (Dublin 1759), p.176-77.

to be explained, which ideas, now unquestioned, were presented as if they were universally valid. On the basis of these two sections, this article will show that in the English public sphere, an earthquake was a spectacle of nature, which attained its significance through a natural philosophical interpretation.

In the eighteenth century, natural philosophy and the spectacle of nature were widespread topics in the British press. Magazines like the *Gentleman's magazine* and the *London magazine* were full of reports about natural curiosities, new inventions and discoveries made in the world of science. In coffee houses, science was performed in shows featuring the air-pump and electric or optical instruments. Those who popularised natural philosophy served the market for popular science, and some of them were able to earn their living exclusively by doing so. While some popularisers were charlatans, most were acknowledged scientists, and several were even fellows of the Royal Society.[3] Apart from shows for entertainment, most of the public lectures focused on the presentation of learning for a practical purpose. Margaret Jacob has demonstrated that applied natural philosophy became one of the sources for the industrial revolution.[4]

In order to reach their customers, the popularisers not only lectured in coffee houses, but also published a wide array of pamphlets and newspaper advertisements. They utilised the new possibilities for communication that came into being during the seventeenth and eighteenth centuries. They and their customers were part of the newly arisen public sphere, which Jürgen Habermas in his basic survey has interpreted as a bourgeois phenomenon.[5] Recent research shows that it was education rather than social class that determined membership of this public sphere,[6] which allowed the 'educated' to distance themselves from the 'vulgar' by accentuating the beauty of their philosophical-scientific knowledge. They contrasted their knowledge with the 'superstition' of the supposedly uneducated masses, who still believed in predictions and omens and were horrified by a passing comet.

It is hard to determine how many people participated in the public sphere. In the mid-eighteenth century, popular newspapers and magazines were read by twenty-five to fifty per cent of the population of London.[7] These readers had access to the information and debates of

---

3. See Larry Stewart, *The Rise of public science: rhetoric, technology, and natural philosophy in Newtonian Britain, 1660-1750* (Cambridge 1992), and Barbara Strafford, *Artful science: enlightenment, entertainment, and the eclipse of visual education* (Cambridge, MA 1994).

4. Margaret Jacob, *Scientific culture and the making of the industrial west* (Oxford 1997).

5. Jürgen Habermas, *The Structural transformation of the public sphere*, translated by Thomas Burger with Frederick Lawrence (Cambridge, MA 1989).

6. Thomas Broman, 'The Habermasian public sphere and "science in the Enlightenment"', *History of science* 36 (1998), p.123-449.

7. See Michael Harris, *London newspapers in the age of Walpole: a study in the origins of the modern English press* (Rutherford, NJ, London 1987), p.190.

the 'enlightened'. Additionally, many illiterates accessed parts of this knowledge by listening to the sermons during services. Accordingly, the public sphere was not a narrow circle but included 'the skilled labouring classes, as well as the middling ranks (shopkeepers, tradesmen, professionals, and merchants) and the social and political elites'.[8]

i. Earthquakes in the public sphere in the 1740s and 1750s

In this public sphere, disasters and especially earthquakes were intensively discussed. Together with thunderstorms, earthquakes were the most frequently reported natural spectacles in the late 1740s and 1750s.[9] We find accounts of them in almost every month's issue of the *Gentleman's magazine* and the *London magazine*. Most of these articles were short and similar to this example from the *Gentleman's magazine*, June 1753: 'Forli, May 12. On Easter Sunday a violent shock of an Earthquake was felt at Citadella, which threw down most of the houses, and a church, and two women perish'd in the ruins. It was felt also at Galliata and some other places, where the damage is very considerable.'[10] Earthquakes are also a recurring element in travel books. Short paragraphs describe how in former times distant countries were shaken by heavy quakes.[11]

In this part of my article, I describe how earthquakes were presented in the 1740s and 1750s in the British public sphere, which elements texts shared, and which epistemological rules the understanding had to follow. I am going to show that the public presentation of earthquakes closely followed that of scientific texts, and emphasise two elements: the role of fear in the presentations and the use of traditional knowledge.

One of the surprising similarities in the texts describing earthquakes is the lack of fear. Enlightened observers in the published texts never showed fear during an earthquake. There are two ways to explain this phenomenon. First, earthquakes could be experienced aesthetically, and represented as sublime. Shortly after the Lisbon earthquake, Edmund Burke

---

8. Bob Harris, *Politics and the nation: Britain in the mid-eighteenth century* (Oxford 2002), p.106-107; see also Margaret Jacob, *The Cultural meanings of the scientific revolution* (Philadelphia, PA 1988), p.106-15.

9. Also in France there was an increasing interest in earthquakes in the 1740s: Grégory Quenet, 'Les tremblements de terre en France aux 17ᵉ et 18ᵉ siècles: une histoire sociale du risque', *Traverse* 10 (2003), p.90.

10. *The Gentleman's magazine* 23 (December 1753), p.290.

11. See for example Joseph Addison, *Remarks on several part of Italy, &c. in the years 1701, 1702, 1703* (London 1745), p.149, 297; George Anson, *A Voyage round the world, in the years MDCCL,I,II,III,IV*, 3rd edn (Dublin 1748), p.78; John Atkins, *A Voyage to Guinea, Brasil, and the West-Indies; in His Majesty's Ship the Swallow and Weymouth*, 2nd edn (London 1737), p.30, 242; Cornelis de Bruyn, *Travels into Muscovy, Persia, and part of the East-Indies. Containing, an accurate description of whatever is most remarkable in those countries* (London 1737), i.117; Patrick Barclay, *The Universal traveller: or, a complete account of the most remarkable voyages and travels of eminent men* (London 1735), p.314, 691, 693.

mentioned earthquakes as fulfilling the conditions of a sublime event: they revealed enormous force, produced horror and destruction.[12] Observers in printed descriptions followed the rules, which the experience of the sublime had to obey. As John Baillie explained in his *Essay on the sublime* (1747), you can only experience the sublimity of nature when you are not afraid.[13] In 1751 this was illustrated in the *London magazine* by the story of the Princess Esterhasi. During an earthquake and an eruption of Vesuvius, the princess stayed in Naples. She went up the mountain every day, 'more intent upon the causes, than frightened at this phænomenon', there she observed the place 'where the ignited substance bent its course, taking with her some persons of learning for her information'; then she followed the stream of lava all the way down till it ended in the sea.[14] Rather than fear, her reaction was curiosity, delight and pleasure upon witnessing the force of nature.

A second possible explanation for the lack of fear in these accounts suggests itself when one notices the scientific detachment of those by whom the information was collected. Here, for instance, is a report in the *Gentleman's magazine* for March 1750:

Between 10 and 11 o'clock at night, on July 1, 1747, being myself in some company at Taunton, we were suddenly surprised with a rumbling noise like distant thunder, which was followed immediately by so considerable motion of the earth, that the chair whereon I sat rocked under me. The noise and shaking seemed to come from distance, and approached gradually, in such a manner, as if a loaded waggon had passed along; and continued nearly the same time as such a waggon would require to go about 100 yards. [... S]ome of us imagined at first the waggon had really gone along, but upon running out and enquiring, we found there had been no waggon.[15]

At this point the author and his companions went outside to see what had taken place.

Other men used the occasion of an earthquake to verify a theory about these events. After an earthquake in London in 1750, for instance, one person systematically gathered descriptions of what all the people in his household had experienced during the shock. Then, for the rest of the day, he conducted experiments on the weather, dropping small pieces of paper out of the window to observe their fall. By doing this, he verified

---

12. [Edmund Burke], *A Philosophical enquiry into the origin of our ideas of the sublime and beautiful*, 3rd edn (London 1761) p.79-82 (Part I, Sect. XVI); p.121-24 (Part II, Sect. V). The first edition of this book was published in 1757.

13. John Baillie, *An Essay on the sublime: by the late Dr. Baillie* (London 1747), edited in *The Augustan Reprint Society* 43 (Los Angeles 1953), p.31; see also Burke, *A Philosophical enquiry into the origin of our ideas of the sublime and beautiful*, Part I, Sect. VII, and Richard Alewyns, 'Die Lust an der Angst', in *Probleme und Gestalten*, ed. Richard Alewyns (Frankfurt 1974) p.307-30.

14. *The London magazine: or Gentleman's monthly intelligencer* 20 (November 1751), p.522.

15. *The London magazine* 19 (March 1750), p.124-25.

that the weather remained calm all day[16] – which was believed to be one of the conditions for a subterranean explosion.

As the effects of an earthquake were similar to the effects of shooting a huge cannon – a rumbling noise and the shaking of the air and the soil – the idea that subterranean explosions produced earthquakes dominated the discussions in the eighteenth century. It was known that all the chemicals necessary for a spontaneous explosion could be found underneath the earth – especially iron, sulphuric matter and water, which are key ingredients in the production of gunpowder. But that was not the only theory and not everyone accepted it. William Stukeley, 'M. D. Rector of St. George's, Queen-Square; Fellow of the College of Physicians, and of the Royal and Antiquarian Society',[17] tried to prove that one of the major conditions for subterranean explosions – a cavernous structure of the underground – did not exist, so he went down under the earth to examine it personally:

I have been myself 2 or 300 feet deep in a solid rock of native salt: I have walked a mile lengthwise directly into the earth, and descending all the way, in the proportion of one yard in five, 'till we came under the bed of the very ocean, where ships were sailing over our heads. This was at Sir James Lowther's coal-pit, at Whitehaven.[18]

Since Stukeley did not discover any openings or caves in the coal-pits, he argued that without holes, subterranean sulphuric vapours could not diffuse and get mixed with iron. Therefore he concluded that underground explosions were impossible.

The men of Enlightenment who described and analysed earthquakes were full of curiosity, and tried to gather as much information as possible regarding these events. They also seemed concerned to describe their behaviour as thoughtful and calm. After the Lisbon earthquake, for example, a merchant wrote a letter to London about how he had experienced the incident. After the first shock he prepared to leave his house: 'I had drest my Legs, and was putting on my Coat and Waistcoat (having first put up my Books in their Case and locked the Doors of it) when I felt the second Shock begin: So I snatched up my Hat, and taking my Wig from a Sconce.' He ran down the stairs, but then stopped, since stones were falling in a yard he had to pass: 'This made me reflect, that by flying from one falling House, I ran the risk of being buried under

---

16. *A Dissertation upon earthquakes, their causes and consequences; comprehending an explanation of the nature and composition of subterraneous vapours, [...]: together with a distinct account of, and some remarks upon, the shock of an earthquake, felt in the cities of London and Westminster, on Thursday, February 8, 1749-50* (London 1750) p.65-66.

17. From the title of the 3rd edn of William Stukeley, *The Philosophy of earthquakes, natural and religious: or an inquiry into their cause, and their purpose: third edition, to which is added, part III. on the same subject* (London 1756).

18. Stukeley, *The Philosophy of earthquakes*, p.11.

the Ruins of many others in the narrow Streets I must be obliged to pass before I could get to any Place of greater Safety.'[19] When he finally reached the square in front of the royal palace, he 'found Numbers of People, of all Nations, collected together; with such Signs of Terror and Distress in every Countenance as can be much better imagined than described'. In contrast to his correctly dressed appearance (he even wore a wig), he told of 'several Persons almost naked' assembled on an open space, 'one of which was an English Surgeon, with nothing on him but a Shirt, Cloak, and Pair of Slippers'.[20] Later in his description he portrayed the behaviour of the masses, who ran in panic back into the narrow streets and got killed by the next shock, while he remained calm in a safe place.[21]

In this and similar reports, the reflected calmness of the enlightened observer was often contrasted with the blind alarm of the uneducated. When something unexpected occurred in nature, the vulgar are portrayed as running away until they came upon an educated person who would protect them from the perilous event. When the tsunami initiated by the Lisbon earthquake reached the British Isles the water of Pibley Dam in the parish of Barlborough rose and fell a couple of feet, making the doors of a boathouse rattle loudly. Because 'not a breeze of wind was heard, nor a wave seen upon its surface' the labourers were so scared by the noise of the water, 'that it was with great difficulty the steward could prevail with any of them to run to the boat-house, and see if any beast was there plunged into the water'. Finally 'a hardy young fellow' went there. But when he reached the house:

he was so shocked with the noise of the water (occasioned, as was presumed, by the water's passing and repassing under the folding doors, as it ebbed or flowed) and by the boat's tumbling about and beating against the sides of the house, that when he returned he was not able at first to give a rational answer to any question that was asked him.

Paul Gemsege, the author of this account, emphasised that it was 're-ceived from two sensible men, and of undoubted veracity (whereof the steward was one)'.[22] Why were the steward in this story and the merchant who wrote from Lisbon not afraid? Or why, if they were afraid, is their fear not mentioned?

As Steven Shapin and Simon Schaffer have demonstrated, in the seven-teenth century the validity of scientific observations depended on cate-gories like confidence and honour. The high social position of a witness to

---

19. *An Account of the late dreadful earthquake and fire, which destroyed the City of Lisbon, the metropolis of Portugal: in a letter from a merchant resident there, to his friend in England* (London 1755), p.13-14.
20. *An Account of the late dreadful earthquake and fire*, p.17.
21. *An Account of the late dreadful earthquake and fire*, p.19-20.
22. *The Gentleman's magazine* 25 (December 1755), p.541.

a scientific experiment was an important element of the credibility of his testimony.[23] In the eighteenth century the categories remained similar. But the honesty of a witness no longer depended mainly on his descent. Rather, every literate person could be trustworthy. But how could one prove that he was well educated? Most eighteenth-century descriptions of happenings in nature contain comparable elements, and it appears that certain rules of narration existed to make sure that one could believe the text and its author. In contrast to religious texts, these texts used a clear grammatical structure with short sentences. The exact location and the weather were mentioned, and the variety of metaphors to describe noise or colours seems to have been limited. The description of the observer's behaviour was particularly important. He had to show indifference regarding the event, and not be blinded by false expectations. He also had to remain calm and free from panic and fear, since only in such a manner could he observe rationally and judge correctly. The terror of the vulgar was used to highlight the enlightened poise of the scientific observer.

The fear of the vulgar also had another function in the texts of the mid-eighteenth century. Accounts of earthquakes suggest that it was only if farmers or their wives ran terrified from their houses that an earthquake, or any other frightening natural event, would be worth investigation by an enlightened person.

Not only did the behaviour of the persons mentioned in reports of earthquakes remain within defined borders, with the enlightened observer reacting calmly, perhaps even with some aesthetic delight, and the vulgar responding with terror. The theories used to explain earthquakes were also limited by the expectations and knowledge of the audience. Although it almost never happens,[24] in the eighteenth century people were often described as being swallowed up by the earth during an earthquake. After the second 1750 earthquake in London, for instance, *Read's weekly journal, or the British-Gazetteer* printed an article about the 1692 earthquake in Port Royal, Jamaica. A man described how he was running in the direction of Morgan's Fort, hoping to be safe, when he reached an open space, 'but, as I made towards it, I saw the Earth open and swallow up a Multitude of People, and the Sea mounting in upon us over the Fortifications, I then laid aside all Hopes of escaping, and resolved to make toward my own Lodging, and there to meet Death in as good Posture as I could'. In this

---

23. See in particular Steven Shapin, *A Social history of truth: civility and science in the seventeenth-century England* (Chicago 1994); together with Simon Schaffer, *Leviathan and the air-pump: Hobbes, Boyle, and the experimental life* (Princeton 1985). For further categories of testimony in this time see R. W. Serjeantson, 'Testimony and proof in early-modern England', *Studies in history and philosophy of science* 30 (1999), p.195-236.

24. Charles James from the Earthquake engineering research center in Berkeley gave me this information.

report the author was not concerned about the causes of earthquakes, but explained the pain, fear and horror he and other people experienced during the disaster.[25]

Charles Wesley similarly used the image of people being swallowed up by the earth to reveal the dread of such an event:

In many Places the Earth would crack, and open and shut quick and fast, of which Openings two or three Hundred might be seen at a Time; in some whereof the People were swallowed up, others the closing Earth caught by the Middle, and squeezed to Death; and in that Manner they were left buried with only their Heads above Ground: Some Heads the Dogs eat.[26]

The image of people, cities and even mountains being swallowed up by the earth was also widespread in less emotional texts about earthquakes. We can find many of these accounts in journals. In Cairo 'streets were swallowed up, and thousands perished';[27] in the city of Cachan an earthquake 'has swallowed up 6000 houses, with all the inhabitants';[28] in the Ecclesiastic State the 'parish church of the village of Padola was entirely swallowed up';[29] in Legoan an earthquake 'swallowed up two large mountains'.[30] In addition, theories of natural philosophy occasionally combined the swallowing of people and cities with subterranean explosions: 'the explosions make large chasms in the earth, and swallow up the whole [city] in a moment'.[31]

Satirical texts on earthquakes also used descriptions of swallowed people. In a fanciful account of how an earthquake had destroyed London in 1750, for example, during the clearing up of the city, 'it was soon discovered whereabouts White's Chocolate House was swallowed up' with the 'great Number of Persons of the first Rank [who] were known to be in it that Night'. The lawyers were also swallowed up: 'The Town received some Comfort upon hearing that the Inns of Court were all sunk, and several Orders were given that no one should assist in bringing any one Lawyer above Ground; but to the great Concerns of all Well-wishers

---

25. *Read's weekly journal, or the British-Gazetteer* 1340 (Saturday 14 April 1750), p.1.

26. [Charles Wesley], *The Causes and cure of earthquakes: a sermon preach'd from Psalm xlvi.8* (London 1750), p.8-9. Other sermons with the description of swallowed people are for example: T. Jones, *Repentance and reconciliation with God recommended and enforced, in two sermons, preach'd at the Parish-Church of St. Saviour, Southwark; on Sunday February the 1st. and on Friday the 6th. Being the day appointed, by His Majesty's proclamation, to be observed as a General Fast. With a serious and affectionate address to the inhabitants of the said parish* (London 1756), p.10; [George Lavington], *A Sermon preached in the Cathedral-Church of Exeter, on the General Fast-day, February 6, 1756. By the Lord Bishop of Exeter* (Exon [1756]), p.6.

27. *The Gentleman's magazine* 24 (November 1754), p.527.

28. *The Gentleman's magazine* 25 (December 1755), p.570.

29. *The London magazine* 20 (September 1751), p.425.

30. *The London magazine* 21 (Feb. 1752), 'Monthly chronologer', p.94.

31. *The Gentleman's magazine* 26 (September 1756), p.422.

to their Country they begin to swarm as usual, and upon Inquiry it seems they have found Holes to creep out at.'[32]

Factual or fanciful reports of swallowed people were not questioned. In the description from Lisbon quoted above, the merchant described in detail what had occurred, without mentioning that the earth had opened and killed people. But when he then added details of places he had not seen himself, he wrote, 'The Earth opened in abundance of Places of the Kingdom.' He listed Alcantara, Scavem, and St. Martinho as examples.[33] Having not seen this phenomenon as an eyewitness, he did not write about it with specificity. But since chasms in the earth were believed to be normal during an earthquake, the merchant incorporated these stories unchecked into his report.

If it hardly ever happened that the earth swallowed up men and houses, why did people believe it? The most probable source of this supposed knowledge may be the Bible, especially this passage from Numbers:

But if the Lord make a new thing, and the earth open her mouth, and swallow them up, with all that appertain unto them, and they go down quick into the pit; then ye shall understand that these man have provoked the Lord.

And it came to pass, as he had made an end of speaking all these words, that the ground clave asunder that was under them:

And the earth opened her mouth, and swallowed them up, and their houses, and all their men that appertained unto Korah, and all their goods.[34]

In the mid-eighteenth century the Bible could still be seen as a reliable source for all kinds of learning, including the interpretation of nature and the proof of natural philosophical theories. When pure observation was not sufficient to explain a phenomenon, or when a theory needed historical data, the stories of the Bible, especially of the Old Testament, were often quoted.[35]

Another example of traditional knowledge and its role in the epistemology of narrations about earthquakes in the English public sphere involves the weather. People knew that the weather was interconnected

32. [Richard Bentley], *A Second letter from a gentleman in town, to his friend in the country, on account of the late dreadful earthquake: containing a list of several more persons that have been since found in the rubbish* (London 1750), p.1-2.

33. *An Account of the late dreadful earthquake and fire*, p.34.

34. Numbers xvi.30-32, *King James Version*. Another example which was often quoted in the eighteenth century is Psalm cvi.17.

35. A good example of using the Bible as a source for natural philosophical conclusions is William Whiston, *Memoirs of the life and writings of Mr William Whiston: Part III, containing his three lectures at the Royal-Exchange coffee-house in London, March 6, 8, and 10, 1749-50: upon occasion of the late remarkable meteors and earthquakes; but much improved by himself since that time* (London 1750). Later in the eighteenth century Tom Paine argued that the Bible could not be a reliable source because it was written by men and it 'had suffered corruption through copying and translation', as John Hedley Brooke explains in his *Science and religion: some historical perspectives* (Cambridge 1991), p.193.

with earthquakes, so it was narrated precisely in the accounts. Earthquakes and lightning were thought to have the same origin. It was believed that down in the earth the exhalations of gunpowder fermented to a vapour which was 'extremely inflammable, and with a little motion, takes fire of it self'. When this 'escapes into the air, it is formed into clouds and becomes the material cause of thunder and lightening; and therefore all the difference between these and an earthquake is, that in the one case it takes fire in the air, and in the other, under ground'. The effects of lightning and earthquakes resembled each other, 'the noise of a violent earthquake to that of thunder' and the smell 'being found in any thing burnt with lightening, as in the waters, &c. cast up by earthquakes, and in the air after both' was recognised as equally sulphuric.[36]

But when Benjamin Franklin showed, by his experiment with a kite in 1752, that lightning was an electrical and not a chemical phenomenon, the logical interaction between lightning and earthquakes had to be revisited.[37] Most commentators on earthquakes simply abandoned the idea that lightning and earthquakes had the same origin. Some natural philosophers, however, tried to preserve the interconnection by integrating electricity into their theories. William Stukeley was the first to use electricity to explain earthquakes. He argued:

In an age when electricity has been so much our entertainment, and our amazement; when we are become so well acquainted with its stupendous powers and properties, its velocity, and instantaneous operation through any given distance; when we see, upon a touch, or an approach, between a non-electric and an electrified body, what a wonderful vibration is produc'd! what a snap it gives! how an innocuous flame breaks forth! how violent a shock! Is it to be wonder'd at, that hither we turn our thoughts, for the solution of the prodigious appearance of an earthquake?[38]

From Franklin's discovery that clouds had diverse electrical charges, which produced lightning, and from the observation that the earth, too, could be charged electrically, Stukeley reckoned, 'that, if a non-electric cloud discharges its contents upon any part of the earth, when in a high electrified state, an earthquake must necessarily ensue'. In addition, he was able to explain the effect of an earthquake: 'The snap made upon the contact of many compass of solid earth, is that horrible uncouth noise, which we hear upon an earthquake; and the shock is the earthquake itself.'[39] Later Joseph Priestley would support this theory by passing an

---

36. For example *The Theory and history of earthquakes* (London [1750]), p.7-8.

37. Shortly before the London earthquake of 1750 Franklin's theory was presented to the London Royal Society; see Stukeley, *The Philosophy of earthquakes*, p. 25. See also *The Gentleman's magazine* 20 (January 1750), p.34.

38. Stukeley, *The Philosophy of earthquakes*, p.22.

39. Stukeley, *The Philosophy of earthquakes*, p.26; see also Bernard Cohen, *Benjamin Franklin's science* (Cambridge, MA 1990), p.145-54.

electrical flash over the surface of ice, and noting that pillars standing on the ice fell down after the electrical shock.[40]

Though this theory connecting earthquakes with electricity was never widely accepted among scholars, the weather remained important for theorists who explained earthquakes as subterranean explosion. For such an event needed to be preceded by a long period of dry weather. So in most reports about earthquakes, one finds descriptions of the weather. An example can be found in the *Gentleman's magazine* for February 1752, when an earthquake and an eruption of a volcano were reported on the Isle of St Domingo. The description starts by reporting that on 18 October 1751, the day of the earthquake, there was 'clearest sunshine, and calmest weather'.[41] The careful description of the weather in these reports exemplifies a general increase of interest in meteorological observation during the early decades of the eighteenth century,[42] but also results from the traditional knowledge that weather was involved in causing earthquakes. In addition, a clear description of the weather, together with a precise report of the location, the date and the time of a natural event, was one of the elements isolated in the early modern conflict between the Catholics and the Protestants over the reliability of reports concerning miracles and divine signs.[43]

Both in the presentation of observations and in the description of the observer's behaviour, the epistemology of public reports about earthquakes widely followed that of scientific texts. Natural philosophy could, and often did, have a mediatory role in giving an earthquake meaning. Earthquakes as an aesthetic or entertaining event were clearly connected with natural philosophy. In fact Princess Esterhazi took 'men of learning' with her, to increase her aesthetic experience when she derived pleasure at the stream of lava on the slopes of Vesuvius. Also the artificial earthquake, quoted at the beginning of this chapter, used scientific knowledge to create an amusement for 'Recreations for gentlemen and ladies'.

ii. Public perceptions of the Lisbon earthquake

The first news about the Lisbon earthquake reached the British Isles at the end of November 1755. It met an interested and well-informed audience, who regarded the earthquake with intense curiosity. For Charles Bulkley, the Dissenter, this was not an appropriate reaction. In one of the first sermons in England about the Lisbon earthquake, he tried

40. Joseph Priestley, *The History and present state of electricity with original experiments* (London 1767), p.687-90.

41. *The Gentleman's magazine* 22 (Historical chronicle, February 1752), p.91.

42. Vladimir Jankovic, *Reading the skies: a cultural history of English weather, 1650-1820* (Manchester 2000), p.90-102.

43. Lorraine Daston and Katherine Park, *Wonders and the order of nature 1150-1750* (New York 1998), p.247-48.

to convince his audience that the 'melancholy and most dreadful event' had to be seen 'not merely as a matter of curiosity and astonishment, but as an awful dispensation of divine providence'.[44]

Apart from curiosity, the initial response to the disaster in Britain was compassion for the Portuguese and British merchants who had lost all their property, and charity. The British king even sent a ship with donations to Portugal.[45] Self-doubt, fear and panic hardly occurred in the early public discussions. Nevertheless, things would change rapidly during the following weeks.

Most newspaper articles on the earthquake in Lisbon simply reported what had happened. Eyewitness accounts by people who had been there were published, and there was discussion about the numbers of dead. (Was the death toll 100,000 or 10,000?)[46] The papers were particularly interested in the fate of the royal family, emphasising that the king had survived unharmed, which made clear there was no lack of power in Portugal. By providing information, these reports satisfied the demands of curiosity. But sometimes an interpretation could be read between the lines, as in reports that only about twenty English Protestants died in contrast to the thousands of Catholics.[47] Sometimes God's anger with the Inquisition was seen as the reason why God had sent the earthquake.[48] But for the most part, the articles printed in newspapers and journals only communicated information from the disaster area itself.

Religious analysis of the catastrophe was primarily made in sermons.[49] It is there that we can find a change in interpretation during the ten weeks from the beginning of December 1755 to mid-February 1756 – the main period during which the Lisbon earthquake was discussed in England.

At first it was seen as a dreadful but local event, a direct divine warning for the Portuguese that had no more meaning for the English than for the rest of the world. This changed towards the end of January 1756, when the problems with France that would culminate in the Seven Years War

---

44. Charles Bulkley, *A Sermon preached at the evening-lecture in the Old Jewry, on Sunday, Nov. 30, 1755, on occasion of the dreadful earthquake at Lisbon, Nov. 1, 1755* (London 1756), p.3.

45. *The London evening post* 4380 (4-6 December 1755), p.1. For an overview of current research on the Lisbon earthquake see Christiane Eifert, 'Das Erdbeben von Lissabon 1755: Zur Historizität einer Naturkatastrophe', *Historische Zeitschrift* 274 (2002), p.633-64.

46. See for example *Read's weekly journal* 2346 (29 November 1755), p.2, to 2343 (6 December 1755), p.4. (The numbering is not uniform in the original.)

47. *The Gentleman's magazine* 26 (February 1756), p.68.

48. *The Whitehall evening-post: or, London intelligencer* 1531 (16-18 December 1755), p.3.

49. Some texts with religious thoughts concerning the earthquake were also published in journals and newspapers, which followed in their arguments those of the sermons, for example, in *The Gentleman's magazine* 26 (February 1756) p.68-70; *The London magazine: or Gentleman's monthly intelligencer* 25 (February 1756), p.67-68; *The Whitehall evening-post: Or, London intelligencer* 1522 (25-27 November 1755), p.3.

began to escalate rapidly. By this time, the Lisbon disaster had become an event with particular significance for Britain:

God is long suffering and merciful, he delays before he kills, and he gives warning before he strikes [...]. Our country has formerly felt the effects of earthquakes; [...] a contagious plague and distemper has raged among the cattle in these kingdoms for several years, and still rages. But, particularly, the dreadful earthquakes sent by God, at this time to our neighbouring nations ought to alarm us, and put us in mind, that as we yield to few nations in wickedness, so we cannot tell, how soon the like calamities may be at our own door.[50]

The earthquake in Lisbon was seen as the last of several divine warnings for the British that God would destroy his chosen people in the coming war. These warnings included the Jacobite Rebellion, the outbreak of a deadly cattle disease that had circulated in Britain since 1746, the London earthquakes in 1750, the Lisbon earthquake, and now the imminent war.

In the sermons, natural philosophy was rejected as the sole explanation of the disaster.[51] The two main religious groups – the Anglican High Church and the Dissenters – differed in the political and moral instructions they drew from the Lisbon earthquake. But their positions concerning the role played by the laws of nature were mostly the same: they insisted that God was the prime mover responsible for the disaster. John Thomas, the Bishop of Lincoln, in his sermon on the official fast day occasioned by the earthquake in Lisbon on 6 February 1756, preached that 'The Infidel looks upon publick Calamities as proceeding from natural Causes: And herein he is not mistaken'; but Bishop Thomas added that it is God with his foreknowledge who is 'regulating the course of nature so as to answer all the ends, and no other ends but those, which he purposes or allows'.[52] The same day the dissenter Joseph Baller expressed the idea of nature as cause of the earthquake in greater detail: 'Now if we do but consider, the different Courses which these Streams of Fire or sulphurous Vapours (which, confined in the Bowels of the Earth, occasioned those horrid Convulsion) [...], if we consider the Courses those Streams took, ere they got Vent, it is truly wonderful, and almost miraculous, that we in this part of the World should escape this sore Visitation.'[53] In explaining the

50. *An Earnest exhortation to repentance: on occasion of the late dreadful and extensive earthquakes: a sermon preached before a congregation on the General Fast-Day: delivered in two parts* (London 1756), p.22.

51. For a short overview of science and religion in the eighteenth century see John Hedley Brooke, 'Science and religion', in *The Cambridge history of science*, vol.iv, *Eighteenth-century science*, ed. Roy Porter (Cambridge 2003), p.741-61.

52. John [Thomas], *A Sermon preached before the House of Lords in the Abby-Church of Westminster, on Friday, February 6th, 1756: being the day appointed to be observed as a general fast, on occasion of the late dreadful earthquake* (London 1756), p.9, p.10-11.

53. Joseph Baller, *Divine alarms and warnings to a sinful people considered and improved: a sermon preached at Barnstaple, in the Country of Devon, on February 6. 1756: being the day appointed for a general fasting and humiliation, on account of the late dreadful earthquakes in divers places; and to implore a divine blessing and success on our counsels and arms against our enemies* (London 1756), p.9-10.

disaster in Lisbon, these preachers see God as the first cause, who used secondary causes such as subterranean explosions to create the earthquake. In the sermons preached concerning the Lisbon earthquake, one can hardly find any discussion questioning the combination of primary and secondary causes.

Six years earlier, when two light earthquakes shook London early in 1750, a fierce, even panic-stricken debate broke out, and the cause of earthquakes was the most intensively discussed topic in the newspapers. Earthquakes were presented as purely natural phenomena without any divine significance; alternatively they were interpreted – in particular by Thomas Sherlock, the bishop of London at this time – as a direct intervention by a furious God who did not need to use secondary causes to shake the earth but 'immediately directed [the earthquake] to these great cities'.[54] The compromise, with God as the primary cause and the laws of nature as secondary causes, did exist in 1750, but it was mostly lost in the fierceness of the conflict.[55]

In contrast, during the first months of 1756 the explanation that earthquakes originated with God acting through natural causes was nearly undisputed. The question of what had happened (an earthquake) was not discussed – neither how it happened (by natural causes), nor why the earth trembled (because of a divine punishment and warning). Instead the popular discussion focused on who was being punished.

As illustrated above, the religious interpretation of earthquakes dominated the debates in winter of 1755 to 1756 (and in spring 1750). As far as most of the lighter or less discussed earthquakes in the 1740s and 1750s were concerned, religious arguments were not very common. But it was sometimes asked how earthquakes could be useful for the natural world, since God would not have created anything useless. Some suggested that earthquakes reduced the subterranean pressure or cleaned the air of bad vapours, interpreting earthquakes as tools to preserve the balance of nature.[56] In the debates about the London earthquakes in 1750, and about the Lisbon earthquake in 1755 and 1756, when religious questions dominated the discussion, it was generally assumed that earthquakes were caused by the laws of nature. But these laws were not used to understand the meaning of the event; instead, these earthquakes were interpreted as negative, alarming signs, which received their meaning from the

---

54. Thomas Sherlock, *A Letter from the Lord Bishop of London to the clergy and people of London and Westminster; on occasion of the late earthquakes* (London 1750), p.4.

55. For a more detailed interpretation of the London earthquakes see Robert G. Ingram, '"The trembling Earth is God's Herald": earthquakes, religion, and public life in Britain during the 1750s', p.97-115 of the present volume, and G. S. Rousseau, 'The London earthquake of 1750', *Cahiers d'histoire mondiale* 11 (1968), p.436-51.

56. *The Whitehall evening-post: or, London intelligencer* 637 (10 March to 13 March 1750), p.1; *The Theory and history of earthquakes*, p.12-13.

Bible. The story of Job was often quoted.[57] Nevertheless there were some attempts to use natural philosophy to ascribe a positive meaning even to the Lisbon earthquake. In his sermon on 6 February 1756, the official fast day, for instance, William Hazeland tried to present the negative consequences of the disaster (10,000 deaths and numberless destroyed houses) as a cheap price when compared to the benefit which creation derived from the earthquake. Drawing on natural philosophical knowledge about the growth of plants, he explained that an earthquake which 'destroys all the Works of Men, overturns and disfigures the whole Surface, operates generally to a beneficial End, by ripening and refining the Mineral Substances, and sending forth that fertile Warmth and Moisture so necessary to the Generation of Vegetables'. Hazeland concluded 'that, if [an earthquake] sometimes deforms the Face of Nature, it is likewise the Origin off all its Beauties'.[58]

In the sermons of 1756 we rarely find long and complex arguments working with the laws of nature (as in Hazeland's sermon), instead it seems that it was sufficient to refer to God's acting through secondary causes, as in the following phrase, and the educated knew what was meant: 'Hast thou entered into the treasures of the nitre, or hast thou seen the beds of sulphur; which GOD hath reserved against the time of trouble, against the day of perplexity and distress?'[59] Or more metaphorically: 'the same Destroying Elements which have been exercised lately, as the fatal Ministers of his Vengeance, upon other Cities (tho' they now sleep in the Bowels of Our Earth) may in this very Hour be call'd forth, by God's Command, to produce the like Dismal Effects in Our Destruction.'[60] In other words, matter laid in the earth produced earthquakes when God determined to exact vengeance. Some sermons referred briefly to the debates of 1750, but in general the secondary causes were mentioned only in a few sentences, and not elaborated explicitly. This suggests that in the British public sphere earthquakes were accepted

57. See for example James How, *A Sermon on occasion of the earthquake at Lisbon, in the Kingdom of Portugal, and the present situation of affairs in Great Britain. Preach'd in the Parish Church of Milton next Gravesend, the sixth of February, 1756. The day appointed by His Majesty for a publick and general fast. By James How, M. A. Rector of Milton in Kent, and St. Margaret's Lothbury in London* (London 1756), p.6; John Pranther, *A Sermon, preached in the Parish Churches of Wath and Pickhill, in Yorkshire, on Friday the 6th of February, 1756; being the day appointed to be observ'd as a publick fast. By John Parnther, M. A. Vicar of Pickhill, and formerly Fellow of Peter-House in Cambridge* (York 1756), p.20; [John Biddulph?], *A Poem on the earthquake at Lisbon* (London 1755), p.7; *The London magazine: or Gentleman's monthly intelligencer* 19 (April 1750), p.176-77.

58. William Hazeland, *The Conclusions of atheists and superstitious persons from public calamities examined, in a sermon preached on the 6th of February, 1756, being the day appointed for a general fast on account of the late earthquakes, &c. By William Hazeland, M. A. Curate of Bishop's Storsford, in Hertfordshire* (London 1756), p.4.

59. John Cradock, *A Sermon preached in the parish church of St. Paul, Covent Garden, on Friday, February 6, 1756: being the day appointed by authority for a general fast* (London 1756), p.14.

60. John Fountayne, *A Sermon, preached in the Cathedral Church of York, on Friday the 6th of February, 1756; being the day appointed for a general fast* (York 1756), p.25.

as natural philosophical events whose causes were known. In 1756 (in contrast to 1750) it was common knowledge that the origin and progress of earthquakes followed the laws of nature, which were the secondary causes, but were initiated by the first cause: the will of God.

The imminent war with France changed the perception of the Lisbon earthquake in Britain and made it especially significant for the British. The Lisbon earthquake, however, changed the general perception of earthquakes in the British public sphere. Before the disaster, enlightened observers had calmly and rationally enjoyed the sublime spectacle of earthquakes, even while the vulgar were terrified. Now both kinds of observers could describe their own panic at such events. After an earthquake in Glowson at the end of December 1755 the author included himself in the group of frightened people and wrote, 'our Fright was such, that we thought the World was at an End'.[61] A similar feeling was expressed by the author of a letter from Tripoli while writing 'we fear that all the city of Syria will experience the fate of Lisbon'.[62] Even more detailed versions of the fear were presented: in *Lloyd's evening post* we can find a report about a gentleman who was so afraid during an earthquake in Cornwall in July 1757 that he lost his senses, fell backwards and 'tumbled into the Court, where he was taken up by his Servants'.[63]

Conclusion

In the British public sphere in the mid-eighteenth century earthquakes were inseparably connected with natural philosophy. It was generally accepted and widely understood that earthquakes were caused by the laws of nature, though there were some disagreements about the precise nature of these causes. In most of the texts concerned with earthquakes, the structure, presentation of observation and description of the behaviour of the observer followed the epistemology of natural philosophy. In reports that presented earthquakes as aesthetic objects or entertaining events, one can detect that natural philosophy played a role in constructing these meanings. Even in the debates about the London and Lisbon earthquakes, where the religious interpretation dominated, earthquakes were presented as natural spectacles of nature. A full understanding might depend on the Bible, but the events were perceived with the inquisitiveness and urge to research fostered by natural philosophy. But after the Lisbon earthquake it seems to have been more difficult, at least momentarily, to view earthquakes with fearless scientific detachment.

61. *The London evening post* 4391 (30 December to 1 January 1756), p.4.

62. 'Letter from Tripoly, Dec. 13', *The Gentleman's magazine* 30 (Historical Chronicle March 1760), p.152.

63. *Lloyd's evening post, and British chronicle* 5 (29 July to 1 August 1757), p.35.

ROBERT G. INGRAM

'The trembling Earth is God's Herald': earthquakes, religion and public life in Britain during the 1750s*

'TODAY, betwixt 12 and 1 o'Clock, the House in which I live in Lincoln's-Inn Fields was shook violently for a Moment', Gowin Knight wrote after the first shock of an earthquake hit London on 8 February 1750. 'Soon after this happen'd, a Servant came from his Grace the Duke of Newcastle, to inquire if we had perceiv'd what had happen'd; and said, that his Grace's House had shook all over.' As Henry Baker walked toward his home on Catherine Street, he found 'people in all the Streets [...] were talking of this Matter; and some of the Women complaining that the Motion had made them sick.'[1] Exactly a month later, another tremor rumbled under London. 'This morning at 25 minutes after 5 we were alarmed with a much severer shock of an Earth Q. than the last', Thomas Wilson recorded in his diary. 'It began with shaking the whole house and every thing in the room and then a Loud report much louder than thunder'.[2] The earthquake that a mad, apocalyptic soldier predicted would destroy London on 8 April 1750 never materialised, but the seismic activity of that winter and early spring unnerved the nation.

It was against this backdrop that Britons understood the catastrophic Lisbon earthquake of 1 November 1755. Detailed news reached Britain slowly.[3] The initial reports, however, sufficiently imparted to Britons that an extraordinary disaster had befallen Lisbon. Tobias Smollett reported at the time that 'the public was overwhelmed with consternation by the tidings of a dreadful earthquake'.[4] 'The affair at Lisbon has made men

* I thank the Center on religion and democracy in Charlottesville, VA, and Ohio University, for the financial support which allowed me to research and write this article. I need particularly to thank Ted Braun, Matthias Georgi, Bill Gibson, Jeremy Gregory, Paul Halliday, Jill Ingram, John Radner, and Josh Yates for their valuable advice in the preparation of this article. All mistakes are mine alone.

1. *Philosophical transactions* 46 (1749-1750), p.602-604. See also G. S. Rousseau, 'The London earthquakes of 1750', *Cahiers d'histoire mondiale* 11 (1968), p.436-51; T. D. Kendrick, *The Lisbon earthquake* (London 1956), p.1-23.

2. *The Diaries of Thomas Wilson, D. D., 1731-7 and 1750*, ed. C. L. S. Linnell (London 1964), p.231.

3. *The Yale edition of Horace Walpole's correspondence*, ed. W. S. Lewis *et al.* (New Haven, CT 1954), xx.511-12.

4. Tobias Smollett, *The History of England* (Oxford 1827), p.421-22.

tremble, as well as the Continent shake, from one end of Europe to another; from Gibraltar to the Highlands of Scotland', William Warburton declared, while Mrs Delany wrote that 'the dismal fate of Lisbon had sunk our spirits to such a degree, that for my part I have not been able to raise them since'.[5] Elizabeth Montagu heard that 100,000 people had died in Lisbon, the kind of estimates that led James Bate to argue that the Lisbon earthquake 'exceeds any Thing in History. No Calamity of so general extent as this, stands recorded either in sacred or prophane History, save only Noah's Flood.'[6]

This chapter examines the ways Britons understood the London and Lisbon earthquakes and the uses to which they put that understanding. In the process, it aims to provide a fuller, clearer portrait of religion's place in public life during the mid-eighteenth century, moving beyond the poles of an *ancien régime* confessional state on the one hand, and a secularised 'polite and commercial' society on the other.[7] The few, such as Jonathan Clark, who have rightly posited religion's continuing importance in public life during the century, have focused almost wholly on political ideology.[8] By way of a study of British responses to earthquakes in the 1750s, this chapter aims to integrate religion more effectively into the broader cultural, intellectual, social, and political histories of the period.

Corporate calamities, particularly natural ones such as earthquakes, were not everyday occurrences, and it might be protested that the ways people responded to them offer little insight into religion's place in everyday public life. Yet their very singularity casts stark light on bedrock values, assumptions and beliefs of people and of a nation: such calamities highlight the areas of shared belief and practice most clearly. Indeed, the London and Lisbon earthquakes show religious beliefs under tremendous stress and, thus, provide a distinctive opportunity to explore religion in mid-modern Britain.[9]

---

5. *Letters from a late eminent prelate to one of his friends* (Kidderminster 1793), p.149; *The Autobiography and correspondence of Mary Granville, Mrs. Delany*, ed. Lady Llanover (London 1861), iii.378-79.

6. *Elizabeth Montagu, the queen of the blue stockings: her correspondence from 1720 to 1761*, ed. E. J. Climenson (London 1906), ii.85; James Bate, *The Practical use of public judgments. A sermon, preached at St. Paul's, Deptford, Kent, on February 6, 1756* (London 1756), p.4.

7. Compare, for instance, John Brewer, *The Pleasures of the imagination: English culture in the eighteenth century* (London 1997) and J. C. D. Clark, *English society, 1660-1832: religion, ideology, and politics during the Ancien Regime* (Cambridge 2000).

8. Clark, *English society*, elucidates the connections between providential theology and political ideologies. I regret that J. C. D. Clark, 'Providence, predestination and progress: or, did the Enlightenment fail?', *Albion* 35:4 (2003), p.559-89, appeared too late for me to take adequate notice of it in this article.

9. Susan Neiman, *Evil in modern thought: an alternative history of philosophy* (Princeton, NJ 2002), p.1 and Susan Neiman, 'What's the problem of evil?', in *Rethinking evil: contemporary perspectives*, ed. Maria Pia Lara (Berkeley, CA 2001), p.41. See also D. K. Chester, 'The theodicy of natural disasters', *Scottish journal of theology* 51:4 (1998), p.485-505.

We should not be constrained by the language of modernisation in this exploration. The notion that Britain became increasingly secular, and thus modern, during the eighteenth century remains axiomatic for many historians. And while the causal language of providence that most Britons used to explain the earthquakes subverts the modernising narrative, to suggest that the eighteenth-century in Britain was as much an age of religion as it was an age of reason, to point out the extent to which Christian belief pervaded and informed Georgian culture and society, merely risks pushing just a little further down the historical timeline the point when *early modern* (religious) Britain gave way to *modern* (secular) Britain.[10] It is a point that needs to be made. But other points about how the language of providence was used also need to be made. For in the midst of a so-called Second Hundred Years War with France, it was the language of providence that public moralists employed to encourage a national reformation of public manners that would, presumably, strengthen the nation in the face of its enemies and give Britons a coherent sense of national identity.

Providence is the longstanding Christian doctrine regarding God's sovereignty over his creation.[11] It is premised on the notion that God is not simply a cosmic watchmaker who created the universe and then left it to run unattended. Rather, the omnipotent, omniscient, and eternal God who created and sustains the universe for supremely good purposes has a plan for mankind. In the way he designed and ordered the universe, he ensured that many of these good purposes would be achieved – this is his general providence. At other times God intervenes directly in natural and human events to secure his divine intentions. These interventions come through fulfilled prophecies, through miracles, and through other non-miraculous acts – this is his particular providence. Early moderns differed as to whether acts of particular providence cancelled or contravened the laws of nature, but all agreed that they were from the hand of God.

While some have shown providential theology's pre-eminence as a language of natural and political causation in post-Reformation England,[12] others have argued that providence's fortunes waned dramatically

10. B. W. Young, 'Religion history and the eighteenth-century historian', *Historical journal* (2000), p.849-68, examines the secularisation of eighteenth-century historiography. Jeremy Gregory, 'Christianity and culture: religion, the arts and sciences in England, 1660-1800', in *Culture and society in Britain, 1660-1800*, ed. Jeremy Black (Manchester 1997), p.102-23, is a useful corrective to Blair Worden, 'The question of secularization', in *A Nation transformed: England after the Restoration*, ed. Alan Houston and Steve Pincus (Cambridge 2001), p.20-40, and C. John Sommerville, *The Secularization of early modern England: from religious culture to religious faith* (New York 1992).

11. This paragraph is drawn from Robert G. Ingram, 'William Warburton, divine action, and enlightened Christianity', in *Religious identities in Britain, 1660-1832*, ed. William Gibson and Robert G. Ingram (Aldershot 2005).

12. Alexandra Walsham, *Providence in early modern England* (Oxford 1999); Blair Worden, 'Providence and politics in Cromwellian England', *Past and present* (1985), p.55-99; John Spurr, '"Virtue religion, and government": the Anglican uses of providence', in *The Politics*

with new developments in science and natural philosophy during the late seventeenth and early eighteenth centuries.[13] It is striking, then, to find providence the hegemonic language of causation for mid-eighteenth-century natural disasters such as the London and Lisbon earthquakes. It was one among a number of languages of causation, to be sure, but it was the language most frequently employed in public debate.

What kinds of evidence support this contention? Certainly England's metropolitan and provincial newspapers widely disseminated the providentialist argument. The *Derby mercury*'s coverage of the 1750 earthquakes is typical. The 16 February edition contained the paper's first sustained reporting on the 8 February earthquake, surveying four possible natural causes of earthquakes and reporting that Newton had predicted 'that in the Beginning of the Year 1750, the Planet Jupiter would in its passage be so near our Globe, as possibly to brush it; if so, it would give the Earth a great Shake'.[14] This was the only issue of the *Derby mercury* that did not discuss the earthquakes as providential signs from God. The edition of 9 March, for instance, published a poem that apocalyptically cautioned:

> But Earthquakes speak louder yet,
> and shake a guilty Shore:
> Ye Fools, who slumber near the Pit,
> Wake now, or wake no more.[15]

Soon afterwards, the paper published a letter pillorying those who fled London to avoid God's wrath as manifested in the earthquakes.[16] Indeed, the *Mercury* ran unusually long lead stories on the front pages of the 30 March, 6 April, and 27 April editions that rejected explanations which focused only on secondary natural causes to the exclusion of primary religious ones. 'How idle and trifling [...] it is to acquiesce in Second Causes, when in reality nothing is properly a Cause, but the First Cause, God Almighty', argued a 'gentleman from London' in late April.[17]

---

of religion in Restoration England, ed. Tim Harris, Paul Seaward, and Mark Goldie (Oxford 1991), p.29-47; Tony Claydon, *William III and the godly revolution* (Cambridge 1996), p.31-52; Craig Rose, 'Providence, protestant union and godly reformation in the 1690s', *Transactions of the Royal historical society* (1993), p.151-69.

13. Patricia Bonomi, *Under the cope of heaven: religion, society and politics in colonial America* (Oxford 1998), p.98; William E. Burns, *An Age of wonders: prodigies, politics and providence in England,1657-1727* (Manchester 2002), p.185-87; Michael P. Winship, *Seers of God: puritan providentialism in the Restoration and early Enlightenment* (Baltimore, MD 1996), p.138-52; Roy Porter, *The Creation of the modern world: the untold story of the British Enlightenment* (New York 2000), p.100, argues along these lines.

14. *Derby mercury* (16-23 February 1750), p.2, 3.

15. *Derby mercury* (9-6 March 1750), p.3.

16. *Derby mercury* (23-30 March 1750), p.2.

17. *Derby mercury* (20-27 April 1750), p.1. *The Bath journal* (February – April 1750, December – January 1756), *The Ipswich journal* (February – April 1750, December 1755 – December 1756), *The Newcastle intelligencer* (December 1755 – February 1756); *The Newcastle journal* (November 1755 – February 1756), for instance, covered the earthquakes similarly.

Other published responses to the earthquakes were also overwhelmingly providentialist. The *English short-title catalogue* (ESTC) returns 138 works directly concerning the London and Lisbon earthquakes; nearly eighty per cent of those were works with a specifically religious orientation. Every one of the published sermons regarding the earthquakes argued that the seismic events were providential warnings from God, and there is no indication that any of the sermons preached in the 12,000 Anglican parishes on 6 February 1756 did not take the providential line.[18]

Providential logic often underpinned even the most influential works of natural philosophy and science. While Christian providential theology had a pedigree dating back to the early church, the physico-theological arguments for earthquake causation in the mid-eighteenth century were not made by those who rejected scientific inquiry. Rather a reading of the earthquake literature illuminates the ways contemporaries reconciled the claims of Newtonian natural philosophy and Christian theology. Except for the followers of John Hutchinson who set out to provide an alternative to the Newtonian worldview, most accepted Newtonianism's basic tenets.[19] This acceptance of Newtonian natural philosophy did not, however, entail a rejection of the idea that God had an active hand in the events of the world.[20] Those making the providential argument tried to show how earthquakes could have both secondary natural and primary divine causes. The boundaries between science and religion were not rigidly fixed during this period.

While geology was not yet a distinctive branch of science, a very few did try to offer naturalistic explanations of earthquakes.[21] Contemporary scientific literature on the earthquakes consisted of the lectures and

18. See, for instance, *The Diary of Thomas Turner, 1754-1765*, ed. David Vaisey (Oxford 1984), p.25.

19. Albert J. Kuhn, 'Glory of gravity: Hutchinson vs. Newton', *Journal of the history of ideas* 22:3 (1961), p.303-22; G. T. N. Cantor, 'Revelation and the cyclical cosmos of John Hutchinson', in *Images of the earth: essays in the history of the environmental sciences*, ed. L. S. Jordanova and Roy S. Porter (Chalfont St Giles 1979), p.4-22; C. B. Wilde, 'Hutchinsonianism, natural philosophy and religious controversy in eighteenth century Britain', *History of science* 18:1 (1980), p.1-24; C. B. Wilde, 'Matter and spirit as natural symbols in eighteenth-century British natural philosophy', *British journal for the history of science* 15:2 (1982), p.99-131; John C. English, 'John Hutchinson's critique of Newtonian heterodoxy', *Church history* 68:3 (1999), p.581-97; and Patricia Fara, 'Marginalized practices', in *The Cambridge history of science*, vol.iv, ed. Porter (Cambridge 2003), p.503-505, provide useful introductions to Hutchinson and his followers.

20. Peter Harrison, 'Newtonian science, miracles, and the laws of nature', *Journal of the history of ideas* 56:4 (1995), p.531.

21. For background, see Roy Porter, *The Making of geology: earth science in Britain, 1660-1815* (Cambridge 1977); Roy Porter, 'Creation and credence: the career and theories of the earth in Britain, 1660-1820', in *Natural order: historical studies in scientific culture*, ed. Barry Barnes and Steven Shapin (Beverly Hills, CA 1979), p.97-123; Roy Porter, 'The terraqueous globe', in *The Ferment of knowledge: studies in the historiography of eighteenth-century science*, ed. G. S. Rousseau and Roy Porter (Cambridge 1980), p.285-324; and Rhoda Rappaport, 'The earth sciences', in *The Cambridge history of science*, vol.iv, ed. Porter, p.400-16.

correspondence gathered in the 1749-1750 and 1755-1756 *Philosophical transactions of the Royal Society* and less than half a dozen pamphlets. While much descriptive literature was written about earthquakes, there were only a limited number of theories on offer that explained their physical causes.

Edward Wortley Montagu's anonymous 1750 pamphlet proffered one conventional scientific explanation, namely that 'subterraneous Fire' and 'subterraneous Vapours' caused earthquakes.[22] Surveying known seismic activity, he identified nine types of earthquakes and concluded that the London earthquake had been developed when, after a dry winter, a rain had 'penetrate[d] very deep into the Earth' where it came in contact with 'Coals in the Earth [...] of a sulpherous kind, [that] might, through their becoming wet in this manner, emit a Vapour capable of producing such a Shock as that which was felt'.[23] Montagu blamed the Lisbon earthquake on subterraneous vapours as well. Noting the melting of ice and snow during a peculiarly hot summer in Greenland and 'the vast Quantity of Sulphur lodged in the Bowels of the Earth' there, he argued that conditions were ripe for seismic activity in the fall of 1755: 'it seems [...] highly probable, that by the soaking in of such excessive Floods of a nitrous Fluid upon these Beds of Sulpher, a prodigious Fermentation might ensue, and the Vapours kindling at a great Depth in the Bowels of the Earth, proceed with such Violence as to heave up that Part of the Sea under which they passed'.[24] The vapours spread out from Greenland towards the European continent, causing tremors where subsidiary streams hit land, but great damage where the main stream hit the Portuguese coast. Though his seismic theories made no mention of God's hand in the earthquakes, Montagu took time at the end of his discourse to acknowledge the providential lessons Christians might divine from them.[25] Providential agency, then, was implicit in his seismic theories.

Contemporaries found a compelling alternative to the 'subterraneous vapours' theory in William Stukeley's electrical airquake theory.[26] Influenced by Benjamin Franklin's electrical experimentations, Stukeley used several lectures to the Royal Society in March 1750, later published as *The Philosophy of earthquakes, natural and religious* (1750), to outline his

---

22. Rousseau, 'The London earthquake of 1750', p.442-43.

23. [Edward Wortley Montagu], *A Dissertation upon earthquakes, their causes and consequences; upon, the shock of an earthquake, felt in the cites of London and Westminster, on Thursday, February 8, 1749-50* (London 1750), p.22-68 (p.66-67).

24. Edward Wortley Montagu, *A Philosophical discourse upon earthquakes, their causes and consequences; comprehending an explanation of the nature of subterraneous vapours, their amazing force, and the manner in which they operate;... to which is prefixed a preliminary dissertation, in which is attempted a rational explanation of the rise, progress, [...] on Saturday, November 1, 1755* (London 1755), p.v.

25. [Montagu], *A Dissertation upon earthquakes*, p.70.

26. Simon Schaffer, 'Natural philosophy and public spectacle in the eighteenth century', *History of science* (1983), p.18.

theory, which held that electrical disturbances 'produce that snap, and that shock, which we call an earthquake; a vibration of the superfices of the earth'.[27] Stephen Hales also argued a version of the airquake theory in his lectures to the Royal Society in April 1750. '[T]he ascending sulphereous vapours in the Earth may probably take Fire, and thereby cause an Earth-Lightning; which is at first kindled at the surface, and not at great Depths, as has been thought', he contended. 'And the Explosion of this Lightning is the immediate Cause of an Earthquake.'[28]

As presented by Stukeley and Hales, the electrical earthquake theory differed from Montagu's seismic theories in being explicitly providential. Stukeley and Hales are illustrative of the unsettled boundaries between natural philosophy and theology during the period.[29] At the time of the 1750 earthquakes, Stukeley was rector of St. George the Martyr in Queen Square, London. But he was not a typical Anglican clergyman; an antiquary, a naturalist, an archaeologist, a Cambridge M. D., and a fellow of the Royal Society, he had practised medicine for nearly two decades before being persuaded by Archbishop Wake to enter into orders.[30] 'Never was there a time in which we wanted all the assistance we can get against the prevailing infidelity of the present wicked age', Wake wrote to the forty-two-year-old doctor in 1729:

> & as our adversaries are men pretending to reason superior to others, so nothing can more abate their pride, & stop their prevalence, than to see Christianity defended by those who are in all respects as eminent in naturall knowledge, & philosophicall enquiries, as they can pretend to be. I am persuaded your education & practice as a Physician, will for this reason enable you to do God & Christianity better service than one brought up to Divinity from the beginning could do.[31]

As Wake had hoped, Stukeley did bring natural philosophy to the defence of Christian belief, especially after the London earthquakes. While he explained the earthquake in naturalistic terms, Stukeley emphasised that his intention was 'to show, how vain, and unmeaning, are all our philosophical inquiries, when destitute of their true view; to lead us into

27. William Stukeley, *The Philosophy of earthquakes, natural and religious. Or an inquiry into their causes, and their purpose* (London 1756), p.22-50 (p.23). See also, *Philosophical transactions* (1749-1750), p.641-46, 657-69, 731-50.

28. Stephen Hales, 'Some considerations on the causes of earthquakes', *Philosophical transactions* 46 (1749-1750), p.677.

29. Brian Young, 'Theological books from *The Naked Gospel* to *Nemesis of faith*', in *Books and their readers in eighteenth-century England: new essays*, ed. Isabel Rivers (London and New York 2001), p.82-86, makes a similar point with regard to theological works and novels during the period.

30. David Boyd Hancock, *William Stukeley: science, religion, and archaeology in eighteenth-century England* (Woodbridge 2002), and Stuart Piggott, *William Stukeley: an eighteenth-century antiquary* (Oxford 1950) are the only scholarly biographies of Stukeley, but neither considers closely Stukeley's writings on earthquakes.

31. *The Family memoirs of the Rev. William Stukeley, M. D., and the antiquarian and other correspondence of William Stukeley, Roger and Samuel Gale, etc.* (1882), p.218-19.

the more engaging paths of religion. That, from speculation of material Causes, we may become adepts in that wisdom which is from above.' He believed that the empirical evidence regarding the earthquakes pointed to 'a plain and notorious proof of God's hand'.[32] Indeed, he argued, 'of all the great and public Calamities which affects us Mortals, Earthquakes claim the first Title to the Name of Warnings and Judgments; none so proper to threaten, or to execute Vengeance'.[33] Why, for instance, did earthquakes 'only destroy great cities' but to show God's displeasure with their sinfulness? Why did Britain suffer unusually heavy rainfall in 1755 but to prevent the kind of electrical disturbances that occurred in the dry spells that caused earthquakes, such as the devastating one in Lisbon? God surely had meant to warn Britons to worship him more fervently.[34] Stukeley believed nature was providence's instrument. Likewise Hales, another Anglican clerical fellow of the Royal Society, failed to see how naturalistic and providential explanations for earthquakes were mutually exclusive. 'God sometimes changes the order of Nature, with Design to chastise Man for his Disobedience and Follies,' he wrote, 'natural Evils being graciously designed by him as moral Goods: All Events are under his Direction, and fulfil his Will.'[35]

The idea that God intervened in human affairs seemingly contradicted Newtonian ideas about the operation of the universe. Conventional wisdom has held that the new science of the seventeenth century promoted the view of an orderly, harmonious, and intelligible universe, which in turn led to the development of natural and rational theologies. Reason became the touchstone of belief so that no truth could be taken merely on authority. Thus armed, the 'enlightened' swept away miracles (particularly regarding Christ's divinity) and other absurdities (such as revealed religion) from Christianity. Orthodox Christian belief thus proved incompatible with the rational Newtonian worldview.[36]

The Thomistic distinction between first and second causes, however, allowed Georgian Britons to accord earthquakes both divine and natural causes. God was the first cause, nature the second. It is the 'Hand of God [...] under whose Government all natural Agents act', Hales argued. 'When he inflicts a Famine on a nation, it is not less the Hand of God,

---

32. Stukeley, *The Philosophy of earthquakes, natural and religious*, p.3, 59.
33. *Philosophical transactions* (1749-1750), p.668.
34. William Stukeley, *The Philosophy of earthquakes, natural and religious*, iii.40.
35. Hales, 'Some considerations on the causes of earthquakes', p.669-70.
36. For classic expressions of this view, see Paul Hazard, *European thought in the eighteenth century: from Montesquieu to Lessing* (1946; Cleveland, OH and New York 1963) and Peter Gay, *The Enlightenment: an interpretation, the rise of modern paganism* (New York 1967). Works like Ernst Cassirer, *The Philosophy of the Enlightenment* (1932; Boston, MA 1966), p.134-96 and Dorinda Outram, *The Enlightenment* (Cambridge 1995), p.31-46, recognise the central place of religious debate in the Enlightenment but nonetheless assume that the purpose of enlightenment as conceived by contemporaries was to reform religion by removing its mysterious and mystical elements.

because we know the natural Causes of it.'[37] This was an approach popularised in dozens of earthquake sermons. 'I cannot conceive, how the Operation of these natural Causes is inconsistent with a religious Acknowledgement of God in such Events', argued Samuel Chandler. 'God is really the proper Agent in these and other like natural Effects, and the Operations of the Laws, which he from the first Origin of Nature fixed, which he by his continued Influence constantly maintains in their Activity.'[38] Edward Bayly assured his audience that 'natural Causes are but Second Causes', while George Horne similarly admonished his listeners in Oxford:

As to nature, no doubt there are second causes made use of in this, as in other judgments; and if the Scripture account of the construction of the earth was accurately examined, philosophers might give a rational and defensible account of them and their agency. [...] But the question to be asked by every one... is, who created these second causes by his power, and directs them by his wisdom, to produce such effects, at such times, in such places, and for such purposes?[39]

That same day in Wolsingham, Durham, William Nowell preached, 'the Elements are not Agents, but merely passive Instruments [... God is] the prime Mover who puts them all in Motion, and directs their Force'.[40] This distinction between primary and secondary causes enabled contemporaries to reconcile the identifiable laws of nature that governed the universe and to accept the interventions of a providential God. Rather than a perversion of Newtonian science for later religious purposes, it was instead a distinction made by Newton and his original religious popularisers.[41]

37. *Philosophical transactions* (1749-1750), p.670.

38. Samuel Chandler, *The Scripture account of the cause and intention of earthquakes, in a sermon preached at the Old-Jury, March 11, 1749-50, on occasion of the two shocks of an earthquake, the first on February 8, the other on March 8* (London 1750), p.7.

39. Edward Bayly, *A Sermon preached at St. James's church in Bath, on Friday, February 6, 1756* [...] *and again,* [...] *on Sunday following, at the abbey-church* (London 1756), p.16; George Horne, *The Almighty glorified in judgment. A sermon preach'd before the University of Oxford, on Sunday, Febr. 15. 1756. Preached before the Mayor and Corporation of the city of Oxford* [...] *on occasion of the late earthquakes and public fast* (London 1756), p.5-6.

40. William Nowell, *A Sermon preached at the parish church of Wolsingham,* [...] *on the 6th of February, 1756, being the day appointed by his Majesty for a general fast, on account of the dreadful earthquake at Lisbon, Nov. 1. 1755* (Newcastle 1755), p.7.

41. Henry Guerlac and Margaret C. Jacob, 'Bentley, Newton, and providence (the Boyle lectures once more)', *Journal of the history of ideas* 30:3 (1969), p.307-18; David Kubrin, 'Newton and the cyclical cosmos: providence and the mechanical philosophy', *Journal of the history of ideas* 28:3 (1967), p.325-46; James E. Force, 'Hume and the relation of science to religion among certain members of the Royal Society', *Journal of the history of ideas* (1984), p.519-26; and Margaret C. Jacob, 'Christianity and the Newtonian world-view', in *God and nature: historical essays on the encounter between Christianity and science*, ed. David C. Lindberg and Ronald L. Numbers (Berkeley, CA 1986), p.238-55 all explore this point. P. M. Heimann, 'Voluntarism and immanence: conceptions of nature in eighteenth-century thought', *Journal of the history of ideas* 39:2 (April – June 1978), p.271-83, argues that this Newtonian voluntarist synthesis was supplanted in the late eighteenth century by

Robert G. Ingram

If contemporary scientific opinion often bore the mark of providential theology, the actions Britons took in the wake of the earthquakes demonstrated a widely shared, if not universal, view of the world in which providence remained an important causal explanation. Consider, for instance, the earthquakes in the winter of 1750. Confusion and wonderment were among the most common initial reactions to the earthquake of 8 February. So too was fear. Elizabeth Montagu complained on 20 February that 'the madness of the multitude was prodigious, near 50 of the people I had sent to, to play cards here the Saturday following, went out of town to avoid being swallowed'.[42] When a more violent tremor rumbled under London on 8 March, the mixed reactions of February turned to widespread panic, especially when a mad soldier predicted that God would destroy London a month later on 8 April with a third earthquake.[43] Many who were able to do so fled London, hoping that distance from the capital would ensure their safety if another earthquake should hit. 'This frantic terror prevails so much, that within these three days 730 coaches have been counted passing Hyde Park Corner, with whole parties removing into the country', Horace Walpole reported on 2 April.[44] 'The terrors & prognostications of the Ignorant and Superstitious have almost emptied Grosvenor Square & its adjacent Streets', John Barker lamented to Philip Doddridge.[45]

Barker pilloried those who fled as 'Ignorant and Superstitious' not because they believed the recent earthquakes were a providential warning from God but rather because they believed they could escape God's providential punishment by removing themselves from London. Lady Bradshaigh was one of those who had fled to Reading, and she later defended her flight by arguing:

I religiously believe God's providence is over all His works; and on that every serious person must depend, whatever situation he may be in. He has also given us means to provide for our safety, and permits us to fly from danger, though, from our erroneous judgement, we may run into a greater. God hath warned us to flee from the wrath to come, and if we take that for a warning, which, in reality, is not one, surely in that we sin not.[46]

Joseph Priestley and James Hutton's theories of activist matter that did not require God's continued sustenance to operate. This was seen by contemporaries as a blow to the idea of an interventionist – and providentialist – God. John Gascoigne, 'Ideas of nature: natural philosophy', in *The Cambridge history of science*, iv.285-304 provides useful background.

42. Climenson, *Elizabeth Montagu, the queen of the blue-stockings*, i.274.
43. See, for instance, *A Series of letters between Mrs Elizabeth Carter and Miss Catherine Talbot from the year 1741 to 1770 [...] in the possession of the Rev. Montagu Pennington* (London 1809), i.332; *Secret comment: the diaries of Gertrude Savile, 1721-1757*, ed. Alan Savile (Devon 1997), p.291.
44. *The Yale edition of Horace Walpole's correspondence*, xx.136-37.
45. *Calendar of the correspondence of Philip Doddridge DD (1702-1751)*, ed. Geoffrey Nuttall (London 1979), p.326.
46. Quoted in Kendrick, *The Lisbon earthquake*, p.13-14.

This was a commonly-expressed sentiment, but one that was also widely criticised.

> Dismay'd, aghast, they fly their own Abodes,
> And throng in dismal Groupes thro' different Roads

declaimed a Military Prophet:

> Wretches! Blush, Kneel down, confess your Shame:
> Providence, is ev'ry where the same.[47]

The *Gentleman's magazine* asked rhetorically of 'those Persons of Distinction' who fled London whether they did 'hope, by a change of place, to flee from the face of that God who is everywhere present?'[48] Religious leaders, both Anglican and dissenter, hammered this message home in print and from the pulpit. Thomas Sherlock, bishop of London, caricatured those who offered naturalistic explanations of the earthquakes as 'Little Philosophers, who see a little, and but very little, into natural Causes'. They had missed the point, Sherlock assured those in the metropolis, because the earthquakes were 'Warnings from God [...] which seems to have been immediately and especially directed to these great Cities, and the Neighbourhood of them'. God had sent the warnings because London was a latter-day Sodom where people had 'unsettle[d] all Principles of Religion':

Lay these Things together [...] and then ask your Heart, whether you have not Reason to fear, that God will visit for these Things [...] But, let us not despair; [...] To him then let us turn with hearty Repentance for our Sins; and with a Resolution to do, each of us in his proper Station, what lies in our power to stem the Torrent of Iniquity which threatens our Ruin.[49]

Thomas Secker, bishop of Oxford, echoed Sherlock's argument in a sermon delivered at the fashionable St James, Westminster, on 11 March 1750. 'Some, I am told, have resolved to fly away from hence upon it: and then imagine, they shall be out of all hazard. But do you hope to fly from God?' he asked. 'Fly from your iniquities to God, if you would be safe. Other precautions will avail you little.'[50] The dissenter Roger Pickering was even more fervid in his address to those who might flee London:

I adjure you, by the Interest of that Gospel you profess, by the Credit of that Faith on which you rest your Souls, that, with humble Hearts, but with Christian Confidence, in your respective Stations on the Spot where Providence has placed

---

47. *A Military prophet: or a flight from providence. Address'd to the foolish and guilty who timidly withdrew themselves on the alarm of another earthquake, April 1750* (London 1750), p.1.

48. *Gentleman's magazine* (March 1750), p.125.

49. Thomas Sherlock, *A Letter from the Lord Bishop of London, to the clergy and people of London and Westminster; on occasion of the late earthquakes* (Dublin 1750), p.4, 6-7, 10-11.

50. Thomas Secker, 'Sermon preached in the parish-church of St. James, Westminster, March 11, 1749-50, on occasion of the earthquake, March 8', in *The Works of Thomas Secker* (London 1825), vol.166.

you, ye wait the Will of God; least the Scoffers at the Power of Godliness rejoice, and the impious Deniers of a Providence triumph.[51]

This clerical notion that God had shown his displeasure with Britain by visiting the nation with a series of earthquakes had its notable detractors, such as the religious sceptic David Hume and the deist Horace Walpole. Sherlock, Hume complained, 'recommends certain pills, such as fasting, prayer, repentance, mortification, and other drugs, which are entirely to come from his own shop'.[52] Walpole was equally dismissive: 'The earth-quake which has done no hurt, in a country where earthquakes ever did any, is sent, according to the Bishop, to punish bawdy prints, bawdy books [...] gaming, drinking [...] and all other sins, natural or not.'[53] Yet Hume and Walpole expressed a minority view. For John Millar felt compelled to delay publishing the second edition of Hume's *Essays concerning human understanding* 'because of the Earthquakes' while Sherlock's pastoral letter was a runaway bestseller, going into six editions and selling over 100,000 copies in less than half a year.[54]

If Hume and Walpole were not in the mainstream of British opinion regarding the causes of earthquakes, their complaints about Sherlock do point to the primary use of providence during the mid-eighteenth century: to promote personal and corporate moral reform, what contemporaries referred to as a 'general' or a 'national reformation'. In almost every jeremiad and fast sermon the providential logic behind the call for a reformation was made clear. This logic had three elements:

(1)

Britain was a latter-day Israel, a nation with whom God enjoyed a special relationship. God, it was believed, had formed a special covenant with Britain.[55] As a sign of that covenant, he had intervened at critical junctures in the nation's history. 'To [God's] immediate interposition we owe the Revolution, the establishment of the Protestant succession, the extinction of the late unnatural rebellion, and [...] the last general peace at Aix-la-Chapelle', Samuel Squire assured his audience at St. Anne, Westminster, while Edward Bayly added the defeat of the Spanish Armada, the Restoration, and the minimal damage done by the 1750

---

51. Roger Pickering, *An Address to those who have either retired, or intend to leave the town, under the imaginary apprehension of the approaching shock of another earthquake: being the substance delivered on the last Lord's-day, the first of this instant April* (London 1750), p.30.

52. *The Letters of David Hume*, ed. J. Y. T. Greig (Oxford 1969), i.141.

53. *The Yale edition of Horace Walpole's correspondence*, xx.133-34.

54. Edward Carpenter, *Thomas Sherlock, 1678-1761* (London 1936), p.286.

55. D. Napthine and W. A. Speck, 'Clergymen and conflict, 1660-1763', *Studies in church history* 20 (1983), p.238. Related to this covenantal idea was the notion that Britain's kings ruled not through indefensible divine right but by providential divine right: Clark, *English society, 1660-1832*, p.115-20.

London earthquakes to the litany.[56] Yet France, popish in its religion, absolutist in its government, now threatened those liberties Britons enjoyed. John Thomas assured the House of Lords that succumbing to the French would mean 'our properties invaded, and our Rights, both civil and religious, infringed by an arbitrary Power'.[57] Likewise Thomas Anguish, preaching on the same day in Deptford, proclaimed 'it more eligible to have the earth open her mouth and take us alive into the pit, than to endure the more base and lingering evils of rapine and slavery from a poor, merciless, insulting Gaul'.[58]

(2)

The only reason Britain now faced threat from popish, absolutist France was because Britons had turned their back on God, despite his special covenant with them. 'We have not so much to fear from the open and avowed violence of foreign enemies', John Cradock assured his listeners at St Paul, Covent Garden, 'as from the secret and formidable attacks of domestic foes, our national impieties.'[59] Topping the list of sins was a thirst for luxury, a common complaint during the period.[60] Samuel Squire saw luxury as the key that unlocked the gateway to unbridled sinfulness: 'this ostentatious manner of life usually surpasses our incomes, and draws us into all the incumbrance of debts, mortgages, and abject dependencies; so the difficulties and perplexities attendant upon so distressful a situation are the most natural introduction to lying, fraud, and oppression; to cheating in our dealings, and treachery in our friendships; to personal underminings, and party-oppositions; to gaming, dueling, and self-murther.'[61] Others complained as well of 'that predominant Love of Pleasures (low, sensual, mean, unmanly Pleasures) that so much infects, effeminates and distinguishes the present Age'.[62] Samuel Chandler fretted

56. Samuel Squire, *A Speedy repentance the most effectual means to avert Gods judgements. A sermon preached at the parish church of St. Anne, Westminster, February 6, 1756* (London 1756), p.11; Bayly, *A Sermon preached at St. James's church in Bath, on Friday, February 6, 1756*, p.24-26.

57. John Thomas, *A Sermon preached before the House of Lords in the abby-church of Westminster, on Friday, February 6th, 1756* (London 1756), p.21.

58. Thomas Anguish, *A Sermon preached at St. Nicholas, Deptford, on the fast day appointed by royal proclamation, on February 6, 1756* (London 1756), p.9.

59. John Cradock, *A Sermon preached in the parish church of St. Paul, Covent Garden, on Friday, February 6, 1756* (London 1756), p.19.

60. My argument here runs counter to Linda Levy Peck, 'Luxury and war: reconsidering luxury consumption in seventeenth-century England', *Albion* 34:1 (2002), p.1-23, and Maxine Berg and Helen Clifford, *Consumers and luxury: consumer culture in Europe, 1650-1800* (Manchester 1999), which posit the de-moralisation of luxury in the mid-modern period. John Sekora, *Luxury: the concept in western thought, Eden to Smollett* (Baltimore, MD 1977), surveys the history of the concept of luxury.

61. Squire, *A Speedy repentance the most effectual means to avert God's judgments*, p.5.

62. John Mason, *The Christian's duty in a time of publick danger. A sermon preached at Cheshunt in the county of Hertford, February 6, 1756* (London 1756), p.30.

that 'Luxury and Love of Pleasure [...] hath infected the Minds, and bewitched the Imaginations of all Degrees of Men; who, when they have no Principles, can have nothing but Instinct and Inclination to govern them, and will madly follow wheresoever that blindly leads them'.[63]

These commentators complained that luxury lived in symbiosis with irreligion, an umbrella term that covered a number of sins, including insufficient observance of the Sabbath and a decline in religious zeal. Philip Doddridge groused that 'great Licentiousness reigns among most of [London's] Inhabitants, and great Indolence and Indifference to Religion even among those that are not Licentious [...] That Assemblies for Divine worship are much neglected, or frequented with little Appearance of Seriousness or Solemnity'.[64] 'there is, a great, and, I fear, a growing indifference amongst us', Charles Bulkeley worried. 'how many are there who seem totally to have forgotten, that they are rational beings, that they have any capacity for religion or any interest depending upon the truth of it?'[65] The third pillar of the nation's licentiousness was a pervasive rationalism. To men of reason, 'The soul is nothing but a peculiar modification of matter; heaven and hell are only dreams, and the Gospel merely a cunningly devised fable', John Allen lamented.[66] Rev. J. Winstanley lambasted 'a self-sufficient Age, like this, when Reason sits sole Arbiter in religious Matters, and arrogantly condemns every Thing, which she cannot perfectly account for, on her own Principles'.[67] Again and again in the fast sermons, preachers, both Anglican and dissenter, inveighed against luxury, irreligion and rationalism. In their thirst for luxury, their irreligious behaviour and their fetishising reason, Britons ran the danger of God destroying their nation.

(3)

Because he loved his people, however, God had sent warnings to Britain in the form of earthquakes. Joseph Baller preached, 'we ought to look upon every evil of Affliction, and that whether public or private, national or personal, as coming from the Hand of God', while Charles Moss argued that 'Public Calamity and Distress are authoritative Warnings of our

63. Chandler, *The Scripture account of the cause and intention of earthquakes, in a sermon preached at the Old-Jury, March 11, 1749-50*, p.36.

64. Philip Doddridge, *The Guilt and doom of Capernaum, seriously recommended to the consideration of the inhabitants of London: in a sermon reached at Salters-Hall, August 20, 1749. Published on occasion of the late alarm by the second shock of an earthquake, March 8, 1749-50* (London 1750), p.35.

65. Charles Bulkeley, *The Nature and necessity of national reformation. A sermon, preached at Barbican, Feb. 6. 1756* (London 1756), p.13.

66. John Allen, *The Destruction of Sodom improved, as a warning to Great Britain. A sermon preached on the fast-day, Friday, February 6, 1756. At Hanover-Street, Long Acre* (London 1756), p.18.

67. J. Winstanley, *A Sermon preached at Conduit-street chapel, in the parish of St. George, Hanover-square. On Sunday, February the 1st, 1756* (London 1756), p.1.

Danger'.[68] Yet these assertions begged answers to potentially disturbing questions of theodicy. Why would God destroy even the righteous in Lisbon just to send a warning to other Christians? Why do bad things happen to good people? These were questions around which preachers tended to dance. One answer to the problem came from William Warburton, who essentially argued that as the moral governor of the universe, God almost had to intervene in human affairs, if he wanted his message to be heard:

the moral Governor of the universe, whose essential character it is, not to leave himself without a witness, doth frequently employ the physical and civil operations of the natural system, to support and reform the moral. For if God indeed be a moral Governor, he must manifest his dominion in whatever world he is pleased to station and to exercise his accountable and probationary creatures. In man's state and condition here, natural and civil events are the proper instruments of moral government.[69]

Others argued that none are innocent because all are sinful. 'God may surely punish whom he pleases, and to what Degree he pleases, and yet be just', J. Winstanley wrote. 'For the best Man upon Earth, is a Criminal in the Sight of Heaven; and, as such, can plead no Right of Exemption from any Sort of Evil whatsoever, which Heaven may think proper to inflict.'[70] This must have proved cold comfort to his listeners.

The more common strategy, to distinguish between general and particular providence, allowed God's ultimate inscrutability to be acknowledged, while nonetheless deriving general messages from disasters. With regard to particular providence, John Thomas argued, 'we cannot use too much care and caution, for fear of wading too far into the divine Judgments, which are, like the great Deep, unfathomable. We are safe, only, while we remain by general conclusions, without descending to particulars.' While it was impossible to determine God's precise plan in causing natural calamities, Thomas did think that God's bigger message could be ascertained from these calamities:

Such are National Calamities, Famines, Pestilences, Deluges, Earthquakes, Wars; which are such alarming events, as must command our attention. And if we acknowledge them to be the works of God, we cannot suppose them wrought without design; and if the moral world be at all concerned in that design, it must lie open to the view of Mankind, or the intended effect be lost. How dark then and intricate soever final Causes in general may be, some of them, at least those for our immediate use, must be so obvious, that we cannot easily mistake them. And although we should be very soon bewildered in the mysterious mazes of

68. Joseph Baller, *Divine alarms and warnings to a sinful people considered and improved: a sermon preached at Barnstaple, in the county of Devon, on February 6. 1756* (London 1756), p.11; Charles Moss, *A Sermon preached at the parish church of St. James, Westminster, on Friday February 6, 1756* (London 1756), p.6.

69. William Warburton, *Natural and civil events the instruments of God's moral government. A sermon preached the last public fast-day, at Lincoln's-Inn-Chappel* (London 1756), p.4.

70. Winstanley, *A Sermon preached at Conduit-street chapel [...] February the 1st, 1756*, p.10.

Providence, yet in the plain indications of divine Favour or Anger we shall not err, if we take Reason and Scripture for our Guides, avoiding to lean on one side towards Infidelity, and on the other side towards Superstition.[71]

Thomas Newman also acknowledged the inscrutability of God's particular providence, but he thought the general import of his providential lessons was clear:

God's end in his visitations is plainly revealed: It is to testify against our sins, and to bring us to testify against them too as evil and bitter; it is to bring us back to his law, which is no other than the dictates of divine wisdom, and the demands of divine sovereignty. His design is to purge away iniquity, to mortify the habits of sin, to reclaim from the practice of it, and by the rectifying of our judgments to turn out fee to this testimonies. This is the fruit, the end, that he proposes.[72]

This approach to the problem of interpreting God's intent was adopted by most contemporaries. Not knowing precisely why God had caused the earthquakes, preachers could nonetheless argue that God was pointing to the obvious need in Britain for a national or general reformation, a recurrent theme in nearly every earthquake sermon. Thus Thomas Hunter's belief that 'Wickedness is and has been, the general Cause of Misery and Ruin the Kingdoms and Nations of the World' led him to argue as well 'That this Kingdom and nation from our present State of Immorality and Impiety, has no Reason to presume it's Security from the like Misery and Ruin.'[73] This approach allowed preachers not to presume to know the inner workings of God's mind, while at the same time linking the cause of national security to moral reform.

The message that God helped shape history and that moral reform would ensure that he continued to intervene on the nation's behalf was one that the king's government particularly attended to during the period. The earthquakes, especially the one in Lisbon, hit at a delicate time in British diplomatic and imperial history. The Spanish war of 1739, the Jacobite Rebellion of 1745 to 1746, and the London earthquake of 1750 suggested to many Britons that the source of these threats to their domestic peace and security might be domestic faults. Now France and Britain were hurtling toward war, and Britain's position in North America looked increasingly vulnerable during the early autumn of 1755. Seeing Portugal, one of Britain's oldest allies, hit by a catastrophic natural disaster struck many with foreboding. Indeed, Bob Harris has noted, 'The call for reform of morals which followed the Lisbon earthquake was significantly greater in scale and had a substantially greater impact, partly because it followed the earlier panic, but also because it

71. Thomas, *A Sermon preached before the House of Lords in the abby-church of Westminster, on Friday, February 6ᵗʰ, 1756,* p.7, 8-9.

72. Thomas Newman, *The Sin and shame of disregarding providences. A sermon preached at Crosby-Square, April 4, 1750. Occasioned by [...] an earthquake* (London 1750), p.16.

73. Thomas Hunter, *National wickedness the cause of national misery. A sermon preach'd at the parish church of Weverham in Cheshire: on Friday, the sixth of February* (Liverpool 1756), p.5.

coincided with the outbreak and early military setbacks of the Seven Years War'.[74] By encouraging the British to think of themselves as God's chosen people, as latter-day Israelites, providentialism also served to forge a sense of national solidarity and identity in the face of a foreign enemy.[75]

George II's government not only sent material relief to the Portuguese, it also proclaimed a day of public fast and humiliation to be held in Britain and Ireland on 6 February 1756.[76] Occasional fasts were popular occasions among both Anglicans and Protestant dissenters, since they fell during national emergencies that frightened nearly everyone.[77] These fast days developed out of the ancient Judeo-Christian practice of fasting, a discipline of penance meant to strengthen one's spiritual life through material self-denial, particularly through abstinence from food. In the early Christian church, fasting was prescribed for Fridays, and sometimes on Wednesdays and Saturdays; Lent, the forty days before the feast of Easter, was also a period of fasting.[78] Royal proclamations of public fast days began in England in 1563, during Elizabeth I's reign, when people were enjoined to leave work and attend a church service on the appointed day. There the preacher would deliver a sermon appropriate to the occasion and, in established churches, would lead a service prescribed by the Archbishop of Canterbury. As Roland Bartel notes, public fasts were special 'because they were proclaimed only in times of national distress, they were nation-wide in scope, and they were both political and religious in character since they were proclaimed by civil authority and administered by the church'.[79] It might be protested that fasts were a normal part of the routine of worship and state occasions in times of natural or man-made crisis, and that there is nothing remarkable about their occurrence.[80] But fasts and thanksgivings were normal in the same way that heart surgery is normal today: although they were royally proclaimed on

74. Bob Harris, *Politics and the nation: Britain in the mid-eighteenth century* (Oxford 2002), p.292.

75. Jeremy Black, 'Confessional state or elect nation? Religion and identity in eighteenth-century England', in *Protestantism and national identity: Britain and Ireland, c.1650 – c.1850*, ed. Tony Claydon and Ian McBride (Cambridge 1998), p.53-74, is the most nuanced account of its subject, though it underplays the cohesive possibilities of providentialism during the mid-eighteenth century.

76. On 18 December 1755, the privy council proclaimed a fast in England and Wales for 6 February; on 31 December 1755, the lord lieutenant proclaimed a fast in Ireland as well: *Bibliotecha Lindesina*, vol.viii: *Handlist of proclamations issued by royal and other constitutional authorities, 1714-1910. George I to Edward VII*, ed. James Ludovic Lindsay (Wigan 1913), p.84.

77. James Joseph Caudle, 'Measures of allegiance: sermon culture and the creation of a public discourse of obedience and resistance in Georgian Britain, 1714-1760', Yale University PhD thesis, 1996, p.262-63.

78. *Oxford dictionary of the Christian church*, p.599-600.

79. Roland Bartel, 'The story of public fast days in England', *Anglican theological review* (1955), p.190.

80. Between 1739 and 1763, the government called twenty-one fasts or thanksgivings (sixteen fasts, five thanksgivings). Between 1714 and 1739, on the other hand, it called only

average every third year during the eighteenth century, and almost annually between 1739 and 1763, they were still notable, and noticed, events.

By most accounts the February 1756 fast proved extremely popular, particularly in London. Sir Roger Newdigate found 'all ye churches crowded' that day, while Mrs Delany also reported, 'The churches are all remarkably crowded. I pray God people's heart may be touched so sincerely by this warning'.[81] Gertrude Savile found 'All the Churches so Crowded that many could not get in'.[82] Having spent the fast day in London, John Wesley rejoiced that 'The Fast Day was a glorious day, such as London has scarce seen since the Restoration. Every church in the city was more than full, and a solemn seriousness sat on every face.'[83] Even in the north, Yorkshireman Ralph Ward recorded in his diary, 'A general Fast, went to Church forenoon which was So Crowded with people as I never See the like before'.[84]

Providential logic clearly underpinned the occasional fast. 'The Conduct of our Legislature hath on this Occasion been truly exemplary,' William Hazeland declared. 'They have taught us by the Appointment of this Day's Solemnity, not to ascribe the late convulsive Throws of Nature to blind, undirected cause; but to the regular Operation of Second Causes executing the inscrutable Counsels of the First.'[85] The wording of the English proclamation of the general fast and humiliation reiterated this message: 'Whereas the manifold Sins and Wickedness of these Kingdoms, have most justly deserved heavy and severe Punishments from the Hand of Heaven, [...] [We] send up our Prayers and Supplications to the Divine Majesty, to avert all those Judgements which We most justly have deserved'.[86] It was a message that got through to many listeners. Thomas Turner noted in his diary that day that his parish priest

endeavoured in a very earnest and pressing manner to show what reason we have to repent of our vicious courses and to turn to the Lord, or else, as he says, how can we expect the favour of the Almighty to be more extensive upon our isle than upon the Portuguese nation and other places which have suffered under this dreadful calamity; and likewise endeavoured to prove that it is impossible for

four (two fasts, two thanksgivings), while between 1764 and 1788, it called only seven (six fasts, one thanksgiving): Caudle, 'Measures of allegiance', p.277-86.

81. Quoted in Harris, *Politics and the nation*, p.292; *The Autobiography and correspondence of Mary Granville, Mrs Delany*, iii.408.

82. *The Secret comment: the diaries of Gertrude Savile, 1721-1757*, p.312.

83. *The Works of John Wesley: journals and diaries (1755-65)*, ed. W. Reginald Ward and Richard P. Heitzenrater (Nashville, TN 1992), iv.41.

84. *Two Yorkshire diaries: the diary of Arthur Jessop and Ralph Ward's journal*, ed. C. E. Whiting (1952), p.188.

85. William Hazeland, *The Conclusions of atheists and superstitious persons from public calamities examined, in a sermon, preached on the 6th of February, 1756* (London 1756), p.14.

86. 'The Proclamation for a general fast [6 February 1756]' (London 1755), p.1. I thank Adrian Jones of the Society of Antiquaries, London, for providing me with a copy of this fast proclamation.

a king to govern a nation and keep his subjects in a steady course of virtue without the assistance of every individual.[87]

Public moralists would have been glad to know that someone like Turner, a reputable resident of East Hoathly, Sussex, took note of the fast day sermon, for it was the middling and elite orders of society to whom the calls for public reform were addressed. Preachers seem to have conceived a national reformation as a kind of trickle-down reform from the top to the bottom of the social hierarchy. Samuel Squire expressed a common view when he argued that the 'nobility, gentry, and large traders have an influence almost irresistible upon their tenants, dependants, and numerous households [...] Wherefore, my brethren [...] let every one of us set about it [reformation], as his particular duty, and his particular interest.'[88]

The earthquakes of the 1750s, then, were not simply seismic events: they were seismic events that conveyed a message from God.[89] That an explanatory model premised upon God's active intervention in the natural world was hegemonic as late as the 1750s fits uneasily into the current historiography of eighteenth-century Britain, which is premised upon increasing secularisation and the relative unimportance of religion during the period. Yet providence was the most common explanation of causation during the period. Like Voltaire, most of the British were horrified by what happened in Lisbon in November 1755, but unlike him they seem to have found a reasonable explanation for this natural evil in traditional Christian theology. 'To suppose these desolations the scourge of heaven for human impieties, is a dreadful reflection', Warburton confided to his friend Richard Hurd, 'and yet to suppose ourselves in a forlorn and fatherless world, is ten times a more frightful consideration.'[90] That most of his countrymen seem to have shared Warburton's view suggests that we have underestimated the extent to which Christian belief pervaded and informed eighteenth-century British culture and society.

87. *Diary of Thomas Turner*, p.26.
88. Squire, *A Speedy repentance the most effectual means to avert God's judgements*, p.17-18.
89. The similarities between the earthquake sermons during the 1750s and puritan earthquakes sermons of the seventeenth century are striking: Maxine van de Wetering, 'Moralizing in Puritan natural science: mysteriousness in earthquake sermons', *Journal of the history of ideas* (July 1982), p.417-38.
90. *Letters from a late eminent prelate*, p.149.

ROBERT WEBSTER

The Lisbon earthquake:
John and Charles Wesley reconsidered

But if our own Wisdom and Strength be not sufficient to defend us, let us not be ashamed to seek
farther Help. Let us even dare to own we believe
there is a GOD: nay, and not a lazy, indolent
Epicurean Deity, who sits at Ease upon the Circle
of the Heavens, and neither knows nor cares what
is done below [...] With Pleasure we own, there is
such a GOD, whose Eye pervades the whole Sphere
of created Beings, who knoweth the Number of the
Stars, and calleth them by their Numes: A GOD
whose Wisdom is as the great Abyss, deep and wide
as Eternity.[1]

Amidst impending plagues and woes,
Extol His saving power:
Earth hath not yawn'd, on us to close,
Or open'd, to devour[2]

I

ON 1 November 1755, in one of the greatest natural disasters of modern
Europe, an earthquake shattered much of Lisbon, killing thousands of
men, women, and children. T. D. Kendrick's history of the catastrophe
noted that 'no one will ever know the number of people who lost their lives
in the Lisbon earthquake'.[3] The disaster received international publicity,
and, as various scholars have shown, precipitated something approaching
seismological shock in the intellectual life of modern society, forcing a
reconsideration of the optimistic strands in Enlightenment ideology.[4]

1. John Wesley, *Serious thoughts occasioned by the late earthquake at Lisbon*, 2nd edn (Bristol
1755), p.25-26.
2. Charles Wesley, 'Hymns occasioned by the earthquake, March 8, 1750. Part II', in
The Poetical works of John and Charles Wesley, ed. George Osborn, 13 vols (London 1870),
vi.42.
3. T. D. Kendrick, *The Lisbon earthquake* (London 1956), p.34.
4. See, for example, Regina Ammicht-Quinn, *Von Lissabon bis Auschwitz: Zum Paradigmawechsel in der Theodizeefrage* (Freiburg 1992), p.217-21; *Die Erschütterung der vollkommenen
Welt: Die Wirkung des Erdbebens von Lissabon im Spiegel europäischer Zeitgenossen*, ed. Wolfgang

Of course, Lisbon was not the only place where devastation occurred through climatic storms and earthquakes in the eighteenth century. London was the scene of several alarming earth tremors in the winter of 1750; the first occurred in early February and the second, which was more serious, in March.[5] Ten days later unusually intense storms passed through Gosport, Portsmouth, and the Isle of Wight. The result was an outbreak of mass hysteria, particularly in London. Certainly, however, the Lisbon earthquake was a horrendous spectacle of ruin which not only encompassed the regions surrounding Lisbon but reached throughout the modern world. Charles Officer and Jake Page write of the pervasive nature of the event:

Severe damage occurred throughout the Iberian Peninsula, including Seville, Cordova, and Granada, Spain, and there was damage in North Africa at Fez and Mequinez. Tremors from the Lisbon earthquake were felt in France, Switzerland, Italy, the Netherlands, Germany, and Great Britain and as far north as Fahlun, Sweden, 1,850 miles away – in all, over a territory of two million square miles. And besides the shocks and the fires, a tsunami struck. The sea first retreated in the harbour, then swept back, engulfing much of the city with waves up to fifty feet high. The tsunami reached several places in the North Atlantic: twelve-foot waves broke on the shores of Antigua in the West Indies, 3,540 miles across the ocean.[6]

With massive wreckage resulting from earthquakes, natural tragedies – their cause and prevention – perplexed modern society. The sheer size of the Lisbon disaster opened debates on various levels. Claudia Sanides-Kohlrausch has correctly noted that, among eighteenth-century European theologians for example, the Lisbon earthquake provided an opportunity for examining the orthodox presuppositions about nature, human nature, and faith. Through these numerous and often volatile debates, modern society came to believe that the issues were complex and one-dimensional answers were neither accurate nor sufficient. Sanides-Kohlrausch concludes: 'It was one important consequence of the discourse about the Lisbon earthquake that it became evident that the aspect of "evil" or "fallen" nature cannot be exterminated from human life by rationalism.'[7] Nowhere was this conclusion more evident than in

Breidert (Darmstadt 1994); Susan Nieman, *Evil in modern thought: an alternative history of philosophy* (Princeton, NJ 2002), p.240-50; and Claudia Sanides-Kohlrausch, 'The Lisbon earthquake 1755: a discourse about the "nature" of nature', in *Is nature ever evil? Religion, science and value*, ed. William Drees (London 2003), p.106-19.

5. John Wesley, 'Journals and diaries III (1743-54)', in *Bicentennial edition of the works of John Wesley*, ed. Richard Heitzenrater, 16 vols at present (Nashville, TN 1980-), xx.320: 'It was about a quarter after twelve that the earthquake began at the skirts of the town. It began in the south-east, went through Southwark, under the river, and then from one end of London to the other'. Hereafter all volumes in the *Bicentennial edition* will be cited as *BEW*.

6. Charles Officer and Jake Page, *Tales of the earth: paroxysms and perturbations of the blue planet* (New York 1993; repr. Oxford 1994), p.53.

7. Sanides-Kohlrausch, 'The Lisbon earthquake, 1755', p.114.

the impassioned religious rhetoric of the eighteenth century; especially as it linked earthquakes with the idea of divine retribution.

In what follows, the writings of John and Charles Wesley on earthquakes will be examined. Leaders of the evangelical revival of the eighteenth century, both men had an important and nuanced approach to the difficulties that earthquakes posed for modern society. John Wesley (1703-1791), the organisational genius of the Methodist movement, published a short tract on the Lisbon earthquake in 1755 and later in 1758 wrote a sermon entitled 'The great assize', where he suggested that an earthquake would usher in God's new kingdom. Charles Wesley (1707-1788), the noted hymn writer and younger brother of John, addressed the phenomena of earthquakes through his poetry and in 1750 wrote a fascinating sermon on 'The cause and cure of earthquakes'. Scattered throughout their respective *Journals* and correspondence are reflections about the providential design of earthquakes, and the Lisbon earthquake in particular. The Wesleys, then, provide a remarkable case study for probing the relationship between faith and reason in the context of natural disasters. In what follows I shall contextualise their thoughts within the theological debates of the day, with the aim of demonstrating that John and Charles Wesley were, despite the accusations of their anti-Methodist opponents, in tune with a particular stream of thought which was influential among the plebeian population. It will additionally be noted that the rhetoric of theological debates gave the Wesleys a means of interpreting natural disasters as egalitarian events with more than natural consequences: a tenet that became critical to their evangelical agenda.

II

When the Bishop of London, Thomas Sherlock, wrote an open letter in 1750 calculating that the people of London had scorned the gospel and consequently impending doom was lurking around the corner, he reached back into a long-standing tradition that had been effective in merging the visible and invisible worlds into a symbiotic organism subject to the providential control of a divine creator.[8] The literary genre of the Jeremiad had a long ancestry that Sherlock and others like him found compatible with their theological orientation. 'We have reason to fear,' declared Bishop Sherlock, 'when we see the Beginning of Sorrows, and the Displeasure of the Almighty manifested in the Calamities we suffer under, and in the Signs and Tokens given us to expect a far more dreadful Judgment.'[9] After Sherlock's open letter to the clergy of London, many

---

8. Alexandra Walsham, *Providence in early modern England* (Oxford 1999), p.116-66.
9. Thomas Sherlock, *A Letter from Lord Bishop of London, to the clergy and people of London and Westminster, on occasion of the late earthquake* (London 1750), p.3.

fled the nation's capital for fear of another earthquake, and the bishop's inflamed rhetoric caused a furore of arguments that addressed the theology and wisdom encompassed in the document.[10]

Sampson Letsome's *The Preacher's assistant* indicated that Sherlock was not alone in his theology or sentiments. Letsome, an obscure indexer of the eighteenth century, gathered information about a variety of sermons from the Restoration to the publication of the first edition of his work in 1753.[11] A cursory evaluation of Letsome's index indicates that the sermons which he catalogued, dealt with – among other things – the existence of storms, earthquakes, and natural disasters. Letsome also listed a diverse assortment of preachers, biblical texts, and homiletic occasions for the sermons. Preachers like Nathaniel Dodge and his *God's voice in the earthquake: or a serious admonition to a sinful world*, sought to locate geological disturbances within an apocalyptic hermeneutic that portrayed earthquakes as ominous signs of God's judicial decree against man's sinful condition. But it was not only within the context of folk religion that individuals were prone to associate earthquakes with God's retributive justice. William Warbarton, no friend to enthusiasts or Methodists in the eighteenth century, wrote an extensive treatise where he endeavoured to demonstrate a divine utilisation to prevent Julian from rebuilding the Temple of Jerusalem in the first century.[12] Thus when clerics addressed the many issues that surrounded the Lisbon tragedy, 'orthodox theologians saw the earthquake as a double gift of Heaven. Not only could it punish particular transgressions; it also would show those who thought

10. On the one hand, representatives of Sherlock's opponents were the Quaker Joseph Besse's *Modest remarks upon the Bishop of London's letter concerning the late earthquakes by one of the people called Quakers* (London 1750), and an anonymous pamphlet entitled *A Serious expostulation with the Right Reverend the Lord Bishop of London on his letter to the clergy and people of London and Westminster* (London 1750). On the other hand, supporters of the Bishop's address included Samuel Hull's *The Fluctuating condition of human life, and the absolute necessity of a preparation for the eternal world, consider'd, in a sermon occasioned by the late shocks of earthquake, preached at Lorriners Hall, March 11, 1750: humbly recommended to the serious perusal of the inhabitants of London and Westminster* (London 1750), and William Stukeley, *The Philosophy of earthquakes, natural and religious. Or an inquiry into their cause, and their purpose* (London 1750).

11. Sampson Letsome, *The Preacher's assistant* (Oxford 1753). See Françoise Deconinck-Brossard, 'Eighteen-century sermons and the age', in *Crown and mitre: religion and society in northern Europe since the reformation*, ed. W. M. Jacob and Nigel Yates (Woodbridge 1993), p.105-21. Sampson Letsome was an indexer who published his compilation of all known sermons since the Restoration, listing well over 13,000 entries along with scriptural text, topic, and homiletic occasion. John Cooke updated Letsome's work in 1783 and included a total of 24,000 sermons.

12. William Warburton, *Julian, or, a discourse concerning the earthquake and firey eruption, which defeated that emperor's attempt to rebuild the temple at Jerusalem. In which the reality of a divine interposition is shewn; the objections to it are answered; and the nature of that evidence which demands the assent of every reasonable man to a miraculous fact, is considered and explained*, in *The Works of the Right Reverend William Warburton*, 7 vols (London 1788), iv.362: 'My chief purpose here is to prove the miraculous interposition of Providence, in defeating the attempt of JULIAN to rebuild the TEMPLE OF JERUSALEM.'

God's works exhausted by the abstract and distant Creation that He still played a role in the world.'[13]

III

When John Wesley came to comment on the Lisbon earthquake in 1755, his thoughts fit comfortably with those of a vast array of cultural and social commentators who viewed nature not only within a framework of connected order but within an arena that housed enigmatic monstrosities. Despite contemporary tendencies to dismiss his view of supernatural intervention, which were not altogether unwarranted, it must be noted that Wesley's knowledge of geology was considerable, and he did therefore not deserve the charge of scientific ignorance so often levelled against him.[14] Not only was he familiar with current geological theory such as Thomas Burnet's (1635-1715) *Sacred theory of the earth*[15] and John Keill's (1671-1721) critique of Burnet in his *An Examination of Dr Burnet's theory*,[16] but his reading also included William Whiston's (1667-1752) controversial *A New theory of the earth*[17] and John Woodward's (1665-1728) *Natural history of the earth*.[18]

John Wesley's ideas about earthquakes were principally found in his *Serious thoughts by the late earthquake at Lisbon* and his sermon entitled 'The great assize', written in 1758.[19] The former went through six editions, the last being published in London in 1756.[20] In the latter, Wesley depicted humanity being ushered into the final judgement by a mighty and terrible earthquake in which 'all the waters of the terraqueneous globe will feel the violence of those concussions [...] The air will be all storm

---

13. Susan Neiman, *Evil in modern thought*, p.243.

14. For example, Sara Schechner, *Comets, popular culture, and the birth of modern cosmology* (Princeton, NJ 1997), p.167-68.

15. Thomas Burnet, *The Sacred theory of the earth: containing an account of the original of the earth, and of all the general changes which it hat already undergone, or is to undergo, till the consummation of all things with a review of the theory, and of its proofs; especially in reference to scripture and the author's defence of the work, from the exceptions of Mr. Warren & an ode to the author by Mr. Addison*, 4th edn, 2 vols (London 1719).

16. John Keill, *An Examination of Dr. Burnet's theory of the earth. Together with some remarks on Mr. Whiston's new theory of the earth* (London 1698).

17. William Whiston, *A New theory of the earth, from its original, to the consummation of all things. Wherein the creation of the world in six days, the universal deluge, and the general conflagration, as laid down in the holy scriptures, are shewn to be perfectly agreeable to reason and philosophy. With a large introductory discourse concerning the genuine nature, stile, and extent of the mosaick history of creation* (London 1696).

18. John Woodward, *An Essay toward a natural history of the earth: and terrestrial bodies, especially minerals: as also of the sea, rivers, and springs. With an account of the universal deluge: and of the effects that it had upon the earth* (London 1695).

19. John Wesley, *Serious thoughts*, Sermons I (1-33), *BEW*, i.355-75.

20. Richard Green, *The Works of John and Charles Wesley. A bibliography: containing an exact account of all the publications issued by the brothers Wesley arranged in chronological order, with a list of the early editions, and descriptive and illustrative notes* (London 1896), p.90.

and tempest, full of dark "vapours and pillars of smoke"; resounding with thunder from pole to pole, and torn with ten thousand lightenings.'[21] In his *Serious thoughts*, however, John Wesley put forward a view of earthquakes that addressed his fundamental belief in divine agency and also addressed human society and its propensity for evil.

A key to understanding Wesley's outlook should begin with a journal entry for 26 November 1755. There he recorded: 'Being much importuned thereto, I wrote *Serious Thoughts on the Earthquake at Lisbon*, directed, not as I designed at first, to the small vulgar, but the great – to the learned, rich, and honourable heathens, commonly called Christians.'[22] In this way, Wesley placed the primary function of *Serious thoughts* in an apologetic framework which used a prescriptive rather than descriptive methodology.

In general, John Wesley was disdainful and suspicious of the elite structures of society. The rich neither understood the fundamental socio-economic plight of the lower classes nor God's regard for the poor.[23] The bulk of modern society had simply ignored God's programme of self-sacrifice and abnegation, opting instead for a separation from plebeian culture.[24] In the opening pages of *Serious thoughts*, Wesley characterised the thinking person of his generation: 'Generous Honesty and simple Truth are scarce any where to be found. On the contrary, Covetousness, Ambition, various Injustice, Luxury and Falsehood in every Kind, have infected every Rank and Denomination of People.'[25] Additionally, he argued, a level of malice had permeated much of Europe with the atrocity of men killing one another in war.[26] By comparison earthquakes and war brought similar, if not equal, results; namely, an irrational and sudden loss of life from the face of the earth. In both London and Lisbon, Wesley saw the signs of a systemic structure where evil had permeated society. From his knowledge of both the Lisbon earthquake and ecclesiastical

21. John Wesley, Sermons I (1-33), *BEW*, i.357.

22. John Wesley, 'Journal and diaries IV (1755-1765)', *BEW*, xxi.35.

23. See John Walsh's 'John Wesley and the community of goods', in *Protestant evangelicalism: Britain, Ireland, Germany and America, c.1750 – c.1950*, ed. Keith Robbins (Oxford 1990), p.255.

24. Theodore Jennings, *Good news to the poor: John Wesley's evangelical economics* (Nashville, TN 1990), p.101, has imaginatively labelled this idea 'economic deism'.

25. John Wesley, *Serious thoughts*, p.3-4. For an examination of the idea of luxury in the eighteenth century, see *Luxury in the eighteenth century: debates, desires and delectable goods*, ed. Maxine Berg and Elizabeth Eger (Basingstoke 2003).

26. John Wesley always considered war the most irrational and wicked of human activities. See, for example, John Wesley, *The Doctrine of original sin: according to scripture, reason, and experience* (Bristol 1757), p.56: 'But there is a still greater and more undeniable Proof, that the very Foundations of all Things, Civil and Religious, are utterly out of Course [...] There is a still more horrid Reproach to the Christian Name, yea, to the Name of Man, to all Reason and Humanity. There is WAR in the World! War between Men! War between Christians! I mean between those that bear the Name of *Christ*, and profess *to walk as He also walked.* Now who can reconcile War, I will not say to Religion, but to any Degree of Reason or common Sense?'

history, John Wesley was quick to highlight that Lisbon, the place of the earthquake, was also the location of the Inquisition, and he noted: 'Where so many brave Men have been murdered, in the most base and cowardly, as well as barbarous Manner, almost every Day, as well as every Night, while none regarded or laid it to heart.'[27] Atrocities of one sort or another had given credence to the doctrine of human depravity in London too, and the seismological reverberations were an indication that all was not morally right in the world. For Wesley, the instability of the earth indicated a supernatural and spiritual unrest that permeated the fabric of an ethos which was disobedient to God: a turbulence which revealed not only the danger of mortal sin but the presence of God's justice in the world. On this point, John Wesley disturbed many educated Christians in the eighteenth century. Archbishop Thomas Herring, for example, in a letter to William Duncombe, characterised Wesley as 'a most dark and Saturnine creature'.[28] An honest evaluation here will find it hard to conceive of John Wesley as a man of the Enlightenment. But it must be remembered that Wesley was not alone in his assertion of God's power to judge humanity in radical and unusual ways. The notion of judgement was affirmed in the continued observance of fast days after national defeats and disasters. In this manner, God's justice and mercy were affirmed under the wider umbrella of providential occurrences, and the hope of restoration became a continued and viable concept in the religious and national imaginations of the people.

At the hub of John Wesley's commitment to such a view was the belief that natural disasters were not particular demonstrations of divine wrath but a universal egalitarian judgement that, by secondary causes, evinced fear and wonder among those who reflected on these matters. The day after the tremor in London on 8 February 1750, he wrote to Grace Bennet: 'This morning my eyes were filled with tears of joy, from a hope that my time here is short.'[29] And, in his *Serious thoughts*, he asserted that the God of Christianity was not a creator who was separated from creation but intensely concerned and connected with it. 'With Pleasure we own,' wrote Wesley, 'there is such a GOD, whose Eye pervades the whole Sphere of created Beings, who knoweth the Number of the Stars,

---

27. John Wesley, *Serious thoughts*, p.4-5. Compare also George Whitefield's *Whitefield at Lisbon. Being a detailed account of the blasphemy and idolatry of popery, as witnessed by the late servant of God, George Whitefield, at the city of Lisbon, during his stay there. Printed verbatim from his account sent to a friend. Also, a narrative of the commencement and continuation of the dreadful earthquake that totally destroyed the above city, with sixty thousand inhabitants, a few months after Mr. Whitefield's visit, on All-Saints Day, being a great festival, and at a time of high mass being performed at all the churches. Printed from an account communicated by an English merchant, residing at that time in Lisbon. With Mr. Whitefield's remarks thereon* (London 1851).

28. Thomas Herring, *Letters from the late Most Reverend Dr. Thomas Herring, Lord Archbishop of Canterbury, to William Duncombe, Esq., deceased, from the year 1728 to 1757. With notes and an appendix* (London 1777), p.173-74.

29. John Wesley, Letters II (1740-1755), *BEW*, xxvi.408.

and calleth them by their Numes: A GOD whose Wisdom is as the great Abyss, deep and wide as Eternity.'[30] The Lisbon earthquake was a dreadful event, but the spectacle of life separated from God was a more horrendous sight.

IV

Charles Wesley too was affected deeply by the Lisbon earthquake and the devastation it caused.[31] Like his brother, he recorded thoughts about earthquakes in his *Journal* and, in 1750, also published a sermon on earthquakes. He also published a collection of nineteen hymns under the title *Hymns occasioned by the earthquake, March 8, 1750*. Divided into two parts, it went through three editions, the last being published in 1756.[32]

Like John Wesley, Charles saw in earthquakes a symbol of God's judicial presence. At the core of Charles Wesley's understanding of human society was a blatant disregard for God's call to holiness. In Hymn III of Part I, he commented:

> But Blinder still, the rich and great
> In wickedness excel,
> And reveal on the brink of fate,
> And sport, and dance to hell.
> Regardless of Thy smile or frown,
> Their pleasures they require,
> And sink with gay indifference down
> To everlasting fire.[33]

Consequently, for Charles Wesley too, the egalitarian structure for interpreting earthquakes was a valid heuristic device which allowed him to address the issue of sin across the board of human existence. His own sermon, originally titled 'The cause and cure of earthquakes', squarely placed the burden of suffering society on the back of sinful humanity: 'But reason, as well as faith', declared Wesley, 'doth sufficiently assure us it must be the punishment of sin, and the effect of that curse which was brought upon the earth by the original transgression. Steadfastness must be no longer looked for in the world, since innocency is banished thence. But we cannot conceive that the universe would have been disturbed by these furious accidents during the state of original righteousness.'[34]

---

30. John Wesley, *Serious thoughts*, p.26.
31. See Thomas Jackson, *The Life of the Rev. Charles Wesley, M.A.: some time student of Christ-Church, Oxford: containing a review of his poetry; sketches of the rise and progress of Methodism; with notices of contemporary events and characters* (New York 1844), p.423-30.
32. Richard Green, *The Works of John and Charles Wesley*, p.70-71.
33. Charles Wesley, *The Poetical works of John and Charles Wesley*, vi.22.
34. Charles Wesley, *The Sermons of Charles Wesley: a critical edition with introduction and notes*, ed. Kenneth Newport (Oxford 2001), p.228.

All humanity was subject to God's justice, because sin had entered man through the wilful choice of Adam and Eve in the Garden. In verse, which was added to the second edition and written in response to the Lisbon earthquake, Charles Wesley enlarged this important concept for the religious imagination:

> The mighty shock *seems now* begun,
> Beyond example great,
> And lo, the world's foundations groan
> As at their instant fate;
> Jehovah shakes the shatter'd ball,
> Sign of the general doom!
> The cities of the nations fall,
> And *Babel's* hour is come.[35]

Judgement and retribution naturally accosted Enlightenment ideology and questioned the presuppositions of the idea of optimism in the eighteenth century.[36] For Charles Wesley, as for his brother John, however, the presence of sin in the world must be realised. The explanation of earthquakes in terms of natural cause and effect did little to satisfy either of the brothers, especially Charles. At the head of his sermon on earthquakes, he contended: 'Now, that God is himself the author, and sin the moral cause, of earthquakes (whatever the natural cause may be) cannot be denied by any who believe the scriptures.'[37] The question of 'how' had little to do with the question of 'why'.

Unlike his brother, Charles Wesley's writings on violent storms demonstrated a pronounced view of suffering which was based on the atonement of Christ. J. Ernest Rattenbury noted sixty years ago that this period of Charles Wesley's life was conditioned not only by national but by personal disasters. The period from 1749 to 1762, Rattenbury observed, 'was one of importance in Charles Wesley's spiritual career. During these years he experienced much trouble: the deaths of children, the serious illness of his wife, disagreements with John, great sorrow of heart because of the increasing divergence of the itinerant preachers from the Church of England.'[38] When he portrayed the victims of the Lisbon earthquake, Charles Wesley keenly and passionately versed:

> By faith we find the place above,
> The Rock that rent in twain;
> Beneath the shade of dying love,
> And in the clefts remain.

---

35. Charles Wesley, *The Poetical works of John and Charles Wesley*, vi.26.
36. See David Spadafora's *The Idea of progress in eighteenth-century Britain* (London 1990).
37. Charles Wesley, *The Sermons of Charles Wesley*, p.227.
38. J. Ernest Rattenbury, *The Evangelical doctrines of Charles Wesley's hymns* (London 1941), p.310.

> Jesus, to Thy dear wounds we flee,
> We sink into Thy side;
> Assured that all who trust in Thee
> Shall evermore abide.[39]

In the second movement of his sermon on earthquakes, too, Charles Wesley went to great efforts to outline the sufferings and tragedies of individuals and nations who had fallen under the disaster of earthquakes. Jamaica and Lima were mentioned by name as examples of locations that had suffered greatly; the personal and national consequences of these disasters were outlined in significant detail. In Charles Wesley's mind, the horror of earthquakes was their swift and immediate nature, which gave little opportunity for escape. In a passionate concluding remark, the hymn writer of the Methodist movement maintained:

In other evils there is some way to escape; but an earthquake encloses what it overthrows, and wages war with whole provinces; and sometimes leaves nothing behind it to inform posterity of its outrages. More insolent than fire, which spares rocks; more cruel than the conqueror, who leaves walls; more greedy than the sea, which vomits up shipwrecks; it swallows and devours whatsoever it overturns. The sea itself is subject to its empire, and the most dangerous storms are those occasioned by earthquakes.[40]

For this reason, Charles Wesley's remedy, like his brother's, was to encourage repentance among individuals and reconstruct a self-identification that conceptualised life within a theatre of natural and supernatural qualifications.[41] For both brothers, a one-dimensional perspective that did not perceive the links between the visible and invisible worlds was myopic and void of truth, security, and hope.

V

Since a primal fear of storms as portents of divine judgement was deeply embedded in English folk religion, Methodist preachers made good use of storms in their evangelical appeal to the populace in the eighteenth century. As Charles Goodwin correctly observes, as many as 700 people were added in 1778 to the Birstal circuit in Yorkshire by 'simple means'; one of which was thunder and lightning.[42] Eighteenth-century Methodists repeatedly found supernatural traces in natural phenomena which caused them to perceive God's providential presence in the midst of judgement. Wesley jibed sarcastically at those sceptics who contended that God had

39. Charles Wesley, *The Poetical works of John and Charles Wesley*, vi.27.
40. Charles Wesley, *The Sermons of Charles Wesley*, p.233.
41. For example, Kendrick, *The Lisbon earthquake*, p.73-19, noted miracles that occurred in Lisbon during and after the earthquake.
42. Charles Godwin, 'The terrors of the thunderstorm: medieval popular cosmology and Methodist revivalism', *Methodist history* 39 (2001), p.101.

nothing to do with earthquakes: 'If thou prayest then [...] it must be to some of these. Begin. "O Earth, Earth, Earth, hear the Voice of thy Children. Hear, O Air, Water, Fire!"'[43]

For both brothers, the important thing about natural disasters was their inclusive scope and man's inability to escape their consequences. The Wesleys, as we have suggested, certainly saw disasters as egalitarian events that positioned all of humanity on an equal plane. At the age of seventy-four, John Wesley wrote to Christopher Hooper: 'There is no divine visitation which is likely to have so general an influence upon sinners as an earthquake. The rich can no more guard against it than the poor. Therefore I have often thought this would be no undesirable event.'[44] The conception of humanity reduced to the level of helplessness before God encouraged the leaders of the evangelical revival, and their agenda of justification by faith alone. Because the Methodists, and especially John Wesley, were also alert to the intersection between the natural and supernatural dimensions of existence, earthquakes provided ample proof that, contrary to the deists and liberal Anglicans of the period, God was integrally concerned and involved in the matrix of creation.

43. John Wesley, *Serious thoughts*, p.21.
44. John Wesley, *Letters of the Rev. John Wesley, A. M.*, ed. John Telford, 8 vols (London 1931; repr. London 1960), vi.284; *Letters of the Rev. John Wesley, A. M.*, vi.150-51, in letter to Thomas Rankin: 'When a land is visited with famine or plague or earthquake, the people commonly see and acknowledge the hand of God.'

GRÉGORY QUENET

Déconstruire l'événement.
Un séisme philosophique ou une
catastrophe naturelle?

LES analyses sur le tremblement de terre de Lisbonne se concentrent habituellement sur la signification de l'événement et la crise qu'il déclenche dans les consciences européennes. Le passage de la catastrophe naturelle à l'événement culturel semble aller de soi, tant le désastre du 1er novembre 1755 est exceptionnel et destructeur. Pourtant, tous les phénomènes naturels meurtriers n'acquièrent pas le statut de catastrophe, et encore moins celui d'événement européen, de 'séisme philosophique'.[1] L'argument quantitatif ne résiste pas longtemps car les 10 000 morts de la capitale portugaise ne suffisent pas à éclipser le grand incendie de Londres de 1666 qui détruit 13 200 maisons, les 100 000 morts de la peste de Provence en 1720, sans parler des centaines de milliers de morts causés par les cyclones en Inde en 1737 et 1789 ou les dix millions de morts de la famine du Bengale de 1770.[2] Voltaire lui-même ne reconnaît-il pas à propos du tremblement de terre de 1699 en Chine qu'il 'fut plus funeste que celui qui de nos jours a détruit Lima et Lisbonne; il fit périr, dit-on, environ quatre cent mille hommes'.[3]

L'intervention de Voltaire et de son 'Poème sur le désastre de Lisbonne' contre l'optimisme dominant est jugée décisive.[4] Pour Theodore Besterman, 'En somme, ce qui a si fortement impressionné les hommes n'a pas été tant le désastre en lui-même que l'événement vu à travers la sensibilité du grand homme. Encore une fois un poète a été le législateur de l'humanité.'[5] Le contexte semble jouer un rôle déterminant car l'apogée de l'optimisme en 1755 masque la fragilité de la justification religieuse et philosophique du mal. Alors, le tremblement de terre du 1er novembre n'est-il

1. Paul Hazard, 'Le problème du mal dans la conscience européenne du dix-huitième siècle', *Romanic review* (1941), p.147-70 (p.159); Bronislaw Baczko, *Job, mon ami. Promesse du bonheur et fatalité du mal* (Paris 1997), p.17.

2. Claude Chaline et Jocelyne Dubois-Maury, *La Ville et ses dangers: prévention et gestion des risques naturels, sociaux, technologiques* (Paris 1994), p.19; *Dreadful visitations, confronting natural catastrophe in the age of Enlightenment*, ed. Alessa Johns (New York 1999), p.xi-xii.

3. Voltaire, *Essai sur les mœurs, Œuvres complètes de Voltaire*, éd. Moland, dorénavant M (Paris 1878), xii.168.

4. Voltaire, 'Poème sur le désastre de Lisbonne', M.ix.470-78.

5. Theodore Besterman, 'Le désastre de Lisbonne et l'optimisme de Voltaire', *La Table ronde* (1958), p.60-74 (p.71).

qu'un exemple exceptionnel parmi d'autres, voire un simple prétexte? Ces arguments ne suffisent pas à expliquer comment un aléa naturel devient un événement historique.[6] Etait-il d'une intensité incomparable à celle des autres désastres? Etait-il imprévisible, bouleversant ainsi les idées reçues? Comment est-il parvenu à la connaissance d'un grand nombre d'Européens? Les contemporains ont-ils eu le sentiment qu'il avait des conséquences majeures?

i. La destruction de Lisbonne

Par quoi les contemporains ont-ils été réellement frappés? Chronologiquement, la destruction de Lisbonne arrive en premier et reste l'événement déclencheur. En 1755, la capitale portugaise est déjà sur le déclin et n'est plus au cœur de l'espace européen depuis longtemps, ne possédant ni force militaire, ni puissance politique, ni rayonnement industriel. La place marchande reste cependant de premier plan, largement dominée par les étrangers: en 1752, près de 500 navires y ont mouillé, ce qui en fait le troisième port après Amsterdam et Londres. Elle demeure aussi une des métropoles de la catholicité, avec pas moins de 131 confréries en 1707, cinquante couvents, 121 oratoires. Tous les Etats d'Europe occidentale entretiennent donc en 1755 un ambassadeur ou un consul, souvent les deux. Le prestige de la capitale portugaise reste fort auprès du public européen, entretenu par les reflets de l'empire colonial. Les récits du tremblement de terre reprennent tous cette image:

Lisbonne étoit l'une des plus grandes villes de l'Europe, bâti sur un terrain fort élevé & montagneux, formant un Amphithéâtre qui procuroit en perspective un très beau coup d'œil. L'on y remarquoit de très beaux édifices, parmi lesquels le Palais du Roi étoit véritablement digne par sa magnificence de loger un souverain [...] On y voyoit de très beaux couvents, grands & spacieux, peuplés d'une multitude de religieux & religieuses, & en si grand nombre que l'on en pouvoit compter près de deux cens dans une seule Communauté. Les ornements des Autels étoient la plupart enrichis d'or, d'argent, de pierres précieuses, de perles fines, & de brillants en quantité.[7]

Lisbonne offre une image ambivalente, mêlant familiarité et distance, ce qui laisse un terrain favorable à l'imaginaire et aux fantasmes. L'or des Amériques continue de faire rêver.[8] La ruine de la ville incarne la figure du déclin des empires et du renversement de la fortune, qui fait partie de l'imaginaire des séismes dans la culture classique.[9] L'archétype de ce bouleversement est le désastre qui, au début du règne de Tibère, ravage l'Asie en une nuit et fait disparaître douze villes entières. Cet épisode est

6. Michel Winock, 'Qu'est-ce qu'un événement', *L'Histoire* (2002), p.32-37.
7. G. Rapin, *Le Tableau des calamités, ou description exacte et fidèle de l'extinction de Lisbonne* ([s.l.] 1756), p.3-4.
8. José Augusto Franca, *Une Ville des Lumières, la Lisbonne de Pombal* (Paris 1965), p.40-41.
9. Grégory Quenet, *La Naissance d'un risque. Les tremblements de terre en France XVIIe-XVIIIe siècles* (Seyssel 2005).

rapporté par Tacite, Sénèque, Strabon, rappelé ensuite dans l'*Histoire romaine* de Coeffeteau, l'*Encyclopédie* de Diderot et D'Alembert et bien d'autres écrits sur les séismes.[10] Le poème de Barthe, un des grands succès de 1756, met en scène, avant l'irruption de la secousse, la puissance de la 'reine du Tage', avec son empire, ses palais, ses temples, ses richesses et ses merveilles de l'art.[11] Sa destruction évoque les villes asiatiques du règne de Tibère, et bien sûr la découverte d'Herculanum (1719) et de Pompéi (1748).[12]

Les tremblements de terre ont une signification anthropologique forte, qui les place à part dans le cortège des fléaux, et les contemporains sont consternés par le spectacle d'une capitale européenne détruite par un phénomène aussi prodigieux. Dans les récits publiés, le tremblement de terre relègue au second plan le tsunami et l'incendie qui causent pourtant la majeure partie des dégâts.[13] Les séismes sont fréquents dans la région de Lisbonne, qui en a subi sept au quartorzième siècle, autant au seizième siècle dont trois violents (en 1531, 1500 maisons détruites; en 1551, 2000 morts; en 1597, trois rues englouties), trois au dix-septième siècle et deux dans la première moitié du dix-huitième siècle (en 1724 et 1750).[14] Pourtant, ces événements sont peu connus hors de la péninsule ibérique et le Portugal ne semble pas considéré comme une région particulièrement sismique. En France, les périodiques, occasionnels et textes littéraires antérieurs à 1755 ne mentionnent pas Lisbonne et le Portugal parmi les zones sismiques, alors que les séismes italiens et de la Méditerranée orientale sont fréquemment cités.[15] Le caractère extraordinaire du désas-tre du 1er novembre en sort renforcé. Pour autant, aucun de ces arguments sur la destruction de Lisbonne n'est décisif.

ii. Les secousses européennes

Les contemporains ont été autant frappés par le séisme à Lisbonne que par les secousses qui ont agité l'Europe pendant des mois. Les effets du séisme du 1er novembre ont été ressentis dans le nord de l'Europe, le

---

10. Sénèque, *Naturales quaestiones*, livre VI, i; Tacite, *Annales*, Livre II, xlvii; Strabon, *Géographie*, livre XII, 8, 16 à 18; Nicolas Coeffeteau, *Histoire romaine* (Paris 1646), p.275; *Encyclopédie ou Dictionnaire raisonné des sciences, des arts et des métiers*, éd. Denis Diderot et Jean D'Alembert (1751-1780), t.xvi.

11. Nicolas-Thomas Barthe, *Ode sur la ruine de Lisbonne* ([s.l.] 1756). Le poème est repris dans l'*Année littéraire* (1756), p.165; le *Journal de Trévoux* (1756), p.1913-17; et le *Journal des savants* (1756), 3e partie.

12. Antoine-Leonard Thomas, *Mémoire sur la cause des tremblemens de terre, qui a remporté le prix 'Accessit' au jugement de l'Académie royale des sciences, belles-lettres et arts de Rouen, le 3 août 1757* (Paris 1758), p.84.

13. J. A. Franca, *Une Ville des Lumières*, p.58-59.

14. J. A. Franca, *Une Ville des Lumières*, p.52.

15. La remarque ne vaut plus après 1755 car les contemporains se plongent dans l'histoire pour chercher la trace de séismes à Lisbonne.

nord de l'Italie, la Catalogne, le sud de la France, la Suisse, en Bohème, aux Açores, sur les côtes du Brésil, aux Antilles, de l'Islande au Maroc, des Etats allemands à Boston.[16] Dans les mois qui suivent, le nombre exceptionnel de séismes permet de parler de la 'crise séismique de 1755-1762 en Europe du Nord-Ouest'.[17] La France est frappée par au moins quarante-quatre séismes du 1er novembre 1755 à la fin de l'année 1756, quatre-vingt-sept au total jusqu'en 1762. Tous les habitants de l'Europe du nord-ouest ont senti à un moment ou un autre un séisme dans les mois qui suivent le tremblement de terre de Lisbonne. A elle seule, une source allemande de la région de l'Eifel en dénombre quatre-vingt-huit entre décembre 1755 et mars 1757, le recteur du collège des Jésuites à Brigue note 135 secousses du 9 décembre 1755 au 26 février 1756, avec seulement vingt-six jours de répit sur un total de quatre-vingt, et pour la journée du 9 décembre une secousse presque chaque demi-heure.[18]

Tous les récits, privés ou publiés, soulignent la fréquence et l'étendue exceptionnelles des secousses des années 1755 et 1756, en les mettant en relation avec l'événement portugais. De nombreux curés français commentent, en marge des registres paroissiaux, la coincidence entre l'ébranlement de leur village et le choc subi par Lisbonne.[19] Ce sont les événements européens qui mobilisent les savants de l'Académie des sciences de Paris: seules deux des quatre-vingt-douze communications sur les séismes effectuées entre novembre 1755 et la fin de l'année 1756 traitent du Portugal.[20] Sur les quatre-vingt-seize correspondances réunies par le géographe Philippe Buache à partir des réseaux académiques, seule une concerne Lisbonne, et encore est-elle datée de 1757.[21] Sur le plan sismologique, la plupart de ces séismes ne sont pas des répliques ni des conséquences des secousses du 1er novembre. Certains sont de forte intensité, tels ceux du 9 décembre 1755 dans le Valais (intensité VIII-IX à Brig), du 27 décembre

16. Paris, Académie royale des sciences, MS registre des procès-verbaux des séances (31 janvier 1756), lxxv, f.55.
17. Pierre Alexandre et Jean Vogt, 'La crise séismique de 1755-1762 en Europe du Nord-ouest. Les secousses des 26 et 27.12.1755: recensement des matériaux', dans *Materials of the CEC project 'Review of historical seismicity in Europe'*, éd. Paola Albini et Andrea Moroni (Milan 1994), ii.143-52.
18. P. Alexandre et J. Vogt, 'La crise séismique de 1755-1762', p.37; Frédéric Montandon, 'Les séismes de forte intensité en Suisse', *Revue pour l'étude des calamités* (1942-1943), v-vi.9-10.
19. Voir par exemple Loire-Atlantique, archives communales de Soudan, registre paroissial manuscrit (1755); Loire-Atlantique, archives communales de Saint Sulpice d'auvergné, registre paroissial manuscrit (1755); Loire-Atlantique, archives communales de Pornic, registre paroissial manuscrit (1755); Haute-Savoie, archives communales de Cernex, registre paroissial manuscrit (1755); Oise, archives communales de Hedencourt, registre paroissial manuscrit (1755).
20. Paris, Académie royale des sciences, MS registre des procès-verbaux des séances (1755-1756), lxxiv-lxxv.
21. Paris, Bibliothèque nationale de France, MS nouvelles acquisitions françaises 20236 et 20237.

1755 dans le Rheinland (intensité VII à Stolberg), du 18 février 1756 dans la même zone (intensité VIII à Stolberg).[22]

De légères secousses qui seraient passées inaperçues sont désormais relevées et commentées parce qu'elles sont rattachées au choc du 1er novembre. Devenus plus attentifs aux phénomènes sismiques qui sont mis en relation les uns avec les autres, enregistrés de manière plus fine, les contemporains ont la conviction que les secousses deviennent plus nombreuses après 1755. Jean-Baptiste Robinet ne fait que reprendre un véritable lieu commun: 'jamais les secousses de tremblement de terre ne furent ni si étendues ni si fréquentes, que depuis quelques années'.[23] Par un mécanisme d'amplification sociale du risque, cet aléa passe au premier plan des préoccupations.[24] Plusieurs sources indiquent l'existence en France d'une mémoire orale sur le tremblement de terre de Lisbonne. Le fait est suffisamment singulier pour mériter d'être souligné, dans un pays où il n'existe pas de mémoire sismique. Lors d'un séisme le 10 octobre 1774 dans les Pyrénées, les habitants de la vallée d'Aspe rappellent qu'une fontaine s'était troublée de la même manière en 1755.[25] Dans les années 1850, ce qui implique une transmission entre générations, on montre encore dans le pays de Foix les traces de dégâts causés dans les montagnes par la secousse de 1755.[26] En 1818, les anciens du village de Saint-Auban en Provence sont capables d'indiquer à un journaliste la source qui est devenue trouble et agitée le 1er novembre 1755.[27]

Le tremblement de terre de Lisbonne n'aurait pas eu un tel retentissement si les contemporains n'avaient ressenti les mêmes secousses, à des milliers de kilomètres de là et au même instant. En 1755 et 1756, la nature crée, de manière tout à fait singulière, un lien entre l'événement lointain et ses spectateurs européens. Ce lien permet une participation à distance et quasi instantanée, caractéristique réservée aux médias modernes selon Pierre Nora.[28] Celui-ci situe en effet l'apparition de l'événement médiatique à la fin du dix-neuvième siècle, quand le progrès des communications, l'intégration croissante des différentes régions du monde (par la

22. *Les Tremblements de terre en France*, éd. Jérôme Lambert (Orléans 1997), p.191. L'échelle MSK est une échelle d'intensité macrosismique, c'est-à-dire qui estime l'intensité d'une secousse à partir des effets sur les hommes et les bâtiments. Elle est utilisée en France et dans la plupart des pays européens pour exprimer l'intensité car elle est adaptée aux régions de faible sismicité. Comportant douze degrés, il ne faut pas la confondre avec la magnitude, introduite par Richter, et qui quantifie la puissance d'un tremblement de terre, représentative de l'énergie rayonnée au foyer sous forme d'ondes sismiques.

23. Jean-Baptiste Robinet, *De la nature* (Amsterdam 1761), p.64.

24. William J. Burns, Jeanne X. Kasperson, Roger Kasperson, Ortwin Renn, Paul Slovic, 'The social amplification of risk: theoretical foundations and empirical applications', *Journal of social issues* (1992), p.137-60.

25. *Journal encyclopédique* (1774), i.350.

26. H. Castillon d'Aspet, *Histoire du comté de Foix* (Toulouse 1852), ii.411.

27. *Journal de Marseille et des Bouches du Rhône* (8 avril 1818).

28. Pierre Nora, 'Le retour de l'événement', dans *Faire de l'histoire, nouveaux problèmes*, éd. Jacques Le Goff et Pierre Nora (Paris 1974), i.285-308.

colonisation, les guerres mondiales, les révolutions, et les transformations économiques) assurent la démocratisation et la participation des masses aux événements. Le tremblement de terre de Lisbonne a donc permis une unification de l'espace européen sans précédent, et peut-être sans équivalent jusqu'à la Révolution française.[29] Dans un système de l'information en progrès mais encore rudimentaire, ces ébranlements unifient soudainement l'espace, offrant une participation inédite à l'événement. De ce fait, le regard sur la nature se modifie, une sensibilité nouvelle aux secousses apparaît, très nette dans de nombreux livres de raisons qui relèvent dix ou vingt tremblements de terre dans l'année.[30] Chacun de ces phénomènes vient s'agréger au séisme de Lisbonne pour constituer un événement-monstre et persuader les contemporains de la multiplication des séismes.

La multiplication des tremblements de terre donne naissance à un nouveau genre d'écrits, les journaux ou tables d'événements telluriques. Anne Amable Augier Du Fot publie en 1756 un *Journal historique, géographique et physique de tous les tremblements de terre et autres événements arrivés dans l'Univers pendant les années 1755 & 1756.*[31] L'année suivante, Laurent-Etienne Rondet accompagne son *Supplément aux réflexions sur le désastre de Lisbonne* d'un *Journal des phénomènes et autres événements remarquables arrivés depuis le 1er novembre 1755.*[32] Citons aussi les *Mémoires historiques et physiques sur les tremblements de terre* d'Elie Bertrand et les tables rédigées par Philippe Buache.[33] A cause des événements de 1755 et 1756, Gueneau de Montbeliard [Guéneau de Montbeillard] commence à rédiger une liste chronologique, souvent considérée comme un des premiers catalogues sismologiques.[34] Le genre est européen car il est incarné par des ouvrages

29. Ana Cristina Bartolomeo de Araujo, '1755: l'Europe tremble à Lisbonne', dans *L'Esprit de l'Europe, dates et lieux*, éd. Antoine Compagnon et Jacques Seebacher (Paris 1993), i.125-30 (p.126).

30. *Jacquemin, cultivateur à Aische en Refail: annotations pour les années 1755-1760*, éd. E. Verhelst, 'Etude de géographie locale: Aische en Refail', *Bulletin de la Société royale de Belgique* (1895), xix.548-49.

31. Anne Amable Augier Du Fot, *Journal historique, géographique et physique de tous les tremblements de terre et autres événements arrivés dans l'Univers pendant les années 1755 & 1756* ([s.l.] 1756).

32. Laurent-Etienne Rondet, *Supplément aux réflexions sur le désastre de Lisbonne. Avec un journal des phénomènes, et autres événements remarquables arrivés depuis le 1er novembre 1755 et des remarques sur la plaie des sauterelles annoncée par saint Jean* ([s.l.] 1757).

33. Elie Bertrand, *Mémoires historiques et physiques sur les tremblemens de terre* (La Haye 1757). Paris, Bibliothèque nationale de France, MS nouvelles acquisitions françaises 20236 et 20237, 'Tables alphabétiques des lieux où l'on a ressenti des tremblements et leur Supplément par Philippe Buache'.

34. Gueneau de Montbeliard [Guéneau de Montbeillard], 'Liste chronologique des éruptions de volcans, des tremblements de terre, de quelques faits météorologiques, des comètes, des maladies pestilentielles, des éclipses les plus remarquables jusqu'en 1760', dans *Collection académique composée des mémoires, actes ou journaux des plus célèbres académies et sociétés littéraires de l'Europe* (Paris 1761), vi.450-700. Voir à ce sujet l'article de Jeff Loveland, dans le présent volume, p.191-207.

hollandais et allemands.[35] Les histoires des tremblements de terre ne sont pas une nouveauté et même plutôt un genre répandu, illustré au seizième siècle et plus récemment par Johann Gottlob Krüger.[36] En 1756, la nouveauté consiste à ne plus rechercher de tels événements parmi les auteurs de l'antiquité et les textes religieux mais dans le présent ou un passé très récent, à partir du dépouillement des gazettes ou de fonds de correspondances. Toutes ces nouvelles alimentent le débat philosophique sur le mal mais sont loin de se résumer à celui-ci.

iii. Le débat physique sur les secousses

Les tremblements de terre suscitent un débat physique passionné à partir de 1756, qui rivalise avec les interrogations sur le mal. Il représente les deux tiers des articles sur les séismes publiés dans le *Mercure de France*, le tiers pour le *Journal de Trévoux*, la moitié pour le *Journal des savants*, plus de la moitié pour le *Journal encyclopédique*, le reste regroupant textes littéraires, philosophiques et religieux.[37] Ce n'est pas un hasard si le mémoire écrit par Kant en 1756 est consacré aux théories sismiques plutôt qu'à la providence.[38] Les interrogations sont toutes centrées sur l'étendue et la diffusion des secousses qui échappent à tous les phénomènes connus jusque-là et bouleversent le rapport à l'espace: comment un événement survenu à Lisbonne peut-il être ressenti au même moment à des milliers de kilomètres de là? Préoccupés avant tout par le rôle des séismes dans l'histoire de la terre, les modèles existants ne permettent pas de répondre à cette question.[39] Comme le souligne l'éditeur de la compilation sismo-logique parue à Londres en 1757, 'the effects of the earthquake [...] were distributed over very nearly four millions of square English miles of the earth's surface: a most astonishing space! and greatly surpassing any thing, of this kind, ever recorded in history'.[40] L'*Encyclopédie* revient

---

35. *Schouwtoneel der akelige en deerlyke verwoestingen, rampen, ongevallen en zonderlinge gebeurtenissen, Sedert den eersten November 1755 zo in Portugal, Spanje, Vrankryk, Italie, Zwitzerland, Duitschland, het Noorden, Engeland en de Nederlanden, als buiten Europa door de Aardbevingen, waterberoeringen Overstromingen en zeldzame Luchtverschynsels verwekt en voorgevallen* (Utrecht 1756); Johann-Friedrich Seyfart, *Allgemeine geschichte der erdbeben* (Francfort, Leipzig 1756).

36. *Discours des causes et effects admirables des tremblemens de terre, contenant plusieurs raisons & opinions des philosophes. Avec un brief recueil des plus remarquables tremblemens depuis la création du monde jusques à present, extraict des plus signalez historiens par V. A. D. L. C.* (Paris 1580); Johann Gottlob Krüger, *Histoire des anciennes révolutions du globe terrestre avec une relation chronologique et historique des tremblemens de terre arrivés sur notre globe depuis le commencement de l'Ere chrétienne jusqu'à present,* traduction de M. F. A. Deslandes (Amsterdam, Paris 1752).

37. G. Quenet, *La Naissance d'un risque.*

38. Emmanuel Kant, 'Histoire et description des plus remarquables événements relatifs au tremblement de terre qui a secoué une grande partie de la terre à la fin de l'année 1755', traduit par Jean-Paul Poirier, *Cahiers philosophiques* (mars 1999), p.85-121.

39. G. Quenet, *La Naissance d'un risque.*

40. *The History and philosophy of earthquakes, collected from the best writers on the subject by a member of the Royal Academy of Berlin with a particular account of the great one of November, the 1st 1755 in various parts of the globe* (London 1757), p.5.

sur la question car 'un des phénomènes les plus étranges des *tremblemens de terre*, c'est leur propagation, c'est-à-dire la manière dont ils se communiquent à des distances souvent prodigieuses, en un espace de tems très-court'.[41]

Dans les mois qui suivent les tremblements de terre européens, des dizaines de théories nouvelles sont écrites et publiées. Elles sont d'une très grande diversité car, par exemple, sur les dix mémoires conservés pour le concours de l'Académie de Rouen en 1756 sur la cause des tremblements de terre, aucun ne propose le même type d'explication. Ces écrits ne se réduisent nullement à la répétition des auteurs antiques: ces derniers sont souvent cités, de nombreux emprunts apparaissent mais ils portent sur des aspects précis, de préférence assez concrets. Aucun traité des années 1750 ne reprend leur conception générale de l'univers ni l'ensemble du système des météores d'Aristote qui était encore omniprésent dans la première moitié du dix-septième siècle. Les tremblements de terre sont un objet de connaissance encore mal constitué car les séismes n'appartiennent à aucune branche de la science en particulier et il est impossible de vérifier les explications proposées:

Nous connaissons la surface de la terre à peu près complètement en ce qui concerne son étendue. Mais nous avons aussi sous nos pieds un monde, avec lequel, encore à notre époque, nous sommes très peu familiers. [...] La plus grande profondeur à laquelle les hommes soient parvenus, à partir des endroits les plus élevés de la terre ferme, ne dépasse pas toujours cinq cents brasses, c'est-à-dire même pas la six millième partie de la distance au centre de la terre.[42]

De plus:

Pour acquérir des connaissances certaines sur les circonstances qui précèdent les tremblemens de terre, et découvrir les signes de leur approche il faudroit que les tremblements fussent ou à peu près périodiques, ou très fréquens, comme la pluie, le vent, la grêle, mais ces tristes événements ont été si rares jusqu'à présent, que qui que ce soit ne s'est appliqué à faire de sérieuses observations.[43]

Les secousses des années 1750 mobilisent des nouveautés scientifiques très différentes, pour les mettre à l'épreuve et tenter de proposer le meilleur modèle théorique. Le champ scientifique n'étant ni totalement professionnalisé ni fermé, le débat public autorise toutes les interventions. Citons les théories minéralogistes sur l'inflammation souterraine, les variantes chimiques sur la fermentation et la dilatation de l'air, les analyses de Philippe Buache sur la propagation par les chaînes de montagne qui structurent le globe, les modèles mécanistes sur la transmission d'une impulsion initiale, sans oublier les mémoires qui invoquent les

41. 'Tremblemens de terre', in *Encyclopédie ou Dictionnaire raisonné* (1751-1780), t.xvi.
42. Kant, 'Histoire et description', p.86.
43. Rouen, Bibliothèque municipale, fonds de l'Académie, MS C 20, 'Concours de 1756 sur les tremblements de terre, mémoire n° 10 par la Sablonnière le Jeune du chapitre d'Evreux'.

mécanismes célestes, la circulation des éléments et de l'air, les cavités souterraines, le phlogistique...[44]

Incontestablement, les théories électriques sont celles qui rencontrent le plus grand succès, remportant avec Isnard [de Grasse] le concours de l'Académie de Rouen tandis que la théorie d'Antoine-Léonard Thomas sur la fermentation et la dilatation obtient un accessit.[45] Ces explications sont elles-mêmes très variées car les tremblements de terre résultent pour certains du contact entre un corps électrique et un autre qui ne l'est pas, pour d'autres d'une impulsion électrique dont les causes restent mystérieuses, ou encore de l'attraction électrique sur le souffre concentré au sein de la terre, jusqu'à provoquer une explosion.[46] En revanche, le mécanisme de propagation des secousses est identique car le fluide électrique se propage instantanément dans tous les corps conducteurs, qui peuvent être des montagnes, des veines de souffre, etc. Pour Isnard, ce principe est le seul à pouvoir expliquer tous les effets singuliers des séismes: l'électricité pénètre les corps sans rien perdre de sa force, frappe les matières intérieurement et extérieurement, produit détonations et scintillations, est une source de lumière, perce d'un trait rapide les corps les plus durs comme la foudre. L'argument le plus fort reste sa capacité de se déplacer à des distances étonnantes, comme les secousses.[47] Il cite Louis-Guillaume Le Monnier qui, le premier, fait en 1746 une estimation de la vitesse de l'électricité: ne trouvant aucun délai détectable pour l'homme entre la vue de l'éclair et la sensation du choc, il en conclut que la décharge va trente fois plus vite que le son. Louis-Guillaume Le Monnier remarque aussi que le choc traverse une pièce d'eau, comme le bassin du jardin des Tuileries, sans perdre de sa force. Des expériences encore plus spectaculaires sont accomplies par Jean Jallabert autour du lac de Genève, par William Watson et d'autres membres de la Royal Society en 1748 pour communiquer le flux à travers des rivières au moyen de deux barres de fer plongées dans l'eau.[48]

iv. A la recherche de nouvelles procédures d'enquête

Le problème posé par les séismes n'est pas seulement théorique mais pratique: les secousses des années 1755-1756 imposent de nouvelles

44. G. Quenet, *La Naissance d'un risque*.

45. Isnard, *Mémoires sur les tremblemens de terre, qui a remporté le prix de physique au jugement de l'Académie des sciences, belles-lettres et arts de Rouen, le 3 août 1757* (Paris 1758); Thomas, *Mémoire sur la cause des tremblemens de terre*.

46. 'Les tremblemens de terre attribués à l'électricité', *Journal encyclopédique* (1er mai 1756), iii.3-18; 'Essai sur les tremblemens de terre', *Mercure de France* (mai 1756), p.93-113; 'Réflexions sur les causes des tremblemens de terre', *Journal de Trévoux* (décembre 1756), p.3012-16.

47. Isnard, *Mémoires sur les tremblemens de terre*, p. 27.

48. John Lewis Heilbron, *Electricity in the 17th and 18th centuries: a study of early modern physics* (Berkeley, CA 1979), p.320.

procédures d'enquête. Pour étudier la répartition et l'étendue de ce phénomène, il faut multiplier les observations et ne plus se contenter d'une seule, fiable en un endroit précis. Les savants doivent donc chacun collecter des informations en mobilisant leurs réseaux de correspondants. A l'échelon parisien se met en place une vue d'ensemble qui tisse des liens entre des points dispersés sur le territoire: Aix, Toulouse, Sedan, Beaune, et d'autres encore. Cette histoire des pratiques commence en fait dans les années 1740, quand les savants découvrent les séismes français. Ces phénomènes, plus nombreux qu'ils ne le pensaient, d'intensité moyenne ou faible, les obligent à construire de nouvelles grilles de lecture et un protocole d'observation approprié.

Dans les procès-verbaux de l'Académie des sciences, ce protocole émerge avant le désastre de Lisbonne, dans les années 1740. En réponse à une demande de René-Antoine Réaumur, Chomel de Bressieu fournit une relation du tremblement de terre ressenti à Annonay en 1740, qui donne l'heure de la secousse, sa durée en secondes, l'aire ébranlée, les effets ressentis et des remarques annexes (les sensations diffèrent selon l'étage).[49] De même, à l'Académie de Toulouse, l'astronome Antoine Darquier lit en 1750 des lettres envoyées de Tarbes par un correspondant de l'Académie sur les séismes survenus en Bigorre.[50] Avec la multiplication des travaux et des observations sismiques en 1755 et 1756, les critères se précisent encore et se fixent. Les récits scientifiques ressemblent alors à cette lettre écrite de Genève par Jean Jallabert, en réponse aux question de Jean-Jacques Dortous de Mairan sur le séisme du 9 décembre:

C'étoit 2 heures 23' après midi. La plupart n'ont senti que deux secousses distantes l'une de l'autre d'environ 30''. Quelques personnes ont cru en avoir remarqué 3. Je les jugeai sur la direction des oscillations de quelques corps suspendus du sud-est au nord-ouest. Le baromètre était à 26 pouces 6 lignes 1/2 le thermomètre a I ^{d} 1/2 au-dessus de o. Le vent très foible à l'ouest, les jours précédents avoient été les plus froids de l'année avec le vent au nord. A 7 heures du matin, j'observai le 6 le thermomètre de M. de Réaumur à 6 1/2; le 7 à 7 1/4, le 8 à 7, et le 9 à o. [...] Tout l'effet du tremblement s'est borné à renverser quelques outils dans des cabinets d'horlogers logés au haut des maisons, et à faire sonner quelques cloches.[51]

Au dispositif initial sont venus s'ajouter le laps de temps entre les secousses, leur direction et des données météorologiques (pression, température, vent) qui précisent, le cas échéant, les coïncidences avec d'autres

---

49. Paris, Académie royale des sciences, MS registre des procès-verbaux des séances (23 mars 1740), lix, f.58.

50. 'Sur un tremblement de terre, & sur des effets singuliers de la foudre', dans *Histoire et Mémoires de l'Académie des sciences, inscriptions et belles-lettres de Toulouse* (Toulouse 1784), ii.15-19.

51. Paris, Académie royale des sciences, MS registre des procès-verbaux des séances (31 janvier 1756), lxxv, f.55.

136

phénomènes exceptionnels (tempête, comète, brouillard...). Avec plus ou moins de rigueur et d'exhaustivité, les observations sismiques envoyées à l'Académie des sciences suivent ce protocole.

Connaître l'heure d'irruption d'un tremblement de terre est primordial. La simultanéité d'une secousse en deux points distincts permet de conclure à l'existence d'un phénomène identique et d'une cause unique. L'existence d'un léger décalage chronologique oriente les interrogations sur les mécanismes physiques: comment peut se diffuser une explosion survenue en un lieu central? A quelle vitesse la transmission s'opère-t-elle? De telles questions exigent une précision accrue, pour renforcer les preuves disponibles, faire des calculs de vitesse, dresser une géographie tellurique. Les récits savants sont attentifs à déterminer l'orientation des mouvements du sol, pour atteindre un niveau global de compréhension. En effet, la direction donne accès à la source des ébranlements, la synthèse de ce type d'informations autorise la mise en relation d'événements éparpillés dans l'espace. La mesure de la durée des secousses offre un élément comparatif de plus, et des pistes supplémentaires pour les théories physiques. Elle est aussi un moyen implicite de qualifier l'intensité de la catastrophe. De manière empirique, les contemporains estiment que la gravité des dommages matériels dépend, entre autres, de la durée de la secousse. Comparant le séisme survenu à Aix le 3 juillet 1756 et le témoignage de personnes qui étaient à Lisbonne le 1er novembre 1755, un témoin explique que 'les secousses furent moins violentes que celles que nous avons ressentis ici, mais qu'à la vérité elles furent beaucoup plus longues. Si celle-ci avoit duré quelques minutes toute la ville auroit été abîmée.'[52] Ce souci n'empêche pas certains témoins de donner des chiffres extravagants, supérieurs à la dizaine de minutes.

La diffusion du protocole d'observation est remarquable et rapide. Le premier cercle concerné réunit les académiciens provinciaux, les correspondants titulaires et les correspondants des académiciens. Les documents réunis par l'Académie des sciences montrent cependant que le protocole touche des acteurs plus divers que les correspondants habituels des académiciens. Lors des événements de 1755, 1756, et ensuite, de nombreuses personnes consignent des observations et les adressent aux savants. Dans l'ensemble du dossier de Philippe Buache on trouve ainsi pêle-mêle une religieuse cordelière du couvent de Saint-Florent-le-Vieil en Maine-et-Loire, un sous-ingénieur des Ponts et Chaussées, un lieutenant d'infanterie, ingénieur à Québec, des académiciens de province ou des correspondants, des Chartreux, des Cordeliers de Salins, un adolescent âgé de quinze à seize ans qui maîtrise sommairement l'écrit, un docteur en médecine correspondant de l'Académie des sciences, un membre de l'oratoire du Portugal, un jésuite, un négociant à la

---

52. Paris, Académie royale des sciences, MS registre des procès-verbaux des séances (4 août 1756), lxxv, f.455-56.

Martinique, un concessionnaire de mines, un contrôleur de la manufacture des Glaces de Saint-Gobain.[53] Parmi les participants au concours organisé par l'Académie de Rouen en 1756, se trouvent un clerc du chapitre d'Evreux, un hobereau breton, un architecte de la ville de Mamers, le procureur royal d'Azay-le-Rideau.[54]

Injustement oublié, le débat physique sur les tremblements de terre doit être considéré comme un des premiers débats populaires sur la science au siècle des Lumières, d'une intensité qui n'a rien à envier à la passion des montgolfières des années 1780. Le peuple n'est pas tenu à l'écart de cette mode tellurique, y compris dans les campagnes. En 1778 s'établit au Mans une 'mécanique de figures mouvantes qui montre la ville d'Orléans assiégée par les Anglais et délivrée par "Jeanne d'Arque" et le tremblement de terre de Lisbonne'.[55] Cette machine, dont la construction a gardé ses secrets, devait circuler dans les foires de la région. Dans tout le royaume, les secousses des années 1750 s'accompagnent de manifestations collectives exubérantes. Voici le tableau que dresse le *Journal encyclopédique*:

Tous les physiciens sont occupés aujourd'hui à chercher la véritable cause des tremblements de terre; les Académies attachent un prix à cette découverte; les Ecoles ne retentissent que des causes de ce cruel phénomène; dans les cercles les plus brillants où l'on ne s'occupe ordinairement que des choses les plus frivoles, on en fait la matière de la conversation; l'ignorant même ose en parler, & suivant de loin le savant qui sait s'arrêter à propos, il se perd bientôt dans les gouffres de la terre entrecouverte de ses pas. Tout le monde en un mot veut pénétrer ce terrible secret de la nature.[56]

Si les sismophiles existent, les sismophobes aussi. Un savant bordelais, M. de Romas, l'apprend à ses dépens en 1759 quand il souhaite faire une expérience publique sur l'électricité, dans un coin du Jardin Royal. Le tremblement de terre du 10 août est, pour lui, l'occasion de démontrer que les théories électriques peuvent expliquer les mouvements de la terre. Le public se persuade cependant que ces maléfices ne sont pas étrangers à la catastrophe qui vient de frapper la ville et se révolte contre le physicien, dont les machines échappent de peu à la destruction.[57] En 1756, Anne-Henriette de Bricqueville attribue la multiplication des secousses aux machines électriques qui provoquent la concentration des souffres dans la

---

53. Paris, Bibliothèque nationale de France, MS nouvelles acquisitions françaises 20236 et 20237.
54. Rouen, Bibliothèque municipale, fonds de l'Académie, MS C 20, 'Concours de 1756'.
55. Jean Queniart, *Culture et société urbaines dans la France de l'ouest au XVIIIe siècle* (Paris 1978), p.126.
56. 'Les tremblemens de terre attribués à l'électricité', *Journal encyclopédique* (1er mai 1756).
57. André Grellet-Dumazeau, *La Société bordelaise sous Louis XV et le salon de madame Duplessy* (Bordeaux 1897), p.262-63.

terre.[58] Dans les mémoires envoyés à l'Académie des sciences de Rouen la même année, un mémoire incrimine lui aussi l'usage de plus en plus fréquent de ces appareils qui agitent la matière électrique du sol et la mettent en communication avec celle du ciel. L'auteur conclut par le souhait 'que les expériances de l'électricité ne fussent pas si fréquantes et même pour parler naturellement, qu'on les supprime entièrement, car pour quoy vouloir contraindre les éléments à produire des effets contraires à ce qui leur est naturel'.[59] Ces enjeux jettent un nouvel éclairage sur le caractère européen de cet événement.

v. L'événement naturel et les réseaux d'information

Le 1er novembre 1755 réussit à cristalliser des thèmes de discussions dont le sens était déjà fixé. Le débat sur le mal est largement antérieur, il avait regagné en acuité depuis la fin du dix-septième siècle. Le débat physique sur les catastrophes naturelles est lui aussi plus ancien et faisait partie d'un sujet plus vaste, la formation de la terre. Dans les deux cas, le retentissement du désastre de Lisbonne a eu pour effet de recentrer les interrogations sur les tremblements de terre et donc de les reformuler. Le pouvoir mobilisateur des séismes s'explique par le contexte des dix dernières années, marqué par la multiplication des informations sur les secousses en France et par plusieurs séismes retentissants tels ceux des 8 février et du 8 mars 1750 à Londres, et ceux de Lima et de Saint-Domingue.[60] Par son pouvoir fédérateur, l'événement a créé un espace de discussion, dont les périodiques sont la vitrine, avec ses tensions personnelles et intellectuelles, ses spécialistes et ses opportunistes, ses thèses, et ses contre-thèses. Cet espace a mis fin à l'isolement des textes pour les insérer dans un système de confrontation où les discours se définissent et se repositionnent les uns par rapport aux autres. Cette confrontation a été d'autant plus forte que le débat a touché l'ensemble de l'opinion éclairée et l'a passionnée, redoublant l'enjeu épistémologique d'un enjeu social: éclairer les interrogations du présent. L'année 1756 inaugure l'intervention des experts au chevet de la terre, que l'on retrouve lors du séisme calabrais de 1783.[61]

Pour les mêmes raisons, un épisode aussi retentissant offre l'occasion de manifester sa différence. La pluralité des lectures est donc une caractéristique de l'événement-monstre, plus que l'unanimisme des commentaires. Selon les sources retenues, le désastre de Lisbonne prend les traits du

---

58. Anne-Henriette de Bricqueville, *Réflexions sur les causes des tremblements de terre, avec les principes qu'on doit suivre pour dissiper les orages tant sur terre que sur mer* (Paris 1756). Compte rendu dans le *Journal de Trévoux* (1756), p.3012-16.

59. Rouen, Bibliothèque municipale, fonds de l'Académie, MS C 20, 'Concours de 1756 sur les tremblements de terre, mémoire n° 10'.

60. Jean Delumeau, *Le Catholicisme de Luther à Voltaire* (Paris 1971), p.307.

61. Augusto Placanica, *Il Filosofo e la catastrofe, un terremoto del Settecento* (Turin 1985).

Dieu vengeur ou de l'anecdote mondaine. A la cour, l'ambassadeur de France au Portugal, le comte de Baschi, fait rire La Pompadour en lui racontant la mort du comte de Peralada, ambassadeur d'Espagne à Lisbonne.[62] Il est vrai que celui-ci a été écrasé par le massif des armes d'Espagne placé sur le frontispice de son palais, qui lui est tombé sur la tête.[63] Le sujet n'est pas non plus totalement futile car, selon Horace Walpole, le cardinal de La Rochefoucault et le père de Sacy, confesseur de Louis XV, ont essayé de jouer sur la superstition du roi face au désastre de Lisbonne pour qu'il reçoive le sacrement à Pâques et renvoie sa maîtresse. Horace Walpole peut facilement tourner en dérision la manière dont La Pompadour se sort du piège: elle sacrifie son rouge à joues en signe de conversion.[64] Même si le danger n'a peut-être pas été très aigu, cette anecdote est un épisode politique qui touche des sujets sensibles. Toujours d'après Horace Walpole, le comte d'Argenson est à l'origine de la cabale pour favoriser le parti de la guerre. La religion du roi est un sujet grave, d'autant plus qu'il ne fait plus ses Pâques depuis 1738. Enfin, l'affaire évoque le précédent humiliant de Metz en 1744 quand le premier aumônier, M. de Fitz-James a obtenu que le roi, au plus mal, chasse sa maîtresse, Mme de Châteauroux.[65] Plusieurs degrés de lecture de la catastrophe se superposent donc dans le même lieu.

La nature du système de l'information amplifie l'intérêt pour les tremblements de terre. Les délais de transmission de l'information entre le Portugal et le reste de l'Europe sont importants: la nouvelle de la destruction de Lisbonne parvient le 4 novembre à Madrid et le 17 novembre à Versailles, pour être annoncée le 22 dans la *Gazette de France*.[66] Ces délais sont doublés d'une irrégularité des flux, ainsi dans la *Gazette de France* pendant près d'un mois et demi, du 29 novembre 1755 au 10 janvier 1756, il n'y a aucune nouvelle de Lisbonne. Le décalage entre les événements dans la capitale du Portugal et les lecteurs de cette gazette est donc au début de janvier de plus de deux mois, alors que les dernières nouvelles dont ils disposent sont alarmantes.[67]

Ces contraintes temporelles ont plusieurs conséquences. Les contemporains ressentent une véritable carence de l'information, que traduit la correspondance de Voltaire. Ce dernier demande de façon insistante à ses correspondants en relation avec le Portugal de lui faire parvenir toutes

---

62. Suzanne Chantal, *La Vie quotidienne au Portugal après le tremblement de terre de Lisbonne* (Paris 1962), p.53.

63. Charles-Philippe de Luynes, *Mémoires du duc de Luynes sur la cour de Louis XV* (Paris 1864), xiv.307.

64. Horace Walpole, *Memoirs of the reign of King George II* (Londres 1847), ii.176.

65. Michel Antoine, *Louis XV* (Paris 1989), p.375, 710-11.

66. Robert Favre, *La Mort dans la littérature et la pensée française au siècle des Lumières* (Lyon 1978), p.63.

67. 'L'épouvantable catastrophe que cette Ville vient d'essuyer. Tous les éléments se sont réunis pour causer la ruine de cette capitale du Portugal', *Gazette de France* (29 novembre 1755).

les informations à leur disposition, pour compléter les gazettes.[68] Ensuite, l'irrégularité des nouvelles accroît la distance qui sépare l'homme des événements portugais, rendant plus aiguës les inquiétudes mais aussi le sentiment d'impuissance et de fatalité. Les contemporains se retrouvent livrés à eux-mêmes, ignorant ce qui se passe autour d'eux et 'on imagine à Genève qu'il y a eu un tremblement de terre en France comme en Portugal, parce que le courrier des lettres a manqué aujourd'hui'.[69] Enfin, la représentation de l'événement devient très irrégulière, au gré des révélations successives, qui n'en deviennent que plus brutales. A trois jours d'intervalle, Voltaire passe ainsi de l'inquiétude ('Mon cher ami, les pucelles, les tremblements de terre et la colique me mettent aux abois') à l'ironie ('la fin du monde et le Jugement Dernier ne sont point encore venus, et puisque les meubles de M. Bachi sont en bon état, tout va bien à Lisbonne').[70] L'événement s'amplifie aussi vite qu'il se dégonfle.

En l'absence d'une information centralisée, les réseaux mis en œuvre sont complexes et de la plus grande diversité. Aux gazettes, qui sont les plus prolixes, s'ajoutent les relations et les correspondances publiées dans les autres périodiques, les récits des nombreux occasionnels, les compléments donnés dans certains ouvrages. La sphère des imprimés n'est qu'une partie du flux de nouvelles car la communication manuscrite est encore très développée au milieu du dix-huitième siècle.[71] Nouvelles à la main, correspondances diplomatiques et privées, copies manuscrites de textes imprimés voisinent avec les publications et les complètent. A l'intérieur du royaume existent de véritables réseaux régionaux, dus aux relations commerciales avec le Portugal et aux familles installées à Lisbonne.[72] Le Briançonnais reçoit de nombreuses lettres grâce à sa colonie de colporteurs-libraires.[73] Les régions proches de la péninsule ibérique sont elles aussi favorisées, le Béarn par exemple.[74] La correspondance des frères Darrot donne un exemple de l'intensité potentielle des échanges, même si toutes les familles ne comptent pas dix-huit enfants.[75] Les lettres

---

68. 'Apprenez-moi, je vous prie, les suites de cette affreuse aventure', dit-il aussi à Tronchin (*Correspondence and related documents*, éd. Th. Besterman, dans *Œuvres complètes de Voltaire*, t.85-135, Genève, Banbury, Oxford 1968-1977; Voltaire à Tronchin, 26 novembre 1755, D6600; Voltaire à Tronchin, 3 décembre 1755, D6613).

69. Voltaire à Sébastien Dupont, 2 décembre 1755 (D6611).

70. Voltaire à Jacques-Abram-Elie-Daniel Clavel de Brenles, 6 décembre 1755 (D6615); Voltaire à Tronchin, 9 décembre 1755 (D6620).

71. François Moureau, 'La plume et le plomb', in *De bonne main: la communication manuscrite au XVIIIᵉ siècle*, éd. François Moureau (Paris, Oxford 1993), p.135-42.

72. Jean-François Labourdette, *La Nation française à Lisbonne de 1669 à 1790. Entre colbertisme et libéralisme* (Paris 1988).

73. 'Lettres sur le tremblement de terre de Lisbonne', dans Fernando Guedes, *O Livro e A Leitura em Portugal* (Lisbonne 1987), p.250-62.

74. Christian Desplat, 'Séismes dans les Pyrénées: contribution à l'histoire des phénomènes naturels (XVIᵉ-XVIIᵉ siècles)', *Revue géographique des Pyrénées et du Sud-Ouest* (1988), lix.99-110.

75. 'Lettres des frères Darrot', *Revue d'Auvergne* (1930), xxxiv.106-17.

envoyées par Claude, marchand établi à Lisbonne, circulent entre Philippe qui habite Paris, un autre frère chanoine à Thiers et d'autres encore. Claude a un beau-frère à Porto, une belle-sœur dont le fils est négociant à Cadix et donne des nouvelles des familles apparentées, établies dans la péninsule ibérique. Toutes ces missives traitent de leurs intérêts commerciaux, des flux d'argents et de marchandises désorganisés par le désastre. Ce sous-ensemble originaire de la péninsule ibérique croise un autre sous-ensemble, européen, rapportant les expériences sismiques de 1755-1756. Par exemple, en un seul article le *Journal historique sur les matières du tems* cite des lettres parvenues de Lisbonne, de l'Algarve, d'un navire d'Amsterdam revenant de Setuval, de Madrid, Tarifa, Cadix, Bordeaux, Angoulême, la région du Havre, Caen, l'Angleterre, la Hollande, l'Italie, et l'Allemagne. Chacune de ces lettres mentionne d'autres lieux, renvoyant à de nouvelles lettres, multipliant les effets d'échos.

Ce véritable écheveau d'informations est aussi nourri par les affabulations et la rumeur. De nombreux occasionnels évaluent le nombre des victimes lisbonnines à 100 000, soit le double du chiffre avancé par la *Gazette de France* dès le 22 novembre 1755, dix fois plus que le chiffre probable.[76] Le chiffre énorme de 100 000 est le premier dont dispose Voltaire et il n'est pas pour rien dans sa révolte contre le tremblement de terre.[77] Quelques semaines plus tard, il reçoit des démentis: 'on exagère toutes les pertes. Les 100 000 hommes péris à Lisbonne sont déjà réduits à 25 000, ils le seront bientôt à 10 ou 12.'[78] Ce désappointement ne l'empêche pas de reprendre ensuite d'autres rumeurs, à propos de 'quelques 100 000 arabes qui ont été engloutis sous la terre' et des Açores ('si les îles Açores sont englouties, comme on l'assure').[79] Cette nouvelle de la disparition d'une île s'est largement diffusée, grâce à certains occasionnels, qui reprennent peut-être des rumeurs.[80] La *Gazette de France* se sent obligée de la démentir, soutenue par un traité nommé *Lettre sur l'impossibilité physique d'un tremblement de terre à Paris*.[81] Une autre rumeur se diffuse de manière extraordinaire, celle des poux volants de Lisbonne. Elle est présente à Paris car Barthélémy Darrot s'enquiert de ce nouveau fléau auprès de son frère qui est dans la capitale portugaise. La réponse de celui-ci indique qu'elle est désormais connue à Lisbonne: 'Les nouvelles publiques qui parlent des poux volant de Lisbonne sont des contes faits à plaisir. Il y a eu, il est vray, beaucoup de maladies, mais elle n'ont été

---

76. Par exemple *Lisbonne abîmée ou idée de la destruction de cette fameuse ville* ([s.l.] 1755).

77. Voltaire à Elie Bertrand, 30 novembre 1755 (D6605).

78. Voltaire à Tronchin, 17 décembre 1755 (D6635).

79. Voltaire à Henault, 13 janvier 1756 (D6688); Voltaire à Tronchin, 29 janvier 1756 (D6709).

80. *Relation du tremblement de terre arrivé à Lisbonne, et d'une ile submergée en Amérique le 1er novembre 1755* (Paris 1755); *Relation du terrible tremblement de terre qui vient d'arriver dans les îles Açores, dépendantes du royaume du Portugal. De Lisbonne, le 1er août 1757* (Paris 1757).

81. *Gazette de France* (17 janvier 1756); *Lettre sur l'impossibilité physique d'un tremblement de terre à Paris* ([s.l.] 1755).

causées par aucun raport avec le tremblement de terre. C'est un effet des saisons comme c'étoit autrefois.'[82]

Enfin, elle a gagné la province car un curé poitevin, Sylvain de La Bussière la consigne sur son registre: 'Maladie qui règne à présent après la destruction totale de Lisbonne, capitale du Portugal; cette cruelle maladie se nomme pédiculaire, dont les effets sont si funestes que la plupart de ceux qui en sont attaqués meurent en désespérés. Ce sont des poux volans qui s'attachent au corps humain et que rien ensuite ne peut faire périr.'[83]

Il est facile d'imaginer l'effet que peut produire dans les campagnes françaises l'évocation d'un tel fléau. D'autres rumeurs encore sont signalées en 1756, par exemple ce tremblement de terre peu vraisemblable dans le Bas-Languedoc à Pont-Saint-Esprit: 'les tremblements de terre ont renversé plusieurs maisons en ces quartiers-là, et des montagnes de 60 toises de hauteur s'y trouvent de niveau aujourd'hui avec la plaine'.[84]

Conclusion

Considérer le désastre de Lisbonne comme une catastrophe naturelle fait surgir de nombreux aspects passés sous silence par le débat sur la providence. Les contemporains, en particulier en France, ont été impressionnés par l'étendue européenne des secousses et leur simultanéité en des points très éloignés, ne correspondant à aucun autre phénomène connu. Les discussions philosophiques et théologiques ont été accompagnées d'un débat scientifique aussi intense, même s'il a laissé moins de traces dans les mémoires. Une profonde unité relie ces différentes interventions car, privé de ses fondements religieux, le mal n'est plus justifié et les Lumières tentent de l'aborder sous toutes ses dimensions, sans aucun esprit de système.[85] En 1755, le degré de risque accepté par les hommes a changé; peut-être faut-il y voir une conséquence du recul des grands fléaux.

La dimension événementielle et naturelle ne se contente pas d'enrichir la compréhension du désastre de Lisbonne, elle permet de la déplacer et de la reformuler. La laïcisation de la catastrophe débute avant 1755, elle est loin d'être généralisée après. En France, l'intérêt pour les tremblements de terre est antérieur car, dès les premières années du dix-huitième siècle, ces phénomènes font l'objet de nouvelles interprétations et deviennent peu à peu un nouvel objet, scientifique, juridique, politique et religieux.[86] En revanche, les tremblements de terre européens de 1755 et 1756 jouent un rôle décisif dans l'émergence de la préoccupation des

---

82. Lettre de Claude Darrot à son frère Barthélémy, de Lisbonne, du 7 septembre 1756, dans 'Lettres des frères Darrot', *Revue d'Auvergne* (1930), xxxxiv.106-17.
83. Vienne, archives communales de Champigny le Sec, MS registre paroissial (1756).
84. *Gazette d'Amsterdam* (6 février 1756).
85. B. Baczko, *Job mon ami*, p.12-14.
86. G. Quenet, *La Naissance d'un risque*.

Lumières pour les catastrophes, donnant aux contemporains le sentiment que les secousses se multiplient, premier cas d'amplification sociale d'un risque à l'échelle européenne. Le retentissement de Lisbonne crée une scène nationale, mettant en rapport pour la première fois l'expérience locale de la catastrophe et les représentations savantes, accélérant ainsi la construction du risque sismique. Enfin, ce débat scientifique populaire et précoce érige la catastrophe en enjeu social, point de rencontre entre des lectures concurrentes et hiérarchisées. La part de l'accidentel et du hasard, celle de l'aléa sismique, ne peut être effacée.

THEODORE E. D. BRAUN

Voltaire and Le Franc de Pompignan: poetic reactions to the Lisbon earthquake

As we commemorate the 250th anniversary of the great Lisbon earthquake, it seems fitting to consider reactions to the event. In this chapter I intend to examine two very different responses to the tremors, both of them expressed in verse. One of these reactions is a well-known poem by Voltaire, the 'Poème sur le désastre de Lisbonne'; indeed, this poem needs little new commentary, and I will situate it with reference to the second poetic reaction, a poem and the book of odes in which it is contained, by Le Franc de Pompignan. Two views of providence are developed in these works, one deistic and the other very Catholic. Both are powerfully and convincingly stated, and – given the religious orientations of the authors – both reach quite opposite conclusions. We hope to demonstrate how or at least to what degree it can be said that the Enlightenment and Christianity affected the authors of these works, Voltaire and Le Franc de Pompignan, and in what manner the two responses reflect attitudes towards life that are if not exactly contradictory then at least contrary.

Voltaire's deism, we should remember, is unimaginable unless we recall the specifically Catholic religious culture in which he grew up and was educated. His enlightenment springs from his struggle against what he saw as the obscurantism and obfuscation of the Catholicism he encountered throughout his life. At home, in school, and in his daily life as an adult, he was surrounded by priests, abbés, and believers, by censors and zealots, with constant reminders of the dominance of Catholicism in his life: theatrical seasons built around religious holidays, even the names of streets and schools, and crucifixes in courtrooms. Fighting what he called *l'infâme* meant fighting religious institutions, the Catholic church in particular, its doctrines, dogmas, practices, and traditions. But – with an irony he would have enjoyed had it happened to an enemy – the harder he fought against *l'infâme*, the harder it was to drive it from his mind. Voltaire's enlightenment can thus be seen as inseparable from Christianity. The choice of subject of his 'Poème sur le désastre de Lisbonne'[1] confirms the truth of this paradox, as does the strong emotion perceptible throughout. In this poem, Voltaire is curiously let down by the memory

---

1. Voltaire, 'Poème sur le désastre de Lisbonne, ou examen de cet axiome: tout est bien', in *Œuvres complètes de Voltaire*, ed. Louis Moland (Paris 1877-1885), ix.465-80. The 'Poème' was first published in March 1756.

of the faith he has lost. When he needs it most, he feels its lack more than ever.

In the 'Poème sur le désastre de Lisbonne', Voltaire proposes to examine the very Christian concept of providence, the idea that God has pre-ordained how events in the cosmos evolve; that is, he wants to examine the doctrine of general providence. But he also intends to do this from the point of view of humanity and of the individual; he wants to analyse the doctrine of particular providence. He specifically mentions Leibniz, Pope, Shaftesbury, and Bolingbroke in the text of his 'Préface' and makes allusion to 'une foule de théologiens de toutes les communions' who have attacked this belief (M.ix.465-66). In particular, he is disturbed by the proposition that all is well: the fatalism inherent in the idea of providence, taken in an absolute sense and without any individual's being able to change his or her pre-ordained fate, is the real target of his satirical attack here (p.468). (This proposition is also attacked in parts of *Candide*, Voltaire's second major response to the destruction of Lisbon; but in this article we are concentrating on Voltaire's poetic reaction to Lisbon.) On the one hand, the axiom that all is for the best in the best of all possible worlds seems to rob humankind of free will and, as a result, of all personal responsibilities for our actions; on the other hand this idea seems to add 'une insulte aux douleurs de notre vie'. The emotion contained in this reaction is easy to see; the poem develops this emotion in such a way as to make us share the author's deep anxiety over this problem, which is basically the problem of physical and moral evil in the world, as we will see later on when we look at Voltaire's poem.

From the point of view of reason, Voltaire believed that pre-determinism leads ineluctably to unorthodox and heretical conclusions: if indeed all is for the best, human nature cannot be thought of as corrupted (Adam and Eve had no choice but to sin), and therefore a redeemer would be unnecessary; and if this world is the best of all possible worlds, we cannot hope for a better one. Furthermore, if all individual evils exist only for the universal good, philosophers are wasting their time looking for the origin of physical and moral evil, because everything that is, is necessary. Such a vision of the world would lead necessarily to atheism in all who opposed it (compare n.2, p.465-67). But Voltaire could not remain for long at this level of abstraction: in order to avoid falling into the absurdities of metaphysics he had to particularise every moral and philosophical consideration. In the objective circumstances of the destruction of Lisbon, how does one bend, become resigned, to the dictates of providence, as if God had wanted to make innocent people suffer? Should we say to the victims of this disaster (p.468): 'Tout est bien; les héritiers des morts augmenteront leurs fortunes; les maçons gagneront de l'argent à rétablir des maisons; les bêtes se nourriront des cadavres enterrés dans les débris; c'est l'effet nécessaire des causes nécessaires; votre mal particulier n'est rien, vous contribuez au bien général'? This *reductio ad absurdum* is how Voltaire poses the problem of the Lisbon disaster in his preface, thoughts he develops in the body of the poem.

Like nearly all his writings relating or alluding to Voltaire in the decades following the virulent attacks of the *philosophes* from 1760 to 1763, attacks that destroyed his literary reputation and severely altered the public judgement of his character, Le Franc de Pompignan's response to the patriarch of Ferney was hidden – in this case in a book of poetry published in the second volume of his *Œuvres complètes* in 1784, the year of his death and six years after Voltaire's death.[2] The fourth book of his Odes, the *Odes chrétiennes et philosophiques*, seems to be arranged in such a way as to respond to certain passages of Voltaire's 'Poème'.[3] The titles of the *Odes chrétiennes et philosophiques* are:

1. La poésie chrétienne (p.143-49)
2. Retour à dieu (p.150-55)
3. Saint Augustin (p.155-63)
4. A M. Racine, sur la mort de son fils (p.163-69)
5. Etablissement, utilité et nécessité du culte extérieur (p.167-75)
6. La Providence, et la philosophie (p.176-86)
7. Le triomphe de la croix (p.187-89)
8. Le triomphe de la religion, aux Carmélites de Saint-Denys (p.189-93)
[9.] Paraphrase de l'oraison dominicale (p.194-96) [unnumbered]

It is not difficult to see the basic Palladian structure of this book of poems. It begins with a three-poem introductory section in which the role and the duty of a Christian poet are explored, a confessional poem in which he acknowledges his past sins and indiscretions, and an exposé of the life and teachings of St Augustine, including the pivotal place of divine providence in Augustinian thought. The second section, also consisting of three poems, is the heart of the poet's discussion of the central theme: providence. It contains the ode to Louis Racine on the death of his son during the Lisbon earthquake, followed by a poem in which the need for an established church and for established places of worship is clearly stated, and finally a poem entitled 'La Providence, et la philosophie'. The third panel of this triptych consists of three poems flowing from the preceding

2. Jean-Jacques Le Franc de Pompignan, *Œuvres* (Paris, Nyon l'aîné, 1784). Our commentary centres on the 'Odes', Livre quatrième, ii.151-96.

3. Oddly, no one up until now appears to have noted the importance of this book to the contemporary criticism of Voltaire's poem. I have been a victim of this oversight, too. Neither in my book nor in my articles and conference papers on Pompignan's poetry or his relations with Voltaire have I ever seen the connections, which are nevertheless obvious once the two works are juxtaposed. An online bibliography of Le Franc de Pompignan can be found at http://www.c18.org/biblio/lefranc.html.

discussions: two acts of faith and a paraphrase of the 'Our father'. The most important responses to Voltaire's poem are the odes to Racine and on providence, but all nine, taken together, comprise a coherent statement of traditional Christian and Catholic thought on this important matter.

The first poem in the fourth book of odes ('La poésie chrétienne') reclaims the rights of religious poetry, which Le Franc avers is inspired not by the Muse Erato but directly by God.[4] He boldly orders profane poets to harken to the music of David (p.143-44):

> Rougissez, s'il se peut, du fruit de vos délires,
> Brisez vos faibles lyres,
> David a pris la sienne, il chante; taisez-vous.

For him, not only does Christian poetry surpass ancient Greek poetry; Judeo-Christian wisdom has a far greater intrinsic value than what he calls (p.145):

> Un bizarre assemblage
> De spectacles honteux et d'infâmes leçons!

He thus establishes, from the very first poem in the book and in opposition to Voltaire's poem, the authority and the superiority of Christian thought over pagan or deistic thought.

Le Franc begins his second ode ('Retour à dieu') by alluding to his own youthful life in Paris where, tempted by the devil, he had sought pleasure with actresses, and to the attacks against him by Voltaire, who is here associated with the demon (p.150):

> Fuis, malheureux ange du crime,
> Esprit rebelle et séducteur.
> Fuis, laisse en paix une victime,
> Que t'arrache un Dieu protecteur.

He goes on to call Voltaire a (p.154):

> citoyen futile
> De ce monde tumultueux

and he declares that God will protect him, Le Franc.

In the third ode ('Saint Augustin'), Le Franc finds in the life of the saint a parallel with his own. He prepares the reader for what he has to say about providence in his ode to Racine, given the importance of providence in Augustinian theology (p.158-59):

---

4. In this regard, we remind our readers that Le Franc had published in 1751 the first edition of his *Poésies sacrées*, the first three books of which (Odes, Cantiques, Prophéties) are translations or paraphrases of biblical texts, more particularly of the Old Testament. See the *Poésies sacrées de Monsieur L* F*****, *divisées en quatre livres, et ornées de figures en taille douce* (Paris, Chaubert, 1751).

Seigneur, que ta grâce est pressante
Pour les âmes de tes élus!
Contre sa force bienfaisante
Augustin ne combattra plus.
Guéri de ses erreurs premières,
Détestant ses fausses lumières,
Tout son esprit est dans sa foi,
Et ne connaît plus de science
Que l'humble et docile croyance
Qui l'attache à ta sainte loi.

It is at this point that the fourth ode ('A M. Racine, sur la mort de son fils') appears, accompanied by two other poems, 'Etablissement, utilité et nécessité du culte extérieur' and 'La Providence, et la philosophie'. These three odes occupy twenty pages right at the centre of the fifty-six page book. Their theme is the central theme of Voltaire's 'Poème sur le désastre de Lisbonne', divine providence, and a subject closely connected to that, the impossibility of our ever knowing the mind of God and the reasons he acts as he does.

Le Franc addressed the ode[5] to his friend Louis Racine, a poet celebrated in his time for two long poems entitled *La Grâce* and *La Religion*, and the son of Jean Racine, the author of tragedies and also of some beautiful Christian odes. Louis Racine's son and daughter-in-law had been killed by a tsunami while on their honeymoon in Cádiz; the ode commemorating their deaths opens this section of the book. The poem seems to have been written immediately after this terrible event, probably as soon as details of the Lisbon disaster became widely known – that is around December 1755 or January 1756.[6] It is therefore contemporaneous with the Voltaire piece, which was published in March 1756. Le Franc's poem was composed shortly afterwards and was published in the *Mercure de France* in May 1756, p.78-82. Le Franc did not have an opportunity to publish it in any of his numerous works until 1784, when he undertook a general, if incomplete, edition of his *Œuvres* a short time before his death. It is not clear whether or not Le Franc had read Voltaire's poem when he was composing his own: in the absence of correspondence on the topic, of manuscripts, or even of marginalia in his extensive library (which was sold to the municipality of Toulouse upon his death, becoming part of the core of works in what is now the Bibliothèque municipale), we do not know if he was familiar with Voltaire's 'Poème' until a later date.

5. Le Franc de Pompignan, *Œuvres*, ii.163-66.
6. The first stanza gives us a clue as to the time of the composition of this poem: 'Il n'est donc plus, et sa tendresse / Aux derniers jours de ta vieillesse / N'aidera point tes faibles pas!' Five stanzas follow in which the son's death is alluded to but never directly except in the line 'Son corps est le jouet des flots' in the third stanza.

Interestingly, in his ode, Le Franc remains calm in the face of disaster. Unlike Voltaire, he neither sheds tears nor appears to be emotionally shaken by the event, nor does he set out to question providence. His goal is very simple: to console a friend for a loss that is difficult to imagine. The poem later gains in force when it becomes part of a larger poetic project and is integrated into a spirited defence of providence.

Le Franc's ode upholds a thesis quite contrary to that of Voltaire in his poem: we must accept our individual fates and bow down before the dictates of providence, precisely because we cannot understand them. The almost total lack of personal emotion in this ode, despite its heart-rending subject matter and the fact that it appears to have been written shortly after the events became known, is striking. Le Franc could not have failed to be deeply moved by the young man's death and by his friend's grief. He must have decided that to console Racine it would be better not to aggravate the pain in his heart, but rather to appeal to the deep faith of his Jansenist friend.

Whenever he attempted to combine Enlightenment (or 'Philosophy', as he called it) and Christianity, Le Franc would, as the Jansenist thinker Pascal had done a century earlier, stop short if his explorations began to lead him to disturbing conclusions.[7] In this instance, he refused to expose himself to the danger of questioning the nature or the existence of God. This attitude is of a piece with the sentiments he had expressed in his 'Epître à Damon', written in 1738 and published in the first book of *Epîtres* (1784):

> Soyons de notre esprit les seuls législateurs.
> Vivons libres du moins dans le fond de nos coeurs:
> C'est le trône de l'homme, il règne quand il pense.
> L'âme est un être pur, fait pour l'indépendance.
> Jugeons, examinons, c'est là notre appanage.
> Cherchons la vérité dans son épais nuage;
> Mais que par la raison nos doutes soient bornés
> Aux objets que le ciel nous a subordonnés.
> Qu'ils ne s'élèvent pas jusqu'au Maître suprême.[8]

He proposes a programme of investigation in all fields (the Enlightenment part of his thought and practice), but in every case subordinated to his Christian faith. His nineteenth-century publisher, Gobet, stated that Le Franc wanted to put a leash on our independence, to limit it to the study of humans and their environment, to establish boundaries beyond which we must never go.[9] Le Franc quite clearly applied this principle to his ode to Louis Racine. In addition, as we have suggested, he wished to console

---

7. See Harcourt Brown, 'Pascal *philosophe*', *SVEC* 55 (1967), p.309-20. We are following rather closely here the argument we presented in the brief article, 'Soyons de notre esprit les seuls législateurs', *SVEC* 303 (1992), p.196-200.

8. Le Franc de Pompignan, *Œuvres*, ii.213.

9. *Œuvres choisies de Le Franc de Pompignan*, ed. Gobet (Paris 1813), i.35.

his Jansenist-leaning friend for the death of his son by confronting the doctrine of divine providence head on. Not needing rational arguments to convince Racine of the truth of Catholicism, he wanted to touch his heart by appealing less to his emotions than to his religious sentiment, to his intuition of the presence of God. Thus the lack of both personal emotions and analytical reasoning can be explained and understood.

In this poem, Le Franc uses an octosyllabic line and six-line stanzas with a light and rather lyric rhyme scheme, aabccb – a good choice for a poet appealing to the spirit or the intuition of a friend. In his poem, Voltaire, looking for an explanation rather than offering consolation, makes use of the traditional rhyming couplet alexandrine line (twelve syllables, with a caesura in the middle); this metric choice is traditional in tragedies, in philosophical works, and generally in all serious poetry, whether addressed to the emotions or to reason. This difference in form establishes a noticeable difference in tone in the two poems.

Voltaire asks, near the beginning of his poem (p.470):

> Direz-vous, en voyant cet amas de victimes,
> 'Dieu s'est vengé, leur mort est le prix de leurs crimes?'
> Quel crime, quelle faute, ont commis ces enfants
> Sur le sein maternel écrasés et sanglants?

The reader can sense the emotion in the third and fourth lines, especially when these are read aloud. The anti-providential line of thought, when Voltaire criticises the Leibnizian theme of the best of all possible worlds, is clear; reading the passage aloud, as was the practice at the time, allows both reader and listener to sense Voltaire's indignation (p.475):

> Leibnitz ne m'apprend point par quels nœuds invisibles,
> Dans le mieux ordonné des univers possibles,
> Un désordre éternel, un chaos de malheurs,
> Mêle à nos vains plaisirs de réelles douleurs,
> Ni pourquoi l'innocent, ainsi que le coupable
> Subit également ce mal inévitable.

A few years later, in chapter 20 of *Candide*, Voltaire illustrated this notion in depicting a ship sinking with a total loss of the crew and passengers. He called divine justice into question while rejecting the doctrine of philosophical optimism.

If Le Franc sees the same devastation and horrors as Voltaire, he responds not with Voltairean doubt but by an act of faith (p.164):

> Ô Lois saintes! Ô Providence!
> C'est bien souvent sur l'innocence
> Que tombent tes coups redoutés.
> Un enfant du siècle prospère;
> L'homme qui n'a que Dieu pour père,
> Gémit dans les adversités.

It is true that the two poets are not speaking of precisely the same thing, for they do not consider the problem from the same perspective. Voltaire demands justice in the here and now, whereas Le Franc accepts that rewards and punishments await us after death (p.164-65). Obviously, Le Franc's response to the event in Lisbon, addressed to a practising and convinced Catholic, could not satisfy a non-believer.

Still, Voltaire does not ask God for reasons or justifications. Instead, he draws up a list of possible explanations of the origin of physical and moral evil in the world (p.475). He finds all of them unacceptable, and his inability to find other explanations is a source of considerable anxiety. Le Franc draws up such a list only by implication. For instance, he seems to believe that non-believers would not even ask if (p.166):

> C'est peut-être la vengeance
> D'un Dieu qu'irritent nos forfaits.

And we have already seen Le Franc's response to Voltaire's questions: God has willed it, and we cannot understand his motives. He sees only providence, only the divine presence, in natural phenomena like the Lisbon earthquake. Thus he says, speaking of the materialist philosophers (p.166):

> Ils écartent ces lois suprêmes,
> Ils s'efforcent par leurs problèmes
> D'anéantir le vrai moteur:
> Recherches pleines d'impostures,
> Qui trouvent tout dans la nature
> Hors le pouvoir de son Auteur.

But Voltaire, rejecting the determinism implicit in the notion of providence, seeks a response that can justify the existence of an infinitely good God. Perhaps that is why, in this poem, he expresses admiration for Bayle, who 'enseigne à douter' (p.476): for human reason has never succeeded in explaining the origin and continued existence of moral and physical evil. That is why Voltaire knows only how to 'souffrir, et non pas murmurer' against providence (p.478). The Christian, by contrast, finds in his faith a sure and comforting response that is unknown by and unavailable to the incredulous. Therefore Le Franc can permit himself to be ironic when he considers the fate of these philosophers before inviting Racine to take refuge in his faith:

> Laissons-les, ces mortels sublimes,
> Traiter d'essais pusillanimes
> Les traits de nos humbles crayons.
> Qu'à leur essor ils s'abandonnent.
> Ce sont des sages, qu'ils raisonnent;
> Nous, esprits vulgaires, croyons.

We do not know if Le Franc succeeded in consoling his friend; but it would certainly be difficult to imagine a more concise contrast between the faith of Christians and the reasoning powers of philosophers.

This contrast points out forcefully the limits of Enlightenment in a Christian philosopher on the one hand and a deistic philosopher on the other. Le Franc wants to impose limits on the subjects of research; Voltaire learns that human reason has its limits; and neither man finds an answer to the problem of evil in nature. We see in Le Franc a calm, a serenity, an assurance of an after life, which come from his unconditional belief. We see in Voltaire the painful search for truth, for knowledge, for understanding, along with doubt and anxiety. If this uncertainty and angst are the price of the quest for truth, the believer does not feel free to permit the application of reason to all domains; but certitude in the face of the questions posed by the deists costs the believer dearly.

Le Franc recalls, at the beginning of his fifth ode ('Etablissement, utilité et nécessité du culte extérieur') that he had rebuilt the chapel on the grounds of his château in Pompignan – which helps to establish the dating of the poems in this book, since the church was erected about 1763.[10] The physical existence of a church is symbolically important to inculcate and retain the faith of the parishioners. Le Franc notes that the (p.167):

> plus beaux tabernacles
> Sont bâtis dans nos coeurs

but he adds that to be sure of the fidelity of men, a visible altar and temple had to make an effect on our minds and eyes (p.168):

> Il fallait qu'un autel et qu'un temple visible
> Fît un effet sensible
> Sur l'âme et sur les yeux.

Pompignan tries to show that God wanted to establish the material edifice of a church ('un temple', 'un autel') and also the spiritual edifice ('l'Eglise'), the institution charged with interpreting God's word to humanity. In this poem, he combats Voltairean deism even if he does not name his adversary explicitly; Voltaire seems to be the 'l'impie', 'l'insensé', one of the 'fameux mortels, prodiges des sciences', 'le blasphémateur' that he attacks repeatedly (p.170, 171, 172, 175).[11]

---

10. See Theodore E. D. Braun, *Un Ennemi de Voltaire. Le Franc de Pompignan. Sa vie, ses œuvres, ses rapports avec Voltaire* (Paris 1972), p.49-55.

11. As in his opera, *Prométhée*, here Le Franc designates Voltaire without naming him. Anyone familiar with the quarrel between the two men in the early 1760s would easily see the allusion to Voltaire in the ode and in the opera. For the opera, see *Aeschylus, Voltaire, and Le Franc de Pompignan's Prométhée*, ed. Theodore E. D. Braun and Gerald R. Culley, *SVEC* 160 (1976), p.137-226.

In the next ode, the third of these central poems ('La Providence, et la philosophie'), Le Franc develops further the ideas he has already set out; but here he addresses Voltaire directly, as always in this book with epithets of disdain but without naming him (p.176):

> esprit volage,
> Toi, qui prétends au nom de sage

'faible mortel' (p.179). In the early stanzas the attack could not be more direct (p.176):

> Et qui ne sait que la nature
> A des loix qu'elle suit toujours [...]
> Qui doute que le seul prestige
> D'un instinct superstitieux,
> Ne métamorphose en prestige
> Tout objet qui surprend nos yeux?

Le Franc continues his attack on Voltaire without respite (p.177):

> Quoi! ce Maître, à présent esclave
> De nos calculs et de nos loix,
> Quand sa créature le brave,
> Sur elle a perdu tous ses droits!

He has his philosopher reply thus (p.179-80):

> Non, réponds-tu, je n'ai pu naître
> Que par l'œuvre d'un créateur;
> Je reconnais ce premier Etre
> Qui de l'univers est l'auteur.

The Christian responds:

> Tu reconnais! vaines paroles,
> Quand tes opinions frivoles
> Gênent sa force et son vouloir.
> Est-ce avouer son existence,
> Que de nier sa providence,
> Et de combattre son pouvoir?

Before offering a long quotation from Lucretius, to show how closely Voltairean thought conforms – in his view – to the Roman poet's atheism, Le Franc makes a rather clear allusion to Lisbon (p.180):

> Tu ne veux pas que le ciel tonne,
> Que les murs tombent, s'il l'ordonne,
> Ni que les flots changent de lieu.

No, for Le Franc, the only philosopher worthy of the name is the docile Christian (p.178):

> Il n'est que le Chrétien docile
> Qui soit philosophe avec fruit.

The docile Christian is a philosopher because he is 'resigned', that is, because he has submitted to the will of providence, which he loves. Someday, he insists (p.186), the false wise men will learn

> qu'il est un trône suprême,
> Où par la sagesse elle-même
> Les philosophes sont jugés.

If we had to choose the single poem in this collection that is the most important direct response to Voltaire's reaction to the Lisbon catastrophe, this poem on providence would stand out from the rest. The message is especially strong when 'La Providence' is coupled with the poem to Louis Racine.

The book ends with its third part, consisting like the others of three poems: an act of faith ('Le triomphe de la croix') presenting the paradox of the death of Jesus and his ultimate resurrection; a declaration of the ultimate triumph of religion over atheism and deism, which is in effect a second act of faith ('Le triomphe de la religion, aux Carmélites de Saint-Denis'); and a prayer ('Paraphrase de l'oraison dominicale'). Given what we have seen above, it is no surprise that Le Franc de Pompignan should have concluded his response to Voltaire in this manner: everything he had written in the first six poems of this book points, through submission to providence, to a public avowal of his faith in God and in Jesus in particular, and therefore to a final prayer. The paraphrase of the prayer of our Lord or the 'Our father', the prayer that Jesus taught to his disciples, is the perfect response to the deist's prayer with which Voltaire ended the 'Poème sur le désastre de Lisbonne', a divine as opposed to a human prayer.[12]

Shortly after the earthquake, Le Franc had tried to console his friend Racine on the death of his son by encouraging him to submit to the will of divine providence. If that poem is a quickly written composition intended to be read by only one person and his family, the *Livre quatrième* of odes is a more public work, a response to the deism that Voltaire expressed in his 'Poème sur le désastre de Lisbonne'. Probably because of the aftermath to Pompignan's 1760 reception speech upon his election to the Académie française in 1759, in which he tried to defend the faith by attacking the *philosophes* head on, he decided to frame his definitive response to Voltaire more indirectly, and to wait until after Voltaire's death and the end of his own life before making it known to the public.

---

12. We might see in the use of this prayer a subtle refutation of charges made by Voltaire, Morellet and others that Le Franc's translation of Pope's 'Universal prayer' proved that he was a deist. See Braun, *Un Ennemi de Voltaire*, p.185-90, and Theodore E. D. Braun and Judy Celano Celli, 'Eighteenth-century French translations of Pope's *Universal Prayer*', *SVEC* 256 (1988), p.297-323.

ANNE-SOPHIE BARROVECCHIO

A propos de Voltaire, de maître André et du *Tremblement de terre de Lisbonne*: histoire d'une supercherie tragique de l'avocat Jean-Henri Marchand

Les roues d'un carrosse servent à le faire marcher;
mais qu'elles fassent voler un peu plus ou un peu
moins de poussière, le voyage se fait également.[1]

En quelque endroit que j'aille, à pied ou en carrosse,
Je me souviendrai du premier jour de ma noce.[2]

Tel vous semble applaudir, qui vous raille et vous joue;
Aimez qu'on vous conseille et non pas qu'on vous loue.[3]

'CÉLÉBRER avec noblesse les événements majeurs suscitant l'émotion de toute une société, c'était alors l'une des fonctions du poète', rappelle Jacqueline Hellegouarc'h dans le chapitre qu'elle consacre au 'Poème sur le désastre de Lisbonne' dans la grande biographie *Voltaire en son temps*, publiée sous la direction de René Pomeau.[4] Ainsi que le précise ensuite J. Hellegouarc'h: 'Voltaire s'en était acquitté naguère par son poème de Fontenoy, et il n'avait pas été le seul, nous le savons.' De fait, on serait tenté de rapprocher Lisbonne de Fontenoy: à dix ans d'intervalle exactement, voilà deux événements qui furent peints par Voltaire, deux épisodes qui frappèrent l'imagination des hommes du milieu du dix-huitième siècle, et qui inspirèrent *a priori* les écrivains du temps. Pourtant, quand on consulte la bibliographie chronologique de Pierre Marie Conlon,

1. Première note de Voltaire au 'Poème sur le désastre de Lisbonne' (1756). En attendant son édition dans les *Œuvres complètes* d'Oxford, on se reportera à l'édition Moland, ix.470 et suivantes. Rappelons que le texte est disponible dans l'édition de Jacques van den Heuvel, dans *Mélanges* de Voltaire (Paris 1961), p.301-309 (notes p.1388-91; note 1 de la p.306, p.1390 pour la citation), et dans l'édition de Jean Dagen, dans Voltaire, *La Muse philosophe, florilège poétique* (Paris 2000), p.93-100.
2. Derniers vers prononcés par M. Du Pont, in *Le Tremblement de terre de Lisbonne*, par Jean-Henri Marchand, acte V, scène viii.
3. Nicolas Boileau, *Art poétique*, cité en exergue du *Censeur hebdomadaire*. Voir ci-dessous, note 36.
4. 'Désastre à Lisbonne (novembre 1755-mars 1756)', dans 'De la Cour au jardin (1750-1759)' *Voltaire en son temps*, éd. R. Pomeau (Paris et Oxford 1995), t.i, part. iii, chapitre xiv, p.824.

l'on ne peut que constater le nombre relativement limité d'écrits publiés sur le tremblement de terre de Lisbonne pour les années 1755 et 1756, par comparaison avec l'effervescence littéraire qui avait immédiatement suivi la victoire du 11 mai 1745.[5]

Les vers de Voltaire mis à part, les réactions poétiques au désastre sont rares. Plus rares encore sont les échos légers ou burlesques de la catastrophe. La chose se comprend aisément. Si les événements heureux, tels que mariages et batailles, pouvaient fort bien donner lieu à toutes les plaisanteries, il ne pouvait raisonnablement pas en être de même d'un événement qui provoqua la consternation générale. L'actualité littéraire s'est ainsi partagée entre interrogations religieuses, relations de témoins oculaires et essais d'explications scientifiques.[6] Par ailleurs, les écrits ont été très vite oubliés; et quelle postérité pouvaient aussi espérer ces tristes productions de circonstance?

Une exception existe cependant. Il s'agit du *Tremblement de terre de Lisbonne*, une tragédie en cinq actes et en alexandrins, publiée par un prétendu André, maître Perruquier, sous l'adresse fictive de Lisbonne et sous la date tout aussi fausse de 1755.[7] Aujourd'hui presque totalement oubliée, la pièce fut pourtant remarquée en son temps. De très nombreux exemplaires en sont toujours conservés dans les bibliothèques, signes, sans aucun doute, de sa très large diffusion passée. Or il se trouve que ce texte ne connut pas seulement un succès éphémère; sa célébrité fut durable, et l'œuvre était encore avidement recherchée, en France, au début du dix-neuvième siècle. En étudiant la tragédie de maître André composée sur le désastre de Lisbonne, c'est en réalité l'histoire d'un texte qui fit les délices des lecteurs du milieu du dix-huitième siècle et des spectateurs du premier dix-neuvième siècle qu'il s'agit de retracer.[8]

Si Grimm écrivait dans la *Correspondance littéraire* en février 1757 que 'cette pièce a eu un grand succès, en ce que maître André l'a très bien vendue. L'extrême absurdité de l'ouvrage devait le faire réussir', ajoutait-il,

---

5. P. M. Conlon, *Le Siècle des Lumières* (Genève 1990), vii.261-559 pour les années 1755 et 1756. Pour un relevé exhaustif, les années suivantes doivent être consultées, complétées, bien entendu, par les journaux du temps.

6. Pour les mentions dans la presse, voir Hans-Jürgen Lüsebrink, 'Le tremblement de terre de Lisbonne dans les périodiques français et allemands du XVIIIe siècle', dans *Gazettes d'information politique sous l'Ancien Régime* (Saint-Etienne 1999), p.301-11. Nous regrettons de n'avoir pas pu consulter l'étude de Robert Arruda, *La Réaction littéraire de Voltaire et ses contemporains au tremblement de terre de Lisbonne de 1775* [*sic*, in Frederick A. Spear, *Bibliographie analytique des écrits relatifs à Voltaire*, Oxford 1992, n° 2373, p.294] (diss. Middlebury College 1977), ni celle de B. Rohrer, *Das Erdbeben von Lissabon in der französischen Literatur des achtzehnten Jahrhunderts* (Heidelberg 1933).

7. De L'Imprimerie du Public, in-8°, 88p.

8. Le texte en a été réédité, avec une notice et plusieurs documents, dans *Voltairomania: l'avocat Jean-Henri Marchand face à Voltaire*, éd. A.-S. Barrovecchio (Saint-Etienne 2004), p.33-104. Désormais, toutes nos références renvoient à cette édition, sauf mention contraire.

craignant 'que ce succès ne tourne la tête à tous les perruquiers';[9] la tragédie 'vous amusera par son extrême platitude', lançait-il, remarquant malignement que 'le curé du Mont-Chauvet a trouvé un rival digne de lui',[10] considérant encore que c'est 'une tragédie fort ridicule'.[11] La pièce n'avait pas été écrite pour être représentée; le texte en fut néanmoins réédité sous la date de 1756[12] et circula aussi en manuscrit.[13] Les critiques du début du dix-neuvième siècle s'accordent à y voir l''une des plus amusantes facéties littéraires du dernier siècle',[14] et en effet, Martine de Rougemont rappelle que la pièce est 'citée jusqu'à la fin du siècle comme un classique de drôlerie'.[15] De quoi s'agit-il?

Le Tremblement de terre de Lisbonne raconte les aventures échevelées d'un jeune gentilhomme de Lisbonne, le Comte, amoureux d'une roturière, Théodora, fille de Don Pedro. Le Comte dévoile ses sentiments à son confident, M. Du Pont, dès la scène i de l'acte I. Quelque temps après, Théodora, voulant sonder Du Pont sur celui qu'elle aime, s'évanouit à ses explications mystérieuses (acte I, scène iii):

> THÉRÈSE, *toute effrayée.*
>
> Est-il possible? Ah! Dieu! ma maîtresse se meurt:
> Au secours, à mon aide, eh! vite des odeurs;
> Mon flacon, où est-il? Tout est-il donc perdu?
> Dans un temps si critique, ah! ah! je n'en puis plus!
> Allons, Monsieur du Pont, tirez votre flacon:
> Vite, j'attends après... mais dépêchez-vous donc!

> M. DU PONT
>
> Je le cherche, mon cœur, avant de le donner.
> Mais bon! je ne l'ai pas; je cours vous le chercher.

Revenant à elle, Théodora explique à sa confidente, Thérèse, la source de son étourdissement. C'est qu'elle est tombée amoureuse du Comte 'Au combat du taureau', 'Le dimanche des Rameaux', quand celui-ci, au péril de sa vie, l'a vaillamment secourue au moment où elle allait 'être écalventrée' par la bête enragée (acte I scène iv); mais elle craint que son

---

9. *Correspondance littéraire*, éd. M. Tourneux (Paris 1879; Nendeln 1968), iii.353.

10. *Correspondance littéraire*, 15 janvier 1757, iii.334-35.

11. *Correspondance littéraire*, septembre 1757, iii.417.

12. A Amsterdam et se vend chez l'auteur, in-8°, 80p. Augustin Thierry précise, dans *Les Grandes Mystifications littéraires* (Paris 1911), i.82: 'En deux mois, trois éditions furent épuisées du *Tremblement de terre*, qu'André débitait lui-même, recevant, avec modestie, félicitations et compliments. Elles lui valurent dans la poche deux mille beaux écus sonnants et trébuchants. La farce rapportait une fortune au berné.'

13. Il en existe un exemplaire conservé à Paris, au département des Arts et du spectacle de la BnF, à la bibliothèque de l'Arsenal, sous le nom de Jean-Henri Marchand, [1755], Rondel ms 314, 1 cahier broché de 88 f°s.

14. Article 'Marchand', *Nouvelle Biographie générale* (Paris 1860), xxxiii.473.

15. M. de Rougemont, *Paradrames, parodies du drame (1775-1777)* (Saint-Etienne 1998), p.130.

amour ne soit pas partagé. Averti du malaise de Théodora, le Comte accourt; les deux amants s'avouent des sentiments réciproques, quoique Théodora s'efforce de ne pas trop se compromettre.

Alors que le Comte vient d'obtenir du père de Théodora la main de celle qu'il aime à l'acte II, il aperçoit son propre père, Don Rodrigues, grand Seigneur Portugais, qui l'aborde avec affabilité. Don Rodrigues a des nouvelles importantes à lui annoncer: il lui a obtenu un 'régiment':

> Et le gouvernement
> De la Ville et de tous les faubourgs de Lisbonne.[16]

Le Comte se confond en remerciements. Mais il déchante rapidement, apprenant que tous ces bienfaits sont liés à son prochain mariage avec Dona Mendoza. Don Rodrigues s'aperçoit du trouble de son fils et tente d'en comprendre les raisons. Le Comte s'efforce d'écarter ses soupçons et se retire. Son père n'est cependant pas dupe de son attitude, et il cherche à se renseigner auprès de M. Du Pont, qui finit par lui avouer que le Comte veut épouser Théodora. Très en colère, Don Rodrigues interdit à son fils de s'unir à 'une fille' dont il sait:

> Que c'est une grisette, et qu'elle n'est pas née
> Pour dedans ma famille entrer par l'hyménée.
> [...]
> Ignorez-vous que Don Pedro, de père en fils,
> Fut toujours roturier; de là vient mon mépris;
> Ce n'est pas pour son nez, par la même raison,
> Que le four aujourd'hui chauffe dans ma maison.[17]

Condamné par son père à s'expatrier s'il s'entête, le Comte, resté seul, s'abandonne à son chagrin, bientôt partagé par Théodora.

Parti pour 'voyager', le Comte fait naufrage près de Constantinople, où se déroule tout l'acte III. Avec M. Du Pont, il parvient néanmoins à échapper à la noyade, et gagne la rive à la nage à la scène i; 'tout mouillé', ils ont aussi tout perdu, mais ils sont vivants. Ils sont alors secourus par un eunuque qui leur apporte mystérieusement 'un gros sac de louis' (scène ii). Il se trouve que la fille du Muphty, Roxane, a aperçu les naufragés de sa fenêtre, comme elle l'explique à sa confidente Nadine (scène v), et qu'elle est immédiatement tombée amoureuse du Comte. Voyant que ce dernier repousse ses avances, elle veut le forcer à l'épouser, mais il résiste et refuse de lui sacrifier sa maîtresse. Devant cet affront, la fille du Muphty lui promet de se venger. Le Muphty, son père, arrive alors, et s'apercevant avec colère que Roxane se trouve seule avec un homme, il ordonne au Comte de se marier ou de se préparer à mourir. Le Comte tente de se justifier, mais le Muphty s'apprête à l'exécuter.

16. Acte II, scène ii.
17. Acte II, scène vi.

Le Comte saisit alors une épée, et son confident, Du Pont, s'apprête généreusement à le seconder (acte III, scène xi):

> M. DU PONT, *l'épée à la main.*
>
> Qu'entends-je? Ah! Ciel! on veut assassiner mon maître!
> A la Garde! z'au guet! ah, scélérat! ah, traître!
> Si tu ne te hâtes vite de décamper,
> Sur le champ, pour le sûr, je vais t'assassiner.

Le Muphty renonce à un combat inégal à deux contre un, et disparaît suivi de sa fille. Sur les conseils de M. Du Pont, le Comte s'enfuit et ils regagnent tous deux Lisbonne.

L'acte IV et l'acte V se déroulent de nouveau dans la capitale portugaise. Théodora confie à Thérèse ses inquiétudes, car elle n'a aucune nouvelle du Comte. Son père veut, par surcroît de malheur, lui faire épouser de force Don Lavaros. Refusant inflexiblement un mariage qui lui fait horreur, Théodora tente de se suicider (acte IV, scène iv):

> Ma chère Thérèse, prête-moi ton couteau;
> L'on t'en rendra un qui sera beaucoup plus beau.
> [...]
>
> THÉODORA, *à elle-même.*
>
> Allons, Théodora, ranime ton courage,
> Et par cet instrument achève donc ta rage.
> Pourquoi hésites-tu? Qu'as-tu qui te retient?
> Ouvre donc ce couteau, et de ta propre main
> Perce-moi de cent coups ce cœur et ce beau sein,
> Pour lequel si longtemps tu as pris tant de soin.
> Adieu, cher Comte, adieu, j'achève mon dessein.

Le Comte arrive juste à temps pour sauver *in extremis* sa maîtresse (acte IV, scène v):

> (*Il arrache le couteau.*)
> [...]
> Malheureux instrument tu ne serviras pas,
> Je jure, de ta vie, à ternir tant d'appas.
> Tu vas être cassé... Crac... Chère reine, hélas!
> Quoi! un instant plus tard, je perdais vos appas!

Théodora lui avoue qu'elle mourait pour échapper à Don Lavaros, neveu de l'Inquisiteur. Le Comte défie son rival, qui est présent: ils se battront en duel. Il relate alors ses aventures à son amante. Comme Don Rodrigues approche, le Comte la quitte. Averti du retour de son fils, il vient s'en plaindre à Théodora. Du Pont arrive et leur annonce que le Comte a tué Don Lavaros au cours du duel. Don Rodrigues reproche alors durement à Théodora d'être la cause des malheurs de son fils; il court demander sa grâce au Roi.

A l'acte V, Don Rodrigues annonce avec satisfaction à Du Pont qu'il vient d'obtenir du roi la grâce du Comte, mais celui-ci est encore menacé par la vengeance de l'Inquisiteur. Du Pont lui apprend alors que le Comte vient d'être fait prisonnier par les archers; tout paraît donc perdu... Don Pedro les rejoint; malgré les attaques de Don Rodrigues, le père de Théodora parvient à lui expliquer qu'il a fait arrêter le Comte afin de le faire conduire en sûreté chez lui. Don Rodrigues se confond en remerciements.

Sur le chemin, Don Pedro reconnaît sa fille, 'habillée en homme'.[18] Découverte, Théodora avoue qu'elle cherchait, par ce costume, à se faire passer pour son amant. Ignorant que le Comte était hors de danger, elle pensait ainsi s'offrir à sa place à l'Inquisition pour le sauver. Don Rodrigues est touché par son courage et propose de marier les deux amants.

Du Pont offre à son tour à Thérèse, qu'il aime, de s'unir en même temps que le Comte et Théodora. Thérèse sort pour aller chez le notaire établir leur contrat; elle doit auparavant envoyer à son futur son 'baigneur'. Resté seul, Du Pont passe en revue tous les tourments récents qui l'ont accablé; heureusement, tout est en passe de s'arranger. Le perruquier arrive; ils échangent les nouvelles qui courent dans Lisbonne, et le perruquier propose à son client de choisir une coiffure à la mode (acte V, scène vi):

> Si vous le voulez bien, je m'en vais vous friser
> Le mieux que je pourrai, j'ose vous l'assurer.
> Vous ne voulez pas être en aile de pigeon,
> Ni en rhinocéros?

Soudain, Du Pont sent que son perruquier l'a coupé; mais ce dernier n'y est pour rien:

> Excusez-moi, Monsieur, je ne sais pas pourquoi,
> Je tremble; assurément, tout me tremble sous moi.
> Je ne sais pas non plus si c'est par vision,
> Je crois voir remuer la chambre et la maison.

Les secousses sont en réalité un effet du tremblement de terre qui est en train de se produire. Du Pont est épouvanté; il s'écrie:

> Grand Dieu! la maison tombe, où vais-je me sauver?
> [...]
> Fallait-il sur le point que j'épouse Thérèse,
> Je me vois écrasé tout comme une punaise?

Le Comte, Rodrigues, Théodora, Du Pont, et Thérèse se retrouvent et décident de gagner le port pour fuir à bord d'un 'vaisseau'. Mais en arrivant, Du Pont assiste, impuissant, à l'engloutissement de son maître et de sa chère Thérèse (acte V, scène viii):

---

18. L'édition de 1805 indique que Théodora est 'couverte d'un voile'. C'est un changement significatif (voir *Voltairomania*, p.90).

M. DU PONT, *seul*.

[...]

A peine êtes-vous donc montés dans le vaisseau,
Que je vous aperçois tout au milieu de l'eau.
Quand je veux avec vous la planche escalader,
D'un coup de vent je vois le vaisseau s'en aller.

Curieuse tragédie, de fait, que cette pièce. Selon le *Dictionnaire de bio-graphie française*, Charles André, 'né à Langres en 1722, était au milieu du XVIIIe siècle perruquier à Paris, rue de la Vannerie. En 1755, on publia sous son nom une tragédie, *Le Tremblement de terre de Lisbonne*, et on fit si bien, paraît-il, qu'il se figura l'avoir écrite.'[19] André aurait donc bel et bien existé; mais il n'en serait pas pour autant le véritable auteur de la pièce. De fait, quoique nous ignorions si 'André fut' 'la victime ou le complice de ces mystifications', 'il semble bien qu'il n'y ait dans l'histoire des poésies de maître André qu'une série de facéties dont l'auteur prin-cipal doit être l'avocat Jean-Henri Marchand', considéré comme 'très capable de ces plaisanteries'.[20]

L'avocat J.-H. Marchand est un homme de lettres à peu près totale-ment oublié aujourd'hui. Ecrivain parisien né à une date inconnue et mort en 1785, il fut avocat en Parlement et censeur; il fréquentait, à en croire Voltaire, la bonne compagnie de la capitale.[21] C'est un de ces *minores* du siècle des Lumières qui avait, comme Pannard ou Piron, choisi de s'illustrer exclusivement dans les parodies et les genres mineurs. Il ne cherchait pas à se faire un nom en écrivant,[22] mais à se divertir. Amateur de littérature gaie 'qui s'est livré surtout à de spirituels badinages en vers et en prose',[23] il était connu pour être un 'plaisant de société'.[24] Quoiqu'il ne soit 'point poète de profession' et qu'il 's'amuse quelquefois à faire des vers négligés qu'il jette sur le papier avec une facilité prodigieuse',[25] Marchand n'en devint pas moins, à partir de 1745, quand il écrivit une *Requête du curé de Fontenoy au Roi* qui fut distinguée par ses contem-porains, un littérateur de renom très apprécié pour 'ses opuscules, qui ne

---

19. Article 'André', *Dictionnaire de biographie française* (Paris 1936), ii.903.

20. *Dictionnaire de biographie française*, ii.903.

21. Voir Voltaire à François-Louis-Claude Marin, le 5 mai 1769 (D14653). La corres-pondance de Voltaire est citée dans *Correspondence and related documents*, éd. Th. Besterman, dans les *Œuvres complètes de Voltaire*, dorénavant *OC*, t.85-135 (Genève, Banbury, Oxford 1968-1977).

22. Voir *Mon Radotage et celui des autres, recueilli par un invalide retiré du monde pendant son carnaval* (Paris 1759), où Marchand lance: 'Et puisque je suis anonyme / Laissez-moi donc dans mon obscurité' (p.224).

23. *Dictionnaire des lettres françaises: le XVIIIe siècle*, du cardinal Grente (1960), nouvelle édition sous la direction de François Moureau (Paris 1995), p.814.

24. Article 'Marchand', *Biographie universelle, ancienne et moderne* (Paris 1820), xxvi.602. Il égayait la société du château de Beaumont (non localisé).

25. *Correspondance littéraire du président Bouhier*, éd. Henri Duranton (dactylographié; Saint-Etienne et Lyon 1974), note 1, p.83. Je remercie M. Dominique Quéro de m'avoir communiqué cette information.

manquent ni d'esprit ni de gaieté'.[26] Quoiqu'ayant publié toutes ses plaisanteries de manière anonyme et que tous ses livres appartiennent à des genres mineurs, Marchand acquit peu à peu une certaine célébrité auprès d'un large public. Il a dû écrire une soixantaine d'ouvrages,[27] comprenant 'de curieuses facéties, des parodies',[28] de ces 'bagatelles littéraires'[29] qui ont 'fait sensation dans la seconde moitié du dix-huitième siècle'.[30]

Marchand usait volontiers, pour publier ses ouvrages, de pseudonymes pittoresques; il pouvait aussi utiliser des prête-noms. Il excellait à déguiser ses autorités narratives, maquillant à l'occasion tout le paratexte de ses écrits afin de faire de ses livres de parfaits objets de fantaisie. C'est ainsi qu'il monta, peut-être avec 'Lasalle de Dampierre, régisseur de l'impôt sur les cartes, et son ami, le "nouvelliste" Ducoin, secrétaire de Pâris de Meyzieu, le fameux bibliophile',[31] ce qui allait devenir une des plus grandes supercheries littéraires du dix-huitième siècle autour du tremblement de terre de Lisbonne et du personnage de Charles André. Tout en romançant sans doute très largement l'affaire, Augustin Thierry résume ce qu'il faut bien désigner, après lui, comme 'La plaisante aventure du perruquier André'.[32] Si 'le dix-huitième siècle a été par excellence le temps des farces grandioses' (p.65), gageons qu'il s'agit là d'un de ses épisodes les plus fameux. A. Thierry poursuit:

> Et puis, un beau jour, l'étonnante tragédie connut les gloires de la rampe. C'était, il est vrai, cinquante années plus tard. Au mois de janvier 1805, la Porte-Saint-Martin donnait la première d'un mélodrame oublié, *Le Désastre de Lisbonne*.
> Aussitôt son voisin, le théâtre des Délassements, de monter en parodie le *Tremblement de terre*, qui reçut un accueil triomphal. La pièce 'spectacle demandée' tint de longs mois l'affiche.[33]

Si *Le Tremblement de terre de Lisbonne* a été repris en 1805, c'est sans doute tout à la fois pour commémorer un triste anniversaire, les cinquante ans du désastre, et disputer à un concurrent son public. L'actualité qui allait se développer autour de la pièce montre qu'elle n'avait pas vieilli. Par

---

26. Lucien Faucou, notice sur Marchand, in *L'Assommoir du XVIIIᵉ siècle, le Vuidangeur sensible*, drame en trois actes et en prose (Paris 1880), p.6.

27. Voltaire écrit au Roi de Prusse, Frédéric II, le 5 avril 1771 (D16091), que cet 'avocat de Paris, nommé Marchand, [qui] régale tous les mois le public d'un ouvrage'. Il exagérait ainsi une formule de Grimm (*Correspondance littéraire*, janvier 1771). Quelques-uns de ses textes furent écrits en collaboration.

28. L. Faucou, *L'Assommoir du XVIIIᵉ siècle*, p.6.

29. L. Faucou, citant les *Mémoires secrets* de Bachaumont, dans *L'Assommoir du XVIIIᵉ siècle*, p.14-15.

30. L. Faucou, *L'Assommoir du XVIIIᵉ siècle*, p.6.

31. A. Thierry, *Les Grandes Mystifications littéraires*, p.66. C'est une information très répandue.

32. A. Thierry, *Les Grandes Mystifications littéraires*, i.61-84.

33. A. Thierry, *Les Grandes Mystifications littéraires*, p.82.

ailleurs, entre 1755 et 1805, la famille de maître André s'était élargie; le perruquier avait eu de nombreux descendants qui avaient assuré la postérité de son œuvre.

Toute une série de textes écrits autour de la figure d'André avait en effet été publiée depuis la tragédie,[34] montrant que les plaisanteries les plus courtes ne sont décidément pas nécessairement les meilleures. Dans la *Correspondance littéraire*, Grimm parlait, en septembre 1757, de ce 'M. Marchand, auteur de plusieurs mauvaises plaisanteries, qui a fait en dernier lieu l'*Encyclopédie perruquière*' (iii.417). Sous le nom de Beaumont, coiffeur dans les Quinze-Vingts, Marchand se dédiait ainsi à lui-même son nouvel ouvrage, développant la supercherie qu'il venait de lancer, s'amusant du dialogue fictif entre deux figures ridicules.[35] Peu après, en 1760, *Deux Lettres de M. André, Maître perruquier, auteur de la fameuse tragédie du Tremblement de Terre de Lisbonne; l'une à M. F***[Fréron]; *l'autre à M. P****[Palissot] étaient publiées par le *Censeur hebdomadaire*.[36] En 1766, un *Poème sur le tremblement de terre de Constantinople*, par un garçon perruquier, ci-devant attaché à la boutique de M. André, était publié sous l'adresse d'Amsterdam.[37] M. de Rougemont note dans *Paradrames* qu''Une famille prend forme: M. l'Allemand, coeffeur qui écrit à M. Doucet, est un neveu de M. André lui-même.'[38] Comme il l'avait fait pour Fontenoy, Marchand a sans doute lancé l'idée des écrits de maître André, étant, par la suite, relayé par ses contemporains qui trouvaient sa plaisanterie féconde.

L'homme de paille supplanta bientôt l'auteur en chair, car 'le barbier prit goût à la versification' et 'composa d'autres poésies dont il mesurait les alexandrins avec une ficelle'.[39] Cette anecdote était célèbre au dix-neuvième siècle. Alexandre Dumas y fait allusion dans les premières

---

34. La pièce aurait même été parodiée par François-Antoine Quétant (1733-1823), dans *Les Muses artisanes ou l'auteur perruquier*, BnF, Ms Fr 9269 [CESAR http://www.cesar.org.uk], ainsi que le signale Catriona Seth dans son article ' "Je ne pourrai pas en faire le récit" ', p.173-90 du présent volume.

35. Voir l'Epître à Monsieur l'illustre et célèbre poète, Monsieur André, perruquier', dans *L'Enciclopédie perruquière, ouvrage curieux à l'usage de toutes sortes de têtes* (Paris 1757); Beaumont, coiffeur, y compose un petit quatrain en l'honneur de son modèle, p.6: 'Alliant aux bons vers, l'état de la tignasse, / André s'est fait un nom parmi nos grands auteurs; / Apollon l'a nommé perruquier du Parnasse, / Il y fait doctement le poil aux doctes sœurs.'

36. Par M. d'Aquin (Utrecht et Paris 1760), iv.112-19. Ces lettres sont éditées dans *Voltairomania*, p.98-101.

37. In-8°, 15p.; voir en particulier l'avertissement et la dédicace, 'A monsieur André, Maître perruquier et poète célèbre', p.iii-viii.

38. M. de Rougemont, *Paradrames*, p.130. Il s'agit du *Parfait Ouvrage, ou Essai sur la coiffure*, traduit du persan, par le sieur L'Allemand, coiffeur, neveu du sieur André, perruquier, breveté du grand roi de Perse, correspondant du grand Turc, de plusieurs sociétés de coiffeurs, perruquiers, baigneurs, etc., etc., etc., à Césarée et en France, chez tous les libraires qui vendent les bons livres, 1776, in-8°, 52p.

39. *Dictionnaire de biographie française*, ii.903.

pages d'*Olympe de Clèves*.[40] Peu à peu André devint donc, à son tour, un personnage de théâtre.[41] L'auteur improbable d'une pièce à succès était devenu un sujet littéraire à part entière.

La célébrité d'André devait-elle finalement conduire à éclipser sa tragédie? Tout au contraire, il semble que la supercherie devait servir la pièce.[42] Le texte du *Tremblement de terre de Lisbonne* n'est pas seulement excentrique, farfelu, fantaisiste, bizarre voire carrément étrange – les qualificatifs ne manquent pas pour tenter de cerner une tragédie si peu commune – il possède indéniablement un intérêt pour lui-même. Sans partager l'enthousiasme du garçon perruquier présumé attaché à la boutique de maître André qui prétendait s'être 'donné la satisfaction' de 'lire' la 'charmante tragédie du *Tremblement de terre de Lisbonne*' 'à peu près plus de vingt fois au moins sans [s]e lasser',[43] ni celui de Beaumont assurant qu'il s'agissait d'une pièce 'capable de faire la barbe aux plus fameux poètes de notre siècle',[44] son texte apprend beaucoup sur les pratiques littéraires de son temps comme sur les idées particulières de Marchand; pour en saisir toute la finesse, il suffit de la replacer dans son contexte.

Il faut alors revenir sur la chronologie. Voltaire composa son 'Poème sur le désastre de Lisbonne' à la fin de l'année 1755, après avoir eu connaissance dans les semaines qui le suivirent, comme ses contemporains, du terrible séisme qui avait ravagé la capitale du Portugal le 1er novembre; ses vers se diffusèrent en manuscrit, avant d'être imprimés par Cramer en mars 1756, le poème se trouvant même réédité plusieurs fois au cours de l'année.[45] Le texte de Marchand, lui, porte la date de 1755 et il se trouve référencé par P. M. Conlon à cette même année dans sa bibliographie; or il est absolument impossible que la tragédie ait été

40. En parlant d''une brochure dont la justification typographique était irrégulière, c'est-à-dire formée de ces lignes inégales qui [...] devaient servir de critérium à maître André pour distinguer les vers de la prose, quand il les mesurait avec une ficelle pour ne les faire ni trop longs ni trop courts' (*Olympe de Clèves*, éd. Claude Schopp avec la collaboration de Jacqueline Razgonnikoff, Paris 2000, p.13).

41. Voir *Maître André et Poinsinet, ou le Perruquier poète*, comédie-anecdote en 1 acte et en vaudevilles, par Théophile Marion Dumersan et Nicolas Brazier, Paris, Théâtre Montansier, 16 pluviôse an XIII (5 février 1805), Paris, Mme Cavanagh, an XIII [1805], in-8°, 30p. (réédition Paris, Barba, 1820, 31p.). Voir aussi Maître André, ou le Perruquier auteur tragique, vaudeville en un acte, par Louis Leconte et Travault l'aîné, Paris, Fages, 1805, in-8°, 24p.

42. Il suffit, pour s'en assurer, de considérer ses rééditions: chez Fages en 1805 (in-8°, 44p.), chez A. Leroux et C. Chantpie en 1826 (in-32, 71p.), chez Barba en 1834 (in-8°, 22p.). Rappelons enfin que P. Bignon a adapté la pièce en 1828, en un acte sans changement de décor, dans un manuscrit conservé sous le nom d'André à Paris, BnF, n. a. fr. 4728, 1 cahier broché de 25 pages.

43. *Poème sur le tremblement de terre de Constantinople*, p.vii.

44. *L'Encyclopédie perruquière*, p.2.

45. Pour toutes ces informations oir J. Hellegouarc'h, 'Désastre à Lisbonne (novembre 1755-mars 1756)', i.816-34. Voir aussi 'Poème sur le désastre de Lisbonne', article de Haydn Mason, dans *Dictionnaire général de Voltaire*, éd. Raymond Trousson et Jeroom Vercruysse (Paris 2003), p.954-56.

publiée à ce moment-là. La mention – parfaitement gratuite – de la prise de Port-Mahon, à la scène vi de l'acte V,[46] est un indice signalant que la fin de la tragédie, à tout le moins, a forcément été rédigée – et imprimée – au plus tôt au cours de l'été 1756,[47] après les succès de Richelieu remportés sur les Anglais à Minorque le 28 juin.[48] L'indication de 1755 s'avère ainsi n'être qu'un effet d'annonce publicitaire, selon une pratique courante à l'époque: il fallait publier l'ouvrage sous la date de l'événement dont il était question. Marchand eut donc tout le loisir de se familiariser avec le 'Poème' de Voltaire avant d'écrire sa contribution; 'la belle Tragédie de Monsieur André qui a fait un si beau bruit dans toute l'Europe et à Paris', 'une pièce si magnifique'[49] prend alors une nouvelle ampleur dès lors qu'on y voit un écho aux vers de Voltaire.

La référence à Voltaire s'affiche d'ailleurs dès l''Epître à Monsieur l'illustre, et célèbre Poète M. de Voltaire'. M. de Rougemont a montré dans *Paradrames* que 'des Epîtres dédicatoires font remarquer au lecteur que de grands personnages s'intéressent favorablement à l'œuvre' (p.12). Ce nouveau geste publicitaire est aussi un signe qui oriente le lecteur vers la piste voltairienne pour saisir tout le 'sel'[50] de la pièce. Bien entendu, l'auteur joint alors, selon la tradition satirique, l'éloge à la critique.[51] Il n'est pas jusqu'à la biographie de maître André donnée dans la préface qui n'entretienne des liens avec la vie de Voltaire.[52]

Les éditeurs de 1826 avaient déjà remarqué:

toute l'estime que maître André avait pour le talent de Voltaire. Son admiration allait si loin à cet égard, ajoutaient-ils, qu'il ne voulait rien composer que d'après ce grand homme. Voilà pourquoi, sans doute, il mesurait avec une ficelle les vers de la *Henriade*, afin que ceux de sa tragédie eussent la même longueur. L'enthousiasme ne saurait aller plus loin.

46. Voir la réplique Du Perruquier, quand '*Il passe M. du Pont au fer.*': 'Notre Bourgeois aussi nous a hier appris / Qu'on lui avait dit que Port-Mahon était pris.'

47. L'on peut ainsi penser que la seconde édition daterait de 1757. Il faudrait mener l'enquête dans les journaux de l'époque recensant les parutions de nouveaux livres.

48. La tragédie s'inscrit ainsi dans une double actualité: elle appartient également à la série des textes écrits sur la victoire de Mahon. Voir *Les Trois Manières*, conte de Voltaire (1763): 'Ainsi, quand Richelieu revenait de Mahon / (Qu'il avait pris pourtant en dépit de l'envie)'. Voir Sylvain Menant, dans Voltaire, *Contes en vers et en prose* (Paris 1992), t.i, note 8 (de la p.374), p.504. S. Menant renvoie également au *Précis du Siècle de Louis XV*, chapitre 31, in *Œuvres historiques*, éd. R. Pomeau (Paris 1968), p.1480.

49. Avertissement au *Poème sur le tremblement de terre de Constantinople*, p.iii.

50. *Correspondance littéraire*, janvier 1771, ix.241.

51. L''écolier' se place ainsi sous la protection de son 'Maître' qu'il appelle familièrement son 'cher confrère'. L'auteur expérimenté doit cautionner les débuts d'un 'novice'. Mais si Voltaire est 'un de nos célèbres', assure André, c'est, lui lance-t-il, parce vous êtes 'toujours reconnu [...] par les pompeux ouvrages que vous avez mis et que vous mettez journellement au jour' (*Voltairomania*, p.44).

52. Ainsi 'des petites rimes satiriques et des chansons' lui ont valu 'quelques bons coups de bâton', qui rappellent la célèbre bastonnade dont fut victime Voltaire par M. de Rohan. Son voyage où il a 'parcouru la terre et un peu la mer' correspond encore au séjour de Voltaire en Angleterre! (*Voltairomania*, p.41.)

La tradition veut que 'ce petit ouvrage' ait même été favorisé du souvenir du grand homme. 'Quant à la lettre que Voltaire écrivit, dit-on, à maître André en réponse à son épître dédicatoire, nous n'hésitons pas à la regarder comme apocryphe, corrigent les éditeurs de 1826. Les quatre pages remplies de ces mots: *faites des perruques, faites des perruques, faites des perruques*, sont une invention de quelque rival jaloux.'[53] Voltaire et André ne s'en trouvaient pas moins désormais associés dans une même plaisanterie. A. Thierry avançait même que 'Voltaire, enchanté, mandait à Pâris de Meyzieu qu'il aimerait mieux avoir fait cette caricature que son *Mahomet* et qu'il voudrait bien avoir la Gaussin pour jouer Thérèse ou Mlle Muphti.'[54]

'Sa pièce! Elle est prodigieuse,' s'exclamait encore A. Thierry. 'Marchand et ses associés s'y sont délectés dans la charge. Toute la saveur de la parodie est dans le sérieux de l'action et le ton des personnages.'[55] Comme le *Vidangeur sensible*, qu'elle devance de plus de vingt ans, la tragédie du *Tremblement de terre de Lisbonne* est inclassable; son texte est 'à la fois puissant et ridicule',[56] accumulant les catastrophes, multipliant les situations invraisemblables ou grotesques,[57] ses personnages contemporains atteignent 'les dernières limites qui séparent le bouffon du grave'.[58] Dans le *Vidangeur sensible*, Marchand pénétrait les artifices du drame; il a su tourner ici en dérision le modèle tragique[59] en le boursouflant de références comiques. Sans nul doute, il s'agit bien ici d'une tragédie 'monstrueuse'.[60] Les mêmes ficelles qui servaient à André à mesurer ses vers

53. Texte édité dans *Voltairomania*, p.102. Jusqu'à preuve du contraire, nous sommes donc dans la tradition.

54. A. Thierry, *Les Grandes Mystifications*, p.81. Information non confirmée.

55. A. Thierry, *Les Grandes Mystifications*, p.76.

56. M. de Rougemont, *Paradrames*, p.127.

57. Comme la scène du flacon, acte I scène iii; le récit du combat du taureau, acte I scène iv; l'appel aux armes de Du Pont, acte III scène xi; la scène du couteau, acte IV scène iv; la scène du perruquier, acte V scène vi. L'épisode où le Comte disparaît, sous le prétexte d'aller uriner, est un des plus inattendus: 'Le Comte, *tout troublé*. / Mon père, permettez, pour un besoin pressant, / Que je m'écarte un peu pour un petit moment' (Acte II, scène ii).

58. M. de Rougemont, *Paradrames*, p.128. L'intrigue amoureuse et le rôle du père sont des motifs que l'on retrouve dans d'autres textes sur le tremblement de terre. Voir Catriona Seth, '"Je ne pourrai pas en faire le récit"' dans le présent volume, p.173-90.

59. On y sent des réminiscences de *Rhadamiste et Zénobie* de Crébillon, mais aussi du *Cid*, etc. D'ailleurs, Marchand remarquait, dans *Les Fruits de l'automne* (Amsterdam [Paris], vve Duchesne et Bastien, 1781, p.58), que 'Corneille, Racine, Voltaire ont produit des chefs-d'œuvre'. Ce n'est donc pas une pièce particulière qui est prise ici pour cible, mais le genre en tant que tel; 'le mouvement d'empathie du pasticheur le mène quelquefois au cœur même d'une écriture', remarque M. de Rougemont dans *Paradrames*, p.128.

60. Dans son *Journal* (ii.75), Charles Collé note qu'il a 'fait relier *Le fils naturel* avec les œuvres dramatiques du Président Hénault et la tragédie du *Tremblement de terre de Lisbonne* parue sous le pseudonyme de M. André sous le titre de *Recueil des monstres dramatiques*'. Cité par Marie-Emmanuelle Plagnol-Diéval dans *Le Théâtre de société: un autre théâtre?* (Paris 2003), p.170, que je remercie très chaleureusement de m'avoir communiqué cette information.

se retrouvent, au sens figuré, dans sa technique dramatique, où l'auteur tire toutes les ficelles de son histoire en recourant à des *trucs* que le genre a galvaudés depuis longtemps. Il fait le procès de tout un genre, dans ce qu'il a d'artificiel et de pompeux.[61]

Une tragédie publiée sans être jouée, la chose commençait à se voir au milieu du dix-huitième siècle, même si cela passait souvent pour un non-sens.[62] L'actualité de la recherche sur le théâtre au siècle de Voltaire montre que l'écriture dramatique est, à l'époque, l'un des laboratoires littéraires les plus actifs et les plus inventifs. Si de nombreux auteurs, comme Crébillon ou Voltaire pour ne citer qu'eux, emboîtent le pas à la dramaturgie classique dont ils perpétuent l'héritage, le théâtre de la Foire, les scènes privées des théâtres de société innovent. Toute une méta-littérature se développe. A la marge, elle instruit le procès des genres et met en question les pratiques d'écriture contemporaine dans un jeu de miroir et de mise en abîme critique. C'est dans cette perspective d'un jeu spirituel engagé avec la littérature que la pièce de Marchand, écrite de *main de maître* et destinée à un public averti, doit être appréhendée. Loin de n'être qu'anecdotiques, le tremblement de terre et les allusions aux vers de Voltaire sont de véritables clés permettant d'interpréter la tragédie de manière approfondie.

Dans une bonne tragédie, le dénouement doit toujours résulter des nœuds que l'intrigue a patiemment élaborés au fil des actes. Dans le *Tremblement de terre de Lisbonne*, il n'en est rien. On serait tenté de dire que le dénouement arrive *comme un cheveu sur la soupe*; de fait, sa fin, *tirée par les cheveux*, défie le bon sens en étant entièrement indépendante de l'action. Le séisme serait donc invraisemblable? Certainement pas: il est, tout au plus, incohérent dans la fiction. Les contemporains de Marchand savent cruellement, depuis le 1er novembre 1755, que le tremblement de terre est tristement réel et qu'il a malheureusement bien eu lieu.

Dans la tragédie, l'improbable arrive contre toute attente. C'est qu'un tremblement de terre ne prévient pas, ne se prévoit pas: il se produit. L'effet accable; reconstituer *a posteriori* l'enchaînement des causes qui l'ont entraîné n'y changerait rien; au contraire, voilà qui dénaturerait les effets de surprise et d'injustice qu'une telle catastrophe suscite. Cette fois, la réalité, justement, a dépassé la fiction. Seule une intrigue contraire à toutes les attentes et à la logique même peut provoquer à nouveau chez le spectateur une forte impression. Il ne s'agit pas de rechercher la terreur et la pitié de la tragédie antique, puisque tout ressort tragique se trouve ici

---

61. Voir les considérations de M. de Rougemont sur le drame, dans *Paradrames*; appliquées à la tragédie du *Tremblement de terre de Lisbonne*, elles sont tout aussi justes: 'Voici, pour tout dire, le drame que les grands dramaturges n'ont pas osé et que les mauvais dramaturges n'ont pas su écrire. Parce que les plus grands, conscients de leur place dans l'histoire de la littérature, ne pouvaient pas aller si loin, et parce que les petits, beaucoup plus violents et libres par rapport aux normes, manquaient de moyens littéraires' (p.128). La pièce fonctionne sur la dissonance, sur le décalage permanent entre la gravité des situations et la bouffonnerie de l'expression des personnages.

62. Voir Grimm, *Correspondance littéraire*, février 1769, viii.273.

désamorcé par la bouffonnerie; la pièce, en revanche, peut restituer, par le rire, le tremblement ressenti alors, physiquement, corporellement, jusque dans ses propres membres, en provoquant une *catharsis* d'une nouvelle espèce.

Dans la tragédie de Marchand, il est interdit d'espérer:[63] alors que tout était en passe de se régler heureusement, une dernière catastrophe se produit; un coup de théâtre, tel un *remords tragique*, précipite tous les personnages dans un gouffre infernal (acte V, scène viii):

> J'ai eu beau le chercher, et partout regarder,
> Le vaisseau n'y était plus: mais un très grand gouffre,
> Qui poussait une odeur toute pleine de soufre,
> L'avait mis tout au fond de ce malheureux trou.
> J'y aurais descendu, si j'avais su par où.
> [...]
> Le trou s'est rebouché, et je ne l'ai plus vu.

Les colères géologiques de la terre se combinent ainsi à une vision traditionnelle des enfers.[64] En dépit des exclamations du langage commun qui émaillent le texte, par Dieu et par le diable,[65] c'est peu dire que Marchand ne se préoccupe pas des décrets de la providence.[66]

L'avocat Marchand s'intéresse certes au drame humain qui fait la triste actualité, mais en montrant, prenant ainsi à contre-pied son modèle, que tout va mal dans la tragédie, mais aussi ici-bas, nul besoin, pour s'en rendre compte, d'en référer à Pope ou à Leibniz. Ouvrir seulement les yeux sur le monde qui nous entoure le prouve. Ses yeux, justement, Du Pont les garde grands ouverts; mais il ne peut pas pour autant croire ce qu'il voit. Il ne lui suffit pas d'ouvrir l'œil et le bon: ses deux yeux sont impuissants à capter le spectacle incroyable auquel il assiste, comme y insistent les redondances comiques de son monologue final (acte V, scène viii):

> Ah! Ciel! qu'ai-je aperçu? Qu'ai-je vu de mes yeux!
> Ah! quel embarquement! Et quel spectacle affreux!
> [...]
> Je cherche partout le Comte de mes deux yeux,
> Je le voyais dans l'eau, puis après dans les cieux.

Seul Du Pont survit au cataclysme. Tel un nouveau Sganarelle à la fin de *Don Juan*, il est le rescapé dérisoire d'une gigantesque catastrophe. Mais même aux dernières extrémités, il cède encore au goût des rimes faciles, provoquant ainsi le rire (acte V, scène viii):

63. Rappelons qu'après plusieurs boutures, Voltaire a décidé d'achever son 'Poème ou examen de cet axiome: tout est bien', sur un souffle d'espérance'.

64. Voir la note 72 de l'édition critique de *Candide* par S. Menant, in *Contes en vers et en prose* de Voltaire, i.468. Les rimes 'soufre' et 'gouffre' sont alors très répandues.

65. Avec respectivement une dizaine et cinq occurrences.

66. Contrairement à Voltaire qui centre son 'Poème' sur l'interrogation religieuse. Une logique, même impénétrable, cède ici le pas à l'absurde. Mais on ne peut guère explorer plus avant la pensée de Marchand, qui compte toujours une part de clandestinité.

> Thérèse, où êtes-vous? Je ne vous verrai plus,
> Mon amour et mon cœur: pour le coup que je meure.
> Que n'ai-je donc aussi péri à la même heure?

Cherchant à peindre ce qu'il voit, Du Pont tente une noble hypotypose qui emprunte ses effets aux élans lyriques du discours en vers de Voltaire, reprenant à son compte les tournures oratoires du 'Poème' (acte V, scène viii):

> Je tremble et je frémis, et je suis si saisi
> Que je ne pourrai pas en faire le récit.
> Non, je ne puis jamais exprimer par mes pleurs
> Le trouble et le chagrin qui causent mes douleurs.
> O malheureux destin! ô fatale journée!
> O dans quel désespoir m'as-tu abandonné?

Cette fois, les vers sont réussis; mais leur effet est d'autant plus ridicule qu'ils sont exprimés par un pleutre qui ne trouve d'issue que dans la fuite. Les héros affrontent les dangers; ils combattent, périssent, et les poètes chantent leurs exploits malheureux avec majesté; les hommes tels que M. Du Pont, eux, ne peuvent que *sauver leur tête* en cédant aux réflexes élémentaires de survie (acte V, scène viii):

> Je fais ce que je peux pour pouvoir l'arrêter [le vaisseau],
> Mais je l'ai lâché; car il allait m'emporter.

La logique est imparable. Et M. Du Pont de s'interrompre:

> Mais je ressens encore un nouveau tremblement.
> Je crains qu'en m'arrêtant en ce lieu plus longtemps
> Je n'y périsse aussi; je m'en vais, si je peux,
> Tâcher de me sauver, m'éloignant de ce lieu.

Du Pont *prend ses jambes à son cou*, ce qui est encore le plus sûr moyen de se tirer d'un mauvais pas et d'échapper à une catastrophe contre laquelle on ne peut rien. Ainsi s'achève la pièce.

Bien entendu, Marchand ne donne pas M. Du Pont pour modèle: personne n'ambitionne d'imiter un valet fuyard donné pompeusement pour un 'confident'. L'objectif de sa pièce n'est certainement pas d'inculquer des normes. La tragédie fonctionne, *in fine*, comme les comédies de Molière: des travers humains sont mis au jour; il s'agit d'en rire, mais le dramaturge ne cherche pas à les réformer ou à leur substituer une leçon moralisatrice.[67] L'écrivain cherche seulement à peindre la catastrophe au naturel. Marchand se garde d'adopter le ton de la déploration, car ce qui l'intéresse, c'est de saisir les répercussions du séisme sur la vie quotidienne, c'est de fixer le moment où les choses communes de l'existence basculent soudainement dans le chaos.

---

67. 'Pour moi, je ne veux ni raisonner, ni réformer, ni critiquer, ni instruire. Je radote pour moi-même et pour l'unique plaisir de radoter', écrivait Marchand dans *Mon Radotage* (p.2-3).

Marchand s'amuse. Comme d'autres *minores* de son temps, il considère que la littérature est un divertissement;[68] il est donc inutile de chercher de nobles justifications à ce qui est et doit demeurer un jeu. Si Marchand s'est plu toute sa vie à imaginer d'originales plaisanteries, différents projets, même en apparence les plus humbles, émaillent sa démarche. Au siècle de Voltaire, siècle philosophique s'il en fût, mais aussi très polyphonique ainsi que l'a déjà montré Theodore E. D. Braun à partir d'un tout autre exemple,[69] Marchand s'affiche comme un moraliste du quotidien.[70] Ce qui n'apparaissait tout d'abord que comme un jeu anodin, l'invention – ou du moins l'exploitation – du personnage d'André, permettait certes des situations cocasses et d'habiles jeux de mots; mais au fil de sa plume, la perruque devient une figure morale. L'ingéniosité de Marchand, un talent que tous ses contemporains lui reconnaissaient, provient précisément de son aisance à trouver des syllepses exploitables à volonté, qui sont signifiantes au sens propre comme au figuré.[71]

Toutefois, ces considérations demeureraient disparates si elles ne s'articulaient autour d'un pivot central. Marchand a, toute sa vie, dialogué avec Voltaire par l'intermédiaire de ses ouvrages. C'est le cas du *Tremblement de terre de Lisbonne*. Mais au lieu d'écrire une critique théorique de ses œuvres,[72] ou de procéder à une transposition vers à vers de son poème sur le mode burlesque, il opère à un autre niveau, et c'est là son originalité. En changeant de registre, des allusions au 'désastre de Lisbonne' se disséminent dans sa pièce,[73] faisant éclater le genre tragique.

---

68. Il notait ainsi dans ses 'Réflexions de l'auteur' en tête des *Giboulées de l'hiver* (Genève et Paris, J.-Fr. Bastien et Guillot, 1782): 'j'avais aussitôt écrit une lettre en vers qu'en prose. Je ne la relisais pas, et je n'aspirais qu'à dérider mon front et celui de mes amis' (p.43).

69. T. E. D. Braun, *Un Ennemi de Voltaire, Le Franc de Pompignan* (Paris 1972), p.6-7.

70. Voir sur ce point notre article sur 'L'avocat Marchand, ou le regard d'un homme du dix-huitième siècle sur son temps', dans 'Images of the eighteenth century', éd. Edward Nye, *SVEC* 2004:07, p.99-110.

71. C'est ainsi que l'apparition du perruquier, personnage qui surgit de manière parfaitement saugrenue dans la scène vi de l'acte V, ne manifeste pas seulement une manie vaniteuse d'un écrivain d'occasion campant les grands auteurs et faisant rire. Elle est surtout symbolique. Voir *L'Encyclopédie perruquière*, p.6-7: 'La nature ne m'a point départi cette abondance de bons dons qu'elle vous a prodigués, écrit le coiffeur au perruquier, cependant j'espère que je passerai ainsi que vous pour un homme de tête, avec la différence cependant que vous en meublez utilement l'intérieur, et que je me borne à en orner agréablement la superficie.'

72. Marchand écrivait ainsi, dans l'Homme agréable', in *Les Giboulées de l'hiver*, p.12: 'Ami, la raison nous attriste; / C'est une sombre coloriste; / Et le meilleur de mes secrets / Est de ne réfléchir jamais.'

73. Les citations en épigraphes sur le 'carrosse' renvoient ainsi à deux conceptions différentes du progrès. Voir sur ce point notre article déjà cité sur 'L'avocat Marchand, ou le regard d'un homme du dix-huitième siècle sur son temps', p.99-110. L'exclamation de M. Du Pont où il se compare à 'une punaise' (acte V scène vi) renvoie à la fourmilière de Voltaire. Par ailleurs, les mauvaises odeurs qui ont permis à maître André de composer sa tragédie, et sans lesquelles il n'aurait jamais écrit son chef-d'œuvre (voir la préface), montrent ici, comme chez l'illustre auteur, qu'il faut 'Un petit mal pour un grand bien.'

A défaut d'avoir un fusil,[74] Marchand fait donc ici *d'une pierre deux coups*. S'il prend, en tout, le contre-pied des choix de l'illustre poète-philosophe, il n'en partage pas moins avec son modèle un même tour d'esprit 'à la française', par un art du dialogue spirituel reposant sur la politesse et la gaieté.[75] Voltaire est bien sa cible, mais il l'est ici en tant qu'auteur officiel affectionnant le ton solennel; les poèmes de circonstance et les genres nobles sont dénoncés ici pour ce qu'ils ont d'inutile et de caduque. C'est bien des pratiques littéraires de certains de ses contemporains dont Marchand s'amuse en écrivant une pièce ridicule; il n'est pas interdit de penser qu'il vise aussi les Le Brun ou les Le Franc. Ainsi, la catastrophe de 1755 fournit à Marchand le prétexte tragique à une réflexion critique sur l'art dramatique du temps, faisant de sa pièce un texte littéraire énergique toujours intéressant.

S. Menant rappelle, dans *La Chute d'Icare*, qu'une contribution de Voltaire sur l'actualité était 'immédiatement mise hors de pair par le public'.[76] 'La situation de Voltaire' n'en est pas moins souvent 'celle d'un suiveur qui cherche, étape après étape, à s'adapter aux transformations de la mode', voulant plaire à ses lecteurs par des pratiques qu'il perfectionnait peut-être plus qu'il ne les inventait.[77] Marchand est toujours du nombre de ses admirateurs; mais il propose à l'occasion, et avec succès, des variations plaisantes sur les événements que Voltaire a décidé de traiter sérieusement. Il met alors les rieurs de son côté, jusqu'à ce que Voltaire contre-attaque. Soulignant, tel un nouveau Démocrite, qu'un philosophe doit rire de tout, le philosophe des Délices donnait bientôt une nouvelle version du tremblement de terre, mais traité cette fois plaisamment et avec ironie, dans *Candide*.[78]

---

74. Allusion à l'étude de Jean Starobinski intitulée 'Le fusil à deux coups de Voltaire', in *Le Remède dans le mal* (Paris 1989), p.123-163.

75. Sur les pratiques comparées de Marchand et de Voltaire, voir notre 'Plaidoyer pour un avocat oublié', dans *Voltairomania*, p.7-20. En jouant le perruquier, ce sont surtout les travers de Voltaire qui sont épinglés.

76. S. Menant, *La Chute d'Icare* (Genève 1981), p.288.

77. S. Menant, introduction à son édition critique des *Contes en vers et en prose* de Voltaire, i.xx.

78. On pourra ainsi mettre en parallèle la tempête dans laquelle Candide est pris avant d'atteindre Lisbonne, au début du chapitre 5, et ses exclamations d'impuissance à la fin du chapitre 6, avec la dernière scène de la tragédie de Marchand où M. Du Pont décrit l'engloutissement du vaisseau; d'autre part, l'entrée dans Lisbonne de Candide peut être rapprochée de l'arrivée du Comte à Constantinople, à l'acte III (*Candide*, éd. R. Pomeau, dans Voltaire, *OC*, 1980, t.48, p.134, 135 et 139-40).

CATRIONA SETH

Pour Marie-Emmanuelle Plagnol-Diéval

'Je ne pourrai pas en faire le récit': le tremblement de terre de Lisbonne vu par Le Brun, Marchand et Genlis

> Le péril passé, où est le poète qui pleurera digne-
> ment sur les cendres de la capitale? Le tremblement
> de Lisbonne, qui n'a duré que quelques minutes, a
> produit plus d'actions fortes que toute la durée des
> siècles n'a produit de belles pages. Voilà Lisbonne
> renversée, et la nature entière est restée stupide et
> muette sur ses décombres.
>
> Diderot, Lettre à Mme d'Epinay [?][1]

ENORME, barbare et sauvage, le tremblement de terre du 1er novembre 1755 l'a certainement été. Il a suscité, chacun le sait, le long 'Poème sur le désastre de Lisbonne' ainsi que des pages célèbres de *Candide*. Mais Voltaire n'est pas le seul Français à avoir écrit à sa façon le terrible événement dans le cadre de textes littéraires. Je voudrais interroger brièvement les œuvres de trois auteurs dans trois genres différents, Le Brun pour la poésie, Marchand pour le théâtre et Mme de Genlis pour la fiction narrative. Leurs évocations de la catastrophe de Lisbonne obéissent, nous le verrons, à des motivations très différentes.

Plus encore que Voltaire, Le Brun a des raisons d'être ému par le cataclysme qui s'est abattu sur la péninsule ibérique le 1er novembre 1755. Le tremblement de terre a été suivi d'un raz-de-marée et deux cents personnes ont péri dans la rade de Cadix. Parmi elles se trouvait l'un de ses proches, le petit-fils du dramaturge Racine et fils du poète Louis Racine.[2] Le Brun avait salué le départ de son camarade dans une ode intitulée 'A mon ami, le jeune Racine, partant pour Cadix, et quittant les

---

1. [novembre 1770?], *Correspondance*, éd. Georges Roth (Paris 1963), x.178-79. Je modernise tous les textes que je cite.

2. Ce dernier, profondément influencé par le jansénisme, évoque avec résignation au détour d'un de ses poèmes religieux la mort de ce fils unique: 'Dieu me l'avait donné, Dieu me l'a ôté. Oui, Dieu me l'a ôté...'. Un autre poète, Le Franc de Pompignan, a également adressé à Louis Racine des vers sur la mort de son fils. En mai 1756, l'on lit dans le *Mercure de France*, p.78-82, l''Ode de M. Le Franc à M. Racine, sur la mort de son fils'. Theodore E. D. Braun étudie les réactions contrastées de Le Franc et de Voltaire au tremblement de terre de Lisbonne au sein de ce recueil. Voir p.145-55 du présent volume.

Muses pour le Commerce'.[3] A l'annonce de la mort du jeune homme, il reprend sa plume. Je voudrais évoquer les deux poèmes concernant directement le désastre qui figurent dans ses œuvres. Le premier, dans l'ordre de l'édition, s'intitule 'Sur la ruine de Lisbonne' (I, ix), le second, publié pour la première fois dès 1755, 'Sur les causes physiques des tremblements de terre, et sur la mort du jeune Racine' (II, xviii).[4] Toutes deux sont des odes écrites selon le schéma malherbien en dizains d'octosyllabes. La première, avec ses plus de deux cents vers, commence en accusant la capitale portugaise d'orgueil, voyant dans la catastrophe naturelle un châtiment divin pour sa superbe. L'autre est plus une déploration sur les malheurs de la terre qui aboutit à un vain appel au salut du jeune Racine. Dans toutes deux, le langage de Le Brun est noble et vigoureux. Il s'agit de dire le malheur de l'homme et son impuissance face à la divinité ou aux forces naturelles.

La première des deux odes, son titre l'indique, s'intéresse au sort de la ville qui fut l'épicentre du tremblement de terre. La catastrophe n'est cependant pas évoquée avant la sixième strophe. Est mis en avant, en revanche, dès le départ, l'hubris de l'homme, du 'mortel superbe', face à une nature qu'il ne saurait contrôler. Voici le premier dizain:

> L'orgueilleux s'est dit à lui-même:
> Je suis le Dieu de l'Univers.
> Mon front est ceint du Diadème;
> J'enchaîne à mes pieds les revers.
> Mes Palais couvrent les montagnes;
> Mon peuple inonde les campagnes;
> La Volupté sert mes festins;
> Les feux brûlent pour ma vengeance:
> L'Onde et les Vents d'intelligence,
> Livrent la Terre à mes destins.

Celui qui se prenait pour un colosse n'est qu'une 'folle argile' et doit tomber. La force du poète est de le montrer avant de dresser face à lui un Dieu Tout-Puissant qui le condamne – et qui, par extension, a châtié Lisbonne. Des échos de passages de l'Ancien Testament surgissent à la lecture de l'évocation de cette puissance:

> Il est un Dieu qui t'environne;
> Son Empire est l'Immensité:
> Il ne doit qu'à lui sa couronne;
> Et son règne est l'Eternité.

3. Ode XIII du livre I (i.38-43 de l'édition posthume des *Œuvres* de Le Brun procurée par Ginguené chez Warée en 1811).

4. La première ode occupe les p.25-32 et la seconde les p.133-39 du tome i de l'édition citée. Conlon signale que l''Ode sur le tremblement de terre arrivé à Lisbonne le premier novembre 1755' a été publiée à Lunéville chez C. F. Messuy sans date dès 1755 et que l'année suivante a vu paraître une réédition intitulée *Odes sur Lisbonne et sur les causes physiques des tremblemens de terre de 1755* (La Haye et Paris). Nous n'avons pu consulter l'ouvrage dont le seul exemplaire répertorié se trouve à Besançon.

Lisbonne, la 'fille du Tage', serait un avatar du mortel orgueilleux, une 'superbe reine des mers' dont les 'vaisseaux impériaux' lui permettent de réclamer le tribut des 'ondes amères' de l'océan et des terres lointaines. Or ce port fier de son commerce a été frappé d'une punition atroce. Le Brun l'appelle:

> Ville superbe et malheureuse,
> De trésors de gloire amoureuse

et revient sur son 'orgueil'. Si ce poème-ci ne prétend pas faire état des causes du tremblement de terre, il en fournit pourtant une analyse morale. Lisbonne aurait été détruite car elle méritait ce sort. Trois strophes sont entièrement consacrées à la description de l'événement en lui-même. Des présages affreux annoncent l'imminence d'une catastrophe. Le dernier soleil qui éclaire la ville 'Pâlit sous des voiles sanglants', les flots de la mer et du Tage, jusqu'alors alliés de Lisbonne, insultent au rivage ou se révoltent.[5] Le Brun a recours aux personnages de la fable pour donner au désastre une portée quasi exemplaire. L'instant fatal aurait été précipité par 'les fières Destinées' et le signal de la chute de Lisbonne serait 'Le cri des Parques mutinées'. Alors, les éléments, ceux que l'homme prétendait contrôler, envahissent l'espace du poème et de la ville impuissante:

> Au bruit des Ondes qui mugissent,
> Des noirs Tourbillons qui frémissent,
> Des Vents dans les airs déchaînés,
> Murs, Tours, Palais, tremblent, s'écroulent;
> Leurs débris se heurtent et roulent
> Sur tes Habitants consternés.

Une adresse à la Ville, par le tutoiement, nous conduit à tous nous considérer comme impliqués, comme susceptibles, du moins, d'avoir les mêmes torts que Lisbonne – la première strophe nous invitait déjà à envisager notre humaine condition. L'accumulation de noms sans déterminants représentent les constructions les plus solides – 'Murs, Tours, Palais' – indique bien que l'individu, décrit plus haut, je l'ai dit, comme une 'folle argile', ne saurait résister à un tel choc. Dans la strophe suivante, Le Brun emploie à nouveau la figure de style de l'accumulation. Il la redouble à la fin d'un vers puis au début du suivant ce qui donne, à première lecture, l'impression d'un enjambement. La structure métrique de ces deux vers fonctionne en chiasme (3/5 – 5/3). L'écho qui unit 'Tout

---

5. Précédée de l'indication 'C'est un Portugais qui parle' et attribuée à M. A. La. La. A Bord, une 'Ode sur les tremblements de terre arrivés à Lisbonne' propose également l'image des mers autrefois domptées: 'Entrant dans le canal du Tage, / Les mers venaient nous rendre hommage, / Et baiser humblement nos bords: / A travers leurs dociles ondes, / Nos flottes aux bouts des deux mondes / Allaient recueillir nos trésors'. Plus loin, le poète ajoute un tour similaire aux 'voiles sanglants' du soleil de Le Brun: 'Déjà, déjà ce jour perfide, / Que la mort s'était destiné, / Lançait sa lumière homicide / Sur ce pays infortuné' (*Mercure de France*, juin 1756, p.6).

périt' en ouverture du distique à 'tout s'éteint' en clôture montre bien qu'il n'est nulle possibilité d'échapper à l'affreux destin:

> Tout périt: arts, beauté, courage;
> Rang, sexe, âge, espoir, tout s'éteint.

Lisbonne, ville caractérisée par sa situation en bord de mer, à l'embouchure d'un fleuve, associée donc à l'eau, devient la proie des flammes, de l'élément inverse. Les repères, en particulier ceux qu'offre la nature, disparaissent:

> La Flamme ondoyante, insensée,
> Du sein des palais élancée
> Roule dans les Cieux obscurcis:
> Et la cendre épaisse et brûlante
> S'élève en nue étincelante
> Que percent d'effroyables cris.

Terre et ciel, cendre et mer se confondent. Les victimes ne sont que cris. Après ces images d'apocalypse, Le Brun change de perspective. Il ramène notre regard du sort de la ville à celui d'un individu. L'image de la flamme revient, sous forme de métaphore filée. Il s'agit alors de dépeindre la passion d'un amant qui a pu épouser celle qu'il aime à la veille du désastre. Des temps du passé introduisent l'anecdote pour bien nous montrer qu'elle est finie mais le poète actualise sa narration en passant par le présent de l'indicatif. Il feint de s'adresser au jeune homme pour lui prédire ce que l'avenir pensera de son sort tragique:

> Toi, dont la touchante aventure
> Consacra ces moments d'horreurs,
> Jeune Amant, la Race future
> Sur ton sort répandra des pleurs.
> Déjà ta Flamme impatiente
> Revolait au sein d'une amante
> Qu'un Père accorde à tes soupirs;
> Déjà tu vois cette journée
> Où le flambeau de l'Hyménée
> S'allume au feu de tes désirs.

Le deuxième tutoiement, après celui adressé à Lisbonne, nous invite à voir l'individu et la ville confondus dans une même horreur. L'anecdote suscite pourtant la sympathie pour le jeune homme et les siens. Un bref passage idyllique nous fait pénétrer dans l'intimité des amants dont la 'brûlante ivresse' trouve 'la nuit promise à leurs feux' longue à venir. C'est l'occasion de souhaiter une autre fin à l'histoire, d'implorer la 'Nuit trop fatale!' de reculer, l'Amour de protéger le sommeil des nouveaux mariés. Un vers, au rythme croissant (3/5), nous fait basculer de l'idylle à l'horreur en désignant de deux façons différentes le jeune homme: 'Tendre Epoux! Amant déplorable!' Le second adjectif nous invite à plaindre celui qui a péri. Après la vision d'ensemble de la catastrophe que Le Brun nous

avait livrée plus haut, il propose de nous la faire voir à échelle individuelle, de l'intérieur, en quelque sorte. 'Les voûtes s'ébranlent,
s'entr'ouvrent'. Il ne s'agit pas simplement de dire l'écroulement des murs
vus de loin, mais bien de remarquer que 'La Mer roule sur les lambris' de
la chambre nuptiale. Nous suivons le jeune homme qui court pour retrouver son épouse:

> ses pas, son cœur, sa vue
> La cherchent parmi les débris.

Le Brun inclut une nouvelle péripétie: une 'barque errante' s'offre aux
amants pour fuir aux 'bords étrangers'. L'Amour ne craint pas le danger.
Par ailleurs, 'L'Espoir, la Voile se déploie'. L'association entre le sentiment et l'objet n'est pas dénuée d'efficacité: le lecteur se prend à compter
sur une fin heureuse 'Mais l'Onde rappelle sa proie'. Un gouffre s'ouvre
devant le couple qui:

> jaloux d'expirer ensemble,
> [...] y tombe en s'embrassant.

Après avoir ému son lecteur par cette histoire individuelle touchante,
Le Brun reprend sa déploration plus générale et son tutoiement s'adresse
une fois de plus à Lisbonne. Ce n'est plus la ville superbe de la veille. Ses
remparts ont disparu. Flammes et eaux se livrent des combats dans les
ruines. Tout est brisé. Tout périt:

> Du jeune époux la Veuve expire;
> Le Vieillard fuit, tombe, soupire,
> Et meurt sur ses fils écrasés!

L'horreur ne peut être dite. Le Brun change une fois de plus d'angle de
vision en nous montrant le retour du Roi du Portugal qui, absent de
Lisbonne, 'Revolait vers ces murs chéris' lorsque la catastrophe a frappé.
Il est 'plein d'un trouble funeste' et, à son arrivée, entouré de quelques
rescapés misérables, il entend des cris: 'Elle n'est plus!' Le pronom n'a pas
d'antécédent grammatical au sein de la strophe. Nous comprenons
cependant bien que c'est de Lisbonne qu'il s'agit. Aucune parole ne
saurait décrire le spectacle, seul le 'silence peint ses malheurs' et l'œil du
roi s'égare 'sur Lisbonne disparue'. Le Brun décrit encore l'horreur du
lendemain de la catastrophe, des besoins, du manque de nourriture, des
plaintes. Il termine sur deux strophes grandioses. La première résume le
sort de la ville et joue sur les temps verbaux pour montrer implicitement
un avant et un après:

> Tu fus, Lisbonne, ô sort barbare!
> Tu n'es plus que dans nos regrets!

Peuple et palais, tout a disparu dans un gouffre 'avare'. La mort et
l'horreur peuplent désormais une solitude atroce et Lisbonne entière est

comme un vaste corps mort qui doit servir d'avertissement aux générations futures:

> Un jour les Siècles, en silence,
> Planant sur ton Cadavre immense,
> Frémiront encor de Terreur.

La dernière strophe change de registre mais rend plus touchante ou du
moins plus immédiate la scène d'horreur. L'exemple est tiré de la nature.
Loin de Lisbonne, Le Brun évoque pour nous un arbre altier, un:

> sapin, dont les ombrages
> Couronnaient la Cime des Monts.

Frappé par la foudre, il tombe et disparaît. Le topos de l'arbre foudroyé,
image plus lisible pour certains que la vision infernale des éléments
déchaînés, clôt le poème et inscrit le passé glorieux de Lisbonne ainsi que
le bonheur éphémère de ses habitants dans notre souvenir:

> Les forêts voisines
> Redisent longtemps aux collines
> Sa chute et la fureur des Cieux:
> Les Vents en dissipent la poudre;
> La seule trace de la foudre
> Le rappelle encore à nos yeux.

L'ode est extrêmement réussie. Le langage vigoureux du poète lui
permet d'avoir recours à plusieurs registres. L'un des aspects remarquables du poème, absent aussi bien de la tragédie de Marchand que de
la nouvelle de Mme de Genlis, est cette variété d'angles de vision qui nous
permet de passer d'une réflexion métaphysique à l'expérience de l'amant
pris dans la tourmente ou à la souffrance du roi retrouvant sa capitale
détruite. On peut se demander si le jansénisme de la famille Racine
n'explique pas, en partie, l'espèce de résignation de Le Brun dans cette
réaction initiale à la catastrophe. Il va changer de point de vue dans sa
seconde ode, celle qui rappelle le sort de son ami Racine. Dans une
tentative de compréhension de l'événement, il y interroge en effet les lois
de la géographie physique.

Bien que son ami soit mort à Cadix, Le Brun évoque dans cette
déploration Lisbonne, l'épicentre du désastre, puis l'étendue des ondes de
choc qui se sont propagées. La première des seize strophes, plutôt que
de se concentrer sur un langage biblique comme la précédente ode, rejoint
la poésie scientifique du temps. Il ne s'agit plus de dire un homme
orgueilleux puni par la divinité, mais de rappeler que le soufre est
'l'aliment du tonnerre' ou qu'à l'intérieur de la terre grondent 'Des sels,
des nitres, du bitume' dont le mélange:

> Fait tonner les cieux sur nos têtes,
> Et mugir l'enfer sous nos pas.

Le Brun rappelle la majesté et l'horreur de la nature. Il s'attarde en particulier sur les volcans, 'Peuple de géants en fureur', dans les flancs desquels bouillonne l'enfer, et qui ravagent les villes jetant:

> de leur bouche foudroyante
> [...] la flamme et la terreur.

Le zeugme est efficace à dire la réalité et sa conséquence. Dieu n'apparaît qu'à la quatrième strophe, comme régisseur des différents changements de l'aspect de la terre. Les éléments en furie se déchaînent:

> Tout naît; tout meurt; tout doit renaître;
> Tout perd la forme de son être,
> Frêle ouvrage des éléments:
> La nature active et féconde,
> Sans cesse reproduit le monde,
> Eternel dans ses changements.

Rien ne saurait résister, 'mer, peuple, rivage' – et on note la place de l'homme entre eaux et terre – subissent la même loi. Pour mieux enraciner ses propos dans une réalité connue de tous, Le Brun avait cité les noms de deux volcans. Viennent ensuite ceux de quatre villes disparues dans des cataclysmes naturels:

> Smyrne, Pompéiane, Héraclée,
> Et toi, Lima, ville des rois.

Ils annoncent le sort de la cinquième ville nommée, Lisbonne, à laquelle, ici encore, le poète s'adresse par un tutoiement.

Afin de montrer la propagation des effets de la catastrophe sur des villes éloignées, en particulier Cadix, Le Brun consacre une strophe à la théorie de la tectonique des plaques, le détachement progressif de terres autrefois reliées entre elles, la France et Albion ou encore l'Espagne et l'Afrique. Les ondes de choc parties de Lisbonne ont été ressenties ailleurs, aux 'îles de Gérion' ou encore:

> De l'Ebre aux sables de Carthage,
> De l'Afrique aux champs d'Albion.

Ici encore eau et feu s'unissent pour semer un désordre terrible. Déchaînés, les éléments semblent engendrer des créatures chimériques et incontrôlables:

> Les deux mers s'appellent, s'unissent;
> Leurs flots se heurtent et mugissent
> Couverts de monstres bondissants;
> Et, du sein des ondes fumantes,
> Le gouffre des mers écumantes
> Vomit la flamme des volcans.

L'univers paraît s'écrouler. Foudre et naufrages guettent les humains. De l'Irlande aux colonnes d'Hercule, la mer se déchaîne. Le nom de la ville dans laquelle le jeune Racine a péri arrive enfin: la 'vague rapide' de l'onde bondissante va 'De Cadix noyer les remparts'. Les quatre dernières strophes s'éloignent de la description de l'événement à l'échelle du continent pour s'attarder sur la mort de l'ami de Le Brun. Pour amener l'évocation de cet accident, raison d'écriture et sujet véritable du poème, nous avons une invocation aux flots en colère:

> Toi, qui grondes sur ces rivages,
> Mer! si tu connais la pitié,
> Epargne au moins dans tes ravages
> L'objet de ma tendre amitié.

Le poète rappelle qu'il a passé sa jeunesse avec cet ami. Tous deux ont été tentés par la poésie. Le sort du jeune Racine paraît incompréhensible; c'est un 'destin bizarre' fomenté par une 'divinité barbare' qui arrache le jeune homme des bras des muses. Dans une strophe très réussie, la ponctuation – de nombreux points de suspension ou d'exclamation – accompagne une irruption du présent de l'indicatif. Nous avons l'impression d'assister à la scène. Un effet d'hypotypose nous rend présent le jeune Racine et le poète s'adresse à lui avant de constater sa disparition et d'en appeler à l'ancêtre célèbre[6] et aux divinités tutélaires du jeune homme:

> Reviens… la mer s'élance… Arrête!
> Vois, crains, fuis ces flots suspendus!
> Ils retombent!… Dieux! la tempête
> L'entraîne à mes yeux éperdus.
> Divin Racine! ombre immortelle!
> Ton fils… il expire, il t'appelle;
> Volez! sa bouche vous implore;
> Toi, déesse plus chère encore,
> Amitié! vole à son secours.

Le rythme saccadé est à l'image de celui des flots qui avancent et se retirent. Un temps, le poète semble suspendre l'issue terrible et imaginer une destinée héroïque pour son ami; l'emploi du futur de l'indicatif l'indique assez. La proposition suivante amène le doute avec son 'si' hypothétique:

> Quels lauriers ceindront sa jeunesse,
> S'il peut vaincre un destin jaloux!

Hélas, ni les 'vertus' du fils Racine, ni la 'tendresse' de Le Brun ne suffisent. Comme Hippolyte, dans la *Phèdre* de son grand-père, le jeune homme périt victime de flots déchaînés et la parque semble regretter de l'avoir pris:

---

6. 'Divin Racine' et la désignation 'ombre immortelle' montrent que, malgré l'indication 'fils', c'est du dramaturge Jean Racine, grand-père de la victime, et non du poète Louis Racine, son père, qu'il s'agit.

> [elle] détourne ses yeux sanglants;
> Ses yeux même en versent des larmes.[7]

Les qualités de la victime rendent sa perte terrible:

> Les amours regrettent ses charmes;
> Et les arts pleurent ses talents.

Le poème se fait alors déploration comme les épigrammes antiques. Ce n'est pas aux néréides, divinités de la mer, mais aux muses qui président aux arts, de recueillir les restes chéris flétris par l'onde et la parque, 'triste et précieux débris'. La fin du poème est une adresse au défunt par-delà les frontières de la vie et de la mort:

> Et toi, dont j'adore la cendre,
> Si tes mânes daignaient entendre
> Des chants consacrés à ta mort,
> Que, pénétrant la rive sombre,
> L'amitié console ton ombre
> Des injustes rigueurs du sort.

Nous avons l'impression de renouer avec les poèmes de l'*Anthologie palatine*. Le jeune Racine rejoint tous ceux qui, morts avant l'heure, n'ont pu tenir leurs promesses. On mesure ici encore le talent du poète qui réussit à passer du général au particulier et de nous intéresser – au sens qu'il aurait donné à ce mot lui-même – au sort de son ami.

Le Brun met en scène dans les deux textes un véritable feu d'artifice verbal. C'est un excellent poète. Entre langage biblique et poésie scientifique, ses odes déploient une vigueur d'imagerie et une variété de tons remarquables. Il réussit à naviguer entre constatations générales et déplorations particulières, suscitant chez son lecteur une admiration horrifiée face aux prodiges de la nature, un sentiment de compassion pour les victimes. Si la première ode offrait une fiction, celle de l'histoire des amants noyés, dans le cadre d'une évocation des causes morales du désastre, la seconde raconte la mort tragique d'un ami du poète en se fondant sur des réalités naturelles.

La première des deux odes de Le Brun s'appuie sur le cas de nouveaux mariés pour nous faire ressentir l'horreur de la catastrophe; le deuxième auteur du corpus se sert, lui aussi, de l'événement malheureux du tremblement de terre pour évoquer le bonheur impossible de deux fiancés. Les parallèles s'arrêtent là. *Le Tremblement de terre de Lisbonne*, attribué au perruquier Maître André, mais dû à Jean-Henri Marchand, publié sous

---

7. On lit, dans le *Mercure*, en avril 1756, p.35, des 'Vers au grand Racine sur la mort du jeune Racine, arrivée à Cadix en novembre 1755' de Le Marié dans lesquels ce parallèle est tracé: 'Quand d'Hyppolite [*sic*] ton pinceau / Crayonnait la triste aventure, / Racine, où prenais-tu les traits de ce tableau, / Le triomphe de la nature? / Ah! de l'avenir en ton cœur / Se peignait l'image touchante, / Et du dernier des tiens ta main tendre et savante, / Sous un nom emprunté, nous traçait le malheur.'

l'adresse fictive de 'Lisbonne, imprimerie du public, 1755',[8] est une tragédie[9] dans laquelle les deux fiancés, héros de l'intrigue, Théodora et le
comte périssent lors de la catastrophe comme tout leur entourage alors
même que le ton goguenard de la pièce laissait espérer une fin heureuse.

La pièce, imprimée plusieurs fois,[10] est attribuée par son auteur à maître André, perruquier. La tragédie est précédée d'une lettre à Voltaire
qui est, bien entendu, un canular. S'adressant à son 'cher confrère', le
'très humble et affectionné serviteur' André s'y présente comme 'un
écolier novice dans l'Art de la Poésie qui s'hasarde à vous dédier son
premier ouvrage'. Il se dit admiratif des 'pompeux ouvrages' que Voltaire
a mis et met 'journellement au jour' et espère obtenir 'un clin d'œil' du
maître. Il ajoute encore ceci: 'Si de votre support vous daignez me
favoriser, je me promets, que franc de toute crainte, je publierai sans cesse
vos louanges, et je rendrai témoignage en tous lieux combien je vous suis
redevable de l'avoir agréé' (2). Une deuxième lettre exploite encore la
veine comique. Elle est adressée, en français, par un Anglais, Cotweyn, à
l'auteur. Elle contient des éloges très flatteurs d'un texte que l'épistolier
ne connaît pas: 'On dit que vous avez fait une tragédie admirable sur le
tremblement de terre de Lisbonne. Je suis très persuadé qu'elle aura le
succès le plus brillant. On m'en a rapporté quelques traits.' Citant en
particulier 'la scène pathétique du couteau' et le 'beau récit du cinquième
acte' (4), Cotweyn demande un exemplaire de la pièce pour la faire
traduire. Les deux lettres se moquent de tout l'appareil des épîtres dédicatoires et pièces documentaires. Elles annoncent au lecteur qu'il est face
à un texte burlesque. La lettre à Voltaire laisse entendre que l'ouvrage,

8. Conlon signale que la tragédie a été faussement attribuée à Jean-Baptiste Paris de
Meyzieu et à Du Coin, son secrétaire, par Joseph de La Porte, *La France littéraire, ou
Dictionnaire des auteurs françois vivans, corrigé et augmenté par M. Formey* (Berlin 1757), iii(3).216
et renvoie à Antoine-Alexandre Barbier, *Dictionnaire des ouvrages anonymes* (Hildesheim
1963), iv.817, et Jean-Marie Quérard, *Les Supercheries littéraires* (Paris 1869-1870), i.346.
Nous citons d'après *La Tragédie de maître André perruquier, ou le Tremblement de terre de Lisbonne,
tragédie en cinq actes et en grands vers, de toutes mesures*, telle que le célèbre M. André, Perruquier, l'a composée et offerte aux Comédiens français (Paris, Fages, an XIII [1805]). Les
numéros de page entre parenthèses revoient à cette édition. L'édition procurée par Anne-
Sophie Barrovecchio au sein de Jean-Henri Marchand, *Voltairomania, L'avocat Jean-Henri
Marchand face à Voltaire*, Coll. 'Lire le Dix-huitième siècle' (Saint-Etienne 2004), apporte des
précisions additionnelles. Voir également, au sein de ce volume, son article 'A propos de
Voltaire, de maître André et du *Tremblement de terre de Lisbonne*: histoire d'une supercherie
tragique de l'avocat Jean-Henri Marchand', p.156-72.

9. CESAR (http://www.cesar.org.uk), la précieuse base de données créée par Barry
Russell, ne donne pas d'indication que la pièce aurait été jouée. Une note MS de
l'exemplaire de Vivienne Mylne, conservé à la Taylorian Library affirme ceci:
'non représentée / V. Léris p. 434'. Anne-Sophie Barrovecchio ('A propos de Voltaire',
p.163) précise que la pièce a été jouée en 1805.

10. Signalons, en plus de l'édition originale et de celle que nous citons *Le Tremblement de
terre de Lisbonne, tragédie, en cinq actes et en vers*, par M. André, perruquier privilégié,
demeurant à Paris, rue de la Vannerie, près la Grève (Amsterdam 1756). CESAR indique
par ailleurs l'existence d'une parodie de la pièce, *Les Muses artisanes ou l'auteur perruquier* de
Quétant, BNF MS FR 9269.

comme tant d'autres de Marchand, s'inscrit en marge des écrits du grand homme et, en l'occurrence, témoigne ici indirectement de la célébrité du 'Poème sur le désastre de Lisbonne'.

La scène, au défi de la règle des unités, va de Lisbonne à Constantinople. Cela permet d'inclure des personnages aussi divers qu'un grand corrégidor portugais et qu'un garçon coiffeur, un muphti ou un eunuque. L'intrigue est simple: le comte et Théodora s'aiment. Le père du jeune homme a prévu d'unir son fils à une jeune femme fortunée et de plus haute naissance que Théodora; le père de celle-ci, Dom Pedro, projette de la marier au riche Lavaros, neveu de l'Inquisiteur. Le comte est envoyé à Constantinople pour l'éloigner de sa dulcinée. Secouru après un naufrage par la fille du muphti, il doit résister à ses avances après avoir accepté son argent. Dupont, son confident, lui dit ainsi (p.26):

> Mademoiselle Muphty de vous est amoureuse,
> Et veut vous épouser en fille vertueuse.

Les deux hommes se voient forcés de fuir Constantinople pour éviter la rage du muphti. Entre temps, Lavaros apprend à Théodora que son père consent à ce qu'il l'épouse et que le comte a péri dans un naufrage. Dom Pedro le confirme et Théodora s'apprête à se suicider. Mais, coup de théâtre, le comte et Dupont arrivent sur ces entrefaites. Après de nombreuses péripéties, leurs pères acceptent l'union de Théodora et du comte. Leurs domestiques conviennent de se marier. Le tremblement de terre a lieu. Tous périssent.

Le ton est souvent railleur et les alexandrins en rimes plates accueillent par endroits des mots de style bas et des expressions familières, ce qui produit un effet comique immédiat. Lorsque le comte prévoit de retourner à Lisbonne malgré son père il dit ceci à Dupont pour légitimer sa conduite (p.29):

> si j'avais resté en ce lieu plus longtemps,
> L'on m'aurait empalé bien sûr, certainement.

La référence au supplice du pal provoque le rire plutôt que l'effroi avec le redoublement des tournures adverbiales. Lavaros, de son côté, tente de forcer Théodora d'accepter sa main (p.32):

> Allons, Théodora, ne vous entêtez pas,
> Consentez, je vous prie, aux ordres du Papa.

Rien n'y fait, La jeune fille tient à sa fidélité envers le comte (p.32):

> Vous avez tort, Monsieur, de vous époumoner,
> Pour, par vos beaux discours, mon Père m'étonner.

Les propos burlesques trouvent un écho dans un acte héroï-comique. Dom Pedro menace de déshériter sa fille au désespoir de sa suivante Thérèse qui interroge ainsi sa maîtresse (p.33):

Chère Théodora, qu'allons-nous devenir?
Sans père et sans amant, il vaut autant mourir.

La jeune femme prend un couteau et veut se suicider devant Lavaros qu'elle refuse. C'est alors qu'intervient le coup de théâtre du retour du comte et de Dupont.

Avant la réconciliation entre les deux familles, les pères s'opposent violemment. Rodrigues accuse Dom Pedro d'être la cause des malheurs de sa famille (p.38):

En voilà, pour mon fils, un qui est manifeste.
Il est dans un cachot, puant comme la peste.
Il n'y serait pas, si votre fille, en l'aimant,
Ne l'avait pas fourré dans tous ces beaux draps blancs.

Expressions éculées ou utilisées à contre-emploi, propos familiers, dictons déformés, alexandrins coupés au défi de l'hémistiche ('Il n'y serait pas, si votre fille, en l'aimant'), Marchand a recours à toutes les ressources du burlesque. Après d'autres épisodes invraisemblables, tout le monde se calme. Les deux unions sont décidées. Dupont, le domestique, appelle un perruquier qui vient le coiffer à la dernière mode – et offre au passage une explication de la raison pour laquelle la pièce est attribuée à maître André! Le coiffeur brûle le fiancé en le frisant. C'est la première indication que quelque chose est pourri au royaume du Portugal (p.42):

Excusez-moi, monsieur, je ne sais pas pourquoi,
Je tremble: assurément, tout me tremble sous moi.
Je ne sais pas non plus si c'est par vision,
Je crois voir remuer la chambre et la maison.

On le voit, nul effort ici pour convoquer une représentation de la puissance des forces naturelles, comme chez Le Brun. On ne peut sentir aucune compassion pour Dupont qui ne sait où fuir. En effet, tout est fait pour rendre la scène cocasse. Le domestique comprend qu'il va mourir et compare son sort à celui d'un insecte misérable (p.42):

Fallait-il sur le point que j'épouse Thérèse,
[que] Je me voie écrasé tout comme une punaise!'[11]

Les événements se précipitent, la didascalie de la scène vi, l'avant-dernière, en fait quelque chose de tout à fait spectaculaire: '*Le fond du théâtre tombe, on découvre la mer et un vaisseau dans le port*' (p.42). La représentation doit montrer ce que les mots ne disent guère: l'horreur et l'énormité. Là encore, la mer déchaînée se fait montagne puis gouffre. Tous les personnages sont noyés, sauf Dupont, à qui il revient de prononcer la dernière tirade avant d'être très certainement engouffré dans

11. A.-S. Barrovecchio souligne ('A propos de Voltaire', p.171) qu'il s'agit certainement d'une allusion burlesque à la fourmilière de Voltaire. Signalons la présence, dans le *Mercure de France* de juillet 1756 (p.43-44) d'une fable d'Aubert intitulée 'Tremblement de terre arrivé chez les fourmis'.

l'abîme.[12] Il dit qu'il se souviendra à jamais de son premier jour de noce... La catastrophe, au sens dramatique, est une catastrophe naturelle. Lisbonne est engloutie avec les personnages sans que le lecteur ne ressente aucune pitié.

Les œuvres de Marchand et de Le Brun paraissent s'opposer sur tous les points. Non seulement la question générique, mais encore la tonalité et l'attitude générale face à un événement tragique les séparent. Bénéficiant de plus de recul que les deux hommes, écrivant par ailleurs après la publication de *Candide* qui incluait, on le sait, une célèbre évocation du tremblement de terre de Lisbonne, Mme de Genlis propose, au sein des *Veillées du château*, un texte qui mérite d'être inclus dans notre corpus.[13] Sous-titré 'conte moral', *Alphonse et Dalinde, ou la Féerie de l'art et de la nature*, occupe plusieurs veillées.[14] Ainsi que l'indique le titre, le désastre de Lisbonne n'est pas au centre du propos. Il occupe en revanche une place essentielle parmi les merveilles et horreurs de la nature dont la découverte par Alphonse est l'un des principes structurants du récit. Ainsi que l'on peut s'y attendre – le texte est censé édifier le lecteur – le conte raconte l'éducation par la vie d'un jeune homme, le héros, Alphonse. A certains égards, le récit de Mme de Genlis est une réécriture de *Candide*. S'il fallait proposer un résumé par mots clefs, l'on inclurait probablement: bijoux, bons nègres, catastrophes naturelles, voyages... Nous avons un texte narratif contraire en tous points à la pièce de Marchand: le tremblement de terre est le début du conte qui se solde par la réunion des amants. Si la tragédie montre l'erreur de l'obstination des géniteurs qui seront forcés de se rendre à la raison des sentiments de leurs enfants, le conte représente une courbe d'apprentissage pour Alphonse comme pour son père et d'autres personnages secondaires qui servent de reflets à l'un ou à l'autre. A l'ouverture, nous apprenons qu'Alphonse est le fils de Dom Ramire, 'l'homme le plus riche et le plus puissant du

12. L''Ode sur les tremblements de terre arrivés à Lisbonne' donne, dans sa dernière strophe (*Mercure de France*, juin 1756, p.11), la parole au dernier survivant: 'Ta faux, ministre de ta haine, / Ô mort! n'épargne donc que moi! / Flamme immortelle et souterraine, / Je vis encor, rallume-toi. / Mer dévorante, qui t'arrête? / Ô Ciel! brise-toi sur ma tête, / Tombe, fond sur elle en éclats; / Et toi, grand Dieu, vengeur du crime, / Sauve ta dernière victime / De l'horreur de ne mourir pas.'

13. Angus Martin, Vivienne G. Mylne et Richard Frautschi, *Bibliographie du genre romanesque français 1751-1800* (London, Paris 1997), n° 99.3, p.424, indiquent l'existence d'un texte dont le seul exemplaire connu se trouve à Oron: *Alphonse, histoire portugaise, arrivée lors du tremblement de terre de Lisbonne* (Paris, Testu, an VII). Ils signalent quatre critiques: *Journal général*, ii.115; *Journal de Paris*, 15 floréal an VII; *Journal typographique*, 15 germinal an VII; *Magasin encyclopédique*, IV (1799), vi.569. Ils fournissent les indications suivantes: '3ᵉ personne, avec une lettre; Portugal, Amérique du Sud; Zulmé, Alphonse, Vestlar, Abarbanela; voyages, intrigue sentimentale, aventures (traite des nègres); ton sentimental et moralisateur.' L'ensemble paraît offrir quelques similitudes avec l'ouvrage de Mme de Genlis.

14. Sur *Alphonse et Dalinde*, on consultera avec profit l'article de Marie-Emmanuelle Plagnol-Diéval: 'Merveilleux ou rationnel: *Les Veillées du château* de Mme de Genlis', dans *Le Partage des savoirs XVIIIᵉ-XIXᵉ siècles*, éd. Lise Andries (Lyon 2003), p.151-62.

royaume' (p.209)[15] qui a réussi à faire carrière grâce à l'ambition et au goût de l'intrigue, malgré une naissance obscure. Le petit Alphonse est l'objet de 'la vile adulation' qui corrompt 'sa première jeunesse'. Son père, trop occupé, confie l'éducation du garçon à des maîtres 'de langues, d'histoire, de géographie, de mathématiques, de musique, de dessin' qui louent ses dispositions naturelles. Alors qu'il se contente d'effleurer des sujets sans importance, Alphonse est décrit par son entourage comme un prodige. Il croit les flatteurs et s'imagine 'profond géomètre, excellent physicien et grand chimiste' (p.210). Cette erreur sur ses propres talents se double d'une certitude inexacte sur ses propres origines. Son père a en effet entrepris de créer une généalogie qui fait remonter la famille à *Lusus*, le premier des Lusitains. Tous s'en gaussent, sauf son fils qui y croit.

A l'aube du 1er novembre 1755, l'on peut résumer ainsi les aspects paradoxaux du caractère du jeune homme: 'quoique enivré d'orgueil, plein d'ignorance, de présomption et de fatuité, gâté par le faste, la flatterie et la faveur, Alphonse n'était pas corrompu sans ressource'. En effet, son naturel est prometteur: 'Il avait du courage, un cœur sensible et de l'esprit.' Les hasards de la vie vont l'obliger à se fier à ces qualités car, comme l'indique l'auteur: 'L'inconstance de la fortune lui préparait la plus utile de toutes les leçons.' Dom Ramire est en train d'apprendre à Alphonse le revers de fortune qu'ils ont subi. En effet, il est ruiné suite à des intrigues. Il ne lui reste que son palais de Lisbonne qui contient encore des richesses immenses en tableaux, meubles, argenterie, et diamants. Les débuts du tremblement de terre se font sentir, on entend des cris, le plancher s'effondre, le mur s'écroule, les deux hommes sont séparés. Alphonse se retrouve au rez-de-chaussée dans le cabinet de son père. Il voit deux coffrets, l'un contenant des diamants, l'autres les titres de noblesse de la famille: 'Alphonse n'hésite pas; voulant du moins, dans ce désastre horrible, sauver ce qui lui paraît le plus précieux, il saisit la cassette où sont les papiers' (p.212). Il se sauve dans le jardin où il aperçoit son père. Mme de Genlis décrit ainsi le parcours du jeune homme: 'Le terrain qu'il parcourt, semblable à la mer agitée par une violente tempête, s'enfonce ou s'élève sous ses pas. Son oreille est frappée d'un bruit souterrain pareil au mugissement des vagues en furie se brisant contre des rochers.' Il:

chancelle, tombe, se relève, retombe encore, et ne pouvant se soutenir sur ses jambes, rampe, roule et se traîne avec effort. Il voit de tous côtés la terre se fendre et former de longs sillons, d'où s'élancent avec rapidité des feux étincelants qui s'élèvent et s'évanouissent dans les airs. Le ciel est obscurci, des éclairs pâles et livides percent les sombres nuages qui le couvrent, le tonnerre gronde, éclate.

---

15. Les numéros de pages entre parenthèses renvoient à l'édition consultée: *Les Veillées du château ou Cours de morale à l'usage des enfants*, nouvelle édition illustrée de dessins par G. Staal gravés par Carbonneau, Delangle, Gusman, Lambert, Leclerc, Manini, Piaud, Vinet, Yon (Paris, Garnier-Frères, [s.d.]), 1 t. in-4°.

La scène est apocalyptique: 'Alphonse voit sur sa tête la foudre mena-çante, et l'enfer entr'ouvert sous ses pas' (p.212-13).

Dom Ramire et Alphonse sont indemnes mais il ne leur reste rien. Le père espère que la cassette sauvée contient les diamants. Le fils annonce fièrement qu'il a su faire la part des choses et a donc préféré garder les papiers. Dom Ramire lève les yeux au Ciel et s'avoue cruellement puni 'd'une ridicule vanité' (p.213). Ses illusions se sont écroulées tout comme sa demeure (p.213):

Ce palais superbe, élevé depuis dix ans, ce palais si neuf, si brillant la veille, n'est plus qu'une ruine! En voyant ces toits écroulés, ces pilastres brisés, ces colonnes abattues, on croirait que le temps seul a pu produire une si terrible révolution; il semble qu'il ait fallu des siècles pour détruire un monument bâti avec tant de magnificence et de solidité; et cependant cette affreuse destruction est l'ouvrage de quelques minutes! [...] Ce jardin, chef-d'œuvre de l'art et de la nature, n'offre plus que l'effrayante image du chaos. Ce n'est plus qu'un amas informe de sable, de boue et de feuilles desséchées. Là, ce matin encore, on admirait une superbe cascade: elle a disparu. A la place de cette montagne artificielle qui coûta des sommes prodi-gieuses, maintenant on n'aperçoit plus qu'un gouffre horrible! Que sont devenus ces bosquets de citronniers, ces statues de marbre, ces vases d'albâtre et de porphyre? On en voit encore quelques vestiges, on en retrouve quelques fragments brisés; le reste est englouti! [...] Dom Ramire tourne de tous côtés ses regards désolés: il est assis près d'un petit bois qu'il a vu naître, et dont les arbres déracinés sont épars, ensevelis ou couchés dans la fange, ces arbres faits pour survivre à la main qui les a plantés, et qui viennent d'être arrachés du sein de la terre.

L'inversion est totale: la montagne artificielle devient gouffre naturel, image du renversement des fortunes de Dom Ramire et de son fils. Le but édifiant de l'auteur n'est jamais caché; pour compléter l'information des lecteurs, dès la fin du dix-huitième siècle, les éditions du texte compren-nent d'ailleurs une note pour expliquer le phénomène du tremblement de terre en général et de celui de Lisbonne en particulier. Chez Mme de Genlis, c'est le premier – et le plus spectaculaire – des cataclysmes natu-rels dont elle fait l'inventaire. Il s'agit, de toute évidence, de mettre en valeur la fragilité de l'homme face à la puissance du monde qui l'entoure. Ici, de plus, la nature reprend le rôle d'une divinité qui serait chargée de châtier Dom Ramire de sa superbe – le même défaut que Le Brun imaginait de reprocher à la ville entière de Lisbonne dans la première de ses odes. Le père et le fils échappent aux ruines et aux pillards grâce à un bateau qui était sur les bords du Tage. Ils seront plus heureux que les fiancés de Le Brun mais ils n'ont rien. Si le père comprend quels ont été ses travers et accepte de vivre modestement en province, le fils forme des projets chimériques et rêve de reconquérir la gloire passée de la famille. Au lieu de se donner des occupations sérieuses, il est oisif: 'Incapable de réfléchir et de s'occuper d'une manière utile et raisonnable, il passait une partie des jours à lire des romans. Cette lecture frivole et dangereuse exaltait, enflammait son imagination, et lui donnait les idées les plus fausses du monde et des hommes' (p.216).

Lors d'une promenade, Alphonse sauve une belle inconnue, Dalinde, poursuivie par un taureau mugissant.[16] Il soupire après la jeune fille qu'il ne revoit plus. Sans avouer son trouble à son père, il l'accompagne en voyage. Il espère retrouver Dalinde à Madrid. Une autre aventure attend Dom Ramire: la rencontre avec un solitaire du fameux monastère de Montserrat. Ce dernier pleure un fils qui s'avère avoir été persécuté par Dom Ramire lui-même. Révélant son identité à l'ermite qui l'a maudit, le père d'Alphonse a la surprise de s'entendre pardonner par un homme exemplaire. Il comprend qu'ayant maltraité le fils du solitaire, il lui reste d'être tourmenté par son propre enfant. Alphonse et Dom Ramire promènent leur ennui, amour fou pour l'un, affres du remords pour l'autre, à travers l'Espagne. Apprenant que Dalinde est à Cadix, le jeune homme abandonne son père. Sur la route, il est confronté à de nouveaux témoignages des pouvoirs de la nature: un météore puis une roche magnétique. Il s'embarque sur le bateau pris par le père de Dalinde et ne découvre que trop tard l'absence de l'adolescente. Il convient d'accompagner le père de celle qu'il aime à travers le monde. Le bon Thélismar lui donne des leçons. Elles mettent en évidence l'insuffisance des acquis du jeune homme. Cet autre père lui démontre que les phénomènes naturels, terrifiants pour le profane, ont une explication rationnelle. Lion blessé, serpent, opossum, Hottentots... Alphonse va faire des rencontres curieuses. Il apprendra également ce qu'est une montgolfière ou globe aérostatique, verra des automates, une éruption volcanique et bien d'autres merveilles. Il visitera des terres éloignées et se rendra notamment à la chaussée des géants sur la côte irlandaise, dans un palais de glace et une mine d'argent.

Un crochet par Surinam est peut-être un clin d'œil aux lecteurs de Voltaire. Nous n'y croisons pas de nègres mutilés mais Alphonse comprend alors qu'il est essentiel de se réconcilier avec son propre père avant de prétendre à la main de Dalinde. Thélismar est parvenu à une résolution similaire. Il prépare un autel à l'amitié et fait ce serment au jeune homme: 'vous êtes mon fils! Vous ne pouvez épouser Dalinde qu'avec le consentement de dom Ramire: mais, quand vous la reverrez, vous ne serez plus forcé de lui cacher vos sentiments!' (p.314). Alphonse, très ému, appelle déjà Thélismar du nom de père. Il lui reste encore des épreuves à surmonter.

Dans un vieux château suédois, le jeune homme, qui n'a pas réussi à retrouver Dom Ramire, doit attendre sa majorité en s'imprégnant de livres qui lui retracent les merveilles de la nature. Intervient alors une descente aux enfers symbolique. Alphonse se rend dans une mine d'argent. Pour le parcours, il a un guide mais est séparé de son père putatif, Thélismar.

---

16. A titre de curiosité, remarquons que Théodora est tombée amoureuse du comte, dans *Le Tremblement de terre de Lisbonne* de Marchand, lorsqu'il l'a sauvée d'un taureau furieux qui pensait l'*écalventrer*.

La scène offre des parallèles avec l'échappée de Lisbonne. Alphonse est obligé de voyager au centre de la terre. Son trajet est un parcours dans 'l'abîme'; le guide a une 'voix lugubre' et fait retentir des 'chants funèbres'. Alphonse l'imagine sous les traits du 'farouche batelier des Enfers'. Les bruits d'eau qu'il entend 'rappellent à son imagination les redoutables fleuves du Tartare'. Si l'univers souterrain est beau avec son magnifique palais d'argent éclairé par des flambeaux, il porte l'empreinte de la tristesse. Les visiteurs sont accueillis par une explosion puis l'obscurité. Thélismar explique à Alphonse ce qui s'est passé: 'La mort [...] a passé sur nos têtes. Tel est l'affreux péril où l'on est souvent exposé dans ces profonds abîmes creusés par la cupidité. Hélas! ce n'est pas ce peuple malheureux, privé de la clarté du soleil, qui jouit des trésors qu'il arrache du sein de la terre! La misère le force à descendre vivant dans ces tombes funestes.' L'auditeur ne peut manquer d'être ému par le récit du sort des mineurs. C'est alors qu'un attroupement attire son regard. Un ouvrier a été blessé par la vapeur méphitique. On annonce même qu'il est mort. Plein de compassion, Alphonse s'approche. Il reconnaît l'homme: 'Mon père! s'écrie-t-il... C'est lui! c'est mon père!... rendez-moi mon père!... Qu'on me conduise à ses pieds... je veux le revoir... je veux mourir près de lui... Dans quels lieux, dans quel état devais-je, ô ciel! le retrouver!... Il n'est plus, et j'existe encore!... je jouissais de la clarté des cieux, et mon père gémissait dans cet affreux abîme!...' (p.322). Fort heureusement, Dom Ramire n'est que blessé. Pendant qu'il délire il imagine Alphonse en vengeur de l'ermite, le fils qui punit pour venger un père affligé. Ayant repris conscience, il explique qu'ayant échoué à retrouver Alphonse, parti avec Thélismar, il a vécu auprès du solitaire dont il a recueilli le dernier souffle et en qui il a lui-même retrouvé un père. Le bon Alvarès est mort en le remerciant des soins 'qu'un père pourrait attendre du fils le plus sensible' et en lui laissant sa 'bénédiction paternelle'. Dom Ramire s'est retrouvé dans la mine à attendre Alphonse qu'il savait auprès de Thélismar. Sous terre, nous avons un accident parallèle à celui de Lisbonne. C'est l'occasion de la deuxième véritable révélation. Le tremblement de terre conduit Alphonse à perdre ses ancêtres fictifs. Dans la mine, il retrouve son père.

La courbe d'apprentissage est complète, pour le père comme pour le fils. L'aîné avait à comprendre ses travers et à expier ses fautes. Il l'a fait en remplaçant le fils qu'il avait ôté à Alvarès et en croyant que son propre enfant l'accablerait. Alphonse est devenu digne de Dalinde en ayant observé la nature et compris sa grandeur; il a racheté sa propre faute vis-à-vis de son père. Chacun a su être le fils d'un tiers, Alvarès ou Thélismar, et a donc travaillé à acquérir l'héritage qui lui manquait, humilité et savoir. Le tremblement de terre de Lisbonne a été la première étape sur ce double chemin de la connaissance. La tragédie a servi de révélateur. Le conte moral paraît être la démonstration du proverbe selon lequel 'à quelque chose malheur est bon'.

Les écrits des trois auteurs tendent à montrer que la nature est plus forte que l'homme. Ils s'élèvent contre les prétentions, l'orgueil d'une ville ou d'un être. Le Brun offre une interprétation morale de l'événement lui-même, proposant une explication de ses causes morales et physiques et examinant ses suites terribles. Néant, déploration et pertes s'inscrivent dans ses vers. Marchand et Mme de Genlis, en revanche, ne s'attardent pas sur l'après du tremblement de terre pour la ville et ses habitants. Ils ne s'intéressent pas à l'ampleur des dégâts. Ils se servent de la catastrophe pour retracer des destinées individuelles, brisées pour le premier, infléchies pour la seconde. Le dramaturge évoque certainement le tremblement de terre par opportunisme. Sa pièce est une plaisanterie d'initiés qui a la particularité de ne pas avoir été écrite pour la scène. Elle s'inscrit dans une actualité récente, en particulier en termes littéraires: elle répond à sa façon au Voltaire du 'Poème sur le désastre de Lisbonne'. Mme de Genlis, quant à elle, utilise l'événement historique, plus présent à l'esprit de ses contemporains que bien d'autres catastrophes naturelles, et donc doué d'une charge émotionnelle supérieure, pour une illustration morale en particulier. Les philosophes, au lendemain du 1er novembre 1755, sont orphelins de certitudes. Les hommes de science se sont intéressés à la tragédie, en témoignent les articles de journaux ou les concours académiques.[17] Au prisme de la littérature, le tremblement de terre s'enrichit de sens nouveaux. Lisbonne conduit à interroger la place de l'homme sur terre. On notera que les textes portent entre autres sur le rapport du père à son enfant, de la créature à Dieu. Lisbonne est un référence partagée. L'horreur qu'inspire la catastrophe s'inscrit dans l'imaginaire collectif. Il le nourrit dans les représentations qu'en livrent les œuvres de Le Brun, Marchand ou Mme de Genlis.

---

17. L'Académie de Rouen a proposé un sujet sur les tremblements de terre à la suite de celui de Lisbonne (concours de 1756). Voir le carton MS Acad. C 20 à la Bibliothèque municipale de Rouen.

JEFF LOVELAND

Guéneau de Montbeillard, the *Collection académique* and the great Lisbon earthquake[1]

IN 1754 Philibert Guéneau de Montbeillard, the author of one article for the *Encyclopédie* and future collaborator on Georges-Louis Leclerc de Buffon's *Histoire naturelle des oiseaux*, assumed the editorship of the *Collection académique*, a series devoted to culling useful publications of European scientific academies and translating them into French. The earthquake in Lisbon in November 1755 moved him not to write poetry or philosophical polemic but to gather data on earthquakes, volcanoes and other potentially related natural occurrences in the hope of making it easier to understand and to survive them. Though the resulting 'Liste chronologique des éruptions des volcans, des tremblements de terre...' hardly fits with the project of the *Collection académique*, he nonetheless published it in volume vi, presumably thinking that the magnitude of the disaster and public reaction to it justified this interruption of his compendium.

Guéneau's 'Liste' was presented as a simple roster of facts, but his choice of some facts and not others indicates a fragmentary theory of earthquakes – a theory worth evoking in this close friend of Buffon. Along with much of the early *Collection*, the 'Liste' also illustrates the limitations of the common eighteenth-century convention of assigning readers rather than authors the prerogative of drawing conclusions from facts. Lastly, the story of Guéneau's 'Liste' is intertwined with the fortunes of the *Collection* as a whole – a series that, despite its resonance with the Enlightenment's ideals, never flourished as much as two other compendia of the mid-eighteenth century, the *Encyclopédie* and the *Histoire naturelle*.

i. Guéneau de Montbeillard and the *Collection académique*

Born in 1720 to a prominent family in Semur-en-Auxois, the son of a noble barrister in *parlement*, Guéneau was schooled locally, in Paris, and in Troyes, twice at Jansenist *collèges*, where he became fervently religious. Later in life he would mingle with atheists and pronounce the afterlife

1. I would like to thank Heather Arden, Theodore E. D. Braun, Kathleen Hardesty Doig, Frank Kafker, and John Radner for their suggestions regarding this article. I am also grateful to Jean-Claude Sosnowski of the Bibliothèque municipale de Semur-en-Auxois and the staff of the Bibliothèque centrale du Muséum national d'histoire naturelle for their help with my research.

a 'fable'.[2] After a year of ill health, he received a degree in law at Dijon in 1742.[3] Soon afterwards he settled in Paris. There he made friends with Diderot and contributed a single article to the *Encyclopédie*, 'Etendue', an ambitious two-page article that distinguishes concepts of space according to the modality of their perception – by touch, the eye, or abstract reflection – and uses them to refute Descartes's view of extension as essential to matter. Leibnizian in its insistence on time and space as relational, 'Etendue' was also broadly influenced by the Enlightenment's sensationism and specifically by Diderot's *Lettre sur les aveugles* (1749) and Buffon's 'Premier discours' (1749). At the end of his article, Guéneau admitted that his contemplations lacked utility, unlike the investigations of practical, 'active' sciences.[4] The ideal of useful knowledge acquired sacred overtones in the French Enlightenment, particularly in the provinces;[5] awareness of this ideal would mark nearly all of Guéneau's intellectual activities.

Meanwhile, around 1752, Jean Berryat (1718?-1754), a physician from Auxerre and correspondent of the Académie royale des sciences, was launching the *Collection académique*.[6] The *Collection* responded to two frequently voiced contemporary concerns. First, as Jean D'Alembert noted in the 'Discours préliminaire' of the *Encyclopédie*, the decline of Latin as an international language of learning posed problems for the Republic of Letters. Specifically, although it made knowledge accessible to a wider

---

2. Guéneau to Bénigne-Elisabeth Potot de Montbeillard, 18 [January 1773?], Fonds Guéneau de Montbeillard, Bibliothèque municipale, Semur-en-Auxois (hereafter FGM-BMS), MS 115 (122), A7; Frank A. Kafker and Serena Kafker, *The Encyclopedists as individuals: a biographical dictionary of the authors of the Encyclopédie*, SVEC 257 (1988), p.167. Spelling, capitalisation and punctuation have been modernised in titles and quotations throughout this article.

3. Bénigne-Elisabeth Potot de Montbeillard, 'Biographie de M. Guéneau de Montbeillard', in *Correspondance inédite de Buffon*, ed. H. Nadault de Buffon (Paris 1860), i.335-38; Kafker and Kafker, *Encyclopedists as individuals*, p.167.

4. 'Etendue', in *Encyclopédie, ou Dictionnaire raisonnée des sciences, des arts et des métiers, par une société de gens de lettres*, ed. Denis Diderot and Jean D'Alembert ([Paris] 1751-1772), vi.45. On the article's Leibnizian or Lockean currents see Fernand Papillon, 'Notice sur Guéneau de Montbeillard, naturaliste et philosophe de l'école de Leibniz', *Séances et travaux de l'Académie des sciences morales et politiques (Institut de France)* 28 (1872), p.245-49; Sylviane Albertan-Coppola, 'De Locke à Helvétius en passant par l'*Encyclopédie*, ou faut-il "casser le XVIII⁰ siècle"?' in *Sciences, musiques, lumières: mélanges offerts à Anne-Marie Chouillet*, ed. Ulla Kölving and Irène Passeron (Ferney 2002), p.370.

5. Daniel Roche, *Le Siècle des lumières en province: académies et académiciens provinciaux, 1680-1789* (The Hague 1978), i.382-84.

6. Guéneau, *Collection académique composée des mémoires, actes, ou Journaux des plus célèbres académies et sociétés littéraires étrangères, des extraits des meilleurs ouvrages périodiques, des traités particuliers, et des pièces fugitives les plus rares; concernant l'histoire naturelle et la botanique, la physique expérimentale et la chimie, la médecine et l'anatomie, traduits en français, et mis en ordre par une société de gens de lettres* (hereafter *CA*), ed. Guéneau *et al.*, 13 vols (Dijon and Paris 1755-1779), i.xlix-l; *CA*, xiii.ii-iii. For a suggestion that Hugues Maret and others founded the *Collection* along with Berryat see 'Nadault (Jean)', in *Biographie universelle ancienne et moderne*, ed. J. Fr. Michaud, reprint edn, 45 vols (Graz 1966-1970), xxx.8.

audience, publication in the vernacular languages prevented scholars from keeping up with discoveries in most other countries and thereby contributed to insularity. While D'Alembert did little but express nostalgia for the old days,[7] Berryat proposed a remedy – to produce a French translation of important texts in other languages, primarily of the best writings from Europe's scientific academies. Second, readers and especially writers across Europe lamented the over-production of books in the early modern period. The publication of so many undeserving texts was bad enough; worse still, the multitude of such texts threatened to conceal the few worth reading. In his utopian *L'An 2440* (1771), Louis-Sébastien Mercier imagined a future society that had dealt with the problem by burning most of its books and distilling the substance of 'a thousand volumes in folio' into a single duodecimo. The *Collection académique* aimed at a similar reduction and revalorisation of European scientific texts: '[Elle] réunira en moins de quarante volumes tous les faits relatifs à son objet, lesquels sont répandus dans plus de huit cents volumes originaux.'[8]

Corresponding to its two goals of translation and abridgment, the *Collection académique* appeared in two sub-series, a sixteen-volume *Recueil des mémoires, ou Collection de pièces académiques* (1754-1787) selected from the publications of the Académie des sciences, and the thirteen-volume *Collection académique* proper (1755-1779), featuring translations of non-French scientific works. Between volumes i and iv the main title of the *Recueil des mémoires* was gradually changed, so that it became simply the 'French part' of the *Collection académique*, but the whole sub-series will be referred to here under its original title. For the 'foreign part' of the *Collection*, Berryat assembled a team of collaborators proficient in languages, all from Burgundy, many with ties to the *Encyclopédie* and the *Histoire naturelle*: Buffon, Louis-Anne Lavirotte, Pierre Daubenton, Edme-Louis Daubenton, Pierre-Henri Larcher, Jean Nadault, Denis Barberet, and Guéneau.[9] Unfortunately, Berryat died before the first two volumes of the *Recueil* were published in 1754. Later that year Guéneau became the editor of the series. Around the same time he abandoned Paris

7. 'Discours préliminaire des éditeurs', in *Encyclopédie*, i.xxx. See also Richard Yeo, *Encyclopaedic visions: scientific dictionaries and Enlightenment culture* (Cambridge 2001), p.54-55.

8. Louis-Sébastien Mercier, *L'An 2440, ou Rêve s'il en fut jamais*, ed. Christophe Cave and Christine Marcandier-Colard (Paris 1999), p.163-66; Guéneau, *CA*, i.xxxvii. See also Yeo, *Encyclopaedic visions*, p.78-98; Suzanne Tucoo-Chala, *Charles-Joseph Panckoucke et la librairie française, 1739-1798* (Pau 1977), p.263-64; *Recueil de mémoires, ou Collection de pièces académiques, concernant la médecine, l'anatomie et la chirurgie, la chimie, la physique expérimentale, la botanique et l'histoire naturelle, tirées des meilleurs sources* (hereafter *RM*), ed. Jean Berryat et al., 16 vols. (Dijon and Paris 1754-1787), i.i-ii.

9. P. Brunet, 'Un centre bourguignon de synthèse scientifique au XVIIIᵉ siècle', *Annales de Bourgogne* 1 (1929), p.107-109; Guéneau, *CA*, i.lii. The physician Jacques Savary, the first of a number of non-Burgundian collaborators, participated in the composition of volume iii. On other early contributors see Jean Nadault to Guéneau, 10 June 1757, FGM-BMS, MS 115 (122), F3.

and returned to Semur, where in 1756 he married Bénigne-Elisabeth Potot de Montbeillard, a local polyglot and future assistant in his research.[10]

To signal his arrival as editor, Guéneau wrote a sweeping 'Discours préliminaire' for the third volume of the series, the first volume of the 'foreign part' and of the *Collection académique* proper. He may have drawn inspiration from the *Encyclopédie* and the *Histoire naturelle*, both of which called attention to themselves with inaugural discourses of great philosophical breadth. Though less commented on than D'Alembert's 'Discours préliminaire' or Buffon's 'Premier discours', Guéneau's 'Discours préliminaire' earned him praise, notably from Diderot in his article 'Encyclopédie' for the *Encyclopédie*.[11] Guéneau, for his part, used his 'Discours préliminaire' to praise Diderot and Buffon, and explore ideas intimately connected with theirs. Amplifying the arguments of 'Etendue', he declared abstractions inevitable but often deceptive. He judged mathematics in particular overrated as a key to nature – a judgement made more notoriously by Buffon and Diderot several years earlier. For this reason, and for lack of public enthusiasm for mathematics, the *Collection* was to concentrate on 'natural philosophy', which in Guéneau's view included experimental physics, natural history and medicine.[12] While endorsing facts and experience as the foundations of knowledge, Guéneau, again like Buffon and Diderot, insisted on the necessity of comparison and generalisation in scientific progress. Still, he declaimed against 'hypotheses' and promised to limit the *Collection* to facts as much as possible.[13] He was ambivalent about the nature of the facts he wished to collect, torn between Buffon's preference for repeated phenomena and Diderot's enthusiasm for singular ones, notably monsters.[14]

Early volumes of the *Collection académique* were organised according to sources. Volume i, for example, presented translated works from the Florentine Accademia del Cimento followed by articles from the *Journal*

10. A. Albrier, 'La famille Daubenton: notice historique et généalogique', *Revue historique, nobiliaire et biographique* 9, new series (1874), p.171; *Correspondence inédite de Buffon*, i.333-35; Pierre Brunet, 'Guéneau de Montbeillard', *Revue de Bourgogne* (September-October 1926), p.518; P. Bernard, 'Notice sur Montbeillard', in *Œuvres complètes de Buffon*, vol.xi (Paris 1801), p.372-75; Guéneau to Potot, [after 11 April 1759], 22 January 1773, FGM-BMS, MS 115 (122), A1, A2.

11. 'Encyclopédie', in *Encyclopédie*, v.645v; see also v.635r-v.

12. *CA*, i.vi-x, xli-xliii. For Buffon's and Diderot's judgements of mathematics see Jeff Loveland, *Rhetoric and natural history: Buffon in polemical and literary context*, SVEC 2001:03, p.127-28.

13. *CA*, i.vi-xii, xxxix; iv.xix-xx. Compare Georges-Louis Leclerc de Buffon, *Histoire naturelle, générale et particulière, avec la description du Cabinet du roi* (Paris 1749-1767), i.3-4; Diderot, *Pensées sur l'interprétation de la nature*, in *Œuvres complètes*, ed. Jean Varloot *et al.*, vol.ix (Paris 1981), p.27-28. See also *RM*, i.iii-iv.

14. *CA*, i.xxii-xxiv, xl-xli, iv.xvii-xix. Compare Loveland, *Rhetoric and natural history*, p.116-18; Andrew Curran, *Sublime disorder: physical monstrosity in Diderot's universe*, SVEC 2001:01, p.3-4, 146-55.

des savants – a rare instance of a French text appearing in the 'foreign part' of the *Collection*. Extracts from particular sources were ordered chronologically, starting almost always from the late seventeenth century, and only advancing beyond 1700 with volume viii. After volume iii, Guéneau organised the *Collection* according to discipline, devoting each subsequent volume to natural history, medicine, or experimental philosophy and chemistry. In the preface to volume iv (1757), he justified his decision not to divide extracts even further by subject; an index, he argued, would achieve the same ends without destroying the advantages of chronological order (*CA*, iv.vii-x). Here and in his preface to volume v (1758), he continued to elaborate on ideas favoured by Buffon and Diderot – specifically regarding reproduction, spontaneous generation, and the creation of new species (*CA*, iv.xv-xvii, v.xi, xix-xxxiii). Like volumes iv and v, on natural history, volumes vi (1761) and vii (1766), devoted to experimental physics and medicine respectively, listed Guéneau as editor as well as among the translators, but he withdrew from both tasks before volume viii (1770). Instead he returned to the *Recueil de mémoires*, dormant since 1754. Unlike the first two volumes, new volumes of the *Recueil* were organised by subject as well as chronology, a change Guéneau announced in volume iv (1770) in a fulsome, six-page dedication to the Académie des sciences which was apparently written too late for volume iii (1769).[15] After 1770 Guéneau's name disappeared entirely from the *Collection*. Both sub-series continued after his withdrawal, even becoming more regular in their instalments, but the *Recueil* ended with volume xvi (1787), and the *Collection* with volume xiii (1779), despite a promise of future translations in the last preface (*CA*, xiii.vi).

One reason for Guéneau's departure is clear. Whether bored with the *Collection académique* or not, he became involved with other projects in the 1760s.[16] In 1766 he attained a degree of celebrity for inoculating his son against smallpox. This was not the first time Finfin, as Guéneau called him, had borne the weight of his father's scientific and philosophical idealism. From Finfin's birth onward, Guéneau measured him at roughly six-monthly intervals. For a brief period in the mid-1770s he measured

15. *RM*, iv.v-vi. As indicated by the subtitle of vol.v of the *Recueil*, the series was also called the *Abrégé de l'Histoire et mémoires de l'Académie royale des sciences*. See Tucoo-Chala, *Charles-Joseph Panckoucke*, p.262, 264.

16. Jacques Roger claims that by 1762 Guéneau was working on a commentary to a series of colour plates for Buffon's *Histoire naturelle des oiseaux*. This is unlikely, since the plates were published with no mention of Guéneau among the contributors, and since the letter cited by Roger refers to Guéneau's 'tirades': an unlikely form of discourse for a study of birds. See Roger, *Buffon: un philosophe au Jardin du roi* (Paris 1989), p.299; Buffon to Guéneau, 20 March 1762, in *Correspondance générale*, ed. H. Nadault de Buffon, reprint edn, 2 vols (Geneva 1971), i.128-29. On Guéneau's frustration with the *Collection* see Pierre Flourens, *Des manuscrits de Buffon avec des fac-simile de Buffon et de ses collaborateurs* (Paris 1860), p.199; P. Brunet, 'Guéneau de Montbeillard', *Mémoires de l'Académie des sciences, arts et belles-lettres de Dijon* (1925), p.126.

Finfin almost hourly to uncover daily variations in height. Though ostensibly empirical, the study seems to have been directed toward proving that Finfin was taller after sleeping and shorter after upright exertion, notably after coming home from a ball after midnight. The results were published in volume iv (1777) of the *Supplément à l'Histoire naturelle*, where Buffon used them to speculate that humans grew faster in summer than winter because of heat's vital powers.[17] The inoculation for smallpox was a riskier matter. Though impressed, Buffon for one was not willing to try it on his own son. Yet the operation succeeded, and Guéneau became a hero to French proponents of inoculation. He read a triumphant report to the Académie de Dijon, to which he had been elected in 1764, dwelling melodramatically on his act as one of patriotism and enlightened paternal love.[18]

Towards 1767 he agreed to write on birds for Buffon's *Histoire naturelle des oiseaux*, and on agriculture for one of Charles-Joseph Panckoucke's encyclopedias.[19] For Guéneau, who was reproached throughout his life for missing deadlines and putting off duties, it must have been difficult to imagine continuing the *Collection* at the same time. His project on agriculture apparently came to nothing, but he flourished as Buffon's collaborator on the *Histoire naturelle des oiseaux*. Many of the articles in the first two volumes of the series were written by him, although Buffon took credit for the whole of both volumes. Finally, in volume iii (1775), five years after the publication of volume i, Buffon revealed Guéneau's participation, notably his responsibility for the celebrated article on the peacock. Though critics later dismissed Guéneau's imitation of Buffon's style as mechanical and affected, it was evidently good enough not to raise suspicions before 1775.

Perhaps encouraged by Panckoucke, who was now publishing both works, Guéneau ended his collaboration on the *Histoire naturelle des oiseaux* after volume vi (1779), and agreed to write for the *Encyclopédie méthodique*. Frustrated by Buffon's deadlines, he asked Panckoucke not to pester him about articles and to give him a year's vacation before expecting anything.[20] He offered to write the sections on quadrupeds and whales as well

17. *Supplément à l'Histoire naturelle*, 7 vols (Paris 1774-1789), iv.376-81; FGM-BMS, MS 115 (122), C3-4.

18. Roger, *Buffon*, p.276-77; Brunet, 'Guéneau de Montbeillard' (1925), p.129-30; Roger Tisserand, *Au temps de l'Encyclopédie: l'Académie de Dijon de 1740 à 1793* (Paris 1936), p.276-79.

19. Guéneau to Buffon, 15 December 1767, 20 January 1768, in *Correspondance générale*, i.164-65. According to Kathleen Hardesty Doig, Guéneau's 'agriculture' was probably intended not for the *Supplément à l'Encyclopédie* (1776-1777) but for a new edition of the *Encyclopédie*, a project that Panckoucke contemplated, abandoned and then revived many years later on a greatly expanded plan as the *Encyclopédie méthodique*.

20. Roger, *Buffon*, p.501; Brunet, 'Guéneau de Montbeillard' (1925), p.127; Guéneau to Thérèse-Marthe Panckoucke, 22 February 1778, Bibliothèque centrale du Muséum national d'histoire naturelle, Paris, MS 1998, vol.ii, letter 174.

as those on insects and on metaphysics, logic and ethics.[21] In the end, Buffon's one-time collaborator Louis-Jean-Marie Daubenton received the former assignment; his *Histoire naturelle des animaux: l'homme, les animaux quadrupèdes et les cétacés* was published in the *Méthodique* in 1782. Meanwhile, in the early 1780s, Guéneau annotated books on insects, observed them himself, and negotiated with Panckoucke and engraver Robert Benard over the plates.[22] In 1785 he died. His wife sent his notes to the new editor of the volumes on insects, Pierre-Jean-Claude Mauduyt de La Varenne, who found them incoherent and managed to use them in a single article, 'Insecte'.[23] Apparently unaided by Guéneau, Pierre-Louis Lacretelle undertook and completed the volumes on logic, metaphysics and ethics.[24]

ii. The 'Liste chronologique'

The Lisbon earthquake took place on 1 November 1755, not long after the first three volumes of the *Collection académique* had been published.[25] Like other French readers, Guéneau was almost certainly apprised of it within a few weeks. A humanitarian reformer who would later draw up plans for reducing poverty and limiting capital punishment,[26] he must have felt the need to react to the tragedy as a *philosophe*. According to the preface of volume vi of the *Collection*, he had started doing research on earthquakes 'almost five years ago' in response to the disaster. Since volume vi had been published by May 1761, he probably began his

21. Christabel P. Braunrot and Kathleen Hardesty Doig, 'The *Encyclopédie méthodique*: an introduction', *SVEC* 327 (1995), p.76; [Guéneau], '[XVIII.] Dictionnaire universel et raisonné de métaphysique, logique, et morale', in the prospectus to the *Encyclopédie méthodique*, in *Encyclopédie méthodique: beaux arts* (Paris 1788), i.xxxvi-xxxvii; Guéneau to [Charles-Joseph Panckoucke], 7 April [1781], FGM-BMS, MS 115 (122), H1. According to the letter, 'il est question de messieurs Bailly et Champfort pour la place de l'Académie' – a reference to the competition between Jean-Sylvain Bailly and Sébastien-Roch Nicolas (Chamfort) for a seat in the Académie française in 1781. The letter was evidently written to Panckoucke – the only person for whom Guéneau was working in 1781.

22. Charles-Joseph Panckoucke to Guéneau, 8 September 1785, FGM-BMS, MS 115 (122), E6; Benard to Guéneau, 11 September 1785, FGM-BMS, MS 115 (122), E7. The Bibliothèque municipale of Semur-en-Auxois holds several books on insects which Guéneau annotated and used as a place for storing his own observations.

23. Mauduyt to Potot, c.1786, 12 December 1786, FGM-BMS, MS 115 (122), D5, D11; Mauduyt, 'Discours préliminaire et plan du dictionnaire des insectes', in *Encyclopédie méthodique: insectes* (Paris 1789), i.i-ii. Compare Brunet, 'Guéneau de Montbeillard' (1925), p.127; Bernard, 'Notice sur Montbeillard', p.366. See also Braunrot and Doig, '*Encyclopédie méthodique*', p.47-48.

24. *Encyclopédie méthodique: mathématiques*, ed. Charles Bossut, 3 vols (Paris 1784-1789), iii.23 (in the separately paginated notice at the head of the volume); Braunrot and Doig, '*Encyclopédie méthodique*', p.76-78.

25. See *Annonces, affiches, et avis divers* (27 August 1755), p.138; *Mercure de France* (September 1755), p.130.

26. Kafker and Kafker, *Encyclopedists as individuals*, p.168.

research within six months of the earthquake in Lisbon.[27] One section of the 'Liste chronologique' to which his labours gave rise, the one detailing the tremors of 1755, is dated 1757 (*CA*, vi.638). His work continued, perhaps fitfully, into 1760; the main body of the 'Liste' deals with events to late September 1760, while a following 'Supplément' continues with events to 5 December 1760. His decision to include the 'Liste' in the *Collection* was apparently made around 1760 when he realised that 'useless' translations proposed for volume vi would have to be cut and replaced with new material.[28]

In some ways the 'Liste chronologique' fits naturally into the *Collection académique*. Much of the data from which Guéneau compiled it had been reported in academic publications. Moreover, he used the preface to volume vi to lay out a plan for an international network of meteorological observers, all sending data to a central academy – a vision closely related to the goals of the *Collection*, as well as to widely shared, partially realised schemes for scientific and academic collaboration. His 'Liste chronologique' was billed as a rough model for meteorological observation, one that interlinked academies would fill out in time.[29] Still, the 'Liste' differed from preceding texts in the *Collection*: compiled from multiple sources, it was also an original creation on the part of the editor. Regarded in this light, it invites comparison with the topical digressions inserted in other multi-year, multi-volume compendia, for example the eulogy for Montesquieu in volume v of the *Encyclopédie* or the vague allusion to the Seven Years War in Buffon's *Histoire naturelle*.[30] Books could not often compete with newspapers or periodicals in breaking news, but the *Encyclopédie* and the *Histoire naturelle* at least made their concessions to the irruptive force of news without much delay. Guéneau, in contrast, missed the vogue for earthquakes by not preparing the 'Liste' for publication in volumes iv (1757) or v (1758) of the *Collection académique*. He may not have prepared enough material in time for these volumes, and he may have expected volume vi to appear on schedule around 1759.[31] In fact it appeared towards May 1761, delayed by 'typographical problems', by publisher François Desventes's construction of a paper mill, and by Guéneau's need to replace many 'useless' sections in his collaborators' translations. He himself probably also contributed to the delay. In 1758,

---

27. *CA*, vi.xi; *Affiches, annonces, et avis divers* (13 May 1761), p.73-74.

28. *CA*, vi.iii. The 'Liste' is not mentioned in the summary of vol.vi in *CA*, v.i.

29. *CA*, vi.v-vi, xiv, xv-xvin. See also James E. McClellan III, *Science reorganised: scientific societies in the eighteenth century* (New York 1985), p.161-62, 220-27; H. Howard Frisinger, *The History of meteorology: to 1800* (Boston, MA 1983), p.99-112; Theodore S. Feldman, 'Late Enlightenment meteorology', in *The Quantifying spirit in the eighteenth century* (Berkeley, CA 1990), p.146-51, 158-77.

30. Buffon, *Histoire naturelle*, xii.xv-xvi.

31. Volume vi was advertised as being in press in the *Journal des savants* (June 1758), p.397. Volumes were originally promised at six-monthly intervals in the *Annonces, affiches, et avis divers* (27 August 1755), p.138.

his collaborator Jacques Savary sent him a letter deploring his failure to reply to several letters, complaining about the insignificance of the material in the *Ephémerides de l'Académie des curieux de la nature d'Allemagne*, and begging him for guidance and more work.[32] In 1760 Guéneau confided to an unknown woman that 'de petits maux et beaucoup de chagrins m'ont empêché de vous écrire depuis; je ne suis plus moi mais je ne veux pas vous attrister'.[33] His wife attributed his withdrawal from the *Collection académique* towards 1770 to a *maladie de nerfs*; at the end of his life he suffered from melancholia.[34] A similar episode of long-term anxiety or depression seems to have helped delay publication of volume vi and thus to have deprived the 'Liste' of some of its relevance.

Guéneau's purposes in undertaking his 'Liste chronologique' were venerable and common to many of those writing on earthquakes in the wake of the disaster of 1755 – namely to understand typical locations and effects of earthquakes, to uncover signs of their approach, and to discover ways of avoiding them or limiting their destructiveness (*CA*, vi.xi). He decided that a list of earthquakes noting their dates, effects, and circumstances might shed light on their workings. The variety of attendant circumstances which he considered potentially important is indicated by his full title, 'Liste chronologique des éruptions de volcans, des tremblements de terre, de quelques faits météorologiques les plus remarquables, des comètes, des maladies pestilentielles, etc., jusqu'en 1760, tirée des mémoires des académies de l'Europe, des ouvrages périodiques, des histoires générales et des relations particulières'. True to its title, Guéneau's 'Liste' is a long one. Along with an attached 'Supplément à la liste chronologique des éruptions de volcans, tremblements de terre, faits météorologiques, etc.', the 'Liste' stretches to 189 pages in quarto, beginning with a comet observed around 2312 BC and ending with a storm that struck the coast of Genoa around 1 pm on 5 December 1760. In between, the 'Liste' chronicles not only the phenomena mentioned in its title but also plagues of animal pests (snakes, caterpillars, rats, locusts, beetles, worms, and so on), wildfires, waterspouts, unusual atmospheric and heavenly appearances ('new stars', the moon's phases, rainbows, eclipses, parhelia, aurora borealis, and so on), and measurements of air pressure and temperature.

Near the end of the 'Liste', occupying fourteen pages – more than any other year – is the entry for 1755. Though it relates many more observations than those for preceding or following years, this entry resembles others in offering an international perspective and in maintaining a detached tone and concentrating on circumstances rather than human suffering. The article could have been very different. On 20 June 1756

32. 4 January 1758, FGM-BMS, MS 115 (122), E3.
33. 2 January 1760, FGM-BMS, MS 115 (122), D4.
34. Potot, 'Biographie de M. Guéneau de Montbeillard', i.339; Bernard, 'Notice sur Montbeillard', p.365-66.

Guéneau send a letter and the five published volumes of the *Collection* and *Recueil* to the Portuguese man of letters Miguel Tiberio Pedegache Brandão Ivo. How the two men became acquainted is unclear, but by 1756 Guéneau was probably hoping to open a Portuguese market for the *Collection* and obtain translated scientific works from Portugal. Having received the letter belatedly, Pedegache replied enthusiastically in 1757, promising to put Guéneau's publisher Desventes in touch with a Portuguese bookseller and to supply Guéneau with any number of short scientific works, some of them his own – all in return for books, for Pedegache had lost almost his whole library in the recent earthquake. He also offered to let Guéneau publish an improved version of his *Nova e Fiel Relação do terremoto que experimentou Lisboa e toto Portugal n° 1 de novembro 1755* (1756) in the *Collection académique*. Apparently rendered into sketches by a certain Paris, Pedegache's *Relação* constituted the basis for a famous series of engravings by Jacques-Philippe Le Bas, published in Paris under the title *Recueil des plus belles ruines de Lisbonne* (1757).[35] Had Guéneau chosen to publish the *Relação* in French, it might have attracted attention as a companion to Le Bas's picturesque images. It would also have overwhelmed the 'Liste' with details regarding the fate of specific buildings and neighbourhoods in Lisbon. In the end the deal foundered, perhaps because of lack of interest on Guéneau's part, perhaps because he was unable to pursue negotiations during his crisis of the late 1750s. Nor did the *Collection* ever publish Portuguese scientific works, by Pedegache or anyone else.

Guéneau declined to name his sources except in a handful of cases, supposedly to avoid making his 'Liste' longer – but he was by no means the first to make such a list. Chronologists since antiquity had listed earthquakes and other natural disasters and oddities, often for their value as signs or miracles. In early modern Europe, earthquakes before and after 1755 provoked flurries of publications, some of which included lists of past earthquakes. One list from which Guéneau borrowed without acknowledgement was in Elie Bertrand's *Mémoires historiques et physiques sur les tremblements de terre* (1757).[36] In the preface (*CA*, vi.xiii) Guéneau claimed to have consulted meteorological and astronomical observations made in scientific academies, Stanislaw Lubieniecki's *Theatrum cometicum* (1666-1668), and Jean-Jacques Dortous de Mairan's *Traité*

35. Pedegache to Guéneau, 12 July 1757, FGM-BMS, MS 115 (122), E11. On Pedegache see T. D. Kendrick, *The Lisbon earthquake* (London 1956), p.58-59. It is usually asserted that Le Bas worked from sketches made by Pedegache and Paris, but the letter here hints that Pedegache merely provided Paris with his *Relação*: 'Je vous avoue, Monsieur, que je verrais avec plaisir cette relation insérée dans la *Collection académique*, non pas telle que je l'ai remise d'abord à Paris, mais telle que je l'ai refaite depuis, parce qu'elle est plus parfaite, plus exacte, plus remplie de faits.'
36. Compare for example the entries for 1534 and 1739 in *CA*, vi.620, 540; Elie Bertrand, *Mémoires historiques et physiques sur les tremblements de terre* (The Hague 1757), p.42, 98.

physique et historique de l'aurore boréale (1733). His use of the latter work is questionable, however, since his lists of aurora do not square with Mairan's in either edition of the *Traité*.

As we have seen, Guéneau hesitated in the 'Discours préliminaire' in his attitude toward monsters and rare events. On the one hand, with Buffon, he saw them as distracting from the more fruitful study of regular phenomena. So persuaded, Buffon followed the majority of eighteenth-century theorists in dismissing volcanoes and earthquakes as superficial happenings in the earth's history.[37] Guéneau, for his part, admitted in his preface that earthquakes were not humankind's greatest scourge, but he was committed to treating them as important events; his 'Liste' was a response to nothing short of a 'disaster' (*CA*, vi.xi, xvi). Behind his work lay the hope that, from a viewpoint encompassing several millennia, earthquakes would turn out to be regular, not accidental. Unlike Buffon, however, Guéneau did not shirk from reporting freakish occurrences associated with earthquakes – for example, the story of a convalescent in Lorraine who contracted gangrene by leaving his leg uncovered during an earthquake (*CA*, vi.571), or instances of rain composed not of water but of wheat (*CA*, vi.516), fish (*CA*, vi.655), hair-like material (*CA*, vi.551), and other things. Occasionally he expressed scepticism, for example about the ability of earthquakes to move land and cities over several miles (*CA*, vi.510, 521) and about the relevance of moonbows and astronomical phenomena to the science of earthquakes (*CA*, vi.xii, 596). The only items in his 'Liste' on which he consistently cast doubt were rains of blood – occurrences long dwelt upon by Christians and others intent on identifying portents and miracles. For Guéneau, there could only be 'supposed' rains of blood, 'red rains', and rains of 'reddish matter'.[38] Though less determined than Buffon to impose order and normality on geological phenomena, Guéneau balked at perpetuating religious symbolism – another sign of his rejection of his earlier Jansenism.

In his preface Guéneau wrote that for lack of time he had been unable to use his 'Liste' in the way he intended, namely to draw conclusions about the nature of earthquakes and make proposals for reducing their damage, but he was publishing the 'Liste' so that others might do so. As Jan Golinski has noted, eighteenth-century collectors of meteorological data may have expected scientific laws to result from their industriousness, but for the most part 'the gratification of that expectation was indefinitely

37. Kenneth L. Taylor, 'Volcanoes as accidents: how "natural" were volcanoes to eighteenth-century naturalists?', in *Volcanoes and history*, ed. Nicoletta Morello (Genoa 1998), p.595-614; Rhoda Rappaport, 'Borrowed words: problems of vocabulary in eighteenth-century geology', *British journal for the history of science* 15 (1982), p.27, 38-44.

38. See for example *CA*, vi.xiv, 489, 496, 504, 506, 522, 529, 541, 544. See also *CA*, vi.519, 525. For an exception see *CA*, vi.511.

deferred'.[39] His own failure, Guéneau added, came with a benefit: 'Les faits passeront par mes mains sans s'y teindre des couleurs d'aucune hypothèse' (*CA*, vi.xi-xiii). Yet even within his insistently secular framework of study, he did not lack convictions regarding the phenomena comprising his 'Liste'. Just as his measurements of his son's height seem to have been driven by a common-sense hypothesis, his selection of data for the 'Liste' pointed to a traditional understanding of meteorology. Exhalations, the causal agent in Aristotle's *Meteorologia*, linked nearly all the phenomena he listed. According to Aristotle, they could cause epidemics, storms, and fright in animals when released from the earth by earthquakes, volcanoes or comets. Guéneau was inclined to accept all these interrelations (*CA*, vi.xii-xiii, xiv-xv). In agreement with eighteenth-century theorists, he saw earthquakes as explosions catalysed by water – hence their location near bodies of water and their frequent appearance after heavy rain. Their shocks, he contended, were transmitted not by contiguous earth but through specific underground channels, as proposed recently by Nicolas Desmarest in his anonymous *Conjectures physico-mathématiques sur la propagation des secousses dans les tremblements de terre* (1756).[40]

If the 'Liste' pointed toward an unremarkable theory of earthquakes through scattered judgements and selective attention to certain phenomena, Guéneau nonetheless offered it to readers as a neutral mass of facts, from which he invited them to make their own theories. This gesture was favoured in the Enlightenment, where to propound one's 'system' explicitly was seen as rash and contrary to the ideal of truth as consensus within a community, whether an academy, the Republic of Letters, or the public sphere. Alphabetically ordered works of reference such as the *Encyclopédie* often advertised their status as simple reservoirs of facts from which independent readers could draw their own conclusions, although the freedom to do so was inevitably limited by editorial choices.[41] The posture of presenting readers with facts instead of theories also lent itself to a form of utopianism. While anyone propounding a system threatened to close the door on further exploration, someone offering facts for future analysis conjured up a future of continued progress. From his position as 'compiler', as we have seen, Guéneau envisioned a worldwide network of empirical philosophers making local meteorological observations under

39. Jan Golinski, 'Barometers of change: meteorological instruments as machines of Enlightenment', in *The Sciences in enlightened Europe*, ed. William Clark, Jan Golinski and Simon Schaffer (Chicago, IL 1999), p.86-91; Feldman, 'Late Enlightenment meteorology', p.150-53, 163, 167, 171-73.

40. *CA*, vi.xi, xv, 636n, 638; Kenneth L. Taylor, 'Nicolas Desmarest and geology in the eighteenth century', in *Toward a history of geology*, ed. Cecil J. Schneer (Cambridge, MA 1969), p.341-42; B. Rohrer, *Das Erdbeben von Lissabon in der französischen Literatur des achtzehnten Jahrhunderts* (Heidelberg 1933), p.53-55. For another theoretical point see *CA*, vi.662n.

41. Wilda C. Anderson, *Between the library and the laboratory: the language of chemistry in eighteenth-century France* (Baltimore, MD 1984), p.35-69.

the watch of a central academy. Among other things, the network would add to and ultimately finish his 'Liste chronologique'. In short, he imagined the *Collection académique* not only as a means of bringing Europe's academies closer together but also as a step toward an international super-academy.[42]

In fact Guéneau's 'Liste chronologique' was in need of further work, whether by an academy or a more concentrated editor. As we have seen, the main 'Liste' is followed by a twenty-five page 'Supplément', also in chronological order. Since their dates overlap through almost their whole length, their existence as separate lists testifies to poor planning and last-minute research. More seriously, the 'Liste' is erratic from a temporal point of view. European chroniclers of natural disasters inevitably found less material in the distant past than in the present, biased as they were by Europe's increasing geographical reach and the growth of record-keeping, especially since the Renaissance. For the most part, Guéneau's 'Liste' conforms to this pattern. But presumably for lack of time, he also neglected the years preceding 1755. The following chart gives the number of pages in the 'Liste' and the 'Supplément' on which there are entries for the seven half-centuries from 1405 until 1754:

1405-1454	3 pages	+	0 pages	=	3 pages
1455-1504	4 pages	+	0 pages	=	4 pages
1505-1554	8 pages	+	2 pages	=	10 pages
1555-1604	10 pages	+	1 page	=	11 pages
1605-1654	15 pages	+	1 page	=	16 pages
1655-1704	33 pages	+	14 pages	=	47 pages
1705-1754	28 pages	+	9 pages	=	37 pages

Above all, Guéneau's data for the years 1751 to 1754 fit on one page and neglect dozens of earthquakes. Nor for these years did he record the readily available observations of weather from the Paris Observatory – observations he used amply in entries for other years.[43]

The inclusiveness of Guéneau's 'Liste' made it more subject to inconsistency than simple lists of earthquakes, since different epochs made different observations of meteorological phenomena. Measurements of barometric pressure entered the list with the entry for 1649; numerical figures for annual and monthly rainfall entered the list with the entry for 1688. In neither case did the new data settle into a definitive, standardised form. In the entries for the years from 1688 to 1708, for example, Guéneau often included a table giving monthly rainfall as measured at the Paris Observatory, but in later entries he contented himself with noting annual

42. *CA*, vi.v-vi, xv-xvin. Compare Anderson, *Between the library and the laboratory*, p.45-47.

43. Compare Jean-Jacques Nicolas Huot, 'Volcan', in *Encyclopédie méthodique: géographie-physique*, ed. Jean-Baptiste-Georges-Marie Bory de Saint-Vincent *et al.*, vol.v (Paris 1828), p.771; *RM*, xi.495-98.

rainfall. His data for rain in Britain varied unpredictably in detail and geographical provenance. Likewise, he provided extensive information on sightings of aurora borealis until 1751, but nothing thereafter. Ultimately, he left his 'Liste chronologique' in a state that discouraged comparison and generalisation.

Readers, however, may not have been interested in trying to make a theory from Guéneau's 'Liste chronologique'. A review in the *Affiches, annonces, et avis divers* paraphrased his invitation to analyse the 'Liste' further but only in passing. A reviewer for the *Journal encyclopédique*, who praised the 'Liste' for inspiring healthy fear and for constituting a 'monument' to which the Lisbon earthquake could be duly consigned, did not even mention its link with a future science of earthquakes.[44] Nor do subsequent writers on earthquakes appear to have taken Guéneau's proposal seriously. Even his close friend Buffon failed to cite the 'Liste' in his treatment of volcanoes in the *Epoques de la nature* (1778). Carl Friedrich Wilhelm Schall neglected to include it (or the *Collection*) in his *Anleitung zur Kenntnis der besten Bücher in der Mineralogie und physicalischen Erdbeschreibung* (1789), a bibliography that cited short articles as well as collections. Likewise Nicolas Desmarest left the 'Liste' out of his bibliography of works contributing to physical geography and the theory of the earth in the first volume of the *Encyclopédie méthodique: géographie physique* ([1795-1798]). Volume v of the same work (1828) included a twenty-one page chronology of earthquakes in a long article on the theory of volcanoes, but it derived from a German source, not Guéneau's 'Liste'. Moreover, the *Encyclopédie méthodique* offered its list with strict caveats about its utility: 'Ce n'est que depuis le commencement de ce siècle [1800] que l'on tient un compte exact des tremblements de terre.'[45] Already in the mid-eighteenth century, partly through Buffon's influence, research on geological history was becoming independent of ancient chronologists; in the second half of the century, the leaders of the emerging discipline of geology focused their observations on the earth itself, keeping their eyes 'on the ground', not on written records.[46] In this climate Guéneau's dream of a science of earthquakes to be based on chronology must have seemed quaint.

44. *Affiches, annonces, et avis divers* (13 May 1761), p.74; *Journal encyclopédique* 5 (August 1761), p.64, 67. See also Elie-Catherine Fréron, *L'Année littéraire* 3 (1761), p.263.

45. 'Volcan', p.763-83. For a theory of earthquakes see 'Volcan', p.717-18. The *Collection*, but not the 'Liste', is cited in Georg Rudolf Boehmer, *Bibliotheca scriptorum historiae naturalis oeconomiae aliarumque artium ac scientiarum ad illam pertinentium realis systematica* (Leipzig 1785-1789), i.87-89.

46. Rhoda Rappaport, *When geologists were historians, 1665-1750* (Ithaca, NY 1997), p.248-49, 260-62; Kenneth L. Taylor, 'Earth and heaven, 1750-1800: Enlightenment ideas about the relevance to geology of extraterrestrial operations and events', *Earth sciences history* 17 (1998), p.86-89; David R. Oldroyd, *Thinking about the earth: a history of ideas in geology* (Cambridge, MA 1996), p.70-85.

Whatever its shortcomings, the 'Liste chronologique' marked a turning point in the history of the *Collection académique*. Evaluations of the *Collection* have varied, Pierre Bernard d'Héry judging it a commercial and conceptual failure, David Kronick calling it 'the most outstanding collection of the eighteenth century'. In between, the *Biographie universelle* is probably realistic in contrasting the 'good idea' with its poor execution.[47] The growing number of books and periodicals also devoted to translating and abridging scientific publications testifies to a need and a market for projects like the *Collection*. The utility of the series can be corroborated with anecdotes about citation and consultation. The opening sub-series of the *Histoire naturelle* cited the *Collection* three times, specifically for its translation of the *Ephémérides*. In two cases Daubenton expressed doubt about anatomical findings announced in the *Ephémérides*; in the third case Buffon drew on it for the first account of the grimme, a West African antelope, to be published in Europe.[48] The *Encyclopédie* cited the *Collection* in the articles 'Pou', 'Sauterelle', 'Scolopendre de mer', 'Scorpion aquatique', 'Seiche', and 'Taon' – specifically volume v of the *Collection*, the only one consisting of a single translated book, Jan Swammerdam's long-unpublished *Biblia naturae*. In 1774, having failed to find a certain volume of the memoirs of the Bolognese Academy, the French astronomer Joseph-Jérôme de Lalande offered to send the Swedish academician Petr-Wilhelm Wargentin volume x of the *Collection académique* instead, which contained at least extracts of the volume in question.[49]

Still, it is striking that the *Encyclopédie* and *Histoire naturelle*, whose editors were Guéneau's friends and among the strongest supporters of the *Collection académique*, cited the series just a handful of times; they cited other compendia much more frequently.[50] Three factors probably contributed to this neglect. First, in attempting to reduce the volume of academic literature by a factor of twenty, the *Collection* inevitably omitted texts intriguing to some. Buffon, for example, cited several articles from the *Philosophical transactions* and the *Ephémérides* which fell within the period covered by the *Collection* but which Guéneau and his collaborators had chosen to omit.[51] Second, by the time the *Encyclopédie* and the opening sub-series of the *Histoire naturelle* were finished in the 1760s, the *Collection* had still not translated anything written after 1700. Older sources were regularly cited in scientific works of the mid-eighteenth century, but the

47. Bernard, 'Notice sur Montbeillard', p.361-62; David A. Kronick, *A History of scientific and technical periodicals: the origins and development of the scientific and technological press, 1665-1790* (New York 1962), p.186; Chaussier and Adelon, 'Berryat (Jean)', in *Biographie universelle ancienne et moderne*, iv.115.

48. Daubenton, *Histoire naturelle*, v.34, viii.95; Buffon, *Histoire naturelle*, xii.307-309.

49. McClellan, *Science reorganised*, p.189.

50. Notice, for example, the citation of the *Histoire générale des voyages* in the *Histoire naturelle* and of the *Histoire naturelle* in the *Encyclopédie*.

51. See, for example, Buffon, *Histoire naturelle*, viii.262n, x.34n. See also Bernard, 'Notice sur Montbeillard', p.361-62.

wonders abundantly reported in seventeenth-century academic publications were becoming less pertinent in the mid-eighteenth century, where utility more than curiosity defined the role of academies.[52] As noted above, Guéneau himself seems to have drawn this conclusion when he reviewed the material submitted for volume vi of the *Collection* – a realisation that led to the publication of his 'Liste chronologique' – but previous volumes were already replete with marvels: a talking dog (*RM*, iv.207), a captured mermaid (*CA*, iv.94), a man who could speak only between noon and one o'clock (*CA*, iii.439-40). Finally, the *Collection* was hampered in its project of becoming a reference work by its instability. Four editorial teams, each with its own projects, oversaw the *Collection* during its lifetime; ownership too passed through a number of publishers. Under Guéneau's direction, the *Collection* was also plagued by delays.

According to Suzanne Tucoo-Chala, the *Collection* earned Panckoucke a sixty-five per cent profit and constituted his third most-advertised title, but these results are vitiated by her failure to distinguish the *Collection* from other academic series, notably the *Mémoires des savants étrangers*.[53] If the *Collection* was so profitable, it is hard to imagine why, unlike the *Encyclopédie* and the *Histoire naturelle*, it ended up being shorter than originally advertised: first projected for 'less than forty volumes', the *Collection* came to be seen by Guéneau as a serial of indefinite proportion (*CA*, iv.x), but it ended abruptly after twenty-nine volumes. A later editor boasted that the opening volumes of the *Collection* had had to be reprinted to meet demand; if so, they may have printed in excess, for by 1771 the early volumes were being offered at a 'nearly fifty per cent' discount.[54] In 1754 Desventes boasted that the series was so far advanced and so obviously useful that he had no need to resort to the 'voie souvent équivoque des *souscriptions*' (*RM*, i.iv); barely three years later, apparently less sanguine about the work's prospects, he and his partners opened an extended campaign to win subscribers (*RM*, iii.ii; *CA*, v.i). In any case, Daniel Mornet's inventory of private libraries in France from 1750 to 1780 casts doubt on the notion that the *Collection* was popular or widely diffused; the series is absent from his list of the fifty-nine 'most read' books on the natural sciences during this period.[55] All in all, it seems clear that the *Collection* fell short of the expectations inspiring and inspired by its creation. The 'Liste chronologique', for its part, reflected and participated in the series' shortcomings: it appeared in the first of two greatly

52. Lorraine Daston and Katharine Park, *Wonders and the order of nature, 1150-1750* (New York 1998), p.329-63; Christian Licoppe, *La Formation de la pratique scientifique: le discours de l'expérience en France et en Angleterre (1630-1820)* (Paris 1996), p.16-17, 218.

53. Tucoo-Chala, *Charles-Joseph Panckoucke*, p.263-64, 267, 270, 398, 409.

54. *CA*, xiii.iii; *Mercure de France* (March 1771), p.153. The reprint in question may have been Desventes's printing of a few copies of early volumes on higher-quality paper. See *Journal des savants* (May 1757), p.318.

55. Daniel Mornet, *Les Sciences de la nature en France, au XVIIIe siècle* (New York 1971), p.247-49.

delayed volumes, it was apparently inserted because of Guéneau's frustration with his materials, and it perpetuated the *Collection*'s reverence for unsynthesised facts, however irregular in order and provenance. Perhaps significantly, the volume of the *Collection* containing the 'Liste' was the first one not reviewed in the *Journal des savants*.

Conclusion

In the history of the ramifications of the great Lisbon earthquake, Guéneau's 'Liste chronologique' is a minor affair and must be counted a failure in many respects. Its empiricism was less radical than Guéneau proclaimed, for its facts were mostly chosen in function of a traditional view of earthquakes and meteorology. Moreover, the historical testimony on which it was based was falling out of fashion in geological research, increasingly replaced by direct observation of rocks and earth. In its inconsistency, the 'Liste' has the look of a rushed, careless effort, yet it still appeared late because of problems with the publisher and because of Guéneau's mental health and resistance to deadlines. Above all, his hopes that the 'Liste' would be augmented by an international super-academy and serve as an springboard for future research on earthquakes were both unfulfilled. Possessing neither the vividness of Pedegache's *Relação* – which might have replaced it in the *Collection* – nor, evidently, much appeal to researchers on geological subjects, Guéneau's 'Liste' soon passed into oblivion.

As we have seen, the *Collection* itself had difficulty fulfilling its promise as a tool for scientific research, but it succeeded as an idea and utopian project, as characterised by Guéneau in his 'Discours préliminaire' and other prefaces. Contemporary reactions to the *Collection* show widespread enthusiasm, particularly among the *philosophes*, for the themes it was premised on: utility, scientific sociability, secularism, international cooperation, and empiricism. In the same way, the 'Liste chronologique' can be appreciated as an example of the good intentions embodied in Guéneau's idealistic career and in list-making and rote empiricism of the Enlightenment. If it no more led to a theory than did the epoch's myriad observations of monthly rainfall or barometric pressure, perhaps it served its author and readers in a different way, as a 'scientific' acknowledgment of the enormity of the disaster, not so different, in the end, from a poem or a prayer. Credible or not as a foundation for a science of earthquakes, the 'Liste chronologique' provided reassurance as testimony to the forces of good will, empirical effort and optimism.

ANNE SAADA
et JEAN SGARD

Tremblements dans la presse

ENVIRON un mois après le tremblement de terre de Lisbonne, la presse ressent tout à coup l'événement, d'une façon soudaine, simultanée, violente. Pendant un mois, les informations vont se succéder par secousses successives, avant qu'au début de janvier, on prenne la mesure de la catastrophe, pour ensuite l'étudier, tenter d'en faire l'histoire et de l'expliquer. Une sorte d'onde sismique parcourt toute la presse d'expression française en Europe, suivie à son tour de répliques, d'accalmies, d'ultimes secousses qui témoignent d'une instabilité et d'une angoisse persistantes. C'est ce phénomène que nous étudierons, du simple point de vue de la construction de l'événement, de la diffusion de l'information et des discours auxquels elle donne lieu. L'événement en lui-même se prête particulièrement à une étude précise: le séisme constitue une nouvelle massive, mais qui se développe dans le temps; on peut en faire aisément la description et le calendrier. Il intéresse toute l'Europe, qui d'ailleurs en ressentira sous des formes multiples les contrecoups; il mobilisera donc toute la presse durant la même période et sur le même territoire. La presse francophone offre ici un corpus relativement cohérent: elle couvre en effet la plus grande partie de l'Europe; elle forme un réseau, parfaitement apte à réagir, comme un sismographe, à des signaux multiples (dépêches, courriers, lettres, relations, etc.). Ce réseau n'est pas totalement homogène: les temps de réaction des périodiques sont évidemment liés à leur rythme de périodicité, et l'on doit tenir compte de la nature de ces rythmes. Les *gazettes* paraissent en général deux fois par semaine, elles transmettent des nouvelles sous forme de bulletins datés, elles les présentent en ordre chronologique selon le degré d'éloignement de la source: les nouvelles de Lisbonne parviendront à Paris avec en moyenne un mois de retard par rapport à l'événement, comme on le verra. Les *mercures* et les revues politiques, le plus souvent mensuelles, prennent leur distance avec l'événement et en analysent la signification avec deux mois de retard; ces revues profiteront du début de l'année 1756 pour en faire une présentation complète. Après quoi viendront les revues savantes, les *bibliothèques*, les journaux scientifiques, dont la périodicité est lente et souvent irrégulière: à elles la charge de fournir des commentaires scientifiques, philosophiques, religieux, durant toute l'année 1756. Nous porterons surtout notre attention sur l'ensemble des gazettes, car ce sont elles qui construisent l'événement et en dégagent déjà, de façon discrète, la signification. Elles constituent en 1755 un ensemble évident, mais dont le fonctionnement reste obscur; dans une certaine mesure, c'est l'événement exceptionnel qui va le révéler.

On compte en Europe, en 1755, une quinzaine de gazettes de langue française, qui couvrent la France et l'Europe du Nord:[1] les Pays-Bas (néerlandais et espagnols), l'Allemagne, la Suède. Leur public est en grande majorité francophone – c'est évidemment le cas pour la *Gazette de France*, les *Affiches de province* et le *Courrier d'Avignon* – mais les grandes gazettes autorisées d'Amsterdam, d'Utrecht, de Bruxelles se partagent une bonne part du marché français de l'information. Cet ensemble de bi-hebdomadaires se montre très réactif au milieu du siècle pour deux raisons: la révolution postale et l'approche de la guerre. Gilles Feyel a montré l'importance de la guerre des tarifs postaux entre 1750 et 1760:[2] Charles Giroud, à Avignon, obtient un accord de faveur pour ses journaux (*Courrier d'Avignon* et *Gazette d'Amsterdam* comprise) dès 1750; la *Gazette de France* obtient le même accord de la Ferme des Postes en 1751; la Ferme, le Ministère des Affaires étrangères et la *Gazette* s'efforcent ensuite d'obtenir le privilège de diffusion des gazettes périphériques, dont le coût d'abonnement baisse régulièrement. En outre, la menace de la guerre, très insistante en 1755, laisse prévoir un fort besoin d'information. En fait, la mobilisation est en cours et les opérations maritimes ont commencé: à consulter la *Gazette d'Amsterdam* ou le *Journal de Verdun*, on peut constater que les prises de bateaux sont continuelles tout au long de l'année 1755. On s'attend à la guerre et tout le réseau informatif des journaux, des ambassades et des consulats, des négociants et armateurs, est en alerte; on pourra même croire un moment que le désastre de Lisbonne était de nature à suspendre ou retarder la guerre; il n'en sera rien.[3] On avait connu par le passé des tremblements de terre – et l'on en fera bientôt l'histoire – mais ils ne concernaient pas un pays aussi proche, une famille royale aussi liée à la couronne de France par son régime, sa religion, sa dynastie, une ville si connue et si prospère, un nœud commercial aussi important, presque une 'ville-monde' pour reprendre l'expression de

---

1. Elles seront désignées, dans nos références, par les sigles suivants: *GA* (Amsterdam), *GB* (Berne), *GBr* (Brunswick), *GC* (Cologne), *GH* (La Haye), *GL* (Leyde), *GS* (Stockholm), *GU* (Utrecht); s'y ajoute le *Courrier d'Avignon* (*CA*). Nous n'avons pas pu disposer d'exemplaire de la *Gazette de Bruxelles*, de la *Gazette de Liège*, ni des *Affiches de Lyon* pour 1755.

2. Voir 'La diffusion des gazettes étrangères en France et la révolution postale des années 1750', dans *Les Gazettes européennes de langue française*, éd. Henri Duranton, Claude Labrosse et Pierre Rétat (Saint-Etienne 1992), p.81-98.

3. Comme le note à plusieurs reprises la *Gazette de Leyde*, le désastre de Lisbonne n'a pas ralenti les préparatifs de guerre; ainsi de Paris le 15 décembre: 'On a d'abord été assez généralement d'opinion que le malheur arrivé à Lisbonne aurait refroidi l'ardeur des Anglais; mais les avis de Londres nous détrompent: ce désastre, loin d'arrêter leur fureur pour la guerre, ne fait que l'augmenter' (*GL*, mardi 23 décembre 1755).

Fernand Braudel.[4] D'où cette attention intense, et cette élaboration passionnée de l'événement, en six séquences pourrait-on dire.

i. Séquences du désastre

a. Premiers signes

Le séisme de Lisbonne a lieu le 1er novembre à 9 heures du matin. Il ne sera pas évoqué avant le 22 novembre; mais la secousse a été perçue beaucoup plus tôt sans qu'on en comprenne l'origine. A Hambourg, selon le Supplément de la *Gazette de Cologne* du 7 novembre, on a ressenti, le 1er novembre, 'une secousse de tremblement de terre qui fut assez gaillarde'. De même à La Haye, selon la *Gazette d'Utrecht* du mardi 4 novembre: '*De La Haye, le 3 novembre.* On ressentit ici une secousse de tremblement de terre, mais qui ayant été assez légère, n'a causé aucun dommage. La même secousse s'est fait sentir dans plusieurs autres endroits de cette province, sans y avoir non plus causé de dommage.' La Trave bouillonne près de Hambourg (*GC*, 14.xi); des secousses sismiques ont été perçues, le 1er novembre, à Bordeaux, mais aussi en Angleterre, en Hollande, en Allemagne, en Groenland, et dans le Supplément de la *Gazette de Cologne* du 18, relayée par la *Gazette d'Utrecht* du 21, puis du 25, l'inquiétude est perceptible:

De Colorne, le 7 novembre. On apprend par une lettre particulière de Bordeaux, qu'on y a eu un tremblement de terre de 2 minutes de durée et très violent le 1er de ce mois à 10 heures un quart du matin. Les secousses d'un tremblement de terre, qu'on a ressenties le même jour à Portsmouth, Rotterdam, Amsterdam, Hambourg et Lübeck, n'ont point été annoncées avec assez d'exactitude pour déterminer si elles se sont rencontrées dans la même heure en évaluant la différence des méridiens.[5]

Cette attention diffuse aux signes sismiques s'explique un peu partout par le souvenir des séismes récents du Mexique, de l'Espagne et de la Suisse.

b. La secousse de Madrid

Entre le 1er et le 20 novembre, les signes précurseurs se sont multipliés, mais si l'on excepte la secousse de Bordeaux, ils viennent tous du Nord, du simple fait de la densité du réseau informatif des gazettes; du même coup, on ne soupçonne pas le lieu du tremblement de terre: de Lisbonne, de Madrid même, rien avant le 21 novembre. Et encore la *Gazette de Cologne* est-elle la seule, ce vendredi-là, à annoncer la nouvelle de la secousse de Madrid, dans son Supplément du 21:

De Madrid, le 3 novembre. Le 1er de ce mois, à 10 heures et 17 ou 18 minutes du matin, nous avons eu ici pendant 4 minutes un violent tremblement de terre, qui a

---

4. *Le Temps du monde* (Paris 1979), p.114 et suiv.
5. 'Colorne' semble bien désigner la Cour de Parme, qui est très liée à l'Espagne.

endommagé plusieurs édifices et coûté la vie à 2 enfants écrasés par la chute d'une croix de pierre du frontispice d'une église. On apprend de plusieurs villes des environs, qu'on y en a aussi ressenti les secousses et qu'en particulier elles ont été très vives à l'Escurial, d'où la Cour partit subitement peu après pour revenir ici.

La *Gazette de Cologne* semble disposer de sources exclusives: le courrier de Madrid est daté du 3, alors que pour la plupart des autres journaux, ce sera un courrier du 4.[6] La *Gazette de France*, qui n'avait encore rien signalé, reçoit coup sur coup une lettre de Madrid du 4 et une autre du 10, ce qui l'amène à publier le samedi 22 un numéro tout à fait exceptionnel:

On essuya ici, le 1er de ce mois, un des plus violents tremblements de terre qu'on y eut éprouvés depuis longtemps. Il commença à dix heures vingt minutes du matin et il dura huit minutes. Cet événement répandit partout une telle épouvante, que la plupart des habitants prirent la fuite et que les prêtres mêmes, qui étaient à l'autel, le quittèrent. Cependant, il n'est arrivé d'autre malheur que la perte de deux enfants, tués par une croix de pierre, qui est tombée du portail de l'église de *Bon Succès*. L'église de Saint André a souffert un tel ébranlement, qu'il s'est fait plusieurs lézardes dans la voûte et dans les murailles. La partie supérieure du portail de la paroisse de Saint Louis s'est fendue.

Les secousses ont aussi été très fortes à l'Escurial, et l'on y eut la première à dix heures dix minutes. La proximité des montagnes donnant lieu de craindre que, s'il survenait un nouveau tremblement, les secousses ne fussent plus dangereuses qu'à Madrid, Leurs Majestés partirent après leur dîner, pour revenir ici. Elles y arrivèrent à huit heures et demie du soir. Le lendemain, par égard pour les alarmes d'une partie de la Cour, Leurs Majestés passèrent toute la matinée sous une tente de la ville. Le soir, le Roi fit chanter le *Te Deum* dans l'église des Hiéronimites, en action de grâce de ce que ce tremblement n'a point eu de suites fâcheuses pour cette capitale. Hier, Leurs Majestés, entendirent dans la même église l'Office des Morts.

Ce bulletin constitue une véritable version officielle; on admirera au passage le style majestueux, la précision et la prudence de l'exposé. Tout est dit: à Madrid déjà, on aura connu le rythme implacable de l'événement, la catastrophe elle-même, le salut de la famille royale, le fait divers pathétique, le bilan qui aurait pu être pire, le *Te Deum* final. Cependant, ce même jour du 22 novembre, la *Gazette de France* publie des lettres de Madrid du 10, qui donnent dans le désordre des nouvelles des grandes villes d'Espagne, notamment de Séville et de Cadix, et enfin de Lisbonne, sous une forme sommaire:

Pour ce qui regarde le Portugal, on a été informé par un courrier dépêché de Lisbonne, et qui est arrivé à Madrid le 8. du courant à quatre heures après-midi, que le 1er. de ce mois, vers les 9. heures du matin, le tremblement s'y est fait sentir d'une façon terrible. Il a renversé la moitié de la ville, toutes les églises et le palais du Roi. Heureusement il n'est arrivé aucun accident à la Famille Royale, qui était à Belem. Le palais qu'Elle habite en ce lieu a souffert. Au départ du courrier, Elle était encore sous des baraques, Elle couchait dans des carrosses, et

---

6. La *GH* du 24 novembre et la *GB* du 29 se réfèrent également à un courrier de Madrid du 3 novembre.

Elle avait été près de vingt-quatre heures sans officiers, et sans avoir presque rien à manger. Le feu a pris dans la partie de la ville, qui n'a pas été renversée. Il durait encore quand le courrier est parti. [...] Comme ce courrier a été uniquement dépêché pour informer Leurs Majestés Catholiques qu'il n'était arrivé aucun malheur à la Famille Royale, on ne sait pas d'autres particularités.

Telle est la première annonce qu'on eut du tremblement de terre de Lisbonne. Ce courrier sans doute expédié par l'ambassadeur de Baschi comporte beaucoup d'approximations, il est marqué d'un certain désarroi; c'est sans doute ce qui a poussé les services de Versailles à le retenir et à n'en donner que des fragments dans la *Gazette* du 22. La *Gazette de Berne*, qui transmettra l'information le 29 novembre, témoigne de l'affolement qui dut régner le 18 dans les couloirs de Versailles:

Paris, 20 novembre 1755. Le Roi reçut, avant-hier, un courrier extraordinaire de la part de son ambassadeur à la Cour de Portugal, avec la nouvelle de l'événement le plus terrible qu'on ait vu jamais en Europe. Il est porté dans les dépêches de cet exprès, que le 1er de ce mois entre les 9 et 10 heures du matin, il y eut à Lisbonne un tremblement de terre de 6 à 7 minutes, occasionné par un ouragan furieux; que dans un si court espace, les 7/8èmes des maisons de la ville furent parties renversées par la secousse du tremblement et parties réduites en cendres par 3 volcans qui ayant subitement paru causèrent un incendie, lequel durait encore le 4, jour du départ du Courrier; que 100 à 130 000 habitants de Lisbonne sont restés ensevelis sous les ruines de cette infortunée ville.[7]

c. Le 28 novembre

Ce jour-là, dans tout le reste de l'Europe, on eut soudain connaissance du désastre. On retrouve à peu de chose près la version de la *Gazette de France* dans la *Gazette d'Amsterdam* du 28. Tous les éléments de la catastrophe y sont résumés, de façon provisoire: tremblement à 9h, ville détruite à moitié, toutes les églises renversées de même que le palais royal, famille royale épargnée, incendie, 50 000 victimes.[8] Si l'on compare cette version avec celle que donne le même jour la *Gazette de Cologne*, on constatera que la base du récit est la même, qu'elle y est cependant complétée par plusieurs sources différentes: une lettre de l'ambassade de France et une lettre en italien du Nonce, entre autres, ont nourri les dépêches du courrier, que la *Gazette d'Utrecht* reprend et complète à son tour; elle les publie le même jour que la *Gazette de Cologne*, ce qui tend à faire croire que les deux journaux ont une source commune, visiblement diplomatique. Peut-être est-ce le fonds commun de toutes les versions publiées ce 28 novembre: une synthèse officielle, une 'lettre écrite de Madrid' rédigée à Buen Retiro le 4, une autre du 10 à partir de l'exprès venu du

7. La *GB* est toutefois la seule à publier la nouvelle de la mort du petit-fils du grand Racine, nouvelle qui sera commentée un peu partout le mois suivant.

8. En réalité pas plus de 15 000, sur un total de 260 000 habitants.

campement de Belém, accompagnées de documents de diverses provenances dont nous parlerons plus tard.[9]

d. Le silence de Lisbonne

De Lisbonne même, rien ne vient après ces premiers échos. La *Gazette de Leyde* (Suppl.) note, le 5 décembre, le côté inhabituel de ce silence:

De Leide, le 5 décembre. Il y a des Lettres de Madrid du 17 du mois dernier, qui disent, qu'on n'y avait rien appris de Lisbonne depuis le 5 novembre: Ainsi nous n'aurons point aujourd'hui 5. Décembre des Lettres de cette dernière ville. Le Courier, qui auroit dû partir le 4. Novembre n'aura pu être expédié à cause de la confusion et de la consternation, où l'on y a été encore probablement ce jour Là. [...] On craint beaucoup pour les Navires qui se sont trouvés sur le Tage, parce qu'il n'est point arrivé de Nouvelles en Angleterre.

Les nouvelles ne passent plus, la *Gazeta de Lisboa* est muette, comme le remarque encore la *Gazette d'Amsterdam* le 16 décembre (nouvelle du 25.xi):[10] 'On n'a encore reçu aucune relation circonstanciée des désastres de Lisbonne. La Gazette de cette ville ne vient plus.'

Cependant le 16 décembre on trouvera dans la *Gazette de Cologne* un récit un peu plus complet de la catastrophe et de ses lendemains. Il y est question non seulement de la fouille des ruines, mais des pillards et de la répression: 'Cinq de ces scélérats, convaincus d'avoir mis le feu aux maisons, qui ont été réduites en cendres, ont été pendus à ces potences.' Le récit est dans l'ensemble précis, très descriptif; pourtant, ce bulletin, qui résume un récit de Lisbonne, a été élaboré à Madrid, et le 19 décembre encore, le même journaliste en fait la remarque: 'On ne reçoit encore en droiture de Lisbonne aucune relation du terrible tremblement de terre, que cette infortunée Ville a essuyé le 1er novembre.' Deux voies seraient possibles pour l'acheminement des nouvelles: la voie de terre, mais les routes sont rompues et les pillards attaquent les courriers, comme le rapporte la *Gazette de Cologne* le 12 décembre:

De Cologne, le 12 décembre. On n'a point encore de lettres de Lisbonne cet ordinaire. Il y en a de France, qui disent que les bandits et autres prisonniers, qui ont recouvré leur liberté à l'occasion du tremblement de terre le 1er de ce mois, se sont répandus dans les grands chemins, qu'ils arrêtent, pillent et dévalisent les courriers et voitures, qu'on envoie de Madrid à Lisbonne ou qui vont de cette ville en Espagne. Selon ces avis, c'est là la cause que les 2 courriers ordinaires du 5 et du 12 ne sont pas arrivés.

---

9. Notons que la même version est donnée par la *GH* du 26.xi, la *GBr* du 6.xii, et sous une forme différente par la *GS* du 12.xii.

10. En réalité, la *Gazeta da Lisboa* a encore publié un numéro le 5 novembre. Voir la thèse dact. d'André Belo, *Nouvelles d'Ancien Régime. La 'Gazeta de Lisboa' et l'information manuscrite au Portugal (1715-1760)*, 1993, ainsi que son article 'A Gazeta de Lisboa eo terramoto de 1755: a margem do nao escrito', *Analise social* 151-52, t.xxxiv (2000), p.619-37. Selon l'auteur, le tirage de la *Gazeta* était de 1500 exemplaires; t.cite les numéros 45 et 46 de novembre 1755.

La voie de mer vers l'Angleterre est traditionnelle; mais un mois après le séisme, aucun bateau n'est signalé en provenance de Lisbonne, comme le note la *Gazette d'Utrecht* (Suppl. 2.xii):

Toutes les nouvelles qu'ils en ont apprises leur sont venues de Madrid et de Paris. L'impatience où sont les négociants est d'autant plus naturelle, que les paquebots de Lisbonne font leur trajet ordinairement en 8 ou 9 jours, et qu'à leur défaut, il devrait au moins être arrivé quelque autre bâtiment anglais, puisque dans le temps du désastre de Lisbonne, il y avait sur le Tage 47 vaisseaux anglais, 50 tant hollandais que danois et suédois, outre plusieurs navires français et espagnols.

Au séisme s'ajoutent donc, comme le dira la *Gazette de Brunswick* du 31 janvier 'l'ébranlement, à l'ébranlement la ruine, à la ruine l'embrasement, à l'embrasement l'inondation'. On en est réduit à scruter les lettres venues d'Espagne par Bayonne, mais cette correspondance officieuse est suspecte, elle est marquée d'exagérations, de terreurs, de fausses nouvelles.[11]

e. Les témoignages

On avait pu entendre déjà des témoignages individuels, mais qui émanaient de personnages officiels; c'était le cas de l'ambassadeur de France, puis de son épouse, la comtesse de Baschi; il y avait encore le personnel de l'ambassade d'Espagne, le nonce du pape, l'envoyé d'Angleterre, etc. Voici le récit de M. de Castres, envoyé de Londres, témoin du désastre, dont il décrit l'ampleur et parfois les détails surprenants (*GC*, 26.xii):

De tous les édifices publics, il n'est resté sur pied que l'Hôtel des Monnaies, où il y a de grandes richesses, qui par l'intrépidité d'un officier subalterne, qui y était en faction et n'a point quitté son poste pendant 3 jours, ont échappé à la scélératesse d'une foule de voleurs, les uns déserteurs français et espagnols, les autres esclaves nègres et matelots anglais etc. qui avaient entrepris de piller, saccager et réduire en cendres tout ce que le tremblement n'avait pas renversé.

A partir de décembre, on va entendre, en ordre dispersé, toutes sortes de récits spontanés de négociants, de marins, d'écrivains qui se trouvaient là par malheur, autant de journalistes improvisés, mais dont la vision va souvent se révéler remarquable dans son désordre et son émotion. M. Pédegache résidait depuis plusieurs années à Lisbonne, où il écrivait une histoire et une description du Portugal. Recruté par le *Journal étranger* et le *Mercure* comme correspondant, il leur adressera un récit très circonstancié, dans lequel paraît sa détresse: il a tout perdu, sa fortune, ses livres, ses manuscrits. Il s'efforce à un compte rendu objectif, mais y parvient difficilement. On est le 11 novembre: 'Je vous écris au milieu de la campagne; car il n'y a pas de maison habitable. Lisbonne est perdue.'

---

11. Le paradoxe veut que la France tienne ses informations de l'Espagne, dont la diplomatie neutraliste lui est suspecte, et que l'Angleterre les reçoive de la France, avec qui elle est presque en guerre.

(*Journal étranger*, décembre 1755; *Mercure de France*, janvier 1756). Toutes ces 'relations' envahissent la presse à la fin de l'année 1755; elles s'imposent dans les grandes rétrospectives de début 1756, avant d'atteindre un public très vaste dans des textes imprimés séparément. En décembre, nous en trouvons dans les gazettes une dizaine, souvent très bien écrites, à la fois précises et dramatiques, telle la grande relation publiée dans la *Gazette de Stockholm* du 23 décembre: 'Le jour de Tous-les-Saints à neuf heures du matin on a senti dans tout le Portugal et surtout dans la ville de Lisbonne, un violent tremblement de terre.' Elles ont souvent eu une double diffusion, dans la presse et dans les brochures. La bibliographie de Pierre Conlon pour 1755 en compte une quinzaine, qui pour la plupart viennent de paraître dans les gazettes. Pour 1756, elle en compte une dizaine; mais déjà, on peut constater que l'on passe du récit événementiel au commentaire religieux, philosophique, politique, scientifique. La peur n'a pas disparu, mais elle se concentre sur les répliques et sur l'étude du phénomène sismique.

f. Le contrecoup culturel

Ce qui surprend le plus, une fois le désastre connu, c'est l'étendue du phénomène, c'est que la secousse ait pris tant de formes sur un territoire aussi vaste. Dès le 1er novembre, il y a eu en Afrique de forts tremblements, ainsi à Ceuta, à Maroc (Marrakech), puis le 18, le 19, le 20 novembre à Tétouan, à Fez et Mequinez (Meknès), où le nombre des victimes paraît considérable; le *Mercure historique et politique*, le *Journal encyclopédique* et le *Mercure* en parlent longuement dans leur numéro de janvier. A Lisbonne même, une seconde forte secousse s'est fait sentir le 8 novembre (*GA*, 23.xii; *GL*, 23.xii; *GS*, 23.xii), et le jour suivant, la même secousse a été ressentie dans le Bugey, à Lyon et en Suisse (*GA* 26.xii). Le *Mercure* se montre très attentif à ces répliques et recueille, à travers la presse européenne, les témoignages les plus lointains. Ces observations, qui viendront de Dalécarlie, de Compostelle, de Prague, de Tarascon et d'Arles ou de Besançon, invitent à une réflexion scientifique. Toute l'année 1756 y sera consacrée; de même, les réflexions sur les causes de la catastrophe, ou sur les moyens de reconstruire Lisbonne, mais elles n'appartiennent plus à l'information directe. Déjà en février, on entre dans l'épilogue du désastre de Lisbonne. C'est le moment où les revues littéraires et les journaux savants vont prendre la relève de l'information immédiate. Leur rythme de publication oblige les revues littéraires ou savantes à une distance par rapport à l'événement; ce qui n'empêche nullement les écrivains et poètes de manifester très tôt leur émotion. Fréron a réagi très vite; il date du 15 novembre dans *L'Année littéraire* une lettre relative au raz de marée de Cadix et à la mort du jeune Racine, unique héritier de Louis, petit-fils de Jean Racine; une 'Ode sur le tremblement de terre arrivé à Lisbonne le 1. novembre 1755 et sur la mort du jeune Racine' par 'M. Guis...' a été soumise au censeur dès le

28 novembre 1755, l'ode de Le Brun et l'ode latine de Bruté de Loirelle, *'in Lisbonense excidium'* le 21 décembre: or le tome vii semble bien avoir paru dès la fin de décembre.[12]

ii. La paralysie du réseau

Délaissons à présent le récit que les gazettes ont donné de l'événement, pour nous tourner vers leur mode d'organisation: comment ont-elles construit leur discours? Les gazettes font souvent allusion à la perturbation de leur réseau d'information du fait du séisme, ce qui nous instruit sur le fonctionnement de ce réseau. Leurs sources sont traditionnellement de quatre sortes. Il y a d'abord les courriers officiels, porteurs d'*exprès*, de *dépêches*, d'*extraordinaires*. On les nomme souvent *Courriers de cabinet*; ils sont envoyés par la Cour, par les ministres et les ambassadeurs; ils se déplacent à cheval, à grande allure, utilisant en cas de besoin les chevaux des relais de postes. En principe, ils ne délivrent leur information qu'aux grands personnages auxquels ils sont dépêchés:[13] c'est ainsi que la Cour de Lisbonne communique avec Madrid, et Madrid (Buen Retiro) avec Versailles; mais dans le cas présent l'information est rapidement et largement diffusée au dehors. Il y a l'*ordinaire*, qui joint les grandes capitales par des voitures circulant à date fixe, ou par des paquebots reliant les grands ports; ce courrier ordinaire contient une ou plusieurs lettres de correspondants attitrés, accompagnées de documents publics; l'*Almanach royal* en donne les dates d'arrivée. Il y a ensuite les *lettres* particulières de lecteurs ou de correspondants du journal, lettres adressées au rédacteur mais souvent récrites par lui, et enfin les *relations* rédigées par des écrivains ou des journalistes de métier, et qui parfois sont publiées séparément; c'est par elles qu'on connaîtra le détail du désastre. Les gazettes de Cologne, d'Utrecht, de Berne témoignent à plusieurs reprises de la tétanisation de ce réseau en novembre (*GB*, 17.xii):

Tout ce qu'on sait du lamentable événement de Lisbonne ne roule jusqu'ici que sur ce qu'on en a appris par le courrier extraordinaire de l'ambassadeur du Roi près de S. M. T. F. lequel en apporta, le 18 du mois dernier, les 1res nouvelles à Versailles. Il en est aussi venu quelques avis par la voie de Madrid, d'où l'on y avait expédié quelques exprès qui par rapport à la difficulté de trouver des chevaux dans les stations ordinaires en Portugal, ont été obligés de faire une partie de leur route à pied. Mais on peut dire que tant ici qu'en Espagne, on n'est informé que du simple fait de la catastrophe; et qu'on manque du côté des particularités qui s'y rapportent, attendu que les courriers ordinaires restent jusqu'à présent en arrière.

12. Le *CA* en signale la sortie dans son numéro du 2 janvier 1756. Remarquons au passage que la nouvelle n'était connue, le 18 novembre, qu'à la Cour, et que Fréron a donc dû en être informé personnellement.
13. Le *CA* signale de place en place ces courriers officiels qui passent sans rien dire (voir le 9.iv.56 et le 15.iv).

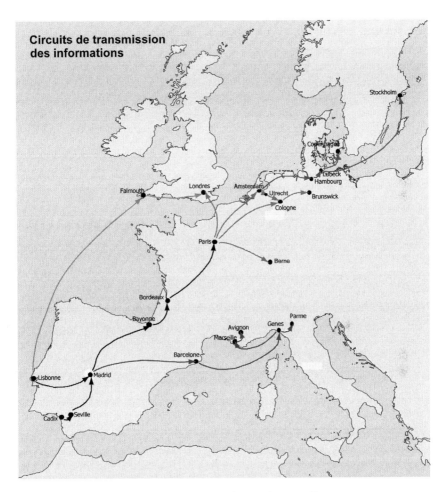

Circuits de transmission des informations

6. Itinéraires de diffusion de l'information en Europe en 1755.

La *Gazette de La Haye* signalera le 22 décembre, que le roi d'Espagne a dû envoyer des escortes armées sur la frontière de Portugal pour protéger les courriers. Les courriers officiels furent les premiers à divulguer l'événement; leurs dépêches se retrouvent à l'identique dans plusieurs gazettes: ainsi, le courrier dépêché de Lisbonne le 4 novembre et arrivé le 8 à Madrid[14] est reproduit, à quelques variations près, entre le 26 et le 29 novembre dans les gazettes de France, de Cologne, d'Utrecht, d'Amsterdam, de Berne (supplément), et de La Haye.[15] Il en va de même de la lettre adressée par le Nonce du Portugal au Nonce de Madrid, citée par les gazettes de Cologne et d'Utrecht conjointement à ce premier courrier,[16] et au milieu d'autres documents par la *Gazette de Berne*. On l'a vu: celle-ci disposait visiblement d'autres sources ou appartenait à un autre réseau d'informations. Dernier document qui apparaît simultanément dans plusieurs gazettes, la relation faite par M. de Castres dans deux lettres écrites de Lisbonne les 6 et 20 novembre, publiées pour la première dans la gazette de la Cour (d'Angleterre) vers le 13 décembre et pour la seconde vers le 18 décembre. Les gazettes de Cologne, de Leyde et de Berne les résumaient fin décembre[17] et celle de Leyde (26.xii) les restituait dans leur intégralité.

Ces sources diplomatiques ne constituent qu'une partie du matériel qui servait à alimenter les gazettes. Une autre source provenait de bulletins accrédités et de lettres des nombreux négociants français, hollandais et surtout allemands et anglais installés au Portugal, documents qui constituaient l'*ordinaire*. Mais celui-ci prit plus de retard encore, comme le signale la *Gazette de Cologne* du 9 décembre:

De trois lettres de Lisbonne, qu'on faisait état de recevoir cet ordinaire, on n'en a reçu aucune, soit que les personnes, dont on les attendait, aient eu le malheur d'être enveloppées dans les ruines de cette ville, soit que le 5 novembre, jour ordinaire de départ du courrier, on n'en ait pas fait partir; ce qui est le plus vraisemblable, attendu que celui que le Roi de Portugal avait envoyé à Madrid le jour précédent, avait trouvé un si grand dérangement dans les premières stations des postes, qu'il avait été obligé de marcher 20 lieues à pieds.

Le réseau de communication que les négociants avaient établi pour transmettre et recevoir rapidement les nouvelles des grandes métropoles avait en effet également été victime des bouleversements engendrés par le tremblement de terre. Les lettres qu'ils adressèrent à leurs confrères mirent ainsi un mois avant de parvenir à leurs destinataires.[18] La *Gazette*

---

14. *GC*, 28.xi.

15. Nous n'avons malheureusement pu consulter la *GL* pour la semaine du 28.xi.

16. La *GU* restitue intégralement la lettre dans son supplément du 28.xi.

17. *GC*, 26.xii, *GL*, 19.xii et 23.xii. La *Gazette de Berne* dans ses suppléments du 27 décembre et du 3 janvier semble s'être inspirée ici des gazettes de Leyde et de Cologne.

18. Un important arrivage de lettres à Londres par voie maritime fut signalé à la mi-décembre. C'est ainsi que l'on apprit que peu d'Anglais avaient péri mais que la factorerie anglaise était ruinée (*GL*, 19.xii, *GC*, 26.xii, *GBr*, 27.xii).

de La Haye reproduisait deux de ces lettres dans ses colonnes le 8 et le 19 décembre,[19] et celles d'Utrecht et de Leyde en imprimèrent chacune une (respectivement le 2.xii et le 30.xii). Ces lettres témoignent de la façon dont leurs auteurs avaient vécu la journée du 1er novembre, décrivent les pertes financières et matérielles terribles qu'ils avaient subies, énumèrent les bâtiments détruits et informent de l'état dans lequel se trouvait la population. Un négociant anonyme envoie à un ami de Paris un récit pathétique (*GU*, Suppl. 2 décembre):

On voit ici la lettre suivante d'un négociant, qui était établi à Lisbonne, écrite à son correspondant en cette ville. Je suis échappé seul de ma maison, et avec l'unique habit que j'ai sur le corps, à l'horrible désastre qui vient d'abîmer Lisbonne. Ma fortune, mes effets, tout ce que je possédais au monde, sont ensevelis sous les ruines d'une ville qui était devenue ma seconde patrie. J'ai vécu jusqu'à l'âge de 72 ans, pour être témoin du plus terrible fléau qui puisse manifester la Colère sur des hommes pécheurs. Du lieu où je m'étais sauvé à la campagne, j'ai vu cette grande et superbe ville, se renverser par des secousses qui soulevaient les bâtiments les plus solides et les agitaient de la même manière que le vent agite les roseaux.

Ces lettres étaient accompagnées de véritables lettres d'information, peut-être rédigées par les services de l'ambassade de France: 'Lettres de Lisbonne' ou 'Lettres écrites des environs de Lisbonne', écrites sur un ton beaucoup moins personnel que les précédentes. Leur différence de statut se montre par le fait qu'une même lettre pouvait être reproduite dans plusieurs gazettes, ce qui ne fut jamais le cas des lettres de négociants. Les gazettes de La Haye et d'Amsterdam citaient ainsi le 1er et le 2 décembre une 'Lettre' datée de Lisbonne du 5 novembre signalant que l'incendie commençait à diminuer. La *Gazette d'Utrecht* ensuite (le 9.xii) reproduisait une 'Lettre de Lisbonne' écrite le 7 novembre, véritable bulletin d'information générale. La même gazette insérait le 16 décembre une lettre du 10 novembre dans laquelle on apprenait que commerçants et habitants commençaient à retrouver leurs effets et où l'on s'interrogeait sur le fait de savoir si 'l'on entreprendra de relever Lisbonne'. Le même jour, la *Gazette de Leyde* renvoyait à des lettres de Lisbonne du 11 novembre qui parlaient de tranquillité retrouvée. Enfin, le 31 décembre, les gazettes de La Haye et de Berne publiaient une longue relation remontant au 25 novembre dans laquelle on apprenait que le roi avait décidé de faire reconstruire la capitale du Portugal à Lisbonne même.

Les lettres de témoins, celles que l'on nomme les 'lettres particulières', par opposition aux 'lettres publiques' (*GB*, 13.xii), se sont multipliées à partir du 28 novembre, comme le signale la *Gazette d'Utrecht*: 'Avant-hier, on a reçu ici, par la voie de France et d'Espagne, un grand nombre de lettres au sujet du désastre arrivé dans le Royaume de Portugal'

---

19. La troisième est mentionnée le 3 décembre.

(Suppl. du 28.xi). Ici, le souci de rassurer ne paraît plus; on y sent plus souvent s'exprimer l'accablement, le désespoir, parfois l'horreur, comme dans cette lettre envoyée de Cadix le 10 novembre au *Courrier d'Avignon* et publiée le 5 décembre:

Des murs renversés, des espaces considérables où l'on ne voit pas pierre sur pierre, des gouffres encore ouverts de toutes parts; une poignée de citoyens sans asile, qui viennent au-devant de leur maître[20] en poussant des cris lamentables; des cadavres mutilés, dont la terre avait vomi des membres, des monceaux de corps humains et des animaux entassés sous les ruines, des petits enfants écrasés dans le sein de leur mère.

Chaque journal semble bénéficier de correspondants bénévoles qui transmettent des lettres, et chacun publie les siennes. Ce que l'on attend pourtant avec le plus d'impatience, ce sont les *relations*, plus complètes, plus descriptives. La *Gazette de Cologne* déplore l'absence de relation complète et fiable:

Suite de Paris, du 29 novembre. Depuis le premier courrier de notre ambassadeur à Lisbonne, on n'a plus reçu aucunes autres particularités du désastre, arrivé à cette Capitale. Il en a cependant déjà paru ici trois relations différentes; mais il n'est guère difficile de s'apercevoir qu'elles ont été fabriquées à Paris.[21]

Elle regrette encore, le 19 décembre, que l'on ne reçoive 'en droiture' de Lisbonne aucune 'relation du terrible tremblement de terre'. Le libraire Scheurleer annonce dans la *Gazette d'Utrecht* du 26 décembre un numéro du *Mercure historique et politique* dans lequel 'on trouvera une relation exacte et très circonstanciée du malheur arrivé à la ville de Lisbonne et à tout le royaume de Portugal, dressé sur les Mémoires les plus authentiques qu'on a eus touchant le sort de cette malheureuse ville'. Le *Mercure historique* publie effectivement en janvier une 'Seconde Relation de la ruine déplorable de Lisbonne, avec toutes les circonstances qu'on en a pu apprendre jusqu'à ce jour', et l'on y perçoit une certaine recherche littéraire (métaphores, présent de narration):

La veille de la Toussaint, on s'aperçut de quelques légers mouvements, qui furent les avant-coureurs de la secousse qui se fit sentir le lendemain à dix heures du matin. Elle ne parut d'abord que comme un ébranlement causé par un carrosse. A ce mouvement la plupart des habitants sortent de leurs maisons.

Au début de janvier, ces relations récrites se multiplient dans la presse comme en librairie; jusqu'à la grande *Relation historique du tremblement de terre survenu à Lisbonne* d'Ange Goudar, elles occuperont le devant de la scène.

---

20. Le Roi du Portugal.
21. *GC*, Suppl. du 5.xii. Même remarque dans la *GB* du 17.xii.

iii. Discours de substitution

Comme on a pu le constater, le trait le plus saisissant de l'effet de Lisbonne sur la presse, c'est d'abord le désarroi: une nouvelle assourdissante est suivie d'un long silence, car le système informatif du Portugal a été détruit et la conjoncture politique rend suspectes les correspondances traditionnelles. Toutes les gazettes déplorent donc le manque d'informations, ce qui leur permet de continuer à parler du tremblement, l'absence d'informations devenant le signe même de l'ampleur de la catastrophe. En dehors du récit du désastre proprement dit, trois types de discours vont se relayer dans les gazettes, contribuant à placer le tremblement au centre de l'actualité. En premier, celui qui rend compte de la consternation éprouvée dans les grandes métropoles. Cet effet est particulièrement sensible à Londres, où l'on se méfie des nouvelles parisiennes, et où l'on a perdu le contact maritime avec Lisbonne (*GB*, 13.12, nouvelles de Londres du 25.xi):

C'est pour accélérer ces avis et s'assurer de relations bien au juste à cet égard qu'à défaut de l'arrivée du paquebot ordinaire qui doit être parti de Lisbonne le 2 ou 3 de ce mois, il y a eu ordre de la Cour au bateau de la Poste d'en dépêcher un extraordinaire auquel il est enjoint de faire toute la diligence possible tant pour aller que pour revenir: et outre les lettres tant publiques que particulières, qu'il est chargé de remettre à ceux des correspondants nationaux qui se trouveront exister, il y a eu quelques négociants qui ont pris le parti de s'embarquer à bord du dit paquebot que l'on présume avoir fait voile hier, de Falmouth.

Cependant la même rupture de communication est ressentie dans les grandes capitales économiques, et en particulier à Amsterdam:

C'est du 26, qu'on sait à Amsterdam la terrible catastrophe de Lisbonne et de la même date, on écrit qu'on en a été consterné généralement à la Bourse, comme un événement qui ne peut qu'être infiniment désastreux pour les négociants tant de Londres que de ces Provinces, et d'une influence au-delà de tout ce qu'on peut imaginer pour tout le commerce de l'Europe.

A l'événement même du tremblement se substitue le tableau de sa réception: c'est elle désormais qui compose en partie le discours des gazettes. On ne doit pas oublier que celles-ci avaient pour objet premier de décrire la conjoncture économique, et toutes les villes d'où émanent nos gazettes entretenaient des liens commerciaux avec Lisbonne. Si le 24 novembre, Voltaire pensait aux 'cent mille fourmis écrasées dans notre fourmilière', il évoquait aussi 'la fortune de cent commerçants' de Suisse, et bientôt la lettre de change de Cadix qu'il voulait négocier au plus vite.[22] Il existe en effet une sorte de sismographe de l'opinion, et c'est la cote des actions de la Compagnie des Indes; notons cependant que les actions de la Compagnie des Indes qui étaient tombées à 1420 £ le

---

22. Lettres au banquier Jean Robert Tronchin le 24 et le 26 novembre, *Correspondence and related documents*, éd. Th. Besterman, dans *The Complete works of Voltaire* t.85-135 (1968-1977), D6600, p.404-405.

28 novembre 1755 sont à 1485 £ en avril 1756 et à 1540 £ en novembre. La secousse boursière a été limitée.

Les gazettes, en second lieu, ne se lassent pas de rapporter les mesures adoptées par les villes pour venir en aide à Lisbonne. Les paroles de compassion et de condoléances, les dons et les envois vers le Portugal du roi d'Espagne, du roi d'Angleterre, du roi de France et des villes marchandes (Hambourg, Amsterdam) figurent au centre de leur intérêt.[23] A partir du mois de décembre, elles se mettent à commenter les paroles et actes de générosité dans chacun de leur numéro, déplorant par ailleurs le manque d'informations directes. Ce genre de discours se fait plus rare à partir de janvier. Parmi les réactions qui retiennent l'attention des gazettes, on note également l'ensemble des cérémonies organisées – jeûnes et prières publiques – à l'occasion du tremblement. Ainsi à Aix-la-Chapelle et à Liège les 27, 30 et 31 décembre, à Bruxelles du 16 au 18 janvier, le 6 février dans les Royaumes d'Angleterre, d'Ecosse et d'Irlande,[24] etc. Au discours sur le tremblement fait place le discours sur les effets provoqués par le tremblement. Pour le dire avec les mots de Pierre Rétat, la gazette 'consacre l'essentiel de son texte à mettre en scène et en échos les multiples annonces de l'événement et les réactions qu'il produit. Ce faisant elle forme l'événement en une surface constamment visible, en une sorte d'image permanente et toujours nouvelle. Elle le déploie dans l'extériorité.'[25]

La dernière façon de parler du tremblement, sans pour autant l'évoquer directement, consiste à mentionner l'ensemble des catastrophes naturelles survenues depuis le 1er novembre. Il faut distinguer ici entre les secousses qui affectèrent Lisbonne après le 1er novembre – notamment entre le 8 et le 20 décembre[26] – et celles qui concernaient le reste de l'Europe et la Nouvelle Angleterre, et enfin l'ensemble des phénomènes naturels advenus depuis cette date. Ainsi, les secousses qui furent ressenties à Bâle, Lyon, Gibraltar, Cadix, au Maroc, en Hollande, à Philadelphie, Boston, etc. depuis le jour de la Toussaint, puis du 9 au 11 décembre, du 25 au 28 décembre et du 8 au 18 février firent l'objet de descriptions détaillées.[27] Les gazettes mentionnent même l'absence de secousses: 'depuis le tremblement de terre du 1er Novembre, on n'a éprouvé ici aucune nouvelle secousse, mais on n'a point été sans crainte qu'il n'en arrivât encore'.[28] Enfin, descriptions d'ouragans, scènes

23. *GU*, 2.xii, 9.xii, 19.xii, 23.xii, 26.xii, 30.xii; *GA*, 2.xii, 9.xii, 12.xii, 16.xii; *GL*, 5.xii; *GC*, 5.xii, 12.xii, 16.xii, 19.xii, 26.xii, 30.xii; *GH*, 8.xii, 10.xii; *GL*, 5.xii, 12.xii, 16.xii, 19.xii, 23.xii, 26.xii.
24. *GC*, 30.xii; *GH*, 19.i; *GU*, 20.i; *GCS*, 30.xii.
25. Voir *L'Attentat de Damiens. Discours sur l'événement au XVIIIe siècle*, éd. Pierre Rétat (Lyon 1979), p.42, ouvrage dont nous nous sommes inspirés.
26. *GU*, 23.xii, *GL*, 23.xii, *GA*, 23.xii.
27. Voir par exemple *GC*, 5.xii, 9.xii, 16.xii, 23.xii, 26.xii, 30.xii; *GU*, 13.xii; *GA*, 26.xii; *GL*, 23.xii, 26.xii 30.xii, etc.
28. *GA*, 06.i.56.

d'agitation des eaux, de formations soudaines de gouffres, d'inondation, de disparition des eaux de fontaines, d'engloutissement de villes entières, de rougissement des eaux, d'apparition de lueurs rouges se succédèrent sans fin dans les colonnes des gazettes.[29] Tous ces événements étaient reliés de façon explicite ou implicite au tremblement de terre de Lisbonne. Celui-ci venait donner sa cohérence à une série de maux qui dérangeaient l'ordre de la nature. Par le biais des gazettes, qui dessinaient les contours géographiques des désordres, toutes les régions touchées par les tremblements de terre, ne fût-ce que légèrement, ont été englobées dans un même mouvement: le tremblement de terre du 1er novembre à Lisbonne est devenu un phénomène général qui concernait l'ensemble des lecteurs européens.

Un seul type de discours est absent de la presse, celui-là même que Voltaire ébauche dans son 'Poème sur le désastre de Lisbonne': le scandale devant le désordre de la création et la mort des innocents, l'interrogation sur la Providence. Le tremblement de Lisbonne était en lui-même un événement sacrilège: il avait eu lieu le jour de la fête de Tous les Saints, dans la capitale d'une nation Très-Catholique, il détruisait les églises dans lesquelles les fidèles s'étaient réfugiés; à Madrid même, les deux premières victimes étaient des enfants atteints par la chute d'une croix. Or personne ne pose la question de la Providence, sinon pour la défendre. Dès le 30 novembre 1755, le pasteur Elie Bertrand prononce dans l'Eglise française de Berne son premier sermon en faveur de la Providence.[30] Ce sermon est suivi de trois autres, à la fin de décembre 1755 et en février 1756; ils seront imprimés plusieurs fois à Genève, puis de nouveau dans la *Bibliothèque des sciences et des beaux-arts* et dans la *Nouvelle Bibliothèque germanique* durant l'été 1756.[31] Ils développent les thèmes de la Providence et de la Cause intelligente, de la Charité pure, de la crainte de Dieu, de son immutabilité, et pour conclure, du bonheur de la Suisse, protégée de la guerre et du malheur par sa foi inébranlable. Dans un *Mémoire pour servir à l'histoire des tremblements de terre de la Suisse, principalement pour l'année 1755*, Elie Bertrand montrera les effets productifs à long terme des séismes, dans un langage qui préfigure parfois celui de Rousseau.[32] Or Voltaire lui-même remercie le pasteur en termes très aimables et lui envoie son propre 'sermon':[33] il n'est pas hostile à la

29. *GCS*, 16.xii, 26.xii; *GUS*, 23.xii, 26.xii.

30. La promptitude de réaction de Bertrand s'explique en partie par le fait qu'il pouvait disposer sur place de la *Gazette de Berne*.

31. *Nouvelle Bibliothèque germanique*, par M. Samuel Formey, juillet-août 1756, art. IV; *Bibliothèque des sciences et des beaux-arts*, avril-juin 1756, art. IV.

32. Sur la *Lettre sur la Providence* de Rousseau, écrite en août 1756, et sur la 'lettre obligeante' que lui envoie Voltaire en réponse, voir les notes d'Henri Gouhier dans les *Œuvres complètes*, éd. Bernard Gagnebin et Marcel Raymond (Paris 1959-1995), iv.1059-75.

33. Lettre à Elie Bertrand du 18 février 1756, D6738. Bertrand fait partie de ces pasteurs libéraux que Voltaire s'efforce de rallier à sa cause en 1756, comme on le verra dans l'article 'Genève' de l'*Encyclopédie* en 1757.

Providence, mais seulement à l'optimisme, ce qui est tout autre chose. Sur la nature de Dieu et sur la Cause intelligente, il ne s'oppose nullement au pasteur, son 'cher philosophe'. Certes Voltaire a ses raisons de ménager le protestantisme libéral, mais on finit par se demander si la presse de 1755 et 1756 n'exprime pas à sa façon, comme elle le fait toujours à l'époque classique, un seul et même consensus religieux et un refus spontané du blasphème. Elle n'exprimera des réserves que sur un intégrisme dont le clergé portugais, à travers l'Inquisition, pouvait donner l'image; c'est ainsi que le *Mercure historique* commente avec sévérité l'*auto-da-fé* d'Evora au cours duquel un homme et une femme sont brûlés pour 'judaïsme'.[34] Mais cette accusation est elle-même de nature religieuse. Le plus véhément anathème nous viendra des jansénistes, dans les *Nouvelles ecclésiastiques*; il porte non contre la Providence, mais contre les jésuites. Pourquoi, nous disent-ils, Dieu a-t-il frappé Lisbonne? Parce que: '1° Lisbonne était une ville d'un grand commerce; 2° Le Portugal et l'Espagne sont des pays d'Inquisition; 3° Le Portugal a été le berceau de la Société des Jésuites', etc. (*Nouvelles ecclésiastiques*, 3.xii.56). Autrement dit, la colère de Dieu est juste; mais les jansénistes seront les seuls à utiliser la Providence contre leurs ennemis, et dans une gazette interdite. Le rôle de la presse à l'époque classique est d'intégrer l'événement aberrant, de justifier la Providence, de rassurer son public, de conforter l'ordre politique, de prononcer finalement ce *Te Deum laudamus* que tout le monde attendait.[35]

---

34. Un article de février s'étendait sur la recrudescence de la foi et les actions de grâces (p.79-85); l'article d'août 1756 fustige l'Inquisition: 'A la honte de la Raison et de l'Humanité, les *autos-da-fé* continuent. Il y en eut un le 20 du mois dernier à Evora' (p.79-80). La GU du 16 décembre et la GS du 30 décembre signalaient qu'un auto-da-fé était prévu à Lisbonne pour le 1er novembre 1755.

35. H. J. Lüsebrink, dans un article intitulé 'Le tremblement de terre de Lisbonne dans les périodiques français et allemands du XVIIIe siècle', dans *Gazette et information politique sous l'Ancien Régime* (Saint-Etienne 1999), p.303-11, fait état d'un non-dit et d'un tardif retour du refoulé à travers les lettres de 1755 publiées dans le *Hannoversches Magazin* en 1779: mais il semble que ces lettres ne soient pas authentiques. Dans la presse de 1755 et 1756, on ne trouve pas trace de révolte ou de millénarisme violent.

GILBERT LAROCHELLE

Voltaire: du tremblement de terre de Lisbonne à la déportation des Acadiens

> Il n'est pour ainsi dire pas de civilisation, pas de conscience individuelle qui ne résonne encore de l'écho lointain d'une catastrophe.
>
> George Steiner, *Dans le château de Barbe-Bleue* (1973)

> Si le pays vit aujourd'hui au rythme des tremblements de terre, c'est parce que nos femmes ne respectent pas les consignes religieuses et se manifestent avec des habits de dévergondées.
>
> 'Des imams d'Alger', *Le Matin* (2 juin 2003)

L'ÉNIGME du mal représente sans doute le plus grand défi qui ne fût jamais posé à la philosophie. Sa persistance dans l'existence humaine déjoue toujours les systèmes de pensée qui en fixent l'origine ou même la signification. Elle revient sans cesse hanter l'esprit à la manière d'un irréductible, mieux d'une provocation qui rappelle toute spéculation aux limites de son projet. Certes, le mal est donné à la réflexion par démesure: il la dépasse et la force dans ses retranchements. A cet égard, trois difficultés surgissent dans la considération de ce phénomène.

D'une part, sur le plan théologique, la tentation de la révolte côtoie l'exubérance divine: comment le mal absolu peut-il naître de la bonté suprême, la souffrance de la bienveillance? Pierre Bayle doutait, dans son *Dictionnaire historique et critique*,[1] de la sagesse du Grand Architecte qui, parce que tout-puissant, eût dû prévoir la chute originelle et épargner l'homme du futile effort de la rédemption. Théoricien de l'optimisme, Leibniz cherchait, dans ses *Essais de théodicée*, à réconcilier les termes de l'aporie et croyait y parvenir. Son problème de départ est bien connu: 'Si Deus est, unde malum? Si non est, unde bonum?'[2] En fait, il se solde par la

---

1. Pierre Bayle, *Dictionnaire historique et critique*, éd. Alain Niderst (Paris 1974). Bayle rappelle qu'Anaxagoras fut le premier philosophe à soutenir qu'une intelligence invisible ordonnait le cours des choses dans le monde physique. Or, cette explication constitue, à ses yeux, 'l'asile de l'ignorance' (p.33), dit-il en reprenant ce mot de la philosophie scolastique. Pour lui, les desseins de Dieu sont incompréhensibles et il refuse donc de croire ce qui surpasse les capacités de son esprit.

2. 'Si Dieu existe, d'où vient le bien? S'il n'existe pas, d'où vient le mal?' Wilhelm Gottfried Leibniz, *Essais de théodicée*, éd. Jacques Jalabert (Paris 1962), p.120.

thèse de la nécessité: le mal doit être pour que le bien advienne, l'un étant enveloppé dans une détermination positive qui le prédestine vers l'autre. Bref, la descente aux enfers porte un principe d'espérance: elle constitue le truchement d'une finalité grandiose à l'œuvre dans le monde et qui se dénoue dans la clairvoyance ultime du *fatum christianum*. Voltaire ironise sur cette bonté assoiffée d'un si lourd tribut de misères humaines comme condition de sa révélation. Dans son 'Poème sur le désastre de Lisbonne' et son roman *Candide*, il marque tantôt le désarroi du philosophe, tantôt l'insolence cultivée du persifleur des desseins de la Providence. Il récuse cette 'ivresse de la causalité' que l'on appelle l'optimisme et l'illusion corollaire consistant à créer une translation entre la brutalité du fait et l'abstraction cosmologique du dogme selon lequel 'tout est bien'.[3] Il n'y a donc pas d'harmonie préétablie qui permettrait de franchir le pas de l'innocence à la faute, du malheur à la félicité. Que Dieu réponde de son acte devant les décombres encore fumants de Lisbonne! Le 'Poème' se décline sous le mode du soulèvement contre toute théodicée:

> Il le faut avouer, le mal est sur la terre:
> Son principe secret ne nous est point connu.
> De l'auteur de tout bien le mal est-il venu?[4]

Bref, au procès du Créateur, le réquisitoire présuppose certes un déisme de référence.

D'autre part, sur le plan épistémologique, l'énormité du mal force l'humilité de la raison. S'il s'abat sur l'homme par un commandement du Très-Haut, le mystère de son origine ne déborderait-il pas toutes les prouesses cognitives de la philosophie? Il trace, en effet, la limite de tout savoir: comment l'infini pourrait-il être soumis à la finitude de la pensée? Le mal n'est donc pas à hauteur d'homme: il lui échappe en tant qu'il comporte une grandeur négative, voire une révélation inversée qui le met hors de portée de l'entendement. Kant rappelle à juste titre que l'appui sur la raison ne permet ni de destituer ni de corroborer les fondements de la théodicée: ces références ne sauraient être justiciables l'une de l'autre. Etablir que le monde est mû par une finalité qui le mène vers la perfection exige 'l'omniscience' d'une raison qui 'méconnaît en cela ses propres bornes'. Démontrer 'l'anti-final' dans l'effectivité de l'expérience humaine implique, en revanche, que l'on sache remettre le mal à sa place et

---

3. Voltaire, 'Poème sur le désastre de Lisbonne ou examen de cet axiome "Tout est bien" ', dans *Mélanges* (Paris 1961), p.304-309; *Candide ou l'optimisme*, dans *Œuvres complètes de Voltaire*, éd. Theodore Besterman, t.48 (Oxford 1980). Quant à l'assertion 'Tout est bien', elle vient du poète Alexander Pope dont Voltaire admirait la poésie davantage que la pensée philosophique. Voir Alexander Pope, *An Essay on man*, éd. Anthony Trott et Martin Axford (Londres 1966). A titre d'exemple, dans l'Epitre 1, X, ces vers de Pope offrent la cible du combat que Voltaire mènera à la lumière des événements de Lisbonne: 'All partial Evil, universal Good: / And, spite of Pride, in erring Reason's spite, / One truth is clear, Whatever is, is right.'

4. Voltaire, 'Poème sur le désastre de Lisbonne', p.307.

l'objectiver par une prétention à la lucidité ultime. La raison: un tribunal incompétent en matière de théodicée.[5] A cet égard, Pascal avait précédé Kant et dénonçait en ouvrant ses *Pensées*: 'Deux excès: exclure la raison, n'admettre que la raison.'[6] Ricœur signale avec justesse, dans sa réflexion intitulée *Le Mal*, l'impasse de méthode qui guette tout savoir sur le sujet: 'Ce que le problème met en question, c'est un mode de penser soumis à l'exigence de cohérence logique.'[7] L'effort de réconciliation entre les assertions 'le mal existe' et 'Dieu est bon' forme, dit-il, ce grand écart que l'on n'enjambe que suspendu à l'idéal de la logique démonstrative et de ses postulats: la non-contradiction, la totalité en tant qu'échelle de la vérité, l'esprit de système, la clarté de l'univoque, la levée du voile de mystère sur le monde.

Quand Voltaire interpelle Dieu en le sommant de s'expliquer sur le destin d'expiation qu'il réserve à Lisbonne, il situe la tâche de la raison dans un horizon pré-kantien et lui confère le mandat de rétablir une commensurabilité entre des grandeurs concurrentes. Son embarras ne s'évalue que par une aspiration à tout comprendre. Il veut ramener l'inexplicable à une pointure humaine: 'On a besoin d'un Dieu qui parle au genre humain. Il n'appartient qu'à lui d'expliquer son ouvrage.'[8] Le 'Poème' en appelle ainsi à un idéal de clarté intellectuelle: le constat de cruauté postule une relation *a contrario* entre la physique (le séisme), la métaphysique (Dieu) et le primat de l'esprit pensant (le jugement négatif): 'Cruels, à mes douleurs n'ajoutez point l'outrage.'[9] La raison s'objecte et le désaveu progresse, comme si Voltaire voulait, par la vir-tuosité d'une contre-preuve radicale, ressaisir le mal en son principe même et s'arroger le droit de 'faire le jeu' de la théodicée en pliant le fait à un devoir de cohérence humaine entre le fini et l'infini, entre l'inopiné et le déterminé. Certes, la rupture de sens lui répugne, parce qu'elle confine

---

5. Emmanuel Kant, *Sur l'insuccès de toutes les tentatives philosophiques en matière de théodicée*, dans *Œuvres philosophiques*, t.ii (Paris 1985), p.1393-95. Ce texte fut écrit en 1791 et constitue une rupture avec le dogmatisme métaphysique par le criticisme. Toutefois, il convient de signaler que la position de Kant avait été jusque-là orientée vers une reconduction de la position de Leibniz. Son *Essai de quelques considérations sur l'optimisme*, rédigé à quelques mois de distance du *Candide* de Voltaire et paru en 1759, reste empreint de la théodicée: 'Depuis que l'on s'est fait de Dieu une notion convenable, aucune idée n'a peut-être été plus naturelle que celle selon laquelle, quand il choisit, il ne peut que choisir le meilleur' (*Œuvres philosophiques*, t.i, Paris 1980, p.167).

6. Blaise Pascal, *Pensées*, dans *Œuvres complètes* (Paris 1954), p.1089.

7. Paul Ricœur, *Le Mal* (Paris 1996), p.13. Sur le même thème, voir aussi: *Où est le mal? Tragique, éthique, politique*, éd. Jérôme Porée et Alain Vergnioux, préface d'André Comte-Sponville (Paris 1994).

8. Voltaire, 'Poème sur le désastre de Lisbonne', p.308. Par ailleurs, pour une excellente description des différents aspects de la vie au Portugal après le 1er novembre 1755, le lecteur pourra consulter l'ouvrage de Suzanne Chantal, *La Vie quotidienne au Portugal après le tremblement de terre de Lisbonne de 1755* (Paris 1962). Pour une analyse philosophique, voir l'ouvrage produit à l'occasion du deux centième anniversaire en 1955: T. D. Kendrick, *The Lisbon earthquake* (Philadelphia, PA 1955).

9. Voltaire, 'Poème sur le désastre de Lisbonne', p.305.

à la tragédie au sens grec du terme. Lisbonne en devient le théâtre par excellence: la chute originelle s'y réédite sans que nulle faute, cette fois, ne fût perpétrée:

> Quel crime, quelle faute ont commis ces enfants
> Sur le sein maternel écrasés et sanglants?
> Lisbonne, qui n'est plus, eut-elle plus de vices
> Que Londres, que Paris, plongés dans les délices?[10]

Enfin, sur le plan ontologique, le monde n'est d'aucun secours pour comprendre l'événement: 'la nature est muette, on l'interroge en vain'.[11] Le 'Poème', avec cette formule, bouscule les fondements de la théologie naturaliste et transfigure l'exaspération en programme: le pari devient alors celui de ressaisir l'être *avant* toute tragédie, de le détacher de l'infini pour le rendre à sa signification indéfinie. Il porte l'exigence du retour à un degré zéro où la nature humaine n'était pas encore déchue par le péché originel. Ainsi, le mal doit sortir du causalisme métaphysique inhérent à l'optimisme:

> Tranquilles spectateurs, intrépides esprits,
> De vos frères mourants contemplant les naufrages,
> Vous recherchez en paix les causes des orages.[12]

Or, si la souffrance n'est plus le destin de l'être ni le langage d'une puissance tutélaire qui parlerait à travers lui, la responsabilité de la Providence dans le tremblement de terre de Lisbonne devient nulle et non avenue. Cependant, pour en découdre avec la théodicée, il faut rompre la complicité de l'être et du mieux-être, de la réalité et de la rationalité. Ni Dieu ni la nature, mais seulement l'homme. Là se réinvestit chez Voltaire une capacité de révélation ontologique. D'abord, sous le mode d'une protestation humanitaire à distance dans laquelle seul l'homme répond de l'homme:

> Mais du sort ennemi quand vous sentez les coups,
> Devenus plus humains, vous pleurez comme nous.[13]

Un sensualisme à l'anglaise entre en scène pour empoigner l'être d'une nouvelle étreinte sans la consolation des voix de l'infâme:

> Quand l'homme ose gémir d'un fléau si terrible
> Il n'est point orgueilleux, hélas! Il est sensible.[14]

Puis, l'espérance vient faire échec une fois pour toutes aux chimères sur l'être-en-soi des choses pour projeter une ambition anthropomorphique:

---

10. Voltaire, 'Poème sur le désastre de Lisbonne', p.304.
11. Voltaire, 'Poème sur le désastre de Lisbonne', p.308.
12. Voltaire, 'Poème sur le désastre de Lisbonne', p.304.
13. Voltaire, 'Poème sur le désastre de Lisbonne', p.304.
14. Voltaire, 'Poème sur le désastre de Lisbonne', p.305.

> *Un jour tout sera bien,* voilà notre espérance;
> *Tout est bien aujourd'hui,* voilà notre illusion.[15]

Deux temporalités se font concurrence: un temps ontologique déjà là; et un temps téléologique sous la responsabilité de l'homme.

Toutefois, comment pareil déplacement de perspective saurait-il rendre le mal à sa signification? A qui l'imputera-t-on désormais? Comment le reconnaître s'il n'est plus un épisode tragique dans l'histoire de l'être? Tel est le thème de ce propos: il s'agit de mettre en question le statut du mal chez l'auteur du 'Poème' et de *Candide.* Car Dieu destitué, subsiste l'homme pour penser l'énigme. Le dilemme se résorbe *prima facie* dans un partage sommaire. D'une part, l'inhumanité et l'avilissement viennent de l'Etre suprême:

> Dieu vous voit du même œil que des vils vermisseaux
> Dont vous serez la proie au fond de vos tombeaux?[16]

D'autre part, au principe tant décrié de la 'raison suffisante' de Leibniz, la suffisance de la raison éclairée permet de jauger le céleste empire:

> L'homme, étranger à soi, de l'homme est ignoré.
> Qui suis-je, où suis-je, où vais-je, et d'où suis-je tiré?
> Atomes tourmentés sur cet amas de boue
> Que la mort engloutit et dont le sort se joue,
> Mais atomes pensants, atomes dont les yeux,
> Guidés par la pensée, ont mesuré les cieux.[17]

Or, Voltaire semble avoir échoué à dire le mal en dehors de son attribution à l'infâme. Une méprise plus grande encore fut de ne pas soupçonner que la raison éclairée pouvait en devenir complice. Les horreurs du vingtième siècle seront, à cet égard, un formidable démenti à l'orgueil des 'atomes pensants' dont la perspicacité rationnelle devait éradiquer l'intolérance et le fanatisme. L'argument retenu ici vise le nœud du problème: l'inacceptation d'un commencement hors de soi, la difficulté à admettre que quelque chose dépasse l'homme. Et pourtant le mal n'est compréhensible que par cette exigence: la protestation d'Antigone, chez Sophocle, devant le refus de sépulture de son frère Polynice l'illustre à merveille. Nulle loi écrite, nulle démonstration, mais une règle informelle et inintelligible pour la pensée objectiviste, parce que le veto de l'être ne sévit plus.

Quant à la raison, 'forme vide et sans substance' (Fichte), 'pliable en tous sens' (Pascal), elle est précédée par des critères qu'elle ne saurait déterminer: calculatrice, elle ne peut rendre l'incalculable et reste aveugle devant l'indignité humaine. A preuve: au moment où la terre tremble à Lisbonne en 1755, l'homme rationnel européen est en train de procéder à

---

15. Voltaire, 'Poème sur le désastre de Lisbonne', p.309.
16. Voltaire, 'Poème sur le désastre de Lisbonne', p.305.
17. Voltaire, 'Poème sur le désastre de Lisbonne', p.308-309.

la déportation du peuple acadien en Amérique. Une épuration ethnique: le mal fondé en raison. Eternelle surdité de l'intellectuel, cécité du maître-penseur dans la controverse:

> De l'Etre tout parfait le mal ne pouvait naître;
> Il ne vient point d'autrui, puisque Dieu seul est maître.[18]

i. Finitude et transcendance

Le 'Poème' commence par une plainte et finit dans un hymne à la lucidité humaine. *Candide* s'ouvre dans le ciel de la métaphysique et se ferme, côté jardin, sur la contingence radicale. L'un pourfend le mal, l'autre l'illustre. Accusation et parodie, humanisme et cynisme, pleurs et rires rivalisent d'ingéniosité pour obturer le passage entre finitude et transcendance. Le point d'appui se situe toujours hors du monde sans être en Dieu. Il fait accueil à un au-delà de l'ordre des choses par la raison, quitte à l'y ramener pour mâter une fois pour toutes le destin et le fatalisme ambiant. Il recoupe les deux lignes de force de la culture occidentale, du moins celles dont le dix-huitième siècle confirmera la primauté. D'abord, le culte de l'examen de conscience qui ramène à soi la mesure du monde: Voltaire incarne plus que quiconque à son époque la capacité de soumettre toute vérité au crible d'une réflexion introspective. Il a rêvé d'une pensée qui puisse penser contre elle-même, d'un sens critique qui sache se maintenir en questionnement sans renoncer à se faire inquiétude pour autrui. De cet impératif éthique, des sensibilités multiples ont surgi: la compassion dans l'affaire Calas par exemple, la haine des tyrannies, le dégoût des impostures, une passion pour la tolérance, etc. Bref, tous ces fronts d'un même combat placent la personne humaine en hauteur et rappellent l'exigence du respect qu'elle commande.

Puis, le souci de l'expérience répond à l'audace de la pensée. Il devient le corollaire d'une conscience souveraine qui, transcendance descendue dans le monde, cherche à se confronter à lui. Le fondement de la raison raisonnante s'appuiera désormais sur quelque chose de solide. L'influence de la philosophie d'outre-Manche est manifeste: elle permet de faire jouer Newton contre Descartes, l'acquis contre l'inné, l'empirisme rationnel contre l'apriorisme métaphysique. L'admiration de Voltaire paraît sans bornes: 'Tout prouve que les Anglais sont plus philosophes et plus hardis que nous. Il faut bien du temps pour qu'une certaine raison et un certain courage d'esprit franchissent le pas de Calais.'[19] Sa rhétorique ne cesse de multiplier les images fortes pour déterminer une échelle de priorité: le 'flambeau de l'expérience' dissipe les envolées 'romanesques' et ténébreuses des spéculations sur le continent. Somme toute, le fait résiste à

---

18. Voltaire, 'Poème sur le désastre de Lisbonne', p.307.
19. Voltaire, *Lettres philosophiques*, dans *Mélanges*, p.32.

l'idée: il peut lui faire objection à la faveur d'une conscience délibérante. Là se situe la cheville du 'Poème':

> L'univers vous dément, et votre propre cœur
> Cent fois de votre esprit a réfuté l'erreur.[20]

Or, le désaveu du réel servira à fragiliser l'idée, tout comme celle-ci libérera en retour le devenir d'un *fatum* à consonance ontologique. La vérité surgit désormais d'une conquête; elle n'est plus donnée, mais construite dans le sillage de l'histoire. Elle se rive à l'entendement philosophique et à un exercice de discernement: à la pomme du jardin d'Eden, le fruit de la tragédie par excellence, la pomme du jardin de Newton indiquera la gravité universelle de la nature, mais aussi de l'esprit. Bref, le mal passe d'un jardin à l'autre. Il perd, chemin faisant, tout sens du tragique: une négativité fusant hors de soi en regard de laquelle nul réconfort, nul allégement n'est possible. La consolation est une douceur étrangère à la tragédie: elle fait partie du lexique de l'espérance. Dans le 'Poème', le narrateur prend le point de vue de la victime pour susciter l'attendrissement du lecteur; dans *Candide*, il donne la parole au persécuteur pour démontrer l'inanité de ses prétentions. Mais le personnage de Candide est tout, sauf tragique. Ses malheurs ne doivent pas faire illusion, puisqu'ils sont portés par une immense promesse dont Cunégonde est à chaque détour le rappel et l'enjeu. Au fond, les ressources de la conscience et la dictée de l'expérience imposent un constat: la source du mal se situe dans l'abstraction. Dès que l'idée n'est plus dans la chose, la persécution commence. Sous-entendu: la raison éclairée par le fait ne peut pas faire souffrir!

Tout système fonctionne en détruisant l'intrigue de l'histoire. Sa vocation consiste à extraire pour unifier, à faire reculer le singulier et le contingent pour imposer une signification panoramique. Son efficacité ne conduit jamais qu'à une double perte dont Voltaire déplore le mépris: celle de la conscience critique et de l'expérience fondatrice. Le résultat se reproduit toujours à l'identique: l'abstrait, l'arbitraire et la violence. Les maillons de la chaîne servant à relier toutes choses et surtout à placer la physique sous la contention de la métaphysique ne constituent rien de moins qu'une entreprise totalitaire. D'entrée de jeu, le décor de *Candide* est campé en Allemagne, pays dont Voltaire déteste la tournure d'esprit vers des spéculations ombrageuses et la langue, symbole d'opacité et dispositif d'embrouillement tout indiqué pour quitter la terre ferme et faire assaut aux cieux éthérés. Westphalie devient ce lieu mythique où semble prévaloir l'idée sans la chose. Et l'Amérique en sera l'exact contraire sous un regard marqué, toutefois, par une même désobligeance: une vague chose sans idée, un faubourg encore inhabité dans la grande patrie de la raison universelle. Même le nom du château paraît volontairement alambiqué

---

20. Voltaire, 'Poème sur le désastre de Lisbonne', p.307.

pour évoquer, par dérision, l'esprit de système: Thunder-ten-tronckh. Maître Pangloss, le praticien de la profondeur, 'le plus grand philosophe de la province, et par conséquent de toute la terre',[21] distribue ses 'oracles' sous bénéfice d'inventaire. Il occupe la cléricature de l'universel au sens où le rappel de l'étymologie peut fort bien côtoyer la désignation d'un combat (*katholikos*: universel). Il est à Voltaire ce que Gorgias fut à Socrate: celui qui sait persuader sur tout par la simple faculté de ramener l'événement à des actes de langage. Prestidigitateur de génie, ses discours sont donc des prodiges d'une cohérence démonstrative subsumant le mal sous l'emprise des lois universelles du bien, sinon du meilleur des mondes possibles en conformité avec la théorie de Leibniz et la poésie de Pope.

L'esprit de système simplifie tout sous l'apparence d'une complexité inouïe. L'adversité surgit-elle que l'ordre reprend aussitôt ses droits. Un doute pointe-t-il qu'une réponse survient, comme si elle était déjà prête d'avance. Le malheur frappe-t-il que l'espérance l'accueille à bras ouverts pour le ramener dans le giron de la totalité bienfaisante. La contradiction ne dure guère sans que l'apaisement ne rétablisse Candide dans la sérénité de la raison suffisante. Bref, l'épine pointe ainsi vers la rose. Il fallait que Candide fût chassé du château après le vol d'un baiser à Cunégonde derrière le paravent: l'allégorie de la chute originelle. La terre devait trembler à Lisbonne, parce que des forces abyssales venues d'Amérique, prouve Pangloss, portent le péril: 'La ville de Lima éprouva les mêmes secousses en Amérique l'année passée; mêmes causes, mêmes effets; il y a certainement une traînée de soufre sous la terre depuis Lima jusqu'à Lisbonne. [...] je soutiens que la chose est démontrée.'[22] L'anabaptiste Jacques devait être englouti dans la rade de Lisbonne, celle-ci ayant été conçue pour qu'il s'y noyât. Il convenait que Candide fut fessé en cadence, 'pendant qu'on chantait' dans la liturgie de l'autodafé et que Pangloss fut pendu, 'quoique ce ne soit pas la coutume.'[23] La vieille perdit une fesse, mais n'était-ce pas pour sauver sa vie? Il devint essentiel que le Juif don Issacar et monseigneur l'inquisiteur s'opposassent pour les faveurs de Cunégonde. Et Candide dut les tuer tous deux pour l'amour de celle-ci. Le Juif et le Chrétien morts, les deux grands symboles de l'esprit de système, cette œuvre, encore inachevée, n'exigeait-elle pas le meurtre du baron jésuite au Paraguay, le frère de la dulcinée, dont la censure aristocratique annihilait l'ambition de Candide d'épouser Cunégonde? Tout est donc nécessaire, même le péché originel dont tout découle: 'La chute de l'homme et la malédiction, dit Pangloss, entraient nécessairement dans le meilleur des mondes possibles.'[24] Satire certes distrayante mais dont la pédagogie vise à faire comprendre une vérité entre deux

21. Voltaire, *Candide*, p.120.
22. Voltaire, *Candide*, p.136.
23. Voltaire, *Candide*, p.139.
24. Voltaire, *Candide*, p.137.

éclats de rire: tout ordre finit par dissoudre les différences. Il détruit l'humain. Il porte le mal comme le vent la tempête et mène à 'l'exercice bulgare':[25] la brutalité et la cruauté.

La clé de l'ordre réside dans le dispositif de l'analogie (*analogon*), le trope de la transcendance. Cette figure de pensée consiste à associer dans une relation de similitude des domaines *a priori* différents. Elle fait se correspondre des idées ou des objets que rien ne liait avant leur déplacement. Son usage permet ainsi de jeter un pont entre des rives séparées et de dépasser les limitations formelles qu'elles comportent. Stipuler le semblable pour abolir le contingent et l'irréductible: 'Chercher le sens', note Michel Foucault, 'c'est mettre à jour ce qui se ressemble.'[26] Or, une telle opération s'effectue, chez Pangloss, par l'imagination qui procure une référence, c'est-à-dire un point d'appui pour solidariser artificiellement une vision et des choses. Bref, il n'y a d'identité que dans l'abstraction. Et même l'énonciation d'un problème ne devient acceptable qu'en regard du potentiel résolutoire de l'analogie où se rencontrent finitude et transcendance: 'Le spectacle de personnes brûlées à petit feu, en grande cérémonie, est, affirment les sages de Lisbonne, un secret infaillible pour empêcher la terre de trembler.'[27] Le sacrifice expiatoire étant une exigence de la séismologie, l'analogie ne produit une concordance métaphysique, ironise Voltaire, que pour distraire la conscience de l'expérience.

Que l'ordre s'établisse ne serait qu'un demi-mal si les concordances qu'il crée ne servaient pas aussi à l'ordonnancement des individus. L'analogie conduit à la croyance, la persuasion à la domination, l'autorité à l'obéissance: seule l'abstraction permet de faire se ressembler les choses pour faire se rassembler les êtres humains. Si la grammaire est la mise en structure du discours, l'*analogon* opère un classement dans le règne du sens, voire des lieux communs de la société. De là tout s'enchaîne: 'Le précepteur Pangloss était l'oracle de la maison, et le petit Candide écoutait ses leçons avec la toute bonne foi de son âge et de son caractère.'[28] Victoire sur autrui et victoire sur les faits: le rapport tient du corollaire: 'Tandis qu'il le prouvait *a priori*, le vaisseau s'entrouvre,'[29] rappelle Voltaire en décrivant l'arrivée de Pangloss à Lisbonne, comme si le récit tombait en syncope pour que le ridicule réponde à l'orgueil du savoir inné. Le déni de l'expérience prévaut chez les figures de l'autorité, mais aussi pour ceux dont l'examen de conscience se limite à l'obéissance: 'Si Pangloss n'avait pas été pendu, déclare Candide, il nous donnerait un bon conseil dans cette extrémité, car c'était un grand philosophe.'[30]

25. Voltaire, *Candide*, p.169.
26. Michel Foucault, *Les Mots et les choses* (Paris 1966), p.44.
27. Voltaire, *Candide*, p.138.
28. Voltaire, *Candide*, p.119.
29. Voltaire, *Candide*, p.134.
30. Voltaire, *Candide*, p.148.

L'épreuve des faits n'y peut rien, parce que le sens est trop fort devant eux.

La métaphysique représente, dans *Candide*, un excès de sens sur le signe. Ne savoir que parler et bâtir le monde à coup de langage (*panglosie*) permet de ne point lire ce qui, dans l'événement, fait signe. Et maître Pangloss reçoit tout signe comme un nouveau territoire se donnant à la colonisation du sens. Mieux, le signe ne constitue jamais que la condition primitive et inachevée du sens. Il est, par définition, en devenir, promis à quelque chose d'autre, comme le mal forme l'en-deçà du bien dans l'harmonie cosmologique de l'optimisme. Il s'ensuit donc une responsabilité illimitée des humains à l'égard du monde non-humain: quand la terre tremble, c'est le fondement symbolique de la société qui doit être reconstruit. Pareille dépendance mène, pour Voltaire, à une condition d'aliénation (*alienus*: être étranger à soi-même). Il faut en chercher la source dans le croisement de la passion et de la religion, notions cousines, du reste, dans le roman. L'échange entre Cunégonde et Candide après le double meurtre du Juif et du prélat l'illustre à merveille. Comment avez-vous fait, 'vous qui êtes né si doux', lui dit-elle, pour être capable de faire autant de mal en deux minutes? 'Ma belle demoiselle, répondit Candide, quand on est amoureux, jaloux et fouetté par l'Inquisition, on ne se connaît plus.'[31] L'aliénation sévit donc dans le règne du signifiant dont Dieu serait l'*exemplum* parfait.

Nulle part davantage que dans les articulations métaphysiques du *religare* la puissance de l'analogie ne se révèle avec autant de force. Dieu représente, pour Voltaire, l'abstraction ultime dont dérivent toutes les autres. Il décrète le principe de tous les liens et gouverne l'événement à sa guise:

> Dieu tient en main la chaîne, et n'est point enchaîné
> Par son choix bienfaisant tout est déterminé,[32]

rappelle le 'Poème'. Esprit au service de l'ordre, volonté libre, le Créateur incréé fit l'homme à sa ressemblance en l'enjoignant de l'imiter. Dès lors, le mal appartient au titulaire de l'*analogon*, celui par qui tout est et advient. Voltaire multiplie à chaque page de *Candide* les indicateurs de l'infâme. Dans la description de la bataille des Bulgares contre les Abares, trois dimensions saillantes se manifestent comme s'il y avait entre elles un rapport de connivence: l'ordre, le massacre et la religion. 'Rien n'était si beau, si leste, si brillant, si bien ordonné que les deux armées. Les trompettes, les fifres, les hautbois, les tambours, les canons, formaient, poursuit Voltaire, une harmonie telle qu'il n'y en eut jamais en enfer.'[33] Si l'ordre fournit l'esthétique par excellence du mal, le décompte de la 'boucherie héroïque', mot qui lie l'hyperbole à un effet de contraste,

---

31. Voltaire, *Candide*, p.149.
32. Voltaire, 'Poème sur le désastre de Lisbonne', p.306.
33. Voltaire, *Candide*, p.126.

'pouvait se monter à une trentaine de mille âmes',[34] chiffre coïncidant – est-ce un hasard? – à celui des victimes du séisme de Lisbonne. Le chaînon déterminant de l'*analogon* ferme la scène à la toute fin: 'Enfin, tandis que les deux rois faisaient chanter des *Te Deum* chacun dans son camp, il [Candide] prit le parti d'aller raisonner ailleurs les effets et les causes. Il passa par-dessus des tas de morts et de mourants.'[35] Conclusion: c'est la religion qui inspire le mal aux êtres humains en les invitant à camper un décor d'enfer sur terre.

A l'inverse, la charité et l'humanisme arrivent davantage par celui sur qui la religion n'a guère influé. Dans sa fuite vers la Hollande, Candide éprouve une grande misère que seuls soulagent ses espoirs de trouver le réconfort auprès des Chrétiens, nombreux en ce pays. Se voyant refuser l'obole demandée, il est menacé et éconduit. Or, comparaison éloquente, un 'homme qui n'avait point été baptisé',[36] l'anabaptiste Jacques, manifestement plus sensible que philosophe, lui offre le secours que sa condition exigeait. Et c'est lui encore qui recueillera le vérolé Pangloss pour le faire soigner à ses frais. Voltaire suggère ainsi que la compassion n'est pas une affaire de religion, mais plutôt d'une extrême réceptivité à la finitude de l'existence humaine.

La dépravation du clergé et son manque d'empathie devant la souffrance complètent l'incrimination du religieux. Le recours à l'éloge paradoxal amplifie l'offensive en servant de promontoire aux valeurs d'une humanité bienfaitrice. Cunégonde ne relate-t-elle pas son aventure à Candide en exposant le carrousel des rôles compromettants que lui firent jouer les caciques de l'Eglise: d'abord victime de la concupiscence de l'inquisiteur 'pendant la messe', puis 'maîtresse' de ce dernier et, enfin, invitée à joindre l'estrade des dignitaires pendant l'autodafé: 'Il me fit l'honneur, dit-elle, de m'y inviter. Je fus très bien placée; on servit aux dames des rafraîchissements entre la messe et l'exécution.'[37] La compassion sous forme de bienséance envers les dames est interposée entre la 'messe' et l''exécution', deux notions dont la juxtaposition évoque une accointance profonde, une complicité symbolique dans le déploiement du fait religieux. La prévarication et la perfidie font loi partout, comme si la foi n'était que le déguisement de l'intérêt. Même l'abstraction théologique se répercute dans l'ordre politique au Paraguay comme en témoigne le féal de Candide, le valet picaresque Cacambo – dont le rôle ressemble à s'y méprendre à celui de l'écuyer Sancho Pança dans *Don Quichotte*. L'administration des Jésuites s'y effectue, déclare-t-il, sous les régimes du glaive et du goupillon: 'C'est une chose admirable que ce gouvernement. [...] Los Padres y ont tout, et les peuples rien; c'est un chef-d'œuvre de

34. Voltaire, *Candide*, p.126.
35. Voltaire, *Candide*, p.126.
36. Voltaire, *Candide*, p.128.
37. Voltaire, *Candide*, p.146.

raison et de justice.'[38] Duplicité des rôles, mais aussi d'une sincérité pour le moins instable: 'Pour moi, poursuit-il, je ne vois rien de si divin que Los Padres, qui font ici la guerre au roi d'Espagne et au roi du Portugal, et qui en Europe confessent ces rois; qui tuent ici des Espagnols, et qui à Madrid les envoient au ciel.'[39] Que dire des péripéties de la vieille dont la déchéance n'a d'égale que l'hypocrisie de son origine: fille du pape Urbain X et, en cela, née des basses œuvres de chair du plus haut clerc de l'Eglise.

Faillite de la conscience et déroute de l'expérience, le tremblement de terre de Lisbonne enseigne, somme toute, que la finitude du mal n'est pas accueillie pour elle-même, mais dans un incessant effet de miroitement vers son point d'origine. Il prouve, pour Voltaire, l'échec de la transcendance à se révéler dans le monde. Le Dieu tout-puissant n'agirait-il que sur le mode de la catastrophe? S'incarnerait-il pour faire excuser son abstraction? Le narrateur de 'Candide' l'insinue en rappelant que 'l'auteur de tout bien', selon les mots du 'Poème', ne peut se soustraire à son destin d'absence surdéterminante et de présence ratée, étant le modèle même de l'esprit de système, le maître de toutes les ligatures entre les ressemblances. Incarnation inaccomplie, peut-être davantage inachevée, puisque le monde créé par Dieu n'offrirait, au fond, qu'un séjour dans le langage, bref comme si Voltaire avait voulu, à travers le risible Pangloss, parodier la célèbre formule de l'apôtre Jean: 'Le Verbe s'est fait chair et il a habité parmi nous.'[40] Le système est la théologie du Verbe.

Point de mal sans cette troublante relation à Dieu. Même le pessimiste Martin, sceptique radical qui ne consent qu'à l'ordre du signifié, ne sait détacher son analyse de la puissance invisible: 'Je vous avoue qu'en jetant la vue sur ce globe, ou plutôt sur ce globule, je pense que Dieu l'a abandonné à quelque être malfaisant.'[41] A qui regarde de près, l'indignité de l'homme paraît congénitale, sa rémission aussi improbable que l'avènement d'une bonté soudaine, dit-il, entre l'épervier et le pigeon dont les relations sont caractérisées de tout temps par une invariable prédation. Le mal traverse, pour Voltaire, les plans théologique (Dieu: le responsable), épistémologique (une indifférence à la raison) et ontologique (une incarnation ratée): l'imputation de l'indignité le cède donc à l'évidence:

> Nous étendons les mains vers notre commun père.
> Le vase, on le sait bien, ne dit point au potier:
> 'Pourquoi suis-je si vil, si faible et si grossier'[42]

rappelle le 'Poème'. Plus éloquente encore la déclaration du derviche à la fin de *Candide*: 'Quand Sa Hautesse envoie un vaisseau en Egypte,

38. Voltaire, *Candide*, p.169.
39. Voltaire, *Candide*, p.169.
40. Jean i.14.
41. Voltaire, *Candide*, p.202.
42. Voltaire, 'Poème sur le désastre de Lisbonne', p.306.

s'embarrasse-t-elle si les souris qui sont dans le vaisseau sont à leur aise ou non?'[43] Les hommes: des 'souris' perdues sur le 'globule'! De viles créatures engagées dans un voyage qui se mène à leur insu. Nulle liberté sur les flots du mal. Leur aise, c'est le chemin frayé par la raison qui leur donne un mot à dire sur la destination. Dès lors, l'optimiste rationnel apparaît comme la nouvelle icône de Dieu sur terre.

ii. L'Amérique: terre de révélation de la condition primitive

Le thème du voyage demeure la seule échappée hors du système. Il constitue, dans *Candide*, la voie royale de sortie du destin. Le scénario se reproduit dans toutes les péripéties du héros principal: les situations se bloquent les unes après les autres sous le double coup d'une cause (abstraite) et d'un effet (violent), puis la fuite vient dégager les horizons. La liberté se situe dans les interstices, l'espoir ne refait son plein qu'avec le signal du départ vers d'autres cieux. Certes, le voyage est, pour Candide, l'unique manière de fragiliser les systèmes contraignants et de déjouer la métaphysique, afin de restaurer, ne serait-ce que pour un temps, le primat de la contingence. Qu'il fît le tour du monde à toute fin pratique pour apprendre à savourer la suffisance de l'expérience relève, au fond, d'une astuce d'écriture pour mettre en scène une réelle pédagogie: seul le mouvement et le potentiel de déstabilisation qu'il porte permettent d'ouvrir le chemin à la conscience critique. L'instabilité est au voyage ce que le désir d'ordre est à la métaphysique. Et au bout du parcours, la promesse d'une nouvelle lucidité qui, tout entière, surgit d'une comptabilisation au passif des virtualités de l'infini. Elle met un terme à l'eschatologie et à l'attente. Si la beauté rêvée de Cunégonde gonflait le goût de la retrouver à chaque revers, si l'épreuve du pire redonnait la force de croire au mieux-être, la neutralisation de l'espérance achève l'histoire au sens hégélien du terme. Non pas qu'elle signe la fin de tout événement dont le simple fait de vivre ne saurait interrompre le cours du reste, mais elle l'accueille dans ce qu'il est pour lui-même, délesté du poids d'une assurance quant à ses liens nécessaires vis-à-vis de l'abstraction.

Le voyage de Candide, une fois exilé de son Allemagne natale, comprend douze étapes qui rythment la douloureuse ascension vers ce Golgotha où l'illusion doit mourir pour que vive l'expérience. Il mène en ces lieux qui forment autant d'épreuves dans un processus de révélation: Hollande, Lisbonne, Cadix, Buenos Aires, Paraguay, Tucuman, Eldorado, Surinam, Paris, Portsmouth, Venise, Constantinople. Le trajet le plus marquant est, toutefois, celui qui s'étale d'est en ouest, la direction, d'ailleurs, par laquelle la civilisation s'est étendue depuis la plus lointaine Antiquité, de la Mésopotamie à l'Amérique. Il s'avère crucial, parce qu'il

---

43. Voltaire, *Candide*, p.257.

symbolise le passage de l'idée vers la chose, alors que le parcours d'ouest en est connote le retour aux abstractions cosmologiques de la vieille Europe. Et l'appareillage vers le nouveau monde élargit la foi en proportion de la distance à franchir: 'Nous allons dans un autre univers', disait Candide; 'c'est dans celui-là sans doute que tout est bien. Car il faut avouer qu'on pourrait gémir un peu de ce qui se passe dans le nôtre en physique et en morale.'[44] Projection de soi dans l'autre pour trouver 'le meilleur des univers possibles.'[45]

La traversée s'effectue, toutefois, en surcharge des aspirations européennes qui, transposées sur les rivages à l'autre bout de la mer, s'amplifient jusqu'à la caricature. Orgueil, arrogance et licence se croisent dans un incessant bruissement d'apparats qui répercutent en les décuplant les vices de la métropole. A peine débarqués à Buenos Aires, les fuyards abordent le nouveau continent à travers un nom dont le déclinement se tuméfie par une imitation maladroite des signes de l'aristocratie du vieux monde: le gouverneur Don Fernando d'Ibaraa, y Figueora, y Mascarenes, y Lampourdos, y Souza. Noblesse oblige! De même, Le Jésuite, frère de Cunégonde et Révérend Père au Paraguay, ne rencontre-t-il pas Candide dans l'exubérance nerveuse des retrouvailles en terre d'Amérique, car ils 'versent des ruisseaux de larmes'.[46] Sitôt l'exaltation passée, une controverse éclate, marquée par une véhémence intraitable: les espoirs de Candide d'épouser Cunégonde. D'un côté, l'objection emprunte aux idées innées, voire à l'impensable mélange des classes sociales: ma sœur 'a soixante et douze quartiers',[47] dit le Jésuite, d'ailleurs baron. De l'autre, la réplique des idées acquises, le nouveau monde devant être celui de l'accomplissement de soi-même contre tous les archaïsmes: 'Tous les quartiers du monde n'y font rien; j'ai tiré votre sœur des bras d'un Juif et d'un inquisiteur; elle m'a assez d'obligations, elle veut m'épouser',[48] répartit Candide. Ce décalage entre l'Europe et l'Amérique montre que le mal n'est point rachetable, fût-ce par l'effort ou le mérite. Il oppose la fatuité de l'homme bien né du dix-huitième siècle à l'égalitarisme que Tocqueville exposera moins de cent ans après Voltaire dans son périple outre-mer.

Le mouvement d'est en ouest constitue certes un acheminement vers le règne des choses. Il dessine la trajectoire de migration du sens dans l'espace et la remontée au stade de l'insignifiance dans le temps. Il fait retour, sur le plan symbolique, au *statu quo ante* de la condition humaine, au stade primitif d'avant toute culture, là où la nature ouvre la course vers la perfectibilité. L'Amérique permet à Voltaire, dans *Candide*, de dépeindre un tableau contrasté de l'Europe. Et la méthode de l'inversion ressortit à

44. Voltaire, *Candide*, p.151.
45. Voltaire, *Candide*, p.151.
46. Voltaire, *Candide*, p.171.
47. Voltaire, *Candide*, p.174.
48. Voltaire, *Candide*, p.174.

une stratégie parmi d'autres pour confirmer la suprématie du vieux monde sur le nouveau. Elle n'aboutit nullement comme chez Rousseau à l'idéalisation du 'bon sauvage' qui aura pour figure, par exemple, le mythe du coureur des bois canadien. L'auteur de la *Lettre sur la Providence* vit, en effet, dans le tremblement de terre de Lisbonne le désarroi provoqué par la vie citadine et, en général, par la modernité: 'La nature n'avait pas rassemblé là vingt mille maisons à six ou sept étages.'[49] La valorisation à rebours du premier homme des Amériques n'est pas une tentation chère à Voltaire. Plutôt préfère-t-il l'ambivalence volontiers cultivée entre celui qui affiche la superbe européenne devant les 'sauvages' et décrie en même temps les méfaits provoqués par la rencontre des deux mondes. D'un côté, il se délecte de l'exotisme, mieux de l'étrangeté de ces peuples indigènes et, somme toute, indignes d'un acte de la Providence: 'Il est assez plaisant que le jésuite Lafitau prétende, dans sa préface de *L'Histoire des sauvages américains*, qu'il n'y a que des athées qui puissent dire que Dieu a créé les Américains.'[50] Puis, de l'autre, il démasque les cruautés du colonisateur et avoue son horreur devant les récits de Bartholomé de Las Casas: 'Ces malheureux sauvages, presque nus et sans armes, étaient poursuivis comme des daims dans le fond des forêts, dévorés par des dogues, et tués à coup de fusil, ou surpris et brûlés dans leurs habitations.'[51] Toutes les scènes de violence dans *Candide* sont, à l'exception de l'anthropophagie chez les Oreillons, un legs de l'Europe: la guerre en Allemagne, la souffrance issue du séisme à Lisbonne, la religion au Paraguay, l'esclavage à Surinam, la vanité à Paris, le chauvinisme en Angleterre, la prostitution à Venise. Seul l'excès de sens porte la barbarie, l'insignifiance étant la contrepartie de la métaphysique.

L'Amérique est une non-coïncidence radicale avec l'idée. Tout simplement parce qu'elle n'en a pas! Voltaire en propose une image cynique en la décrivant comme ces espaces infinis qui effrayaient tant Pascal. S'agissant de la folie propre à l'Angleterre et de celle, non moins sévère, de la France, un mot, dans *Candide*, conjugue l'insulte et la condescendance: 'Vous savez que ces deux nations sont en guerre pour quelques arpents de neige vers le Canada', fait-il dire à Martin, 'et qu'elles dépensent pour cette belle guerre beaucoup plus que tout le Canada ne vaut.'[52] De plus, au lieu d'élever l'homme, l'Amérique le tue et le mange selon les lois sauvages de la nature. L'*Essai sur les mœurs et l'esprit des nations* (1756) confirme le jugement: 'Ce qu'il y avait de plus horrible chez les Canadiens, est qu'ils faisaient mourir dans les supplices leurs ennemis captifs, et qu'ils les mangeaient. Cette horreur leur est commune avec les Brésiliens, éloignés d'eux de cinquante

---

49. Jean-Jacques Rousseau, lettre à Voltaire, le 18 août 1756, dans *Lettres philosophiques* (Paris 2003), p.94. On reconnaît dans ce passage la tentative de Rousseau de faire le procès de la civilisation moderne et d'incriminer au passage le mésusage de la liberté humaine.
50. Voltaire, *Essai sur les mœurs et l'esprit des nations* (Paris 1962), p.71.
51. Voltaire, *Essai sur les mœurs*, p.251.
52. Voltaire, *Candide*, p.223.

degrés.'[53] A preuve, dans *Candide*, quand Cacambo négocie un sauf-conduit à l'extérieur du territoire des Oreillons, l'argument tombe sous le coup d'une ironie mordante: 'Vous comptez donc manger aujourd'hui un jésuite: c'est très bien fait; rien n'est plus juste que de traiter ainsi ses ennemis. En effet, le droit naturel nous enseigne à tuer notre prochain.'[54] L'homme ne devient une chose, comestible par surcroît, que dans un moment de révélation de sa condition primitive. Sa réduction à la consistance d'un objet suggère que son statut véritable avoisine celui de l'animalité. Après tout, l'esclave de Surinam ne déclare-t-il pas: 'Les chiens, les singes et les perroquets sont mille fois moins malheureux que nous.'[55] En conséquence, rien n'indique que le mal en Amérique soit bâti sur la transcendance. En fait, il n'est pas lié, au sens de *religare*, à l'idée selon un axe vertical qui le subsumerait sous la chape de plomb d'un esprit de système. Au contraire, il émane de la pulsion naturelle des bêtes dont l'action semble commandée par l'instinct, par les passions qui se déploient sous la dictée du *bios*.[56] Il constitue alors le contrebas symbolique de la civilité européenne qui, posée en promontoire offert à l'escalade de la raison, vient confirmer *a contrario* les valeurs de référence.

Non-sens du mal et non-lieu (*u-topos*) de son théâtre d'opération: il n'est pas inopportun d'observer que la neige et l'or sont des matériaux parfaitement antithétiques en principe, mais tout à fait similaires dans *Candide*. La neige évoque la désolation du désert froid et inhospitalier. Elle est la toute première résistance que l'homme rencontre au sortir du jardin d'Eden: 'Candide, chassé du paradis terrestre, marcha longtemps [...]; il se coucha sans souper au milieu des champs entre deux sillons; la neige tombait à gros flocons.'[57] La déveine du pécheur le conduit aux rigueurs de l'hiver qui annonce l'ère glaciaire des valeurs. De même, la topographie de l'Eldorado, quoique fort différente des 'quelques arpents de neige', se découpe sur le fond de 'montagnes inaccessibles' et de rivières torrentueuses dans le décor desquelles Voltaire plante une société semblable à la république de Platon ou à celle de Cicéron. La recension des signes du mal indique qu'il ne peut y advenir: absence de prêtres pour rappeler la hiérarchie sociale interposée entre Dieu et les hommes, point de moines pour faire brûler les hérétiques, accord parfait des esprits en tous points, bref la transcendance elle-même s'effondre, parce qu'elle est ramenée à une religiosité immanente. La destitution des formes de subordination ou plutôt de classement se reconnaît même dans le règne

53. Voltaire, *Essai sur les mœurs*, p.278.
54. Voltaire, *Candide*, p.179.
55. Voltaire, *Candide*, p.196.
56. Dans l'*Essai sur les mœurs*, Voltaire écrit clairement, en parlant des 'sauvages' de l'Amérique, que le mal qu'ils commettent résulte des passions: 'La guerre, ce crime et ce fléau de tous les temps et de tous les hommes, n'avait pas chez eux, comme chez nous, l'intérêt pour motif; c'était d'ordinaire l'insulte et la vengeance qui en étaient le sujet comme chez les Brésiliens et chez tous les sauvages' (p.278).
57. Voltaire, *Candide*, p.122.

minéral, l'or y étant un caillou dérisoire et sans valeur. Devant la 'boue jaune' de l'Eldorado, la cupidité des étrangers apparaît aussi ridicule que la combativité de la France et de l'Angleterre pour conquérir 'quelques arpents de neige'. Seule la matière diffère dans le parallélisme du non-sens. Cette figure burlesque de l'Européen est inoffensive, dès lors qu'elle se développe en terre d'utopie plutôt que sous le rayonnement du flam-beau de l'expérience.

La cité idyllique de l'Eldorado ne connaît donc point le mal. Elle constitue le meilleur des mondes possibles, d'autant plus facile à accepter qu'il n'existe pas. Et on ne raisonne pas devant l'idéal, parce que le fait n'est pas opposable à la pensée. Ainsi, l'utopie accrochée à un flanc de montagne chez les Incas reste un baroud d'honneur que la fiction rend à Pangloss. Son impact dans la narration est de fournir un redoutable moyen de transport des préjugés européens. De même, à l'inverse, l'exhibition d'une nature inerte dans les steppes endormies sous les flocons de l'hémisphère nord comporte un effet interchangeable. Certes, elle suggère qu'il ne vaut pas la peine de s'y attarder, la matière nue étant un point de chute futile pour l'esprit. Il devient alors difficile de s'empêcher de faire le rapprochement entre le 'Poème' et une certaine image de l'Amérique dans *Candide* où l'extravagance de la nature procède de son insignifiance constitutive: 'la nature est muette, on l'interroge en vain',[58] rappelons-le, comme si la pensée n'avait guère de prise sur un fait brut. Entre l'idée (parfaite) et la chose (muette), le problème de la liberté dans la commission du mal aurait-il buté en Amérique sur ces deux extrêmes? Et l'interrogation si chère à Voltaire n'aurait-elle pas coincé le thème de la responsabilité entre des 'aveuglements réfléchis' autant pour escamoter la question de la source du mal que pour soustraire l'homme à l'admission de toute participation dans la construction de sa propre indignité?

Mil sept cent cinquante cinq ne marque pas seulement l'*annus horribilis* de la miséricorde divine dans le développement de la philosophie sur l'origine et sur les causes du mal. L'émotion suscitée à l'échelle de l'Europe devant le cataclysme de Lisbonne coïncide aussi, de manière curieuse, avec un abaissement du seuil de l'indignation: la tentation de la révolte contre le Tout-Puissant n'effleure même pas l'esprit de Voltaire lorsqu'il considère avec détachement les tragédies humaines qui ont cours hors de son monde de référence. En Amérique, au moment précis où la bonté divine trébuche sur les rives du Tage, les Acadiens subissent l'épreuve fondatrice de leur histoire, le fer rouge de leur mémoire et de leur civilisation qui, pour employer les mots de Georges Steiner, 'résonne encore de l'écho lointain d'une catastrophe'.[59] Leur traumatisme n'a nullement ébranlé le philosophe de la tolérance dont la conscience cri-tique et le souci de l'expérience devaient pourtant servir de leviers pour

---

58. Voltaire, 'Poème sur le désastre de Lisbonne', p.308.
59. George Steiner, *Dans le château de Barbe-Bleue* (Paris 1973), p.14.

déraciner le mal. Un sens de l'étonnement fut perdu quelque part entre l'ancien et le nouveau monde et son absence se fait remarquer par une appréciation différentielle du malheur des hommes. Moment crucial dans la bataille entre les Français et les Anglais en Amérique, la déportation des 12,617 Acadiens sur un nombre de 15,000 environ équivalait à une mise à mort ou même à l'extinction rationnellement planifiée d'un peuple sur la base d'une catégorie raciale.[60] Elle représente encore aujourd'hui la tache originelle de l'identité acadienne, la chute hors de soi dans un voyage sans retour pour la plupart, où le mal fait à l'homme par l'homme sera achevé par les ravages de la petite vérole, maladie commune à Pangloss et aux déportés.

Le traité d'Utrecht (1713) avait commencé ce que la déportation va tenter poursuivre: la mainmise, lente mais décisive, de l'Angleterre sur les colonies d'expression française en terre d'Amérique. Il stipulait que l'Acadie, un établissement de colons fondé en 1604 et marqué par un esprit d'indépendance à l'égard des puissances européennes, passait sous contrôle britannique. Il fut décidé que les Acadiens auraient alors le choix de prêter serment à la Couronne anglaise ou bien de quitter leurs terres, rebaptisées Nova Scotia par la signature du traité. La résistance des Acadiens aux décisions prises en Europe s'explique par leur désir de préserver leur liberté religieuse au nom d'un principe de tolérance en vertu duquel la foi dût être détachée de la loi. Un certain *modus vivendi* entre les Acadiens et les Britanniques fut possible jusqu'à la recrudescence de la tension vers 1750 entre les deux belligérants du vieux continent. Une solution définitive vint à l'esprit des Anglais quant au sort des Acadiens: un déplacement forcé vers les autres colonies d'Amérique.

Le mal subi sous la forme d'une dévastation à nulle autre pareille ne peut être nommé par le recours au langage de la transcendance ni imputé à l'indifférence d'un Dieu négligent. Au contraire, il provient d'un programme réfléchi, sinon de la raison elle-même à l'œuvre dans une histoire produite par l'action humaine: destruction des habitations, confiscation des terres et du cheptel, mise à feu des villages, battues pour arrêter les fuyards, séparation des familles, expédition des hommes, des femmes et des enfants vers des horizons respectivement différents pour défaire les liens naturels. Certes, le voyage constitue une déstabilisation des univers de référence, disions-nous déjà. Par contre, il illustre, dans le 'grand dérangement',[61]

60. Bien que le nombre exact des déportés soit difficile à établir et que les auteurs font généralement preuve de prudence, Robert A. Leblanc fournit, dans une étude sur le sujet, le chiffre cumulatif de 12,617 entre la période s'étalant de 1755 à 1763. Il faut signaler que la déportation débute en 1755 mais qu'elle se poursuit sur une période de plusieurs années. Voir son article: 'Les migrations acadiennes', *Cahiers de géographie du Québec* 23:58 (avril 1979), p.99-124.
61. Expression consacrée pour désigner la déportation des Acadiens. Quant au mot 'Acadie' lui-même, il provient du nom grec 'Arcadie' attribué à l'origine selon un jugement de ressemblance géographique. Ce nom aurait été donné par le navigateur italien Giovanni da Verrazano qui fit une reconnaissance de la côte est de l'Amérique en 1524.

l'esprit de système expulsant hors de lui un corps étranger, l'abstraction en quête d'homogénéité, une révélation du libre arbitre dans l'abcès même du mal. Le 1ᵉʳ novembre 1755, jour de la Toussaint, une flottille de navires quitte Chignectou dans les brumes matinales avec plus de 1,500 détenus entassés dans des cales insalubres. De Lisbonne à l'Acadie: fallût-il, de plus, qu'un Dieu vengeur, dans la démesure de sa colère, dans l'*ubris* de sa fureur, fasse encore d'une tragédie le moyen pour en occulter une autre: celle commise par l'homme?

La déportation des Acadiens constitue la première épuration ethnique de l'homme blanc par l'homme blanc en Amérique: 'Tout prouve que les Anglais sont plus philosophes et plus hardis que nous',[62] ne disait-il pas Voltaire? Faut-il recevoir cette admiration *in extenso*? A tout événement, elle présente les signes d'une mauvaise foi. Quand paraît l'*Essai sur les mœurs et l'esprit des nations* en 1756, ouvrage publié quelques mois à peine après le 'Poème sur le désastre de Lisbonne', le drame de l'Acadie est connu de l'auteur. Il l'évoque dans ses causes et dans ses conséquences. Parlant de la paix d'Utrecht (1713), il écrit que 'les ministres qui firent ce traité, n'ayant pas déterminé les limites de l'Acadie, l'Angleterre voulant les étendre, et la France les resserrer, ce coin de terre a été le sujet d'une guerre violente en 1755 entre ces deux nations rivales'.[63] Singularité cruciale entre toutes, l'affrontement n'eut pas pour seul objectif d'assurer les conditions de la conquête selon le schéma d'une guerre classique, mais de pratiquer une véritable 'hygiène sociale' destinée à balayer le territoire de la présence de ceux dont la foi représentait une tare atavique. Du reste, éparpillés dans les colonies britanniques, les déportés se rapprochèrent des esclaves avec lesquels ils firent parfois cause commune, tout comme ils avaient bénéficié, avant leur départ, du support des Amérindiens, deux alliances qui, pour les Anglais, leur conférera un statut biologique avoisinant celui des Noirs et des Rouges.

Lisbonne ou la liberté de l'homme victime de la religion. L'Acadie ou la liberté de religion victime de l'homme. Les catastrophes synchrones de la Toussaint sont certes des occasions pour interroger le régime de causalité dont chacune d'elles procède, mais peut-être également pour prendre la mesure de leur réception dans le monde des idées, surtout dans celui de Voltaire. Le recul de l'indignation chez lui se double d'une sélectivité manifeste dans le traitement des faits: le flambeau de l'expérience ne projette pas ses lumières dans toutes les régions de la réalité. Quant à la conscience, le génie de l'humanisme rationnel, elle inspire des émotions discriminées. On n'imagine pas l'affaire Calas en Amérique: la mobilisation de toute l'Europe pour dénoncer l'injustice commise contre un individu. La contention géographique de l'indignation prouve, par ricochet, que la dignité humaine se définit dans un lieu quelque part,

---

62. Voltaire, *Lettres philosophiques*, dans *Mélanges*, p.32.
63. Voltaire, *Essai sur les mœurs*, p.279.

tout comme l'insistance à dévoiler la dimension tragique du séisme de Lisbonne pointe vers une topographie de l'espérance. Ainsi, les signes d'une nouvelle théodicée ne surgissent plus dans l'arithmétique du mal si chère à Leibniz:

> Tristes calculateurs des misères humaines
> Ne me consolez point, vous aigrissez mes peines,[64]

clamait encore le 'Poème'. Ils se révèlent dans un axe horizontal est–ouest où l'Amérique représente une terre adamique incarnant la désolation originelle, une nature demandant à devenir une culture, à la limite une faute qu'il faudrait amender par un acte de civilisation. Après tout, la petite vérole dont souffre Pangloss ne vient-elle pas de l'Amérique où aurait été consommé le fruit défendu dans un temps primordial? Or, si l'apport à l'Europe du 'chocolat et la cochenille'[65] atténue l'amertume du péché originel par une dérisoire consolation, la nécessité du rachat ne commande-t-elle pas la tâche de discriminer ce qui, dans l'espèce humaine, ne peut être mis en relation d'équivalence? Ainsi, l'Amérique reste un défi, un monde d'étrangeté que nul poème ne saurait ébranler.

Voltaire n'a pas vu que le mal pouvait être une bouture de la raison dans l'arborescence intellectuelle européenne. Il n'a pas dénoncé l'expulsion des Acadiens ni ne s'est intéressé réellement à leur sort, parce que ceux-ci n'avaient pas d'importance dans les débats du vieux monde et ne commandaient donc pas l'indignation qui eût été nécessaire au redressement de leur abjecte condition. Le silence de Voltaire n'a d'égal que celui des immensités neigeuses, comme si une telle attitude devait correspondre à la nature elle-même. Virtuose du dévoilement des ruses de *l'analogon* dont procède toute pensée symbolique, il s'est pourtant révélé incapable de relier, au sens de *religare*, des variables dont le croisement historique semble, à l'analyse, probant, mieux avéré: le mal et la raison. Eût-il fait le rapprochement que l'optimisme humaniste et la confiance infinie au pouvoir de l'esprit humain se fussent rétrécis jusqu'à compromettre la culture même des Lumières. D'ailleurs, l'heure était, à la fin du dix-huitième siècle, à l'expansion de la connaissance et non pas à l'admission de ses limites. Il fallait plutôt sortir par tous les moyens de la situation tragique de l'homme et domestiquer l'incompréhensible en l'inscrivant dans l'espérance d'une rédemption sans Dieu. Même Kant définissait le mal comme cette hétéronomie qui place l'être humain hors des maximes de la raison, tout en présupposant l'existence d'un 'mal radical' que seule la volonté déterminée peut surmonter en le soumettant à la clairvoyance de la pensée. Mais la rhétorique de l'espérance se bute, chez lui, à quelques soupçons qui percent çà et là sur les chances de la raison de viser des fins glorieuses: 'Le bois dont l'homme est fait est si

---

64. Voltaire, 'Poème sur le désastre de Lisbonne', p.306.
65. Voltaire, *Candide*, p.131.

courbe qu'on ne peut rien y tailler de bien droit',[66] comme si l'idée ne pouvant être l'*ultima ratio* des faits.

Conclusion

Raison et religion métabolisent toutes deux la violence. Ni l'une ni l'autre n'opèrent selon quelque négativité intrinsèque dont elles seraient secrètement dépositaires. Tout dépend du champ d'application où elles sont convoquées. Point de solidarité entre l'incalculable et l'intolérable selon ce que Voltaire crut; guère de divergence par nature non plus entre le rationalisme et l'obscurantisme. L'Acadie et Lisbonne offrent des théâtres de réflexion sur le mal que l'on distingue par l'imputation de l'origine. La première sert à rappeler la responsabilité de l'homme et le privilège de sa liberté sans lesquels le mal reste complètement absurde. La seconde a permis à Voltaire d'innocenter l'homme en référence à une volonté cosmique qui porterait le mal comme un legs venu d'ailleurs. Or, la véritable question n'est pas de savoir si l'on doit croire ou refuser la thèse du péché originel à partir de laquelle tout se joue dans le 'Poème' et *Candide*. Plus cruciale encore est l'attitude consistant à prendre acte de l'existence *en fait* des tragédies qui rééditent à chaque fois l'épopée de la chute dans le fil de l'expérience humaine. Au-delà de l'allégorie religieuse et de sa réfutation rationaliste, l'accueil du mal au cœur de l'histoire suffit à démontrer que nul ne peut recommencer à sa guise et que la trame des événements dans laquelle il s'insère est faite du poids de tous les hommes. Ainsi, l'historicité à l'aube de ce siècle est marquée par la 'toute-brûlure' (Steiner) que fut Auschwitz et on ne peut pas penser comme si cette faute absolue n'avait pas été. Dans cet esprit, il faut reconnaître que l'homme ne vient pas au commencement. Il n'inaugure pas le monde, il le continue et s'inscrit dans une histoire qui le dépasse et pour laquelle il est un être à la fois constituant et constitué, libre et déterminé, le mal devenant pour lui une possibilité inhérente à son action, fût-elle gouvernée par la raison. C'est peut-être ce que Pascal signifiait en écrivant que 'l'homme passe infiniment l'homme'[67] et en posant ainsi l'énigme au cœur de l'existence.

La barbarie est constitutive de l'humanité: elle en participe de l'intérieur comme un germe qui peut à tout moment se développer.[68] Vouloir être à soi-même son propre commencement, le principe ultime de cohérence entre le fini et l'infini, constitue un décret qui immole à son tour des pans de l'expérience humaine sur l'autel de l'abstraction. Peut-être est-ce cela le péché originel: la désignation de soi comme l'origine de toute chose, le bris de solidarité avec la mémoire et l'histoire déjà faite. Et la

---

66. Kant, *Idée d'une histoire universelle d'un point de vue cosmopolite* (Paris 1985), p.195.

67. Pascal, *Pensées*, p.1207.

68. Voir à ce sujet l'ouvrage de Jean-François Mattéi, *La Barbarie intérieure: essai sur l'immonde moderne* (Paris 1999).

tragédie, c'est l'homme dans le refus de tout lien, détaché de tout et séparé de tous, comme Camus l'a illustré dans *La Peste*. Ou est-ce Kirilov qui, dans *Les Possédés* de Dostoïevski, se tue pour se prouver qu'il est son propre principe de raison. Aussi Voltaire, qui ne compte que sur l'homme, n'aurait-il pas introduit par là le plus grand malentendu de l'humanisme contemporain? Malgré tout, il faut continuer de réfléchir avec et contre lui, surtout quand, depuis le minaret, sonne encore aujourd'hui l'appel du muezzin pour convoquer les fidèles devant l'imam dont le prêche tente de les convaincre que le débraillé vestimentaire des femmes en Algérie soulève la colère de Dieu que répercutent les tremblements de terre. Point d'effet sans cause, disait Pangloss.

MONIKA GISLER

Optimism and theodicy: perceptions of the Lisbon earthquake in protestant Switzerland

Introduction

ASSESSMENTS of major natural disasters usually emerge long after the event, in larger contexts of interpretation. Yet we might ask whether such events did not also act as structural, transcending moments, transferring semantic structures or breaking them up. The reaction to the 1755 Lisbon disaster is key to this discussion. Researchers today generally believe that not only did the earthquake in Lisbon unsettle the optimism of the early Enlightenment, but that it may have destroyed it altogether. The earthquake, it has been stated, marked the turning point from optimism to pessimism in eighteenth-century thought.[1] To underline the argument, the reader is usually referred to Voltaire's works after the Lisbon earthquake, the 'Poème sur le désastre de Lisbonne',[2] published in 1756, and the novel *Candide ou l'optimisme*[3] of 1759.

Reconsideration of Voltaire's working process and the reactions to his works reveals that Voltaire's renunciation of theological optimism was itself criticised. Non-specialists seldom recognise that the version of the 'Poème' published in May 1756 does not represent the first draft, but a modification. The 1756 release was written after profound criticism of the first versions. The writings became the object of fierce disapproval by Rousseau, but also by less prominent critics: Swiss clerics, magistrates and scholars were among their many detractors.

---

1. Carl-Friedrich Geyer, 'Das Jahrhundert der Theodizee', *Kant-Studien* 4 (1982), p.393-405; Horst Günther, *Das Erdbeben von Lissabon erschüttert die Meinungen und setzt das Denken in Bewegung* (Berlin 1994); Peter Gould, 'Lisbon 1755: Enlightenment, catastrophe, and communication', in *Geography and Enlightenment*, ed. David N. Livingstone and Charles W. J. Withers (Chicago, IL and London 1999), p.399-413; Theodore Besterman, 'Voltaire et le désastre de Lisbonne: ou, la mort de l'optimisme', in *SVEC* 2 (1956); with a more critical perspective Ruth Groh and Dieter Groh, 'Religiöse Wurzeln der ökologischen Krise. Naturteleologie und Geschichtsoptimismus in der frühen Neuzeit', in *Weltbild und Naturaneignung. Zur Kulturgeschichte der Natur*, ed. Ruth Groh and Dieter Groh (Frankfurt 1996), p.11-91 (p.49-50).
2. Voltaire, 'Poème sur le désastre de Lisbonne', reprint in Wolfgang Breidert, *Die Erschütterung der vollkommenen Welt. Die Wirkungen des Erdbebens von Lissabon im Spiegel europäischer Zeitgenossen* (Darmstadt 1994), p.58-73.
3. Voltaire, *Candide ou l'optimisme*, ed. René Pomeau, in *The Complete works of Voltaire* (henceforward *OC*), vol.48 (Oxford 1980).

Voltaire's correspondence and that of his contemporaries allow us to delineate responses to the 'Poème' which undermine the hypothesis of pessimism after the Lisbon earthquake.[4] Reactions from Swiss protestants to the earthquake, on the contrary, demonstrate a variety of interpretative patterns.[5] I will show that, rather than shifting to a metaphysical pessimism, the optimistic concept of the early Enlightenment – best delineated in Leibniz's dictum of the 'best of all possible worlds'[6] – was perpetuated throughout the second half of the eighteenth century. By exploring the responses to Voltaire's 'Poème' within protestant Switzerland I will show that the hypothesis of a decreasing optimism by the 1755 earthquake is too narrow a focus on the intellectual elite of Europe. The reactions to Voltaire's 'Poème' rather refer to a strong concern to maintain optimism. To emphasise my point, I will then outline different patterns of interpretation of the Lisbon earthquake.

i. The Lisbon earthquake and Switzerland

The great earthquake occurred on Saturday 1 November 1755, All Saints Day, coinciding with the celebration of high mass in Spain and Portugal. It was felt throughout the Iberian peninsula and northwest Africa, as well as in some areas of western Europe such as southern France and northern Italy. At distant locations on the European continent where the earthquake was not felt, several associated phenomena were observed. Since the most important damage occurred in Lisbon (caused by a tsunami and a fire that followed), this event is widely known as the 'Lisbon earthquake', although its epicentre was in the Atlantic Ocean,

---

4. Two contributions have already raised the subject. While Haydn Mason, 'Voltaire and Elie Bertrand', in *De l'humanisme aux lumieres, Bayle et le protestantisme. Mélanges en l'honneur d'Elisabeth Labrousse*, ed. Michelle Magdelaine, Maria-Cristina Pitassi, Ruth Whelan, and Antony McKenna (Oxford 1996), p.715-26, focused on the reaction of Swiss clerics, Martin Stuber, 'Divine punishment or object of research? The resonance of earthquakes, floods, epidemics and famine in the correspondence network of Albrecht von Haller', *Environment and history* 9, special issue: *Coping with the unexpected – natural disasters and their perception*, ed. Michael Kempe and Christian Rohr (2003), p.173-93, discussed the reaction in the Haller correspondence.

5. Concerning the reactions in German-speaking regions (mainly Germany) see Ulrich Löffler, *Lissabons Fall – Europas Schrecken. Die Deutung des Erdbebens von Lissabon im deutschsprachigen Protestantismus des 18. Jahrhunderts* (Berlin and New York 1999).

6. Gottfried Wilhelm Leibniz, 'Die Theodizee von der Güte Gottes, der Freiheit des Menschen und dem Ursprung des Übels', *Philosophische Schriften*, Bd. 2, ed. H. Herring (Frankfurt 1996). Leibniz's concept of metaphysical optimism understood evil as an unavoidable consequence of a decree by the most perfect being over the creation of an optimal world. In this respect, each evil is embedded into a universal harmony, preestablished by God. Thus this world, which also includes the evil, due to the universal harmony is good – the best of all possible worlds.

southwest of Cape San Vicente, at a distance of several hundred kilometres from the city.[7]

Unusual natural phenomena were recorded in detail and most of the information was published. Most reports date from one month or more after the event. Data on the Lisbon event were connected with characteristic observations in the respective regions. In Switzerland the earthquake was observed mainly in the movement of bodies of water. Several observers described how lakes and rivers swelled in a most unaccustomed manner: 'The dreadful earthquake of the 1st of November last has been perceived even in this country, though very faintly. It turned some of our rivers on a sudden muddy, without any rain, and swelled our lake of Neufchâtel to the height of near two feet above its natural level, for the space of a few hours.'[8] Large water movements were observed in the lakes of Zurich and Geneva, as well as in Lago Maggiore.[9] In Biel spring water was made turbid, despite the pleasant weather.[10] News of the event and its local effects was disseminated via journals, and also through sermons. We suppose that the people were able to contextualise their own observations only when they had news from Lisbon and its surroundings. After hearing about what happened in Iberia, people were able to connect their own impressions with other information on the great earthquake. It was the perception of the quake as a shared natural experience, not just a Portuguese event, which made it a European disaster.[11]

The depiction of streets and places full of dead and dying people emphasised the essential horror of that All Saints Day. Immediately after the disaster, a figure of more than 100,000 dead was announced; it had to be scaled down later.[12] Today the number of victims is estimated at between 15,000 and 20,000.[13] Emotional repercussions followed for those

---

7. J. M. Martínez Solares and A. López Arroyo, 'The great historical 1755 earthquake. Effects and damage in Spain', *Journal of seismology* 8 (2004), p.275.

8. Vautravers, 'Letter from Mons. de Vautravers F. R. S. to Thomas Birch D. D. Secr. R. S.', *Philosophical transactions giving some accounts of the ingenious, in many considerable part of the world* 49 (1756), p.436-38.

9. Gian Antonio Barazzi, 'Il terremoto del 1755 a Locarno', *BSSI* 4:8 (1882), p.214-15; Trembley, 'Letter from Mons. Trembley to his Brother', *Philosophical transactions* 49, p.438-39; Zurich, Staatsarchiv, Männedorf, Pfarrbuch 1721-1762.

10. Neuhaus to Haller, 4 December 1755, Bern, Burgerbibliothek, N Albrecht von Haller Korr.

11. Christiane Eifert, 'Das Erdbeben von Lissabon 1755. Zur Historizität einer Naturkatastrophe', *Historische Zeitschrift* 274 (2002), p.633-63, sees in the establishing of a common ground of experience the reason for the reception and engaged participation when the Lisbon event was interpreted.

12. For example Voltaire to Tronchin, 17 December 1755, *Correspondence and related documents* (henceforward D), ed. Th. Besterman, in *The Complete works of Voltaire* v.85-135 (Geneva, Banbury, Oxford 1968-1977), D6635.

13. Martínez Solares and López Arroyo, 'The great historical earthquake', p.278-79.

who suffered and also for those who were spared. Astonishment over the unaccustomed movements of Swiss waters gave way to relief over surviving. Many reports on the earthquake and its consequences appeared, beginning with observations of the quake and its effects, followed by treatises on its possible causes – a topic that had been of no interest in Switzerland for thirty years. Several essays dealt with questions of theological and religious interpretation.

ii. Voltaire's 'Poème' against optimism

Philosophical discourse about the end of optimism and a new debate on theodicy received essential impetus from Voltaire who, having read the first newspaper reports,[14] wrote his famous 'Poème sur le désastre de Lisbonne, ou examen de cet axiome "Tout est bien"' (1756).[15] Voltaire criticised the philosophy of Gottfried Wilhelm Leibniz (1646-1716) and Alexander Pope (1688-1744); a criticism that he intensified a few years later with his novel *Candide*. The Lisbon earthquake served Voltaire in both writings as an example of the world's evil and absurdity.

As is well known, by the time of the disaster the author of the 'Poème' had settled in Switzerland, in Geneva. He arrived there at the end of 1754, since a return to Paris after a three-year stay abroad was not possible. At the end of 1755 he moved near to Lausanne, a territory of the federal state of Bern, although he regularly returned to Geneva.[16]

On 24 November 1755, Voltaire first mentioned the earthquake in a letter to his friend and physician Théodore Tronchin, who was living in Geneva at the time. Voltaire outlined his concerns regarding the earthquake: 'Voylà monsieur une phisique bien cruelle. On sera bien embarassé à deviner comment les loix du mouvement opèrent des désastres si effroiables dans le *meilleur des mondes possibles*.'[17] Shortly afterwards, in another letter, he described similar doubts to Elie Bertrand (1713-1797),[18]

14. Berthold Rohrer, *Das Erdbeben von Lissabon in der französischen Literatur des achtzehnten Jahrhunderts* (Heidelberg 1933), p.9.
15. The exact date of the composition of the 'Poème' is difficult to determine. Besterman, 'Voltaire et le désastre de Lisbonne', p.177, proposes that Voltaire wrote the 'Poème' within a week after he learned of the disaster and thus finished a first draft at the beginning of December 1755. This is particularly likely in view of the fact that early drafts of the 'Poème' seem to have been circulating near the beginning of December 1755. Francis J. Crowley, 'Pastor Bertrand and Voltaire's Lisbon', *Modern language notes* 74:5 (1959), p.430-33, argues that this estimation is based on wrong assumptions.
16. On Voltaire's relations to Switzerland, the Swiss theologians, and the county of Bern see Graham Gargett, *Voltaire and protestantism* (Oxford 1980); Mason, 'Voltaire and Elie Bertrand'; Louis-Edouard Roulet, *Voltaire et les Bernois* (Neuchatel 1950).
17. Voltaire to Tronchin, 24 November 1755, D6597, original emphasis.
18. Elie Bertrand (1713-1797) studied Latin, Greek, philosophy, mathematics and theology; in 1740 he was ordained. He held memberships in diverse academies such as Berlin, Leipzig and Göttingen. He was a contributor to the *Encyclopédie* of Diderot and

main priest in the French church of Bern, and for some time correspondent and confidant to Voltaire.[19] At the time of the earthquake, Bertrand had already published some writings on natural philosophy, mainly in geology.[20] We can suppose that Voltaire addressed himself on the subject to Bertrand as both a theologian and naturalist: 'Voicy la triste confirmation du désastre de Lisbonne et de vingt autres villes. C'est cela qui est sérieux. Si Pope avait été à Lisbonne aurait il osé dire, tout est bien?'[21] Facing the suffering of Lisbon, Voltaire questioned Pope's axiom 'Whatever IS, is RIGHT'[22] as well as Leibniz's dictum of 'the best of all possible worlds', declaring the philosophy of optimism wrong: 'La ville de Lisbonne engloutie par un tremblement de terre; cent-mille âmes ensevelies sous les ruines: [...] voilà un terrible argument contre *l'optimisme*.'[23] He repeated his criticism in a second letter to Bertrand on 18 February 1756, arguing that optimism is the only philosophy in human history that refuses to acknowledge the existence of evil: 'Les hommes de tous les temps et de touttes les relligions ont si vivement senti le malheur de la nature humaine, qu'ils ont tous dit que l'œuvre de dieu avait été altérée. [...] Il faut avouer que l'ouvrage de Pope détruit cette vérité, et que mon petit discours [the 'Poème'] y ramène.'[24] If everything is right, then nothing can ever become any better. But a philosophy that would not allow any hope of improvement, of betterment, had to be called cruel:

Hélas! si tout est bien quand tout est dans la souffrance, nous pourons donc passer encore dans mille mondes, où l'on soufrira, et où tout sera bien. On ira de malheurs en malheurs, pour être mieux. Et si *tout est bien*, comment les leibnitiens

D'Alembert, but above all to the *Encyclopédie* of Yverdon; see Marc Weidmann, *Un Pasteur-naturaliste du XVIIIe siècle: Elie Bertrand (1713-1797)* (Lausanne 1986).

19. Since Voltaire's arrival in Geneva, he and Bertrand had established contact via correspondence. We know of 104 letters from Voltaire to Bertrand for the period from 1754 to 1773; from Bertrand to Voltaire only six letters exist; the number of lost letters is unknown. A first culmination of the exchange was in September 1755 after Bertrand had visited Voltaire. Mason, 'Voltaire and Elie Bertrand', p.715-16, states that the correspondence served both *savants*. Voltaire approved Bertrand's wide knowledge and strong interest in natural history.

20. Elie Bertrand, 'Memoires sur la structure interieure de la terre', in Elie Bertrand, *Recueil de divers traités sur l'histoire naturelle de la terre et des fossiles* (Avignon 1766), p.1-103; Elie Bertrand, 'Essai sur les usages des montagnes', in *Recueil de divers traités sur l'histoire naturelle de la terre et des fossiles*, p.105-222. Bertrand later received from Voltaire more records concerning earthquakes (mainly from other parts of the world) for his own earthquake compilation; Voltaire to Bertrand, 20 April 1756, D6841.

21. Voltaire to Bertrand, 28 November 1755, D6603.

22. Alexander Pope, *An Essay on man*, part I, i.294.

23. Voltaire to Bertrand, 30 November 1755, D6605, original emphasis.

24. In this regard Voltaire failed to understand Leibniz's argument, which did not deny evil. The concept of metaphysical optimism rather understood evil as an unavoidable consequence of a decree by the most perfect being over the creation of an optimal world; see Stefan Lorenz, 'Theodizee', in *Lexikon der Aufklärung*, ed. Werner Schneiders (Munich 1995).

admettent ils un mieux? Ce mieux n'est il pas une preuve que tout n'est pas bien?[25]

The concept of optimism was thus 'désespérant', 'une philosophie cruelle'. At that time, the 'Poème' had already faced criticism. In December, the first drafts were in circulation and provoked serious objections.[26] Voltaire himself had sent parts of the 'Poème' to friends and acquaintances, or read it to distinguished circles in his home. In January 1756 he wrote to his friend Nicolas Claude Thieriot with the request 'd'aller chez mr d'Argental avec ce petit billet; il vous communiquera le sermon, et vous verrez ensemble s'il est possible que cela soit communiqué'.[27] Even more clearly he addressed himself to d'Argental: 'si cecy n'est pas une tragédie, ce sont au moins des vers tragiques. Je vous demande en grâce de me mander s'ils sont orthodoxes. Je les crois tels; mais j'ay peur d'être un mauvais théologien.'[28] From February onwards several different versions of the 'Poème' circulated in Paris anonymously, some of them wrongly attributed to Voltaire.[29] The 'Poème', which clearly expresses the shock that the earthquake had released in Voltaire,[30] drew strong reactions from many readers, dividing them into two groups.[31] From some it evoked unconcealed enthusiasm;[32] in others it provoked intense denial.[33] The first group praised its narrative beauty; the second profoundly rejected its free thinking.

Serious early criticism also came from Voltaire's Swiss environment, where the clerics and bourgeois of Bern and Geneva objected to the pessimism in the 'Poème'. Afraid that too many people would be deterred by its dark view, Voltaire was ready to revise some of the verses: 'Il a fallu

25. Voltaire to Bertrand, 18 February 1756, D6738.

26. 'un certain Poëme qui fait beaucoup de bruit & qu'on luy attribue', Bruyset to de Lamoignon de Malesherbes, 12 December 1755, D6624.

27. Voltaire to Thieriot, 2 January 1756, D6671.

28. Voltaire to d'Argental, 15 February 1756, D6734.

29. In numerous letters Voltaire complained about the unpleasantness that emerged; see for example Voltaire to de Chennevières, 1 February 1756, D6713, and Voltaire to Capperonnier de Gauffecourt, 1 February 1756, D6714.

30. Voltaire sent to the duchesse de Saxe-Gotha a copy of the 'Poème' with the comment that he was very angry ('fâché') at the earthquake when writing the 'Poème', Voltaire to Meiningen de Saxe-Gotha, 1 January 1756, D6666. Yet in December 1755 Voltaire noted that manmade wars by far exceeded natural catastrophes in the number of fatalities they caused; see for example Voltaire to Allamand, 16 December 1755, D6629.

31. Approximately twenty reprints appeared in the first year after publication; see Breidert, *Die Erschütterung der vollkommenen Welt*, p.57.

32. See for example Thieriot to Voltaire, 19 January 1756, D6695.

33. Perhaps the best known criticism came from Jean-Jacques Rousseau. In a letter to Voltaire he answered Voltaire's 'Poème' by defending optimism as a comforting concept, and declaring the causes of evil as originating from human action and the ruinous condition of civilisation rather than a world that was good *per se*; Rousseau to Voltaire, 18 August 1756, D6973; see also Erhard Oeser, 'Das Erdbeben von Lissabon im Spiegel der zeitgenössischen Philosophie', in *Elementare Gewalt. Kulturelle Bewältigung. Aspekte der Natur-katastrophe im 18. Jahrhundert*, ed. F. Eybl, H. Heppner and A. Kernbaumer (Vienna 1999), p.185-95 (p.185-88).

dire ce que je pense et le dire d'une manière qui ne révoltât ny les esprits trop philosophes ny les esprits trop crédules.'[34] As a consequence, he rewrote several passages, particularly at the end. Late in February 1756 a new version was available which contained a more conciliatory gesture with a stronger emphasis on hope. In May 1756, the 'Poème' on Lisbon and the poem 'La religion naturelle' dating from four years earlier, were printed.

Mason agrees with Havens that revising the 'Poème' represented a gesture of goodwill from Voltaire towards his hosts.[35] In 1756 Voltaire was still very hesitant about openly expressing his frank opinion on important religious doctrine.[36] Although the revised 'Poème' contained softer statements for the critics, such changes did not reflect Voltaire's real view. In a letter of March 1756 he describes his restraint in the revision: 'Je n'ay peur que d'être trop ortodoxe, par ce que cela ne me sied pas. Mais la résignation à l'être suprême sied toujours bien.'[37]

Havens underlines his argument with a discovery he made in a Leningrad archive: an example of Voltaire's own copy of the 'Poème', to which Voltaire has added some remarks.[38] The final passage of the 'Poème' reads:

> *Un jour tout sera bien*, voilà notre espérance;
> *Tout est bien aujourd'hui*, voilà l'illusion. [...]
> Mais il pouvait encore ajouter l'espérance.[39]

Voltaire sharply modified line 118, '*Un jour tout sera bien*, voilà notre espérance' changing the final words to 'quelle frele espérance!' For the phrase 'voilà l'illusion' he appended: 'c'est qu'elle illusion!' And the last line of the 'Poème' Voltaire amended with a question mark: 'Mais pouvait-il encore ajouter *l'espérance?*'[40] Based on this annotated copy, Havens concludes: 'Hence, it would be entirely unsafe to quote Voltaire's final published lines as representing accurately his real opinion.'[41]

Despite this modified end passage, research literature has taken Voltaire's 'Poème' as a point of reference for criticising optimism after the

---

34. Voltaire to Cideville, 12 April 1756, D6821.
35. May to Haller, 6 January 1756, Bern, Burgerbibliothek, N Albrecht von Haller Korr, and Seigneux de Correvon to Haller, 27 March 1756, Bern, Burgerbibliothek, N Albrecht von Haller Korr. See Haydn Mason, 'Voltaire's "sermon" against optimism: the "Poème sur le désastre de Lisbonne"', in *Enlightenment essays in memory of Robert Shackleton*, ed. Giles Barber and C. P. Courtney (Oxford 1988), p.189-203, and George R. Havens, 'Voltaire's pessimistic revision of the conclusion of his "Poème sur le désastre de Lisbonne"', *Modern language notes* 44:8 (1929), p.489-92.
36. Havens, *Voltaire's pessimistic revision*, p.491.
37. Voltaire to d'Argental, 22 March 1756, D6798.
38. After Voltaire's death his niece left his library to the tsarina Catherine of Russia; see Georg Holmsten, *Voltaire* (Reinbek bei Hamburg 2002), p.152.
39. Voltaire reprinted in Breidert, *Erschütterung der vollkommenen Welt*, p.72-73.
40. Havens, *Voltaire's pessimistic revision*, p.491-92.
41. Havens, *Voltaire's pessimistic revision*, p.491.

Lisbon earthquake as well as a trigger for renewed debate over theodicy.[42] In doing so, we are ignoring that the criticism of the 'Poème' was just as significant as enthusiasm for it. As mentioned above, the revised ending was the result of numerous and local discerning voices.[43] In particular the pessimistic testimony of the 'Poème' was heavily questioned. Ever since his arrival in Switzerland, Swiss protestants had distrusted Voltaire, and his affinity with deism and materialism was criticised. After publishing the 'Poème', he was abandoned by some of his contemporaries. I will elucidate this with some examples from the correspondence network of the scholar Albrecht von Haller (1708-1777) from Bern (Switzerland).[44]

At the beginning of December 1755, Voltaire, now living in Montriond near Lausanne, started reading early versions of his 'Poème' in small lecture circles of acquaintances. One of Haller's friends from Bern, Beat Ludwig May,[45] then living in exile, received notes on the end passages of the 'Poème' via an acquaintance who had heard Voltaire personally. On 2 January 1755, May sent comments to Haller.[46] Usually an admirer of Voltaire, May expressed great concern over the materialistic and pessimistic thoughts in the 'Poème': 'Mr de Voltaire [...] à fait un Pöeme sur Lisbone, qu'il n'a fait que lire à ses convives, l'on m'en à envoyé les 8. vers que je joins icy. Come J'ay bien de croire que c'est de son aveu, et qu'il m'a paru que les Vers (fort admirés à Lausanne) sentent fort le matérialisme.'[47] May compared the 'Poème' with Haller's 'Über den Ursprung des Übels' (1734),[48] which he translated into French and sent to Voltaire: 'J'ay risposté par quelques fragments de ma traduction de Vostre [Haller's] Origine du mal, qui me paroissent à peu près Convenir pour réponse. Vous y trouveres peûtêtre un peu de bonne volonté, mais un fort

42. See references in note 1.

43. 'Les tremblements de terre qui ont ruiné Lisbonne ont fait dire à notre poëte [Voltaire] que tout n'est pas bien; il fit un poëme sur cet événement terrible, et lorsque ce poëme n'était encor qu'une ébauche il eut la bétise de le lire à quelques suisses. Ces suisses s'imaginant que le poëte combattait l'axiome de Pope, crurent qu'il n'admettait que la proposition contraire, savoir que dans ce monde *tout est mal*. Cette bévue de quelques suisses n'a pas laissé de lui faire quelque petite tracasserie. Le poëte se plaint à la vérité que nous habitions un globe qui parait miné et que nous soyons exposés à des événements si affreux, mais il se résigne à la volonté de Dieu', Collini to Dupont, 21 March 1756, D6797.

44. Albrecht von Haller (1708-1777), physiologist, naturalist and *savant* in Bern and Göttingen. Haller was professor of anatomy, botany and surgery at the newly funded university of Göttingen. Through his teaching and publishing, he actively contributed to improving the university. Thanks to Haller the *Göttingische Gelehrte Anzeigen* gained significantly. After 1745 he was a magistrate in Bern and in this function was very important to Voltaire, who lived in that state. Concerning the topic of earthquakes in Haller's correspondence see Stuber, *Divine punishment*, p.173-93.

45. Beat Ludwig May (1692-1758), magistrate, Bern and Chexbres VD.

46. 'Que fautyl O' Mortel? Mortel, Il faut Souffrir. Se soumettre en Silence, adorer et mourir', May to Haller, 2 January 1756, Bern, Burgerbibliothek, N Albrecht von Haller Korr.

47. May to Haller, 2 January 1756, Bern, Burgerbibliothek, N Albrecht von Haller Korr.

48. Albrecht von Haller, 'Über den Ursprung des Übels', in Albrecht von Haller, *Versuch Schweizerischer Gedichte* II (Vienna 1793), p.1-49.

médiocre Poete; mais que M^r. de V: fasse des vers Allemands Nous serons aux Niveaux.'[49] May judged Haller's poem as a didactic piece which discusses the problem of theodicy from a much firmer standpoint than Voltaire. In this poem Haller tried to sidestep the problem of theodicy with an argument about the glorification of God (*doxologia*).[50] May cites the part of Haller's poem which speaks of the teleological aim of nature to justify a boundless confidence in God and the accuracy of his creation, and proposes Haller's poem as an antithesis to Voltaire's.

Another scholar with access to a provisional version of Voltaire's 'Poème' was the aforementioned cleric Elie Bertrand. He, like May, had criticised the ending of the 'Poème' as overly pessimistic. In a response of 18 February 1756, Voltaire announced revisions. He informed Bertrand that he was ready to accept the moment of hope and willing to integrate it into the 'Poème':

Vous me direz que je ne tire pas cette conséquence, que je laisse le lecteur dans la tristesse et dans le doute. Eh bien! il n'y a qu'à ajouter le mot d'espérer à celui d'adorer, et mettre '*mortels il faut souffrir, Se soumettre, adorer, espérer et mourir*'.[51]

And in a letter of 7 March he added: 'je compte venir vous aporter à Berne et soumettre à votre jugement et à celui de M. le b. de Freidenrick mes rêveries dont vous avez voulu voir l'ébauche. Vous verrez que j'aurai profité de vos sages et judicieuses réflexions.' The letter includes a new version of the last passage of the 'Poème'. Voltaire comments with the words: 'Voilà à peu près comme je voudrais finir, mais il est bien difficile de dire en vers tout ce qu'on voudrait.'[52]

Another correspondent of Haller's, Gabriel de Seigneux de Correvon (1695-1775),[53] had the opportunity to attend one of Voltaire's readings along with other people, who were most respected because of their religion and morality.[54] He later expressed towards Haller his pleasure regarding the 'Poème', which, he announced, was as beautiful as Voltaire's other works. He said that Voltaire read it very well, although the manuscript was completely fragmented due to many changes, amendments and deletions. In the new final sequence, which Seigneux de Correvon sent to Haller, the verses that had been criticised by May and Bertrand were replaced by a longer new passage. It was more or less the final version,

---

49. May to Haller, 2 January 1756, Bern, Burgerbibliothek, N Albrecht von Haller Korr. See also May to Haller, 6 January 1756 Bern, Burgerbibliothek, N Albrecht von Haller Korr, where he once again notes the problem of theodicy, which he sees better answered by Haller than Voltaire. May, however, strove in vain to receive a complete version of Voltaire's 'Poème'.

50. Haller, 'Ursprung des Übels', p.48.

51. Voltaire to Bertrand, 18 February 1756, D6738, original emphasis.

52. Voltaire to Bertrand, 7 March 1756, D6766.

53. Gabriel de Seigneux de Correvon (1695-1775), solicitor and magistrate in Lausanne.

54. 'L'après-midi il eut la Complaisance de nous lire lui même sa belle et grande pièce sur les malheurs de Lisbonne', Seigneux de Correvon to Haller, 27 March 1756, Bern, Burgerbibliothek, N Albrecht von Haller Korr.

which was later published. Seigneux de Correvon added to the letter an account of the conversation that followed the reading. He emphasised that Voltaire never questioned Pope's axiom 'Tout ce qui est est bien', but rather criticised its misuse. Voltaire even stated that he could agree with the concept, saying that in the future everything might be good; but he criticised the ability of human reason to recognise the wisdom of the system. Moreover, Voltaire had emphasised that only the Christian religion might arrive at truth and serenity. The enthused Seigneux de Correvon closed with the words: 'Je n'entreprendrai point de vous rendre toutes les belles choses qu'il nous dit à la gloire du Christianisme; il les dit avec une chaleur qui persuade et de la réalité des choses et de la créance que leur donne celui qui parle.'[55]

Voltaire's now cautious stance in the 'Poème' as well as his acclamation of Christianity had tactical reasons. Voltaire had to assume that everyone in Bern was noticing his remarks. Among them was Haller who, since December 1755, had been a correspondent of his. All the same, Voltaire's efforts had no positive effect on Haller. In Haller's correspondence with Charles Bonnet (1720-1793),[56] heavy criticism of the Lisbon 'Poème' can be found. On 18 December 1756, Bonnet inquired of Haller whether or not the latter would be satisfied with Voltaire's 'Poème' on the Lisbon earthquake: 'Est-ce là entendre *l'Optimisme*? Mais voilà Mr Voltaire; il veut toujours manier le Philosophique, et presque toûjours il le manie mal.' Bonnet even denies Voltaire's philosophical competence and notes: 'S'il n'avoit point écrit sur la Philosophie, on l'auroit cru plus Philosophe. Il a parlé Philosophie et il n'a point été trouvé Philosophe.'[57] Haller too gave Voltaire no credit for philosophical competence. He accused him of having too narrow a focus on the divinely restricted age of a human being. All people are supposed to be divine creations ('DIEU leur createur') and God alone decides upon life and death. It was the destiny of human beings to die; this was not a question of contingency. Why should God prevent them from dying by marvels?[58] Who – Haller asks – would envy the creator for having to decide about life and death. Haller declared absolutely unphilosophical the way Voltaire spoke of the numerous dead in Lisbon.[59]

55. Seigneux de Correvon to Haller, 27 March 1756, Bern, Burgerbibliothek, N Albrecht von Haller Korr.

56. Charles Bonnet, 1720-1793, solicitor and magistrate, naturalist and philosopher in Geneva.

57. Bonnet to Haller, 18 December 1756, *The Correspondence between Albrecht von Haller and Charles Bonnet*, ed. Otto Sonntag (Bern, Stuttgart, Vienna 1983), p.90-92 (p.91), original emphasis.

58. Haller, *Briefe ueber einige Einwuerfe nochlebender Freygeister wider die Offenbarung* (Bern 1775-1776), i.29.

59. Haller to Bonnet, 8 January 1757, *Correspondence between Albrecht von Haller and Charles Bonnet*, p.92-94.

After the publication of Voltaire's satirical novel *Candide*, Bonnet once again brought up the 'Poème' with its criticism of optimism:

[Voltaire] êst à mon avis un des Etres les plus malheureux qui soyent sur la surface du Globe. Il le seroit désja par sa triste incrédulité. Un homme qui peint l'Univers, comme il est peint dans le Poëme sur Lisbonne et dans *Candide*, voit toute la Nature tendue de noir. Mais ce que je ne lui pardonne pas, c'êst de nous la montrer ainsi.[60]

Bonnet vehemently rejected the pessimism represented by Voltaire's two works (despite the modification of the Lisbon 'Poème'). Haller also designated the Lisbon 'Poème' as the decisive moment when he recognised Voltaire's true nature: 'J'ai reconnu a l'ocasion de la ruine de Lisbone les vues de ce Poete: Le mal domine, un Dieu bon et sage ne gouverne donc pas.'[61] Henceforth Haller saw in Voltaire one of his greatest opponents.[62]

Haller always adhered to the idea of nature as a divine creation provided with divine laws. His reasoning went like this: since God is the source of all natural laws and the human being is an image of God, an individual is able to comprehend natural laws. Haller's argument is based on physico-theological assumptions: each reference to nature brings the human being closer to God. Both the poetic and scientific depiction of nature reveal God's wisdom, for God demonstrated goodness and omnipotence in and through nature. Consequently, God did not distinguish between good and bad phenomena in nature. Rather he selected the necessary required remedies for instructing human beings: 'Gott, der durch Erdbeben ganze Reiche umstuerzt, [...], eben der allweise, der gerechte Gott, der die Tage der sterblichen Menschen gezählt hat, [...] es war seiner Weisheit gemaess, daß sein unmittelbar durch ihn beherrschtes Volk wissen mueßte, kein Zufall, keine sogenannte Gesetze der Natur, sondern einzig der Befehl ihres wahren Koeniges, waere die Ursache ihrer Bestrafung.'[63]

iii. Interpretative patterns in Swiss protestantism

Swiss protestant records that appeared after the Lisbon earthquake provided a variety of interpretation patterns. Theological descriptions of natural phenomena insisted on God as the one who created and governs

---

60. Bonnet to Haller, 27 March 1759, *Correspondence between Albrecht von Haller and Charles Bonnet*, p.160-62 (p.161), original emphasis.

61. Haller to Bonnet, 16 March 1759, *Correspondence between Albrecht von Haller and Charles Bonnet*, p.158-60 (p.159).

62. See among others Haller, *Briefe*, which was written particularly against Voltaire's philosophical ideas.

63. 'God, who destroys entire empires through earthquakes, the almighty and just God, who counted the days of the mortal being; [...] it was in accordance with His wisdom that His people would have to know that no contingency, no so-called laws of nature, but rather the command of their true king was the cause of the punishment', Haller, *Briefe*, i.95-96.

the earth, and recognised in the earthquake a divine act that had to be interpreted. Earthquakes were seen as an occasion to do penance before God, confess all sins and change one's life. But natural explanations were no longer denied in Swiss protestantism; even quite a few theologians accepted common earthquake theories, albeit their insistence on moral intentions behind the natural phenomena. But the most important pattern was the physico-theological concept that recognised natural phenomena as God's voice speaking through nature: earthquakes were no longer to be understood as human suffering but as proof of the divine *doxa*.[64] Physico-theology, based on the older natural theology, sought to demonstrate that if the mechanical notions were handled well, it would still be possible to accept God as an active ruler of the world. The physico-theological proof of God was saying that traces of divine wisdom could be discovered in nature. In this understanding, physico-theology used science theologically so as to demonstrate divine providence. A common feature of all patterns was the amalgamation of 'cosmological optimism' – nature formed by God and free of the human being is good – with 'ethical pessimism' – evil has its place within human nature. In this way the problem of theodicy was outlined.

The theologians that presented their opinion to the public were an important group. They generally took the Lisbon event as an opportunity to speak of human sin in dominical and penance sermons. Earthquakes were most frequently interpreted in protestant sermons as a divine sign.[65] It was the task of pastors to read this sign and communicate it, and in so doing, they placed their sermons in the context of a catastrophe communication, which often diffused knowledge of earthquakes. The descriptions of the earthquake usually remained very general, with little detail. The main purpose of these sermons was to show that earthquakes were justified by human action. The theologians did not deny human suffering; rather they offered good reasons for its existence. They proclaimed that earthquakes punished human evil and invited sinners to confess and change their lives. The clerics' main concern was to admonish and create an effective remembrance. People were supposed to recognise God as the main cause of the dreadful events, acknowledge his power in the world, and take his warning to heart. Earthquakes were signs by

---

64. Groh and Groh, *Religiöse Wurzeln*, p.50-59; Löffler, *Lissabons Fall*, p.96-97; Wolfgang Philipp, *Das Werden der Aufklärung in theologiegeschichtlicher Sicht* (Göttingen 1957); Helga Dirlinger, 'Das Buch der Natur. Der Einfluss der Physikotheologie auf das neuzeitliche Naturverständnis und die ästhetische Wahrnehmung von Wildnis', in *Individualisierung, Rationalisierung, Säkularisierung. Neue Wege der Religionsgeschichte*, ed. Michael Weinzierl (Vienna, Munich 1997), p.156-85.

65. 'Wie wohl wird uns kommen, wenn wir auch wissen und verstehen, was der damit zu uns hat sagen wollen!' ('We would be happy so as to understand what He was going to say!'), Jakob Valentin, *Waechterstimme Des Allmaechtigen, Welche ER zu unserer Warnung gegen das Ende des 1755. und Anfang des 1756. Jahrs zu verschiedenen mahlen in Europa und andern Welttheilen durch starke Erderschütterungen hat hoeren lassen* (Zurich 1756), p.8.

which God announced his dwindling patience with human sin. He thus intended either to warn or punish.[66] Human beings must not question divine will, because they are miserable and imperfect; only God is eternally perfect.[67] This argument was commonly used against those who criticised suffering from the earthquake. Human beings should never judge or question God, because they must not raise themselves above Him.[68]

Human beings who lost faith in God as the creator and guide of the world's order had to be warned or punished. But if they lived a God-fearing life, they could protect themselves from further disasters. In the cases where God warned but did not punish, such as in Switzerland during the Lisbon earthquake, God was willing to show patience. Such a warning hence included a chance: 'Vielleicht schonet der Herr unser noch eine Weile mit denen Plagen, welche der grossen Noth nur ein Anfang sind, warnet und loket uns zur Buss und Glauben an seine H[eiligen] Verdienste, durch Exempel seines Eifers die Er uns noch hin und wieder an andern vorstellet.'[69] Other clerics expressed the hope that these signs might be seen as requests for awakened spirit and recognition of sins.[70] People should take to heart the impressions of such events and acknowledge God's omnipotence and justice in order to be saved from future judgement.[71]

The question of why earthquakes happen was posed not to challenge theodicy (for God was not to be challenged) but to recognise God's intent.[72] Assuming God's wisdom, the concern was to read his signs. One of the clerics, the Pietist Jakob Valentin, gave a threefold reading of earthquakes: they are a divine judgement on those directly involved in

66. Johann Kaspar Ziegler, 'Erschreklicher Untergang der Stadt Lisabon, sammt denen zu gleicher Zeit anderswo geschehenen fast allgemeinen Erdbeben, und ausserordentlichen Bewegungen des Wassers, zur Erwekung einer tieffen Ehrfurcht vor GOtt vorgestellt', in *Monatliche Nachrichten einicher Merkwuerdigkeiten, in Zuerich gesammlet und herausgegeben* (Zurich 1755), p.1-8; Johann Caspar Pfenninger, *Das Erdbeben, ein Beweis der Heiligkeit, Gerechtigkeit, Weisheit und Macht des Grossen Gottes* (Zurich 1756).

67. Pfenninger, *Das Erdbeben*, p.11.

68. Pfenninger, *Das Erdbeben*, p.8-11, Elie Bertrand, 'La considération salutaire des malheurs publics. Ou sermon sur Jérémie XXII.v.8', in *Memoire sur les tremblemens de terre avec quatre sermons* (Vevey 1756), p.1-22.

69. 'Perhaps God still prevents us from troubles, which would be the beginning of the misery; he warned and asked to penance and to believe in his holy merits; and he introduces his passion by showing it through others', Valentin, *Wächterstimme*, p.4.

70. 'Die rufende, lokende und warnende Stimme des HErrn, auf die Zeichen der Zeiten, nicht behöriger Massen gemerket und Acht gegeben' ('The calling voice of God and his signs, not having been acknowledged'), Hans Conrad Wirz, *Drey Busspredigten, ueber den ausserordentlich gefeyrten Baettag gehalten* (Zurich 1756), p.67.

71. Hans Jacob Friess, *Schriftmaeßige Anweisung, wie man sich foerchterliche Gerichte GOttes, die ueber andere Menschen ergehen, zu seinem Heyl zu Nutz machen solle. In einer Predigt über Luc. XIII.v.4.5. vorgetragen, und auf instaendiges Begehren zum Druck uebergeben* (Zurich 1756), p.4-8.

72. 'Erkanntnuß von denen absichten GOttes [zu] verstehen, was der HErr damit zu uns hat sagen wollen!' ('Insight of God's intent, in order to understand what He was going to say'), Valentin, *Wächterstimme*, p.7.

the punishment; a warning voice calling those who have been saved to do penance and convert; and a sign to predict other important events. Events in the Old Testament, especially the flood and the destruction of Sodom and Gomorrah, were used to illustrate how natural disasters were divine judgements of the godless. Human sins, such as impenitence, indifference to the divine and contempt of God, were the main reason for these divine tribunals. Since the remedies used so far obviously did not suffice, God had to use a more extraordinary corrective. In Valentin's understanding earthquakes belonged among these heavy punishments. The Lisbon earthquake was only a warning for the Swiss people, since God did not destroy their regions and towns. Those so warned who now atoned would be helped, for God will accept the penance. But if the warnings were not recognised, affliction was certain.[73] Valentin addressed himself explicitly to the atheists too, who in his opinion neither recognised the divine *providentia* nor the punishment of the sins after death. Even though it is not outlined explicitly in the sermon, we can assume that Valentin saw the Catholic inhabitants of Portugal as unbelievers who needed to be punished. But even usually pious people had to remember regularly to relearn humility and modesty.[74]

In contrast to those clerics who saw earthquakes only as divine interventions, other theologians were ready to accept natural explanations, even though they insisted on the first cause of all natural phenomena, which was of course God. The cleric Daniel Stapfer, for example, integrates contemporary earthquake theory into his argument and connects it with theological interpretation. In the introduction to the sermon Stapfer describes the world as 'allervollkommenste Maschine'.[75] Evidently he orientates himself to Christian Wolff's (1679-1754) philosophy of optimism.[76] Yet neither Wolff nor Stapfer intended to draw a deistic concept of the machine; they interpreted the world rather as a well-organised creation under the domination of God, effective even at this time. Stapfer first describes the world as teleologically structured, according to the wise plan of God. In this plan everything had its purpose, nothing was without avail. Enclosed fires in caves – which, he assumed, were a main cause of earthquakes – were most important for the prosperity and fertility of the soil, the production of metals and minerals. If earthquakes served this invention, they were not to be called evil but important to serve life on earth, they were part of God's providence, as were all other phenomena.[77] Stapfer then connects natural with moral intentions. Everything happens

---

73. Valentin, *Wächterstimme*, p.7-17.

74. Johann Jakob Zehnder, *Die Absicht GOttes in der Offenbahrung seiner Gerichten bey den Einwohneren des Erdkreisses* (Bern 1755), p.24-30.

75. 'absolutely perfect machine', Daniel Stapfer, *Betrachtung des Erdbebens* (Zurich 1756), p.14.

76. See Löffler, *Lissabons Fall*, p.489-91.

77. Stapfer, *Betrachtung des Erdbebens*, p.48-57.

after the course of nature, which is embedded within the wise providence that leads the course steadily. Yet, earthquakes are to warn and punish, in order to improve the human being. Here lies the moral intention of Stapfer's sermon: when earthquakes help to improve the human being, they are needed, equal to their utility in the course of prosperity. The correlation of all things has been wisely described as a pre-established harmony, created by God. By calling the believers' attention to God's wise plan, Stapfer praises the creator's perfection.

Even though it was probably not his intention, we can call Stapfer's consolidation of natural and moral concepts physico-theologian. Physico-theologians in general tried to connect scientific and theological explanations of natural phenomena. This allowed them to maintain philosophical optimism even with regard to catastrophes. The physico-theological coping emphasised a positive conversion of the negative, assuming that God or nature did nothing in vain if one searched for the metaphysical and practical utility of all apparent evil. Divine wisdom and power were to be acknowledged and demonstrated in divine acts, because God creates only what serves to recognise his wisdom. This is in opposition to the assumption of an ethical pessimism, which defines evil as part of human nature.

The physico-theological concept is also largely present in the works of Elie Bertrand, who includes natural analyses of earthquakes with theological interpretations.[78] His sermons as well as his natural philosophical writings reveal him to be very religious,[79] but that in his priestly function he did not deny the insights of the scientific community. At the time of the Lisbon event he had already published several books on natural philosophy.[80] In the four sermons Bertrand preached and published within four months after the quake, he asks for the raison d'être of the disaster.[81] The first sermon attacks the non-belief of those who think of such catastrophes as mere natural events and who do not see the possibility of recognising God within. Bertrand wrote his first sermon under the principle of Jeremiah xxii.8: 'Plusieurs Nations passeront près de cette Ville, & chacun dira à son Compagnon de voyage, pourquoi l'Eternel a-t-il fait ainsi à cette grande Ville?' When God created the world, he had predicted all events as well as all the effects that would follow. God therefore

---

78. Bertrand's writings after 1755 were not only a reaction to the Lisbon earthquake but also to an earthquake of 9 December 1755 in the Valais region (Switzerland), the largest seismic event in Switzerland in the eighteenth century; see Monika Gisler, Donat Fäh and Nicholas Deichmann, 'The Valais earthquake of December 9, 1755', *Eclogae geologicae Helvetiae (Swiss journal of geosciences)* 97 (2004). Bertrand's interest in physico-theological concepts started long before 1755.

79. Bertrand's faith was broadly discussed in Mason, 'Voltaire and Elie Bertrand', Gargett, *Voltaire and protestantism*, and Roulet, *Voltaire et les Bernois*.

80. Mason, 'Voltaire and Elie Bertrand', has already pointed out the importance of Bertrand's writings. One must not see Bertrand as a typical example of Swiss protestantism, however.

81. Elie Bertrand, *Mémoire sur les tremblemens de terre avec quatre sermons* (Vevey 1756).

knew, and even wanted, such unfortunate cities to be destroyed by an earthquake. For God's action is never without a reason: 'Dieu étant un Etre sage, qui ne veut, qui n'ordonne rien sans raisons, il doit avoir ses vuës dans ces dispensations extraordinaires, dans ces tristes subversions.'[82]

God is a creator and therefore established the consistent order of the world. To recognise the will of God, however, one would need to be divine. The question of God's wise providence in allowing earthquakes was thus not acceptable to Bertrand. Rather he understood earthquakes as a divine lesson.[83] Misfortune is not sorrow, but a training process. Bertrand reminded the believer that God must have had moral intentions in destroying Lisbon by an earthquake:

Voulez-vous cependant savoir, Mes Fréres, quelques-unes des raisons pour les-quelles *l'Eternel a fait ainsi à cette grande ville*? Raisons morales, qui sont les seules à notre portée, les seules aussi qu'il nous importe de savoir, car nous sommes ici-bas, non pour spéculer, mais pour agir. Dieu veut nous apprendre que nous ne sommes pas faits pour cette terre, qui peut crouler sous nos pas; que notre ame immortelle n'est pas formée pour être possédée par des richesses que la terre peut engloutir.[84]

Human beings are not supposed to be taken by the desire to possess goods, but to remember that mortal life is only preparing them for life in heaven. Consequently, by sending earthquakes God does not want to punish, but to remind human beings to be prepared for death. This is also the main topic of the second sermon, where Bertrand demonstrates these ideas at length. It is all a question of acknowledging God's wisdom and fearing Him: 'Craignons Dieu, & nous l'aimerons, nous le servirons, nous l'imi-terons.'[85] Bertrand differed radically from his fellow believers; he did not understand earthquakes as a divine punishment nor did he see an angry God within natural disasters. God sends grief and sorrow to improve and convert human beings. Earthquakes are signs of God; not of an evil God, but of a wise and benevolent regent who seeks to guide and perfect human beings. Evil is not denied in Bertrand's sermons, but redefined. Harmony in God's creation is not jeopardised; rather human beings are guided to change for the better. God is not to be questioned, nor opti-mism to be denied; on the contrary, Bertrand's deepest concern was to bring people closer to a caring God. Bertrand answered the theodicy question by asserting that God or nature would do nothing in vain. With this argument he outlines an interpretation pattern that can be read as a preventive scheme. If people heeded the call to a more God-fearing

82. Bertrand, 'La considération salutaire', p.7.
83. Elie Bertrand, 'La crainte du seigneur est la vraye sagesse. Ou sermon sur Job XXVIIIv.28', in *Memoire sur les tremblemens de terre avec quatre sermons* (Vevey 1756), p.23-47 (p.35).
84. Bertrand, 'La considération salutaire', p.8, original emphasis.
85. Bertrand, 'La crainte du seigneur', p.46.

existence, future catastrophes would be averted. This position calls for a God that is not deistic but the world's providence (*providentia*) and governor (*gubernatio*).

In his sermons, however, Bertrand did not entirely abandon the physical explanations of earthquakes; rather he tried to unite them with theological interpretations. At the beginning of his first sermon, he confronted philosophers who tended to interpret earthquakes as natural phenomena only: 'Ainsi parlent ceux qu'on nomme Philosophes, & qui se glorifient de l'être. Esprits supérieurs, votre philosophie est bien bornée si elle s'en tient là! Voila la mechanique; où est l'Esprit moteur?'[86] Bertrand did not deny natural laws, but he emphasised the basic cause of all natural laws. He explained earthquakes as the effects of winds enclosed in caves and then enflamed by underground fires or through fermentation. By bringing physical explanations into a metaphysical context, Bertrand declared the fundamental laws as divine.

These arguments are to be found not only in his sermons, but also in his philosophical writings on earthquakes.[87] Here he repeated that all natural events were created by God to instruct and direct human beings. The more impressive the phenomena, the more the people are called to find God: 'Ne doutons point que ces agitations de la terre n'ayent leur usage physique aussi bien que leur destination morale.'[88] For God is the first and only reason for these phenomena: 'N'est-il donc pas la prémière cause de ces tremblemens & de leurs suites?'[89] On a physical level, earthquakes announce (and help produce) fruitful years.[90] By shifting natural catastrophes into positive concepts, Bertrand celebrated God's wisdom, which created the movement and stable order of the world, and wisely formed the caves that were necessary for the production of earthquakes. It was essential to recognise that the fundamental laws were divinely made, and that the world's mechanism needed everything God had created, since this insight led to praising God. This was Bertrand's motivation in seeking the natural and moral reasons behind seismic activity. The more exact the acquired knowledge ('les idées'), the more this would humble the limited human being.

Conclusions

With his work, Bertrand popularised natural philosophy and provided the foundation for moving beyond merely metaphysical interpretations.

---

86. Bertrand, 'La considération salutaire', p.5.

87. Elie Bertrand, *Mémoires historiques et physiques sur les tremblemens de terre, Recueil de divers traités sur l'histoire naturelle de la terre et des fossiles* (Vevey 1756).

88. Bertrand, *Mémoires historiques*, p.12-13.

89. Bertrand, 'La considération salutaire', p.6.

90. 'Elles annoncent la fertilité pour les années suivantes', Bertrand, *Mémoires historiques*, p.13.

In the theological sermons he interpreted earthquakes as calls to conversion, as warning signs to offer renewed reverence to God. In his scientific writings, he investigated the reasons behind earthquakes not to doubt God or the perfection of the world, but to appreciate God's design. Only God as *première cause* could know the basic fundamentals for all natural phenomena. This was also the argument of the cleric Stapfer, who described the world as teleologically structured, according to God's wise plan. In this plan everything had its purpose, because God did nothing in vain. The human intellect could learn something about God's plan by using scientific knowledge. An enlarged understanding of physics would enable recognition of God, a common position of physico-theology. Natural phenomena, even the disastrous ones, could be explained by noticing their utility.

This theological understanding of evil allowed transcending the question of theodicy. By changing the negative into the positive, the reactions of Swiss protestantism to the Lisbon earthquake dealt with the inhuman effects of the catastrophe by referring to God's perfectly designed order. The interpretation patterns of Bertrand and others underline the direct reactions to Voltaire's 'Poème', which questioned and deterred – even though not homogeneously – the pessimistic view of Voltaire's intention. The responses to the 'Poème' were much more diverse than disrupting the optimistic philosophy of the early Enlightenment. We have seen in Haller's correspondence network that the pessimistic impact of the 'Poème' was largely rejected. Haller instead spoke of the teleological aim of nature to justify a boundless confidence in God. The Lisbon disaster confronted the belief in harmony and expedience of the divine order but was unable to reject it. The question of why such earthquakes happen was not posed to dispute theodicy but to recognise God's intent. The catastrophe served as an occasion to remind people of the omnipotence of God. If people tried to live a more God-fearing existence, future catastrophes could be averted. It would then be possible to shift this ethical pessimism to a physico-theological optimism that asserted that the world was good. Because of its magnitude, the event had an impact on philosophical and religious discourses; but religion and philosophy had their effects on how the event was understood.

LUANNE FRANK

No way out:
Heinrich von Kleist's *Erdbeben in Chile*

THE literary focus of this study is a German work entitled *Das Erdbeben in Chile* (The earthquake in Chile), a brief, disturbing, improbably concentrated novella by Heinrich von Kleist, dated 1807.[1] The eponymous event of Kleist's novella is an earthquake of a century earlier (1647),[2] on another continent. It may even, according to a recent re-inquiry into the matter, claim as part of its provenance a still earlier (and possibly also a later) Peruvian natural disaster (1538 and 1666 respectively).[3] But it is widely accepted that the primary origin of the novella's focal event was in fact the Lisbon earthquake.[4] Thus does a nineteenth-century work featuring a seventeenth-century Chilean earthquake figure in a volume of studies focusing on an eighteenth-century event, the great earthquake in Lisbon in 1755. This, however, is not all.

Part of what remains, and what the present study undertakes, is the following: first, to review, in addition to the geological, further sets of originating events for the novella – broadly cultural events, and spiritual, psychic events, each of which also points to Lisbon; second, to use these cultural and spiritual events to suggest Kleist's possible identity as a hinge

1. Heinrich von Kleist, *Das Erdbeben in Chile*, *Sämtliche Werke und Briefe*, ed. Helmut Sembdner (Munich 1965), ii.144-59. Titles and quotations from Kleist henceforward are to this edition, as is the quotation from Goethe cited below (n.24).

2. It is identified as such in the novella's opening sentence: 'In Santiago, [...] Chile, [...] just at the moment of the great earthquake of the year 1647.'

3. These were volcanic eruptions, one of which figures in Jean-François Marmontel's *Les Incas* (1777 in French and German), still popular in Kleist's time. See Gisela Schlüter, 'Kleist und Marmontel: Nochmals zu Kleist und Frankreich', *Arcadia* 24 (1989), p.13-24.

4. The novella's setting in Chile has been attributed to Kleist's possible need for a 'more primitive, quasi-mythic and exotic setting than the sophisticated city of Lisbon in 1755', in order 'to develop his theme of the malevolence of [an] enraged mob'. See Alfred Owen Aldridge, 'The background of Kleist's *Das Erdbeben in Chili*', *Arcadia* 4 (1969), p.180. This would be a mob capable of the gruesome acts that, after the quake, are the novella's most salient features. For additional information on the topic of Lisbon as the novella's source see also Aldridge, 'Background', p.173-80; Kleist, *Werke und Briefe in vier Bde*, ed. Peter Goldammer (Berlin 1978), iii.654; Thomas E. Bourke, 'Vorsehung und Katastrophe: Voltaires "Poème sur le désastre de Lisbonne" und Kleists *Erdbeben in Chile*', in *Klassik und Moderne* (1983), p.228-53; Susanne Lendaff, 'Kleist und die Beste aller Welten: *Das Erdbeben in Chile* gesehen im Spiegel der philosophischen und literarischen Stellungnahmen zur Theodizee im 18. Jahrhundert', *Kleist Jahrbuch* (1986), p.125-49; and Dirk Grathoff, 'Die Erdbeben in Chili und Lissabon', in *Kleist: Geschichte, Politik, Sprache: Aufsätze zu Leben und Werk Heinrich von Kleists* (Opladen 1999), p.96-111.

figure between the Enlightenment and the modern *epistèmes*, as Michel Foucault describes them;[5] and, finally, to explore how it might be that Kleist should be caught between these *epistèmes*, with no way out – unable fully to embrace the new, even as his work helped to shape it, and similarly unable any longer to credit the old, though to be thus able would seem the fulfilment of the deepest of his desires.

If, geologically speaking, *Erdbeben*'s primary originating event was the Lisbon earthquake, culturally speaking its originating events also focus on Lisbon. They are, as it were, Lisbon once removed: Lisbon thought, Lisbon given meaning. They have been shown to be certain of Lisbon's literary, philosophical and theological reverberations, among which figure prominently Voltaire's well-known 'Poème sur le désastre de Lisbonne' of 1756 (completed in 1755),[6] and his *Candide* of 1759,[7] as well as comments by Immanuel Kant, to whose first critique Kleist owed the most stunning insight of his life, an insight to which we shall return. It is in a much earlier work, however, that Kant made a series of comments focusing on earthquakes that are held to have riveted Kleist. In Kant's 'History and natural description of the noteworthy events of the earthquake that at the end of 1755 shook a large part of the Earth' (1756),[8] he notes that a tale of an earthquake, that most devastating of events (Kant has Lisbon in mind, as is evident from his title), could be moving enough to lead its readers to (presumably moral-spiritual) betterment. But he adds that he will leave the writing of such a tale to more capable hands. Forty-five years later, with natural catastrophes still on his mind, and now celebrating the moral capacity of humans, he writes in his third critique that it is in their confrontation with natural disasters – in measuring themselves against nature's overwhelming might – that humans become capable of sublime acts.[9]

---

5. Michel Foucault, *The Order of things: an archaeology of the human sciences* (New York 1970; French original 1966).

6. Voltaire, 'Poème sur le désastre de Lisbonne, ou examen de cet axiome: tout est bien', in *Œuvres complètes de Voltaire*, ed. Louis Moland (Paris 1877-1885), ix.465-80.

7. See Bourke, 'Vorsehung und Katastrophe'; Werner Hamacher, 'Das Beben der Darstellung', in *Positionen der Literaturwissenschaft*, ed. David E. Wellbery (Munich 1985), p.149-73 (esp. p.151-54 and n.6, p.188); and Saskia Herrath, 'Zurück zum Ursprung oder das kultivierte Paradies: Voltaires *Candide* und Kleists *Erdbeben in Chili*', in *Kleine Lauben, Arcadien und Schnabelewopski: Festschrift für Klaus Jeziorkowski*, ed. Ingo Wintermayer (Würzburg 1995), p.27-39.

8. 'Geschichte und Naturbeschreibung der merkwürdigen Vorfälle des Erdbebens, welches an dem Ende des 1755sten Jahres einen grossen Theil der Erde erschüttert hat', in *Kants gesammelte Schriften* (Berlin 1910), i.456-58.

9. In 'On nature as a power', para. 28 of the *Critique of the power of judgment*, Kant makes the following point: examples of nature such as volcanoes and hurricanes (among others) 'are powers we call sublime because they elevate the strength of our soul above its usual level, and allow us to discover within ourselves a capacity for resistance of quite another kind, which gives us the courage to measure ourselves against the apparent all-powerfulness of nature'. *Kants gesammelte Schriften* (Berlin 1908), v.261; translation by Paul Guyer and Eric Matthews, in *Critique of the power of judgment* (Cambridge 2000), p.144-45.

Such acts are what Kleist's story, in its 'idyllic' middle section, describes occurring, before the idyll turns to tragedy. In the hours immediately following the earthquake, ordinary people perform extraordinary deeds – courageous, selfless, heroic deeds, exemplarily moral in a Kantian sense. And Kleist appears to take no chances that these not uncommon people's uncommon heroism, seen as prompted by the earthquake, will be missed by the reader.[10] In the face of the earthquake, these people become extraordinary, and in becoming extraordinary, they become who they have never been.

In Kleist's case an additional quake, one of a very different order, had just such an effect. It brought about a new, undreamt-of Kleist, one whose work becomes increasingly prominent on the world-literary stage, as the age Kleist helped to inaugurate becomes increasingly accustomed to itself and the range of scholarly disciplines continues to expand. I am referring here to the sudden focus on Kleist at the end of the twentieth century and since, especially in women's and film studies, by scholars not led to Kleist by Germanistik,[11] to which Kleist studies prior to the 1970s had been essentially restricted;[12] to the widespread coverage by the English-language popular press of the German films of certain of Kleist's works;[13] and to the publication of a new English translation of Kleist's *Penthesilea* – the most original, powerful, and unrelenting of his dramas (one that Goethe turned from in revulsion) – appearing in a special collectors' edition.[14]

10. Although Kleist seems clearly to indicate this heroism and even suggests that *Erdbeben* be considered a 'moralische Erzählung' [moral tale] (to G. A. Reimer, May 1810, ii.895), critics have questioned whether he saw any figure in the work as unequivocally heroic. See Karl Otto Conrady, 'Das Moralische in Kleists Erzählungen: Ein Kapitel vom Dichter ohne Gesellschaft', in *Literatur und Gesellschaft vom 19. bis ins 20. Jahrhundert*, ed. Hans Joachim Schrimpf (Bonn 1963), p.56-82; John M. Ellis, 'Kleist: *Das Erdbeben in Chili*', in *Narration in the German novelle: theory and interpretation* (Cambridge 1974), p.46-76 (esp. p.73-75); Richard L. Johnson, 'Kleist's *Erdbeben in Chili*', *Seminar* 11 (1975), p.33-45; Robin A. Clouser, 'Heroism in Kleist's *Das Erdbeben in Chile*', *Germanic review* 58 (1983), p.129-40; and Hamacher, 'Das Beben der Darstellung', esp. p.157-62.

11. See for example the numerous studies unrelated to Germanistik proper listed in Mary Rhiel, *Re-viewing Kleist: the discursive construction of authorial subjectivity in West German Kleist films* (New York 1991), p.139-55.

12. In a review of an English translation of selected letters and short pieces by Kleist appearing in the 1980s and reported on exceptionally widely in the popular press (*An Abyss deep enough*, ed. and trans. Philip B. Miller, New York 1982), Richard Leiter takes special note of the usual restriction of interest in Kleist to a German public. See 'Kleist's Kant crisis', *American scholar* 51 (1982), p.561-63. This restriction may not be obvious to Germanists, for whom Kleist is an ongoing preoccupation.

13. See the numerous popular reviews of the films *Die Marquise von O* and *Prinz Friedrich von Homburg* cited in *Readers' guide to periodical literature* and *Film literature index* in the late 1970s and early 1980s. Eric Rohmer's *Marquise* (1975) appeared at the New York film festival only in October 1976, yet the *Index* for 1976 alone (iv.247) lists for it forty-two entries excluding newspapers. A single example, one that drew scholarly response, was Pauline Kael's unappreciative assessment of this otherwise much celebrated film. See 'No id', *The New Yorker* 25 (1976), p.67-68. See also John Gerlach. 'Rohmer, Kleist and *The Marquise of O*', *Literature film quarterly* 8 (1980), p.84-90

14. Heinrich von Kleist, *Penthesilea: a tragic drama*, translation and introduction by Joel Agee, illustrations by Maurice Sendak (New York 1998).

The additional earthquake noted above marks a third originating event for the novella, in this case a spiritual, psychic – in short, intimately personal – event. This was Kleist's well-known Kant crisis of 1801. The crisis was the immediate result of Kleist's encounter with the shocking, forever inassimilable fact, dredged from Kant's first critique, that all possibility of arriving at certainty through reason was forever closed to humankind: that there was no secure, certain, indisputable rational guide to action, no certain means of identifying truth.[15] A satisfactory term for this shock – for Kleist and his critics perhaps the only adequate term – is 'earthquake'. And earthquake for Kleist and his countrymen, as well as for his critics, means Lisbon.

Thus does *Erdbeben* become recognisable as a radically overdetermined literary work, each of whose earthquake-related instigators points to Lisbon. That this should be so has partly to do with the fact that each encounter with the word earthquake in a western cultural-literary context, whether in Kleist, Kleist criticism, or elsewhere, brings to mind immediately, even for those only vaguely familiar with Europe's literature, philosophy, theology, or social, intellectual history, the earthquake in Lisbon. The importance of this as a physical, intellectual, emotional, and spiritual event, and its dynamism as a force for change, although already much examined, even now, on its 250th anniversary, demands further attention. For Europe, earthquake and Lisbon are synonymous: earthquake is Lisbon first and foremost, however conscious we may be of San Francisco, 1906 and 1989; Skopje, 1963; Bhuj, 2001; Bam, 2003; the Indian Ocean tsunami, 2004, and others.

Kleist's Kant crisis was for him an intellectual and spiritual earthquake. This has been recognised by his critics, who have repeatedly turned to the word earthquake or its synonyms to signal the force and imply the aftershocks – also a word often used – of Kleist's psychic devastation in the face of what he found in, or interpreted into, Kant. This earthquake vocabulary has persevered even through the sweeping changes that western literary criticism underwent in the mid- and late twentieth century, widening what had been a limited number of traditional approaches to discrete literary objects; altering the objects 'themselves', their face, apparent essence, and meanings; and thus challenging as misguided the idea of any work's 'itselfness'. (Examined in the terms of some contemporary thought systems, for example, Kleist's works sometimes scarcely recognise themselves.)

But despite these sometimes amazing transformations, earthquake continues to be an indispensable word for representing Kleist's experience,

---

15. Viewed as the key event in Kleist's development as an author, the Kant crisis receives continuing scholarly attention. Recent readings of Kleist across Kant are Bernhard Greiner's *Eine Art Wahnsinn: Dichtung im Horizont Kants. Studien zu Goethe und Kleist* (Berlin 1994), and also his *Kleists Dramen und Erzählungen* (Tübingen 2000).

which is typically referred to as '[ein] Beben des Bewusstseins' (a quaking of consciousness),[16] or 'eine Erschütterung des Seins' (a convulsion of being). Kleist's mind as affected by Kant becomes 'der erschütterte Sinn' (the violently shaken sensibility).[17] Under Kleist's pen, representation 'quakes'.[18] Kleist's abandonment of the general for the particular becomes 'der Zusammensturz des Allgemeinen' (the collapse-in-upon-itself of the general).[19] For one critic, earthquake in Kleist is 'a paradigm for human life'.[20] Another argues that Kleist's Kant crisis and his earliest resulting narrative, *Erdbeben*, indeed represent earthquakes for Kleist, but so do all the other novellas as well, 'for in all of these [...] the earth quakes'.[21] The dramas too, one might add, feature psychic earthquakes, earthquakes of being – inexplicable, reason-defying, consciousness-arresting events. In this sense, each is a literary Lisbon.[22]

The characters in Kleist's works experience – and the works themselves emphasise – the collapse of conventional understandings, values and relationships. These collapses, together with Kleist's dense, often breathless language, the distressing harshness of some of the events depicted, and the typically 'excessive' ways of being and acting of certain characters in confronting these events, led Kleist's works to be placed more often than not outside the parameters of the German-, not to mention the world-literary canon. Although a few of Kleist's contemporaries immediately recognised his genius, his works' otherness was rejected or shied away from by numerous other contemporaries, who preferred a literature conforming to the sometime Apollonian literary norms of Kleist's own time, as well as by later critics still spiritually attuned to Greek classicism's 'noble simplicity and quiet grandeur' (Winckelmann's well-known phrase) as the *sine qua non* of great literature.

16. Karlheinz Stierle, 'Das Beben des Bewusstseins: Die narrative Struktur von Kleists *Das Erdbeben in Chili*', in *Positionen*, ed. Wellbery, p.54.

17. Norbert Altenhofer, 'Der erschütterte Sinn', in *Positionen*, ed. Wellbery, p.39.

18. Hamacher, 'Das Beben der Darstellung', p.149.

19. Helmut J. Schneider, 'Der Zusammenstürz des Allgemeinen', in *Positionen*, ed. Wellbery, p.110.

20. Hilda Meldrum Brown, '*Das Erdbeben in Chile*', in *Heinrich von Kleist: the ambiguity of art and the necessity of form* (Oxford 1998), p.144-61.

21. Hermann A. Korff, *Geist der Goethezeit* (Leipzig 1953), iv.86.

22. Kleist's most performed and one of his most popular dramas, *Prinz Friedrich von Homburg*, corresponds to this characterisation only in a muted way, but it so distressed ('infuriated') certain members of its initial audiences, who had heard it read aloud by Kleist in Berlin in 1810, or heard of it, that performances of it, scheduled that year and in that city at the home of Prince Anton Heinrich von Radziwill and at the National Theatre, were banned. See Joachim Maass, *Kleist: a biography* (New York 1983), p.203, 208. Even ten years after the early readings, a 'widely anticipated Berlin production was cancelled' and 'at the same time, a production planned by the Vienna Burgheater' (Maass, *Kleist*, p.249). These events of 1910 and later are but two of a cloud of reversals that beset Kleist throughout his life. It could not be said of his work, as August Wilhelm Schlegel said of Friedrich de La Motte-Fouqué's, that it suffered only from the fact that 'no real misfortune ha[d] ever befallen [its author]' (Maass, *Kleist*, p.211).

Goethe himself, and the early twentieth-century critic Friedrich Gundolf are two cases in point. Kleist presents *Penthesilea* to Goethe 'auf den Knieen meines Herzens' (on the knees of my heart).[23] Goethe's reaction is measured and somewhat cool.[24] His comments about the work to others, however, are characterised by revulsion. His outspokenly negative responses to Kleist's works persist for years (he somehow finds even *Amphitryon* – a gentle drama, relatively speaking – deplorable), extending long after Kleist's suicide.[25]

Gundolf recognises Kleist as 'the most original dramatist of Germany',[26] but, unable to perceive a literary precedent for *Penthesilea*, he labels the drama un-human.[27] He views *Erdbeben* and all the other novellas excepting *Kohlhaas* as examples of sensation-mongering.[28] In short, German classicism had no room in its schemes for the violence inflicted and endured by the characters in such works, or for the psychic lacerations that the works themselves inflicted on their readers. Eric Blackall, to whom we shall return, does not mention Kleist at all in his landmark study of the rise of German literary language by Kleist's time, not even as a topic he might wish to examine closely in a subsequent work. Apparently bound by certain language norms in his appreciation, Blackall finds that the German language reaches its zenith with Goethe.

The objections of Goethe and others notwithstanding, Kleist's works do join the German Olympian's, and Voltaire's as well, as recognisably major events in the history of western literary art. And precisely due to Voltaire's and Kleist's placing Europe's quintessential earthquake under the aegis of their art, Lisbon embarks on a literary afterlife different from, and possibly longer-lasting than, its purely historical, social, scientific, philosophical, and theological afterlives. One critic suggests as much when he observes that art marks the only available access to eternity. Art, he says, 'is the only eternity there is'. Perhaps for this very reason more of us will read the literary Voltaire and the literary Kleist (Kleist was an essayist-theorist before he was a dramatist-storyteller) than we will Kant. Lisbon, if not guaranteed immortality by art is, as part of art's order, arguably less subject to the vicissitudes of historical memory than the purely

---

23. To Goethe, 28 January 1808 (ii.806).

24. His response (1 February 1808): 'I can't yet make friends with Penthesilea. She is of so wondrous a race and moves in such a strange region that it will take me time to find my way around in both' (ii.806).

25. Katharina Mommsen, *Kleist's Kampf mit Goethe* (Heidelberg 1974). On the longevity of Goethe's revulsion, see p.194.

26. Friedrich Gundolf, *Heinrich von Kleist* (Berlin 1922), p.152.

27. Gundolf, *Heinrich von Kleist*, p.108. He insists that 'the world's reason, which we honor in Goethe and Shakespeare, is deaf and dumb in Kleist', *Penthesilea* being 'the first drama [...] in world literature to achiev[e] its effects without participation in the laws and ideas of human beings up to its time' (p.108).

28. Gundolf, *Heinrich von Kleist*, p.165.

historical, philosophical, theological event it might otherwise have remained. In addition, perhaps because the literary artistic text engages us simultaneously on increasingly numerous cognitive levels,[29] not to mention emotional and visceral levels (we are thrown into a sort of shock by *Erdbeben* and not first of all aesthetic or philosophical shock), the work of art keeps us focused, in ways that the texts of other disciplines cannot, on the massive dislocations that – as Lisbon itself may have first convinced us – now seem part of the order of things.

Some of the above – the theological questions raised by the earthquake and Voltaire's opposition to Leibnizian optimism – has been clearly enough laid out in the scholarship linked to Lisbon, a certain amount of this scholarship having been brought together nearly half a century ago by T. D. Kendrick in his work on the event.[30]

But I should like to go beyond the particular lives and afterlives of the quake already excavated, and to do so first by noting what before his Kant crisis had typically been Kleist's unquestioning, highly optimistic certainty of certainty – he had even written an essay entitled 'Essay on the *certain* way of finding happiness' (emphasis added, ii.301-15); second, by noting the collision between that certainty and what Kleist also came to see as an irrefutable argument demonstrating certainty's *in*accessibility; and, finally, by moving from these observations to possibly new recognitions. I should like to read Kleist's disastrous experience as more than merely an apparently obsessive reaction – within a single model of understanding – to a loss of belief in the rational accessibility of certainty.

The key word is certainty, and the recognition of its impossibility is, for Kleist, an earthquake-like experience.

I wish to suggest that the collision Kleist experiences between his certainty of certainty on the one hand and its sudden opposite on the other, a collision he experiences as earthshaking (causing the reader's mind to reverberate with western notions of the massive, world-changing, culture-altering event of Lisbon), is at the same time a collision, as experienced by a single individual, between the *épistèmes* Foucault labels classical, on the one hand, and contemporary (or 'modern') on the other, that is, between the *épistème* of the Enlightenment, on the one hand, and that which identifies our contemporaneity on the other. This collision identifies Kleist as a quintessential hinge figure between the two, as Don

---

29. Jurij Lotman, *The Structure of the artistic text, Michigan Slavic contributions* 7 (Ann Arbor, MI 1977), p.4, 59-60, 67-68, notes art's special capacities for storing information, generating knowledge, and generating new disciplinary 'languages', by virtue of its ability to sponsor a multiplicity of different interpretive systems simultaneously and to call forth others: (in part) by virtue of its ability to enter into potentially innumerable extra-textual relations. The literary text, Lotman argues, is thus multiplanar and continuously generative, as opposed to the generally uniplanar, static scientific text.

30. T. D. Kendrick, *The Lisbon earthquake* (London 1956; New York 1957).

Quixote was for Foucault between the classical *episteme* and the *episteme* of the Renaissance that preceded it (Foucault, *The Order of things*, p.46-50). It is perhaps no accident that if Kleist finds himself positioned between two conflicting *epistemes*, inhabiting each in part and neither fully, that he should, as he does, conceive characters sometimes hilariously reminiscent of Foucault's Quixote, in that they are befuddled by a world they, too, necessarily misconstrue. Comical Sosias, in Kleist's *Amphitryon*, perplexed at his displacement by the strange 'double' bearing his name, is such a character. Misconstrual for Kleist, however, most typically precipitates tragedy, its impact described by him and his critics as earthquake.

I would identify Kleist as the simultaneous inhabiter of both the classical and the contemporary *epistemes*, a figure with one foot planted in the old and the other in the new. I would identify him as an altogether reluctantly but nonetheless resolutely Janus-faced inhabitant of each: the classical, suffused with permanence, sameness and space, and the contemporary, suffused with change, difference and temporality. One of his faces turns, with hope, expectancy and longing, but also despair, towards a displaced past in which there is no salvation, security or certainty, although there once seemed to have been. The other turns equally resolutely and despairingly, even when it makes comedy of its despair, into a wind blowing out of nowhere, a noplace with only uncertain futures, and from which there is no way out, only different directions one can take, which become but temporary journeys beset by accidents without end, and endless reversals, each again exhaustingly followed by its opposite. Both faces typically exhibit a tragic, though sometimes a comic mien.

Like Kafka – who greatly admired Kleist, and a century later was trapped by a similar and similarly terrible insight into the uncertainty and inexplicability of the human condition – Kleist is not unable to generate humour from his predicament. Kafka, for example, dissolved in laughter as he read aloud from *The Trial*. Kleist wrote the greatest of German comedies, *Der zerbrochene Krug*, and an equally great tragicomedy, *Amphitryon*, scene after scene of which pitches its audiences into helpless laughter. But *Amphitryon* does not take its comic place beside *Krug*, since it is a seesaw of a drama, always potentially tragic. It ends with Alkmene's single syllable, 'Ach!', expressing her awareness, although she will go on living, of the awful order of things from which there is no way out, no path to the bright meadows of Enlightenment certainty. This is the order of things that patterns the unpredictable negative – accident, reversal, disaster – in sequential alternation or simultaneous contradiction with the equally unpredictable positive, turning one into the other, or pulling the one out of the other – whether incomprehensibly (as in *Die heilige Cäcilie* and *Der Zweikampf*) or partly explicably (as in *Erdbeben* and *Die Marquise von O*). The uncertainty and fragility of this order are demonstrated by its repeated and inevitable shattering, for inexplicable or monstrously explicable reasons. Implying its tendency to shatter, Kleist calls it 'die gebrechliche Einrichtung der Welt'.[31]

Kleist's intellectual disaster, which soon resulted in *Die Familie Schrof-fenstein*, a tragedy completed by November 1802, and eventually also in *Erdbeben*, his first novella, immediately elicited from him the unforgettable, 'Mein einziges, mein höchstes, Ziel ist gesunken, und ich habe nun keines mehr' (My own, my highest goal has sunk away, and I have no goal any longer), of 22 March 1801.[32] This is a shattering cry from a man once so certain of his goals and of the means to reach them. The Kant crisis brought him almost instantly to reconfigure himself – philosophically – into an unblinking inhabitant of an altered world, formerly undreamt-of aspects of which he found already confronting him, other aspects of which he created or added to, even to the point of tightening the new age's thumbscrews on himself. This was a world whose way of knowing, almost unquestionably, Lisbon had already done much to alter. (Thus may the onset of Foucault's third *episteme*, despite his insistence to the contrary, be rendered in part historically explicable, as it long has been by students of the Lisbon catastrophe and its aftermaths.) Kleist was willing to see what he saw, and to lay it out in narrative and drama; indeed, perhaps he was unable not to do so. But he was unwilling, finally, to accept what he saw.

I would even argue that Kleist becomes recognisable as one of the poetic forgers of the new world, as Foucault recognises it, in the sense of the altered nature both of the events this new world suddenly generates, and of its altered language-oriented domains. These are the features by which we, living among works of art using a similar language, and travelling Foucault's path, have come to perceive it. They are the unpredictability and often hard, often violent, and persistently inexplicable nature of its events; the frequent, breathlessly bold rashness, the manic nature, even, of some of its characters; the specific density that words again assume, as signifiers, after having long been rendered invisible, transparent, possessed of no material weight, no density; language's often reversed relations between signifier and signified; and the excessiveness of a given word, a given signifier, over the dimensions of its signified (the way a given signifier exceeds its signified, existing beyond it as a sometimes broad and unmapped potential for understanding).[33] Thus not only by way of event and character, but in his metamorphoses of Enlightenment language as well, in the role-expanding revelations of its potentials he guides it to explore and realise, Kleist is also effectively an originator of the new *episteme*.

31. The fragile arrangement of the world (ii.143).

32. To his fiancé, Wilhelmine von Zenge (ii.634).

33. Foucault, *The Order of things*, p.209-11 (harshness, violence, savagery); p.117-18, 300, 303, 306 (language). Numerous words and phrases chosen by Foucault to characterise the new *episteme*'s effect on or relation to the old bring Kleist's experiences and emphases to mind: 'reversal' (p.209), 'disintegration' and 'rupture' (p.221), 'shatter' (p.239), and 'dissolution' (p.243), to name a few.

He brings the old language into the new ways of being Foucault describes, as no longer exclusively representational (as in the classical *episteme* as Foucault describes it), but possessed again of 'its own enigmatic density',[34] and of a sudden richness of remainder, as it had been in the Renaissance and in the ancient Greek dramatists the Renaissance rediscovers, and on whose works Kleist tutors himself.

Thus the actions of Kleist's characters are not the only adventures in his works, nor are his plots merely figuratively embellished, essentially pure representational accounts of the acts of human characters. Rather, the language undertakes character- and action-determining adventures of its own. What had formerly been regarded as merely decoratively enhancing, essentially empty, figurative language now determines character and event. On a typical occasion, a given metaphor, though apparently merely elicited by and descriptive of a given character, and thus apparently merely a vehicle according to the conventional understanding of the tenor-vehicle relation, instead itself – without ceasing to be a vehicle – effectively determines the nature and eventual deeds of a given tenor. In effect, it brings the tenor into being, becomes it. That it can do so demonstrates a revolution in literary language, a startling change from the long-depleted possibilities of Enlightenment representation as Foucault understands it, a massive expansion beyond its former limitations. In this way Kleist's language often exemplifies the radical predominance, and excessiveness, of the signifier over the signified. In his hands an Enlightenment language that regarded itself as essentially pure, the signifier rendering the signified approximately exactly, without remainder, their relation the conventional one of master and slave, can become more the determiner of the signified than the signified's essentially empty, transparent echo.

I shall cite a single example. It must come from *Penthesilea*, rather than *Erdbeben*, since, while the novella exemplifies important aspects of the new *episteme* in the violent acts of certain of its characters, in its sheer excessiveness, and in the incomprehensible reversals of its other events, the language reporting these events remains studiedly objective. Its signifiers precisely, crisply, even on occasion coldly, match its signifieds.

It is otherwise in the drama, which matches excessiveness of event with excessiveness of language. When, at the outset of Kleist's *Penthesilea*, we hear Odysseus' astonished reports of the Amazon queen, apprehending her and her army and that of the Greeks as two raging wolves, the teeth of each possibly soon to be sunk in the throat of the other, then of Penthesilea herself as cataclysm, whirlwind, flood, and something inexplicable even beyond the categories that order human apprehension (i.323-24), it may seem that these are but instances of overblown figurative language, exaggerated signifiers soon to be displaced when their tamer, more mundane signified appears, the latter an instance of the real.

34. Foucault, *The Order of things*, p.297, 304.

But the dynamism of these signifiers, both in themselves and tumbling over one another in their headlong delivery, is as significant a part of the drama's action as what conventionally goes by that name. Not a mirroring, mimesis, echo, or afterimage, this is the forging of a dramatic character by language. Long before the drama plays out, this Penthesilea, who in the form of these burgeoning images emerges before she has yet appeared on stage, will have been accurately recognised as cataclysm and ravening animal rather than merely human figure. Kleist's achievement in generating her in these tumbling images, tightly packed and possessed of a material density of their own, is what makes the stage portrayal of her all but sure to fail, unless massive projections of her metaphorical-literal outlines are thrown onto the stage's backdrops before she appears, and throughout the staging, as she explodes into the consciousness of the Greeks. These are outlines of a polyvalent psychic immensity, a sort of cosmic fury that leaves every opponent with whom it comes into contact diminished, even when it lies unconscious and supposedly dead – as Penthesilea does at one point.

Eventually, but not without radical reversals, this figure fills out the predictions of catastrophe that the language, ostensibly about but in fact creating her, implied – her teeth sunk in the flesh of the beloved, slaughtered out of love. In such a work, Kleist unmistakably belongs to the contemporary *episteme*, and he may be the first such German dramatist. It is interesting but not surprising that Blackall, in his indispensable *Emergence of German as a literary language*,[35] does not examine Kleist's language, instead concluding his investigations with Goethe. For, viewed in hindsight, Blackall's exploratory boundaries are immediately recognisable as those of Foucault's classical *episteme*, whose limits Kleist bursts as the condition of his art.[36] At the time Blackall was writing, Foucault and his literary and philosophical contemporaries were not yet on the horizon, nor, to Blackall's knowledge at least, were eastern European semioticians' understandings of the convention-breaking imperatives of great art (although Kleist himself observed that beauty was never conventional). Thus the now-commonplace extremes of the contemporary *episteme* – its altered language, its harsh events, its violence of character – are for Blackall yet to be accommodated in theory.

35. Eric A. Blackall, *The Emergence of German as a literary language* (Cambridge 1959).

36. I want to emphasise here that Kleist is apparently not attempting to distinguish his work by means of sheer, alien otherness for its own sake, though he does seek distinction. But he seeks it in the tradition of greatness that he knows, that of the Greek tragedians, though to achieve it he follows the dictates of extraordinary situations as he encounters or uniquely (*v.* traditionally) imagines them under the influence of his own dynamic personality, thunderstruck by Kant. In doing so, he generates that otherness that this study recognises as characterising the contemporary *episteme*, for which, in Arthur O. Lovejoy's words, 'diversity itself [is] the essence of excellence', the 'attack upon [...] differentness having been the central and dominating fact in the intellectual history of Europe' during the preceding *episteme* (Arthur O. Lovejoy, *Great chain of being*, New York 1936, p.293).

Kleist can also also be regarded as a part forger of the new *epistème* in another sense, one growing more directly out of Lisbon and its aftermaths, which first convince him of the world's essential *Gebrechlichkeit*. But Lisbon and after had been the work of Seismos, and then of Voltaire and Kant. Kleist becomes part forger in the sense that, having been denied Leibniz by Voltaire, rational certainty by Kant, and the world's predictability by Seismos, and having become convinced of any presiding deity's indifference, he himself closes off the only other possible avenue to certainty.

In earlier asserting the no-way-out convictions of Kleist as lived by his characters, and referred to repeatedly in his correspondence in lines prophetic of this one, written to his sister Ulrike on the morning of his suicide (22 November 1811): 'Die Wahrheit ist, dass mir auf Erden nicht zu helfen war' (The truth is that there was no help for me on earth; ii.887), I intentionally left unsaid that there had indeed seemed to be an alternative route to certainty for Kleist apart from reason, and that, for better or worse, his characters often settled on it.

This was Kleist's much vaunted *Gefühl*, or feeling, intimate personal intuitiveness, its reliability ostensibly demonstrated by his best-known essay, 'On the marionette theatre' (ii.338-45). The marionette doesn't think, doesn't reason her way through her dance; her flawless moves are guided by the equivalents of human intuition. Several decades of potential Kleistians, from the early 1930s until the 1960s, were taught by the existentialist critics Gerhard Fricke and Günter Blöcker[37] to see that Kleist did have faith in a certainty – in *Gefühl*. But these scholars failed to admit, perhaps even to see, what character after Kleistian character learns – that *Gefühl*, too, can be an uncertain guide to action, though perhaps not as uncertain as reason, and much closer to the heart. This is especially evident in *Erdbeben*, in which *Gefühl* repeatedly fails, and in failing leads to multiple brutal deaths, one of them ghastly. Eventually Walter Müller-Seidel clarified the matter by showing that *Gefühl*, too, was unreliable.[38]

Thus for Kleist there was and would be no way out. Not, at least, into certainty, if this implies a definitive *modus operandi*, or a definitive, finally satisfactory, unchanging response to any situation. When Foucault refers to time – and, implicitly, to unpredictable change – as characteristic of the new *episteme*, he does not speak merely in the abstract. His words are closely reminiscent of what the criticism regards as Kleist's concrete experience. Foucault notes, for example, the era's being 'restored to the irruptive violence of time', its being subjected to time's 'perpetual disruption[s]'.[39] These observations are reminiscent of Lovejoy's description, in his *Great chain of being*,[40] of the change from Enlightenment to

---

37. Gerhard Fricke, *Gefühl und Schicksal bei Heinrich von Kleist* (Berlin 1929), and Günter Blöcker, *Heinrich von Kleist oder das absolute Ich* (Frankfurt 1954).
38. *Versehen und Erkennen: eine Studie über Heinrich von Kleist* (Cologne 1967).
39. Foucault, *The Order of things*, p.132, 113.
40. Lovejoy, *Great chain of being*. See ch.2, ch.9-11.

Romantic thought as a move from other-worldliness to this-worldliness, from a refusal of temporality to an embrace of time and its discontents. Chief among these discontents are change and uncertainty. It seems clear, although Lovejoy wrote three decades before *epistèmes* and paradigm shifts became part of an everyday scholarly vocabulary, that he was recognising a shift of the sort Foucault would later see moving western ways of knowing, emphatically including his own, from his second to his third *epistème*. Repeatedly in writings and interviews after *The Order of things*, Foucault viewed change as a rule of his own thought, on which he often enough reversed himself, and thus of his own *epistème*: he saw that whatever solutions could be arrived at would already have generated new problems. He said: 'I am trying to [...] grasp the implicit systems that determine our most familiar behaviour without our knowing it [...] and to show how one could escape.' But, having extricated himself from any given system, he saw that he was already entangled in another, in a sense its opposite.[41] Truth was reversible. Foucault rang on it more than a few of its reversals. And he did not flinch. Nor do we, born, as it were, into the contemporary *epistème*. We in fact generate expressions of our tolerance of uncertainty and the inexplicable, or of our mild fortitude in facing them. These expressions are more accepting than Alkmene's 'Ach!', but, like it, issue from people who, unlike Kleist, do go on living. They are expressions of humans come too late in the world for simple happiness, or for explanations. One such expression has been the much-celebrated 'Catch 22'. Another is the now ubiquitous 'Whatever'.

Why, then, seeing – as he all too clearly does – the inevitability of endless reversals brought home to him by Lisbon, its cultural aftermaths, and its earthquake predecessors, is Kleist unable to assimilate this insight? How can he help inaugurate and apparently revel in one aspect of the new age (its no longer merely representational language), sponsor another (its literature's emphasis on violence in character and event), and see and confirm a third (the age's sharp questioning of the certainty of reason), but at the same time refuse, finally, to accept the loss of certainty, as Kafka was able to do a century later, becoming, as it were, the self-effacing high priest of the uncertain and the inexplicable, of humans' subjectedness, as radically opposed to their much vaunted, individualistic, and wilful, subjectivity?

I should like to consider a possible answer: for Kleist the refusal of certainty was not an option, despite Lisbon, despite Kant, despite the demise of *Gefühl*. That it was not, in the face of all evidence to the contrary, was the source of Kleist's tragic vision. I am speaking of tragedy not in the modern sense in which routes to success or survival may indeed seem to have been available had a given hero but 'made the right choice',

41. See my 'Michel Foucault', in *Twentieth-century rhetorics and rhetoricians: critical studies and sources*, ed. Michael G. Moran and Michelle Ballif (New York 2000), p.168-84.

but rather in the ancient Greek sense in which whatever the given decision, it is a route to disaster.[42] Kleist is caught in such a vise. He is literally overcome by his recognition of the inevitability of the uncertain. Again and again he dramatises this recognition in narrative and in works written for the stage. But he retreats each time to the haven of certainty. His suicide is the last such retreat. His choice stands on his tombstone: 'Nun, O Ewigkeit, bist du ganz mein' (Now, oh eternity, you're completely mine). These words lend special meaning to that comment to his sister from his final day, stating that 'mir auf Erden nicht zu helfen war' (on earth there was no help for me, ii.887). Earth was uncertainty; but oh, eternity...

Why, for Kleist, was uncertainty not an option? Martin Heidegger's *Parmenides*, a winter semester 1942-1943 seminar, which first saw print in 1982, may offer an idea worth considering: the culture Kleist inherited was hardwired for certainty.

Kleist could not refuse to acknowledge uncertainty, change, the decisive challenge of the temporal and its exigencies to the permanencies of Enlightenment faith. Rationally speaking, he could see that there was no certainty. He had Chile, Lisbon, Kant, and the errors of *Gefühl* as proof. At the same time, he could not relinquish certainty, anchored as he was in an *epistème* grounded in its faith in this concept – an *epistème* for which certainty was the very meaning of truth.

In his seminar, which he calls a 'meditation' on the meaning of truth, Heidegger lays out the modern period's understanding of truth, which for him was the gravest possible misunderstanding. In doing so he offers insights that, had they not been invisible to Enlightenment thought and to certain of its post-Socratic Greek predecessors, could have left us bereft of a Kleist, and of much else. For Heidegger here argues emphatically and specifically that truth is precisely not certainty (his word of choice for what he views as the misconstrual of truth's meaning), is not *certitudo*, the narrow and erroneous channel into which – though the inclination in this direction had begun much earlier (with Plato and Aristotle) – Roman culture in particular and definitively (if not, as Heidegger hopes, irrecoverably) forces pre-Socratic truth, depriving it of its essence (we shall shortly see how) and of rich stores of established and potential meaning,[43] and thus grounding what would become the Enlightenment's, as well as the contemporary West's, way of knowing.

Heidegger's entire 243-page meditation is, at its most transparent, primarily an attempt to translate the Greek designation for truth, the single word *alétheia*, adequately. In doing so he opens to thought the

42. Martin Heidegger makes this distinction in *Parmenides*, translated by André Schuwer and Richard Rojcewicz (Bloomington, IN 1992), p.73. The ultimate disastrousness of any available course can be illustrated, for example, by the potential outcomes of Agamemnon's 'choices' when he is called on to sacrifice his own child.

43. Heidegger, *Parmenides*, p.39-58.

possibilities for understanding available in this word, and suggests, in passing, the nature and range of the losses that over two millennia result for the West from the long concealment of what he uncovers.

Heidegger points out that the name Alétheia (designating a Greek female deity) consists of the Greek *a* privative (meaning 'non' or 'un') plus *léthe* (meaning 'concealment'). The single word 'un-concealment' thus contains within itself the opposition 'concealment–unconcealment'. Hence for Heidegger the essence of truth is not *certitudo* or any of its close Latin relatives such as *rectitudo* and *justitia*. Instead, the essence of truth is conflictual, is conflict,[44] as the opposition of the concepts 'concealment' and 'unconcealment', which together make up truth's name, indicates.

Carefully heeding this Greek word, *alétheia*, its constituents, its counterwords, and their uses and thus meanings in Ancient Greek, Heidegger sees that in moving from Greece to Rome, the meaning of truth also moves – from the opposition concealment–unconcealment to the stark abstraction *veritas* (the form in which *alétheia* is received and apprehended by Roman culture) and thence to its fellows *certitudo*, *rectitudo* and *justitia* (the several forms and meanings it takes on thereafter). In the Roman translation of *alétheia* as *veritas*, the meaning of truth is no longer determined at all on the basis of concealment–unconcealment and the conflict between them. Indeed, 'for the Romans, the realm of concealment does not at all come to be [...] the essential realm determining the essence of truth' (p.48).[45] Instead, 'the essence of truth is determined on the basis of [...] assurance and certitude. The true becomes the assured and certain. The *verum* becomes the *certum*' (p.51).[46]

For Heidegger, 'the inception of the metaphysics of the modern age rests on the transformation of the essence of *veritas* into *certitudo*' (p.51).[47] Roman and Christian '*veritas* [...] *rectitudo animae*, *justitia*, provides to the modern essence of truth its character as [...] certainty and assurance [...] The true, *verum*, is what [...] vouches for certainty' (p.52).[48] In Heidegger's view, the shift of *alétheia* to *veritas* and thence to *certitudo* brings about a wholesale but clandestine metamorphosis of western culture. This metamorphosis is still underway in Heidegger's time (as in the present), having reached its philosophical zenith in the thought of Friedrich Nietzsche and his doctrine of the will to power: 'In Nietzsche's thought,

44. Heidegger, *Parmenides*, p.17.

45. 'Der Bereich der Verbergung und der Entbergung kommt im Römischen [...] überhaupt nicht dazu, der massgebende Wesensbereich zu werden, aus dem sich das Wesen der Wahrheit bestimmt.' Heidegger, *Parmenides* (Frankfurt 1982), p.71.

46. 'Das Wesen der Wahrheit bestimmt sich aus [ein gewisser] Sicherheit und Gewissheit. Das Wahre wird zum Gesicherten und Gewissen. Das verum wird zum certum.' Heidegger, *Parmenides*, p.75.

47. 'Der Beginn der neuzeitlichen Metaphysik beruht darin, dass das Wesen der veritas sich zur certitudo wandelt.' Heidegger, *Parmenides*, p.76.

48. 'Die christlich verstandene veritas als rectitudo animae [...] gibt dem neuzeitlich Wesen der Wahrheit das Gepräge [...] der Sicherheit.' Heidegger, *Parmenides*, p.76.

where the metaphysics of the Occident reaches its peak, the essence of truth is founded on certitude' (p.52),[49] and in Nietzsche's hands, 'the basic feature of reality is will to power' (p.52).[50]

For Heidegger, the transformation of the meaning of truth has cultural ramifications extending all the way from rudimentary levels of language-recorded perception, to the identity and destiny of man, to conceptions of deity (p.40, 104, 122), the latter everywhere much in question after Lisbon, and with the nature of which Kleist himself was not unconcerned, after the earthquakes of his experience, both geological and spiritual. Heidegger calls the transformation of the essence of truth, of which he here writes the history, the primary historical event of the West, 'the genuine event of history' (p.42).

For Heidegger, the essence of truth is conflict. As a result of this conflict, concealment may indeed give way to unconcealment, or the reverse may take place, but the two do not coincide. Conflictual they remain: in conflict. And this conflict is the first level at which truth might be said to be apprehendable. This first level would reveal truth at its most concrete: conflict. A second level would be the appearance or disappearance (unconcealment or concealment, disclosure or covering over) that takes place as a result of the conflict. Should unconcealment prevail, what gets unconcealed, what undergoes unconcealment, emerges, and becomes present. Should concealment prevail, what undergoes concealment gets obscured, covered over, disappears.

Truth, at ground level, can be understood as conflict. Had Kleist but known – had he but been born to this insight!

Thus I conclude this consideration of the mother of earthquakes and its aftermaths, among which number Kleist the writer; the decisive event of his life showing him there was no way out; and, beginning with *Schroffenstein* and famously including *Erdbeben*, his creative works from first to last, each of which was written under the long shadow of Lisbon.

Postscript: Kleist and Goya: sharing the hinge

In November 2003, a month after the conference for which this study had been completed, Robert Hughes' book, *Goya*, appeared,[51] recognising the Spanish painter as 'a true hinge figure [between periods in art]' (p.10). Much of what Hughes says about Goya, a contemporary of Kleist, is reminiscent of Kleist himself. Hughes writes, for example, of Goya's 'remaking himself from top to bottom, into so apparently different an

---

49. 'Nietzsche, durch dessen Denken die abendländische Metaphysik ihren Gipfel ersteigt, [gründet] in seinem Denken das Wesen der Wahrheit in die Sicherheit.' Heidegger, *Parmenides*, p.77.

50. 'Das Wirkliche hat den Grundzug des Willens zur Macht.' Heidegger, *Parmenides*, p.77.

51. Robert Hughes, *Goya* (New York 2003).

artist [than he had been earlier: from court artist to recorder of the atrocities and grisly human sufferings of war], and with such compulsive force' (p.13); of his 'gasp of recognition at the sheer, blood-soaked awfulness of the world' (p.6) and his willingness to represent it (p.282); of his ability to 'se[e] through the official structures of society' (p.10), including the church, as Kleist does in *Erdbeben*; and of his 'persistent scepticism that [...] tends, above all, to take little for granted' (p.10). Goya's works bearing 'witness to [...] almost unspeakable facts' (p.7) lie temporally close to Kleist's. Goya's depiction of the execution of the Spanish patriots on 3 May 1808, is done in 1814; 'And it can't be helped' (male figures staked for execution), in 1810-1811 (the latter, noted earlier, as the year of Kleist's suicide); and the agonies of 'The pilgrimage to San Isidro', from 1820 to 1823. Hughes speaks only of Goya's hingeing 'the old world' (p.11), which Hughes does not identify by name, to the Enlightenment, but it seems clear from his descriptions, if one's reference is Foucault, that Goya will have painted acutely aware of, if not precisely as a participant in, the ways of knowing of the Renaissance *épistème* (his 'Caprichos' and 'Pinturas Negras' [Black Paintings] are Renaissance-linked, with 'their fascinat[ion with] witchcraft and absorption [in] the ancient superstitions that surrounded the Spanish witch cult, which he illustrated again and again', p.11). But he flourished as a fully-fledged participant in the Enlightenment *épistème* with his court paintings (p.11), and worked as an early inhabitant of the contemporary *épistème* with his later, great portrayals of war and their 'scenes of atrocity and misery' (p.5), brutality and horror (p.272-99, 307-19). Hughes speaks of Goya's 'stripping the human animal to its most primitive essences [in these portrayals ...] a process of which he was', Hughes adds, 'the supreme tragic poet' (p.312-13); Kleist engages in such a process in *Erdbeben* when he describes a member of the Santiago mob smashing a child's head against a pillar, where it bursts. It was in the latter two *épistèmes* that Goya lived, as did Kleist, and these that he perhaps more properly 'hinged'. Since Kleist and Goya were contemporaries, and each experienced the seismic shift between *épistèmes*, the question arises as to why Goya was able to endure the shift – to go on working – and Kleist was not. An answer would be purely speculative, but Goya appears to have been endowed with a more even temperament than Kleist, whose highs were exceedingly high and whose lows were exceedingly low and frequent – too low and too frequent, finally, for him to go on. Moreover, Goya's life appears not to have been characterised by the innumerable reversals that plagued Kleist's, and he remained somewhat more the observer of the scenes he depicted than a figure, like Kleist, who had himself endured, if not comparable sufferings, then at least the strains, setbacks and reversals that inspired and informed his presentations of them.

ESTELA J. VIEIRA

Coping and creating after catastrophe: the significance of the Lisbon earthquake of 1755 on the literary culture of Portugal

Two hundred and fifty years later, scholars and scientists from a range of fields continue to reflect on the Lisbon earthquake of 1755. This natural catastrophe, often referred to as a world-shaking event, had massive physical consequences which reached far beyond Lisbon. Records claim that the earthquake, estimated to have attained approximately 9.0 on the Richter scale, destroyed a third of Portugal's capital city, resulted in three aftershocks, fires and a tsunami, and killed tens of thousands of people. The Lisbon earthquake is also considered a world-shattering event on a metaphorical level because it changed the way people interpreted their surroundings. The tragedy and its aftermath sparked a great deal of intellectual debate in politics, religion, art, and philosophy. The earthquake was not only a source of inspiration for many philosophers and artists of the Enlightenment, but across time thinkers and analysts return to it as a paradigm of disaster. Never before in history did a natural catastrophe produce such an extensive international reaction and organisation, nor result in such perceptible conceptual change. Many different elements influenced the outcome and created the meaning of the event, including the geographic, economic and political position of Lisbon at the time, the historic moment and its ideas, and the individuals and powers involved in the events. The historical and aesthetic experience was stimulated and shaped by all these different elements. But the ongoing significance of the earthquake is also a result of the historical and imaginary constructions of the episode over time.

A recent and striking theoretical and philosophical work by Susan Neiman is a perfect illustration of how this unforgettable event continues to fuel new ideas. In *Evil in modern thought* (2002) Neiman traces the development of ethical and theological attitudes toward evil. In order to understand what resources remain for thinking about contemporary evil, as represented by Auschwitz and also by destructive natural events of the latter half of the twentieth century, the author turns first to Lisbon for an event paradigmatic of evil in its time. She shows that the conceptually shattering earthquake produces a shift in consciousness and that, since Lisbon, 'natural evils no longer have any seemly relation to moral evils;

hence they no longer have meaning at all. Natural disaster is the object of attempts at prediction and control, not of interpretation.'[1] Although many theologians at the time interpreted the earthquake as God's punishment, what actually takes over in the aftermath is the idea that God's ways are not mysterious. Part of becoming modern is turning to practical concerns and proceeding forward to prevent human evil, as King D. José's ministry or Pombal's government endeavoured to do. The author connects the evolution of thought with the decisive shift that takes place with the earthquake: 'Theory proceeded much as Pombal did. It focused on eradicating those evils that could be reached by human hands.'[2] The earthquake not only serves as a model for recent theoretical and philosophical discourse, but also begins to appear as a fundamental topos in contemporary literature.

The recent trend in Portuguese historic novels, led by two of the country's foremost authors, José Saramago and António Lobo Antunes, is also taken up by Hélia Correia, who in *Lillias Fraser* (2001) recounts the events of 1 November.[3] This is one of the few contemporary fictional representations of the national tragic event, and it opts to have the earthquake experienced by a foreigner. The protagonist is an exiled Scottish adolescent who, upon surviving the bloody battle of Culloden, is sent to Lisbon. The violent and catastrophic character of the battle foreshadows the earthquake. As we will see later, prefiguring the tragedy is a ubiquitous narrative strategy in national literary representations of the earthquake. A type of *Bildungsroman*, this novel also narrates aggressive encounters between Lillias and local elements and characters, both historical and fictional. These events and characters serve as witnesses to the chaos of the disaster and its aftermath. Nobel prizewinner José Saramago's work *Memorial do convento* (1982), translated into English as *Baltasar and Blimunda*, informs Correia's novel in more ways than one.[4] Mafra serves as one of the settings in both novels, and Lillias' ability to foresee people's death reminds us of Blimunda's power, when on an empty stomach, to see through and inside others. There is a first-person narrator, who probably represents the perspective of Correia herself, who interrupts the third-person narrative every so often. This is one of the narrative techniques that the author employs in order to turn away from a strict approach to a historical novel.[5]

---

1. Susan Neiman, *Evil in modern thought* (Princeton, NJ 2002), p.250.
2. Neiman, *Evil in modern thought*, p.250.
3. Hélia Correia, *Lillias Fraser* (Lisbon 2001).
4. José Saramago, *Memorial do convento* (Lisbon 1982).
5. Since traditionally the third-person narrator represents a historical perspective, the first-person narrator challenges this point of view. There is an engagement in the work with the historical experience, but the novel also asks questions that stand outside the specific time period.

This current literary re-evaluation is significant because it reinforces the idea that the earthquake is an event with enduring semantic implications. The evolution of history and the onset of other catastrophic events also redefine the original shock of the Lisbon earthquake. The destructive events surrounding the collapse of the World Trade Center on 11 September 2001 provide a key point of reference. The global impact of the Lisbon earthquake in its era is comparable to the upshot of the recent disaster in New York. It would be premature to elaborate on the current events, since catastrophes prove more meaningful once a significant chronological distance has been established, but both represent catastrophic moments whose aftermath and consequences significantly outweigh the events themselves. Not surprisingly, a recent project first recollects Lisbon in order to look at the recent disaster in New York from different points of view.

Out of ground zero (2002) is a compilation of different case studies in urban reinvention that analyses how various cities, devastated by natural or manmade catastrophes, coped with disaster.[6] The series of essays puts the rebuilding of Ground Zero into historical and cross-cultural perspective. Kenneth Maxwell, author of *Pombal: paradox of the enlightenment* (1995), a rigorous historical account of the Marquês de Pombal's government and its effect on the capital's reconstruction, writes the portion on the Lisbon earthquake.[7] Maxwell focuses on Pombal's efforts to transform Lisbon into a modern bourgeois and commercial city embodying the Enlightenment. The author elaborates on the paradoxical elements that are part of the reorganisation of Lisbon, explaining how an authoritative government successfully restructured and reformed society. Architecture is the underlying art form that rose to the occasion immediately after the earthquake because it stressed pragmatism and efficiency. This form of expression coped productively with the tragedy by allowing the possibility of starting from scratch with modern structures and by constructing a city that would anticipate future progress and similar emergencies.

Expectedly, then, the earthquake generated innovation and originality primarily in architecture, engineering, sculpture, and the technical arts. From among the different aesthetic expressions cultivated locally, architecture became the most immediate and utilitarian art form during the years after the devastation of Lisbon. The earthquake destroyed a city but also provided an opportunity to rebuild and recreate a new space. The new modern city promised to be equipped for a future of commercial activity and a habitat for a rising bourgeoisie. Perhaps this is why the

---

6. *Out of ground zero: case studies in urban reinvention*, ed. Joan Ockman (Munich and New York 2002).

7. Kenneth Maxwell, *Pombal: paradox of the Enlightenment* (Cambridge 1995).

most important national intellectual reflections on the earthquake are the indispensable scientific works written by one of Portugal's leading architectural and art historians. *Lisboa Pombalina e o iluminismo* (1977) by José-Augusto França is one of the most important of his works on the events surrounding the earthquake. In it, the author traces the history of the reconstruction of Lisbon, exploring how the new city took part in a dialogue with the European Enlightenment, and the extent to which the reconstructive efforts shaped the new society and ideas governing Portugal.[8]

All these retrospective approaches reveal not only that the Lisbon earthquake continues even today to serve as a fundamental point of comparison, but also that disasters are motifs that provoke discursive reflection. This is intensified when removed from the event by geographical or chronological distance, or both. For this reason many thinkers outside Portugal lead and stimulate dialogue regarding the earthquake, and the imaginative interpretations and representations of the event are late in coming. If there is one characteristic that stands out in the published discourse, especially philosophical and theoretical, it is the external focus and perspective. Naturally, the earthquake is a more appealing topic on theoretical terms than in reality. From the exterior there is an epistemological distance that turns violence and catastrophe into cultural topoi of critical and political relevance. The curiosity to observe destruction turns the place of suffering into a stage, a space emptied of content for the interpretative mind to transform. The scope of the inflated popular reaction to the earthquake suggests this was the first modern catastrophe to be represented and interpreted sensationally, especially from abroad.

Outside Portugal public reactions are widespread, and great thinkers and artists develop individual and stimulating thoughts and points of view. Local history and knowledge are often neglected. The universal aspirations of the philosophical discourse of the Enlightenment further eclipse regional forms of coping with the earthquake. But studying the national literary and intellectual developments and focusing on local events and accounts is also a significant task. This essay explores for the first time certain Portuguese texts and authors together and within the context of the earthquake. Furthermore, it attempts to read the event as a traumatic episode for the local and immediate culture. A careful study of Portuguese writing can reveal the consequences of calamity on local writing, while advancing our understanding of the relationship between disaster and intellectual development.

To trace the effect of the earthquake on Portuguese literature and literary culture it is important first to turn to the immediate aftermath and

8. José-Augusto França, *Lisboa Pombalina e o iluminismo* (Lisbon 1977). Also see *A Reconstrução de Lisboa e a arquitectura Pombalina* (Lisbon 1989).

analyse what sort of discourse it aroused and when. During the period after the disaster, the Portuguese literary world was characterised by silence and evasion. Although countless letters were written, usually by foreigners to their families and friends back home or by the Portuguese giving accounts to friends abroad, these narratives are often embellished descriptions of the day's events, but not conscious literary constructions inspired by the earthquake. The calamity also motivated religious leaders in their sermon writing, and all across the world parishioners listened to emotional diatribes about God's wrath, sin and the Apocalypse in the context, sometimes distorted, of the Lisbon earthquake. These theological but also very political texts reveal the interesting and often biased perspectives that foreign societies had of Portugal and Catholicism. Meanwhile in Portugal what seems to happen in the literary realm corresponds more closely to twentieth-century theories of trauma, and allows us to read the earthquake at least in part as a traumatic event.

Trauma studies and definitions of trauma have evolved and become flexible to such a degree that it is possible to read the earthquake as a traumatic experience for Portuguese writers. One general definition of trauma, given by Cathy Caruth in her recent work *Unclaimed experience* (1996), applies partly to the events in Lisbon. The author writes: 'trauma describes an overwhelming experience of sudden and catastrophic events in which the response to the event occurs in the often delayed, uncontrolled repetitive appearance of hallucinations and other intrusive phenomena'.[9] Elements of this experience manifest themselves in the silences and responses of Portuguese writing immediately following the earthquake. Caruth's argument that trauma is also present in the voice of the wound, then transferred to the listener of that voice, is also relevant to the experience of the earthquake. This was an event that took place in Lisbon yet had a stronger emotional and intellectual resonance in other cultural centres, to the point that the significance of the earthquake as a disaster or traumatic moment evolved and took shape abroad. Inside Portugal the government quieted the voices of the traumatised. The disaster was replaced by opportunities and new beginnings and words by the stones of the new buildings. Listeners outside heard via letters the voice of the wounded in Lisbon. Another of Caruth's observations further reinforces the experience of the earthquake as a traumatic one. Since history is related to the traumatic experience because it is never individual or single but often implied in other people's trauma, then the earthquake too stands out for the traumatic effect it had on individuals who did not experience the events. This is illustrated in the anxiety the incident produced abroad. If such an event could happen in Lisbon, it might happen anywhere and to anyone. People across Europe were

9. Cathy Caruth, *Unclaimed experience: trauma, narrative, and history* (Baltimore, MD 1996), p.11.

traumatised because what was once an inconceivable and incomprehensible experience became a possibility.

Although writers managed to write after Lisbon, and the world had a distinct conceptual structure in the eighteenth century, we can still observe that the nationals invested in the tragedy were hesitant to write. Many of the national poetic accounts that recap the tragedy admit first their reluctance to recount the events. Some of the authors of this poetry begin their composition with outright frustration at finding themselves obliged to fulfil a foreigner's request to put the earthquake into writing. One poem that begins with exactly this angst and reveals an internal conflict with writing and with coping with the tragic event is Nicilao Mendo Osório's *Oitavas ao terremoto* (1756).[10] The author communicates his dissatisfaction at being obliged to dwell on the tragedy because it renews the pain. Writing is not a healing process, but a constant renewing or repetition of the traumatic event. The verses plead forgiveness for putting in writing what they argue no words can describe or express. On various occasions Osório compares his text to a mere shadow of the real event, one that is swiftly fleeing from his memory. His verses resemble a dark illusion that haunts and surprises the individual involved, just like the black shadow that follows one.

The national poetic constructions present the conflicts involved in writing about the earthquake while suggesting that it is impossible to put the suffering in words. Portuguese poetic works contrast dramatically with Voltaire's famous 'Poème sur le désastre de Lisbonne' (1755). As Rita Goldberg explains, Voltaire makes suffering the subject of his poem and the locus of truth. She writes that Voltaire 'devotes himself entirely to the victims of the earthquake in his poem; his audience is not his subject'.[11] Voltaire's and other external accounts give a voice to the local silences. Without literally observing the events, this writing gives us the literary version of the earthquake that the sufferers and actual witnesses were incapable of supplying. The Portuguese poetic accounts, on the other hand, transmit the shock and silence produced by the event. This writing avoids detail and turns away from the narration of pain. Instead the authors quickly change the subject to any and all positive consequences.

The difficulty or impossibility of giving meaning to the earthquake in literature probably resulted from both the traumatic effect of the catastrophe and the change in the political environment. The individuals in power discouraged attributing any negative significance to the event that might impede the reconstruction process. Instead, there was an attempt to move society and people away from pain and suffering. For those in

10. Joaquim de Fóios and Miguel Rodrigues, *Oitavas ao terremoto, e mais calamidades que padeceo, a cidade de Lisboa, no primeiro de Novembro de 1755 por Nicilao Mendo Osório* (Lisbon, Of. de Miguel Rodrigues, 1756).

11. Rita Goldberg, 'Voltaire, Rousseau, and the Lisbon earthquake', *Eighteenth-century life* 13:2 (May 1989), p.1-20 (p.1).

Portugal, it was preferable to confer no sense at all to the earthquake than debate or ask unanswerable questions about whether or not it represented divine punishment or announced the fatal destiny of a people. It was not only the unsettling character of the disaster, but also the efforts of those in power that promoted a silencing and controlling of emotions and ideas that might have caused social disorder. We only have to remember two famous national cases where the government made it clear that points of view contrary to optimism, pragmatism, and stability would not be tolerated. In 1761 Francisco Xavier de Oliveira was condemned to being burned in effigy for his *Discours pathétique au sujet des calamités présentes arrivées en Portugal*.[12] The same 1761 *auto-da-fé* killed the Jesuit priest Gabriel Malagrida, who in *Juízo da verdadeira causa do terremoto que padeceu a corte de Lisboa no primeiro de Novembro de 1755* (1756), and in other writings and sermons, prophesied future earthquakes and condemned to hell anyone working for the reconstruction of Lisbon.[13]

The silence on a local level is nowhere more dramatic than in the *Gazeta de Lisboa*, where reporting in the post-earthquake years illustrates this silencing and the significant traits of the discursive and political reactions to the disaster. Other European gazettes for months dedicated columns to accounts and letters about the earthquake. In contrast, Charles Ralph Boxer describes the brief reference to the earthquake in the *Gazeta de Lisboa* as 'a masterpiece of understatement'.[14] On 6 November 1755 it published the following brief announcement: 'O dia primeiro do corrente mês ficará memorável em todos os séculos pelos terramotos e incêndios que arruinaram uma grande parte desta cidade, mas tem havido a felicidade de se acharem entre as ruínas os cofres da fazenda real e da maior parte dos particulares.'[15] Such a reduction of events can only suggest a mixture of trauma and a wish to restore confidence at a local level. André Belo has studied how the *Gazeta de Lisboa* evolved in the years following the earthquake.[16] His argument is that the journalism of the time reveals more by what is not published, and by what is silenced in the gazettes. He claims, in other words, that there is also a story on the margins of the *Gazeta de Lisboa* that tells how the earthquake affected society and culture. It fills up its pages with distant and international news and information,

12. Cavaleiro de Oliveira, *Discours pathétique au sujet des calamités présentes arrivées en Portugal* (Coimbra 1922).

13. Gabriel Malagrida, *Juizo da verdadeira causa do terremoto que padeceu a corte de Lisboa no primeiro de Novembro de 1755* (Lisbon, Of. de Manoel Soares, 1756).

14. Charles Ralph Boxer, *Some contemporary reactions to the Lisbon earthquake of 1755* (Lisbon 1956), p.4.

15. Cited in Ana Maria Magalhães and Isabel Alçada, *O Dia do terramoto* (Lisbon 1989), p.212. 'The first of this month will remain memorable for all the centuries because of the earthquakes and fires that ruined a large part of this city, but fortunately the chests of the royal family and of the majority of the citizens were found among the ruins.'

16. André Belo, 'A *Gazeta de Lisboa* e o terramoto de 1755: a margem do não escrito', *Análise social* 34 (2000), p.619-37.

but omits local and immediate developments. Belo identifies a 'horror da actualidade' apparent in the form of reporting in the *Gazeta de Lisboa*.[17] Society was horrified by the present or the immediate. Part of the reason for this was political, and clearly the director of the gazette received orders from the monarchy to keep disruptive elements out of print and instead promote repetition and continuity. But beyond these intentions, the changes in the discourse of the *Gazeta de Lisboa* also point to a disenchantment with the possibilities of the journalistic word. There is a reduction of numbers published, diminished page length, and the periodical takes a step backwards in form, presentation, and quality, considering the advancement it had seen before 1755. An attempt to soften emotional reactions to the earthquake could be read in the literary culture and published discourse, but they also reflect the ambiguity and confusion these emotions produced in the public figures and intellectuals.

When authors choose to write about the earthquake instead of remaining silent, they do not depict its pain as the external accounts did, but focus instead on the optimistic emotions stirred by the reconstructive energy. This positive view of events is also imbued with nationalistic ideology, and not surprisingly the epic is the genre of choice. The earthquake seems to have stimulated a revival of a national literary tradition that begins with *The Lusiads* (1572), the renaissance classic epic poem by Luís de Camošes. The three epic works that take the events surrounding the earthquake as their context are *Lisboa reedificada* (1780) by Miguel Maurício Ramalho, *Lisboa restaurada* (1784) by Vicente Carlos de Oliveira, and *Lisboa destruída* (1803) by Teodoro de Almeida.[18] The titles alone of the first two works reveal their primary intention to celebrate the new city. A misreading of Camošes' classic epic would interpret the poem as solely the glorification of the country's historic and future feats. To a certain extent this is the reading of the national classic reflected by these epics when they adopt it as their model. The epic had served in the past to tell of the glorious conquest by the Portuguese, and the earthquake presents yet another grand episode in national history. These writings, unlike some of the more immediate poetic accounts, examine the earthquake from a constructive perspective. In Camošes' classic Portugal's history and seafaring adventures and conquest act as a pretext for its more important aesthetic intentions. These poems also use the Lisbon earthquake as an excuse to recreate yet another epic. The revival of this classical genre then serves to glorify the earthquake as a monumental event in Portuguese history, and shows that literature coped and reacted to the disaster by returning to the national classics. Furthermore, in these

17. Belo, 'A *Gazeta de Lisboa*', p.624, 'A horror of the present time'.
18. Vicente Carlos de Oliveira, *Lisboa restaurada pelo grande* (Lisbon, Of. de Fernando José dos Santos, 1784), Teodoro de Almeida, *Lisboa destruída poema* (Lisbon, Of. de António Rodrigues Galhardo, 1803), Miguel Maurício Ramalho, *Lisboa reedificada poema épico* (Lisbon, Régia Of. Typographica, 1780).

poems the Portuguese individual is the epic hero and Portuguese society is whole and unified. These elements are especially interesting because of what they reveal about the relationship between catastrophe and local artistic production.

The objective of the poems seems to be to use writing to remedy culture during a fragile chapter of Portugal's history. Although the reconstruction was exciting, it was accompanied by conflicts, delays, and many difficulties. Progress was not in all cases smooth and efficient, and Portuguese society, culturally recuperating, paralleled the massive construction site of downtown Lisbon. These authors employ literature as a cathartic form of expression that serves as reconciliation for the survivors and a scaffold for society. Certain common structural characteristics in these poems reveal their shared interest in lessening the importance of the disaster and focusing on the constructive outcomes. The earthquake appears only halfway through the long poems, and the description of the disaster is minimal. Because the earthquake in the poems lasts no longer than the tremors did on 1 November, it does not have quite the same destructive impact. The first part of each poem consists of a long history of the Portuguese monarchs and national glories and conquest. Emphasising the idyllic and glorious past underlines a sense of stability in the present. After a brief description of the events on 1 November, the third and final part is devoted to praising the reconstructive efforts and the important figures who contributed to the rebuilding of the city. Each of these epic writers attempts to transform the tragedy of the earthquake into something bearable, to utilise the event for the benefit of strengthening the established discourse, and to give a sense of stability to a delicate state of affairs.

A closer look at one of the poems reveals these objectives more clearly. *Lisboa reedificada* is similar to Camošes' classic because of its incorporation of mythical figures and gods. Each of the nine cantos is narrated from the perspective of a different mythical god, who sings the worth of the Portuguese along with their suffering. This pain appears as a noble sacrifice that the Portuguese must endure. The author writes:

> Choras por ver hum povo castigado,
> Que a sua mesina culpa a tanto obriga,
> E não ponderas bem, que com cuidado
> A quem o Ceo mais ama, mais castiga:[19]

This point of view helps people cope with the pain by attaching to it a transcendental purpose. The author makes frequent references to classical history and compares these episodes to Lisbon. Ramalho writes that as Rome acquired its glory from a burned Troy, Lisbon too will be a city superior to what it was before the earthquake.

---

19. Ramalho, *Lisboa reedificada*, p.26. 'You cry at seeing a people punished, / whose petty guilt obliges her to be, / And you do not ponder well, that with care / Heaven punishes the most those it loves the most.' All translations are mine unless otherwise noted.

> Tambem essa verás, Cidade amante,
> Reproduzir das cinzas mais formosa;
> Do pranto nascerá perla brilhante,
> D'entre agudos espinhos será rosa:
> O mesmo estrago seu significante
> Será da sua gloria portentosa;
> Mais não chores, socega a tua queixa,
> Alenta o coração, a mágoa deixa.[20]

Besides looking to the prosperity of the city, the author also considers its pain and suffering. He compares the earthquake to a war, whose victory requires torment and misery. He recognises that the suffering is reflected in silence. He claims that silence is the 'língua do queixume' (p.69), or the language of lament. In Portuguese, however, 'queixume' communicates not only suffering but also a sense of protest, which further reinforces a traumatic reading of the event by suggesting that the silence was unconsciously a form of protest. Even though it was now possible to confront the disaster, reminiscences of the difficulties of telling the story were still present.

It is important to note that these epic re-enactments of the earthquake were written years after the event. *Lisboa destruída* by Teodoro de Almeida appeared as late as 1803 and is particularly interesting because the author claims a further purpose for his writing. Since he was a priest, it would be expected that Almeida's goal would also be to defend Catholicism. More notable, however, is how he anticipates that his narrative will also correct the confusion created by the various and disordered accounts of the earthquake. In this way the canonical genre guarantees the text's authority over other writing and ideas. As an eyewitness his testimony promises to reconstruct the event accurately. He claims that at the time it was futile to give literary shape to the earthquake, but now that the nation has begun to look at the disaster in retrospect, the account becomes necessary. These works construct the interpretation or the meaning of the earthquake as a glorious episode in Portuguese history and also reveal different cultural strategies for coping with the disaster.

Besides the revival in the epic genre, the literary practices in place after the earthquake reveal how writers and artists more often escaped the topic and retreated into a space removed from the immediate reality. Evasion of the topic of the earthquake is evident in the institutional foundation of the Arcádia Lusitana, which turned the focus of literary expression away from political and social events towards a universal, classical, and purely literary poetic form. The Arcádia Lusitana was founded four months after

---

20. Ramalho, *Lisboa reedificada*, p.32. 'That one too you will see, loving City, | Reproduce from the ashes more beautiful; | From the wail will be born a shining pearl, | From among the sharp thorns there will be a rose: | Its very ruin will be its significance | From its glory it shall be portentous; | Do not cry any more, calm your lament, | Comfort your heart, abandon your pain.'

the earthquake, in March 1756, by a group of recent university gradu-
ates. This group of poets and dramatists, besides discussing and theorising
about tragedy, poetry, and drama, as defined by Aristotle and the classics, also reveal through their focus and personal experience some of the
earthquake's structural changes. The antecedents and the European
models for this trend in literature were already in place prior to 1755, but
the tragedy thrust the movement and organisation forward. As António
José Saraiva and Óscar Lopes explain in their *História da literatura Portuguesa*, personal merit and virtue were given top priority when selecting
members of the Arcádia. These new literary organisations and tendencies
reformed national literature and marked the future generations of Portuguese letters. The earthquake resulted in permanent changes in the
make-up of society, blurring class differences and giving precedence to
self-worth, while shifting the social focus of art.

The most significant Arcadians, Pedro António Correia Garção,
Domingos dos Reis Quita, António Dinis da Cruz e Silva, and Manuel de
Figueiredo, all came from either middle- or low-class backgrounds. These
writers avoided the topic of the earthquake by focusing their criticisms on
the decadent nobility and simultaneously promoting a moralising point
of view in their writing that defended the interests of the bourgeoisie.
This reveals their partial ideological identification with the governmental regime's politics and concept of the nobility. Pombal's personal
participation in these literary assemblies was short-lived, but the Arcadian
activity was to a certain point in tune with his social and political values.
This is especially evident in the development of Arcadian drama, since
Pombal personally commissioned various dramatic pieces. The three
known dramatic pieces commissioned by Pombal, written by Figueiredo,
and published in 1775, are *O Avaro dissipador*, *O Indolente miserável*, and *O
Fidalgo da sua própria casa*. These works, as the authors of *História da literatura* write, 'contrastam o tipo do Fidalgo, quixotescamente anacrónico,
ignorante, e inútil, com a pequena burguesia rural, que exaltam, numa
linguagem por vezes afim da dos fisiocratas, sustentando a seguinte
moralidade: fidalgos autênticos, "de homens-bons / o Rei é que os faz"'.[21]
The plays oppose the decadent nobility with an authentic emerging self-
made bourgeois individual, whose moral values gain him nobility.

The new social framework that evolved out of the earthquake and took
literary and social shape during the Arcadian period had a long-term
impact on the literary culture of the nation. The aesthetic preoccupation
of the poets and dramatists of the neoclassical era prepares Portuguese
romanticism. A century later, romantic works begin to reconstruct the

---

21. António José Saraiva and Óscar Lopes, *História da literatura Portuguesa* (Porto 2000),
p.618. 'they contrast the hidalgo type, quixotically anachronistic, ignorant, and useless,
with the small rural bourgeoisie, which they exalt with a language at times similar to that
of the physiocrats, sustaining the following morality: authentic hidalgos, "of good-men /
the King is the one that makes them"'.

historic events from similar perspectives. The best known authors of the nineteenth century do not rewrite the earthquake but focus instead on the Pombal dictatorship, reinforcing the important role this period had in Portuguese history. Almeida Garrett's dramatic piece, *Sobrinha do Marquez* (1848) deals with the political and social situation that characterises the earthquake's aftermath.[22] The character types represent the different social classes, with their political and religious interests, and the plot concentrates on the struggle between these. Another important romantic author, Camilo Castelo Branco, writes a work critical of Pombal titled *Perfil do Marquês de Pombal* (1883).[23] In this cross between a personal essay and a biography, Camilo criticises the absolutist qualities of Pombal, refutes arguments that credit the Marquês' government with the political reformation of the country and the reconstruction of Lisbon, and instead constructs romantic figures out of Pombal's enemies, defending the Távora family and the religious orders. This is not a rigorous biographical study of the Marquês, but it clearly outlines the opposing views that have surged around the personality of Pombal and that still remain. As Maxwell explains, 'To some Pombal, who to all intents and purposes ruled Portugal between 1750 and 1777, is a great figure of enlightened absolutism, comparable to Catherine II in Russia, Frederick II in Prussia and Joseph II in the Austrian monarchy; to others he is no more than a half-baked philosopher and a full-blown tyrant.'[24]

If these important romantic writers focused more on Pombal and less on the earthquake, they were nonetheless part of the literary movement characterised by a fervent cultivation of the historic novel. They themselves wrote many historic works. Their younger contemporary, Manuel Joaquim Pinheiro Chagas, an important literary critic and also the author of many historic novels, published in 1874 *O Terremoto de Lisboa*.[25] The text, perhaps the first truly novelistic version of the earthquake written by an acclaimed Portuguese author, reveals how the relationship between the catastrophe and art had evolved over time. The earthquake is now the ideal setting to narrate the changing social structure of the country. The author maintains a before and after narrative structure, also common in the earlier poetic and epic reconstructions of the event, although the pre-earthquake period receives the most attention, and the earthquake functions as the climax of the work. There is also an important scene that prefigures and further builds suspense for the important catastrophic moment. The fire at the Hospital de Todos os Santos prefigures the earthquake. This tragic event already describes the desperation, suffering, and pain of the Lisbon inhabitants to such an intense degree that the reader is led to believe that nothing could possibly be worse than

22. J. B. de Almeida Garrett, *Sobrinha do Marquez* (Lisbon 1848).
23. Camilo Castelo Branco, *Perfil do Marquês de Pombal* (Porto 1981).
24. Maxwell, *Pombal*, p.1.
25. Manuel Joaquim Pinheiro Chagas, *O Terremoto de Lisboa* (Porto 1937).

this, only to discover later that this is just the beginning of a long tragedy awaiting the characters.

It is interesting that the author describes as much pain in the fires as he does in the earthquake, thereby linking the event of 1755 to previous struggle and experience. At this fire, Teresinha, an orphaned young woman, is saved from the flames by the main character, Luiz Correia, a noble young man whose mother ends up adopting Teresa. She grows up among a world of art and culture, and Luiz falls in love with her. Carlos, Luiz's opposite in moral qualities, a bastard of the late King D. João V, opportunistic and revengeful, seduces Teresa. To her misfortune she runs away with him only to return devastated to her adopted home on 1 November begging her loved ones for forgiveness. The catastrophic events of the day are also the culminating actions of the plot; Carlos and Teresa discover that they are siblings and both die on the day of the earthquake. While directly after the earthquake literature portrayed the bourgeois individual as having superior moral qualities to the decadent nobility, here Carlos is corrupt and Luiz, the noble, is also noble in character. Still, Teresa is the more complex figure, who makes the transition between the two social and moral worlds. While still characterising the social positions, therefore, the new historical novel begins to explore the complexities of the relationship between the different social and subjective frameworks. But the conclusion seems to suggest that the earthquake is a tragic event that brings an end to these rising and corrupting forces in society. What will happen after the earthquake is left open, creating for the first time a mystery concerning what the events will stimulate. The text invites readers to explore the imaginary realms that a tragedy, such as the Lisbon earthquake, can open.

At the same time that some of the leading literary figures were reflecting on the important historic moment surrounding the earthquake, the event was featured in more popular literature, especially in romantic, sentimental historical novels. The earthquake figures at the forefront of an 1850 popular novel with no identified author, *O Premio da virtude ou terremoto de Lisboa em 1755*.[26] In telling an alluring, well-structured story of Lisbon before and after the earthquake, and especially in prefiguring the earthquake with massive fires that attack the city, the work has a similar format to *O Terremoto de Lisboa*. But unlike Pinheiro Chagas, the author of this work also ties political issues and loves stories to the catastrophic events. The narrator's perspective embellishes and inflates Pombal's efforts and heroism, and the detailed description of the new buildings and squares suggests a sincere admiration for the creativity and intelligence involved in Lisbon's reconstruction. The novel's real appeal, however, is the personal story of the nobleman Fernando and his love for Maria,

---

26. *O Premio da virtude ou terramoto de Lisboa em 1755: novela portuguesa* (Lisbon, Typ. de L. C. da Cunha, 1850).

a woman of the middle-class. Fernando also saves Maria from the fires that ruined city buildings only months prior to the earthquake. This prefiguration gives disaster a form of continuity, diminishing the quality of unexpectedness that catastrophe seems to have for the individuals who experience the events. Instead of emphasising the rupture the destruction creates, the plot gives meaning to the disaster through continuity and normality. Although of noble blood, Fernando's personal actions are what demonstrate his worth and win Maria's love. His father is criticised for narrow-mindedness, since he imprisons his son upon discovering his secret marriage to Maria. A happy ending brings together King D. José I and his minister, who, having freed Fernando and joined the couple, ultimately correct Rodrigo's outdated thinking. The plot seems to emphasise the aftermath of the earthquake as a time when personal actions outweighed social class in significance, and destructive events provided a chance for individuals and groups to demonstrate their qualities. The word 'or' in the title of this work, *O Premio da virtude ou terremoto de Lisboa em 1755, The Prize of virtue or the Lisbon earthquake of 1755*, seems to couple the one thing with the other, implying that the earthquake was not only an opportunity to start from the beginning, but also a chance to test and reward one's virtuous qualities. In this novel the earthquake functions to stimulate love, politics, architecture, and virtue in a positive way.

These two romantic novels emphasise the social consequences that resulted from the natural catastrophe and model their characters on the individuals who gained social status and even emotional happiness from such a misfortune. A century afterwards, the Great Earthquake becomes the focus of romantic novels that do not have difficulties in expressing and manipulating the events to tell a story around them. The distance in time has allowed these authors, who did not directly experience the events, to feel inspired by them. This gives these narratives fluidity and a sense of easiness with the topic that is not apparent in earlier work. Furthermore, romanticism, as Isabel de Campos shows in her book, *O Grande terramoto*, is intimately tied to the earthquake.[27] Her work studies how the Lisbon earthquake provoked sentiments and subjective responses to disaster that are widespread in German romantic poets and writers. She concludes that these feelings and sentiments disclose early signs of Romanticism, as subjective responses to disaster led to changes in arts and ideas. If the earthquake abroad triggered German Romanticism, it is not surprising that writers of the Portuguese Romantic era would also have been impressed by the event, and it was during this time that literature took up the earthquake above all for its novelistic possibilities.

The earthquake also makes a subtle appearance in the work of Eça de Queirós, one of Portugal's most important nineteenth-century writers. In his novels, different characters disillusioned by their native land and

---

27. Isabel Maria Barreira de Campos, *O Grande terramoto* (Lisbon 1998).

enthusiasts of foreign influences appeal to the earthquake in a particular way. For these characters, the national situation is so dreadful that only two possible events could salvage the state of affairs. Both solutions are quite drastic: the divine bring either another Spanish invasion, as had occurred in the sixteenth century, or another earthquake, like the one on All Saints Day in 1755. At the end of *O Primo Bazilio* (1878), Bazilio and his travelling companion return by train from Paris to Portugal, where they experience all the inconveniences of a backward transportation system. Reinaldo, after the exhausting trip, complaints to the hotel clerk that for a year his prayer has always been the same: ' "Meu Deus, manda-lhe outra vez o terramoto!" Pois todos os dias leio os telegramas a ver se o terramoto chegou [...] e nada! Algum ministro que cai, ou algum barão que surge. E de terramoto nada! O Omnipotente faz ouvidos de mercador às minhas preces [...] Protege o país! Tão bom é um como outro!'[28] What stands out here is the humorous and ironic approach of Reinaldo, who wants the earthquake to punish and destroy a country he believes is incapable of reform, and also his misreading of the original event. If the earthquake did bring reform and stimulate the country to adopt more modern infrastructures and ideas, then the earthquake was not simply a bad thing for Portuguese society. This of course is a perspective possible only after some time, or when ideas are removed from the space of suffering, which is the modern and distant approach to a catastrophic event. These responses will also lead to more constructive analysis of disaster and more complex interpretations of the events. Furthermore, the fact that Reinaldo waits for the telegram also reminds us of the thousands of letters that were sent out with the news, some of them arriving months later. The telegram is also an appeal to the modernity of a historic event, an appeal to make the past relevant to thinking about the present situation.

The Lisbon earthquake of 1755, memorable throughout history and across cultural boundaries, is referred to time and again by renowned authors. Considerable critical work analyses the writings of canonical authors such as Voltaire and Rousseau, Kant and Kleist, among others. In other European countries, the earthquake impressed mostly philosophical writers, whose interest often rested in the melodramatic nature of the events and how this affected reason, religion, the role of nature, and human will. Basically, it gave way to theoretical debates about ideas. Up until the twentieth century the earthquake still inspired critical rethinking. In Germany, it has been an especially widespread topic for intellectual discussion. In Thomas Mann's *The Magic mountain*, for instance,

---

28. José Maria Eça de Queirós, *O Primo Bazilio* (1878; Lisbon 2001), p.446. 'For a year now, my one prayer has been: "Please, God, send another earthquake!" Every day I read the news to see if the earthquake has arrived [...] but no! A minister has fallen or a baron has risen. But no earthquake! The Almighty turns a deaf ear to my prayers. He protects this country. Well, all I can say is that they deserve each other!' Eça de Queirós, *Cousin Bazilio*, translated by Margaret Jull Costa (Cambridge 2003), p.435.

Settembrini brings up the earthquake with the clear pedagogical purpose of explaining the triumph of reason over nature. Of course, what is most interesting here, as in Eça, is the humour and irony that using the event produces. Settembrini asks Hans Castrop: '"Haben sie von dem Erdbeben zu Lissabon gehört?"', and Hans responds, '"Nein, – ein Erdbeben? Ich sehe hier keine Zeitungen."'[29] Hans is ridiculed because he does not know the earthquake took place during the eighteenth century; but considering the indefinite role of time in this novel, and its relationship to place and reality, the humour in the scene is also significant because in reality it makes absolutely no difference when the earthquake took place. The debate it inspires is still relevant, and the questions it raises are timeless. We can see from these modern approaches that the earthquake is an event with an established discourse and meaning, a collection of associations that come along with it. Evidently literature often challenges these associations.

On a local level, the significance and function of the earthquake are also multiplied at different time periods. The nature and moment of a catastrophe often transform the national literary and cultural production. Literary evidence marks how the Portuguese cultural tradition responded to the disaster immediately following the earthquake and how the event was a turning point that still has reverberations in Portuguese cultural production. While the outside world used the earthquake enthusiastically, local artists coped with the tragedy by avoiding the topic, returning to it only after it was distanced in time. Those that tackled the event did so with confounded attitudes. While confronting the historic circumstances and extracting significance from the disaster, authors preferred to be positive and idealistic rather than critical. Disaster then, on the one hand, encouraged escapism and continuity in literature. On the other hand, it stimulated critical thinking that, although not directly engaged with the event, marked shifts in the literary arts.

But the Lisbon earthquake also reveals that the nature of the catastrophe and the political circumstances surrounding it are inseparable from cultural and intellectual development. The paradoxical yet authoritative political structure that modernised Lisbon is apparent in the cultural and discursive forms of coming to terms with the disaster. Writing that confronts disaster, rupture, and tragedy, has the inconsistent double effect of silencing its voices while anticipating a modern response to disaster in creative thinking.

29. Thomas Mann, *Der Zauberberg*, ed. Michael Neumann (Frankfurt 2002), p.379. '"Do you know about the Lisbon earthquake?" and Hans responds, "No... an earthquake? I've not been reading newspapers here"'. Thomas Mann, *The Magic mountain*, translated by John E. Woods (New York 1996), p.246.

Summaries

MALCOLM JACK

Destruction and regeneration: Lisbon, 1755

The essay examines the physical damage caused by the earthquake of 1755 to the public buildings, collections and private houses of the city of Lisbon, as recorded in eye-witness accounts, subsequent travellers' reports and as established by modern research. It considers the death toll and general destruction of a considerable area of the city against the background of the political effort – especially of the Marquês de Pombal – to re-establish order and begin the rebuilding of the seafront or Baixa area of Lisbon. Pombal's dominance in the regeneration of the capital and the enlightened despotism by which he subsequently ran the country (with royal protection), continue the post-earthquake story. Pombal's handling of the Aveiro conspiracy, the Jesuit Order and his modernisation of the administrative and educational systems are described in the closing parts of the essay.

CHARLES D. JAMES *and* JAN T. KOZAK

Representations of the 1755 Lisbon earthquake

In the morning of 1 November 1755 a massive earthquake (or rather three successive earthquakes) struck Portugal, Spain, and Morocco. Lisbon was the hardest hit of the major cities, and the quake has always been referred to as the great Lisbon earthquake. This article begins with a physical description of the earthquake, its causes and its effects, and then moves on to examine some representations of the damage. The many artistic images of the 1755 great Lisbon earthquake may help illustrate currents of thought that appear to emerge with the disaster. A theme, continued by contemporary earthquake reconnaissance, of empirical investigation and scientific conjecture spawned by the enormous damage and the wide area of perceptibility of the earthquake shaking is discernible in detailed architectural drawings and maps following the earthquake. Artistic depictions of ordinary citizens suffering death and misery as a result of a powerful, inaccurately illustrated natural disaster, suggest the arrival of modern themes of social responsibility for the welfare of ordinary citizens and the power of nature and of human life freed from a dominantly religious interpretation. Several digital images taken from the Kozak collection of historical earthquake images at the Earthquake engineering research center, University of California, Berkeley are used to illustrate these broad themes.

RUSSELL R. DYNES

The Lisbon earthquake of 1755: the first modern disaster

The earthquake in Lisbon, perhaps the fourth largest city in Europe at that time, occurred when Portugal hoped to develop a modern state to catch up with its neighbours. An earthquake in the capital city was a severe blow to trade with its colonies and with its neighbors. A minister, later to be known as the Marquês de Pombal, was given the responsibility by the king for the emergency response and for reconstruction. Pombal created twelve district leaders with strong emergency powers, disregarded traditional burial rites, controlled prices, and initiated plans for massive reconstruction. To speed up reconstruction, materials were prefabricated and standardised. Wooden frames with greater flexibility to future earthquakes were mandated and a standardised façade was required for all new buildings. Finally, a new square, placed on the old Royal plaza, was renamed the Praca do Comercio, reflective of Pombal's vision for Portugal's future. This unprecedented scope of governmental responsibility is what makes the Lisbon earthquake the first modern disaster.

DIEGO TÉLLEZ ALARCIA

Spanish interpretations of the Lisbon earthquake between 1755 and the war of 1762

Portugal, Spain and Morocco suffered a powerful earthquake on All Saints Day 1755. Its epicentre was located at the southwest of Lisbon. Its magnitude (8.5 to 9) killed 30,000 people in Lisbon, and destroyed the most important part of the city. The Spanish ambassador in Lisbon, count of Peralada, died with them. Since the queen of Spain was Portuguese (Doña Barbara de Braganza), Spain tried to help Portugal and sent the count of Aranda, one of the most important Spanish nobles. During the war of 1762, Spanish interpretation of Lisbon earthquake became more political. With some brief data of the physical damage as starting point, this study aims: to determine the nature of the cultural impact of the earthquake; to analyse the diachronic evolution of the interpretation of the earthquake in Spain between 1755 and 1762; and to highlight the political, social and religious factors that conditioned this interpretation between 1755 and 1762.

CARMEN ESPEJO CALA

Spanish news pamphlets on the 1755 earthquake: trade strategies of the printers of Seville

This paper addresses the Lisbon earthquake of 1755 and its relevance as a news item in the Spanish journalistic scenario. Spanish popular press dramatically increased its output over the following months. To further elaborate this point, we have collected all the works on the earthquake published in Seville, one of the cities most severely hit in Spain. In all, sixty-eight works have been considered, the majority of which were published in 1755. An in-depth analysis of the works shows them as popular journalistic narratives or *relaciones de sucesos*. Printers' strategies to arouse and maintain the interest of the public are also considered in this paper.

MATTHIAS GEORGI

The Lisbon earthquake and scientific knowledge in the British public sphere

This article examines the representation of earthquakes in the British public sphere in the middle of the eighteenth century. It shows how earthquakes were portrayed in the 1740s and 1750s, and which epistemological rules the understanding of explanations for earthquakes had to obey. The article will show that earthquakes were inseparably connected with natural philosophy. I argue that earthquakes were generally accepted as caused by the laws of nature. They attained their significance for example as a divine sign, an entertaining event or an aesthetic experience through a natural philosophical explanation. Even in the debates about the London and Lisbon earthquakes, when religious interpretations dominated, earthquakes were presented as natural spectacles of nature. A full understanding might depend on the bible, but the events were perceived with the inquisitiveness and urge to research fostered by natural philosophy.

ROBERT G. INGRAM

'The trembling earth is God's herald': earthquakes, religion and public life in Britain during the 1750s

This article examines the ways Britons understood the London and Lisbon earthquakes of the 1750s, anatomising the primary language of causation, providence, and exploring its complementary relation to Newtonian natural philosophy. This article also examines the uses to which Britons put their understanding of the earthquakes. In the process, the article aims to provide a fuller, clearer portrait of religion's place in public life during the mid eighteenth century, moving beyond the poles of an *ancien régime* confessional state on the one hand, and a secularised 'polite and commercial' society on the other. The few, such as Jonathan Clark, who have rightly posited religion's continuing importance in public life during the century, have focused almost wholly on political ideology. By way of a study of British responses to earthquakes in the 1750s, this article aims to integrate religion more effectively into the broader cultural, intellectual, social, and political histories of the period.

ROBERT WEBSTER

The Lisbon earthquake: John and Charles Wesley reconsidered

This article offers an evaluation of the Wesleys' writings on violent storms and the Lisbon earthquake, in particular. John Wesley, the organising genius of the evangelical revival and Charles Wesley, the prolific hymn writer of the eighteenth century, addressed various moral issues that the Lisbon earthquake created for modern society. John Wesley wrote a short tract on the Lisbon earthquake and also addressed the apocalyptic nature of earthquakes in a sermon ('The great assize'). Charles Wesley, for his part, wrote a sermon on earthquakes and also composed a collection of nineteen hymns that dealt with the London tremors of 1750 and the Lisbon earthquake of 1755. Additionally, the Wesley brothers commented on violent storms throughout their respective journals and letters. Throughout, therefore, they tackled issues such as nature, human nature and faith, which was a prevalent trend in the religious rhetoric of the Enlightenment. Additionally, the essay argues, John and Charles Wesley saw violent storms as egalitarian events that positioned both rich and poor on equal grounds with regard to the relationship of creation to the Creator. The thesis of the essay maintains that the Wesleys' view of storms not only reveals their anti-elite sentiments but also served the evangelical agenda of the Methodist movement in the eighteenth century.

GRÉGORY QUENET

Déconstruire l'événement. Un séisme philosophique ou une catastrophe naturelle?

L'intensité du débat philosophique suscité par le désastre de Lisbonne prouve son caractère exceptionnel. Pourtant peu de commentaires se sont penchés sur la nature de cet événement: est-ce un simple hasard si une catastrophe naturelle est devenu un élément fondateur de la conscience européenne? L'opinion publique européenne a été ébranlée par les nouvelles de la destruction d'une des villes les plus riches d'Europe et le chiffre de 100 000 morts avancé dans les premiers mois. Mais, plus encore, les contemporains ont été saisis par une forme de participation à l'événement tout à fait inédite, en l'absence d'un système médiatique contemporain. La secousse du 1er novembre a en effet été ressentie de l'Islande à l'Afrique du Nord, des Etats allemands à Boston; durant toute l'année 1756, des dizaines de séismes sont relevés en Europe. Rapportés par les gazettes, à un moment où s'accélère la diffusion des informations, ils suscitent les interrogations des contemporains et relient des espaces enclavés. Lisbonne a aussi suscité un débat scientifique, oublié aujourd'hui alors qu'il a eu un retentissement aussi grand que le volet philosophique. Le problème central est de comprendre comment un séisme produit en un lieu peut se diffuser presque immédiatement à des milliers de kilomètres de là. L'académie de Rouen organise un concours sur le sujet, des dizaines de théories sont proposées, dont des modèles électriques. Ce débat passionne les contemporains et constitue un des premiers succès 'populaires' de la science, avant les montgolfières et le mesmérisme des années 1780. En amont du siècle, il rejoint les interrogations des savants qui, depuis les années 1740, avaient 'découvert' les tremblements de terre français. En aval, il annonce les projets des para-tremblements de terre et para-volcans des années 1780.

THEODORE E. D. BRAUN

Voltaire and Le Franc de Pompignan: poetic reactions to the Lisbon earthquake

This article examines Le Franc de Pompignan's immediate reaction to the death of his friend Louis Racine's son in Cádiz during the Lisbon earthquake of 1 November 1755 ('A M. Racine, sur la mort de son fils'), which he later incorporated into a longer reaction to Voltaire's 'Poème sur le désastre de Lisbonne' in the final edition of his *Œuvres* (Paris, Nyon l'aîné, 1784) as the *Odes*, IV, ii.151-96. In the ode to Racine he opposes what he sees as the *philosophes*'s rejection of Providence in a simple expression of faith addressed to his Jansenist-leaning friend. Later, in book IV of his *Odes*, he constructs a strong rebuke to Voltairean beliefs in nine odes that both reaffirm his belief in Providence and castigate Voltaire and his followers for their disbelief. Although composed around 1763, this book of poems was never published separately, and was first made public the year of Le Franc's death.

ANNE-SOPHIE BARROVECCHIO

A propos de Voltaire, de maître André et du *Tremblement de terre de Lisbonne*: histoire d'une supercherie tragique de l'avocat Jean-Henri Marchand

L'avocat parisien Jean-Henri Marchand est un de ces *minores* par choix du siècle de Voltaire qui, sans être auteur de profession, publia de nombreux ouvrages, dont plusieurs furent de grands succès de librairie. Certains sont écrits en relation avec des œuvres ou avec la figure de Voltaire, ainsi que notre anthologie *Voltairomania* le montre. Quand Voltaire écrit son 'Poème sur le désastre de Lisbonne' (1755), ses vers fournissent à Marchand l'idée d'une tragédie burlesque, *Le Tremblement de terre de Lisbonne* (1755 [1756]) publiée sous le prête-nom de maître André, perruquier. Sa pièce, comme la plupart de ses écrits, propose plusieurs niveaux de lecture. Le premier repose sur le spectacle tragique de deux amants malheureux qui meurent au cours d'une catastrophe qui émut toute l'Europe; le second résulte du dialogue que la parodie entretient discrètement avec les vers de Voltaire; le dernier enfin invite à une réflexion générique et à une analyse des pratiques littéraires du milieu du dix-huitième siècle, où les auteurs se répondent les uns aux autres dans un jeu d'échos spirituels et d'inspirations mutuelles, et où les ouvrages même en apparence les plus anodins peuvent développer des vues hardies.

CATRIONA SETH

'Je ne pourrai pas en faire le récit': le tremblement de terre de Lisbonne vu par Le Brun, Marchand et Genlis

Si les écrits de Voltaire sur le désastre de Lisbonne sont connus, il n'en va pas de même d'autres textes sur la catastrophe. Le Brun écrit deux belles odes, ému par la mort d'un de ses proches amis. Rappelant le langage des psaumes, son style est vigoureux. Il célèbre la puissance de Dieu et de la Nature. L'avocat Marchand réagit moins au tremblement de terre qu'au poème de Voltaire. Sa pièce se veut burlesque et déploie toutes les ressources du burlesque, culminant avec la destruction de Lisbonne. Cet événement sert de point de départ à un conte moral de Mme de Genlis. Un jeune homme et son père apprennent la valeur des choses confrontés à la majesté des éléments et à l'amitié de leurs semblables. Poème, pièce et fiction narrative disent chacun à leur façon l'importance d'une tragédie dont les effets se sont prolongés bien au-delà de la ville de Lisbonne et du 1er novembre 1755.

JEFF LOVELAND

Guéneau de Montbeillard, the *Collection académique* and the great Lisbon earthquake

In 1754 Philibert Guéneau de Montbeillard assumed the editorship of the *Collection académique*, a series devoted to culling publications of European scientific academies and translating them into French. The earthquake in Lisbon in 1755 moved him to gather data on earthquakes, volcanoes and other potentially related natural occurrences in the hope of making them understandable and more safely bearable. Though the resulting 'Liste chronologique...' hardly fitted with the project of the *Collection*, he published it in volume vi, presumably thinking that the magnitude of the disaster justified this interruption of his compendium. His 'Liste' was presented as a roster of facts, but the choice of some facts and not others indicates a fragmentary theory of earthquakes – a theory worth evoking in this friend of Buffon. Along with much of the early *Collection*, the 'Liste' also illustrates the limitations of the common eighteenth-century convention of assigning readers rather than authors the prerogative of drawing conclusions from facts. Lastly, the story of Guéneau's list is intertwined with the fortunes of the *Collection* as a whole – a series that, despite its resonance with the Enlightenment's ideals, fell short of the expectations inspiring and inspired by its creation.

ANNE SAADA *and* JEAN SGARD

Tremblements dans la presse

Le tremblement de terre de Lisbonne a provoqué pendant plusieurs mois une onde de choc qui nous éclaire sur le fonctionnement de la presse d'Ancien Régime. En examinant les articles publiés dans une quinzaine de gazettes de langue française, on observe d'abord la façon dont se construit le récit d'un événement qui a duré au total six minutes. Il est pressenti par de petites secousses ressenties un peu partout le 1er novembre, mais on n'apprend que trois semaines plus tard la réplique de Madrid; quant au séisme de Lisbonne, on en attend le récit près d'un mois; les témoignages détaillés n'arrivent qu'à la fin de décembre; le contrecoup de la catastrophe se propage ensuite dans la presse littéraire, religieuse, scientifique, pendant six mois. Le séisme de Lisbonne a commencé par détruire le réseau d'information, qui se reconstitue lentement; cette reconstruction nous éclaire sur la nature des sources d'information: courriers officiels, courrier ordinaire, bulletins accrédités et lettres, publiques ou particulières, relations complètes de correspondants. Différents points de vue se juxtaposent pour donner enfin une vue globale de l'événement. Ce silence de Lisbonne pendant plus d'un mois alimente différents discours de substitution: discours de désarroi, qui insiste sur la réception de l'événement et sur la presse elle-même, discours compassionnel, qui développe le tableau d'une solidarité européenne, discours scientifique sur les désordres de la nature, qui englobe peu à peu tout le territoire européen. Seule est esquivée l'interrogation sur la Providence: la presse entretient un immense consensus, intègre la catastrophe à un ordre immanent et développe son propre *Te Deum*.

GILBERT LAROCHELLE

Voltaire: du tremblement de terre de Lisbonne à la déportation des Acadiens

Le tremblement de terre de Lisbonne signe, dans l'esprit de Voltaire, la défaite de la transcendance et l'illusion de la miséricorde divine pour soutenir l'action des hommes. La catastrophe naturelle de 1755 secoue la scène intellectuelle de toute l'Europe par les ondes de choc que crée la plume indignée du grand philosophe: comment un Dieu de bonté a-t-il pu être à l'origine de tout ce mal? Une théologie négative est alors pressentie comme le signe inversé de l'espérance sans limite dont l'homme devient le porteur, voire l'unique titulaire. Or, une telle explication, si chère à l'optimisme humaniste du dix-huitième siècle, finit par escamoter le problème de la responsabilité humaine. Le propos de cette réflexion consiste à rappeler que Voltaire, même s'il a pris sur lui 'la douleur des hommes' comme disait Michelet, s'est rendu incapable de penser l'hypothèse de leur indignité et du mal qui leur incombe. Si Voltaire ne peut absoudre Dieu du drame de Lisbonne, comment peut-il ignorer celui que les hommes créent en Amérique avec la déportation des 10 000 Acadiens exactement au même moment en 1755? La coïncidence des événements fournit des indices significatifs sur les sensibilités respectives qu'ils déclenchent. Le culte de l'homme comme être de Raison ne paraît d'ailleurs pas compatible, chez lui, avec l'intolérance et le fanatisme dont il voit la cause dans la religion. La question de l'indignité humaine serait-elle le point aveugle de la philosophie voltairienne? La conjonction de la Raison et de l'inhumain y aurait-elle été une possibilité mésestimée, sinon ignorée?

MONIKA GISLER

Optimism and theodicy: perception of the Lisbon earthquake in protestant Switzerland

Assessments of major natural disasters usually emerge long after the event, in larger contexts of interpretation. Yet we might ask whether such events did not also act as structural, transcending moments, transferring semantic structures or breaking them up. The reaction to the 1755 Lisbon disaster is key to this discussion. Researchers today generally believe that not only did the earthquake in Lisbon unsettle the optimism of the early Enlightenment, but that it may have destroyed it altogether. To underline the argument, the reader is usually referred to Voltaire's works after the Lisbon earthquake. Reconsideration of Voltaire's working process and the reactions to his works reveals that Voltaire's renunciation of theological optimism was itself criticised. Reactions from Swiss protestants to the earthquake demonstrate a variety of interpretative patterns. I will show that, rather than shifting to a metaphysical pessimism, the optimistic concept of the early Enlightenment was perpetuated throughout the second half of the eighteenth century. The study of regional patterns of philosophical and religious answers to the Lisbon earthquake will allow us to go beyond a simple interpretation in the realm of religious dogma and exegesis of holy texts. The reactions to Voltaire's 'Poème' were much more diverse than disrupting the optimistic philosophy of the early Enlightenments. Because of its magnitude, the event had an impact on the philosophical and religious discourses; but religion and philosophy affected how the event was understood.

LUANNE FRANK

No way out: Heinrich von Kleist's *Erdbeben in Chile*

This study focuses on one of the best-known literary 'remainders' of the Lisbon earthquake of 1755, Heinrich von Kleist's *Das Erdbeben in Chile*, by identifying certain of its earthquake-related instigators: geological (the Lisbon earthquake itself), cultural (the literary and philosophical reactions to the earthquake and its aftermaths on the parts of Voltaire and Kant); and psychic-spiritual (Kleist's earthquake-like shocks at discovering the uncertainty of either reason-based or feeling-based knowing and the certainty of always impending, unpredictable, and incomprehensible reversals). The study theorises Kleist's insight into the inevitability of uncertainty, and its conflict with the certainty on which he had based his life's plan as determining him as a quintessential hinge figure between the Foucauldian classical and the contemporary *épistèmes*, forced to inhabit but unable to accommodate both, experiencing the conflict between them as tragic, and this tragedy, though unavoidable, as unacceptable. The study then asks why Kleist could not accommodate the uncertainty he found evidence of everywhere, and posits as an answer that he was grounded in an *épistème* that saw certainty as a supreme value, as the very name and form of truth, the more basic form of truth – conflict – having been lost with the eclipse of pre-Socratic thought.

ESTELA VIEIRA

Coping and creating after catastrophe: the significance of the Lisbon earthquake of 1755 on the literary culture of Portugal

Starting with a brief survey of some contemporary reflections on the Lisbon earthquake to mark the event's continued significance, this essay reconsiders the importance of the catastrophe from a national perspective and explores how the earthquake affected Portugal's literary and intellectual development. The immediate discourse, especially the poetic reconstructions of the day's experiences, suggests that the catastrophe produced a traumatic effect on Portuguese letters. Changes in the *Gazeta de Lisboa* indicate the impact that the political environment had on Portuguese literary culture after the earthquake. The dramatic and poetic production that comes of the post-1755 Arcadian societies reveals how the political and social make-up evolved. The national revival of the epic stimulated by the earthquake further illustrates forms of coping with the disaster in literature. The epics' authors return to the canonical model to give authority to their version of the incidents and to emphasise their optimistic interpretation of these. In Portugal's late Romantic period there were numerous novelistic representations of the earthquake, using love stories and pre-figuration to narrate their fictional representations of the earthquake. In modern Portuguese writing the earthquake seldom appears as the main focus, but authors often refer to the episode and complicate with irony the event's possible semantic inferences. Therefore, the earthquake, like the authoritarian government that ruled post-earthquake Portugal, had a powerful if paradoxical impact on the country's literary creation.

Bibliography

An abstract of the form of prayer to be used on Friday the 6ᵗʰ of February, 1756, being the day appointed by proclamation for a general fast, and humiliation, for imploring the blessing of God upon our fleets and armies, and for humbling ourselves before Him in a deep sense of his late visitation, by most dreadful earthquakes (London 1756).

An account of the earthquake which destroyed the city of Lisbon, on the first of November, 1755 [...] *illustrative of the great picture of the earthquake at Lisbon, now exhibiting at the Lyceum, Strand. The landscape painted by C. J. Pugh; the figures by R. K. Porter. Selected from the London Gazette* (London 1800).

An account of the late dreadful earthquake and fire, which destroyed the city of Lisbon, the metropolis of Portugal. In a letter from a merchant resident there, to his friend in England (London 1756).

An account of the late dreadful hurricane, which did so much damage to our West India fleet, [...] *Also, an account of the late alarming earthquake, which happened in various parts of the kingdom* (London 1750).

An address to the inhabitants of Great Britain, occasioned by the late earthquake at Lisbon (London 1756).

Adventures under-ground: a letter from a gentleman swallowed up in the late earthquake to a friend on his travels (London 1750).

Advice to England; or, resolution. A poem. Occasioned by the late earthquake. And seriously recommended to all families; more especially, to those who intend to depart London (London 1750).

Affiches, annonces, et avis divers (Paris 1751-1811).

Aguilar Piñal, Francisco, *La Biblioteca de Jovellanos* (1778; Madrid 1984).

– *La Biblioteca y el monetario de Cándido M. Trigueros* (1798; Seville 1999).

– 'Conmoción espiritual en Sevilla por el terremoto de 1755', *Archivo hispalense* 171-173 (1973), p.37-53.

– *Historia de Sevilla: siglo XVIII* (Seville 1989).

– *Romancero popular del siglo XVIII* (Madrid 1972).

A. La. La. A Bord, M., 'Ode sur les tremblements de terre arrivés à Lisbonne', *Mercure de France* (juin 1756), p.6.

Albertan-Coppola, Sylviane, 'De Locke à Helvétius en passant par *l'Encyclopédie*, ou faut-il "casser le XVIIIᵉ siècle"?' in *Sciences, musiques, lumières: mélanges offerts à Anne-Marie Chouillet*, ed. Ulla Kölving and Irène Passeron (Ferney 2002), p.367-74.

Albrier, A., 'La famille Daubenton: notice historique et généalogique', *Revue historique, nobiliaire et biographique* 9 (1874), p.152-81.

Alcock, Thomas, *A Sermon of the late earthquakes, more particularly that at Lisbon; part whereof was preached December 31. 1755, and the other part February 4. 1756, in the parish church at St. Andrew, Plymouth: wherein the subject is considered both in a philosophical and religious light* (Oxford 1756).

Aldridge, Alfred Owen, 'The background of Kleist's *Das Erdbeben in Chili*', *Arcadia* 4 (1969), p.173-80.

Alembert, Jean D', 'Discours préliminaire des éditeurs', in *Encyclopédie, ou Dictionnaire raisonnée des sciences, des arts et des métiers, par une société de gens de lettres*, ed. Denis Diderot and D'Alembert ([Paris] 1751-1772), i.i-xxxiv.

Alexandre, Pierre, and Jean Vogt, 'La crise séismique de 1755-1762 en Europe du Nord-ouest. Les secousses des 26 et 27.12.1755: recensement des matériaux', in *Materials of the CEC project 'Review of Historical Seismicity in Europe'*, ed. Paola Albini and Andrea Moroni (Milan 1994), ii.143-52.

Allen, John, *The Destruction of Sodom improved, as a warning to Great Britain. A sermon preached on the fast-day, Friday, February 6, 1756. At Hanover-Street, Long Acre* (London 1756).

– *The Nature and danger of despising repeated reproofs, considered; in a sermon preached at Hanover-Street, Long-Acre, March 11. 1749-50. On occasion of the two late earthquakes* (London 1750).

Almeida, Teodoro de, *Lisboa destruída poema* (Lisbon, Of. de António Rodrigues Galhardo, 1803).

Altenhofer, Norbert. 'Der erschütterte Sinn: Hermeneutische Überlegungen zu Kleists *Das Erdbeben in Chile*', in *Positionen der Literaturwissenschaft: Acht Modellanalysen am Beispiel von Kleists 'Das Erdbeben in Chili'*, ed. David E. Wellbery (Munich 1985), p.39-53.

Ammicht-Quinn, Regina, *Von Lissabon bis Auschwitz: Zum Paradigmawechsel in der Theodizeefrage* (Freiburg 1992).

'André', in *Dictionnaire de biographie française* (Paris 1936), ii.903.

André, Charles, Mᶜ perruquier, prête-nom de Marchand, Jean-Henri, *Le Tremblement de terre de Lisbonne* (Lisbon, de l'Imprimerie du Public, 1755).

– *Le Tremblement de terre de Lisbonne* (Amsterdam, et se vend chez l'auteur, 1756).

– *La Tragédie de Maître André perruquier, ou le Tremblement de terre de Lisbonne* (Paris, Fages, An XIII [1805]).

– *Le Tremblement de terre de Lisbonne* (Paris, A. Leroux et C. Chantpie).

– *Le Tremblement de terre de Lisbonne* (Paris, Barba, 1834).

Anguish, Thomas, *A Sermon preached at St. Nicholas, Deptford, on the fast day*

appointed by royal proclamation, on *February 6, 1756* (London 1756).

Anker-Mader, Eva-Maria, *Kleists Familienmodelle: Im Spannungsfeld zwischen Krise und Persistenz* (Munich 1992).

Anonymous, *An account by an eye-witness of the Lisbon earthquake of 1ˢᵗ November 1755* (Lisbon 1985).

Anonymous, *A Serious expostulation with the right reverend the Lord Bishop of London on his letter to the clergy and people of London and Westminster* (London 1750).

Anderson, Wilda C., *Between the library and the laboratory: the language of chemistry in eighteenth-century France* (Baltimore, MD 1984).

Annonces, affiches, et avis divers (Paris 1751-1811).

Antoine, Michel, *Louis XV* (Paris 1989).

Arruda, Robert, *La Réaction littéraire de Voltaire et ses contemporains au tremblement de terre de Lisbonne de 1775*, 1977, dissertation.

Arx, Bernhard von, 'Heinrich von Kleist und die Novelle', in *Novellistisches Dasein: Spielraum einer Gattung in der Goethezeit* (Zurich 1953).

Ashton, Thomas, *A Sermon preached on occasion of the general fast appointed by royal proclamation, on February 6, 1756* (London 1756).

Augier Du Fot, Anne Amable, *Journal historique, géographique et physique de tous les tremblements de terre et autres événements arrivés dans l'Univers pendant les années 1755 & 1756* ([n.p.] 1756).

An Authentick view of the city of Lisbon in Portugal, at the time of the dreadful earthquake, which entirely destroyed that city, on the 1st of November, 1755, and as it ended; drawn from the other side the Tagus, by one of the best artists for those things in that country (London 1755).

Azevedo, J. Lucio, *O marquês de Pombal e a sua época* (Porto 1990).

Baczko, Bronislaw, *Job, mon ami: promesse du bonheur et fatalité du mal* (Paris 1997).

Baller, Joseph, *Divine alarms and warnings to a sinful people considered and improved: a sermon preached at Barnstaple, in the county of Devon, on February 6. 1756. Being the day appointed for a general fasting and humiliation* (London 1756).

Barazzi, Gian Antonio, 'Il terremoto del 1755 a Locarno', *BSSI* 4:8 (1882).

Barreira de Campos, Isabel Maria, *O Grande terramoto* (Lisbon 1998).

Barrovecchio, Anne-Sophie, 'L'avocat Marchand, ou le regard d'un homme du dix-huitième siècle sur son temps', *SVEC* 2004:07, p.99-110.

– 'Hylaire, cousin de *Bélisaire*: une parodie pour rire de l'avocat Jean-Henri Marchand (1767)', *Le Rire des moralistes*, ed. Jean Dagen (Paris, forthcoming).

– ed., *Voltairomania: l'avocat Jean-Henri Marchand face à Voltaire*, Coll. 'Lire le dix-huitième siècle' (Saint-Etienne 2004), p.33-104.

Bartel, Roland, 'The story of public fast days in England', *Anglican theological review* (1955).

Barthe, Nicolas-Thomas, *Ode sur la ruine de Lisbonne* ([n.p.] 1756).

Bartolomeo de Araujo, Ana Cristina, '1755: l'Europe tremble à Lisbonne', in *L'Esprit de l'Europe: dates et Lieux*, ed. Antoine Compagnon et Jacques Seebacher (Paris 1993), i.125-30.

Bate, James, *The Practical use of public judgments: a sermon, preached at St Paul's, Deptford, Kent, on February 6, 1756* (London 1756).

Bayle, Pierre, *Dictionnaire historique et critique*, ed. Alain Niderst (Paris 1974).

Bayly, Edward, *A Sermon preached at St James's church in Bath, on Friday, February 6, 1756 [...] and again [...] on Sunday following, at the abbey-church* (London 1756).

Bearcroft, Philip, *A Sermon preached before the Right Honourable the Lord-Mayor, the Alderman and citizens, at the Cathedral-Church of St Paul, on Friday, February 6, 1756. Being the day appointed by his Majesty's proclamation for a general fast* (London 1756).

Beaumont (coiffeur dans les Quinze-Vingts), pseudonym of Jean-Henri Marchand, *L'Enciclopédie perruquière, ouvrage curieux à l'usage de toutes sortes de têtes* (Amsterdam [Paris] 1757).

Beckmann, Beat, *Kleists Bewusstseinskritik: Eine Untersuchung der Erzählformen seiner Novellen* (Bern 1978).

Behme, Hermann, *Heinrich von Kleist und C. M. Wieland* (Heidelberg 1914).

Beissner, Friedrich, 'Unvorgreifliche Gedanken über den Sprachrhythmus', in *Festschrift Paul Kluckhohn und Hermann Schneider* (Tübingen 1948), p.427-44.

Belo, André, 'A *Gazeta de Lisboa* e o terramoto de 1755: a margem do não escrito', *Análise social* 151-152 (2000), p.619-37.

– *Nouvelles d'Ancien Régime. La 'Gazeta de Lisboa' et l'information manuscrite au Portugal (1715-1760)*, 1993, doctoral thesis.

Bennett, Edwin Keppel, 'The metaphysical novelle: Kleist', in *A History of the German 'Novelle'*, ed. H. M. Waidson (Cambridge 1961), p.37-46.

Berg, Maxine, and Helen Clifford, *Consumers and luxury: consumer culture in Europe, 1650-1800* (Manchester 1999).

Berg, Maxine, and Elizabeth Eger, ed., *Luxury in the eighteenth century: debates, desires and delectable goods* (Basingstoke 2003).

Bernard, P., 'Notice sur Montbeillard', *Œuvres complètes de Buffon* (Paris 1801), xi.361-76.

Berryat, Jean, *et al.* ed., *Recueil de mémoires, ou collection de pièces académiques, concernant la médecine, l'anatomie et la chirurgie, la chimie, la physique expérimentale, la botanique et l'histoire naturelle, tirées des meilleurs sources* (Dijon and Paris 1754-1787).

Bertrand, Elie, 'La consideration salutaire des malheurs publics. Ou sermon sur Jérémie XXII.v.8', in *Memoire sur les tremblemens de terre avec quatre sermons* (Vevey 1756), p.1-22.

– 'La crainte du seigneur est la vraye sagesse. Ou sermon sur Job XXVIII.v.28', in *Memoire sur les tremblemens de terre avec quatre sermons* (Vevey 1756), p.23-47.

– 'Essai sur les usages des montagnes', in *Recueil de divers traités sur l'histoire naturelle de la terre et des fossiles* (Avignon 1766; first edition Zurich 1754), p.105-222.

– 'Mémoires historiques et physiques sur les tremblemens de terre', in *Recueil de divers traités sur l'histoire naturelle de la terre et des fossiles* (Avignon 1766; first edition Vevey 1756), p.227-495.

– *Mémoires historiques et physiques sur les tremblemens de terre* (The Hague 1757).

– 'Memoires sur la structure interieure de la terre', in *Recueil de divers traités sur l'histoire naturelle de la terre et des fossiles* (Avignon 1766; first edition Zurich 1752), p.1-103.

– *Memoire sur les tremblemens de terre avec quatre sermons* (Vevey 1756).

Besse, Joseph *Modest remarks upon the Bishop of London's letter concerning the late earthquakes by one of the people called Quakers* (London 1750).

Besterman, Theodore, 'Le désastre de Lisbonne et l'optimisme de Voltaire', *La Table ronde* (1958), p.60-74.

– 'Voltaire et le désastre de Lisbonne: ou, la mort de l'optimisme', in *SVEC* 2 (1956), p.7-24.

Bevis, John, *The History and philosophy of earthquakes, from the remotest to the present times: collected from the best writers on the subject [...] By a member of the Royal Academy of Berlin* (London 1757).

Bibliotecha lindesina, vol.viii: *Handlist of proclamations issued by royal and other constitutional authorities, 1714-1910: George I to Edward VII*, ed. James Ludovic Lindsay (Wigan 1913).

Biddulph, Joseph, *A Poem on the earthquake at Lisbon* (London 1755).

Blackall, Eric, *The Emergence of German as a literary language* (Cambridge 1959).

Black, Jeremy, 'Confessional state or elect nation? Religion and identity in eighteenth-century England', in *Protestantism and national identity: Britain and Ireland, c.1650-c.1850*, ed. Tony Claydon and Ian McBride (Cambridge 1998), p.53-74.

Blanco Martínez, Rosa M., and Carmen Rubalcaba Pérez, 'Sueño de una sombra: escritura y clases populares en Santander en el siglo XIX', in *Cultura escrita y clases subalternas: una mirada española*, ed. Antonio Castillo Gómez (Oiartzun 2001), p.128-31.

Blankenagel, John C., 'Heinrich von Kleist: "Das Erdbeben in Chili"', *Germanic review* 8 (1933), p.30-39.

Blöcker, Günter, *Heinrich von Kleist oder das absolute Ich* (Frankfurt 1977).

Boehmer, Georg Rudolf, *Bibliotheca scriptorum historiae naturalis oeconomiae aliarumque artium ac scientiarum ad illam pertinentium realis systematica* (Leipzig 1785-1789).

Bolt, Bruce, *Earthquakes* (New York 2000).

Bonafous, R., *Henri de Kleist* (Paris 1894).

Bonomi, Patricia, *Under the cope of heaven: religion, society and politics in colonial America* (Oxford 1998).

Borkowski, Heinrich, *Kleist und Kant* (Königsberg 1935).

Bossut, Charles, ed., *Encyclopédie méthodique: mathématiques* (Paris 1784-1789).

Bourke, Thomas E., 'Vorsehung und Katastrophe: Voltaires "Poeme sur le désastre de Lisbonne" und Kleists "Erdbeben in Chile"', in *Klassik und Moderne* (1983), p.228-53.

Bouza, Fernando, *Corre manuscrito: una historia cultural del Siglo de Oro* (Madrid 2001).

Bowman, Thomas, *A Sermon preached in the parish-church of Holbeach, Lincolnshire, on Friday the 6th day of February, 1756* (Cambridge, 1756).

Boxer, Charles Ralph, *The Portuguese seaborne empire: 1415-1825* (Oxford 1963).

– *Some contemporary reactions to the Lisbon earthquake of 1755* (Lisbon 1956).

Braga, María Luísa, 'O terremoto de 1755: sua repercussão, a nível ideológico, em Portugal e no estrangeiro', in *História de Portugal e dos tempos pré-históricos aos nossos dias*, ed. Joao Medina (Lisbon 1997), p.347-70.

Branco, Castelo Camilo, *Perfil do Marquês de Pombal* (Porto 1981).

Braunrot, Christabel P., and Kathleen Hardesty Doig, 'The *Encyclopédie méthodique*: an introduction', *SVEC* 327 (1995), p.1-152.

Braun, Stefan, 'Heinrich von Kleist/ Helma Sanders: "Das Erdbeben in Chili". Eine vergleichende Analyse der Erzähleingänge von Film und Novelle' in *Erzählstrukturen Filmstrukturen*, ed. Klaus Kanzog (Berlin 1981), p.59-89.

Braun, Theodore E. D., *Un Ennemi de Voltaire, Le Franc de Pompignan* (Paris 1972).

– '"Soyons de notre esprit les seuls législateurs"', *SVEC* 303 (1992), p.196-200.

–, and Judy Celano Celli, 'Eighteenth-century French translations of Pope's *Universal prayer*', *SVEC* 256 (1988), p.297-323.

Bravo, Juan, *Compendio geográfico y histórico del Reyno de Portugal, dividido en 5 provincias y el Algarve, en el que se da puntual noticia de todas las plazas y fortalezas que hay en dicho Reyno, su graduación, vecindario, parroquias y personas* (Madrid, Andrés Ortega, 1762).

Breidert, Wolfgang, ed., *Die Erschütterung der vollkommenen Welt: Die Wirkungen des Erdbebens von Lissabon im Spiegel europäischer Zeitgenossen* (Darmstadt 1994).

Brewer, John, *The Pleasures of the imagination: English culture in the eighteenth century* (London 1997).

Bricqueville, Anne-Henriette de, *Réflexions sur les causes des tremblements de terre, avec les principes qu'on doit suivre pour dissiper les orages tant sur terre que sur mer* (Paris 1756).

Broman, Thomas, 'The Habermasian public sphere and "science in the Enlightenment"', *History of science* 36 (1998), p.123-49.

Brooke, John Hedley, *Science and religion: some historical perspectives* (Cambridge 1991).

Brors, Claudia. *Anspruch und Abbruch: Untersuchungen zu Heinrich von Kleists Ästhetik des Rätzelhaften* (Würzburg 2002).

Brown, Harcourt, 'Pascal *philosophe*', *SVEC* 55 (1967), p.309-20.

Brown, Hilda Meldrum, *Heinrich von Kleist: the ambiguity of art and the necessity of form* (Oxford 1998).

Brunet, Pierre, 'Un centre bourguignon de synthèse scientifique au XVIIIe siècle', *Annales de Bourgogne* 1 (1929), p.104-24.

– 'Guéneau de Montbeillard', *Mémoires de l'Académie des sciences, arts et belles-lettres de Dijon* (1925), p.125-31.

– 'Guéneau de Montbeillard', *Revue de Bourgogne* (1926), p.516-32.

Buch, Hans Christoph, '"Das Erdbeben in Chile": Eine wahre Geschichte', in *Kleists Erzählungen und Dramen*, ed. Paul Michael Lützeler and David Pan (Würzburg 2001), p.11-14.

Buffon, Georges-Louis Leclerc de, *Correspondance générale*, ed. H. Nadault de Buffon (reprint edition Geneva 1971).

– *Supplément à l'Histoire naturelle* (Paris 1774-1789).

– and Louis-Jean-Marie Daubenton, *Histoire naturelle, générale et particulière, avec la description du Cabinet du roi* (Paris 1749-1767).

Bulkeley, Charles, *The Nature and necessity of national reformation. A sermon, preached at Barbican, Feb. 6. 1756. Being the day appointed for a general fast* (London 1756).

– *A Sermon preached at the evening-lecture in the Old Jewry, on Sunday, November 30, 1755, on occasion of the dreadful earthquake at Lisbon, November 1, 1755* (London 1756).

Burillo, Pedro, *Descripción histórico-geográfica y chronológica del Reino de Portugal* (Zaragoza, Francisco Moreno, 1762).

Burnet, Thomas, *The Sacred theory of the earth* (reprint of the 1691 edition Carbondale, IL 1965).

– *The Sacred theory of the earth: containing an account of the original of the earth, and of all the general changes which it hat already undergone, or is to undergo, till the consummation of all things with a review of the theory, and of its proofs; especially in reference to Scripture and the author's defence of the work, from the exceptions of Mr. Warren & an ode to the author by Mr. Addison* (London 1719).

Burns, William E., *An Age of wonders: prodigies, politics and providence in England, 1657-1727* (Manchester 2002).

Burns, William J., Jeanne X. Kasperson, Roger Kasperson, Ortwin Renn, and Paul Slovic, 'The social amplification of risk: theoretical foundations and empirical applications', *Journal of social issues* (1992), p.137-60.

Byass, William, *Christ's instructions to his followers concerning the suffering Galileans; a sermon preach'd in the parish-churches of Storrington and Parham in Sussex, on Friday, February 6, 1756. Being the day appointed for a public fast* (London 1756).

Cabezas, Fray José, *Historia prodigiosa de la admirable aparición y milagrosos portentos de la imagen soberana de María Santísima Nuestra Señora de la Soterraña de Nieva, especialísima defensora de truenos, rayos, centellas y terremotos* (Mexico, Imp. del Nuevo Rezado, 1748).

Cantor, G. T. N., 'Revelation and the cyclical cosmos of John Hutchinson', in *Images of the earth: essays in the history of the environmental sciences*, ed. L. S. Jordanova and Roy S. Porter (Chalfont St Giles 1979), p.4-22.

Carpenter, Edward, *Thomas Sherlock, 1678-1761* (London 1936).

Carter, Elizabeth, *A Series of letters between Mrs. Elizabeth Carter and Miss Catherine Talbot from the year 1741 to 1770* (London 1809).

Caruth, Cathy, *Unclaimed experience: trauma, narrative, and history*, (Baltimore, MD 1996).

Carvajal y Lancáster, José de, *La Diplomacia de Fernando VI. Correspondencia entre Carvajal y Huéscar, 1746-1749*, ed. Didier Ozanam (Madrid 1975).

Cassirer, Ernst, *Heinrich von Kleist und die kantische Philosophie, Kantgesellschaft* 22 (1919). Reprinted in *Idee und Gestalt: Goethe, Schiller, Hölderlin, Kleist: Fünf Aufsätze* (Berlin 1921) p.153-200.

– *The Philosophy of the Enlightenment* (Boston, MA 1966; originally published in 1932).

Castillo Gómez, Antonio, '*No pasando por ello como gato sobre ascuas. Leer y anotar en la España del Siglo de Oro*', *Leituras. Revista da Biblioteca Nacional* 9-10, special issue *O livro antigo em Portugal e Espanha séculos XVI-XVIII* (2002), p.99-121.

Castillon d'Aspet, H., *Histoire du comté de Foix* (Toulouse 1852).

Caudle, James Joseph, 'Measures of allegiance: sermon culture and the creation of a public discourse of obedience and resistance in Georgian Britain, 1714-1760', Yale University PhD thesis, 1996.

Chagas, Manuel Joaquim Pinheiro, *O Terremoto de Lisboa* (Porto 1937).

Chaline, Claude, et Jocelyne Dubois-Maury, *La Ville et ses dangers: prévention et gestion des risques naturels, sociaux, technologiques* (Paris 1994).

Chandler, Samuel, *The Scripture account of the cause and intention of earthquakes, in a sermon preached at the Old-Jury, March 11, 1749-50, on occasion of the two shocks of an earthquake, the first on February 8, the other on March 8* (London 1750).

Chantal, Suzanne, *La Vie quotidienne au Portugal après le tremblement de terre de Lisbonne* (Paris 1962).

Chaussier and Adelon, 'Berryat (Jean)', in *Biographie universelle ancienne et moderne*, ed. J. Fr. Michaud (reprint edition Graz 1966-1970), iv.115.

Chester, D. K., 'The theodicy of natural disasters', *Scottish journal of theology* 51:4 (1998), p.485-505.

Church of Ireland, *A Form of prayer, to be used in all churches and chapels throughout the kingdom of Ireland, upon Friday the sixth of February next, being the day appointed by general proclamation for a general fast and humiliation* (Dublin 1756).

Clark, J. C. D., *English society, 1660-1832: religion, ideology, and politics during the Ancien Regime* (Cambridge 2000).

– 'Providence, predestination and progress: or, did the Enlightenment fail?', *Albion* 35:4 (2003), p.559-89.

Clark, Samuel, *A Sermon preached at Daventry, December 7, 1755, on occasion of the late earthquake at Lisbon, November 1, 1755* (London 1756).

Claydon, Tony, *William III and the godly revolution* (Cambridge 1996)

Clergyman at London, *A Letter from a clergyman at London to the remaining disconsolate inhabitants of Lisbon. Occasioned by the late dreadfull earthquake [...] To which is added, a faithful account of Mr. Archibald B—Wr's motives for quitting his office of Secretary to the Court of Inquisition* (London 1756).

Clergyman of Gloucestershire, *An Exhortation address'd particularly unto the people of London, occasion'd by the late proclamation, for a fast &c. on the 6th of February next* (London 1756).

Clergyman of the Church of England, *The Late uncommon and terrible shocks of our earth considered as alarming and awakening calls to a national repentance. Occasioned [...] by the last dreadful earthquake that was felt in and about the county of Northampton, on Sunday, September 30, 1750* (Northampton 1750).

Climenson, Emily J., *Elizabeth Montagu, the queen of the blue-stockings: her correspondence from 1720 to 1761* (New York 1906).

Clouser, Robin A., 'Heroism in Kleists "Das Erdbeben in Chile"', *Germanic review* 58 (1983), p.129-40.

Coeffeteau Nicolas, *Histoire romaine* (Paris 1646).

Conlon, Pierre Marie, *Le Siècle des Lumières* (Geneva 1990), vii.261-559 for years 1755 and 1756.

Conrady, Karl Otto, 'Kleists "Erdbeben in Chili": Ein Interpretationsversuch', *Germanisch-Romanische Monatsschrift*, NF 4 (1954), p.185-95.

– 'Das Moralische in Kleists Erzählungen: Ein Kapitel vom Dichter ohne Gesellschaft', in *Literatur und Gesellschaft vom 19. bis ins 20. Jahrhundert*, ed. Hans Joachim Schrimpf (Bonn 1963), p.56-82.

– 'Notizen über den Dichter ohne Gesellschaft', in *Kleist und die Gesellschaft: Eine Diskussion*, ed. Walter Müller-Seidel (Berlin 1965), p.67-74.

Corkhill, Alan, 'Kleists "Das Erdbeben in Chili" und Brechts *Der Augsburger Kreidekreis*: Ein Verlgeich de Motivik und des Erzählstils', *Wirkendes Wort* 31 (1981), p.152-57.

Correia, Hélia, *Lillias Fraser* (Lisbon 2001).

Correspondance littéraire du président Bouhier, ed. Henri Duranton (Saint-Etienne, Lyons 1974).

Correspondance littéraire, par Grimm, Diderot et al., ed. M. Tourneux (Paris 1879; Nendeln 1968), vol.iii, viii and ix.

Couto, D., *Historia de Lisboa* (Lisbon 2003).

Cox, James, *God's mercies slighted and neglected, a challenge to his justice. A sermon preached at Hampstead Chapel, March the 25th, and at Kensington, April the 1st, 1750* (London 1750).

Cradock, John, *A Sermon preached in the parish church of St. Paul, Covent Garden, on Friday, February 6, 1756, being* the day appointed by authority for a general fast (London 1756).

Crowley, Francis J., 'Pastor Bertrand and Voltaire's Lisbon', *Modern language notes* 74/5 (1959), p.430-33.

Curran, Andrew, *Sublime disorder: physical monstrosity in Diderot's universe*, *SVEC* 2001:01.

Daston, Lorraine, and Katharine Park, *Wonders and the order of nature, 1150-1750* (New York 1998).

Davidts, Hermann, *Die novellistische Kunst Heinrich von Kleists, Bonner Forschungen*, NS 5 (Berlin 1913).

Deconinck-Brossard, Françoise, 'Eighteenth-century sermons and the age', in *Crown and mitre: religion and society in northern Europe since the Reformation*, ed. W. M. Jacob and Nigel Yates (Woodbridge 1993), p.105-21.

Delaforce, A., *Art and patronage in eighteenth-century Portugal* (Cambridge 2002).

Delany, Mary Granville, *The Autobiography and correspondence of Mary Granville, Mrs. Delany*, ed. Lady Llanover (London 1861).

Del Barco, Antonio Jacobo, 'Carta del Doctor Barco satisfaciendo algunas preguntas curiosas sobre el terremoto del primero de noviembre de 1755', in Juan Enrique de Graef, *Discursos mercuriales* 3, 13 (21 April 1756), p.566-605.

Delumeau Jean, *Le Catholicisme de Luther à Voltaire* (Paris 1971).

Desplat Christian, 'Séismes dans les Pyrénées: contribution à l'histoire des phénomènes naturels (XVIᵉ-XVIIᵉ siècles)', *Revue géographique des Pyrénées et du sud-ouest* (1988), lix.99-110.

Deux Lettres de M. André, Maître perruquier, auteur de la fameuse tragédie du Tremblement de Terre de Lisbonne; l'une à M. F** [Fréron]; l'autre à M. P*** [Palissot], in *Le Censeur hebdomadaire* (Utrecht, Paris, Cuissart, 1760), iv.112-19. Ces lettres sont éditées dans *Voltairomania*, p.98-101.

Diderot, Denis, *Correspondance*, ed. Roth (Paris 1963).

– 'Encyclopédie', in *Encyclopédie, ou Dictionnaire raisonnée des sciences, des arts et des métiers, par une société de gens de lettres*, ed. Denis Diderot and Jean D'Alembert ([Paris] 1751-1772), v.635-48.

– *Pensées sur l'interprétation de la nature*, vol.ix of *Œuvres complètes*, ed. Jean Varloot et al. (Paris 1981), p.1-111.

Dioguardi, Gianfranco, *Un Aventurier à Naples au XVIIIᵉ siècle* (Castelnau-le-nez 1993).

Dirlinger, Helga, 'Das Buch der Natur. Der Einfluss der Physikotheologie auf das neuzeitliche Naturverständnis und die ästhetische Wahrnehmung von Wildnis', in *Individualisierung, Rationalisierung, Säkularisierung. Neue Wege der Religionsgeschichte*, ed. Michael Weinzierl (Vienna, Munich 1997), p.156-185.

Discours des causes et effects admirables des tremblemens de terre, contenant plusieurs raisons & opinions des philosophes. Avec un brief recueil des plus remarquables tremblemens depuis la création du monde jusques à present, extraict des plus signalez historiens par V. A. D. L. C. (Paris 1580).

A Dissertation upon earthquakes, their causes and consequences; [...] Together with a distinct account of, and some remarks upon, the shock of an earthquake, felt in the cities of London and Westminster, on Thursday, February 8, 1749-50 (London 1750).

Divine of the Church of England, *A Form of prayer, for the use of private families, and particular persons. Compos'd on occasion of the late dreadful earthquakes, and now publish'd pursuant to His Majesty's pious order, for a general fast, to be religiously kept on the 6ᵗʰ of February, 1756. To which is added, an hymn* (London 1756).

Dodd, William, *The Nature and necessity of fasting. Being the substance of two sermons preach'd in the parish churches of West Ham, Essex, and St. Olave's, Hart-street, London. By the Rev.*

William Dodd [...] *To which are added, two solemn acts of private devotion, proper for that day, from the pious Bishop Ken's Practice of divine love* (London 1756).

Doddridge, Philip, *Calendar of the correspondence of Philip Doddridge DD (1702-1751)*, ed. Geoffrey Nuttall (London 1979).

– *The Guilt and doom of Capernaum, seriously recommended to the consideration of the inhabitants of London: in a sermon reached at Salters-Hall, August 20, 1749. Published on occasion of the late alarm by the second shock of an earthquake, march 8, 1749-50* (London 1750).

Dodge, Nathanael, *God's voice in the earthquake, or, a serious admonition to a sinful world. A sermon* (York 1756).

Dodwell, William, *The Doctrine of a particular providence stated, confirmed, defended and applied. In two sermons preached before the University of Oxford, at St. Mary's, on Sunday April 20. 1760* (London 1760).

– *The Doctrine of the divine visitation by earthquakes illustrated, confirmed, and applied. In two sermons preached on the fast-day and the preceding Sunday* (London 1756).

Dumas, Alexandre, *Olympe de Clèves*, ed. Claude Schopp and Jacqueline Razgonnikoff (Paris 2000).

Dumersan, Théophile Marion, and Nicolas Brazier, *Maître André et Poinsinet, ou le Perruquier poète* (Paris 1805).

Dyer, Denys, 'The imagery in Kleist's *Penthesilea*', *Publications of the English Goethe society* 5 (1952), p.191-201.

– *The Stories of Kleist: a critical study* (New York 1977).

Dynes, Russell R., 'The dialogue between Voltaire and Rousseau on the Lisbon Earthquake: the emergence of a social science view', *International journal of mass emergencies and disasters* 18 (2000), p.97-115.

An Earnest Exhortation to repentance on occasion of the late [...] Earthquakes.

A sermon [on Luke xiii.5 ...] *on the General Fast-Day*. (London 1756).

Eccles, Samuel, *National sins the cause of national judgements: a sermon, on the account of the late infection among cattle, and the present sickness among the horses. Preached at St. Matthew's, Bethnal-Green, November 18, 1750* (London 1751).

Edwards, Thomas, *A Sermon, preached in the Parish church of St. Michael, in Coventry, on February 6, 1756* (Coventry 1756).

Eideker, Martina E., 'Unmittelbarkeit als Illusion: Heinrich von Kleists "Das Erdbeben in Chili"', *New German review* 10 (1994), p.61-76.

Eifert, Christiane, 'Das Erdbeben von Lissabon 1755. Zur Historizität einer Naturkatastrophe', *Historische Zeitschrift* 274 (2002), p.633-64.

Elias, N., *Power and civility: the civilizing process*, vol.ii (New York 1982).

Ellis, Christopher, and Pedro de Alba. 'Acceleration distribution and epicentral location of the 1755 "Cape Ann" earthquake from case histories of ground failure', *Seismological research letters*, 70:6 (1999), p.758-73.

Ellis, John M., 'Kleist's "Das Erdbeben in Chili"', In *Narration in the German Novelle*, (Cambridge 1974), p.46-76.

Enciso Recio, Luis Miguel, *La Gaceta de Madrid y el Mercurio Histórico Político, 1756-1781* (Valladolid 1957).

English, John C., 'John Hutchinson's critique of Newtonian heterodoxy', *Church history* 68:3 (1999), p.581-97.

Ermatinger, Emil, *Das dichterische Kunstwerk* (Leipzig 1921).

Escalante, Fernando, 'Voltaire mira el terremoto de Lisboa (1)', *Cuadernos hispanoamericanos* 600 (2000), p.69-82.

– 'Voltaire mira el terremoto de Lisboa (2)', *Cuadernos hispanoamericanos* 601-02 (2000), p.139-52.

'Essai sur les tremblemens de terre', *Mercure de France* (mai 1756).

Ettinghausen, Henry, 'Hacia una tipología de la prensa española del siglo XVII: de *hard news* a *soft porn'*, in *Studia Aurea*, ed. I. Arellano, M. C. Pinillos, F. Serralta, M. Vitse (Navarra 1996), p.51-66.

– 'Política y prensa 'popular' en la España del siglo XVII', *Anthropos* 166-67, special issue *Literatura popular*, ed. M. C. García de Enterría (1995), p.86-91.

Eyre, John, *Religion, a nation's safety. A sermon preached at Epsom, on Sunday, February 8, 1756* (London 1756).

Falkenfeld, Hellmuth, 'Kant und Kleist', *Logos* 8 (1919-1920), p.303-19.

A False prophet detected: being a particular account of the apprehending John Misavan, a trooper in Lord Delawar's troop of Horse Guards, who villainously pretended to prophecy, that there would be another shock of an earthquake, on Thursday, the 5th day of April [...] With his whole examination before [...] Justice Fielding (London 1750).

Fara, Patricia 'Marginalized practices', in *The Cambridge history of science*, vol.iv: *Eighteenth-century science*, ed. Roy Porter (Cambridge, 2003), p.485-507.

Faucou, Lucien, *L'Assommoir du XVIIIe siècle, Le Vuidangeur sensible* (Paris 1880).

Favre, Robert, *La Mort dans la littérature et la pensée française au siècle des Lumières* (Lyon 1978).

Feldman, Theodore S., 'Late Enlightenment meteorology', in *The Quantifying spirit in the eighteenth century* (Berkeley, CA 1990), p.143-77

Feijoo, Fray Benito, *Copia de carta escrita por el Ilmo y Rmo P. Mro. Fr. Feijoo a cierto caballero de la ciudad de Sevilla en que apunta algunas noticias pertenecientes a los terremotos* (Seville, José Navarro y Armijo, 1756).

– *Nuevo Systhema sobre la causa physica de los terremotos, explicado por los phenómenos eléctricos y adaptado al que padeció España en el primero de noviembre de 1755. Su autor el Ilmo y Rmo Sr. D. Fr. Benito Feijoo. Dedicado a la Muy erudita, Regia y esclarecida Academia*

Portopolitana por D. Juan Luis Roche (Puerto de Santa María, Casa Real de las Cadenas, 1756).

– *El Terremoto y su uso. Dictamen del Rmo P. M. Fr. Feijoo explorado por el Licenciado Juan de Zúñiga* (Toledo, Francisco Martín, 1756).

Feyel, Gilles, 'La diffusion des gazettes étrangères en France et la révolution postale des années 1750', in *Les Gazettes européennes de langue française*, ed. H. Duranton, C. Labrosse and P. Rétat (Saint-Etienne 1992), p.81-98.

Figueredo y Victoria, Francisco José, *Pastoral letter, exorting penitence, sent by Don Francisco Joseph de Figueredo, y Victoria, the Archbishop of this Holy Metropolitan Church, to the clergy, in the city of Guatemala, and to the people of his diocese, in connection with the earthquake that had such a devastating effect on the City of Lisbon, in Portugal, and on other parts of Europe and the Coasts of Africa last year on 1 November 1755* (Guatemala, Joachim de Arévalo, 1756).

Fischer, Bernd, 'Fatum und Idee: Zu Kleists "Erdbeben in Chili"', *Deutsche Vierteljahrsschrift für Literatur und Geistesgeschichte* 58 (1984), p.414-27.

Fischer, Ernst, 'Heinrich von Kleist', *Sinn und Form* 13 (1961), p.759-844.

Fischer, Ottokar, 'Mimische Studien zu Heinrich von Kleist' *Euphorion* 15 (1908), p.488-510, 716-25; *Euphorion* 16 (1909), p.62-92, 412-25, 747-72.

Fitschen, Irmela, 'Antithetische Züge in Kleists Erzählung "Das Erdbeben in Chili"', *Acta Germanica* 8 (1973), p.43-58.

Flourens, Pierre, *Des manuscrits de Buffon avec des fac-simile de Buffon et de ses collaborateurs* (Paris 1860).

Fludger, John, *The Judgments of God considered. In a sermon preached in the parish church of Putney, December 7, 1755; occasioned by the late earthquakes in Spain and Portugal* (London 1755).

Fóios, Joaquim de, and Miguel Rodrigues, *Oitavas ao terremoto, e mais calamidades que padeceo, a cidade de Lisboa, no primeiro de Novembro de 1755 por Nicilao Mendo Osório*, (Lisbon, Of. de Miguel Rodrigues, 1756).

Fombuena Filpo, Vicente, 'El terremoto de Lisboa: un tema de reflexión para el pensamiento ilustrado', *Espacio y tiempo* 9 (1995), p.9-22.

Force, James E. 'Hume and the relation of science to religion among certain members of the Royal Society', *Journal of the history of ideas* (1984), p.519-26.

Fothergill, George, *The Proper improvement of divine judgments. A sermon preached before the Mayor and Corporation, at St. Martin's in Oxford, on Friday, February 6, 1756* (Oxford 1756).

Foucault, Michel, *Les Mots et les choses* (Paris 1966).

– *The Order of things: an archaeology of the human sciences* (New York 1970). Translation of *Les Mots et les choses*.

Fountayne, John, *A Sermon, preached in the cathedral church of York, on Friday the 6th of February, 1756; being the day appointed for a general fast* (York 1756).

Foxcroft, Thomas, *The Earthquake a divine visitation. A sermon* [on Is. xxix.6] (Boston, MA 1756).

França, José-Augusto, *Lisboa Pombalina e o Iluminismo* (Lisbon 1977).

– *Lisbon Pombalina e o Ilumimismo* (Lisbon 1983).

– *A Reconstrução de Lisboa e a Arquitectura Pombalina* (Lisbon 1989).

– *Une Ville des Lumières, la Lisbonne de Pombal* (Paris 1965).

Francis, D., *Portugal 1715-1808* (London 1984).

Fréron, Elie-Catherine, *L'Année littéraire* (Paris 1754-1776).

Fricke, Gerhard, *Gefühl und Schicksal bei Heinrich von Kleist* (Berlin 1929).

Fries, Albert, *Stilistische und vergleichende Forschungen zu Heinrich von Kleist mit Proben angewandter Ästhetik, Berliner Beiträge zur germanischen und romanischen Philologie* 30 (1906).

Friess, Hans Jacob, *Schriftmaeßige Anweisung, wie man sich foerchterliche Gerichte Gottes, die ueber andere Menschen ergehen, zu seinem Heyl zu Nutz machen solle. In einer Predigt über Luc. XIII.v.4.5. vorgetragen, und auf instaendiges Begehren zum Druck uebergeben* (Zurich 1756).

Frisinger, H. Howard, *The History of meteorology: to 1800* (Boston, MA 1983).

Gambold, John, *The Reasonableness and extent of religious reverence: a sermon preached at the Brethren's Chapel in Fetter-Lane, on the afternoon of the fast-day, Feb. 6, 1756* (London 1756).

García Colorado, Francisco, *La Voz de Dios oída en el terremoto acaecido el día primero de Noviembre* (Madrid, Francisco Javier García, 1755).

Gargett, Graham, *Voltaire and protestantism* (Oxford 1980).

Garrett, Almeida, *Sobrinha do Marquez* (Lisbon 1848).

Gascoigne, John, 'Ideas of nature: natural philosophy', in *The Cambridge history of science*, vol.iv: *Eighteenth-century science*, p.285-304.

Gausewitz, W, 'Kleists "Erdbeben"', *Monatshefte* 55 (1963), p.188-94.

Gay, Peter, *The Enlightenment: an interpretation, the rise of modern paganism* (New York 1967).

A Genuine letter to Mr. Joseph Fowke, from his brother near Lisborn, dated November 1755. In which is given a very minute and striking description of the late earthquake (London [1755])

Geyer, Carl-Friedrich, 'Das Jahrhundert der Theodizee', *Kant-Studien* 4 (1982), p.393-405.

Gibbons, Thomas, *A Sermon preached at Haberdashers-Hall, November 30th, on occasion of the tremendous earthquake at Lisbon, November 1, 1755* (London 1756).

Gilbert, Robert, *The Terms of national happiness stated and recommended. A sermon delivered at Northampton, Feb. the 6th M.DCC.LVI* (London 1756).

Gittins, Daniel, *A Serious and earnest address to all orders and degrees of men amongst us. Being a sermon preached on occasion of the late general fast, February 6th, at the churches of South-Stoke and Leominster. By Daniel Gittins, L. L. B.* (London 1756).

Glendinning, Nigel, 'El padre Feijoo ante el terremoto de Lisboa', *Cuadernos de la Cátedra Feijoo* 18:2 (1966), p.353-65.

God's wrath made manifest. Being a mournful copy of verses on the late dreadful earthquake at Lisbon (London 1750)

Godwin, Charles, 'The terrors of the thunderstorm: medieval popular cosmology and methodist revivalism', *Methodist history* (2001), p.99-107.

Goldammer, Peter, 'Kleist und Goethe', *Weimarer Beiträge* 23:9 (1977), p.25-44.

Goldberg, Ana Maria, and Isabel Alçada, *O Dia do terramoto* (Lisbon 1989).

Goldberg, Rita, 'Voltaire, Rousseau, and the Lisbon earthquake,' *Eighteenth-century life* 13.2 (1989), p.1-20.

Golinski, Jan, 'Barometers of change: meteorological instruments as machines of Enlightenment', in *The Sciences in enlightened Europe*, ed. William Clark, Jan Golinski and Simon Schaffer (Chicago, IL 1999), p.69-93.

Gómez Urdáñez, José Luis, *Fernando VI* (Madrid 2001).

– *El proyecto reformista de Ensenada* (Lérida 1996).

– and Diego Téllez Alarcia, '1759. El "Año sin rey y con rey": la naturaleza del poder al descubierto', in *El Poder en Europa y América: Mitos, tópicos y realidades*, ed. E. García Fernández (Bilbao 2001), p.95-109.

González, Juan, *Nueva Chorographica descripcion de todas las provincias, villas, obispados, arzobispados, puertos, fortalezas, y considerables lugares del Reyno de Portugal [...] con los principales rios, bahías, mares, montañas, llanuras, sierras, y collados, sobre que estàn situadas: obra utilissima, para la inteligencia de la historia deste Reyno, y politico systema presente* (Madrid, Joseph Padrino, 1762).

Goudar, Ange, *Profecía política verificada en lo que está sucediendo a los portugueses por su ciega afición a los ingleses. Hecha luego después del terremoto del año de 1755*, translated by Bernardo Iriarte and Nicolás de Azara (Madrid, Imp. de la Gaceta, 1762).

– *Profecía política, verificada no que está succedendo aos Portuguezes pela sua céga affeicão aos Inglezes. Escrita depois do terremoto do anno 1755 e publicada por ordem superior no anno de 1762, em Madrid, traduzida do hespanhol* (Lisbon, Typografia Rollandiana, 1808).

– *Relation historique du tremblement de terre survenu à Lisbonne le premier Noviembre 1755 avec un detail contenant la perte en hommes, eglises, palais, couvens, maisons, meubles, marchandises, diamans, etc. Precedée d'un Discours politique sur les avantages que les portugais pourroient retirer de leur malheur et dans lequel on développe les moyens que l'Angleterre avoit mis on usage pour ruiner le Portugal* (The Hague, Philantrope, 1756).

Gould, Peter, 'Lisbon 1755: Enlightenment, catastrophe, and communication', in *Geography and Enlightenment*, ed. David. N. Livingstone and Charles W. J. Withers (Chicago, IL, London 1999), p.399-413.

Graham, Ilse, *Heinrich von Kleist: word into flesh, a poet's quest for the symbol* (Berlin 1977).

Graham, Robert, *The Power of God over the constitution of nature. A sermon preached on the general fast, February 6, 1756* (London 1756).

Grathoff, Dirk, 'Die Erdbeben in Chili und Lissabon', in *Kleist: Geschichte, Politik, Sprache: Aufsätze zu Leben und Werk Heinrich von Kleists* (Opladen 1999), p.96-111.

Green, Richard, *The Works of John and Charles Wesley. A bibliography: containing an exact account of all the publications issued by the brothers Wesley arranged in chronological order, with a list of the early editions, and descriptive and illustrative notes* (London 1896).

Gregory, Jeremy, 'Christianity and culture: religion, the arts and sciences in England, 1660-1800', in *Culture and society in Britain, 1660-1800*, ed. Jeremy Black (Manchester 1997), p.102-123.

Greiner, Bernhard, *Eine Art Wahnsinn: Dichtung im Horizont Kants. Studien zu Goethe und Kleist* (Berlin 1994).

– 'Kant und Kleist: Die Krisis erhabener Interpretation des Zufalls in der Kunst ("Das Erdbeben in Chili")', in *Kontingenz und Ordo: Selbstbegründung des Erzählens in der Neuzeit*, ed. Bernard Greiner and Maria Moog-Grünewalt (Heidelberg 2000), p.177-89.

– *Kleists Dramen und Erzählungen* (Tübingen 2000).

Grellet-Dumazeau André, *La Société bordelaise sous Louis XV et le salon de madame Duplessy* (Bordeaux 1897).

Grigg, J., *The Voice of danger, the voice of God. A sermon preached at St. Albans, and at Box-Lane, chiefly with a view to the apprehended invasion* (London 1756).

Groh, Ruth, and Dieter Groh, 'Religiöse Wurzeln der ökologischen Krise. Naturteleologie und Geschichtsoptimismus in der frühen Neuzeit', in *Weltbild und Naturaneignung. Zur Kulturgeschichte der Natur*, ed. Ruth Groh and Dieter Groh (Frankfurt 1996), p.11-91.

Guedes, Fernando, *O Livro e a Leitura em Portugal* (Lisbon 1987).

Guéneau de Montbeillard, Philibert, 'Etendue', in *Encyclopédie, ou Dictionnaire raisonnée des sciences, des arts et des métiers, par une société de gens de lettres*, ed. Denis Diderot and Jean D'Alembert ([Paris] 1751-1772), vi.43-45.

– letters and unpublished papers, fonds Guéneau de Montbeillard, Bibliothèque municipale, Semur-en-Auxois, France; Bibliothèque centrale du Muséum national d'histoire naturelle, Paris.

– 'Liste chronologique des éruptions de volcans, des tremblements de terre, de quelques faits météorologiques, des comètes, des maladies pestilentielles, des éclipses les plus remarquables jusqu'en 1760', in *Collection académique composée des mémoires, actes ou journaux des plus célèbres académies et sociétés littéraires de l'Europe* (Paris 1761), vi.450-700.

Guéneau de Montbeillard, Philibert, et al., ed., *Collection académique composée des mémoires, actes, ou journaux des plus célèbres académies et sociétés littéraires étrangères, des extraits des meilleurs ouvrages périodiques, des traités particuliers, et des pièces fugitives les plus rares; concernant l'histoire naturelle et la botanique, la physique expérimentale et la chimie, la médecine et l'anatomie, traduits en français, et mis en ordre par une société de gens de lettres* (Dijon and Paris 1755-1779).

Guenther, Beatrice Matina, *The Poetics of death: the short prose of Kleist and Balzac* (Albany, NY 1996).

Guerlac, Henry, and Margaret C. Jacob, 'Bentley, Newton, and providence (the Boyle lectures once more)', *Journal of the history of ideas* 30:3 (1969), p.307-18.

Gundolf, Friedrich, *Heinrich von Kleist* (Berlin 1922).

Günther, Horst, *Das Erdbeben von Lissabon erschüttert die Meinungen und setzt das Denken in Bewegung* (Berlin 1994).

Habermas, Jürgen, *The Structural transformation of the public sphere*, translated by Thomas Burger and Frederick Lawrence (Cambridge, MA 1989).

Hales, Stephen, *Some considerations on the causes of earthquakes. Which were read before the Royal society, April 5, 1750* (London 1750).

Hall, Clifton D., 'Kleist, catholicism, and the Catholic Church', *Monatshefte* 59 (1967), p.217-26.

Haller, Albrecht von, *Briefe ueber einige Einwuerfe nochlebender Freygeister wieder die Offenbarung* (Bern 1775-1776).

– 'Über den Ursprung des Übels', in *Versuch Schweizerischer Gedichte* vol.ii (Vienna 1793), p.1-49.

– and Charles Bonnet, *The Correspondence between Albrecht von Haller and Charles Bonnet*, ed. Otto Sonntag (Bern, Stuttgart, Vienna 1983).

Hallifax, James, *A Sermon preach'd in St. John's chapel in the parish of St. Andrew, Holborn, on Sunday February 8, 1756, being the Sunday after the day appointed by proclamation for a general fast and humiliation, on account of the dreadful earthquake at Lisbon* (London 1756).

Hancock, David Boyd, *William Stukeley: science, religion, and archaeology in eighteenth-century England* (Woodbridge 2002).

Harding, Robert, *Reflections on the late extraordinary events of Providence, and the proper influence they ought to have on Man. A sermon* [on Ps. xviii.8] *occasioned by the late publick fast* (London 1756).

Harris, Bob, *Politics and the nation: Britain in the mid-eighteenth century* (Oxford 2002).

Harris, Michael, *London newspapers in the age of Walpole: a study in the origins of the modern English press* (London 1987).

Harrison, Peter, 'Newtonian science, miracles, and the laws of nature', *Journal of the history of ideas* 56:4 (1995), p.531-53.

Hartley, Thomas, *God's controversy with the nations. Addressed to the rulers of Christendom* (London 1756).

[Hastings, Thomas], *The Military prophet's apology* (London 1750).

[–], *A Military prophet: or a flight from Providence. Address'd to the foolish and guilty, who timidly withdrew themselves on the alarm of another earthquake, April 1750* (London 1750).

Hauc, Jean-Claude, *Ange Goudar: un aventurier des lumières* (Paris 2004).

Havens, George R., 'Voltaire's pessimistic revision of the conclusion of his *Poème sur le désastre de Lisbonne*', *Modern language notes* 44:8 (1929), p.489-92.

Hazard, Paul, *European thought in the eighteenth century: from Montesquieu to Lessing* (Cleveland, OH, New York 1963; originally published 1946).

– 'Le problème du mal dans la conscience européenne du dix-huitième siècle', *Romanic review* (1941), p.147-70.

Hazeland, William, *The Conclusions of atheists and superstitious persons from public calamities examined, in a sermon, preached on the 6th of February, 1756* (London 1756).

Heilbron John Lewis, *Electricity in the 17th and 18th centuries: a study of early modern physics* (Berkeley, CA 1979).

Heimann, P. M., 'Voluntarism and immanence: conceptions of nature in eighteenth-century thought', *Journal of the history of ideas* 39:2 (1978), p.271-83.

Helbling, Robert, *The Major works of Heinrich von Kleist* (New York 1975).

Hellegouarc'h, Jacqueline, 'Désastre de Lisbonne (novembre 1755 – mars 1756)', in 'De la cour au jardin (1750-1759)', *Voltaire en son temps*, ed. René Pomeau (Paris, Oxford [1985-1994] 1995), i.816-34.

Heller, Erich, 'The dismantling of a marionette theatre: psychology and the misinterpretation of literature', *Critical inquiry* 4 (1978), p.417-32.

Herrath, Saskia, 'Zurück zum Ursprung oder das kultivierte Paradies: Voltaires *Candide* und Kleists "Erdbeben in Chili"', in *Kleine Lauben, Arcadien und Schnabelewopski: Festschrift für Klaus Jeziorkowski*, ed. Ingo Wintermayer (Würzburg 1995), p.27-39.

Herring, Thomas, *Letters from the Late Most Reverend Dr. Thomas Herring, Lord Archbishop of Canterbury, to William Duncombe, Esq., Deceased, from the Year 1728 to 1757. With Notes and an Appendix* (London 1777).

Herzog, Wilhelm, *Heinrich von Kleist: sein Leben und sein Werk* (Munich 1914).

The History and philosophy of earthquakes, collected from the best writers on the subject by a member of the Royal Academy of Berlin with a particular account of the great one of November, the 1st 1755 in various parts of the globe (London 1757).

Hoffmeister, Johannes, 'Beitrag zur soganannten Kantkrise Heinrich von Kleists', *Deutsche Vierteljahreschrift für Literatur und Geistesgeschichte* 33 (1959), p.574-87.

Holmsten, Georg, *Voltaire* (Hamburg 2002).

Holz, Hans Heinz, *Macht und Ohnmacht der Sprache: Untersuchungen zum Sprachverständnis und Stil Heinrich von Kleists* (Frankfurt 1962).

Honest Briton, *A Directory for the due improvement of the approaching fast: or, an honest Briton's pathetick address to his countrymen, on the present fashionable vices, and the decay of true patriotism and pubick spirit* (London 1756).

Horne, George, *The Almighty glorified in judgment. A sermon preach'd before the University of Oxford, on Sunday, Febr. 15. 1756* (Oxford 1756).

Horn, Peter, 'Anarchie und Mobherrschaft in Kleists "Erdbeben in Chili"', *Acta Germanica* 7 (1972), p.77-96.

How, James, *A Sermon preached on occasion of the earthquake at Lisbon, in the kingdom of Portugal, and the present situation of affairs in Great Britain. Preach'd in the parish of Milton next Gravesend, the sixth of February, 1756* (London 1756).

Hughes, Robert, *Goya* (New York 2003).

Hull, Samuel, *The Fluctuating condition of human life, and the absolute necessity of a preparation for the eternal world, consider'd, in a sermon occasioned by the late shocks of earthquake, preached at Lorriners Hall, March 11, 1750* (London 1750).

Hume, David, *The Letters of David Hume*, ed. J. Y. T. Greig (Oxford 1969).

Hunter, Thomas, *An historical account of earthquakes, extracted from the most authentick historians [...] With many other particulars. And a sermon preached at Weverham, in Cheshire, on Friday the 6ᵗʰ of February last* (Liverpool 1756).

– *National wickedness the cause of national misery. A sermon preach'd at the parish church of Weverham in Cheshire: on Friday, the sixth of February* (Liverpool 1756).

Huot, Jean-Jacques Nicolas, 'Volcan', vol.v of *Encyclopédie méthodique: géographie-physique*, ed. Jean Baptiste Georges Marie Bory de Saint-Vincent et al. (Paris 1828), p.656-817.

Ingenious Gentleman, *The General theory and phaenomena of earthquakes and volcanoes: wherein the several systems of M. Amontons, Dr. Lister, M. de Buffon, Dr. Woodward and others are exhibited and considered, with remarks; in which the natural causes of these astonishing effects are assigned; To which are added, an historical account of the various appearances and effects [...] and a particular history of the Lisbon earthquake* (London 1756).

Ingram, Robert G., 'William Warburton, divine action, and enlightened christianity', in *Religious identities in Britain, 1660-1832*, ed. William Gibson and Robert G. Ingram (Aldershot, forthcoming).

Isnard, *Mémoires sur les tremblemens de terre, qui a remporté le prix de physique au jugement de l'Académie des sciences, belles-lettres et arts de Rouen, le 3 août 1757* (Paris 1758).

Jacob, Margaret C., 'Christianity and the Newtonian worldview', in *God and nature: historical essays on the encounter between Christianity and science*, ed. David C. Lindberg and Ronald L. Numbers (Berkeley, CA 1986), p.238-55.

– *The Cultural meanings of the scientific revolution* (Philadelphia, PA 1988).

– *Scientific culture and the making of the industrial west* (Oxford 1997).

Jacquemin, cultivateur à Aische en Refail: annotations pour les années 1755-1760, ed. E. Verhelst, 'Etude de géographie locale: Aische en Refail',

Bulletin de la Société royale de Belgique (1895), xix.548-49.

Jackson, Thomas, *The Life of the Rev. Charles Wesley, MA: some time student of Christ-Church, Oxford: containing a review of his poetry; sketches of the rise and progress of methodism; with notices of contemporary events and characters* (New York 1844).

Jankovic, Vladimir, *Reading the skies: a cultural history of English weather, 1650-1820* (Manchester 2000).

Jennings, Theodore, *Good news to the poor: John Wesley's evangelical economics* (Nashville, TN 1990).

Jessop, Arthur, and Ralph Ward, *Two Yorkshire diaries: the diary of Arthur Jessop and Ralph Ward's journal*, ed. C. E. Whiting (1952).

Johns, Alessa, ed., *Dreadful visitations, confronting natural catastrophe in the age of Enlightenment* (New York 1999).

Johnson, Richard L., 'Kleists "Erdbeben in Chili"', *Seminar* 11 (1975), p.33-45.

Jones, Thomas, *Repentance and reconciliation with God recommended and enforced, in two sermons, preached at the parish-church of St. Saviour, Southwark; on Sunday February the 1st and on Friday the 6th [...] with a serious and affectionate address to the inhabitants of the said parish* (London 1756).

Journal des savants (Paris 1665-1792).

Journal encyclopédique (Liège and Bouillon 1756-1794).

Jung, Georg, 'Dialogische Bilder in Kleists Verssprache', *Die Sammlung* 13 (1958), p.578-79.

Jung, Gustav, 'Der Erotiker Kleist', *Zeitschrift für Sexualwissenschaft und Sexualpolitik* (1925), p.208-13.

Kade, Richard, 'Heinrich von Kleist und seine Sprache', *Zeitschrift für den deutsch Unterricht* 2 (1888), p.193-208.

Kael, Pauline, 'No id', *The New Yorker* 25 (1976), p.67-8. (Review of Eric Rohmer's film, *Die Marquise von O*, 1975.)

Kafker, Frank A., and Serena Kafker, *The Encyclopedists as individuals: a biographical dictionary of the authors of the Encyclopédie, SVEC* 257 (1988).

Kant, Immanuel, 'Geschichte und Naturbeschreibung der merkwürdigen Vorfälle des Erdbebens, welches an dem Ende des 1755sten Jahres einen grossen Theil der Erde erschüttert hat', in *Kants Gesammelte Schriften* vol.i (Berlin 1910), p.456-58.

– 'Histoire et description des plus remarquables événements relatifs au tremblement de terre qui a secoué une grande partie de la terre à la fin de l'année 1755', translated by Jean-Paul Poirier, *Cahiers philosophiques* (1999), p.85-121.

– *Idée d'une histoire universelle d'un point de vue cosmopolite* (Paris 1985).

– 'On nature as a power', in *Critique of the power of judgment*, ed. Paul Guyer and translated by Paul Guyer and Eric Matthews (Cambridge 2000), p.261.

– *Sur l'insuccès de toutes les tentatives philosophiques en matière de théodicée*, in *Œuvres philosophiques* (Paris 1985), ii.1393-95.

Kaufmann, F. W., 'Kleist und Fichte', *Germanic review* 9 (1934), p.1-8.

Keene, Benjamin, *The Private correspondence of Sir Benjamin Keene*, ed. Richard Lodge (Cambridge 1933).

Keill, John, *An Examination of Dr. Burnet's theory of the earth, together with some remarks on Mr. Whiston's new theory of the earth* (London 1698).

Kendrick, Thomas Downing, *The Lisbon earthquake* (London 1956).

Kidgell, John, *A Discourse preach'd at Somerset-Chapel on Friday, February the 6th, 1756, being the day appointed for a general fast* (London 1756).

Kilner, James, *The Perpetual inter-agency of providence in all things. A sermon preached at the parish-church of Lexden in Essex, on the sixth of February, 1756 (being the day appointed for a general fast)* (London 1756).

King, Arnold, *A Sermon* [on Ps. cxxvii.2] *preached [...] on [...] the day appointed for a general fast* (London 1756).

Kircher, Hartmut, *Heinrich von Kleist: Interpretationen* (*Das Erdbeben in Chili, Die Marquise von O*) (Munich 1992).

Klein, Johannes, 'Heinrich von Kleist', in *Geschichte der deutschen Novelle von Goethe bis zur Gegenwart* (Wiesbaden 1954), p.49-70.

– 'Kleists "Erdbeben in Chili"', *Deutschunterricht* 8 (1956), p.5-11.

Kommerell, Max, 'Die Sprache und das Unaussprechliche: Eine Betrachtung über Heinrich von Kleist', in *Geist und Buchstabe der Dichtung: Goethe, Schiller, Kleist, Hölderlin* (Frankfurt 1956), p.243-317.

Konersman, Ralf, 'Das Versprechen der Wörter: Kleists erste und letzte Dichtung', *Text und Kritik* (Sonderband 1993), p.100-24.

Koopmann, Helmut, *Freiheitssonne und Revolutionsgewitter: Reflexe der Französischen Revolution in literarischen Deutschland zwischen 1789 und 1840*, (Tübingen 1989).

Korff, H. A., *Geist der Goethezeit* (Leipzig 1953), vol.iv.

Kozak, Jan, and Charles James, 'Historical depictions of the 1755 Lisbon earthquake' and 'Images of historical earthquakes: the Kozak collection', online at http://nisee.berkeley.edu.

Kozak, Jan, and Marie-Claude Thompson, *Historical earthquakes in Europe* (Zurich 1991).

Kraft, Helga W., *Erhörtes und Unerhörtes: Die Welt des Klanges bei Heinrich von Kleist* (Munich 1976).

Kratz, Guillermo, *El Tratado hispano-portugués de límites de 1750 y sus consecuencias* (Rome 1954).

Kronick, David A., *A History of scientific and technical periodicals: the origins and development of the scientific and technological press, 1665-1790* (New York 1962).

Kubrin, David, 'Newton and the cyclical cosmos: providence and the mechanical philosophy', *Journal of the history of ideas* 28:3 (1967), p.325-46.

Kuhn, Albert J., 'Glory of gravity: Hutchinson vs. Newton', *Journal of the history of ideas* 22:3 (1961), p.303-22.

Kühnemann, Eugen, 'Kleist und Kant', *Jahrbuch der Kleist Gesellschaft* 2 (1922), p.1-30.

Kunz, Erich., 'Die Gestaltung des tragischen Geschehens in Kleists "Erdbeben in Chili"', in *Gratulatio: Festschrift Christian Wegner*, ed. Maria Honeit and Matthias Wegner (Hamburg 1963), p.145-17.

Labourdette, Jean-François, *La Nation française à Lisbonne de 1669 à 1790: entre colbertisme et libéralisme* (Paris 1988).

Lambert, Jérôme, ed., *Les Tremblements de terre en France* (Orléans 1997).

Lavington, George, *A Sermon preached in the cathedral-church of Exeter* (London 1756).

Leblanc, Robert A., 'Les migrations acadiennes' in *Cahiers de géographie du Québec* 23:58 (1979), p.99-124.

Leconte, Louis, et Travault l'aîné, *Maître André, ou le Perruquier auteur tragique* (Paris 1805).

Lee, Henry, *God's summons after despised forbearance, enforced in a sermon on Amos iv.12, preached at St. Olave's, Southwark, February 8, 1756* (London 1756).

Le Franc de Pompignan, Jean-Jacques, 'Ode de M. Le Franc à M. Racine, sur la mort de son fils', *Mercure de France* (mai 1756), p.78-82.

– *Œuvres* (Paris, Nyon l'aîné, 1784).

– *Poésies sacrées de Monsieur L* F****, divisées en Quatre Livres, Et ornées de Figures en taille douce* (Paris, Chaubert, 1751).

– *Prométhée*, in *Aeschylus, Voltaire, and Le Franc de Pompignan's Prométhée*, ed. Theodore E. D. Braun and Gerald R. Culley, *SVEC* 160 (1976), p.137-226.

Leibniz, Wilhelm Gottfried, *Essais de théodicée*, ed. Jacques Jalabert (Paris 1962).

Leiter, Richard, 'Kleist's Kant crisis' (review of *An Abyss deep enough*, ed. and translated by Philip B. Miller,

New York 1982), *American scholar* 51 (1982) p.561-63.

Leland, John, *A Sermon preached at Eustace-Street, on February the 6th. 1756. Being the day appointed* [...] *for the general fast* (Dublin 1756)

Le Mari, 'Vers au grand Racine sur la mort du jeune Racine, arrive à Cadix en novembre 1755', *Mercure de France* (April 1756).

Lendaff, Susanne, 'Kleist und die beste aller Welten: "Das Erdbeben in Chile" esehen im Spiegel der philosophischen und literarischen Stellungnahmen zur Theodizee im 18. Jahrhundert', *Kleist Jahrbuch* (1986), p.125-49.

Letsome, Sampson, *The Preacher's assistant* vol.i: *A Series of the texts of all the sermons published since the restoration*, vol.ii: *An Historical register of all the authors* (London 1753).

Letters from a late eminent prelate to one of his friends (Kidderminster 1793).

'Lettres des frères Darrot', *Revue d'Auvergne* (1930), xxxiv.106-17.

Lettre sur l'impossibilité physique d'un tremblement de terre à Paris, ([n.p.] v.1755).

The Lisbon earthquake of 1755: some British eye-witness accounts, ed. J. Nozes (Lisbon 1987).

Lisbon in the Renaissance (Urbis Olisiponis Descriptio by Damião de Góis) translated by J. S. Ruth (New York 1996).

Lisbonne abîmée ou Idée de la destruction de cette fameuse ville ([n.p.] 1755).

Livermore, Harold Victor, *A New history of Portugal* (Cambridge 1976)

Löffler, Ulrich, *Lissabons Fall – Europas Schrecken. Die Deutung des Erdbebens von Lissabon im deutschsprachigen Protestantismus des 18. Jahrhunderts* (Berlin, New York 1999).

López de Amezua, Fernando, *Historia de los Phenómenos observados en el terremoto que sintió esta Península el día 1 de noviembre de 1755*, in Juan Galisteo, *Diario philosóphico, médito, chirúrgico. Colección de selectas observaciones y curiosos fragmentos sobre la Historia*

Natural, Physica y Medicina (Madrid, Antonio Pérez de Soto, 1757).

López, Pilar, Miguel Arranz, Carme Olivera, and Antoni Roca, 'Contribución al estudio del terremoto de Lisboa del 1 de noviembre de 1755: observaciones en Cataluña', in *Materials of CEC project review of historical seismicity in Europe*, ed. P. Albini and A. Moroni (Milan 1994).

López-Vidriero, María Luisa, *Los Libros de Francisco de Bruna en el Palacio del Rey* (Seville 1999).

Lorenz, Dagmar, 'Väter und Mütter in der Sozialstruktur von Kleists "Erdbeben in Chili"', *Etudes germaniques* 33 (1978), p.270-81.

Loveland, Jeff, *Rhetoric and natural history: Buffon in polemical and literary context*, SVEC 2001:03.

Lucas, R. S., 'Studies in Kleist II: "Das Erdbeben in Chili"', *Deutsche Vierteljahrsschrift für Literaturwissenschaft und Geistesgeschichte* 44 (1970), p.145-70.

Luis, A. B., *Sebastião José* (Lisbon 1984).

Lüsebrink, Hans-Jürgen, 'Le tremblement de terre de Lisbonne dans les périodiques français et allemands du XVIIIᵉ siècle', in *Gazettes d'information politique sous l'Ancien Régime* (Saint-Etienne 1999), p.301-11.

Luther, Bernhard, *Heinrich von Kleist: Kant und Wieland* (Biberach an der Riss 1933).

Luynes, Charles-Philippe de, *Mémoires du duc de Luynes sur la cour de Louis XV* (Paris 1864).

Licoppe, Christian, *La Formation de la pratique scientifique: le discours de l'expérience en France et en Angleterre (1630-1820)* (Paris 1996).

McClellan, James E., III, *Science reorganised: scientific societies in the eighteenth century* (New York 1985).

McGlathery, James M., *Desire's sway: the plays and stories of Heinrich von Kleist* (Detroit, MI 1983).

Malagrida, Gabriel, *Juízo da verdadeira causa do terremoto que padeceu a corte de*

Lisboa no primeiro de Novembro de 1755 (Lisbon, Of. de Manoel Soares, 1756).

Mallet, Robert, *Great Neapolitan earthquake of 1857* (London 1862).

Mann, Thomas, 'Heinrich von Kleist und seine Erzählungen', in *Gesammelte Werke in zwölf Bänden*, vol.ix: *Reden und Aufsätze* (Frankfurt 1960), p.823-42.

– *The Magic Mountain*, translated by John E. Woods (New York 1996).

– *Der Zauberberg*, ed. Michael Neumann (Frankfurt 2002).

Man of Business, *A Satirical review of the manifold falsehoods and absurdities hitherto publish'd concerning the earthquake. To which is annext, an authentic account of the late catastrophe at Lisbon* [...] *The whole interspersed with reflections* [...] *and a set of new characters drawn from the life* (London 1756).

'Marchand', article in *Biographie universelle, ancienne et moderne* (Paris 1820), xxvi.602.

'Marchand', article in *Dictionnaire des lettres françaises, le XVIIIe siècle*, ed. cardinal Grente (1960), ed. François Moureau (Paris 1995), p.814.

'Marchand', article in *Nouvelle Biographie générale* (Paris 1860), xxxiii.473.

Marchand, Jean-Henri, *Les Fruits de l'automne* (Amsterdam [Paris], vve Duchesne et Bastien, 1781).

– *Les Giboulées de l'hiver* (Geneva, Paris, J.-Fr. Bastien et Guillot, 1782).

– *Hylaire par un métaphysicien*, [parodie du *Bélisaire* de Marmontel], (Amsterdam [Paris] 1767).

– *Mon radotage et celui des autres, recueilli par un invalide retiré du monde pendant son carnaval* (Paris 1759).

– *Le Tremblement de terre de Lisbonne*, Département des Arts et du Spectacle of the Bibliothèque nationale de France, bibliothèque de l'Arsenal, Rondel ms 314.

Mariano Nipho, Francisco, *Descripción historica y geographica del reyno de Portugal, con la serie y panegyrico de todos sus Reyes: La población repartida por provincias, comarcas, corregimientos, intendencias, y oidorías, dando circunstanciado el vecindario, y situación de sus ciudades, villas y lugares, que con un índice geográfico, para mayor claridad extracto de varios Autores y particularmente del P. Luis Cayetano de Lima, clérigo reglar, etc* (Madrid, Gabriel Ramírez, 1762).

– *Explicación physica y moral de las causas, señales, diferencias y efectos de los terremotos: con una relación muy exacta de los mas formidables* [...] *que ha padecido la tierra desde el principio del mundo hasta el que se ha experimentado en España y Portugal el dia primero de noviembre de* [...] *1755* (Madrid, Herederos de Agustín de Gordejuela, 1756).

Martin, Angus, Vivienne G. Mylne, and Richard Frautschi, *Bibliographie du genre romanesque français 1751-1800* (London, Paris 1997).

Martínez Solares, José Manuel, *Los Efectos en España del terremoto de Lisboa de 1 de noviembre de 1755* (Madrid 2001).

– and A. López Arroyo, 'The great historical 1755 earthquake: effects and damage in Spain', *Journal of seismology* 8 (2004), p.275-94.

Martin, George M., 'The apparent ambiguity of Kleist's stories', *German life and letters* 31 (1978), p.144-57.

Mascareñas, Jerónimo, *Campaña de Portugal por la parte de Extremadura: el año de 1662* (Madrid, Imprenta de Fco Javier García, 1762).

Mason, Haydn, 'Voltaire and Elie Bertrand', in *De l'humanisme aux Lumières, Bayle et le protestantisme*, ed. Michelle Magdelaine, Maria-Cristina Pitassi, Ruth Whelan, and Antony McKenna (Oxford 1996), p.715-26.

– 'Voltaire's "sermon" against optimism: the *Poème sur le désastre de Lisbonne*', in *Enlightenment essays in memory of Robert Shackleton*, ed. Giles Barber and C. P. Courtney (Oxford 1988), p.189-203.

Mason, John, *The Christian's duty in a time of publick danger. A sermon preached at Cheshunt in the county of Hertford, February 6, 1756* (London 1756).

Mattéi, Jean-François, *La Barbarie intérieure: essai sur l'immonde moderne* (Paris 1999).

Mauduyt de La Varenne, Pierre-Jean-Claude, 'Discours préliminaire et plan du dictionnaire des insectes', in *Encyclopédie méthodique: insectes* (Paris 1789), i.i-cclxxxviii.

Maxwell, Kenneth, 'Pombal', in *Out of Ground Zero: case studies in urban reinvention*, ed. Joan Ockman (Munich, New York 2002), p.20-45.

– *Pombal: paradox of the Enlightenment* (Cambridge 1995).

Mayer, Hans, *Heinrich von Kleist: Der geschichtliche Augenblick* (Pfüllingen 1962).

Menant, Sylvain, *La Chute d'Icare* (Geneva 1981).

Merchant of Lisbon, *A Second letter from a merchant of Lisbon to his friend in England, on the late destruction of that city by an earthquake and fire* (London 1756).

Merchant resident there, *An Account of the late dreadful earthquake and fire, which destroyed the city of Lisbon* (London 1755).

Mercier, Louis-Sébastien, *L'An 2440, ou Rêve s'il en fut jamais*, ed. Christophe Cave and Christine Marcandier-Colard (Paris 1999).

Mercure de France (Paris 1724-1791).

Michell, John, *Conjectures concerning the cause, and observations upon the phaenomena, of earthquakes; particularly of that great earthquake of the first of November 1755, which proved so fatal to the city of Lisbon* (London 1760).

Millares Carlo, Agustín, *Ensayo de una bio-bibliografía de escritores naturales de las Islas Canarias* (Madrid, Tip. de Archivos, 1932).

Miller, Philip B, *An Abyss deep enough* (New York 1982).

Milner, John, *Ruin prevented by repentance, applied to civil societies [...] Occasioned by the late dreadful earthquake at Lisbon, and the apprehension of nearer threatening calamities* (London 1756).

Modern, R. E., 'Sobre "El terremoto en Chile" de Kleist', *Torre* 10 (1962), p.151-55.

Molina Cortón, Juan, *Reformismo y neutralidad. José de Carvajal y la diplomacia de la España Preilustrada* (Badajoz 2003).

Mommsen, Katharina, *Kleists Kampf mit Goethe* (Heidelberg 1974).

[Montagu, Edward Wortley], *A Dissertation upon earthquakes, their causes and consequences; upon, the shock of an earthquake, felt in the cites of London and Westminster, on Thursday, February 8, 1749-50* (London 1750).

– *A Philosophical discourse upon earthquakes, their causes and consequences; comprehending an explanation of the nature of subterraneous vapours, their amazing force, and the manner in which they operate [...] to which is prefixed a preliminary dissertation, in which is attempted a rational explanation of the rise, progress [...] on Saturday, November 1, 1755* (London 1755).

Montagu, Elizabeth, *Elizabeth Montagu, the queen of the blue stockings: her correspondence from 1720 to 1761*, ed. J. Climenson (London 1906).

Montandon, Frédéric, 'Les séismes de forte intensité en Suisse', *Revue pour l'étude des calamités*, (1942-1943), v-vi.9-10.

Moreira de Mendonça, J. J., *História universal de terramoto* (Lisbon 1758).

Mornet, Daniel, *Les Sciences de la nature en France, au XVIIIᵉ siècle* (reprint edition New York 1971).

Moss, Charles, *A Sermon preached at the parish church of St. James, Westminster, on Friday, February 6, 1756 being the day appointed by His Majesty for a general fast, on occasion of the late earthquakes, and the present situation of public affairs* (London 1756).

Moucha, Pamela, 'Verspätete Gegengabe: Gabenlogik und Katastrophenbewältigung in Kleists "Erdbeben in Chili"', *Kleist Jahrbuch* (2000), p.61-88.

Moureau, François, 'La plume et le plomb', in *De bonne main: la communi-*

cation manuscrite au XVIIIe siècle, ed. François Moureau (Paris, Oxford 1993), p.135-42.

Mourinho, Antonio María, *Invasão de Trás-os-Montes e das Beiras na guerra dos sete anos pelos exércitos bourbónicos, em 1762, através da correspondência oficial dos comandantes-chefes Marqués de Sarriá e Conde de Aranda* (Lisbon 1986).

Müller-Salget, Klaus, 'Das Prinzip der Doppeldeutigkeit in Kleists Erzählungen', *Zeitschrift für deutsche Philologie* 92 (1973), p.85-211.

Müller-Seidel, Walter, 'Kleist's Weg zur Dichtung', in *Die deutsche Romantik: Poetik, Formen, und Motive*, ed. Hans Steffen (Göttingen 1967).

– *Versehen und Erkennen: Eine Studie über Heinrich von Kleist* (Cologne, Graz 1967).

Muth, Ludwig, *Kleist und Kant: Versuch einer neuen Interpretation*, Kant Studien 68 (1954).

'Nadault (Jean)', in *Biographie universelle ancienne et moderne*, ed. J. Fr. Michaud (Graz 1966-1970), xxx.7-9.

Napthine, D., and W. A. Speck, 'Clergymen and conflict, 1660-1763', *Studies in church history* 20 (1983), p.231-51.

Nef, Ernst, 'Die Bedrohlichkeit des Zufalls in den Novellen H. v. Kleists', in *Der Zufall in der Erzählkunst* (Bern 1970), p.18-28.

Neiman, Susan, *Evil in modern thought: an alternative history of philosophy* (Princeton, NJ 2002).

– 'What's the problem of evil?', in *Rethinking evil: contemporary perspectives*, ed. Maria Pia Lara (Berkeley, CA 2001), p.27-45.

Newman, Thomas, *The Sin and shame of disregarding providences. A sermon preached at Crosby-Square, April 4, 1750. Occasioned by [...] an earthquake* (London 1750).

Nieto, Ishac, *A Sermon preached in the Jews Synagogue, on Friday, February 6, 1756; being the day appointed by authority for a general fast* (London 1756).

Nora, Pierre, 'Le retour de l'événement', in *Faire de l'histoire: nouveaux problèmes*, ed. Jacques Le Goff and Pierre Nora (Paris 1974), i.285-308.

Norwell, William, *A Sermon preached at the parish church of Wolsingham [...] on the 6th of February, 1756, being the day appointed by his Majesty for a general fast, on account of the dreadful earthquake at Lisbon, Nov. 1. 1755* (Newcastle 1756).

Oellers, Norbert, '"Das Erdbeben in Chili"', in *Kleists Erzählungen*, ed. Walter Hinderer (Stuttgart 1998), p.48-54.

Oeser, Erhard, 'Das Erdbeben von Lissabon im Spiegel der zeitgenössischen Philosophie', in *Elementare Gewalt. Kulturelle Bewältigung. Aspekte der Naturkatastrophe im 18. Jahrhundert*, ed. F. Eybl, H. Heppner and A. Kernbaumer (Vienna 1999), p.185-95.

Officer, Charles, and Jake Page, *Tales of the earth: paroxysms and perturbations of the blue planet* (New York 1993; reprinted Oxford 1994).

Ohmann, Fritz, 'Kleist und Kant', in *Festschrift für Berthold Litzmann zum 60. Geburtstag*, ed. Carl Enders (Bonn 1920), p.105-31.

Oldroyd, David R., *Thinking about the earth: a history of ideas in geology* (Cambridge, MA 1996).

Oliveira, Cavaleiro de, *Discours pathétique au sujet des calamités présentes arrivées en Portugal* (Coimbra 1922).

Oliveira Marques, *História de Portugal* (Lisbon 1985).

Oliveira, Vicente Carlos de, *Lisboa restaurada pelo grande* (Lisbon, Of. de Fernando José dos Santos, 1784).

Ortiz Gallardo de Villarroel, Isidoro Francisco, *Lecciones entretenidas y curiosas physico-astrológicas sobre la generación, causas y señales de los terremotos y especialmente de las causas, señales y varios efectos del sucedido en España en el día primero de noviembre del año passado de 1755* (Salamanca, Antonio José Villagordo, 1756).

Orton, Job, *Noah's faith and obedience to divine warnings and his preservation from the deluge, considered and improved. A sermon preached at Shrewsbury on Friday, February 6, 1756* [...] *To which is added a prose-translation of a poem, by Carlo Maria Maggi, on the same subject* (Salop 1756).

Ossar, M., 'Kleist's "Das Erdbeben in Chili" and "Die Marquise von O"', *Revue des langues vivantes* 34 (1968), p.151-69.

Outram, Dorinda, *The Enlightenment* (Cambridge 1995).

Pan, David, 'The aesthetic foundation of morality in "Das Erdbeben von Chile"', in *Kleists Erzählungen und Dramen*, ed. Paul Michael Lützeler and David Pan (Würzburg 2001), p.49-60.

Papillon, Fernand, 'Notice sur Guéneau de Montbeillard, naturaliste et philosophe de l'école de Leibniz', *Séances et travaux de l'Académie des sciences morales et politiques (Institut de France)* 28 (1872), p.235-50.

Le Parfait Ouvrage, ou Essai sur la coiffure (à Césarée et en France, chez tous les libraires qui vendent les bons livres, 1776).

Parnther, John, *A Sermon, preached in the parish churches of Wath and Pickhill, in Yorkshire, on Friday the 6th of February, 1756* (York 1756).

Pascal, Blaise, *Pensées*, in *Œuvres complètes* (Paris 1954).

Patrocinio admirable del glorioso patriarcha y perfectíssimo modelo del Estado Eclesiástico San Phelipe Neri, segundo thaumaturgo y especial avogado en tiempo de terremotos. Sácalo a la luz pública la devoción de sus hijos para excitar al Pueblo Sevillano acudan a su Patrocinio en semejantes calamidades (Seville, Imp. de los Recientes, 1755).

Peckard, Peter, *A Dissertation on Revelations, xi.13. And the same hour was there a great Earthquake, and the tenth part of the city fell, and in the earthquake were slain of men seven thousand. In* which is attempted to be shewn, that there is some reason to believe this prophecy is completed by the late earthquake (London 1756).

Pereira de Figuerido, Antonio, *Commentário Latino e Portuguez sobre o terramoto e incendio de Lisboa* (Lisbon 1756).

– *A Narrative of the earthquake and fire of Lisbon by Antony Pereria, of the Congregation of the Oratory, an eyewitness thereof* (London 1756).

Petit, Peter (vicar of Royston), *Natural occasions of terror considered as international warnings of providence: or an enquiry how far we, of this nation, may be concerned to attend to the late extraordinary and alarming events* (London 1756).

Pfenninger, Johann Caspar, *Das Erdbeben, ein Beweis der Heiligkeit, Gerechtigkeit, Weisheit und Macht des Grossen Gottes, Nach Anleitung der Worten des frommen Jobs Capitel ix:1-6. Bey Anlass des, Dienstags den 9. Christmonat 1755. Abends um halb 3. Uhren, sich zu Zuerich und dasiger Enden ereigneten Erdbebens, Dem Volk Gottes in einer Predigt Sonntags den 14. Christmonat dieses Jahrs vorgetragen* (Zurich 1756).

Philipp, Wolfgang, *Das Werden der Aufklärung in theologiegeschichtlicher Sicht* (Göttingen 1957).

Pickering, Roger, *An address to those who have either retired, or intend to leave the town, under the imaginary apprehension of the approaching shock of another earthquake: being the substance delivered on the last Lord's-day, the first of this instant April* (London 1750).

Pieper, Renate, *La Real Hacienda bajo Fernando VI y Carlos III, 1753-1788* (Madrid 1992).

Piggott, Stuart, *William Stukeley: an eighteenth-century antiquary* (Oxford 1950).

Pinnell, Peter, *A Sermon preach'd in the parish-church of Eltham in Kent, on Friday, February 6, 1756, being the day appointed by authority for a general fast* (London 1756).

Pitts, Joseph, *Turning to God, an effectual way of escaping threatened judgments. A sermon preach'd in New-Court, February 6, 1756* (London 1756).

Placanica, Augusto, *Il Filosofo e la catastrofe, un terremoto del Settecento* (Turin 1985).

Plagnol-Diéval, Marie-Emmanuelle, 'Merveilleux ou rationnel: *Les Veilles du château* de Mme de Genlis', in *Le Partage des savoirs XVIIIe-XIXe siècles*, ed. Lise Andries (Lyon 2003), p.151-62.

– *Le Théâtre de société: un autre théâtre?* (Paris 2003).

Pöder, Elfriede, *Interpretation zwischen Theorie und Praxis: Diskursanalyse und feministische Theorie: Eine Untersuchung am Beispiel zweier Interpretationen von Kleists "Erdbeben in Chili"* (Innsbruck 1994).

Poème sur le tremblement de terre de Constantinople (Amsterdam 1766).

A Poem on the earthquake at Lisbon (London 1755).

A Poem on the late earthquake at Lisbon. To which is added, thoughts in a churchyard (London 1755).

Pope, Alexander, *An Essay on man*, ed. Anthony Trott and Martin Axford (London 1966).

Porter, Roy, 'Creation and credence: the career and theories of the earth in Britain, 1660-1820', in *Natural order: historical studies in scientific culture*, ed. Barry Barnes and Steven Shapin (Beverly Hills, CA 1979), p.97-123.

– *The Creation of the modern world: the untold story of the British Enlightenment* (New York 2000).

– *The Making of geology: earth science in Britain, 1660-1815* (Cambridge 1977).

– 'The terraqueous globe', in G. S. Rousseau and Roy Porter, ed., *The Ferment of knowledge: studies in the historiography of eighteenth-century science* (Cambridge 1980), p.285-324.

Potot de Montbeillard, Bénigne-Elisabeth, 'Biographie de M. Guéneau de Montbeillard', in *Correspondance*

inédite de Buffon, ed. H. Nadault de Buffon (Paris 1860), i.335-41.

The Power of God over the constitution of nature: a sermon [on Is. xlviii.13] *preached on the General Fast, February 6, etc.* (London 1756).

Prellwitz, Gertrude, 'Heinrich von Kleist und Goethe,' *Jahrbuch der Goethe-Gesellschaft* 8 (1921), p.88-94.

O Premio da virtude ou terramoto de Lisboa em 1755: novela portuguesa, (Lisbon, Typ de L. C. da Cunha, 1850).

'The proclamation for a general fast [6 February 1756]' (London 1755).

Queirós, José Maria Eça de, *Cousin Basilio*, translated by Margaret Jull Costa, (Cambridge 2003).

– *O Primo Bazilio* (Lisbon 2001).

Quenet, Grégory, *La Naissance d'un risque: les tremblements de terre en France XVIIe-XVIIIe siècles* (à paraître).

– 'Les tremblements de terre en France aux 17e et 18e siècles: une histoire social du risque', *Traverse* 10 (2003), p.90.

Queniart, Jean, *Culture et société urbaines dans la France de l'ouest au XVIIIe siècle* (Paris 1978).

Quétant, François-Antoine, *Les Muses artisanes, ou l'auteur perruquier* (Paris n.d.), BnF, Ms Fr 9269.

Ramalho, Miguel Maurício, *Lisboa reedificada poema épico* (Lisbon, Régia Of. Typographica, 1780).

Rapin G., *Le Tableau des calamités, ou description exacte et fidèle de l'extinction de Lisbonne* ([n.p.] 1756), p.3-4.

Rappaport, Rhoda, 'Borrowed words: problems of vocabulary in eighteenth-century geology', *British journal for the history of science* 15 (1982), p.27-44.

– 'The earth sciences' in *The Cambridge history of science*, vol.iv: *Eighteenth-century science*, p.400-16.

– *When geologists were historians, 1665-1750* (Ithaca, NY 1997).

Rattenbury, J. Ernest, *The Evangelical doctrines of Charles Wesley's hymns* (London 1941).

Razón de entrar en Portugal las tropas españolas como amigas y sinrazón de recibirlas como enemigas. Reducido a las memorias presentadas de parte a parte (Madrid, Imp. de la Gaceta, 1762).

Rector, Martin, 'Johann Georg Zimmermanns Gedicht "Die Zerstörung von Lissabon" (1756)', in *Johann Georg Zimmermann-königlich grossbritannischer Leibarzt*, ed. H. P. Schramm, *Wolfenbüttler Forschungen* 82 (Wiesbaden 1998), p.83-92.

Reeves, Robert K., 'The Lisbon earthquake of 1755: confrontation between the church and the Enlightenment in Eighteenth Century Portugal', thesis online at http://www.dickinson.edu/~quallsk/thesis_reeves.doc.

Reflections physical and moral upon the [...] *uncommon phenomena in the air, water, or earth, which have happened from the Earthquake at Lima to the present time. In a series of* [...] *Letters from a Member of Parliament* (London 1756).

'Réflexions sur les causes des tremblemens de terre', *Journal de Trévoux* (décembre 1756), p.3012-16.

Reid, Harry Fielding, 'The Lisbon earthquake of November 1, 1755', *The Bulletin of the Seismological society of America*, 4:2 (1914), p.53-80.

Relación de los patronatos que tiene San Francisco de Borja en varios Reynos y Ciudades de la Christiandad contra los Terremotos, y beneficios que con dichos Patronatos recibieron sus habitantes: sacada de varios autores (Madrid, Imprenta de la viuda de Manuel Fernández, 1755).

Relation du terrible tremblement de terre qui vient d'arriver dans les îles Açores, dépendantes du royaume du Portugal. De Lisbonne, le 1er août 1757, Paris, 1757.

Relation du tremblement de terre arrivé à Lisbonne, et d'une ile submergée en Amérique le 1er novembre 1755 (Paris 1755).

Reske, Hermann, 'Die kleistische Sprache', *German quarterly* 36 (1963), p.219-35.

Rétat, P., ed., *L'Attentat de Damiens: discours sur l'événement au XVIIIe siècle* (Lyon 1979).

Reuss, Roland, '"Im Freien"? Kleists "Erdbeben in Chili": Zwischenbetrachtung "nach der ersten Haupterschütterung"', *Brandenburger Kleist-Blätter* 6 (1993), p.3-24.

Rhiel, Mary, *Re-viewing Kleist: the discursive construction of authorial subjectivity in west German Kleist films* (New York 1991).

Richards, Thomas, *National repentance urged from the prospect of national judgments. A sermon preach'd at the parish-church of All-Saints in Northampton, on February 6, 1756* (London 1756).

Ricœur, Paul, *Le Mal, labor et fides* (Paris 1996).

Ridley, Glocester, *God's threatnings against sinful nations exemplified, and improved. A sermon preached in the chapels of Romford and Poplar* [...] *April 1, and 8, 1750* (London 1750).

Ringleb, Heinrich, 'Heinrich von Kleist: das Ende der Idyllendichtung', *Jahrbuch der deutschen Schiller Gesellschaft* 7 (1963), p.313-51.

Ritzler, Paula, 'Zur Bedeutung des bildlichen Ausdrucks im Werke Heinrich von Kleists', *Trivium* 2 (1944), p.178-94.

Roberts, David, 'Kleists Kritik der Urteilskraft: Zum Erhabenen in "Das Erdbeben in Chili"', in *Heinrich von Kleist und die Aufklärung* (New York 2000), p.46-57.

Robinet Jean-Baptiste, *De la nature* (Amsterdam 1761).

Roche, Daniel, *Le Siècle des Lumières en province: académies et académiciens provinciaux, 1680-1789* (The Hague 1978).

Rodríguez de Campomanes, Pedro, *Noticia geográfica del Reino y Caminos de Portugal* (Madrid, Joachim Ibarra, 1762).

Rodríguez Sánchez de León, Ma. José, 'El terremoto lisboeta de 1755 en las relaciones de sucesos', in *Las Relaciones de sucesos en España*

(1500-1750), ed. M. C. García de Enterría, H. Ettinghausen, V. Infantes, and A. Redondo (Alcalá de Henares 1996), p.305-13.

Roger, Jacques, *Buffon: un philosophe au Jardin du roi* (Paris 1989).

Rohrer, Berthold, *Das Erdbeben von Lissabon in der französischen Literatur des achtzehnten Jahrhunderts* (Heidelberg 1933).

Romaine, William, *An Alarm to a careless world. A discourse occasioned by the late earthquakes, preached November 30, 1755* (London 1755).

Rondet Laurent-Etienne, *Supplément aux réflexions sur le désastre de Lisbonne* ([n.p.] 1757).

Rose, Craig, 'Providence, protestant union and godly reformation in the 1690s', *Transactions of the Royal Historical Society* (1993), p.151-69.

Roulet, Louis-Edouard, *Voltaire et les Bernois* (Neuchatel 1950).

Rousseau, George S., 'The London earthquake of 1750', *Cahiers d'histoire mondiale 11* (1968), p.436-51.

Rousseau, Jean-Jacques, *The collected writings of Rousseau*, ed. Roger D. Masters and Christopher Kelly (Hanover 1990).

– letter to Voltaire, 18 August 1756, in *Lettres philosophiques* (Paris 2003), p.94.

Samuel, Richard, 'Heinrich von Kleists Novellen', in *Deutsche Weltliteratur, Von Goethe bis Ingeborg Bachmann: Festgabe für J. Alan Pfeffer*, ed. Klaus W. Jonas (Tübingen 1972).

Sánchez-Blanco Parody, Francisco, *El Absolutismo y las Luces en el reinado de Carlos III* (Madrid 2002).

– *La Mentalidad ilustrada* (Madrid 1999).

San Cristóbal, Francisco, *Vida, martyrio y milagros del apóstol de Ascoli, el sr.. S.. Egmidio, especialísimo protector en los terremotos* (Seville 1756).

Sanides-Kohlrausch, Claudia, 'The Lisbon earthquake 1755: a discourse about the "nature" of Nature', in William Drees, ed., *Is nature ever evil?*

religion, science and value (London 2003), p.106-19.

San Juan, E., Jr., 'The structure of narrative fiction', *Saint Louis quarterly* 4 (1966), p.485-502.

Saraiva, António José, and Óscar Lopes, *História da literatura Portuguesa* (Porto 2000).

Saramago, José, *Memorial do convento* (Lisbon 1982).

Savile, Gertrude, *Secret comment: the diaries of Gertrude Savile, 1721-1757*, ed. Alan Savile (Kingsbridge 1997).

Schaffer, Simon, 'Natural philosophy and public spectacle in the eighteenth century', *History of science* (1983), p.1-43

Schechner, Sara, *Comets, popular culture, and the birth of modern cosmology* (Princeton, NJ 1997).

Schlagdenhauffen, Alfred, 'Kleist et Goethe', *Etudes germaniques* 16 (1961), p.321-34.

Schlüter, Gisela, 'Kleist und Marmontel: Nochmals zu Kleist und Frankreich', *Arcadia* 24 (1989), p.13-24.

Schneider, Helmut J., 'Die Blindheit der Bilder: Kleists Ursprungszenarien', in *Bildersturm und Bilderflut um 1800: Zur schwierigen Anschaulichkeit der Moderne*, ed. Ralf Simon and Thomas Wirtz (Bielefeld 2001), p.289-306.

Scholz, Ingeborg, *Heinrich von Kleist: "Über das Marionettentheater"; Das Käthchen von Heilbronn; "Das Erdbeben in Chili"; "Die Marquise von O": Interpretationen und methodisch didaktische Hinweise* (Hollfeld 1984).

Schouwtoneel der akelige en deerlyke verwoestingen, rampen, ongevallen en zonderlinge gebeurtenissen, Sedert den eersten November 1755 zo in Portugal, Spanje, Vrankryk, Italie, Zwitzerland, Duitschland, het Noorden, Engeland en de Nederlanden, als buiten Europa door de Aardbevingen, waterberoeringen Overstromingen en zeldzame Luchtverschynsels verwekt en voorgevallen (Utrecht 1756).

Schrader, Hans-Jürgen, 'Spuren Gottes in den Trümmern der Welt:

Zur Bedeutung biblischer Bilder in Kleists "Erdbeben'", *Kleist Jahrbuch* (1991), p.34-52.

Scott, Douglas F. S., 'Heinrich von Kleist's Kant crisis', *Modern language review* 42 (1947), p.474-84.

Secker, Thomas, *The Works of Thomas Secker* (London 1825).

Sekora, John, *Luxury: the concept in western thought, Eden to Smollett* (Baltimore, MD 1977).

Sem razão de entrarem em Portugal as Tropas Castelhanas como amigas, e razão de ferem recebidas como Inimigas: Manifesto reduzido as memorias presentadas de parte a parte (Lisbon, Offic. de Miguel Rodrigues, 1762).

A Serious and affectionate address to the cities of London and Westminster; occasioned by the late earthquake (London 1750).

Serjeantson, R. W., 'Testimony and proof in early-modern England', *Studies in history and philosophy of science* 30 (1999), p.195-236.

Seward, Thomas, *The Late dreadful earthquakes, no proofs of God's particular wrath against the Portuguese: a sermon* [on Luke xiii.4, 5] *preached Dec. 7, 1755* (London 1756).

Seyfart, Johann-Friedrich, *Allgemeine geschichte der erdbeben* (Frankfurt, Leipzig 1756).

Shapin, Steven, *A Social history of truth: civility and science in the seventeenth-century England* (Chicago, IL 1994).

– and Simon Schaffer, *Leviathan and the air-pump: Hobbes, Boyle, and the experimental life* (Princeton, NJ 1985).

Sherlock, Thomas, *A Letter from Lord Bishop of London, to the clergy and people of London and Westminster, on occasion of the late earthquake* (London 1750).

Shower, John, *Practical reflections on the earthquakes that have happened in Europe and America, but chiefly in the islands of Jamaica, England, Sicily, Malta, &c. With a particular historical account of them, and divers other earthquakes* (London 1750).

Silz, Walter, '"Das Erdbeben in Chili'", *Monatshefte* 53 (1961), p.210-38.

Smollett, Tobias, *The History of England* (Oxford 1827).

Smyth, Arthur, *A Sermon preached in Christ-church, Dublin, on Friday the 6th of February, 1756, being the day appointed for a general fast* (Dublin 1756).

Sommerville, C. John, *The Secularization of early modern England: from religious culture to religious faith* (New York 1992).

Spadafora, David, *The Idea of progress in eighteenth-century Britain* (London 1990).

Spälti, Jakob, *Interpretationen zu Heinrich von Kleists Verhältnis zur Sprache* (Bern, Frankfurt 1975).

Spengler, Joseph J., *French predecessors of Malthus* (Durham 1942).

Squire, Samuel, *A Speedy repentance the most effectual means to avert Gods judgements. A sermon preached at the parish church of St. Anne Westminster, February 6, 1756; being the day appointed for a general fast and humiliation* (London 1756).

Stallings, Robert, 'Disaster and the theory of social order' in *What is disaster? Perspectives on the question*, ed. E. L. Quarantelli (London 1998).

Stebbing, Henry, *A Discourse preparatory to the religious observance of the day of publick fasting and humiliation, appointed by authority, to be kept on Friday the sixth of February 1756* (London 1756).

– *A Sermon preached at Gray's Inn Chapel, on Friday, February 6, 1756. Being the day appointed by authority for a public fast* (London 1756).

Steiner, George, *Dans le château de Barbe-Bleue* (Paris 1973).

Steinhauer, Harry, 'Heinrich von Kleists "Das Erdbeben in Chile'", in *Goethezeit: Studien zur Erkenntnis und Rezeption Goethes und seiner Zeitgenossen: Festschrift Stuart Atkins* (Munich 1981), p.281-300.

Stillingfleet, Benjamin, *Some thoughts occasioned by the late earthquakes. A poem* (London 1750).

Stockum, Theodorus C. van, 'Heinrich von Kleist und die Kant-Krise', in *Neophilologus* 39 (1955), p.65-66.

Streller, Siegfried, *Das dramatische Werk Heinrich von Kleists* (Berlin 1966).

Stukeley, William, *The Philosophy of earthquakes, natural and religious, or an inquiry into their cause, and their purpose* (London 1750).

'Sur un tremblement de terre, & sur des effets singuliers de la foudre', in *Histoire et Mémoires de l'Académie des sciences, inscriptions et belles-lettres de Toulouse* (Toulouse 1784), ii.15-9.

Taylor, Charles, *Sources of the self: the making of the modern identity* (Cambridge 1989).

Taylor, John, *The Inefficacy of the greatest national strength to secure from the divine judgments* (London 1756).

Taylor, Kenneth L., 'Earth and heaven, 1750-1800: Enlightenment ideas about the relevance to geology of extraterrestrial operations and events', *Earth sciences history* 17 (1998), p.84-91.

– 'Nicolas Desmarest and geology in the eighteenth century', in *Toward a history of geology*, ed. Cecil J. Schneer (Cambridge, MA 1969), p.339-56.

– 'Volcanoes as accidents: how "natural" were volcanoes to eighteenth-century naturalists?' in *Volcanoes and history*, ed. Nicoletta Morello (Genoa 1998), p.595-618.

Téllez Alarcia, Diego, 'El caballero D. Ricardo Wall y la conspiración antiensenadista', in *Ministros de Fernando VI*, ed. José Miguel Delgado Barrado and José Luis Gómez Urdáñez (Córdoba 2002).

– 'Guerra y regalismo a comienzos del reinado de Carlos III. El final del ministerio Wall', *Hispania* 209 (2001), p.1051-90.

– 'El joven Campomanes y el ministro Wall (1754-63)', in *Campomanes doscientos años después*, ed. María Dolores Mateos Dorado (Oviedo 2003), p.417-31.

– 'D. Ricardo Wall, el ministro olvidado', online at http://www.tiemposmodernos.org/ricardowall.

Terrick, Richard, *A Sermon preached before the Honourable House of Commons, at St. Margaret's, Westminster, on Friday, February 6, 1756* (London 1756).

Thierry, Augustin, *Les Grandes Mystifications littéraires* (Paris 1911).

Thomas, Antoine-Leonard, *Mémoire sur la cause des tremblemens de terre, qui a remporté le prix "Accessit" au jugement de l'Académie royale des sciences, belles-lettres et arts de Rouen, le 3 août 1757* (Paris 1758).

Thomas, John, *A Sermon preached before the House of Lords in the abby-church of Westminster, on Friday, February 6th, 1756* (London 1756).

Thomas, Peter David Garner, *George III: King and politician, 1760-1770* (Manchester 2002).

Tisserand, Roger, *Au temps de l'Encyclopédie: l'Académie de Dijon de 1740 à 1793* (Paris 1936).

Tobriner, Stephen, 'Earthquakes and planning in the 17th and 18th century', *Journal of architectural education* 33:4 (1980), p.11-15.

– *The Genesis of Noto: an eighteenth-century city* (London 1982)

Torriano, Nathaneal the younger, *A Sermon preached at Hooe and Ningfield in Sussex, on Sunday, February 1st, 1756* (Lewes 1756).

Torrubias y Ponce, José de, *Descripcion geografica-historica del Reyno de Portugal: en la qual se dara mas gustosa y cabal inteligencia a los mapas* (Madrid, Joseph Estevan Dolz, 1762).

Totton, William, *Two sermons preached in Layton-Stone chapel, Essex, I. On Friday, February 6, 1756, being the day appointed [...] for a general fast. II. On Sunday, February 15, following* (London 1756).

'Tremblemens de terre', in *Encyclopédie ou Dictionnaire raisonné des sciences, des arts et des métiers*, ed. Diderot and D'Alembert (1751-1780), vol.xvi.

'Les tremblemens de terre attribués à l'électricité', *Journal encyclopédique* (1er mai 1756), iii.3-18.

Trembley, 'Letter from Mons. Trembley to his brother', *Philosophical transactions, giving some accounts of the ingenious, in many considerable part of the world* 49 (London 1756), p.438f.

A True and particular account of the late dreadful earthquake at Lisbon (London 1756).

Tucoo-Chala, Suzanne, *Charles-Joseph Panckoucke et la librairie française, 1739-1798* (Pau 1977).

Turner, Thomas, *The Diary of Thomas Turner, 1754-1765*, ed. David Vaisey (Oxford 1984).

United States Geological Survey (USGS), *Information about past and historical earthquakes*, online at http://earthquake.usgs.gov/activity/past.html.

Valentin, Jakob, *Waechter-Stimme Des Allmaechtigen, Welche ER zu unserer Warnung gegen das Ende des 1755. und Anfang des 1756. Jahrs zu verschiedenen mahlen in Europa und andern Welt-Theilen durch starke Erd-Erschütterungen hat hoeren lassen* (Zurich 1756).

Van de Wetering, Maxine, 'Moralizing in puritan natural science: mysteriousness in earthquake sermons', *Journal of the history of ideas* (1982), p.417-38.

Vautravers, de, 'Letter from Mons. De Vautravers F. R. S. to Thomas Birch D. D. Secr. R. S.', *Philosophical transactions, giving some accounts of the ingenious, in many considerable part of the world* 49 (1756), p.436-38.

Vicente, Gemma, 'El terremoto de Lisboa y el problema del mal en Kant', *Themata, revista de filosofía* 3 (1986), p.141-52.

Vilanova, Susana, Catarina Nunes and João Fonseca. 'Lisbon 1755: a case of triggered onshore rupture?', *Bulletin of the Seismological society of America* 93:5 (2003), p.2056-68.

Voltaire, *Candide ou l'optimisme*, ed. René Pomeau, in *Œuvres completes de Voltaire*, vol.48 (Oxford 1980).

– *Candide: or Optimism*, translated by J. Butt (Middlesex 1947).

– *Contes en vers et en prose*, ed. Sylvain Menant (Paris 1992).

– *Correspondence and related documents*, ed. Theodore Besterman, in *Œuvres complètes de Voltaire*, vol.85-135 (Geneva, Banbury, Oxford 1968-1977).

– *Essai sur les mœurs* (Paris 1878).

– *Lettres philosophiques*, in *Mélanges* (Paris 1961).

– 'Poème sur le désastre de Lisbonne' (1756): ed. Moland, M.ix.470 and following; ed. Jacques van den Heuvel, in Voltaire, *Mélanges* (Paris 1961); ed. Jean Dagen, in Voltaire, *La Muse philosophe, florilège poétique*, (Paris 2000), p.93-100.

– *Précis du Siècle de Louis XV*, in *Œuvres historiques*, ed. René Pomeau (Paris 1968).

Walker, Samuel, *Prepare to meet thy God: two sermons preach'd at Truro in Cornwall, on Friday, February 6, 1756* (London 1756).

Wallin, Benjamin, *The Christian's duty and confidence in times of public calamity. Being several discourses occasioned by the late dreadful earthquakes and the apprehensions of a French war* (London 1756).

Walpole, Horace, *Memoirs of the Reign of King George II* (Londres 1847).

– *The Yale edition of Horace Walpole's correspondence*, ed. W. S. Lewis *et al.* (New Haven, CT 1954-).

Walsham, Alexandra, *Providence in early modern England* (Oxford 1999).

Walsh, John. 'John Wesley and the community of goods', in *Protestant evangelicalism: Britain, Ireland, Germany and America, c.1750-c.1950*, ed. Keith Robbins (Oxford 1990), p.25-50.

Warburton, William, *A Critical and philosophical enquiry into the causes of prodigies and miracles, as related by* historians. *With an essay towards restoring a method and purity in history* (London 1727).

- *Julian, or a discourse concerning the earthquake and fiery eruption, which defeated that Emperor's attempt to rebuild the temple at Jerusalem* (London 1750).
- *Julian*, in *The Works of William Warburton* (London 1788), iv.333-531.
- *Natural and civil events the instruments of God's moral government. A sermon preached the last public fast-day, at Lincoln's-Inn-Chappel* (London 1756).

Watkins, Richard, *A Sermon preach'd on the fast-day, at Clifton Campvill in Staffordshire* (Oxford 1756).

Webster, William, *The Nature, causes, and designs of God's judgments. Set forth in a sermon preached at Ware, in Hertfordshire, on Friday, February 6, 1756, being the fast day* (London 1756).

Weidmann, Marc, *Un Pasteur-naturaliste du XVIIIe siècle: Elie Bertrand (1713-1797)* (Lausanne 1986).

Wellbery, David E., ed. *Positionen der Literaturwissenschaft: Acht Modellanalysen am Beispiel von Kleists "Das Erdbeben in Chili"* (Munich 1985).

Wesley, Charles, *The Cause and cure of earthquakes. A sermon preach'd from Psalm xlvi.8* (London 1750).
- *Hymns occasioned by the earthquake, March 8, 1750: part I*, in *The Poetical works of John and Charles Wesley*, ed. George Osborn (London 1870).
- *The Sermons of Charles Wesley*, ed. Kenneth Newport (Oxford 2001), p.225-37.

Wesley, John, *The Bicentennial edition of the works of John Wesley*, ed. Richard Heitzenrater (Oxford, Nashville, TN 1980-2004).
- *The Doctrine of original sin: according to scripture, reason, and experience* (Bristol 1757).
- *Hymns occasioned to the earthquake, March 8, 1750. Part I* (Bristol 1756).
- *The Letters of the Rev. John Wesley*, ed. John Telford (London 1931; reprinted London 1960).

- *Serious thoughts occasioned by the late earthquake at Lisbon* (Bristol 1755).
- *Serious thoughts occasioned by the earthquake at Lisbon, to which is subjoin'd an account of all the late earthquakes there, and in other places* (London 1756).
- *The Works of John Wesley: journals and diaries (1755-1765)*, ed. W. Reginald Ward and Richard P. Heitzenrater (Nashville, TN 1992).

Wetzel, Michael. 'Geben und Vergeben: Vorüberlegungen zu einer Neudeutung der Ambivalenzen bei Kleist', *Kleist Jahrbuch* (2000), p.89-103.

Whiston, William, *A New theory of the earth, from its original, to the consummation of all things* (London 1696).

Whitefield, George, *A Letter from a clergyman at London to the remaining disconsolate inhabitants of Lisbon, occasioned by the late dreadful earthquake, by which the great and populous city hath been laid in ruins* (London 1755).
- *Whitefield at Lisbon, being a detailed account of the blasphemy and idolatry of popery, as witnessed by the late servant of God, George Whitefield, at the City of Lisbon, during his stay there* (London 1851).

[Whitehead, Paul] P. D., *A Full and true account of the dreadful and melancholy earthquake, which happened between twelve and one o'clock in the morning, on Thursday the fifth instant, with an exact list of such persons as have hitherto been found in the rubbish. In a letter from a gentleman in town, to his friend in the country* (London 1750).

[Whitehead, Paul], *A Second letter from a gentleman in town, to his friend in the country, on account of the late dreadful earthquake. Containing a list of several more persons that have been since found in the rubbish* (London 1750).

White, Thomas, *A Sermon preached in St. Andrew's church, Dublin, before the Honourable House of Commons, on Friday the 6th of February, 1756. Being the day appointed for a general fast, on account of the late dreadful earthquakes* (Dublin 1756).

Wiese, Benno von, *Die Deutsche Novelle von Goethe bis Kafka* (Düsseldorf 1965).

– 'Heinrich von Kleist: "Das Erdbeben in Chili"', *Jahrbuch der deutschen Schiller-Gesellschaft* 5 (1961), p.102-17.

Wilde, C. B., 'Hutchinsonianism, natural philosophy and religious controversy in eighteenth century Britain', *History of science* 18:1 (1980), p.1-24.

– 'Matter and spirit as natural symbols in eighteenth-century British natural philosophy', *British journal for the history of science* 15:2 (1982), p.99-131

Williams, John, *Awful providences, calls to repentance. A sermon preached at Stamford, in the county of Lincoln, on the 6th of February, 1756, being the publick fast day appointed by authority* (London 1756).

Wilson, Thomas, *The Diaries of Thomas Wilson, D. D., 1731-1737 and 1750*, ed. C. L. S. Linnell (London 1964).

Winock, Michel, 'Qu'est-ce qu'un événement?', *L'Histoire* (2002), p.32-37.

Winship, Michael P., *Seers of God: puritan providentialism in the restoration and early Enlightenment* (Baltimore, MD 1996).

Winstanley, J., *A Sermon preached at Conduit-street chapel, in the parish of St. George, Hanover-square. On Sunday, February the 1st, 1756* (London 1756).

Wirz, Hans Conrad, *Drey Buss-Predigten, ueber den ausserordentlich gefeyrten Baett-Tag gehalten; Samt einem, bey gleichem Anlase, an die Ehrwuerdige Kirchen-Diener auf der Landschaft abgelassenen Brief* (Zurich 1756).

Wittkowski, Wolfgang, 'Skepsis, Noblesse, Ironia: Formen des Als-ob in Kleists "Erdbeben"', *Euphorion* 63 (1969), p.247-83.

Wolff, Hans M., *Heinrich von Kleist: Die Geschichte seines Schaffens* (Bern 1954).

Woloch, Isser, *Eighteenth-century Europe: tradition and progress* (New York 1982).

Woodward, John, *An Essay toward a natural history of the earth: and terrestrial bodies, especially minerals: as also of the sea, rivers, and springs. With an account of the universal deluge: and of the effects that it had upon the earth* (London 1695).

Worden, Blair, 'Providence and politics in Cromwellian England', *Past and present* (1985), p.55-99.

– 'The question of secularization', in *A Nation transformed: England after the Restoration*, ed. Alan Houston and Steve Pincus (Cambridge 2001), p.20-40.

Xylander, Oskar, *Heinrich von Kleist und J. J. Rousseau* (Berlin 1937).

Yeo, Richard, *Encyclopaedic visions: scientific dictionaries and Enlightenment culture* (Cambridge 2001).

Young, B. W., 'Religion history and the eighteenth-century historian', *Historical journal* (2000), p.849-68.

Young, Brian, 'Theological books from *The Naked gospel* to *Nemesis of faith*', in *Books and their readers in eighteenth-century England: new essays*, ed. Isabel Rivers (London, New York 2001), p.79-104.

Zehnder, Johann Jakob, *Die Absicht Gottes In der Offenbahrung seiner Gerichten bey den Einwohneren des Erdkreisses. Vorgestellt In einer Predigt ueber die Worte bey dem Profeten Jesaias in dem XXVI. Cap. in dem letzteren Theile des 9. Verses. Sonntags den 14. Christm. 1755* (Bern 1755).

'Zeit anderswo geschehenen fast allgemeinen Erdbeben, und ausserordentlichen Bewegungen des Wassers, zur Erwekung einer tieffen Ehrfurcht vor Gott vorgestellt', in *Monatliche Nachrichten einicher Merkwuerdigkeiten, in Zuerich gesammlet und herausgegeben* (Zurich 1755), p.1-8.

Index

STUDIES ON VOLTAIRE AND THE

SVEC

2005:02

SVEC

INDEX

A fully searchable index to over
fifty years of research published in *SVEC*
http://www.voltaire.ox.ac.uk/svec_index

Manuscripts should be prepared in accordance with the *SVEC* style sheet, available on request and at the Voltaire Foundation website (www.voltaire.ox.ac.uk). One paper copy should be submitted to the *SVEC* general editor at the Voltaire Foundation, 99 Banbury Road, Oxford OX2 6JX, UK; an electronic version, with a summary of about 750 words, should be sent to jonathan.mallinson@trinity.ox.ac.uk.